10-32

THE
PRIVATE
PRESS

Printing at the Dun Emer Press. Miss Elizabeth Yeats and her companions.
Photograph: Courtesy of St. Bride Printing Library.

THE PRIVATE PRESS

Second Edition, Revised and Enlarged

RODERICK CAVE

R. R. BOWKER COMPANY
NEW YORK AND LONDON, 1983

Published by R. R. Bowker Company
205 East Forty-second Street, New York, NY 10017
Copyright © 1983 by Xerox Corporation
All rights reserved
Printed and bound in the United States of America

LIBRARY OF CONGRESS CATALOGING IN PUBLICATION DATA

Cave, Roderick.
    The private press.

    Bibliography: p.
    Includes index.
    1. Private presses—History. I. Title.
Z231.5.P7C37 1983   686.2'09   83-7163
ISBN 0-8352-1695-0

Designed by Philip Grushkin

The press marks on the dust jacket are from the following presses:
Row 1—Village Press, Kelmscott Press, Eragny Press;
Row 2—Officina Bodoni; Row 3—Doves Press, Strawberry Hill Press,
Grabhorn Press, Nonesuch Press; Row 4—The Oriole Press,
The Sign of the George, Golden Cockerel Press, Daniel Press;
Row 5—Laboratory Press, Gregynog Press, The Essex House Press, Ashendene Press.

FOR MY WIFE, DAWN

CONTENTS

PREFACE
TO THE SECOND EDITION

"WHAT IS A PRIVATE PRESS?" is a question that has never been answered altogether satisfactorily. The fact is that no simple or concise definition is possible. Every writer on private printing has his own definition: for the French bibliographer Anatole Claudin, writing on early private presses in France, it was a press "set up in a monastery, a palace, a residence or a private house, not the residence of a professional printer"—in other words, a printing establishment that did not exist for commercial gain.

This is a useful definition for the period of which Claudin was writing, but when one considers later periods in which government printing offices, university presses, and captive printing plants in many kinds of organizations came into existence, his definition becomes far too broad to be of use. Other printing historians, particularly on the Continent where strict regulation of the printing trade continued far longer than in Great Britain, have often regarded as private any press set up beyond the number permitted under license. Edmond Werdet, for example, in his *Histoire du Livre en France* (1862), included in his list of prerevolutionary presses in France one set up in the Department of War by government decree in 1768, which was considered a private press by French standards at that time. But to Werdet's English contemporaries, this press would have been considered purely an official press and not a private one, since to them a private press was one owned by a private individual, who used it to print whatever he chose, with no thought of making it pay its way.

So narrow a definition as this, however, excludes William Morris's work at the Kelmscott Press, as well as the work of such later presses as Doves or Golden Cockerel, which most twentieth-century collectors regard as *the* private presses, even though they operated on an increasingly commercial scale. For these presses a more suitable definition is that of C. R. Ashbee, who described a private press as one "whose objective is an aesthetic one, a press that, if it is to have real worth, challenges support on a basis of standard, caters for a limited market, and is not concerned with the commercial development of printing by machinery." Ashbee's definition in turn excludes some who regard their presses as private. A good rule of thumb is in the dictum of the late John Carter. In his introduction to the catalogue of the exhibition of the *English Private Presses 1757 to 1961* held at the Times Bookshop in London in 1961, Carter wrote of

> the fundamental principle of private press printing; the principle that, whether
> or not the press has to pay its way, the printer is more interested in making a
> good book than a fat profit. He prints what he likes, how he likes, not what
> someone else has paid him to print. If now and then he produces something
> more apt for looking at and handling than for the mundane purpose of reading,
> remember he is concerned as much with his own pleasure and education as with
> yours.

Pleasure and education: it is now about 30 years since my own pleasure in private presses was first awakened, growing originally from an interest in the work of Eric Gill. The early 1950s were not a time when there was much general enthusiasm for private press work in Great Britain; in many ways the idea of fine printing, of the production of handsome editions that were deliberately small in size and necessarily high in cost, was out of tune with the times. The spirit that in the 1920s and the 1930s had resulted in so much private press activity had ebbed; the day of the private press seemed to be over. With hindsight, one can see clearly enough that the tide was turning; my own interest, like that of many others who dabbled with printing, was part of a new flow that has led to more widespread activity in private printing today than ever before.

When the text of the first edition of this book was written in 1969–1970, it came as the culmination of 10 or 12 years in which I had been concerned with private presses. As editor of *The Private Library,* and as founding editor (with Thomas Rae) of the annual bibliography *Private Press Books,* I was very close to the current movement in private and pastime printing. My reasons for writing the book were twofold: first, a belief that the new private presses that had emerged since World War II were doing interesting work that deserved description and discussion, and that their books needed to be judged in appropriate terms, not necessarily those applied to the great private presses of the Arts and Crafts Movement. Second, I believed that the work of these contemporary private presses and of the earlier generation needed to be viewed in historical context. So far from the idea of the private press having been invented by William Morris, or even Horace Walpole, my own reading and research clearly indicated that the printing of books by private individuals outside the regular book trade dated back to the earliest days of printing from movable types—indeed, in some ways, the private presses were heirs to some traditions of the manuscript book, as the commercial book trade was to others.

Since the first edition was published in 1971, my own professional activities and avocational interests have led me far from the centers of private press activity, both physically and intellectually. To prepare this new edition has been a little like meeting an old flame: would I find that what had intrigued or charmed me in the past would still stir me? Would I find that the many changes in my old love were changes I liked, or regretted? The reader will no doubt discover that my old enthusiasm has not died.

There are some very real differences between the private press scene of the late 1960s and that of today. Changes in printing technology have vastly increased the difference in the ways trade books and private press books are printed. Many more books from private presses are being published, sometimes at prices that run into four figures. There has also been very much more published on private presses since the first edition. In addition to the journals *The American Book Collector* and *The Private Library,* there are articles and reviews in the newer *Fine Print* and *Matrix.* There have been many bibliographies of individual presses, exhibition catalogues, and studies of individual presses. Such books as Susan O. Thompson's *American Book Design and William Morris,* Colin Franklin's *The Private Presses,* Dorothy Harrop on Gregynog, and John Dreyfus on Nonesuch have provided much additional material or different points of view, which have enabled me to amplify or amend my text.

When first planning the second edition I intended little more than a revision and updating of those chapters dealing with the private press scene in the United States and Great Britain from the 1960s onward. In practice, the rewriting has been much more extensive, with new material (where I have additional information or I have changed my opinions) in nearly every chapter. In addition to the rewritten chapters on the United States and Great Britain, there are many other chapters with considerable changes from the first edition: for example, the section dealing with Morris's American followers, and my revised estimate of the importance of the Vale Press, and the introduction of discussion of the Shakespeare Head Press. Chapters dealing with the presses of Canada, Australia, and New Zealand have been added. Many new illustrations have also been provided.

As before, I have attempted to show some of the different types of presses that have been owned or operated by amateurs who have worked outside conventional book trade channels in the past 500 years of the printed book. Some of them do not fit altogether easily into the section in which they are described; any classification for such irrational and eccentric undertakings can be little better than a procrustean bed. By no means have all private presses been discussed: The selection has necessarily been a personal one, quite deliberately excluding some (like James Guthrie's Pear Tree Press) that have produced substantial work. Particularly in dealing with recent private press activity, I have been highly selective and omitted all reference to some presses producing delightful work. If my choice is found odd, I can only plead that waywardness and eccentricity are in the traditions of the material. Working within the framework of the original edition, I have not attempted to deal with some aspects of contemporary press work—for example, the effect that funding by the National Endowment for the Arts has had in the United States, the role of dealers like Serendipity Books and the Basilisk Press and Bookshop, or the emergence of artists' books, which can perhaps be regarded as an extension of conventional private press work. Nor, based in New Zealand, have I felt competent to discuss the work of the contemporary private presses of Germany, the Netherlands, and other European countries, delightful and stimulating though the books of, for example, the Raamin-Presse and Grillen-Presse are. Concentration has been on the English-speaking world, and the only recent Continental work described is that of presses such as the Plain Wrapper Press, which form part of the Anglo-American tradition.

As with the first edition, I could not have prepared the text of this revision without substantial help from many institutions and individuals. I am very glad to be able to acknowledge the advice, information, and help given by so many. In New Zealand, the staff and collections of Victoria University Library, Auckland University Library, and particularly the Alexander Turnbull Library have been of great assistance. I am grateful to the Council of Victoria University of Wellington for granting me leave to undertake further research in Great Britain and the United States, without which this revised edition would not have been possible. Of particular help in England have been the Birmingham City Libraries, the Bodleian Library, the British Library Reference Division, the St. Bride Printing Library, and the Victoria and Albert Museum; in the United States, The New York Public Library, The Pierpont Morgan Library, the Watkinson Library at Trinity College, the Lewis Walpole Library at Farmington (Connecticut), Fairleigh Dickinson University Library, University of Pennsylvania Library, Hunt Institute for Botanical Documentation, the King Library at the University of Kentucky, the Newberry Library, the Gleeson Library at the University of San Francisco, and the Research Library UCLA; and in Canada, the University of Alberta Library. For permission to reproduce work in their collections, I am grateful to the Lewis Walpole Library, the University of Alberta Library, The Pierpont Morgan Library, The New York Public Library, Birmingham City Libraries, St. Bride Printing Library, and Alexander Turnbull Library.

In addition, I should like to thank the following colleagues and friends for their help: Anna-Lou Ashby; Charles Aston; Brian Baumfield; Martha Birchfield and James Birchfield; Carol Blinn; David Butcher; Bernadette Callery; Simon Cauchi, David Chambers; Kathleen Coleridge; Steven Corey; Dame Hildelith Cumming; Victoria Dailey; Emma-Joy Dana; James Davis; Joan Davis; John DePol; Paul Hayden Duensing; Harry Duncan; Geoffrey Farmer; Jerome Frank; Colin Franklin; James Fraser; Jeannine Green; Penny Griffith; Philip Grushkin; Carolyn Reading Hammer; J. Hill Hamon; Robin Heyeck; Richard J. Hoffman; Andrew Horn; Jeffrey Kaimowitz; Sandra Kirshenbaum; Peter Koch; J. Ben Lieberman; Alan Loney; D. F. MacKenzie; Paul Morgan; James Mosley; Mary Parry and Nicholas Parry; Michael Piech; Rose Randle and John Randle; W. Gay Reading; Ward Ritchie; Robert Rosenthal; Leonard Seastone; Philip Sperling; Michael Taylor; Diana Thomas; Susan O. Thompson; Daniel Traister; J. E. Traue; Claire Van Vliet; Frances Wakeman and Geoffrey Wakeman; Kathy Walkup; Renee Weber; Berthold Wolpe; and Lili Wronker and Erich

Wronker. A special debt of gratitude is due to Terry Belanger, for his help in organizing my tour in the United States, and to Jean Peters, whose assistance has gone far beyond what an author expects from an editor. Being on the other side of the globe from my publisher could have made production a nightmare; Jean Peters ensured that it was not. To my wife, Dawn, to my daughter, Rowena, and to Helen Bark for reducing my often chaotic manuscript to clean copy, to Elsje Van Den Munckhof and Dorothy Macdonald for assistance with the index, and to John Casey for his photographic work, I am also grateful. Errors of fact and judgment remain my own.

RODERICK CAVE

Wellington, New Zealand
Easter Day, 1983

PART ONE

—

THE PRIVATE PRESSES

Chapter 1

THE ORIGINS OF
THE PRIVATE PRESS

IN 1639, THE DEAN OF MUNSTER, Bernard von Mallinckrodt, in his important *De Ortu ac Progressu Artis Typographicae, Dissertatio Historica* made the first reference in literature to the private press. Much of the text of this handsome volume was concerned with presenting the documentary evidence on the invention of printing two centuries earlier, but the learned dean also paid tribute to some of the great printers—Aldus Manutius, Froben, Plantin, and others—whose work had assisted the cause of scholarship. To this list of scholar-printers Mallinckrodt included almost as an afterthought a brief note on some individuals "who had sometimes their hired printers and set up their peculiar and private presses."

Ironically, none of Mallinckrodt's examples would at a later date have been regarded as private presses (in the sense that, say, Horace Walpole, William Morris, or Francis Meynell would understand the term), but it was, nevertheless, an early recognition by an acute mind that in the field of printing the amateur had a role more significant than in most other arts and occupations. Their role was more significant if only because their work, books, would survive and be identifiable in a way that few other artifacts can be as readily identified and assigned to their makers.

Today we are used to the idea of the amateur in many fields, whether the craft potter, the narrow-gauge railway enthusiast, the brewer of strange wines, or the home moviemaker. For more than a century manufacturers have been catering to the hobbyist, to the dabbler in printing no less than in other crafts, and it calls for some effort to put ourselves into the position of those who lived at a time when it was by no means so easy.

> The possession of a private printing press is, no doubt, a very appalling type of bibliomania. Much as has been told us of the awful scale on which drunkards consume their favoured poison, one is not accustomed to hear of their setting up private stills for their own individual consumption. There is a Sardanapalitan excess in this bibliographical luxuriousness which refuses to partake with other vulgar mortals in the common harvest of the public press, but must itself minister to its own tastes and demands. The owner of such an establishment is subject to no extraneous caprices about breadth of margins, size of type, quarto

or folio, leaded or unleaded lines: he dictates his own terms; he is master of the situation, as the French say, and is *the true autocrat of literature*.

When John Hill Burton wrote these extravagant lines in *The Book Hunter* in 1862 he was thinking of some of the amateur presses that had flourished at the start of the century rather than the burgeoning hobby-printers of his own time. Like Mallinckrodt, he saw the private press in relation to the printing and publishing trades, as a deliberate, even willful, eccentricity. Certainly eccentricity and willfulness have contributed not a little to the private press scene at times. But so many individuals have "set up their peculiar and private presses" throughout the whole period of printing that it becomes clear that they form a distinct undercurrent, of continued, though varying, significance for the past 500 years. To trace their origin it is necessary to consider them not simply in relation to society or the book trade in these 500 years, but to go back beyond Gutenberg and the era of typographic man.

Most of us have a fairly clear picture of the production of books before the transformation instituted by Gutenberg's invention of printing from movable types. From early childhood reading we will have gained an impression of the monastic scriptorium, with tonsured monks busily writing and limning manuscripts to the greater glory of God. For some of us, the charming simplicity of this picture will be spoiled by the realization that a good many medieval manuscripts can never have been anywhere near a monastery and that there must also have been many scribes who worked outside the religious houses. We do not often think of there being the regular production and sale of books in the way that there is a book trade today.

As with all the hazy half-forgotten images acquired at school, this picture is far from being accurate. It is commonplace that the production of books was a well-established and flourishing business long before printing. No doubt the time needed to write out a lengthy manuscript was a limiting factor in books' availability, and there is plenty of evidence to show that they were very expensive. But for the wealthy man books were certainly readily available in fifteenth-century Italy, as is shown by the purchases made by Duke Humphrey of Gloucester, John Tiptoft of Worcester, and by other English humanists.

Naturally enough, the scarcity and cost of manuscripts meant that nearly all libraries were very small; Cambridge University Library in 1424 had just 122 volumes. Individuals only rarely possessed more than one or two books. It was the dream of Chaucer's Clerk of Oxenford to own 20, but Chaucer certainly does not suggest that his clerk's dream was likely to be fulfilled.

For the man of learning there were several ways books could be acquired if he wanted to own them rather than consult them in libraries. This can be seen from the monk Thorirus Andreae. While attending the Council of Constance he took the opportunity to transcribe some manuscripts himself, had others copied for him by professional scriveners, bought some books on the spot, and gathered still more through purchases from a number of booksellers elsewhere.

The professional production of books was undertaken in the monastic scriptoria (some of which were large, like that of the Dominicans in Basel with over 30 copyists in the 1430s) and by lay copyists like those working for Vespasiano da Bisticci, Diebold Lauber, or John Shirley, and by the semiprofessionals—the university students who worked their way through college by copying manuscripts for others. This was the established "professional" book trade, but, as Curt Bühler has shown so well in his penetrating study *The Fifteenth Century Book: The Scribes, the Printers, the Decorators* (Philadelphia, 1960), this trade production was certainly dwarfed by amateur production, by the number of manuscripts scholars copied out for their own use. Petrarch, Chaucer, and many others are known to have worked in this way, and some of them managed to build up very respectable collections. In 1444, for instance, Johann Sintram of Würzburg presented to a Franciscan library in his native city 61 manuscripts containing texts he had copied in libraries as widely scattered as Ulm and Oxford, Strasbourg, and Reutlingen. Many of the volumes were *Sammelbände*, a collection of short texts by different authors, that Sintram compiled to suit his own needs and tastes. These are precisely the sort of work that a modern scholar may undertake for his research, although he is likely to rely on interlibrary loan and the photocopier to achieve the same end.

A man will turn over half a library to make one book, as Dr. Johnson observed. In the period before the spread of printing had created ideas of ownership of intellectual property or copyright, the nature of authorship and publication was totally different from what it later became. A writer might quote a passage here, garner an idea there, or mix what he had read with his own original contributions with splendid abandon. When he published his book, he did so simply by permitting others to read what he had written. If the first readers approved the text, copies would be made and the work would circulate to a wider audience. Such an idea of publication was not quickly to be superseded by publication in printed form. Widespread circulation of manuscript copies continued for a very long time, and the printing of texts for private circulation is commonplace.

It is scarcely exaggeration to say that in the production of books before Gutenburg's time one can see the foundations of the private press as clearly as one can see the foundations of the commercial printing and publishing industries. In a sense, the monastic scriptoria with their devotion to the duty of preserving and passing on works of real importance were the ancestors not only of the modern academic publisher, but also of the many private presses that at different times have been devoted to the production of works of scholarship. The production of a copy or two of a manuscript for circulation to friends of the author laid the way for a great deal, perhaps the majority of later private publishing. In the work of some of the professional scribes of the renaissance, producing manuscripts of outstanding calligraphy, we can find the ancestors of those modern amateur printers whose concern was the "Book Beautiful." The outstanding example is the manuscripts produced under the direction of Vespasiano da Bisticci, of which E. Ph. Goldschmidt observed that they were textually poor, being

> written with extraordinary slovenliness. Whole lines are left out, mistakes
> abound, repetitions are left uncorrected rather than spoil the beautiful page.
> Vespasiano's manuscripts are written for people who wanted to possess these
> books, not to read them, and the scribes knew it and were much more attentive
> to the evenness of their letters than to the sense of what they were writing.

The similarity between Goldschmidt's comments, and those made on some later fine printing (Holbrook Jackson on Kelmscott, for instance) is remarkable. What is clear is that in concern for the book as art form, or as vehicle for art, modern fine printing and *livres d'artiste*—and the customers for them—are in direct descent from these calligraphic manuscripts.

It is by no means unreasonable to regard the first printing in France as being more of a private nature than an innovative move in the book trade. When in 1469–1470 Johann Heynlin, who had been Rector and Librarian of the Sorbonne, together with Guillaume Fichet the Professor of Philosophy and Rhetoric (and also a former Rector and Librarian) invited three German printers to come to the Sorbonne to set up a press, one may certainly regard their enterprise as an early instance of academic publishing. In the following two years the printers produced several books of academic interest, deriving naturally from their patrons' work. Undoubtedly some of the work was of a more private nature, produced entirely in the way that Fichet required, and at his own cost; of the edition of Cardinal Bessarion's oration in favor of a crusade against the Turks that was printed in 1471, at least 45 copies are known to have been presented to various potentates by Fichet. Very much the same happened, though on a less lavish scale, with Fichet's own *Rhetoric*.

It is also possible to regard the earliest English printing as of a private nature. The bibliographer G. P. Winship argued that William Caxton ought not to be regarded just as Britain's prototypographer, as William Blades had depicted him, but, in fact:

> The man who introduced economical bookmaking into England was a well-to-do retired wool merchant who enjoyed translating French romances and who provided himself with a private press because this was cheaper than having copies made by hand for the many friends who asked him to give them his translations.

Winship was persuaded by the famous words Caxton included in his translation of Raoul le Fèvre's *Recueil des Histoires de Troies:*

> For as much as in the writing of the same my pen is worn, mine hand weary and not steadfast, mine eyes dimmed with overmuch looking on the white paper . . . and also because I have promised to diverse gentlemen and to my friends to address them as hastily as I might this said book. Therefore I have practiced and learned to my great charge and dispense to ordain this said book in print after the manner and form as ye may see here . . . to the end that every man may have them at once.

These are persuasive words, but modern Caxton scholarship has shown clearly enough how astute a businessman Caxton was, and we would be wrong to regard his essay into printing as noncommercial. Nevertheless, even this instance shows the difficulty at the time in distinguishing the professional from the amateur, the commercial from the noncommercial. Certainly the invention of printing produced no sudden change in the normal pattern of book production. The scribe continued to flourish for many years in competition or collaboration with the printer.

The new invention was beset with difficulties. To set up as a printer demanded considerable capital. The demand for books was difficult to predict, and even in university towns and important trading centers the market could become saturated very rapidly.

Histories of the book were for centuries—at least as late as the *History of Printing* published by the Society for the Promotion of Christian Knowledge (SPCK) in 1862—enlivened with a delightful legend, which seems to derive from Joannes Walchius, in his *Decas Fabularum,* published in Strasbourg in 1609. In this, Walchius repeats a story told to him by Henricus Schorus about the earliest days of printing. In it, Johann Fust took some volumes of the Bible to sell in Paris. At the time the price for a manuscript copy of the Bible was 400 or 500 crowns, but Fust sold his books for 60 crowns. When the demand slackened, he, like any good merchant, sold them for 50 crowns, then for 40, and at last for still less. By this time the early purchasers, who had been wondering how it could be that each copy was identical, realized that he had a method of producing the books "by an easy art," and those who had paid the higher price demanded their money back. They became so troublesome to Fust, Walchius continues, that he was compelled to leave Paris.

This is no more than a legend. But until there was some standardization of prices, improved channels of distribution, and knowledge by the printers of what could or could not be sold, the printer who attempted to earn his living by selling on the open market would not find life easy.

> We first among the Germans brought the art of printing to Rome, at great labour and expense. We struggled against difficulties which others refused to face, and in consequence our house is filled with unsold books, but empty of the means of subsistence. Broken in strength we crave your gracious help.

This was the gist of the plea that Sweynheym and Pannartz addressed, not unsuccessfully, to Pope Sixtus IV in 1472.

The history of printing in the fifteenth century is full of competent printers who were unsuccessful in business: Johann Zainer, Ulrich Zell, Johann Neumeister—the list could be lengthened almost indefinitely. Competition in the larger cities and the dire threat of bankruptcy (nothing to view lightly in those days) compelled printers like other craftsmen to take to the roads, settling in one place for a few months to produce works demanded locally before moving on. Work of this kind was seldom of a normal commercial nature undertaken as a speculation; instead, the printer contracted to print a book or books at the order and expense of a patron.

The most common work of this sort was probably in the field of missals and breviaries for church use. During the first 20 years of printing bishops seem often to have looked askance at printed books, and it was not until 1474 that a printed missal was placed on an altar. When the new method had become acceptable, several different methods of commissioning the printing developed. The policy of the German bishops was to commission the best printer they could find to undertake the work; they permitted him to charge an agreed price, and they required each church in their diocese to provide itself with a copy before a certain date. This method was to be followed very closely with the printing of Bibles in England.

In France there were several instances in the fifteenth century of an approach that cut across normal commercial printing to a very much greater extent. About 1478, for example, a wealthy Canon of St. Hilaire, Poitiers, named Bertrand de Brossa installed Stephen des Grez, a printer from Paris, in his own home. Grez printed a *Breviarum Historiale,* a quarto of some 326 leaves, in 1479. Another book printed at the canon's orders, Cardinal Torquemada's *Expositio Brevis . . . Super Toto Psalterio* was completed two years later. Similarly in 1482 Pierre Plumé, Canon of Chartres, invited the Paris printer Jean du Pré to produce a missal for use in the cathedral, and installed his equipment and lodged him in the canon-house while it was being printed. A breviary for use at Chartres followed in 1483. Perhaps these were not true private presses, and we should think of the canons as amateur publishers rather than amateur printers with hired men to do the heavy or tedious work. It would certainly be a mistake to regard them only as customers who took printers into their households for want of a better alternative. They knew what they wanted, and by having the work done under their immediate supervision they were able to ensure that they got it.

Probably much the same was true of Johannes Trithemius, Abbot of Sponheim, in the Hunsrück mountains between Trier and Mainz in Germany. Trithemius is a very interesting figure among the German humanists at the turn of the fifteenth century, because he obviously recognized the merits of the printed book as well as those of the manuscript. Trithemius wrote persuasively in favor of continued copying in monastic scriptoria in his *De Laude Scriptorum* (1494), giving as one reason that parchment manuscripts would last a thousand years, whereas the life of the paper of the printed book would be very much shorter. He also made extensive use of printed books, not least of which was offering them to other monastic libraries in exchange for their manuscripts, which were added to the Sponheim Library.

De Laude Scriptorum was only one of many books printed to his order at the printing house of Peter von Friedberg at Mainz. A modern editor of his work in praise of scribes has commented that Friedberg's shop could almost be called the Sponheim Abbey Press: Of the 25 editions he printed in the fifteenth century, no fewer than 13 had Trithemius as author, while another six came from his immediate circle of friends. The close correspondence between the manuscripts and the printed text, and the meticulous proofreading indicate the active part that the abbot took in the preparation and production of the books printed by Friedberg.

Such patronage was extremely common at the end of the fifteenth century, so that the distinction between the commercial and private printer became very slight. To give one more instance drawn from Spain, shortly after Granada had been taken from the Moors, Juan Varela de Salamanca is known to have been summoned there from Seville by the energetic Archbishop Hernando de Talavera. Between 1504 and 1508 he printed several books at the order and expense of the archbishop. They included a breviary, a gradual, an antiphonary, and an Arabic grammar and dictionary that the archbishop had instructed to be prepared as an aid to those engaged in the conversion of the recently conquered Moors. That these books were special commissions and not produced for trade is sufficiently shown by Varela's handing over the stocks of the books he had printed to the cathedral authorities when he left Granada soon after his patron's death in 1508.

Chapter 2

THE QUASI-OFFICIAL
OR PATRON'S PRESS

For a wealthy or powerful man who wished to have particular books printed in the manner he chose, to take a printer into his employ for a while, as Bertrand de Brossa had done at Poitiers, was a natural enough course in the fifteenth and sixteenth centuries. From Benvenuto Cellini's *Autobiography* one can gain a good picture of the pattern that operated between patrons and craftsmen in other arts. Sometimes the craftsmen would be under the protection of a particular patron but would undertake other work as well as their commissions for him; in other cases, the craftsmen would work exclusively on books ordered and paid for by their protector, and, in those cases, there can be no doubt that their work has to be regarded as private.

Many, but by no means all, such ventures were for the production of church books. Toward the end of 1484, for example, Robert Fouquet and Jean Cres set up a press in the little town of Brehan-Loudéac in the Duchy of Brittany. The town was on the estates of Jean de Rohan, and in all but the last book Fouquet and Cres printed they stated that they worked under Rohan's protection. It seems very likely, if not certain, that the work was done at his expense as well, for the publications were of a sort one would not have expected: books of poetry instead of the devotional works that would have been the natural choice for printers in such a religious country. When they had printed their seventh book in 1485, Fouquet departed—war had broken out between France and Brittany—and the Breton Cres continued to print alone, having prudently removed himself to the greater safety of the Benedictine Abbey of Lantenac about 10 miles away. There he printed an edition of Mandeville's *Travels* in 1488, and is believed to have followed it with a number of liturgical works for the abbey, of which only *Le Doctrinale des Nouvelles Mariées* (1491) has survived.

Jean Cres was a peripatetic printer. When such printers settled in one place to work wholly on work ordered by a particular patron, then the first main group of private presses began, those semiofficial or court presses that were at once private and the forerunners of the modern government printing offices. The earliest printer to receive official recognition, by virtue of his appointment as court printer to the Emperor Maximilian I, was Johann Schönsperger the elder (1481–1523); and in the works printed for the emperor—the emperor's prayer book (1512–1513) of which only 10 copies were pulled, and the *Theuerdank* completed in 1517—no expense was spared in the quest for magnificence. Similarly, the splendid Complutensian Polyglot Bible that was printed by Arnaõ

Guillen de Brocar at Alcalá in Spain at almost exactly the same time is said to have cost Arnaõ's patron Cardinal Ximenes the sum of 50,000 gold ducats to produce. The cardinal's establishment for the production of the Polyglot was of course far more than a printing house alone. Work on printing the Polyglot did not occupy all of Brocar's time since he continued to produce books at his own risk as well. But for the Polyglot, and a series of six splendid folio service books for the cardinal's cathedral at Toledo the expenses were borne entirely by Ximenes.

One may argue that such presses are far too princely to be regarded as private presses, but that they had evolved into something far less humble. Guillen de Brocar was in effect running a university press. Nevertheless, the continuity was there in the involvement and interest of the patrons in the work that was done for them; an involvement that one can find more easily and frequently in the field of the fine arts.

In the sixteenth century, as A. W. Pollard has said:

> The enthusiasm with which the new art had at first been received died out.
> Printers were no longer lodged in palaces, monasteries and colleges; Church
> and State, which had at first fostered and protected them, were now jealous and
> suspicious, even actively hostile. . . . Printing had sunk to the level of a mere
> craft.

The appointment of court printers and the work that they produced became very much less the personal concern of the monarch. But this was in the typographically developed countries of western Europe; in the less settled territories of eastern Europe they survived very much longer. In Transylvania, for example, Prince Johann Sigismund Zapoly summoned the printer Raphael Hofhalter to Carlsberg in 1566 to take charge of his private press, a press that continued to be run by Hofhalter's widow and children after his death the following year. When their patron died they were unable to support themselves by commercial printing and had by force of circumstances to leave the country. Subsequently in 1637 George Rakotsky reestablished a private press; the celebrated *Officium Ragotzianum* written by his son after he had succeeded to the throne was, according to Jacques Charles Brunet, printed under his personal supervision.

A far more romantic story is told by Brunet of another of these semiofficial presses in Transylvania, that of Count Wolfgang Bethlen at the castle of Kreisch. The count's printer, Michael Székesi, was in 1687 engaged in printing a large folio, the *History of Transylvania* written by the count. Some 800 pages had been printed when the Turkish army arrived; the castle was besieged and taken, and the count and his men taken and sold into slavery. A century later, when the castle was being rebuilt after the territory had been recaptured from the Turks, the workmen uncovered a cellar that had been bricked up; when it was opened it was found to contain a mass of rotting paper that turned out to be the sheets of the book abandoned so hastily. Only two nearly complete copies of this *liber rarissimus rarior* could be made up.

To an even greater extent than in eastern Europe the spread of printing overseas in the wake of European expansion was at first usually of a noncommercial nature. Printers might be called to undertake printing for official or missionary purposes; in more than a few cases mission presses were operated by priests with no training as printers, like the Jesuits' press in Paraguay described in Chapter 24. In Iceland, to give one example, the fifteenth-century French pattern reappears. It is remarkable that although printing (introduced into Denmark in 1482, and Sweden the following year) did not reach Finland until 1642 or Norway until 1643, the art was introduced to Iceland at a remarkably early date. The initiative came from Jón Arason, the last Catholic Bishop of Hólar (the ancient capital of the island) who about 1530 organized the establishment of a printing office run for him by a Swede, Jón Matthíasson. Only fragments survive of the *Brevarium Holense* that he printed

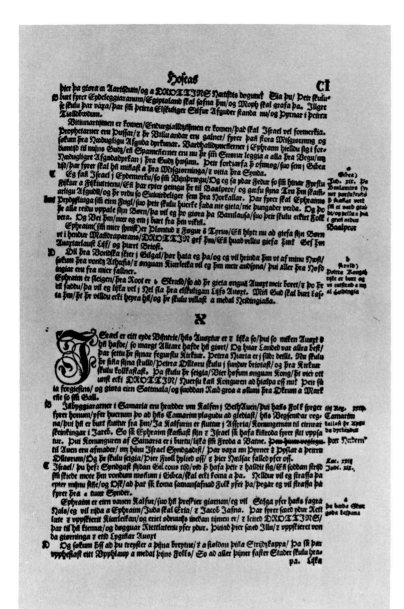

ILLUS. 1. Jón Jónsson, Hólar, Iceland. Page from Guthbrandsbiblíar printed at the Bishop's press, 1584. Note the correction hand-stamped into the text.

for the bishop about 1531. Jón Matthíasson may have printed an Icelandic translation of the New Testament for Bishop Jón. After Arason's death, he continued work for his Lutheran successor in the see until his own death in 1567. Thereafter, particularly under Bishop Guthbrandur Thorláksson the son and grandson of the first printer continued to print work at Hólar (Illus. 1). Not until the late eighteenth century did the economic condition of Iceland permit the operation of a normal commercial press.

It is perhaps stretching the point to regard all early Icelandic work as private, but there can be no doubt about the private nature of the earliest printing in another Danish colony, Greenland. The modern settlement of the country from Europe came relatively late; it was not until 1721 that a post was established at Godthaab. A few years later Moravian missionaries from Herrnhut in Saxony started evangelizing the Greenlanders, and it was one of these missionaries, Jesper Broderson, who was responsible for the introduction of the printing press.

TUKSIAUTIT

AKIOREEKSAUTIKSET,

MAKPERSÆGANGOEESA

I

NÛngme. 1793.

Jo: Neuherrnhut u. Groonland graduit.

ILLUS. 2. Jesper Broderson, Greenland. Title page of the *Choral Songs* printed on the Missionary's press at Nongme (Godthaab) in 1793.

Only one work printed by Broderson has survived, a collection of choral songs in Greenlandic published in Nongme (Godthaab) in 1793 (Illus. 2). It appears that while attending a synod in his own country, Broderson on his own initiative equipped himself with a small "Handbuchdruckerey" that he took back with him to Greenland. There he set himself to learn how to print and painfully produced his little 68-page book using a very small type. It seems that it was not his intention to use the press for any extensive work, or perhaps he found the results did not justify the labor involved, and the headquarters of the mission in Saxony knew nothing of it. In the year following the publication, Broderson had to leave Greenland because of severe illness, and his press and type were abandoned. They remained unused and forgotten for over half a century.

In the middle of the nineteenth century Hinrich Rink was appointed Crown Inspector of southern Greenland. This was a post roughly comparable with that of district commissioner in the old British colonial service, and Rink, like so many district officers, devoted himself to the service and study of the country and its people. In 1855 he discovered Broderson's printing equipment that was neglected for so long, and in the autumn and winter of that year he used it to good effect on a number of small publications.

The first of these was a little handbill in Greenlandic Rink printed on October 21, 1855. It proclaimed:

> Exciting news! The ship has arrived and will make two voyages this year. England
> and Russia are at war with one another, but there is no fighting in the North [i.e.,
> Denmark]. When the King was out riding recently he had a fall and was injured,
> but is recovering. The reindeer hunting has been poor, but seals are plentiful.
> Praise God, there is little illness. The Danes in Godthaab wish you well!

As well as this quaint newssheet, five other pamphlets were printed. They included a note on the school syllabus; news of the Crimean War; a Christmas hymn; and *Aid for the Sick,* a 32-page handbook on diet, hygiene, and similar topics.

Rink printed these "Godthaab pamphlets" as they came to be known, in order to establish that it would be practicable and useful to set up a proper printing press in the country to be run by the Greenlanders themselves. He had already used a woodcut in one of the pamphlets that had been cut by the Greenlander Rasmus Berthelsen, whom Rink taught to print and who was probably almost entirely responsible for the production of the pamphlets. Armed with his work as an example of what could be done, Rink was in a position to approach the authorities in Copenhagen for a grant to purchase equipment for his press.

While on leave in the capital in the winter of 1856–1857, Rink managed to persuade the government that his proposals were reasonable, and with the modest allowance of 250 rix-dollars he purchased type, a small handpress, and an even smaller lithographic press that he took back to Greenland and installed in his house in Godthaab in the spring of 1857.

There can be no doubt that even according to the strictest of definitions Rink's work had previously been that of a private press. From 1857 it was private no longer, as it was officially financed and approved. Although an increasing number of publications came from the inspector's press during the 1860s and 1870s as his assistants became more skilled, and many of them are unmistakably official printing, but a good many of its productions still bore the stamp of private enthusiasm rather than of public policy. At least one of the earliest, a 34-page booklet on *Hans Egede,* seems from the crudity of its production not to have been printed on a press at all. Tradition has it that it was produced by pupils in the Godthaab school by impressing the paper by hand on to the inked type (Illus. 3).

The first real book printed on the new press was *Pok: A Greenlander Who Has Travelled Abroad,* which was set and printed under Rink's supervision by Rasmus Berthelsen and his assistant Lars Møller (or Arqualuk, as he became known throughout Greenland) in 1857. This little 18-page book was illustrated with woodcuts by Berthelsen (and in some copies with lithographs perhaps drawn by Rink himself) and tells of the adventures of the first Greenlanders to visit Denmark in 1723.

Through pressure of official duties Rink's personal involvement in the work of his press became much less during the 1860s. By the time that ill-health forced him to leave Greenland for good in 1868 the operation of the "South Greenland Press" was in the capable hands of Lars Møller, who had in the winter of 1861–1862 been sent on a short training course to Denmark. With the subsequent development of this press down to the present day we are not concerned, but that it should have grown so successfully through the difficult circumstances of its early years can only make us marvel at the determination of the printers. For the press was essentially a winter occupation (the summer was spent in hunting and fishing and gathering fuel), and printing in the Greenland winter was not easy. The press was housed in an icy stone workshop in the grounds of the inspector's house, and the dampened paper often froze stiff while being used. Supplies of ink often ran out, and fresh ink of a sort had to be made by boiling soot and varnish. It was not until the turn of the century that the press was more suitably housed.

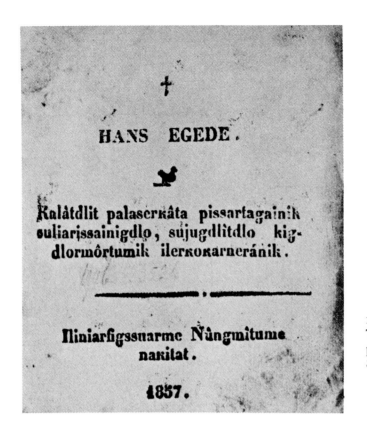

ILLUS. 3. Hinrich Rink, Greenland. Title page of *Hans Egede,* a booklet printed by pupils in the Godthaab School, 1857.

At about the time that Rink was experimenting with Broderson's old press, a Herrnhuter missionary named Samuel Kleinschmidt also became interested in printing, probably through seeing some of Rink's experimental pieces. In 1856 Kleinschmidt wrote to his half-brother in Holland asking him to send him a press. The press arrived in 1857, and from then until his death in 1886 Kleinschmidt used it constantly. The books that he printed on the press at Neu Herrnhut during the first two years were *Nunalerutit,* a primer of geography completed in 1858, and an outline of world history the following year. Both volumes were produced in their entirety by Kleinschmidt who was author, compositor, pressman, binder, and distributor. For the work of one entirely self-taught, they are of a very high standard.

After the production of the world history there was a lull in the press's activity. Kleinschmidt broke with the Herrnhuter mission and became a teacher in the Danish school in Godthaab. He was, in fact, moving closer and closer to a personal identification with the Greenlanders and adopted the Greenland costume of anorak and sealskin trousers (and the old Eskimo aversion to washing) and built himself a log cabin of the traditional pattern. In the cabin he installed his press, which the Herrnhuters had allowed him to take on condition that they received free copies of anything he printed. Kleinschmidt (or Samualé as he became known to the Greenlanders) produced many books of an educational or missionary flavor from his press, entirely at his own expense. The most important was a translation of the Bible into Greenlandic that was issued in parts between 1864 and the late 1870s, a fantastic labor for one man to undertake. Samualé regarded his version only as a first draft to be revised and improved by other missionaries, but, nevertheless, his Old Testament text remains the standard to this day. Of an entirely different nature was a little book *About Animals* that he wrote and printed in 1863. Here Samualé described various animals previously unknown to the Greenlanders, and for which, of course, no names existed in their language. The names he invented—"he who noses around and tears things up" for the rhinoceros, "the one without joints" for the elephant—have now become the standard Greenlandic names for these creatures. But Samualé's contribution to the language was far greater than this; with a grammar and dictionary that he had published before he acquired his press he virtually created Greenlandic as a written language.

Greenland was unusual in the importance that private printing assumed in the development of the press, but it is not too exceptional to serve as an example of the importance of the amateur in spreading the craft of printing.

The subject of missionary printing is fascinating. Buried in the archives of missionary societies and elsewhere are a host of stories illustrating the spread of printing into many parts of Asia, Africa, and the Pacific area through missionary zeal.

Sometimes the effort was deliberately planned by the society concerned. For instance, for New Zealand the Church Missionary Society (CMS) in London decided in 1833 to send out a trained printer and equipment that they ordered through their London printers. When the printer, William Colenso, arrived in the Bay of Islands in December 1834 and unpacked the equipment, he found that although he had a press, type, and ink, his supplies did not include cases, galleys, ink slab, ink balls, imposing stone, or furniture! As an experienced printer, Colenso was able to surmount these "little" difficulties (as well as the temptation the type presented to Maoris in search of lead for casting musket balls) and proof an edition in Maori of St. Paul's Epistles to the Philippians and the Ephesians by February of the following year.

By no means all missionaries were trained as printers. In Uganda the pioneer missionary Alexander Mackay had the distinct advantage that as a child of the manse in Aberdeenshire he had possessed a small press as an educational toy, and, according to his sister's memoir, at the age of 10 amazed visitors by his skill in setting type and the accuracy of his proof sheets.

Mackay was a man of pronounced mechanical skills whose original aim had been to go as an engineering missionary to Madagascar, where 40 years earlier printing had been introduced by the London Missionary Society—but that is another story. Eventually Mackay found his life work in Uganda, where he had a small press and small font of type that he used to produce portions of the scriptures in Swahili and Luganda. But for the majority of Ugandans who came to the mission school, the first need was to teach them to read. The small size of the type supplied with the press was unsuitable, and Mackay therefore cut large wooden types for use in reading sheets, and even contrived to cut and cast lead types for this purpose.

In his journal, Mackay recorded some of the difficulties entailed in printing. In October 1882 he wrote of the problems experienced with an invasion of soldier ants:

> The smell of the ink seemed to attract them, for in they came swarming all over
> the wall against which my table stood. I removed the press to the other side of
> the room and continued my work, getting ashes strewn all over the side where
> they were. But in ten minutes they had swarmed through the wall of straw
> round to my new position, and on to the press and all over the papers. It
> seemed that the ink took their fancy. I had to remove to another room, but
> there they came also, in spite of fire, ashes and all. I did not get entirely rid of
> them till I had finished the impression.

In many instances in Africa and in the South Seas, missionary work required that the native languages first be reduced to a written form before any printing could be undertaken. In New Zealand, Colenso was to devise a layout of the case designed especially for the restricted Maori alphabet, leaving the unused letters in parcels on the floor—a method that worked well until he was required to set matter also in English—when it must have taken all his Christian forebearance not to curse the CMS for failing to supply him with proper cases! Elsewhere, missionaries who themselves

Η ΠΡΟΟΔΟΣ

ΤΟΥ ΧΡΙΣΤΙΑΝΟΥ ΑΠΟΔΗΜΗΤΟΥ

ἐκ

ΤΟΥ ΠΑΡΟΝΤΟΣ ΚΟΣΜΟΥ

μέχρι

ΤΟΥ ΜΕΛΛΟΝΤΟΣ.

Ἀποδειχθεῖσα ἐν ὀπτασίας μορφῇ· μετὰ
προσθήκης σχολίων τινων, ἐξηγητι-
κῶντε καὶ ψυχωφελῶν.

▬▬▬▬▬

ΜΕΤΑΦΡΑΣΘΕΙΣΑ ΑΠΟ ΤΟ ΑΓΓΛΙΚΟΝ,

ΠΑΡΑ

Σ. Σ. ΒΙΛΣΩΝΟΣ

ΤΟΥ ΦΙΛΕΛΛΗΝΟΣ.

Ἀπὸ τὴν ἐξ Ἀμερικῆς Τυπογραφίαν·
ΕΝ ΜΕΛΙΤΗ
1824.

ILLUS. 4. American Mission Press, Malta. Title page of one of its works produced for circulation among the Greeks, 1824.

lacked any typographical understanding could put impossible demands on their printer colleagues. The missionaries' aim for a simple orthography—a single letter for a single sound—produced work with a different value for the symbols than that used in English. In Tonga in 1835, the Wesleyan missionary, David Cargill, went too far in his request to their printer, John Hobbs, for a leaflet that was to be printed in Fijian. As Hobbs reported:

> Mr. Cargill said, "I want you to cast me some Greek thetas." I said "The *Th* in Fijian is flat and I am not a type founder: take one of our spare letters and make that do." In a short time I got the thing printed giving C the sound of Th.

And today, C is still used for *Th* in Fijian.

Missionary printing was undoubtedly private in the sense of being completely uncommercial, and even when operated by trained printers (as in the New Zealand case), the presses called for a degree of improvisation more common with the amateur than the professional. But to do them justice, much more space is required than can be given here.

Chapter 3

————

THE SCHOLARLY PRESS

THE PRESSES OPERATING under the control of a patron or as a part of missionary endeavor from time to time printed scholarly texts, but the production of such books was usually not the central reason for their establishment. In many respects they can be regarded as the ancestors of the modern official and religious publishing houses that exist today. For the precursors of the modern academic publishers whose function is to publish scholarly texts we have to look elsewhere. The vast majority were, of course, produced for trade by ordinary commercial printers, and one cannot stress too highly the importance of those scholar-printers—Aldus Manutius at Venice, Froben at Basel, the Estiennes at Paris and Geneva, to name only some of the most distinguished—in providing a model for the university presses' quest for excellence. Nevertheless, the private press also had a part to play.

In two areas of scholarship the private press has been of real significance: in what could be called Near Eastern studies and in astronomy. There are excellent reasons for this. Work on the Near East and its languages calls for Arabic and other types and for compositors able to work with these languages. The availability of typefaces and craftsmen has always been a problem, and, before the emergence of university and other specialist printers with the resources for this work, several scholars found their best solution in having types cut to their own order, and in having printers work under their direct supervision. (The same is true of scholarly work calling for other "exotic" faces. Whether Amharic or Anglo-Saxon, at times similar personal endeavor has been needed.) Some of this work is discussed in Chapter 24.

The reasons for private work in astronomy are not very different. Astronomy is nothing if not an exact science, and the printing of the research results, of astronomical tables and so forth, calls for a care and knowledge which was all too rare among commercial printers. For the astronomer who had sufficient means at his disposal a press that was operated under his constant personal supervision was an obvious solution, particularly as such an arrangement removed all risk of the loss or theft of his work.

Perhaps the first scholarly private press of any importance was that of Johannes Müller, or Regiomontanus. Born in 1436 in Königsberg (from the Latinized form of which his name is taken), he went to Vienna at the age of 16 to study under George Peuerbach, one of the foremost astronomers of the time. After some years in Italy and Hungary he settled in Nuremberg about 1471. Among his pupils there was the wealthy Bernhard Walther who assisted him financially so that he was able to build an observatory and construct astronomical instruments. This was not all: Walther provided Regiomontanus with a printing press from which he published a number of astronomical books. Its activity ceased in 1475 when Regiomontanus was called to Rome to advise Pope Sixtus IV on calendar reform and was not resumed: The astronomer was murdered while in Rome.

Among the books printed at this press were an edition of Peuerbach's *Theoricae Novae Planetarum,* a series of annual almanacs, and a volume of ephemerides for the years 1475 to 1506. The ephemerides was of particular importance, because the volume contained the method of "lunar distances" Regiomontanus had discovered, which enabled mariners at sea to fix their position whenever the moon was visible. It is more than possible that Columbus navigated with these ephemerides; certainly they were used by Amerigo Vespucci on his voyage to the New World.

In his *Calendarium* of 1474 Regiomontanus made use of a volvelle, that is, paper disks cut out and fastened with threads, a sort of two-dimensional geometric substitute for the astrolabe. It was not the first publication to include movable disks, but Regiomontanus's use of volvelles was to be repeated by later astronomical writers with private presses, notably Petrus Apianus and Johann Hevelius.

Two of the Regiomontanus's publications are of a different nature from his other work: editions of Vegius's *Philalethes* and of St. Basil's *Opusculum ad Juvenes.* It has been suggested by Victor Scholderer that these may have been printed at the request of Regiomontanus's patron-pupil Walther. It is possible that the astronomer had at times to adapt his program to suit Walther's wishes.

Another important early press concerned with astronomy was that of Peter Bienewitz of Leisnig, better known as Petrus Apianus (1502–1552). Apianus was Professor of Mathematics at the University of Ingolstadt. From the press operated under his direct supervision in his own house, he issued several important and handsome books. These included his *Instrument Buch* (1533) (Illus. 5) and *Astronomicum Caesareum* (1540), which was lavishly equipped with volvelles—no less than 37 full-page examples (Illus. 6). For Apianus and his contemporaries, these were more useful than mathematical tables; despite the time consumed in their production (and the obviously greater risks to a book with movable parts) they were desirable and far more easily produced in private press work than in the commercial book trade.

Like most scholars of the time, Apianus was no narrow specialist. As a printer he is remembered no less for his contribution to classical studies in the collection of classical inscriptions, *Inscriptiones Sacrosanctae Vetustatis* (1534), edited by himself and Bartholomeus Amantius.

For this handsomely produced folio, which has been described as the finest example of early private press printing, the expenses of production were borne by Apianus's patron Raimund von Fugger. Fugger was also instrumental in obtaining the privilege (equivalent to today's copyright protection) that was bestowed on the work by the Emperor Charles V.

Both Regiomontanus and Apianus were to some extent dependent on the support of a patron. The next significant private press publishing astronomical work, that of the Dane Tycho Brahe, was not subject to the control of anyone but the astronomer himself. Tycho had been born into a noble family in 1546. By no means a typical member of the Danish nobility of the time, he had from a very early age been fascinated by the heavens, and when as young as 17 he was, despite discouragement, making skillful observations. After studying at the university in Copenhagen, he traveled to Germany, became friendly with the Landgrave William of Hesse, and had thoughts of settling in Basel. But King Frederick II of Denmark was intelligent enough to recognize Tycho's potential and granted him the little island of Hveen in Äresund, together with a sufficient income to build an observatory there.

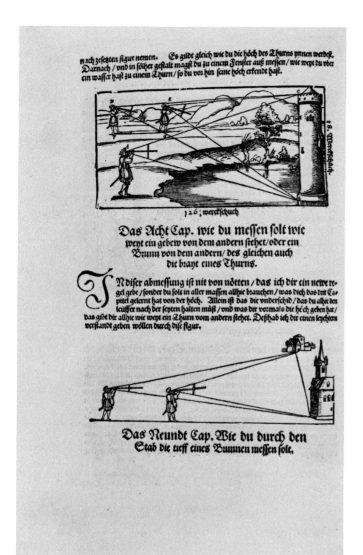

ILLUS. 5. Petrus Apianus, Ingolstadt.
A page from Apianus' *Instrument Buch*
printed at his private press, 1533.

In 1576 work on the observatory, Uraniburg, or "Castle of the Heavens," was started. The building of his great observatory, and the construction and installation of his sextants, armillae, and other instruments naturally absorbed Tycho's energies for a time. When this work had been completed, Tycho and his assistants were able to settle down to methodical observations, observations that were fuller and more exact than any made before. The idea of writing a book, a *Theatrum Astronomicum,* which would cover his entirely new theory of astronomy, then occurred to him. There were considerable difficulties in the way. Tycho doubted whether the printers in Copenhagen were competent to be entrusted with exacting work of this nature, but to go further afield and send his book to Hamburg for printing would increase the risk of loss or theft (throughout his life Tycho was almost pathologically afraid of having his work stolen). The solution was to have the printing done under his own supervision at Uraniburg; but it was not until 1584 that his printing office came into being. Its establishment was not a simple matter, as all necessary supplies and equipment—printer, presses, type, paper—had to come from abroad. Tycho was fortunate enough to be able to engage Christopher Weida, a capable German printer, to manage the press for him. In a letter written to his friend Heinrich Bruceus at Rostock Tycho explained why the press was essential: He

ILLUS. 6. Volvelle used by Petrus Apianus in *Astronomicum Caesareum,* 1540. Photograph: Courtesy of the Rare Books and Manuscripts Division, The New York Public Library, Astor, Lenox, Tilden Foundations.

was engaged in writing two books, and because plague had broken out in Copenhagen it was impossible for him to get any work done there. He was, therefore, he wrote, sending his man Joachim to Wittenburg to buy equipment. A small building to the south of the observatory was converted into a printing office, and work started in 1585. To his friend and kinsman Henrik Rantzau, Governor of Holstein, Tycho wrote enthusiastically offering to print anything he wished, and he soon followed his offer with the gift of the first work from the press, some Latin poems addressed to various friends.

The equipment of the printing office was modest: a press, a few sizes of roman and italic type, to which as time went by were added some engraved blocks of astronomical instruments and of views of the observatory. Publications such as *Diarium Astrologicum et Meteorologicum,* a calendar for the year 1587, appeared fairly rapidly. From the beginning there were difficulties in obtaining sufficient supplies of paper from Germany. Although King Frederick issued instructions that, "Our man and servant Tyge Brahe of Knudstrup must be given as many *cartas cosmographicas* or as much paper as is to be found in Our library in Our castle of Copenhagen or in Our Danish or Norwegian kingdoms or in any of Our possessions in order to assist him in his undertakings," the situation did not improve. It must have seemed to Tycho that he would never get his great work printed.

Characteristically, he decided that he would build his own paper mill at Uraniburg. He was not unfamiliar with the craft, having assisted an uncle in establishing the first paper mill in Scandinavia at Herrevad in 1572. In October 1590 he recorded that "our first book, on the most recent heavenly phenomena, is receiving its last touches from the printer. But the failure of the paper supplies has caused some delay, and prevented the work from being finished. Although I have taken the trouble to erect a papermill (at no small expense) I am without a suitable papermaker, and so this has not yet been of any use." He invoked the assistance of the Landgrave William, who offered to try to engage assistants for him at Frankfurt, but in the end Tycho managed to find the staff for himself. The paper mill had been expensive because of the elaborate system of reservoirs necessary to ensure an adequate supply of water to the mill in summer, but it worked satisfactorily. The supply of raw materials for papermaking was ensured by Tycho's influence at court: "Rag sermons" were preached throughout Denmark exhorting the people to send their rags to his paper mill.

Tycho's book, which had been held up for lack of paper, *De Mundi Aetherii Recentioribus Phaenominis,* had been started in 1588. It is a substantial quarto and was intended to form the second volume of his *Theatrum Astronomicum.* As events turned out he did not live to complete either the first or third volumes, and it remained for his greatest pupil, Johannes Kepler, to finish the work.

Even before the paper mill had been completed, the end of the Uraniburg observatory was in sight. In 1588 King Frederick II died, and the court of his successor Christian IV was filled with those jealous of the special favor in which Tycho had been held. At first King Christian continued to support the observatory, but by 1597 Tycho had been so far disgraced that the whole of the royal subsidy of his work had been withdrawn. It was in great part his own fault. He was no courtier (his pride and choleric temper prevented that), and he had neglected all other duties for his beloved astronomy; but the slander of jealous rivals also played a considerable part.

So, his income gone, Tycho abandoned Uraniburg. Determined to quit Denmark, he moved to Rostock, then to Wandesburg near Hamburg, and finally, at the invitation of the Emperor Rudolph II, to Prague.

Although Uraniburg had been abandoned, astronomy had not, and Tycho took with him all his more portable instruments and the printed sheets of his uncompleted books. According to some early accounts, he also took his printing equipment. He was certainly soon printing again. At Henrik Rantzau's home, where he stayed for a little more than six months, he continued his observations and had his handsome folio *Astronomiae Instauratae Mechanica* printed by Philip de Ohr, a printer whom he had summoned from Hamburg to work under his supervision. When Tycho moved to Prague and refounded his observatory at Benatek, the various incomplete books again followed with the baggage. After his death in 1601 many of the sheets came into the hands of a Nuremberg bookseller, G. Tambach, by whom several of the books were reissued.

Tycho Brahe's press was not the last significant private undertaking in the field of astronomy. At Danzig, the wealthy Johann Hevelius (1611–1687) established an observatory in 1641, which in its time was the best equipped in Europe. Inspired by Brahe's astronomical work, he improved on Tycho's star catalogue, made the first accurate study of the moon's surface, and produced the first systematic study of all recorded comets. It was natural for one who so admired Tycho's work to imitate his methods of publication and take a printer into his permanent employ. This printer, Simon Reininger, also served as an assistant in Hevelius's observatory and appears to have become his most accurate and valued helper. Several books of considerable importance were produced at the press, and for at least one of them, *Selenographia* (in which the chief features of the moon were named), Hevelius engraved the map himself. In 1679 the observatory, the printing house, and all the instruments were destroyed by fire. Despite the disastrous losses that Hevelius suffered as a result of the fire, including the loss of most copies of the books he had printed, the observatory was rebuilt, but the printing office does not appear to have been revived.

Hevelius's press at Danzig had not been the first to be inspired by Tycho Brahe's example. In Denmark itself, while the Uraniburg press was still active, the Dean of Ribe, Anders Sorensen

Vedel, set up a printing house with royal approval. This Liljebjerget press in 1591–1592 produced a number of scholarly texts written or edited by Vedel, of which the most important was probably his *Hundrede Udvalgde Danske Viser* (1591).

On a similar though even grander scale than the presses of Tycho and Hevelius was that started in Sweden by Hevelius's contemporary, Count Per Brahe. Lord High Steward, Governor of Finland, and the greatest landowner of the country, the count was one of the most important figures of the Swedish Golden Age. In contrast to most Continental princes of the time, he was a benevolent magnate, and while away from his own province of Visingborg he kept in constant correspondence with his officials there. In 1634 he established a high school at Visingō; 10 years later he started a paper mill. In 1666 he started a printing press, a step he had long contemplated. The printer appointed to direct it, Johann Kankel (1614–1687), was a Pomeranian who had in 1663 attempted unsuccessfully to obtain the directorship of the royal printing office in Stockholm and was eking out a living in the city. He seems to have been recommended to Per Brahe by Chancellor de la Gardie. It appears that Kankel's appointment was to the staff of the school in Visingō, but he was first and foremost printer to the count (a survival of the earlier, semiofficial presses, which is scarcely surprising because there were only nine printers in the whole of Sweden at that time).

The press was set up in a specially built house near the school. The equipment purchased was limited to a single press and a few small fonts of type, but Kankel was a competent typefounder and was well able to supplement his slender typographical resources. The count had appointed a bookbinder to assist him, and he had an apprentice who did much of the presswork, but Kankel could not have had time on his hands. Also at that time his marriage was not proving satisfactory, as the earliest surviving piece from the press shows—a letter sent to his wife (whom he was attempting to divorce) that he printed "because I know you can never read handwritten letters."

The records that have survived enable us to form a very good picture of the working of Per Brahe's press. The count would give Kankel instructions on what was to be printed or would send them to him through his secretary, and frequently he corrected the proofs of the more important books himself. Kankel was left to exercise his own initiative to a considerable extent, however, and many of the slighter pieces seem to have been printed without any specific instructions from Brahe. Now and again there were difficulties over the supply of paper, but on the whole production ran very smoothly.

Rather more than 50 works from the count's press have survived. Of the more substantial works ordered by Brahe were a number of voyages of Swedish mariners to Japan, the West Indies, and other countries; a translation of Icelandic sagas, the *Norlantz Chronicles*; and an old Swedish rhymed chronicle of Alexander the Great. There was a genealogy of the Brahe family; an edition of *Œconomia*, a household book for young noblemen which had been written by the count's grandfather in 1581; and a medical manual prepared by one of the count's army surgeons. There were probably several books printed especially for the use of the school, but of these only a song book, *Piae Cantiones*, has survived.

The works printed by Kankel on his own initiative seem usually to have been ephemeral pieces, such as verses of homage and verses in memoriam. The count made it his regular practice to spend Christmastide in his castle at Visingborg among his own people, and for his arrival Kankel prepared elaborate broadsides. Several of those that survive are in the form of maze prints (Illus. 7), typographic tours de force in the troublesome preparation of which Kankel seems to have taken special delight. In the production of these maze prints Kankel had no rival in Sweden. In other respects his work was little better than that of his contemporaries and like theirs shows German influence very markedly.

In 1680 Per Brahe died, and the government of his province was reorganized and taken over by

ILLUS. 7. Count Per Brahe, Visingo, Sweden. A maze-print made by the count's printer Johann Kankel, 1674.

the Crown. The new count, Nils Brahe, seems to have intended to pension Kankel off, but when the school was taken into the patronage of the Crown he was permitted to continue in his office, where he continued printing until at least 1685. In 1686 he was offered the appointment of university printer at Uppsala, but declined the post on the grounds of age and infirmity. When he died the following summer, the printing equipment was sold and used for the first press to be established in the town of Jönköping.

The presses of the two Brahes, Tycho and Per, represent the patron's press of the sixteenth and seventeenth centuries in their finest form. Although private presses were seldom maintained on so lavish a scale as these, there were many of them throughout Europe. Sometimes they were used for the production of provisional texts in the way that today we would resort to the photocopier. About 1600, for example, Cardinal du Perron maintained a private press in his château at Bagnolet for the express purpose of printing a preliminary edition of his works for circulation to his friends; then, having received their comments and criticisms, a revised edition would be prepared for general publication. Bossuet resorted to a similar method for his *Exposition de la Doctrine de l'Eglise Catholique,* and one can indeed find a faint echo of it in the production of Sir Winston Churchill's *History of the Second World War,* for which a first draft was set in type, and the text then largely rewritten on the basis of the proofs.

Archbishop Parker's *De Antiquitate Britannicae Ecclesiae* is sometimes said to have been the first book privately printed in England. The basis for this tradition is to be found in a note written by the archbishop's son John on the flyleaf of one of the Bodleian copies: "liber iste et collectus et impressus est propriis in aedibus Lamethiae positie" [this book was both compiled and printed in his own house at Lambeth]. There is no other evidence for the existence of a private press in Lambeth Palace, but, as Parker explained in a letter to Cecil, he intended to have the book always beside him so that he could amend the text whenever the need arose. The work exists in so many "states" that it seems possible that the archbishop had no intention of producing a final text. It would, therefore, have been convenient for the printer John Day, who printed several other books at the archbishop's expense, to have transferred one of his presses temporarily to Lambeth to carry out the printing. The edition was a small one; Parker recorded that he had not sent the book to more than four people in the kingdom, but "some men smelling the printing of it, seem to be very desirous cravers of the same."

The great Richelieu was another who both took considerable official interest in printing—he was responsible for the establishment of the Imprimerie Royale in 1640—and had sufficient personal interest to set up his own private press at the Château de Richelieu in 1633. The press was put under the direction of Estienne Migeon (or Michon) and employed a small type, *petite sédanoise,* which is thought to have been cut by Jean Jannon at Sedan and which closely resembled the fonts used by the Elzevirs. Richelieu's press had considerable virtues, and the books produced there rivaled those of the Elzevir family in quality of presswork. After Richelieu's death the press seems to have been continued by his brother, and its publications to have included a Bible and a translation by J. Desmarets of extracts from Plato, Epictetus, Plutarch, and other classical authors, published in 1653. The later history of the press is confused, however. The type appears to have passed into the hands of Protestant printers at Charenton, who used it to print surreptitious editions of various books bearing Desmarets's name and the Elzevir pressmark. An interesting account of some of these later "Richelieu" pieces appears in Charles Nodier's *Mélanges Tirées d'une Petite Bibliothèque* (Paris, 1829).

Almost exactly contemporary with Richelieu's press was that of another French statesman, Maximilien de Béthune, Duc de Sully. While he was in retirement in his Château de Sully, in the Orleanais, he had a printing office installed in the château, on which in 1637 the first two volumes of his political memoirs were printed.

In general, private presses with a scholarly purpose became less common, particularly with the growth of university presses. Nevertheless, even in university towns one finds the occasional instance of printing undertaken more privately. At Oxford in 1688, for example, Abraham Woodhead's *Motives to Holy Living* was printed as a large quarto by Obadiah Walker on the private press he had in University College. Such presses continued to be set up from time to time into the eighteenth century or even later.

We find an amusing account of one such in Casanova's *Memoirs,* with Casanova's record of a visit he paid to Count Mosca Barzi at Pescaro in 1766. When he called on the count, he was shown his library, and presented with a four-volume set of comments on the Latin poets from Ennius to the twelfth century, which the count had printed at his own press. Casanova was not impressed with the count's work. "There was nothing of his own in it," he wrote in his *Memoirs,* "all he had done was to classify each fragment in chronological order. I should have liked to see notes, comments. . . . In addition the type was not elegant, the margins were unsatisfactory, the paper of poor quality and misprints common. . . . As a consequence the book was not profitable and as the Count was not wealthy, his wife often reproached him with the money he had squandered on it." G. Natali's study in his *Idee Costumi Uomini dell Settocento* (Turin, 1926) confirms the general accuracy of Casanova's account and adds considerable extra details on Count Mosca Barzi's life and publications. Casanova's own story of his visit, as given in the authoritative Brockhaus-Plon edition of his *Histoire de Ma Vie,* differs in many ways from that given in earlier editions, such as that in Machen's translation.

At much the same time that Count Mosca Barzi was squandering his money on his Latin poets, the antiquary Edward Rowe Mores (1730–1778) ran a press of very considerable interest in England. Mores, a typical antiquary of his time, a saxonist, and one of the earliest figures in the field of life insurance, seems to have bought a small press soon after taking his degree at the Queen's College in 1750. A number of slight pieces from his press that he printed after his move from Oxford to London and later to Low Leyton in Essex in 1759 are preserved in the Bodleian Library. The chief work printed at his press, which is the principal reason for his name being remembered by printing historians today, was his *Dissertation upon English Typographical Founders and Founderies* (1778), the pioneer history of typefounding in Britain. Eighty copies of the book were printed, and it is evident from the quirks of style and eccentricity of arrangement that the type was set by Mores himself.

Mores died in November 1778 "of a mortification in his leg, which he suffered to reach his vitals, sitting in an arm-chair, while the workmen passed through the room to repair the next. He would not admit physician or nurse; and scarcely his own mother." The copies of the *Dissertation* passed into the hands of John Nichols, who added an eight-page appendix and published it, at a price of six shillings, in 1779. The edition prepared by Harry Carter and Christopher Ricks (Oxford, 1961) contains a considerable amount of information on Mores's press and a list of its equipment and the prices realized when it was sold by auction after Mores's death, information of a kind that is all too rare for early private presses.

Chapter 4

———

THE PRESS AS AN
EDUCATIONAL TOY

And Frederick William he, of Saxony the lord
A private press maintain'd, with Printers round his board.

So WILLIAM BLADES TRANSLATED a passage written by Johann Rist in his *Depositio Cornuti Typographici* (1677). The Friedrich Wilhelm II, Duke of Saxe-Altenburg, of whom he was writing, maintained a private press of the quasi-official kind we have already described, from which a sumptuous edition of Luther's works was published between 1661 and 1664. Even before this time rulers of Saxony had been interested in printing; another Friedrich Wilhelm had set up a press at Torgau in 1596. At this press operations were under the direction of a printer, Jakob Popperich, and a schoolmaster, Johann Wankel, and it is possible that it was an early example of many presses maintained by royalty as toys to be used in the education of their children.

Such use of the press for the education of princes did not, of course, necessarily call for the special establishment of a private press. In 1648, for example, the 10-year-old Louis XIV was taken on a visit to the Imprimerie Royale and "helped" with the production of an edition of the *Mémoires* of Philippe de Commines. The Imprimerie Royale had been established only eight years earlier and, because of the serious interest taken by the Bourbons in its work, was to become the supreme example of a royal press. Rather similarly, although making the mountain come to Mahomet, on February 15, 1731, "a printing press and cases for composing were put up at St. James's house for their majesties to see the noble art of printing," reported the *Gentleman's Magazine*. "His Royal Highness the Duke [of Cumberland] wrought at one of the cases, to compose for the press a little book of his own writing, call'd, *The laws of Dodge Hare*. The two youngest princesses likewise compos'd their names, &c., under the direction of Mr. S. Palmer, printer in this city."

Nevertheless, there are more than a few instances of private presses being set up deliberately because of their usefulness in making education attractive. One can probably dismiss the toy press exhibited at the 1877 Caxton Celebration, which was purported to have been used by Charles I as a child, since it seems very likely that it was made much later than the early seventeenth century. On

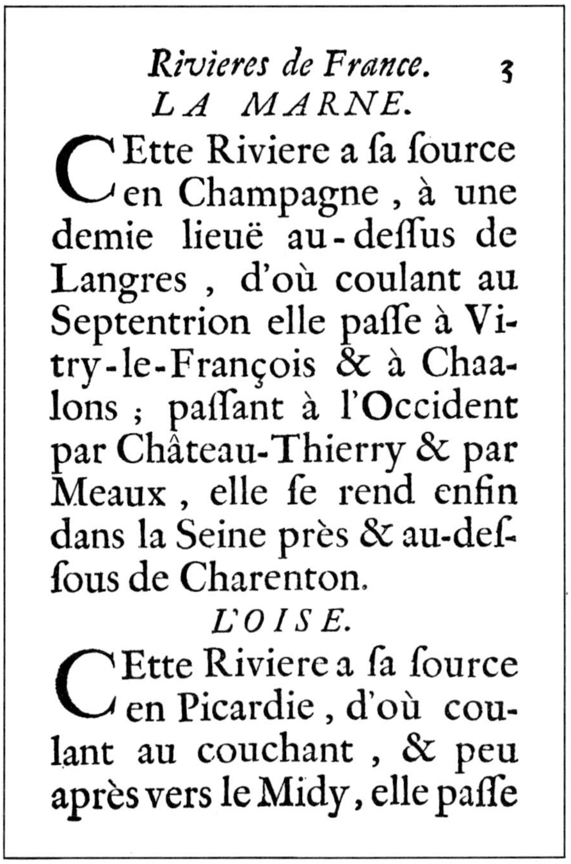

> *Rivieres de France.* 3
> *LA MARNE.*
>
> CEtte Riviere a ſa ſource en Champagne , à une demie lieuë au-deſſus de Langres , d'où coulant au Septentrion elle paſſe à Vitry-le-François & à Chaalons ; paſſant à l'Occident par Château-Thierry & par Meaux , elle ſe rend enfin dans la Seine près & au-deſſous de Charenton.
>
> *L'OISE.*
>
> CEtte Riviere a ſa ſource en Picardie , d'où coulant au couchant , & peu après vers le Midy, elle paſſe

ILLUS. 8. Imprimerie du Cabinet du Roi, Paris. A page from *Cours des Principaux Fleuves et Rivières de l'Europe,* 1718. Set up, and perhaps printed, by Louis XV.

the other hand, a miniature printing office installed in the Tuileries in 1718 is well authenticated. The press was set up for Louis XV, and the little boy, then eight years of age, was taught the rudiments of the craft by a distinguished Paris printer, Jacques Collombat. Louis set the type and may even have printed one or two copies of some lessons in geography entitled *Cours des Principaux Fleuves et Rivières de l'Europe. Composé & Imprimé par Louis XV . . . À Paris, dans l'Imprimerie du Cabinet de S.M* (Illus. 8). The press survived until 1730, and nearly 50 pieces were issued from it, though not many, one imagines, produced by the king's hand!

Louis XVI, when Dauphin, was also taught how to print by A. M. Lottin, and in 1776, at the age of 12, produced an edition of *Maximes Morales et Politiques Tirées de Télémaque, Imprimées par Louis Auguste, Dauphin.* A curious and well-authenticated story is told of this book by Charles Nodier in his *Mélanges Tirées d'une Petite Bibliothèque:* When the Dauphin had finished printing the 25 copies of his book, he bound them up for presentation. The first copy was naturally for his grandfather, the king, who took the book, opened it, and read the first maxim his eye chanced upon. For a man as preoccupied with thoughts of future revolution as Louis XV is known to have been, what he read was profoundly significant. It was a passage stating that once rulers broke the barriers of good faith and of honor, they could not restore the confidence necessary to them or reestablish a respect for the principles of justice in their subjects; they would become tyrants, and their subjects rebels, and only through revolution would an equilibrium be restored. It was too much for the king. "M. le Dauphin," he observed, "votre ouvrage est fini, *rompez la planche.*" As Nodier says, since the book was already complete the king could only have been playing on words to refer to the future.

Louis XVI never lost his interest in printing. A year or two before the Revolution he was shown the new press that Philippe-Denis Pierres had devised and was so pleased with it that he printed many sheets on it himself.

In England royal presses of this sort were much less common. Despite the interest shown by Charles II in the sciences, his direct experience of printing seems to have been limited to a visit he paid shortly before his death to the "frost fair," which was set up on the frozen Thames in January and February of 1683–1684. The royal party included the queen, the Duke of York and his wife, Princess Anne and her husband Prince George of Denmark. A fly sheet recording their visit was printed on a press on the ice. Presses producing keepsakes were regular sideshows at these frost fairs, of which there were others in 1739–1740, 1788–1789, and 1813–1814. As stated in John Evelyn's diary, in 1683–1684, "the Thames before London was . . . planted with boothes in formal streetes, all sorts of trades and shops furnish'd and full of commodities, even until a printing presse, where the people and ladyes took a fancy to have their names printed. . . . The humour took so universally, that 'twas estimated the printer gain'd £5 a day for printing a line onely, at sixpence a time."

It is not untypical that in France the merits of the press for teaching should have been exploited, whereas in England printing was regarded as little more than a rude trade suitable for fairground sideshows. Nevertheless, there was at least one royal press in England in the nineteenth century— that at Frogmore Lodge, Windsor. It was set up during the residence there of Queen Charlotte in 1809. Her companion, Miss Ellis Cornelia Knight, was closely concerned in its operations, editing a volume of translations from the German, and contributing (with Samuel Rogers) to a volume of miscellaneous poems in 1812. Most of its work was uninteresting (abridged chronologies of the history of various European countries, evidently for the use of children) and wretchedly produced. The printer employed, E. Harding, appears to have been a jobbing printer in Windsor.

The use of the press in education was not limited to royalty, and there is plenty of evidence of small presses being used by the aristocracy in this way, particularly in eighteenth-century France. An interesting and very little-known press of this sort belonged to the last Marquis de Bercy, although it is far from typical in that it was operative at the height of the French Revolution in 1791. That the press is little known is scarcely surprising, because only one title was produced, and that is of extreme rarity: *Fables et Oeuvres Diverses,* by Maximilian-Emanuel-Charles Malon, Marquis de Bercy (Illus. 9).

This book was originally issued in parts, and was never completed, printing being brought to a halt after four parts had been produced. It was printed by the marquis's 11-year-old son a year after his father's death in 1790, on a press set up in the Château de Bercy, which then stood on the outskirts of Paris, near to the Porte de Charenton. In the preface, addressed to his uncle and aunt, his godparents, the young printer gave this engaging account of the book:

> What! do we read the name of Charles Malon on the titlepage of a book? And
> has our nephew, our little cousin, turned printer? This is indeed a puzzle . . . I
> can well understand your surprise, my dear Godparents, and I hasten to give
> you the explanation.
>
> My good friends M de Praslin and M de Montesquiou had been given little
> English printing sets as New Year gifts. With these they could print a few lines.
> This gave them very great pleasure, which they were not slow in letting me
> share. After I had played with them, my enthusiasm showed my tutor how
> much I would like to have a printing press of my own. Always anxious to
> satisfy my wishes when they were reasonable, he sought a way of enabling me
> to print more complete and accurate than these toys. Without saying anything
> to me about it he had little cases made which were perfect models of

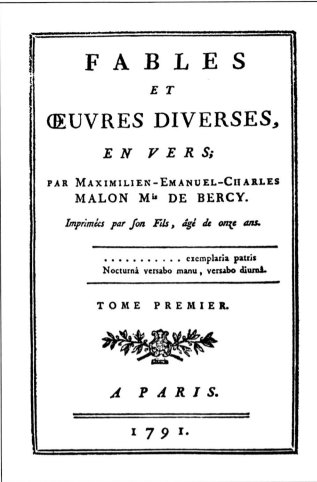

ILLUS. 9. Imprimerie de Bercy, Paris. Title page of the book printed by the 11-year-old Marquis de Bercy, 1791.

compositors' cases—to be brief, a complete small printing office was made of which I knew nothing until it was brought to me. You will be able to imagine what a marvellous surprise I had! My tutor had paid all the costs, which I am paying back out of my pocket money.

It was necessary to learn how to use my equipment, and that demanded much practice. As with Renard in the fable,

D'abord je m'y pris mal, puis un peu mieux . . .

At last, thanks to the efforts of my tutor (and you will be able to guess how much he has contributed to my success) I have been able to embark on a project very dear to my heart, and I have the double satisfaction of knowing through and through the writings of my dear father . . . and of offering them to you, my Godparents. May I, in sending them to you, remind you of the love you had for him, and hope that (as I long to resemble him in every way) I may succeed to this love?

As it was entirely for you that I have printed this book (of which I have produced thirty copies) I was in a hurry to reap the fruits of my labours, and so have adopted the method of sending it to you in parts. Because I can spend only my free time on the work, and because I have only enough type to print four pages at a time, its completion will be slow. And I shall be afraid of losing heart if I do not receive your approbation.

The young printer's godparents evidently did approve of his work, since four parts of the book, a total of 144 pages, were completed. But in 1791 revolutionary fervor in Paris was at its height. It was probably only thanks to the protection of the Jacobin Jean Tallien, who was later to secure the downfall of Robespierre and was himself a printer and the son of a former family steward, that the marquis had remained undisturbed so long. It could not last, and in 1792 the Château de Bercy was decreed state property.

Chapter 5

THE ARISTOCRATIC PLAYTHING

The *Gentleman's Magazine* had not been the only periodical to report on Samuel Palmer's demonstration of printing at St. James's Palace in 1731. A fuller report appeared in *The Craftsman,* which concluded with the observation that:

> It must be the greatest Mortification to *Those,* whose guilt makes Them enemies
> to this useful Invention, to see it encouraged by their Majesties, in such a
> Manner, and even to behold some of the Royal Family initiating Themselves in
> the noble Arts of *Writing* and *Printing.*—We could wish that our *Nobility* and
> *Gentry* would follow this Royal Example, and set up a *Printing-Press* in their
> Houses; which, we apprehend, would be a much more polite, as well as a more
> instructive Amusement for Themselves and their Heirs, than the modern fash-
> ionable Diversions of *Billiard-Tables* and *Fox-hunting.*

A cutting of this passage was to be pasted at the beginning of the journal of the most famous of eighteenth-century private presses, that of Horace Walpole at his Gothic villa Strawberry Hill.

The Strawberry Hill Press, which was set up in one of the outbuildings of Walpole's house in 1757 (Illus. 10), was, in the words of Wilmarth S. Lewis:

> for his own pleasure and convenience; he would bring out only books and
> trifles by his friends and himself and unpublished manuscripts of antiquarian
> interest. He would control their distribution. He let Dodsley, the leading
> London publisher, sell some; others he sold for charity—the poor of
> Twickenham, a learned and indigent tailor, his friend Bentley—but most he
> gave away. His political pieces continued to appear anonymously in London.
> Strawberry was not to be defiled by them.

The first stage was the appointment of a printer and the installation of equipment. In his first printer, William Robinson, who started work on June 25, 1757, Walpole had chosen moderately well; during the two years that he worked for Walpole he printed competently and extensively, if not exceptionally well. But Robinson left in a huff in March 1759: "My printer, who was a foolish

ILLUS. 10. The Printing Office at Strawberry Hill. Photograph: Courtesy of The Lewis Walpole Library, Yale.

Irishman, and who took himself for a genius, and who grew angry when I thought him extremely the former and not the least of the latter, has left me," Walpole wrote to Lord Zouch. His next few appointments to the position were most unsuccessful, and the record in Walpole's *Journal of the Printing Office* reads very amusingly:

1759 March 5th	Robinson the Printer went away
29th	My new printer, Benjamin Williams, came
May 25th	He went away
June 19th	James Lister, a new Printer, came; staid but a week.

Eventually, after a number of printers had departed rapidly, leaving debts or pregnant girls behind them, Walpole appointed Thomas Kirgate as his printer in 1765. Kirgate was no more skilled at his craft than his predecessors, but he fitted into the Strawberry Hill household well enough to become Walpole's secretary, librarian, and curator of prints, remaining in his employ until Walpole's death in 1797. Yet he too was not an altogether desirable servant, abusing Walpole's confidence in his secretarial capacity and as printer issuing several forgeries of Strawberry Hill books.

Wilmarth S. Lewis has claimed that the press "has to its credit the first editions of more books of lasting interest than any other private press in England before or since." Certainly the publishing program started splendidly, with an edition of two of Gray's *Odes* (Illus. 11). "On Monday next the Officina Arbuteana opens in form," wrote Walpole to Chute on July 12, 1757. "The Stationers' Company, that is Mr. Dodsley, Mr. Tonson, &c. are summoned to meet here on Sunday night. And with what do you think we open? *Cedite, Romani Impressores*—with nothing under *Graii Carmina*. I found him in town last week: he had brought his two Odes to be printed. I snatched them out of Dodsley's hands, and they are to be the first-fruits of my press."

The books printed at the Strawberry Hill Press during the 32 years of its life included a good number from Walpole's own pen, including his *Catalogue of the Royal and Noble Authors of England* (1758), *Anecdotes of Painting in England* (1762–1763), *Hieroglyphic Tales* (1785), and *The Mysterious Mother* (1768), the least bad of tragedies in a period of bad tragedy; but not, surprisingly, his *Castle of Otranto*. The press also produced guides to the contents of Strawberry Hill and tickets of admission to view the house and similar pieces, but it was in no sense a vanity press. Much important material by other authors was also produced: editions of Lucan, of the autobiography of Lord Herbert of Cherbury, of Hamilton's *Memoirs of the Count de Grammont,* and several others of lasting importance.

Walpole's press had another much less serious side that fitted better with his claim that "present

ILLUS. 11. Strawberry Hill Press, Twickenham. Title page of Gray's *Odes*, the first book printed at Walpole's Press, 1757.

amusement is all my object"; this was a side much more characteristic of the aristocrat's plaything. On May 17, 1763, for example, Walpole recorded in his journal that "Mesdames de Boufflers and Dusson, two French Ladies who came to England this year, breakfasted at Strawberry Hill, and were carried to see the Printinghouse; where desiring to see something printed, the following lines which had been set ready, were taken off."

> *The Press speaks.*
> *For Madame de Boufflers.*
> *The gracefull Fair, who loves to know,*
> *Nor dreads the North's inclement Snow;*
> *Who bids her polish'd accent wear*
> *The British diction's harsher air;*
> *Shall read her praise in ev'ry clime,*
> *Where types can speak or Poets rhyme*

Strawberry Hill produced a good many of these trifles, which were typical of the eighteenth-century private press, in France as much as in England. There is a story of Louis XV visiting a press and finding a pair of spectacles lying on a sheet of paper. On examining the sheet through them, he found that it contained "a panegyric of his person as majestic as it was delicate. 'Ah,' exclaimed the King, 'these lenses are too strong. They make everything appear larger than life!' " Although such pieces today fetch very high prices, it was not through these that Strawberry Hill achieved the fame it had in its own time. And of its fame there is no doubt. As early as 1759 broadsheets were being hawked in the London streets with the imprint of Strawberry Hill on them to make them sell, and in 1792 Walpole wrote that "some years ago Count Potocki brought me a message from the present King of Poland . . . desiring my *Anecdotes of Painting*. It distressed me as they were out of print. . . . I was reduced to buy a second-hand set . . . and, though the original set sold for less than thirty shillings, I was forced to pay thirteen guineas from their scarcity."

During the nineteenth century Walpole himself was extraordinarily misunderstood and undervalued—"a gentleman-usher at heart," said Macauley—and Strawberry Hill books were also attacked, although they never lost their value to book collectors. In 1854, for example, Bolton Corney commented in *Notes and Queries* on Walpole's edition of the *Memoirs of the Count de Grammont*, "In reprinting the dedication to Madame du Deffand, I had to insert *eight* accents to make decent French of it! The *avis* is a mere medley of fragments: I could not ask a compositor to set it up!" And so on, and so on. All this would not have worried Walpole. Writing to his friend Mason in May 1773, he had confided, "I have not the patience necessary for correcting the press. Gray was ever reproaching me with it, and in one of the letters I have just turned over, he says, 'Pray send me the proof-sheets to correct, for you know you are not capable of it.' It is very true; and I hope future edition-mongers will say of those of Strawberry Hill, they have all the beautiful negligence of a gentleman."

From the point of view of book design, modern authorities have not been flattering. Stanley Morison conceded that the press encouraged interest in typography but insisted that much finer work was done by commercial printers of the day. D.B. Updike was more forthright: "Among its rather indifferent printing the . . . Lucan is worthy of moderate praise," was the best that he could find to say. Yet the books have a certain modest elegance of their own and are without doubt a pleasure to handle and read.

The Strawberry Hill Press was almost the only private press of any importance in England in the eighteenth century. In France *The Craftsman*'s recommendation to the nobility and gentry would have been entirely superfluous, as in the seventeenth and eighteenth centuries there were many such aristocratic playthings. These presses were particularly common at Versailles, where the mother of Louis XVI had a little press in the 1750s that the Duc de Bourgogne continued to run in the following decade. In her apartments *"au nord"* Madame de Pompadour also had a small press from which an edition of Corneille's *Rodogune*, with an etching by her hand, was issued in 1770. Nearly all of these were serious presses, and their work had a high moral tone about it. The Duc de Bourgogne's edition of a prayer book for the use of the royal family is typical. In complete contrast was another earlier royal press. In 1730 the Duchesse de Bourbon-Condé, aided and abetted by the unsavory Abbé Grécourt, had a little press ("L'Imprimerie du Vourst") installed in the Palais de Bourbon, from which she issued an odd little volume called *Maranzaciniana*. This was a collection of strange sayings and *sottises* (a perfect parody of the typical *ana* of the period, in fact) of a certain Maranzac, who had formerly been an equerry in the service of Louis XIV's son, and after the latter's death had been taken into the duchess's household as a sort of court buffoon. A chapter in Nodier's *Mélanges* is devoted to this piece of nonsense.

Not only the royal family and courtiers at Versailles had their own presses, but many presses were also scattered in the homes of the nobility around France at different times in the eighteenth century. In 1720 at the Château de Fresne Chancellor d'Aguesseau printed a memorial volume on the life, death, character, and manners of his father for circulation among members of his family; and in 1735 the Marquis de Lussay issued a *Recueil de Differentes Choses, 1663–1726*. In 1778 Bochart de Saron had a press in his house in Paris; and in 1778 the Duc de Choiseuil printed his *Memoires* in his Château de Chanteloup.

Such volumes of memoirs, family histories, and the like have been characteristic of private presses at all times, but they seem to typify the aristocratic amateurs of the *ancien régime* in particular. How many of these were set or printed by the owners of the presses is questionable, and their work is not generally of much interest today. Two such amateur enterprises stand out as being much closer in spirit to modern private presswork. The first is the press of Capperonnier de Gauffecourt, a friend of Voltaire and of Madame d'Epinay, who had a press of her own at Geneva. In 1763 de Gauffecourt printed his own *Traité de la Relieure des Livres* in an edition of 25 copies for presentation to his friends (Illus. 12). As a bookbinding manual it is not very good, but it was the first separately published account of the craft. The other was that of the papermaker Léorier de Lisle, who in 1784 produced 50 copies of Pelée de Varennes's *Les Loisirs des Bords du Loing ou Recueil des Piéces Fugitives* at Montargis. De Lisle's book is a delightful example of eighteenth-century French typography, for which he had made the paper using grass, lime-tree bark, and other fibers. For subsequent experiments with unusual fibers de Lisle went elsewhere to have his sheets printed. The *Oeuvres du Marquis de Villette* was printed in London in 1786 in two editions (one on paper from lime-tree bark, the other on marshmallow fibers) at the back of which were bound single sheet specimens of papers made from many other unfamiliar fibers, from dandelion roots to hops. (In this

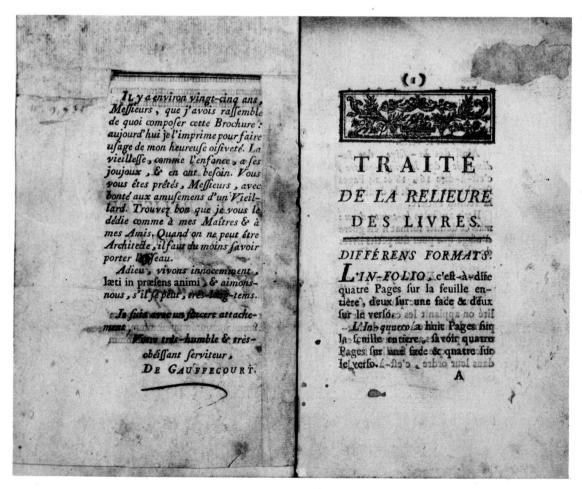

ILLUS. 12. Capperonnier de Gauffecourt, Switzerland. *Traité de la Relieure des Livres*, 1763; the first separately printed account of bookbinding—written, printed, and bound by an amateur.

use of outside printers, de Lisle was anticipating John Mason's Twelve by Eight Press, with its employment of outside printers to complement his own papermaking experiments.)

It was into such a situation that Benjamin Franklin entered when he was appointed the first American minister to the French court in 1776. It was natural indeed that a man who thought of himself first and last as a printer should install a press in his residence at Passy. The conventional picture is of the old man (he was then in his seventies) using his press as a relaxation from the cares of public service, to teach his grandson Benjamin Franklin Bache how to print, and producing the series of "bagatelles" that charmed the French salons of the time. Yet there was a much more serious side to Franklin's work at the Passy Press. As well as the bagatelles, which were propaganda of the subtlest sort for the American cause, Franklin produced a range of official documents—blank passports, orders against American bank balances in France, promissory notes and bonds, regulations about the capture of prizes at sea, and similar pieces. All of these demonstrate how much Franklin had to work on his own initiative as the American Minister Plenipotentiary; the Passy Press was virtually a government printing office as well as the hobby of an aged man. How much more than this Franklin's press was still remains to be discovered. The bagatelles and official pieces were small pieces, and the first dated document from the Passy Press was a dinner invitation in July 1779. Yet in 1777 and 1778 large purchases of type were made; in 1780 Franklin had at least three presses, and in the same year he bought typefounding equipment extensively. Four employees, a foreman and three assistants, were engaged full time in typefounding at this time, and even allowing for the fact that some of this type was produced for American printers cut off from their normal English sources of supply, the Passy Press was obviously operating on a much larger scale than can be explained by the pieces known to have been produced.

The French Revolution naturally put a stop to much of the amateur printing of the aristocracy, but such presses did not necessarily disappear straight away, as we have seen from the Marquis de Bercy's little press. In at least one case the Revolution was the principal cause of such a press's being set up.

The events of the Revolution in France, which compelled so many of the aristocracy to become *emigrés,* persuaded the Duc de Luynes that it would be wise to retire to the country. He and his wife and family spent the troubled years of the 1790s living quietly and discreetly at the Château de Dampierre. His wife, Guyonne de Montmorency-Laval, had at court been a lady-in-waiting to Marie-Antoinette, a post for which she seems to have been singularly ill suited and which she disliked heartily. She was something of a bluestocking and was a strong masculine character, who always dressed in an extraordinarily unfashionable manner and, at times, in men's clothes. Country life must have wearied her. When, in company with Madame Récamier, she visited the printing house of Ballanche, she was unable to restrain her enthusiasm. Hoisting up her skirts, she set herself before a case of type and quickly and accurately set up a passage, to the amazement and admiration (so we are told) of all the workmen. She had found the ideal hobby.

A press and equipment were quickly installed at Dampierre, and in 1797 the first book from the press was issued, *Robinson Crusoe,* with an interlinear French translation by the duchess. From then until 1810 a steady stream of books came from the press—translations of Gray's *Elegy,* of the life of Dean Swift, anthologies of verse "for the use of friends living in the country," and many others. The duchess appears to have done most of the typesetting and presswork as well as editing the texts herself. She was not interested in binding, and the books were sewn into paper covers by an Irish lady, Madame Felz, who lived at the château. In 1810, however, an imperial decree by Napoleon forbade all such private presses, and the duchess was compelled to abandon her hobby. Instead of printing she devoted herself to writing, and more than 40 volumes of her manuscripts survive at Dampierre.

Another private press that disappeared as a result of Napoleon's decree was that owned by the Baron de Villenfagne, a historian. While he was Burgomaster of Liège in the 1790s the baron had had a press erected in his house from which he published his *Histoire de Spa* among other works. This press fades into insignificance beside another Belgian private press of about the same period, that of the Mareschal Prince de Ligne. In his magnificent Château de Bel Oeil the prince set up a small press about 1780, on which it amused him to print small editions of books, mainly from his own hand, for presentation to his friends. So enthusiastic was the prince, in fact, that some authorities have suggested that he had a second press in his house in Brussels. Among the books he printed by far the best known is his *Coup d'Oeil sur Bel Oeil* of which 50 copies were produced in 1781 (Illus. 13). Some of his other works, such as his *Mélanges de Litterature,* published with the imprint "à

ILLUS. 13. Imprimerie de Bel Oeil, Belgium. Title page of the most famous of the books from the Prince de Ligne's private press, 1781.

Philisopolis" in 1783, are of equal interest. It seems that much of the printing was done by the prince himself, with assistance from his son and perhaps from his chaplain. It has been surmised that he also bound the books, so far do surviving copies fall below professional standards!

In 1794 the events of the Revolution compelled the prince to leave his country, his home, his fortune, and his press, and he retired to Vienna where he set up house in the suburbs, living in straitened circumstances. Here he once more set up his press, and between 1795 and 1811 a collected edition of his works, *Mélanges Militaires, Litteraires et Sentimentaires,* was issued.

The most richly endowed of all eighteenth-century private presses was the one that Frederick the Great of Prussia maintained "*au donjon du château*" in Berlin. Even before he succeeded to the throne, Frederick had been contemplating the operation of a press at Rheinsberg, in order to print an edition of Voltaire's *Henriade.* His original idea was not to print the work at his own press but to have it produced by the English engraver John Pine. He had been greatly impressed by Pine's *Horace,* published between 1733 and 1737, and dreamed of a *Henriade* engraved by Pine with decorations by the Prussian artist Knobelsdorff. Pine was busy with other work, and demanded seven years in which to produce the book. Neither Voltaire nor Frederick was willing to wait so long, and so they turned to the idea of a carefully printed edition to be produced under Frederick's personal supervision. In October 1739 Frederick wrote to Voltaire to say that a printing office was to be installed in the tower he was having built to house his library at Rheinsberg. Soon afterwards Algarotti was asked to find out the cost of purchasing printing equipment in England, Frederick wrote a preface, and the artist's preliminary sketches for the designs were well advanced. "No matter what the cost, we shall create a masterpiece, worthy of its text," Frederick wrote. But the *Henriade* was never to appear. On the death of his father, Frederick had to leave Rheinsberg for Berlin, and for some years afterwards cares of state prevented him from contemplating his own personal press.

Eventually, however, Frederick found the leisure to return to his dreams of having books for private circulation printed under his personal direction. As a result of researches by Hans Droysen and Paul Seidel in the Hohenzollern archives at the beginning of this century, it has become clear that in 1748 the official royal printer Christian Friedrich Henning was instructed to equip a printing office in the king's residence. The engraver George Friedrich Schmidt, who in 1743 had been tempted to return from a brilliant career in Paris to become court engraver, was placed in charge of the press's operations.

The first book to be printed by the new press was, appropriately enough, an edition of Frederick's own literary pieces: *Œuvres du Philosophe de Sans Souci,* published "*au donjon du château, avec privilège d'Apollon, MDCCP*" (Illus. 14). The first part of the first volume, a mock-epic poem about the French ambassador Valory entitled *Palladion,* had in fact been printed in 1749, but the king could not bring himself to pass proofs without changing and expanding his text. As he wrote to Algarotti, "Vous faites bien plus sagement que moi, avec vos ouvrages; vous les limez et après vous imprimez; pour moi j'imprime, je me repens et puis je corrige."

Despite the secrecy with which *Palladion* had been printed, knowledge of its existence leaked out, and Frederick was considerably embarrassed by a request, which Valory transmitted from the French court, for a copy—so embarrassed, in fact, that even his friend Voltaire was told that if he wished to see a copy he could do so only in Berlin. This was not an outright refusal, for Voltaire was already planning to come. When Voltaire arrived in July 1750 he found the press's second book, Frederick's *Mémoires pour Servir à l'Histoire de la Maison de Brandebourg,* already well advanced. After Voltaire had read through the sheets, covering them with his characteristic ironic comments (Illus. 15), printing was interrupted so that the book could be rewritten. The corrected edition (Illus. 16), was completed the following year, and copies were distributed to Valory and others. Meanwhile, the

ŒUVRES

DU

PHILOSOPHE

DE

SANS-SOUCI.

Au Donjon du Chateau.

Avec Privilége d'Apollon.

M. DCC. L.

ILLUS. 14. Au Donjon du Château, Berlin. Title page of one of Frederick the Great's works, printed at his private press, 1750.

scandal of *Palladion* was still alive, and in order to put an end to it the king decided to suppress the offending edition of his *Œuvres* and to reprint it in a single volume, removing some pieces and adding others, such as his essay on the art of war. A copy of the new edition, completed in 1751, was sent to Valory: "Je ne saurais vous envoyer ce que votre politesse vous engage de me demander avec tant d'instance," wrote Frederick. "Je n'ai fait tirer que très peu d'exemplaires de la dernier édition et les anciennes sont si imparfaites et si incomplètes que je me propose d'en faire bruler tous les exemplaires." As far as he was concerned, the affair was now closed.

These early books were not different in essence from the work produced by other aristocratic presses, although undertaken on a grander scale. Frederick's press had another more serious side to it, just as Franklin at Passy was more than a printer of bagatelles. In 1752 a small octavo manual, *Principes Généraux de la Guerre Appliqué à la Tactique et à la Discipline des Troupes Prussiennes,* was printed under conditions of the strictest secrecy and circulated to some (though it seems not all) of the generals commanding his forces. Their silence on the book was ordered, and to confuse the issue

FRÉDÉRIC-GUILLAUME,
LE GRAND ELECTEUR.

RÉDÉRIC-GUILLAUME nâquit à Berlin, le 6. de Février 1620. Il reçut le nom de GRAND, & il étoit effectivement. Le Ciel l'avoit formé exprès, pour rétablir, par fon activité, l'ordre, dans

N 3

[Voltaire's handwritten suggestions for changes]

ILLUS. 15. Au Donjon du Château, Berlin. Proof page from Frederick the Great's *History of the House of Brandenburg,* with Voltaire's suggestions for changes.

FRÉDÉRIC-GUILLAUME,
LE GRAND ELECTEUR.

RÉDÉRIC-GUILLAUME nâquit à Berlin le 6. de février 1620. Il étoit digne du nom de GRAND, que fes peuples & fes voifins lui ont donné d'une commune voix. Le ciel l'avoit formé exprès

O   pour

ILLUS. 16. Au Donjon du Château, Berlin. Page from Frederick the Great's *History of the House of Brandenburg,* as published, 1751.

in the event of a leak an octavo edition of another military work, selections from the commentaries of the Chevalier de Folard on Polybius "pour l'usage d'un officer," was prepared for circulation to his commanders.

Only one more book was to be printed "*au donjon du château,*" the king's *Réflexions sur les Talens Militaires . . . de Charles XII*. Frederick was unable to supervise the printing personally, since he was away in the battlefield, but this did not prevent him from finding fault with the edition sent to him in November 1759 by the Marquis d'Argens to whom he had entrusted the production. "Les Huns et les Visigoths s'ils avaient eu des imprimeurs, n'auraient pas plus mal fait," he commented acidly. A corrected edition was hastily prepared and accepted without comment by the king in January 1760. By now the Seven Years' War was well under way, and Frederick had no more time for such pleasures. Even after the end of the war, the king had no heart for printing, and his press was never revived.

Occasionally such presses were to be found in the unlikeliest places. Robinson, in his *Last Days of Bishop Heber,* recorded that the Rajah of Tanjore in south India had a good library and philosophical instruments and adds, "that of which he is justly proud, as the rarest curiosity of an Indian court, is an English printing press worked by native Christians, on which they struck off a sentence in Mahratta in the Bishop's presence, in honour of his visit."

Chapter 6

———

PRIVATE PRINTING AND THE BIBLIOMANIA

THE EARLY YEARS of the nineteenth century in England, the period of the Napoleonic wars, were also a period in which book collecting was to boom. An aristocratic interest in early printed books, assiduously fanned by Dr. Dibdin in his *Bibliomania* (1809, enlarged edition 1811) reached its height at the celebrated sale of the library of the Duke of Roxburghe, which spread over some six days in May and June 1812, and at which the Marquis of Blandford paid the previously unheard-of price of £2,260 for the famous Valdorfer *Boccaccio*.

It was in celebration of this sale that the Roxburghe Club was founded. Dibdin and some 17 like-minded friends agreed to meet for a celebration dinner annually, at which toasts were to be drunk to "the immortal memory of John Duke of Roxburghe, Christopher Valdarfer, Gutenberg, Fust and Schoeffer . . . and to the cause of bibliomania all over the world." In this it probably did not differ from many convivial meetings arranged to celebrate prize fights, race meetings, and the like. Had this been all there was to the Roxburghe Club it would probably have survived only a few years, but at the first anniversary dinner on June 17, 1814, it was proposed and agreed, as James Markland recorded in the *Gentleman's Magazine*, that "upon each successive anniversary, one of the members is to produce a reprint of a scarce and curious tract, or to print some original manuscript, and the number of copies will be confined to that of [the members of] the Club." With the first of these books, Bolland's reprint of the Earl of Surrey's translation of Virgil (1814), the Roxburghe Club became the first of the many publishing societies that were so prominent a feature of nineteenth-century England.

The idea of reprinting early works was by no means new in 1813; it was at least a century old. The Gothic spirit that Horace Walpole understood so well, and the reprints of early ballads in Percy's *Reliques* and in the work of Ritson and Sir Walter Scott must all have stimulated the interest of the original Roxburghe members and of other contemporary book collectors.

Few of the Roxburghe Club's publications were printed at private presses, although they were usually well printed and were for a restricted audience in the private press tradition. In any case, a further account of its work has been rendered superfluous by Nicolas Barker's *The Publications of the Roxburghe Club, 1814–1962* (Cambridge, for presentation to members of the Roxburghe Club, 1964). Its work was closely akin to that of a number of private presses that flourished in the early years of the nineteenth century, particularly of presses owned by wealthy book collectors who used them for reprinting scarce works or manuscripts never before printed. These were not the elegant playthings of Walpole and others; they had a serious scholarly purpose.

"Present amusement is all my object," Walpole had written of Strawberry Hill. Much the same could be said of the presses of the bibliomania, with the difference being in the antiquarian pursuits from which their owners derived their amusement. The earliest such pursuit in fact preceded the foundation of the Roxburghe Club by a generation and represents amateur enterprise in transition from the aristocratic toy to the bourgeois hobby of Victorian times. This was the Grange Press of George Allan (1736–1800) of Darlington.

Allan was an attorney by profession and an antiquary by avocation, who in 1769 "commenced Printer . . . to amuse an idle hour," as he wrote to a friend enclosing a copy of his first publication, *Collections Relating to St. Edmund's Hospital, at Gateshead.* Many of the pieces Allan was to print over the next 20 years were other similar antiquarian tracts based on copies of records he had transcribed. This first piece was printed a page at a time on a small portable press, not an easy way to produce good work. For six or seven years he resorted to another method of getting the works he had compiled and composed printed, namely, taking the forms to the town printer to be worked off, but about 1776 he took the final step of having a common-press built for him in London.

All this was done in the time he could spare from his professional activities, and Allan was compelled to seek assistance. The first such assistant, a certain George Smith whose name appears in the imprint of *The Legend of St. Cuthbert* (1777), proved no more satisfactory than Walpole had found some of his printers and was dismissed. By April 1780 Allan had "taught a young Gent to manage it in my absence."

As well as his antiquarian tracts, Allan's Grange Press was used for "a great variety of fugitive satirical pieces . . . particularly Election-squibs," for printing a variety of documents needed in his professional work as attorney, and in a number of books and slighter pieces undertaken for friends. One of these was the Welsh antiquary Thomas Pennant, for whom Allan completed 30 copies of Pennant's *Miscellanies* in 1783, and 50 copies of his *Of the Patagonians* in 1788. At one time Pennant was contemplating purchasing a press of his own, and Allan's letters of advice were filled with valuable information, including the recommendation that he purchase Baskerville's types "as they are not above a penny a pound dearer than other founders."

Pennant did not set up a press of his own, but there was another private press in North Wales at the end of the eighteenth century, that of Paul Panton of Plas Gwyn, Anglesea. The only surviving evidence for this is in two letters from Luke Hansard to Panton, which survive in the National Library of Wales. They show that Hansard had provided Panton with a common-press, cases, types, and other impedimenta, and, like Allan's letters to Pennant, contain many useful tips on how to keep his ink balls in good condition, and so forth. What Panton printed, like the ultimate fate of his press, is shrouded in oblivion.

Strangely enough, the first of the private presses that one can associate closely with the mood of the bibliomania was also set up in remotest Wales. This was the Hafod Press, which Colonel Thomas Johnes, a Cardiganshire squire, set up at Hafod House near Aberystwyth in 1803. For some years before this Johnes had been engaged in translating Froissart's *Chronicles,* of which there had been no translation since that made by Lord Berners in 1523–1525. The problems of supervising its printing in London without neglecting his Cardiganshire interests had troubled him sorely. Perhaps inspired by the example of Lewis Morris, who in 1731 had attempted to print specimens of Welsh poetry in the locality, he eventually decided the best solution was to have his own printing house in Wales. Two printing presses and enough type for five folio pages were purchased, and early in 1803 a printer was brought down from London. Despite good working conditions and wages, this printer could not settle in the quiet Welsh countryside. An appeal for help to a Scottish friend produced a more satisfactory employee, however, and the printer his friend suggested, James Henderson, was to continue as Johnes's printer until the Hafod Press closed in 1810. It seems to have been an ideal partnership; Henderson's pride in his craft made the production of the books slower than Johnes would have wished, but the colonel had the good sense to bow to his printer's feelings, with the result that the publications of the Hafod Press compare well with commercial printing of the time.

The first volume of the Froissart appeared by Christmas 1803, the fourth in 1805. Despite some reservations by reviewers, the book sold well. Even at the 10 guineas charged for each set sold, Johnes lost money on his venture, but he had been seized with the urge to continue with translations. Froissart was followed by an edition of the *Chronicle* of Joinville in 1807, of the travels of Bertrandon de la Brocquiere in the same year, the *Chronicles* of Monstrelet in 1808–1809, and a final volume of Froissart in 1810. In the intervals of producing these very substantial volumes Henderson was engaged in printing reports for the Cardiganshire Agricultural Society, a *Cardiganshire Landlord's Advice to His Tenants* and other works of the same sort. On occasion his work was interrupted by Johnes's visitors who, in the good old manner of the preceding century, would be invited to try their hand at the press.

In 1810 Johnes decided to call a halt to his printing activities. A disastrous fire at Hafod in 1807 had destroyed much of his library, and the death of a favorite daughter three years later seems to have overwhelmed him. The press was closed.

A few years later, in 1813, Sir Egerton Brydges started a press at Lee Priory near Canterbury, which was far more typical of these nineteenth-century scholarly presses than Hafod had been. One of the original members of the Roxburghe Club, Brydges had for some years before its establishment been issuing antiquarian reprints, which were printed for him by the firm of Thomas Bensley in London.

Brydges was a strange figure with his Gothic-romantic melancholy, his fondness for picturesque solitude, and his interest in the books and literature of the past. However much in period he was in these tastes, he was profoundly out of sympathy with his times in his passionate antidemocratic prejudices, which were only made worse by his failure in his claim to the ancient Barony of Chandos and by his almost feudal extravagance which caused him considerable financial embarrassment. He became a soured and despairing man. It was almost a matter of course that when he set up his press it should prove a source of vexation and worry to him.

To start with, all went well. In 1813 Brydges enticed two of Bensley's workmen, John Johnson (the author of *Typographia*) and John Warwick, with a novel proposal. If they provided presses, type, paper, and labor he would find them premises, supply them with copy, and undertake the editorial work; the profits of the venture would be shared. First there was an experimental edition of the poems of the Duchess of Newcastle produced for private circulation in 1813. In the next book, the first placed on sale, Brydges's own *Sylvan Wanderer,* the policy of the press was defined as "furnishing the literary collectors with reprints of some of the most curious tracts of former days, in which there shall be an attempt to add beauty of typography and wood-engraving, to the interest of the matter selected from the rarities of the Black Letter Stores."

Modern writers have tended to damn the Lee Priory books with faint praise, and certainly the quality of their production was overshadowed by the commercial printing of Bulmer and later of William Pickering. Yet the books have an agreeable elegance, and at the time of their publication they were highly admired and advance-subscribed with a speed characteristic of periods of book market inflation. All was apparently going sweetly, with reprints of Raleigh, of Nicolas Breton, of Wither, and others appearing rapidly. In May 1816 there was a serious quarrel between Brydges and Johnson, which eventually led to Chancery proceedings. The press carried on under Warwick alone,

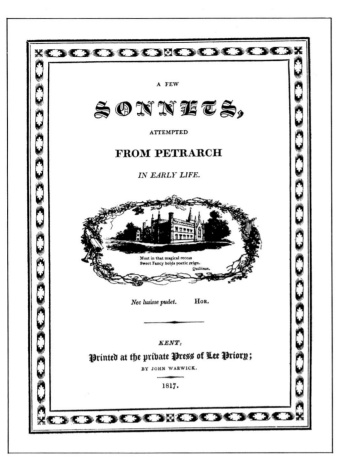

ILLUS. 17. Lee Priory Press, Kent. *Sonnets from Petrarch,* 1817. One of the more successful of Sir Egerton Brydges's private press books.

but it is clear that Johnson had been responsible for whatever typographical excellence the earlier books possessed, and the later publications are far inferior. Brydges himself left England to live on the Continent in 1818, but the press continued to work at Lee Priory until 1822. Some 45 books and pamphlets were produced in all.

Contemporary with the Lee Priory Press was that set up at Auchinleck by Sir Alexander Boswell, the son of Johnson's biographer, in 1815. Like Brydges's press, it was concerned in reprinting early literature (although in this case Scottish literature) and had the distinction of printing one of the early Roxburghe books. In Dibdin's *Bibliographical Decameron* (1817), Sir Alexander's own account of the establishment of the press is given. Having resolved to reprint the text of the disputation between John Knox and Fr. Quentin Kennedy of which he possessed the only surviving copy:

> I was constrained to purchase two small founts of black letter, and to have punches cut for eighteen or twenty double letters and contractions. I was thus enlisted and articled into the service, and being infected with the *type* fever, the fits have periodically returned. In the year 1815, having viewed a portable press invented by Mr John Ruthven, an ingenious printer in Edinburgh, I purchased one, and commenced compositor. At this period, my brother having it in contemplation to present [a volume of the poems of] Barnfield to the Roxburghe Club, and not aware of the poverty and insignificance of my establishment, expressed a wish that his tract should issue from the Auchinleck

> Press. I determined to gratify him, and the portable press being too small for general purposes, I exchanged it for one of Mr Ruthven's full-sized ones; and having increased my stock to *eight* small founts, roman and italic, with the necessary appurtenances, I placed the whole in a cottage, built originally for another purpose . . . not a quarter of a mile from my house.

In the three years of its life from 1815 to 1818 the Auchinleck Press produced some 15 or 16 booklets, mostly in editions limited to 40 copies. Although John Hill Burton exaggerated in claiming in *The Book Hunter* that Boswell "alone and singlehanded, set the example of printing the kind of books which it was afterwards the merit of the book clubs to promulgate," the work of the Auchinleck Press is unjustly neglected today.

Undoubtedly the private press that should have been preeminent among these bibliographical and antiquarian undertakings was that which belonged to Sir Thomas Phillipps, the world's greatest book collector. "I wish to have one copy of every book in the world," he said, and his immense collection of manuscripts and printed books is not yet completely dispersed. Phillipps started collecting books seriously while an undergraduate at Oxford in 1812. By 1822, the year in which he started his own press, his obsessive book buying had got him into such financial straits that a period of retrenchment on the Continent had become necessary. His reasons for starting his press were unexceptionable: "The public is probably aware that I do not print for profit," he wrote in one of his prefaces. "My object is to preserve information which is lying in [manuscripts possessed by] public libraries; and to put it in the power of those who desire that information to have it in their own house, without the trouble and expense of having copies made." And in another he wrote, "Twenty-

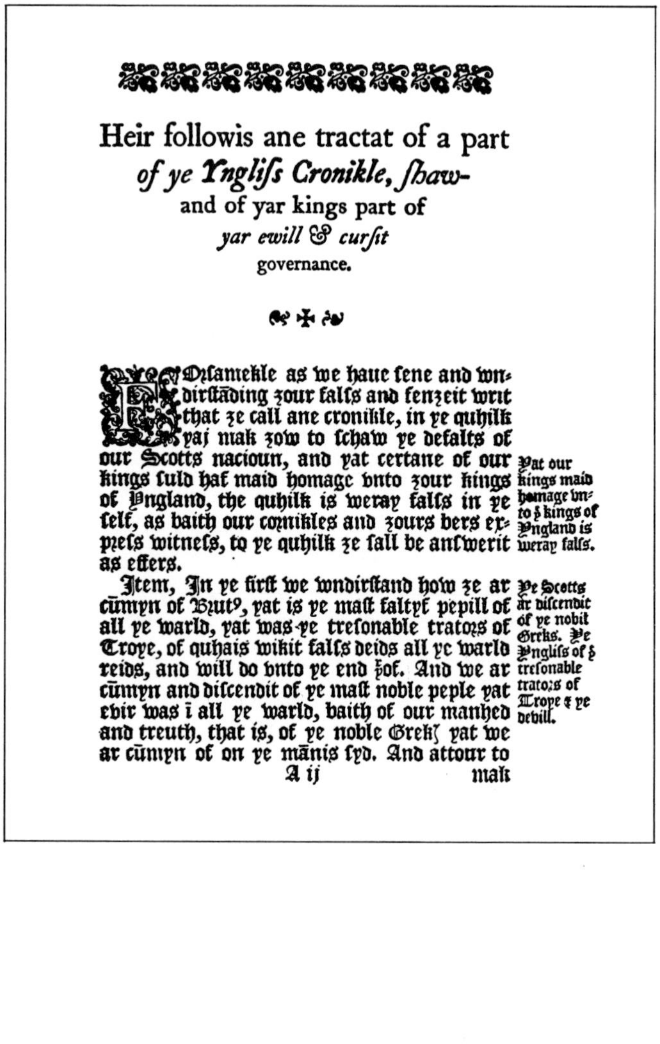
Heir followis ane tractat of a part
of ye Ynglifs Cronikle, fhaw-
and of yar kings part of
yar ewill & curſit
governance.

Forsamekle as we haue sene and wndirstāding zour falss and fenzeit writ that ze call ane cronikle, in ye quhilk yai mak zow to schaw ye defalts of our Scotts nacioun, and yat certane of our kings suld haf maid homage vnto zour kings of Yngland, the quhilk is weray falss in ye self, as baith our cronikles and zours bers express witness, to ye quhilk ze sall be answerit as effers.

Yat our kings maid homage vnto ye kings of Yngland is weray falss.

Item, In ye first we wndirstand how ze ar cūmyn of Brut9, yat is ye mast faltyf pepill of all ye warld, yat was ye tresonable tratoris of Troye, of quhais wikit falss deids all ye warld reids, and will do vnto ye end yof. And we ar cūmyn and discendit of ye mast noble peple yat evir was ī all ye warld, baith of our manhed and treuth, that is, of ye noble Grekz yat we ar cūmyn of on ye mānis syd. And attour to

Ye Scotts ar discendit of ye nobil Greks. Ye Ynglifs of ye tresonable tratoris of Troye & ye devill.

A ij mak

ILLUS. 18. Auchinleck Press, Scotland. Page from one of Sir Alexander Boswell's antiquarian reprints, 1818.

five copies only are printed, my object being merely to prevent unique records from being utterly destroyed by a single accident." In these ways, Phillipps's antiquarian zeal was reminiscent of George Allan's policy of printing historical documents at the Grange Press. There were also less creditable private reasons as well as these public statements of his aims in setting up his private press. For several years before 1822 Phillipps had employed commercial printers to print the texts of manuscripts in his collection and had found that they were expensive, and, worse still, they expected to be paid promptly, at which he was particularly bad. Soon after Phillipps had left England in 1822, John Agg, an Evesham printer to whom he owed money, nearly sent the bailiffs into Phillipps's house Middle Hill, Broadway; only prompt action by his father-in-law prevented the distraint. Phillipps may well have considered that a private press, operated by a printer in his own service, would be cheaper as well as more convenient.

Cheaper and more convenient it was to prove—for Phillipps, less so for his unfortunate printers. The story of the first, a young man from Bungay in Suffolk named Adolphus Brightley, was to be only too typical. Brightley had been engaged by Phillipps, before he went abroad, and had been promised quarters in Broadway Tower. When Brightley arrived in August 1822 he found the conditions considerably less than ideal. Phillipps's agent wrote to his absent master:

> My dear Sir, your printer is come to the Tower & I am very sorry for him
> indeed he seems so much Distress'd & disappointed in the Place; it is he says
> impossible for him to think of Living there neither do I think it fit for him or
> any one else, in the state it is now in, the Windows are so bad Broken that the
> wet when it rains floods every Room, & runs through the floors & Ceilings so
> that the Plaistering is coming down in many places, & as there is but one
> Lodging room it wou'd never do for him & his Sister, therefore he cannot
> think of having her come down. Another Objection to the Place as being unfit
> for the Business, is that there is no Water, which he shall be often wanting; I
> really am very sorry for the Young Man he seems so much Distress'd & says
> that he had but little Money & he has laid it all out in types & one thing or
> another that he knew he shou'd want for the Business, that will never be of any
> use to him or any other Printer only for this work of yours. Therefore hope
> you will give me an Order to assist him with a little Money to Pay him for
> what he has laid out & the Expense of his coming Down.

Through the agent's good offices, Brightley's living and working conditions in the tower were gradually improved, and for a year or two he seems to have enjoyed his position. "I am still in the Tower," he wrote in the spring of 1823, "now Summer is approaching I find it the most delightful situation imagination can conceive." He set himself conscientiously to learning Latin and Anglo-Saxon in order to perform his work the better. When Phillipps had gone abroad he had left a good deal of copy for his printer, but it was frequently illegible and always ill arranged, and Brightley was often at a loss to know how to proceed. Worse, Phillipps was either unable or unwilling to pay his employees regularly, and by the end of 1825 the arrears due to his wretched printer were over £200. Eventually Brightley decided to cut his losses and gave notice to leave. After vainly advertising for a successor able to compose types in "Saxon, Greek, Latin, French, German, Persian, Arabic and Domesday characters," Phillipps engaged a London printer, F. T. G. Crees, who remained only six months. He was replaced by a local boy, Edwyn Offer, who had been an assistant to Brightley. He lasted until 1829. "I am not aware," he wrote to Phillipps, "whether you imagine that the refusal of any pecuniary remuneration for nearly six years of faithful service will stimulate me to any fresh exertions—*I should think not*."

48

ITINERARIUM
AD
TERRAM SANCTAM:
PER
PETRUM DE SUCHEN,
A. D. M.CCC.XXXVI.
SCRIPTUM A. D. M.CCC.L.

EX MANUSCRIPTO ANTIQUO, IN BIBLIOTHECA FRATRUM
EREMITARUM ORDINIS SANCTI AUGUSTINI,
APUD FRIBURGAM, IN HELVETIA,
Nunc primum edidit
D. THOMAS PHILLIPPS, BARONETTUS.

TYPIS MEDIO-MONTANIS
IN TURRE LATIVIENSI
IMPRESSUS.
1823.

ILLUS. 19. Middle Hill Press, Worcestershire. *Itinerarium ad Terram Sanctam*, 1823. Early, well-designed work printed by Adolphus Brightley.

For some years the press lay idle, and much of Phillipps's printing was done away from Middle Hill. In his commendable endeavor to multiply copies of important texts in the public records, Phillipps was a customer of Rudolph Appel, and from the early 1850s until the end of his life he had a number of works produced by the anastatic printing process. At one time Phillipps seems to have tried to tempt Appel to become his printer at Middle Hill. Perhaps fortunately for himself Appel declined, but there were at least seven other printers who worked at the press at different times before Phillipps's death in 1872. The only one of them to last for long was James Rogers who with his sons worked for him from 1854 to 1872.

In such circumstances it is scarcely to be wondered at that the productions of the Middle Hill Press were of a sort which, as A. N. L. Munby has observed, "it would be charitable to describe as mediocre." The most important work of the press was the catalogue of Phillipps's manuscripts produced over the period 1824 to 1871, which was abominably printed on paper of different colors and sizes with uncorrected as well as corrected sheets used in different copies (Illus. 20). In several of his publications the list of errata was fantastically long, as Phillipps was always prone to rush into print and was a very careless editor. He printed his books in very small editions, which he then

CATALOGUS LIBRORUM MANUSCRIPTORUM IN BIBLIOTHECA PHILLIPPICA;

LITERATIS APERTA. 1828.

———*000*———

Ex Bibliotheca Mac Carthy.

1 Livy. [*Gallice.*] 4 vols. folio. vel. sæc. xv. [*With many illuminations.*]
2 Do.   Do.   3 vols. folio. vel. sæc. xiv. [*With many illuminations.*]
3 Thucydides. [*Latine*] folio. vel.
4 Sallust. [*Scriptura Italica.*] vel.
5 Suetonius. vel. sæc. xii.
6 Virgil. [*Beautifully illuminated.*]
7 Lactantius. [*Italian.*] vel. sæc. xv.
8 Liber Precum.

Debure.

9 Ordonnances Religieuses. vel. sæc. xiv.
10 Apicius. vel. sæc. x.
11 Hippocrates. vel. sæc. x.
12 Cristine de Pise Mutation de Fortune.
13 Extraits de Seneque. vel.
14 Plato sur l'Immortalité. vel.
15 Berosus. vel. sæc. xiv.

Royez.

16 Croniques de Jean de St Tre.
17 Ordre de St Michel. vel. sæc. xvi.
18 Galfrid Monumetensis. vel. sæc. xiii.
19 Cartularium de Fontevraud. vel. sæc. xiii.
20 Do.   Saumur. vel. sæc. xi.
21 Do.   Laon. vel. sæc. xiii
22 Do.   Sauve Majeur. vel. sæc. xiii.
23 Do.   S. Severini de Bourdeaux. vel. sæc. xiii.
24 Do.   Metz. vel. sæc. xiii.
25 Do.   Laudun or Laon. vel. sæc. xiii.
26 Do.   S André de Bourdeaux. vel. sæc. xiii.
27 Do.   Belver. vel. sæc. xiii.
28 Cronique de St Denis. vel. sæc. xiv.
29 Revenues de l'Archeveché de Bourdeaux. vel.
30 Romant de la Rose. vel. sæc. xiv. (1375.)
31 Cronique de France. vel. sæc. xiv.
32 Calendarium Benefactorum Sti Petri Salmuri. vel. sæc. xiii.
33 Tresor des Histoires. vel. sæc. xiii.
34 Tresorerie de la Marine. vel. sæc. xv.
35 Revenues de diverses Abbayes &c. folio.
36 Cossa's Livre des Temps. Vel.
37 Croniques de Gennes. Vel.
38 Loi Salique et Miroir Histoire de France. Vil.
39 Chemin de Paradis. Vel.
40 Entrevues des Roys.
41 Custumale Andegavense. vel. sæc. xv.
42 Terrier du Captal de Buch. vel. sæc. xiv.
43 Computus Monetæ receptæ in Andegavia. vel. sæc. xiii.
44 Rentale Domini de Gastines. vel. sæc. xiii.
45 Statuta collegii de Marche.
46 Repertorium Cartarum de Champagne.
47 Juvenal et Persius.
48 Vitæ Amici et Caroli Magni. Vel.
49 Confessio Soliloqua. Vel.
50 Registrum Precedentium Legis Ecclesiasticæ. Vel.
51 Fiefs de la Ville de Craon.
52 Traites des Roys de France avec les Papes.
53 Histoire de Du Guesclin. vel.

Royez or Paris.

54 Æsopi Fabulæ. vel.
55 Nobiliaire de Normandy.
56 Mich. de Vouges Collection de Prieres. vel.
57 Lectionarium Ecclesiæ S. Germani. vel. sæc. xvii.
58 Galfridus Monumetensis
59 Alexandri de Villa Dei Doctrinale. vel. sæc. xv.
60 Hippocratis Opera. vel. sæc. xiv.
61 Horloge de Sapience. sæc. xv.
62 Legende Doree. vel.
63 Psaulmes en Plein Chant. Vel.

64 Leonard Aretino de Bello Gothico.   Vel.
65 La Spina Rosa.
66 Pelerinage de la Vie Humaine.   Vel.
67 Christine de Pise Debut sur le Roman de la Rose.   Vel. sæc xv.
68 Bernard de Humilitate.   Vel.
69 Generalités de France.
70 Interpretatio Nominum Hebraicorum.   Vel.
71 De Oculo Morali.   Vel.
72 Raymundi Lullii Opera.   Vel. sæc. xiv.
73 Vita Christi.   Vel.
74 Marci Evangelium.   Vel.
75 Petri de Alliaco ———.   Vel.
76 Comment. in Apocalyps.   Vel.
77 P. Gregorii Dialogi.   Vel.
78 Villare Gallicum.
79 Pupilla Oculi Johannis de Burgh.   sæc. xv.
80 S. Anselmi Opus quoddam.   Vel.
81 Ligues de la Suisse.   Vol. 2. vel. sæc. xvi.
82 Do.   Universelle.
83 Jean Cara Vita sur les Constitutions des Chevaliers de Malta. 2 vols. folio. ch.
84 Sti Thomæ Aquinatis Opera. vel. 4to.

Brodie and Dowding, Salisbury.   ☞ Ex Insulâ Jersey.

85 Histoire des Arabes. folio. ch.
86 Do. de Malthe. folio. ch.
87 Brantome's Memoires des Hommes Illustres. Vol. 1. folio. ch.
88 Job cum Glossis. vel. sæc. xiii.
89 Turrecremata de Potestate Ecclesiæ. folio. ch.
90 Principes de Marine. folio. ch.
91 Remarques sur l'Isle de Malthe. folio. ch.
92 Principia Cartesiana. folio. ch.
93 Bonifacii VI. Decretalium. vel. sæc. xiv. folio.

Thorpe.

94 Catalogue of American Books. 5 vols. 8vo. ch.
95 Stevens' Collectanea de Monasteriis, &c. 3 vols. folio. ch.
96 Review of Parliaments. ch.
97 Rules of the House of Commons. ch.
98 Journal of   Do.   Do.   in 1640. ch.
99 Judicature in Parliament. ch.
100 Cotton's Remonstrance of the House of Commons to James I. ch.
101 Pedigrees of Berkshire Families.
102 Account of the Peshall Family. folio. ch.
103 Do. of the Argyle Do. ch.
104 Do. of the Navy. ch.
105 History of Edward IV. ch.
106 Parliamentum Pacificum. ch
107 Exactions on the State. ch.
108 General Assembly of ———. vel.
109 Of the Irish Plantations. ch.
110 Valor Beneficiorum. folio. ch.
111 St George's Grants of Arms. 18mo. ch. sæc. xvii.
112 Cases of Habeas Corpus. folio. ch.
113 Curia Wardorum. folio. ch. [*Olim Comitis Grey de Stamford.*]
113 Snelling's View of Silver Coinage. folio. ch.
114 Burlington and Gainsbro' Pedigrees.
115 Maffei de Republica Venetiæ.
116 Flower's Derby Visitation. folio.
117 Norfolk   Do.   12mo.
118 York (query ?)   Do.
119 Leicester   Do.   [*Query from Nichols?*]
120 Cambridge   Do.   1620.
121 Benolt's Devon Visitation. [*Query ?*]
122 Sir Peter Thomson's History of Poole.
123 Alphabet of Arms, [*Query?*]
124 Arms of Knights of the Bath.
125 Do   Do.   of the Round Table.
126 Pedigree of Sydenham. [*Query.*] vel. Roll.
127 Do. of Bullen.   Do. Do.
128 Do. of Gifford of Wilts.   Do. Do.
129 Do. of Botiler of Sudely.   Do. Do.
130 Do. of Bagge. *Paper roll.*

ILLUS. 20. Middle Hill Press, Worcestershire. Proof page of Sir Thomas Phillipps's *Catalogue of Manuscripts,* 2nd ed., printed for him by Edwyn Offer, 1828.

distributed in an utterly unsystematic manner. The result has been that many of the works that Phillipps had put into print for the first time are today almost as inaccessible to the scholar as if the Middle Hill Press had never existed.

Not many private presses were so ill organized, or their owners such bad employers as Sir Thomas Phillipps. For contrast, there is the account given by Charles Manby Smith in his *The Working Man's Way in the World* (1851–1852, reprinted by the Printing Historical Society, 1967) in which the author reminisced about his life in the printing trade. In this remarkable book the author recorded that in the summer of 1830 he was taken into the service of a Rev. Dr. D——e who had retired to Prospect Villa, near F——d in Somerset, and wanted to have his sermons printed. Smith tells an idyllic story of his two years spent living as a member of the family, spending his days in printing, and his evenings in fishing for trout with his employer, or in winter in teaching him the violin, or playing chess with his wife. It is a charming story in what seems an authoritative and authentic personal account of a printer's life in the 1820s and 1830s. Unfortunately a thorough investigation by Simon Nowell-Smith has shown that the story of Prospect Villa is pure romancing, and we must regard the account of Dr. D——e's press and the edition of the sermons more as the sort of work a printer would have enjoyed than as a record of a real enterprise.

To return from the ideal to the real, an interesting late press inspired by the bibliomania was that which the antiquary E. V. Utterson set up at Beldornie House, near Ryde in the Isle of Wight, in 1840. Utterson was an early member of the Roxburghe Club, presenting books to it in 1820 and again in 1836, and had edited two volumes of *Early Popular Poetry* for general publication in 1817. His decision to set up his own press came late in life, and its productions seem to have been exclusively type-facsimiles of books in his own collection, with the original woodcuts and ornaments carefully copied from the originals. Between 1840 and 1843 he reprinted such pieces as Samuel Rowlands's *Looke to It: For Ile Stabbe Ye* (1604) (Illus. 21A and 21B), Patrick Hannay's *Songs and Sonnets* (1622), and, echoing the Auchinleck Press, Barnfield's *Cynthia*. All were well printed on good paper, in editions limited to 12 or 15 copies for presentation to fellow book collectors. The press seems to have been a summer amusement, because in November 1841 Utterson told Philip Bliss, the Oxford book collector, that he had discharged his printer for the winter but hoped "to set tympan and fresket to work again in the Spring."

In what was perhaps the last of these scholarly private presses to be established, that of Prince Louis-Lucien Bonaparte, we find a reversion from the antiquarian bibliophile presses of the Lee Priory or Beldornie pattern to the more purely learned presses of an earlier era.

Prince Louis-Lucien, nephew of the emperor, had been born in England in 1813 (when his father was a prisoner of state) and spent most of his long life in England or Italy. He devoted his time to philological studies, and, although later regarded by F. J. Furnivall, James Murray, and others in the Philological Society as too superficial in his dialectical research, he deserved his considerable reputation for developing philological studies at a time when Britain had lagged behind Germany in the field. The prince's method included the collection of versions of the parable of the sower put into various languages and dialects, which he then printed for distribution to scholars. A good deal of this work was farmed out to commercial printers and represents private publishing rather than private printing (as with Sir Thomas Phillipps's activities). In the mid-1850s he had a press of his own at his home in Norfolk Terrace, Bayswater. "J'ai une petite imprimerie chez moi," he wrote to a friend in 1856, "uniquement pour les Evangiles de St.-Matthieu en Basque et pour d'autres raretés bibliographiques." In 1857, 10 works were produced at his press, and in the following year 5 more. These varied in length from single sheets to books of over 150 pages, all in editions of no more than 250 copies. The earliest bore no indication of printer, but most carry the name of the prince's employees, W. H. Billing or, more rarely, E. Billing.

TYRANT KINGES.

YOU high Imperious crowne-contending Kings,
Who for Earth's glory (not *Religions* good)
Turne human bodies into bloudy springs,
And die the ground with flaught'red Chriftians blood;
That for the gayning of an earthly Crowne,
Will toffe a spatious Kingdome vpfide downe.

You that deuorce the hufbands from their wiues,
By fatall warre, the endleffe foe to peace:
You that denye poore new-borne Babes their liues,
And will not graunt sweet life an howers leafe:
That care not how, or by what meanes you raigne,
So you the golden Crowne and Scepter gaine.

ILE STABBE YEE.

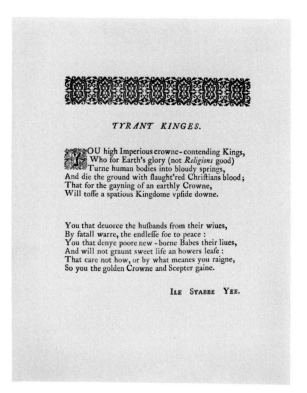

ILLUS. 21A. Beldornie Press, Isle of Wight. Text page from its type-facsimile of *Looke to It*. 1841. Photograph: Birmingham City Libraries.

VEREOR NE HÆC FORTE NIMIS ANTIQUA, ET JAM OBSOLETA VIDEANTUR. *Cicero in Verrem.*

Reprinted at the Beldornie Prefs, by J. N. Lydall, for Edwd. V. Utterfon, in the year MDCCCXLI.

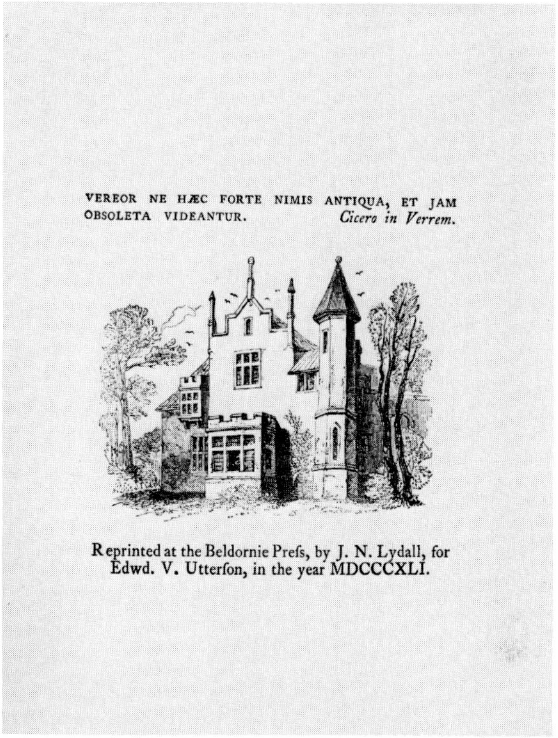

ILLUS. 21B. Beldornie Press, Isle of Wight. Colophon page from *Looke to It,* 1841. Photograph: Birmingham City Libraries.

The Billings' work had no special typographic merit, and Prince Louis-Lucien may have been disappointed by the quality of their printing. He confided to a friend working on Basque dialects that they were not sufficiently skilled for him to consider printing on vellum. It was, of course, convenient to have the Billings on the spot, so that the proof correction so vital in this work could be done easily. Nevertheless, the prince found it difficult to organize a regular flow of work from his correspondents who had undertaken to provide texts in the various dialects and found it necessary to remind one of the tardier contributors that the printer "was paid by the day, and was often idle for lack of copy." Other private press owners might attempt to fill these gaps in serious work by setting the printers to the production of bagatelles, election-squibs, and other ephemera, but not Prince Louis-Lucien. After 1858 he abandoned his private press and reverted to the use of trade printers. The pure scholarly private press had become an unnecessary luxury.

Chapter 7

—

THE AUTHOR AS PUBLISHER

FEW OF THOSE OWNING the many different private presses described in earlier chapters would as a matter of course have been their own printers. They had presses operated for them by printers whom they employed for reasons that to them seemed sufficient. Sometimes they would set the type or undertake the presswork themselves; had they instead chosen to have their work printed in the usual way, they could have done so easily enough, at any rate after the craft of printing was well established.

Relationships between authors and publishers have often been uneasy. In the nineteenth century it was not uncommon for an established successful writer to contract with his publisher for the production of a book entirely at the author's expense, thus securing to him a profit far greater than that coming from outright sale or from royalties. In such cases, the publishers received a commission on sales. A great proportion of "privately printed" books have for one reason or another been produced to cut out the middleman, the publisher.

Sometimes authors have gone as far as cutting out both printer and commercial publisher, as they felt that to produce their work privately would be more rewarding. In this class was the lawyer Charles Viner, who had prepared a *General Abridgment of Law and Equity* on which he is said to have started work soon after he had been admitted to the Middle Temple in 1700. When the work was eventually completed in 1738 it was offered to a commercial publisher, but Viner regarded his offer of £500 for the work as "very trifling" and decided not only to publish the book himself, but print it as well. He had presses and other equipment installed in his house at Aldershot, had paper manufactured with a special watermark, and between 1742 and 1753 his printers produced a 23-volume edition of the *Abridgment* which was sold at £26 the set (Illus. 22). Although it has been aptly described as "a vast and labyrinthine encyclopaedia . . . ill arranged and worse digested," the work was by no means unsuccessful. To be sure, such a method called for considerable financial outlay, but no doubt the ease with which the detailed checking of proofs for such a work could be done was a boon for the man who could afford it. Viner's self-confidence in his work paid off handsomely. It was in part from the profits of his *Abridgment* that the Vinerian Professorship of Common Law at Oxford was endowed after his death in 1756.

Another writer to adopt a similar method was the great anatomist and surgeon John Hunter

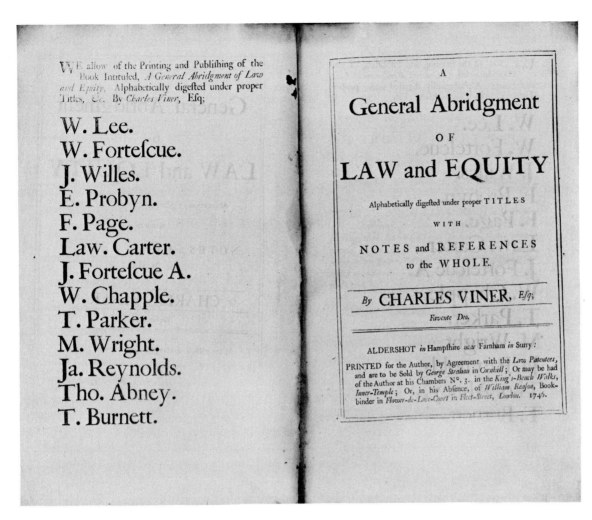

We allow of the Printing and Publishing of the Book Intituled, *A General Abridgment of Law and Equity*, Alphabetically digested under proper Titles, &c. By *Charles Viner*, Esq;

W. Lee.
W. Fortescue.
J. Willes.
E. Probyn.
F. Page.
Law. Carter.
J. Fortescue A.
W. Chapple.
T. Parker.
M. Wright.
Ja. Reynolds.
Tho. Abney.
T. Burnett.

A

General Abridgment

OF

LAW and EQUITY

Alphabetically digested under proper TITLES

WITH

NOTES and REFERENCES
to the WHOLE.

By CHARLES VINER, *Esq;*

Favente Deo.

ALDERSHOT *in* Hampshire *near* Farnham *in* Surry:

PRINTED for the Author, by Agreement with the *Law Patentees*, and are to be Sold by *George Strahan* in *Cornhill*; Or may be had of the Author at his Chambers Nº. 3. in the *King's-Bench Walks*, *Inner-Temple*; Or, in his Absence, of *William Reason*, Bookbinder in *Flower-de-Luce-Court* in *Fleet-Street, London.* 1746.

ILLUS. 22. Charles Viner, Hampshire. Title opening from Viner's *Abridgment*, 1746.

(1728–1793). Hunter's first work, *The Natural History of the Human Teeth,* had been published in 1771 by Joseph Johnson, and it is said that Johnson's generous payment was used to pay the costs of Hunter's wedding two months later. A second volume of the treatise on teeth was issued by Johnson in 1778, and this was followed rapidly by a reissue of the first volume and by Latin, Dutch, and German editions produced on the Continent. In arranging for these, Johnson was behaving like a sensible businessman, but it has been surmised that Hunter was not well pleased because he received no further profit.

At any rate, Hunter's two next books were not published by Johnson. When they appeared in 1786 his *Observations on Certain Parts of the Animal Economy,* which consisted of amended texts of previously published papers, and *A Treatise on the Venereal Disease,* simply stated that they were "sold at No. 13 Castle Street, Leicester Square," Hunter's own house. That the books were not only published by Hunter but also printed in his home is confirmed by a memorandum book (now in the Hunterian Museum at Glasgow) belonging to his secretary William Clift and by some of the observations of Hunter's first biographer Jesse Foot. Foot recorded that proof correction was undertaken by a synod of distinguished medical men and recounted how he came to Castle Street to buy one of the books and found John Andree, one of Hunter's ablest pupils, folding the sheets while women were sewing them.

It is clear from Clift's memoranda that the press in Castle Street was an active one. Directed by John Richardson who was assisted by two pressmen, the first edition of *Venereal Disease* sold its 1,000 copies quickly enough for a second reset edition of 500 to be produced in 1788. *Animal Economy* was a slower seller, and not until 1792 was a second reset edition produced. Hunter's *Treatise of the Blood* was also printed by Richardson, being completed in November 1794 after Hunter's death. For these later works printed at the Castle Street press, distribution was arranged with Johnson and George Nicol to supplement the retail sales from Hunter's house. Cutting out the middleman had not proved as easy or profitable as Hunter had hoped, although the press was certainly profitable and had not prevented the rapid appearance of pirate editions. Hunter had prevented the cheap Dublin reprint, which was the bane of London publishing at the time, but French, German, and American editions of *Venereal Disease* appeared in 1787.

A good many other medical men have from time to time printed their own books. One slightly mysterious instance is that of William Turton (1762–1835), now remembered chiefly as a conchologist. Most of his publications on medicine or natural history were issued through the London book trade and printed by commercial printers; nevertheless there survives *A Treatise on Cold and Hot Baths* in the second edition, with the imprint "Swansea: Printed at the Author's Private Press, 1803." At the time Turton had a medical practice in Swansea, and his edition of Linnaeus (1802–1804) was being printed commercially in that town. Was his private press an attempt to secure greater financial rewards for himself? No other work is known from it, and one can only surmise that he found it easier to work through the commercial printing trade as the need for printing arose.

These men were all able to have their work printed and published through trade channels if they so chose, but other authors were unable to persuade any publishers to accept their work and too poor to have their work printed at their own cost by vanity presses or to commission a printer to produce it. For them a private press often seemed the only way to give their work the greater authority and power that print confers.

Probably the most famous example of this usually misdirected endeavor was in the printing activities of William Davy at Lustleigh in Devon at the end of the eighteenth century. Born to poor parents near Tavistock in 1744, and educated at Exeter Grammar School and later at Balliol College, Oxford, Davy took holy orders and at his examination "Received great encomiums for his Biblical knowledge." For a few years he was a curate at Moretonhampstead and later at Drewsteighnton, where his sermons were "of so disagreeable a nature that the most respectable part of his parish could not, without painful feelings, attend his ministry." Or so they complained to his bishop. Summoned to Exeter to explain, Davy took with him some 12 volumes of a "System of divinity" on which he had started work while still at Oxford, and the explanation became clear. The sermons complained of had been on the "Vices of the Age"; a previous series on the "Virtues of the Age" had been received with approval by his parishioners. The bishop inspected his sermons carefully and praised his zeal, adding that when a living became vacant Davy would not be forgotten.

Filled with enthusiasm, Davy determined to publish his system of divinity, incomplete as it was. An impressive list of subscribers was collected, and in 1785–1786 six duodecimo volumes were printed for the author by the proprietors of the *Exeter Flying Post*.

Davy's sanguine hopes were soon shattered. A good many of the subscribers failed to pay for their copies, and the public received his book with complete indifference. He was left with a debt of £100 to his printer, a very serious matter for him as the annual stipend of the perpetual curacy of Lustleigh, to which he had been appointed in 1786, was only £40. He was determined not to abandon his work, being convinced of its practical usefulness in making his parishioners "willingly attend the Church, when they found they had some *Equivalent* for their money." By 1795 Davy had as he thought perfected his work, which had grown to such proportions that the proprietor of the

Flying Post estimated that it would cost £2,000 to have it printed. Even if Davy had been able to find patrons, it would have been very difficult to raise such a sum, and the archbishop and bishops whom he attempted to interest in his project were emphatic in their refusal.

With most men the projected book would have been abandoned, however regretfully, but Davy was a man of pronounced mechanical ability. At the age of eight he had watched carpenters building a watermill and had carved himself a scale model that worked better than its original. It seems probable that what little he had seen on his visits to the Exeter printer's shop convinced him that he could easily overcome his problem by printing a specimen volume of his work himself. Armed with this, he probably reasoned, he could no doubt attract enough support to continue with his original plan of having the whole work printed commercially.

Accordingly, "he resolved *to do what he could*. He borrowed money to purchase a fount of castaway types of a printer in Exeter." The proprietor of the *Flying Post* received him tolerantly, and sold him a case of battered type, but could not resist saying, "I expect that in less than a month you will come and entreat me to take all again from you." Yet before the month was up, Davy had built himself a press, which his son many years later described as being "of a very substantial and convenient form, and on a principle very different from those in general use" and had taught himself enough of composition and presswork to produce a specimen that he showed his supplier in triumph. The printer "remarked with evident surprise 'Well Sir, if you have done this, you will do anything.' "

How substantial the "anything" was to prove would have astonished him even more. Within five months Davy had succeeded in printing 40 copies of a volume of some 328 pages, an altogether remarkable achievement when one remembers that he had at this time only sufficient type to set and work off a page at a time. Once more with high hopes he sent 26 copies to the two universities, to the Archbishop of Canterbury, to the Royal Society, to a number of literary reviews, and to individuals he thought might be willing to help his work. Once more he was disappointed. Most of the recipients ignored the book; the reviews were at best patronizing. The Secretary of the Royal Society got as far as sending a letter of thanks, but he failed to send the letter postage paid so Davy was obliged to pay the postage himself, no mean consideration for so poor a man in the days before the penny mail.

Even this disappointment did not deter him; he was a very dogged man. He still had 14 copies of the first volume, and he determined to finish the work as he had started it, at his own press. He managed to reduce the extent of his own labors by training a housemaid, Mary Hole, to act as compositor, while he cut the paper, read the proofs, printed the sheets, and bound the completed volumes. A welcome increase of his stipend (to £60 per annum!) made the expense of the undertaking a little less burdensome, but it was only Davy's indomitable spirit that enabled him to produce three volumes in 1796 (it is perhaps scarcely coincidence that there were no entries in the Parish Register that year), another two volumes in 1797, and so on until the twenty-sixth and final volume was finished in 1807.

A System of Divinity was not a handsome example of printing. The presswork was very poor, with some lines being starved of ink and others blurred with an excess of it. The work abounded in additions and afterthoughts, which were printed on slips and pasted in, and Davy's lack of Greek and Hebrew types, and the consequent additions in manuscript, did not help the effect. But Davy's long years of work were not without reward: Isaac D'Israeli gave the book a favorable notice in the *Quarterly Review,* and the bishops of Durham and Gloucester wrote to express their appreciation. Not all the recipients of copies were so polite. His own Bishop of Exeter observed, presumably in reply to an inquiry from Davy on whether he had received his set, via his secretary, "that he could not be supposed to be able to notice every trifle that appeared in print." This was more than Davy could take: "If his Lordship considered 26 volumes octavo, the labour of fifty years in collecting, compiling, and printing, a *trifle,*" he retorted, "he certainly could not allow himself to expect from his Lordship either approbation or encouragement."

One might have expected that after all these labors, which were so ill rewarded, Davy would have had more than enough of printing for a lifetime and that, as he was now in easier financial circumstances, he would have turned to commercial printers for anything further he wished to publish. For 10 or 15 years his press seems to have lain idle, but in 1823, at the age of 80, he once more set to work with a volume of selections from his *System.* Without any assistance whatsoever, he produced another octavo volume of 480 pages. This time the worth of his work was recognized by the new Bishop of Exeter, and in December 1825 he was presented with the living of Winkleigh. He was not to enjoy it long; he died there the following June. In his will he remembered Mary Hole, "my old and faithful servant." Although his life may have been one of misguided application, there can be little doubt that in the labors of printing he had shared with her for so long he had probably been happier than most men are in their work.

It would be difficult to find other instances of such devotion as Davy's, but it is by no means hard to find other examples of authors turning printer. In his *Typographical Gazetteer,* the Reverend Henry Cotton mentions the case of the young Irish scholar Patrick Lynch, who was born in 1757 and educated at Ennis by Donough au Charrain from whom he had an excellent grounding in the classics. Family misfortunes compelled him to give up his studies, but after five years as a small farmer he settled at Carrick-on-Suir, Tipperary. Having turned author, and compiled a Chronoscope he "had no means of publishing it. In concert with a barber in the town he procured some types, and by means of a bellows press, he actually set and printed his first work with his own hands and established the first printing-press ever seen in that place."

The private press seems to have had considerable fascination for the clergy in the past, to judge from the numbers who possessed them in the eighteenth and nineteenth centuries. Often it was probably because more than other educated men they had sufficient leisure and insufficient funds for commercial printing. Sometimes the books that they printed on their presses were in the field of local history, like the Reverend Francis Blomefield's *History of Norfolk* of which the first volume was printed on his own press at Fersfield in 1739 (the presswork proved so unsatisfactory that the second volume was printed in Norwich) or like *The History of Lacock Abbey,* which was compiled and printed at Lacock by the chaplain to the Countess of Shrewsbury in 1806 and is another unsatisfactory example of bookmaking. More usually they were concerned with religious or church matters, like that operated at Wisbech by the Reverend Henry Burrough in the 1770s, or that at Whitburn, near Linlithgow, by the Reverend Archibald Bruce in the 1800s, or the Reverend Frederick Nolan's press at Prittlewell in Essex in the 1820s. Sometimes these presses were run with true missionary zeal. Between 1852 and 1875 the Reverend George Hay Forbes, the Episcopal minister at Burntisland, operated a press that produced a monthly magazine, *The Gospel Messenger,* and his own liturgical writings. After his death the Pitsligo Press, as it was called, was continued for some years by a trust set up by his will.

Such presses were to be found in the British colonies as well. In 1824, for example, George Wilson Bridges the Rector of St. Ann's, Jamaica, printed a little *Statistical History of the Parish of Manchester,* where he had previously been rector. Three years later he followed it with *A Service for the Parochial Church of St. Ann,* in which the few pages of letterpress were followed by 10 leaves of music that he had lithographed; this was the earliest use of lithography in the island. Bridges does not appear to have dabbled further in printing himself, but in the 1840s he was experimenting with photography, a hobby to which many amateur printers turned. His continued interest in fine

ILLUS. 23. Francis Blomefield, Norfolk. Bookplate for his Parish Library, 1736.

printing is attested by his *Outline and Notes of Twentynine Years* (1862), itself a good instance of the Caslon revival.

Quite often these clerical presses were also used for more frivolous work, as for example that of the Reverend John Fletcher at Madeley, Shropshire. As well as printing the usual series of sermons, in 1792, Fletcher produced Dr. Beddowe's *Alexander's Expedition Down the Hydaspes,* a book that has been described as "in every way a curiosity, having been printed by a woman and illustrated with woodcuts by a Parish Clerk." The poem itself is very strange, having apparently been written with the twofold object of demonstrating the possibility of imitating Erasmus Darwin's *Botanic Garden* and of denouncing English expansionism in India.

The clergy did not, of course, have a monopoly on printing their own books. At least one volume of poems by Lewis Way was printed by the author at Stansted in 1822. In the middle of the nineteenth century Albany Wallace, a wealthy eccentric who lived at Worthing, had a press on which he printed a number of books he had written or translated. Wallace had originally had his press in London, where he produced *The Reigns of the Stuarts Dramatised* in six parts between 1835 and 1843. He moved to Worthing some time before 1850 when he printed his *Elfrida,* following this with translations of Voltaire and Racine in 1854 and 1861. One of his prefaces is amusing:

> A certain picture was said by a connoisseur to be "very well painted for a
> *gentleman!*" a species of negative praise which gave but little satisfaction to the
> artist.—Should the *Amateur-Printer,* however, meet with as much, he will be
> very well contented.—All he can say himself for his work is, "that it is legible";
> and his type being of a pretty tolerable rotundity, he does not think it will need
> an additional pair of spectacles to be made out.

Something of the carefree attitude of those who regarded themselves as amateur authors as well as amateur printers, and had few illusions about the importance of their work, can be obtained from this preface. A very engaging picture of another earlier press is given by Martin in his *Catalogue of Books Privately Printed* (1834) in which he quotes a letter from a correspondent:

> I was acquainted for many years with Charles Dickinson Esq. of Somerset-
> shire, . . . He, during a portion of his life, devoted himself to auto-printing; he
> kept presses and types in his apartments, and composed in a leaden style—I
> mean to say, that the patriotic, ultra-liberal principles which he professed he
> embodied in excellent poetry, and as Apollo gave him the verse, he printed, but
> wrote not his poem. Mr. Dickinson read his poems to me, portions indeed, for
> they formed some volumes quarto, of perhaps eight hundred pages each, in
> large type and with some margins to receive corrections.

For contrast, there was another poetic amateur active on the other side of the globe in mid-Victorian times. An early settler in the Wellington region of New Zealand, William Golder (1810–1876) was a very different man from Charles Dickinson. Golder was a writer of rough ballads, which transferred to this pioneer community in the southern hemisphere many of the features of the street literature of early Victorian Britain. Golder initially followed the old balladmonger's tradition of personally canvassing for subscribers and hawking his books for sale. In this way his *New Zealand Minstrelsy* (1852), the first book of verse published in the colony, and two other epic poems were published. These were all printed for him by commercial printers, but the final effusion of this "poetaster of large ambitions and unequalled verbosity," as he has been described, was printed by himself "at his amateur press, Mountain Home, Hutt" in 1871. This book, *The Philosophy of Love [A Plea in Defence of Virtue and Truth!]: A Poem in Six Cantos,* makes a substantial volume of over 200 pages. In the *New Zealand National Bibliography* it is noted as being "execrably if worthily printed by Golder," a judgment that could stand as an epitaph for many works from amateur presses of this kind.

Modern examples of the author-turned-printer are not uncommon. A few years ago in New York City Rex Benedict set and printed by hand, a page at a time, the 300-odd pages of his *Fantasano, a Romance* and some lesser pieces of prose and prose poetry. Relatively few authors of substantial prose works will still turn to hand setting and letterpress printing of their work today, unless they have typographical interests. The greater ease and convenience of offset litho reproduction from typewriter script will be preferred. I have no doubt that this would have been the solution which would have been chosen by one of the more "successful" authors-turned-publisher, Charles Reis.

Reis was a Trinidadian lawyer who in the late 1920s wrote a *History of the Constitution of Trinidad.* There were at that time no commercial publishers in the island who might have been willing to publish it, and Reis's inquiries at the offices of the *Port of Spain Gazette,* at Yuille's Printerie, and other commercial firms showed him that it would cost him far too much to consider having it printed at his own expense. So while on leave in London he bought himself a small treadle press and a small font of Cheltenham type, and on his return home he printed the book himself, completing it in 1929. After finishing the book, still the standard text in its field, he used his press for some years to produce ephemera for the Portuguese Club in Port of Spain, but it was essentially a one-book press.

Trinidadian history, and the difficulties of getting the source materials for its study into print, were to be responsible for the establishment of another private press some years later. When the Historical Society of Trinidad and Tobago was founded in the early 1940s, one of its principal objects was the publication of documentary sources, but the difficulties caused by the Second World War together with the rising cost of printing threatened to put an end to its work. Professor K. S. Wise, who was retiring from the Imperial College of Tropical Agriculture to live in England, bought a handpress and occupied his retirement by selecting, translating, editing, and printing some hundreds of pieces for publication by the society. Like Reis, Wise made no money from his work, and, in fact, he must have subsidized the society to a considerable extent. He had, however, the satisfaction of collecting and making available the materials from which Eric Williams and others have subsequently drawn for their historical studies, and sets of his documents form an important part of all collections of West Indiana.

The presses so far described in this chapter all existed for the single purpose of getting material dear to the owner into print. In this way they are not so far from the private presses of the bibliomania, except that they were for the most part printing material of less intrinsic importance; the owner was himself the printer and not an employer of printers; and the quality of production was a matter of relatively minor importance to the owners, although few of them were worse than the Middle Hill Press. As long as the books were put into print it was enough. There were and are presses operated by authors who deliberately choose this method of production for aesthetic reasons. In some cases an author has felt that only if he can personally design and decorate the vehicle for his texts can the full artistic aim of his work be realized.

The outstanding example of such work—so outstanding that it is almost an impertinence to discuss it briefly in the present context and so far above most private press work that it is seldom recognized as such—is to be found in the "illuminated" poetic and prophetic books that were printed by William Blake. Blake's earliest published verse, *Poetical Sketches,* was printed at the expense of his friends in the conventional way in 1783. Blake was not himself satisfied with this method of production. When about 1788 he began to collect some of the poems that had originally been included in the manuscript of his burlesque novel *An Island in the Moon* he was unsure at first how they could best be presented. By this time Blake was fully aware that he was a *complete* artist; he knew that poetry and design are different forms of the same thing and that he possessed the originality and craftsmanship both demand. He was not contented therefore to have his poems only in written or printed form. He wished to clothe them so that they were more than poems; they would be poem-pictures forming an artistic whole.

The methods used by Blake for his "illuminated printing" have been the subject of considerable speculation over the past century. Blake himself believed that this method of producing his poetry was communicated to him in a dream by his dead brother Robert, but it was not until the experiments made by S. W. Hayter and Ruthven Todd in the 1940s that anyone had a clear understanding of his methods. That Blake's books were produced by a method of relief etching had been clear enough, but the means by which he had written his poems in reverse on the surface of the plate before etching had never been explained satisfactorily. Todd and Hayter's investigations revealed that Blake probably got his ideas from a suggestion on methods of transferring writing from paper to the surface of a copper plate in Alexander Browne's *Ars Pictoria* (1675). Blake improved on Browne's method, and it seems that he wrote the text of his poems and drew the outlines of the decorations on paper in a mixture of bituminous and resinous varnish. When the paper was pressed into contact with a heated copper plate, the varnish was transferred to the surface of the plate, and very little retouching was necessary. The plate was then etched in the usual way, leaving the text and decorations, which had been protected by the varnish resist, in relief. To ink and print these plates, as for normal intaglio copper engravings, would not have been possible. Todd's experiments suggest that a plain unengraved plate would have been painted over with a special ink compounded from egg yolk and water color, which pressed into contact with the etched plate would take the ink on the raised areas and could then be printed in the usual way. After printing, Blake added further decoration in watercolor with pen or brush to each print, varying them on each copy he made.

The series of Blake's now famous illuminated books was started with his *Songs of Innocence,* dated 1789. His method of illustration was elaborated in the course of time through *The Book of Thel,*

The Marriage of Heaven and Hell, and other works; and the contrast in style between the decoration of the *Songs of Innocence* and the *Songs of Experience,* with which it was issued from 1794 onward, is most marked.

Blake's technique was too slow for him to be able to produce many copies of his books, and it was not until many years after his death, and largely because of the enthusiasm of such men as Richard Monckton Milnes and Alexander Gilchrist (whose *Life* of Blake was first published in 1863), that his poems were extensively reprinted. When they were reprinted, they normally appeared as ordinary letterpress printed pages; it is only in the last few years that the work of the William Blake Trust and the Trianon Press has made it possible for many readers to see Blake's poetry in the form in which Blake wished it to be seen.

Among the enormous number of writers and artists who have been inspired by Blake's work a few have worked in the tradition of Blake's private printing. On Iona in the 1880s J. W. Cormick and W. Muir produced small lithographic editions of Gaelic poetry—*The Blessing of the Ship* (1887) and *The Death of Fraoch* (1888) are the only two known to me, although they may have produced more— in the design of which the style of the prophetic books was followed closely. In this century there have been two other presses that are also in Blake's tradition, unlike most other modern private presses whose owners normally owe their inspiration (however indirectly) to William Morris and the Arts and Crafts Movement.

The first of the two to be established was that of Ralph Chubb, himself a mystic and very conscious of following Blake. In a prospectus called *My Path,* which he issued in 1932, he said that "Blake, faced with an almost identical problem solved it in almost the same way. I accept his tradition, and am grateful, and own my obligation; still, I am no copier nor follower. Rather I take up the thread where he left it and develop the plan." This was a very bold claim, but one that had the support of at least one critic, P. G. Konody. Chubb, he wrote, "is not an imitator of Blake, but his mind dwells in the same spirit regions, and he is technically better equipped to give pictorial form to his visions." Looking back over 50 years one may reasonably judge that this was an absurd exaggeration; nevertheless Chubb's career as printer has much of interest in it.

Ralph Chubb (1892–1960) was educated at St. Alban's Grammar School (memories of which recur constantly in the last books he printed) and at Selwyn College, Cambridge. After serving in the First World War, he studied at the Slade School of Art, and formed a close friendship with the artist Leon Underwood, through whose support and influence he had a number of exhibitions at Chenil's and the Goupil Galleries and had pictures hung at the Royal Academy. Despite this support and the judgments of critics like Konody, his work did not sell, and to secure an income he took a part-time position teaching art at a boys' public school.

From early childhood he had been obsessed with the idea of making books, and in 1924 he turned to printing. He could not afford a press, but his elder brother Lawrence (the "practical" member of the family and later a distinguished geologist) built him a primitive press out of a carpenter's screw and some odd pieces of timber. Lawrence also provided type and chases, showed Ralph how to make wood engravings, and how to print. The first production from the press, in fact, was Lawrence Chubb's macabre poem *A Vision* of which together they printed 27 copies (Illus. 24).

With this press Chubb produced three volumes of his own work. Of these only his *Sacrifice of Youth* (1924) was set and produced entirely by himself; he disliked typesetting and his eldest sister, Ethel, set the type for the other two. For his next books he turned to commercial printers, whose bills were paid by his long-suffering family. And there is no doubt they were long suffering: Chubb was a homosexual at a time when homosexuality was not tolerated by English society. The failure of his paintings and other studies of adolescent male nudes to sell was partly due to their ambivalence, but this was the least of the Chubbs' worries. Various indiscretions demanded not just his resigna-

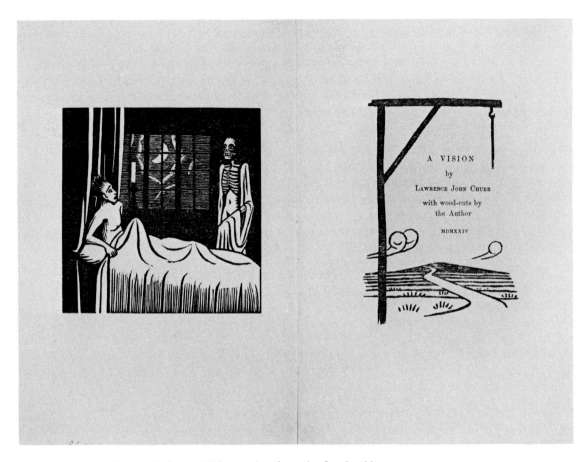

A VISION
by
LAWRENCE JOHN CHUBB
with wood-cuts by
the Author
MDMXXIV

ILLUS. 24. Ralph Chubb, Berkshire. Title opening from the first booklet
printed on the press made for Chubb by his brother Lawrence, 1924.

tion from his teaching post, but a total move for the whole family to a district where they were not
known.

It was, in fact, as a result of his homosexuality that Chubb turned eventually to lithographic
work. Printers refused on moral grounds to touch his manifesto, *An Appendix* (1929), and he
resorted to duplicating by writing out the text himself on stencils. The pamphlet was without any
artistic merit, but it pointed the way for his later printing. He bought a lithographic press, so that he
could "combine poetic idea, script, and designs, in free and harmonious rhythm—all unified together—so as to be mutually dependent and significant." At the same time, he decided to renounce
painting and engraving entirely except in the production of his books, so that it was with some
justification that he wrote, "My object is ideal, my work is not a pastime even to the extent that it
was with William Morris, but is the living output of one who labours for humane ends content in
humble circumstances."

During the 1930s Chubb was to produce four books lithographically, with the text written out
in a highly formalized script, which, though lacking the clarity and elegance of Edward Johnston's
school of calligraphy, harmonized excellently with the illustrations. The books were received warmly
by a small group—necessarily small, as Chubb seldom printed more than 30 to 40 copies, although
the nature of his work was such that its appeal would be restricted. Critics were cautious in their
notices of work so far out of the ordinary, but a reviewer in the *Times Literary Supplement* observed
that "no one could suspect Chubb's work of being a mere literary imitation [of Blake]; it is

obviously an instance of the parallel working of a similar mind." In the last book completed in the 1930s, *The Secret Country* (1939) (Illus. 25), and in *The Child of Dawn* (1948) and *Flames of Sunrise* (1953) Chubb moved some way from his philosophical and mystical preoccupations. The volumes included a number of stories of occult adventure and Gothic tales, which would not have disgraced "Monk" Lewis. At the same time he reached his peak as an illustrator. The themes were still markedly more homosexual than British society was prepared to tolerate, and it was no doubt only the fact that the books were produced in such small editions for subscribers that saved him from prosecution; he was warned that no more books of this kind would be tolerated. (Even in 1958, when I first became interested in Chubb's printing, the intellectual climate was such that the British Museum kept some of his work in the "private case" of erotica, which was not entered in the catalogues. Chubb had told me they were there, and after some inquiries I found myself being interviewed by the Superintendent of the Reading Room, who had to assure himself that I had a serious purpose and would not be depraved by having them issued to me! How times have changed.)

ILLUS. 25. Ralph Chubb, Berkshire. Prospectus for *The Secret Country*, lithographed in Chubb's characteristic style, 1939.

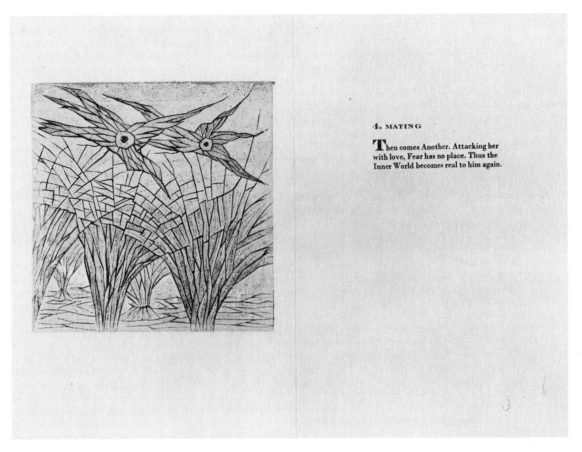

4. MATING

Then comes Another. Attacking her with love, Fear has no place. Thus the Inner World becomes real to him again.

ILLUS. 26. Gogmagog Press, London. *A Bird's World*, 1959. Double spread from this never-published book.

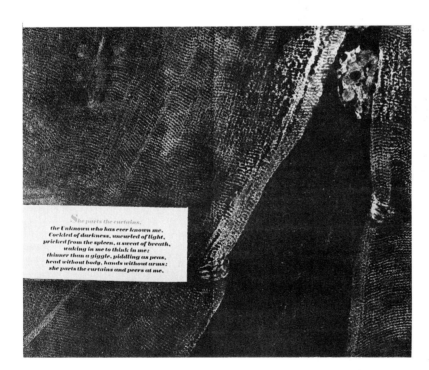

She parts the curtains,
the Unknown who has ever known me.
Cockled of darkness, uncurled of light,
pricked from the spleen, a sweat of breath,
waking in me to think in me:
thinner than a giggle, piddling as peas,
head without body, hands without arms;
she parts the curtains and peers at me.

ILLUS. 27. Gogmagog Press, London. Opening from *The Curtain*, 1960.

His sister Muriel, with whom he was then living, found a way to save him from despair. In an attic she found a box of stories and poems that he had written in childhood and that were full of childhood innocence for which there could be no persecution. For his two last books, *Treasure Trove* (1957) and *The Golden City* (1960), he drew on this material. He was by then a sick man, and his eyesight was failing badly, so he had to resort to a simplified script and manner of illustration; this style accorded well with the nature of the texts.

Toward the end of his life, Chubb presented much of his artistic work to galleries and libraries in Britain, in the hope that posterity would afford him the recognition denied him in his own time. Since his death, his executors have had some fragmentary work completed at the Cuckoo Hill Press for similar presentation, and a Memorial Collection of his archives, artistic works, and books has been formed.

It is a relief to turn from this story of misbegotten endeavor to another contemporary private press, one at which the owner has (like Blake) been much more of an innovator in the art of producing the book beautiful. This is the Gogmagog Press of Morris Cox. In some respects Cox's reasons for starting his press were more like those of William Davy than those of Blake. The magazines in which his stories and poems had been published had closed, and the publishers of his first book of verse, *Whirligig* (1954), were not convinced that the style of his work would interest

ILLUS. 28. *Left:* A Gogmagog illustration. The trial print. *Opposite page left:* The block. *Opposite page right:* The final print.

more than a very limited circle of readers and were not prepared to lose money on future books. Cox was, therefore, presented with a classic problem: to abandon writing altogether, to attempt to adapt his style to one that might have more sales appeal, to go to a firm of vanity publishers, or to take up printing himself. In this there was nothing except the high quality of his poetry to distinguish him from a host of other writers; the difference was that he was an artist who since the 1920s had been experimenting with autographic illustration processes and had achieved a considerable measure of success in printmaking. So in 1956, already in his 50s, he bought his first font of type, modified a press that he had made for printing linocuts, and set to work. His first book, *Yule Gammon,* was completed early in 1957. Of the 20 copies printed only a few had been sold before Cox decided that the standard of production was too low and scrapped the remainder. A fresh start was made with *The Slumbering Virgin,* a blank-verse interpretation of the old tale of the sleeping princess, which was published under the imprint of "The Gogmagog Press."

The aims he should pursue with his press were now clear to Cox: to publish original texts supported in full by his own illustrations. The philosophy he developed for the Gogmagog Press was a severe one, demanding that all the tasks involved in the production should be undertaken by the author/artist. One of his beliefs is that "no serious work should be attempted which can be done

ILLUS. 29. Gogmagog Press, London. A range of Morris Cox's bindings.

as well or better by the average commercial printer."* In consequence, he regarded his earliest work as unsatisfactory in production. One difficulty was in the quality of paper. Of two books printed in 1959, one, *A Bird's World* (Illus. 26), was never issued, while the other, *Nine Poems from Nature*, nearly suffered the same fate. With his next book, *The Curtain*, Cox was very much better pleased, and it remains one of the most completely satisfying of all Gogmagog books (Illus. 27).

The Curtain employed for the first time some of Cox's highly individual techniques in printing. These sometimes call for a combination of direct and offset printing, in which the sheets of soft pliable Japanese paper are printed on both sides; the face is offset from a rubber blanket while the printing block is impressed into the reverse side of the sheet. For this type of work Cox modified an office press to be capable of use for direct or offset use, or a combination of both. His blocks are often works of art in themselves, being built up from cardboard, lace, wire netting, dried leaves and other objects into a surface impossible to print by any conventional means (Illus. 28). Whether complex or simple—and some of his most effective blocks have been very simple—much of the success of Cox's work lies in the inking: hand dabbing of color in the Japanese manner to produce subtle multicolored prints of a kind achieved by no other private printer. The success of this technique can be seen most effectively in such works as his series *An Impression of the Seasons* (1965–

*In the first edition of this book, following an earlier writer I quoted this tenet as "no serious work should be attempted which *cannot* . . . ," which I had interpreted as a deliberate double negative, a paradox on the lines of Oscar Wilde's "anything worth doing is worth doing badly." Cox concedes that such an interpretation is possible but prefers the straightforward assertion that his approach to the private press demands that he only tackle work that is of a kind the commercial printer could not print as well.

ILLUS. 30. Gogmagog Press, London.
Morris Cox at work on *Conversation Pieces*
at his Adana flatbed platen modified
for offset printing, c.1961.

1966) in which the nature prints have a tactile quality otherwise found only in some of the French *beaux-livres* with their *estampilles*.

Printing by these methods is extremely slow, each impression demanding perhaps 15 or 20 minutes to make. Because Cox also binds his books (achieving a harmony with the content all too rare even when the printer is also the binder), his output has always been small (Illus. 29). After the distribution of Gogmagog books was taken over by Bertram Rota, Cox has had more time to concentrate on the making of his highly individual books. Some of them, like the landscape panoramas of *An Impression of the Seasons* or his *Winter Trees* (1977), are virtually without text, while in others, like his poems *Intimations of Mortality* (1977), the text has been printed by another private press allowing Cox to concentrate on his illustrative work that he does so well.

The Gogmagog Press was set up to permit Cox to print his own work, and although he has occasionally printed work written by others, such as *A Mediaeval Dream Book* (1963), these have in general been less successful than those in which the whole conception has been Cox's own. To the typographical purist, harking back to Cobden-Sanderson or some other such august figure, Cox's work can be a considerable irritation. On the choice of type he is undoubtedly heretical:

> There is no ideal type. Perhaps type faces should be one's own, with a character
> of one's own. However, better an ugly face married to the mood of the work
> than one which sits pretentiously in a vacuum.

Sometimes he has used faces of pronounced ugliness—Matura, Rockwell, Playbill, and so on—and done so in layouts that flout all the conventions, whether of the symmetric or asymmetric school. Yet his books undoubtedly *work,* not as imposing examples of fine typography, not as witty pieces of the moment whose appeal lies in their novelty, but as genuinely fresh contributions to our conception of what the book can be. Gogmagog has been aptly described as "the most poetic and creative private press in England"; like Blake's illuminated printing it represents the author as printer in a way that few could hope to emulate.

Chapter 8

CLANDESTINE PRESSES I: MORAL

"WITH TWENTY-SIX SOLDIERS of lead I shall conquer the world" is an old boast of the printer. It was not long after the introduction of printing into western Europe that rulers began to realize the power that producers of the printed word could wield—power that could be harnessed (as in the case of the Emperor Maximilian, with his ambitious program of over 100 books that were to broadcast the glories of the house of Habsburg) but that could be disastrous in the hands of the opposition. A solution to the problem was sought in censorship. It was not a new idea, for in the late Middle Ages the ecclesiastical authorities, particularly in the universities, had attempted to control the written word and, naturally, extended their censorship to the printed book. It was not until 1501, however, that the Pope (Alexander VI) attempted to impose preventive censorship on nontheological books (previously the church has been interested only in the suppression of heresy). This position was to harden the attacks of the Protestant Reformation and of the increasing power of the secular rulers until the first *Index Librorum Prohibitorum* was promulgated by Pope Paul IV in 1559. Meanwhile temporal rulers were also claiming the right of censorship as their own prerogative. The first secular censorship office had been set up by the electorate of Mainz and the imperial city of Frankfurt as early as 1486.

The result of such action was not to silence those presses publishing material unwelcome to the secular or ecclesiastical authorities but to drive it underground, and clandestine presses have flourished whenever and wherever there has been political, religious, or moral oppression.

Not all such presses have been operated by amateurs, of course, however private they may have been. Some of them have covered up their traces so successfully that the true identity of the printers, or the very existence of the press, remains in doubt. The most common subterfuge in evading the attentions of the censor was the use of false imprints on the books printed, and these were used extensively by reputable publishers. In London, J. Charlesworth had enough courage to publish the revolutionary tracts of Giordano Bruno, but he compounded it with prudence by making the books appear as if printed in Venice and Paris. On occasion the lack of censorship was a trouble to printers. The laxity of the Dutch censorship in the seventeenth century made any book on a controversial subject that declared its Dutch origin more than usually suspect to foreign censors;

and so, for example, when the Elzevirs in Amsterdam published Pascal's *Provinciales* in 1657 they used the imprint "Cologne, chez Pierre de Vallée."

The path of the bibliographer is made treacherous by these false imprints, and many writers have been deceived by them. For generations it had been believed that Ulrich von Hutten, the political publicist of German humanism, maintained a press in his castle of Stekelberg, a place from which he could with impunity publish his attacks on the Duke of Wurtemberg. Cotton, Peignot, Brunet, and other authorities all support the story, and only modern bibliographical examination of type and ornaments has shown that the books with this imprint were produced by a commercial printer elsewhere and that the imprint *in arce Stekelberk* was used only to mislead the censor.

In England the religious and political controversies of the sixteenth and seventeenth centuries provided an excellent field for such presses to flourish. One of the most famous of these was that of the Jesuit martyr Edmund Campion. In the course of his work in rallying the spirits of the persecuted English Catholics, early in 1581 he wrote his famous *Decem Rationes,* "Ten reasons for the confidence with which Edmund Campion offered to dispute with his adversaries on behalf of the Faith." The difficulties of producing the book were great: It was essential that the textual references with which the work was copiously endowed should be given accurately, as any slip would have been pounced upon eagerly by his opponents and quoted as evidence of dishonesty. It was originally intended that the book should be printed in secret by Stephen Brinkley, who had installed a surreptitious press at Greenstreet House in East Ham some time in 1580, and had printed several works for Campion's fellow-missionary Robert Persons in 1580 and 1581. Campion, therefore, came up to London to supervise its production. The search that was being made for him was closing in; Walsingham's government spies were very efficient, and when one of the servants of Ronald Jenks, a stationer who had supplied many of the materials, turned informer, it was obviously unsafe to continue where they were. The press was quickly moved to Stonor-on-Thames, where Dame Cecilia Stonor had put her house at the missionaries' disposal. It was an ideal spot, easily accessible by river from London and Oxford, and yet well hidden from prying eyes in dense beech woods. Here under Brinkley's supervision four workmen printed the *Decem Rationes,* and the completed copies were sent to a Father Hartley at Oxford, who in time for university commencement on June 27, 1581, placed copies on the benches in St. Mary's Church.

Viewed as an example of book production, Campion's tract shows relatively few signs of the haste and difficulties of its production. The presswork is good, the composition correct. Yet there are indications that it was produced with very limited typographical resources. There was a shortage of some sorts—Æ had at times to be represented by Æ or by E; the question mark is from a black letter font; and the Greek quotations had to be represented in italic type. In its day, however, the design of the book was of no interest; the romantic manner of its appearance in St. Mary's, and Campion's polished and urbane style caused a great effect in the university. Lord Burghley regarded its publication as a matter of gravity, and enlisted the aid of the Bishop of London and of the Regius Professors of Divinity at the two universities to produce replies to the book. The hunt for Campion was intensified, and in July he was taken. Offered his life if he would abjure his faith and offered the prospect of high advancement if he would enter the Protestant ministry, he refused. On December 1, 1581, he was hung, drawn, and quartered in Tyburn.

After the seizure of the Stonor press it seems that Richard Rowland (or Verstegan, as he was later known), a printer in Smithfield, intended to carry on with Catholic printing. But soon after his first clandestine book, *A True Report of the Death and Martyrdome of M. Campion,* had been printed, his press also was seized. Rowland evaded capture and managed to flee the country, to continue printing recusant books in Paris and later in Antwerp.

Although these presses were troublesome enough to the authorities (as were to be the later secret presses of Robert Southwell and others), it was not only on the Catholic side that clandestine presses were at work. In the 1580s the danger to the English church from the rising tide of Puritanism was very great, and Archbishop Whitgift found it necessary to adopt the most stringent methods to keep the Puritans in check. In 1586 he obtained a decree from the Star Chamber that forbade the publication of any book unless authorized by himself or the Bishop of London, limited the number of printing presses, and revived an old law imposing the severest penalties for the publication of slanderous or seditious works. One result was the rise of what has become known in literary history as the Marprelate controversy.

Among those who suffered most severely from Whitgift's policy was the printer Robert Waldegrave. He had already had several terms of imprisonment for printing unauthorized tracts, when in April 1588 he printed John Udall's *The State of the Church of Englande,* an attack on the church far more dangerous and outspoken than earlier works that had been savagely prosecuted. At Whitgift's order his house was raided by officers of the Stationers Company on April 16, and a press, types, and copies of Udall's tract were seized and confiscated. Waldegrave himself managed to escape, but his occupation was gone and he had a wife and children to support. With nothing further to lose, he conveyed some type he had rescued to the London home of a certain Mistress Crane, while he himself seems to have moved to Kingston-on-Thames, where a new edition of Udall's book was printed with equipment belonging to John Penry, "the father of Welsh non-conformity," who had previously suffered under Whitgift and been associated with Waldegrave. Probably by June Waldegrave had moved to Mistress Crane's country house in the nearby village of East Molesey, where the type had been conveyed from London. He was soon at work on another pamphlet by Udall, and by October was engaged on the first of the Marprelate tracts, commonly called *An Epistle.*

An Epistle burst on the world with startling effect. The work of "Martin Marprelate" was devastating in the success with which it covered the bishops with ridicule while at the same time leading the reader on into the traps of Puritan doctrine. The stir the tract caused was so great that by November 14, Burghley was writing urgently to Whitgift telling him to spare no time in arresting those responsible. But this was not to be too easy. As early as June Whitgift's pursuivants had searched for Waldegrave at Kingston, and by November he had moved to the greater safety of Northamptonshire, setting up his press once more in the house of Sir Richard Knightley, a friend of Penry. Here the second Marprelate tract, *The Epitome,* was printed before December. Early in January 1589 the press had moved again to Coventry, where more tracts, *The Minerall Conclusions* and *Hay Any Work for Cooper,* were also produced. Waldegrave was tiring of his work; quite apart from the very considerable personal danger involved he seems, like a good many Puritans, to have disliked Martin Marprelate's methods. He is next to be heard of in La Rochelle where he retired for safety and where he seems to have printed some other pamphlets by Penry and by Job Throckmorton, another of the Marprelate writers. They took some time to find another printer to replace him, but early in the summer of 1589 John Hodgkins, "a salt-petre man," was engaged. He printed two further pamphlets, *Theses Martinianae* and *The Just Censure and Reproof of Martin Junior,* on the press belonging to Penry, which had been moved to a new home in the house of a Mistress Wigston in a village some miles south of Coventry. Hodgkins disliked the press and moved to Manchester, where there was another press, to work on *More Work for the Cooper.* He and his assistants were caught while engaged on this work in late August and carried off to London for examination under torture.

This was not to be the end of Martin Marprelate, however. Penry's old press in Mistress Wigston's house was still undiscovered, and it was quickly moved to Throckmorton's house at Hasely and used to print the last Marprelate tract, *The Protestation,* in September 1589. The first half-sheet of the book is very obviously amateur work (perhaps that of Penry and Throckmorton), but the rest shows all the marks of a skilled printer; it has been conjectured that it was completed by Waldegrave, who had returned to England. Soon after the book had been finished Penry and Waldegrave left for Scotland. They were just in time: In October an informer gave away the secret of the press and all those concerned were arrested and imprisoned. A few years later Penry returned from Scotland and was seized on a trumped-up charge of treason, paying with his life for the part he had played in the affair. Waldegrave more prudently stayed in Scotland, where he became King's Printer, until King James succeeded to the English throne.

As well as the recusant printing carried on openly abroad at Douay and elsewhere, there seems to have been at least one long-lived Catholic press at Birchley Hall in Lancashire, operated by members of the Anderton family from about 1608 until 1642. With the later increase of religious and political tolerance in Britain, there was naturally a decline in the number of clandestine presses of this sort. One of the last in England was a Jacobite press that printed *A Collection of Loyal Songs* with the imprint Ragland Castle in 1750. In Ireland such presses flourished very much later, particularly in the troubled years after 1916, when work was ably directed by Michael Collins. Much of this printing was undertaken in secret by commercial printers who were sympathetic to the cause of Irish independence—the bonds and promotional literature produced for the "National loan," for example, which were printed at Dollard's Printing House near Dublin Castle. Collins did not consider it sufficient to rely only on the services of sympathizers; special printing equipment was also obtained and secreted in Aungier Street, where Dick McKee was engaged in setting up and printing *An tOglách,* the newssheet of the Republican Army, in the intervals he could find from his work as a member of the Dublin Brigade.

The British Isles have had their share of surreptitious printing. In the early years of the nineteenth century there was a substantial production of underground literature by those opposed to the status quo, and the punitive legislation and enforcement measures employed by those in authority in an attempt to root out "undesirable" literature, particularly the unstamped newspapers, represent some of the uglier aspects of Britain's history. Not many of those producing this material were amateurs, although Julian Hibbert's rather innocuous private press (whose Greek types are described in Chapter 24) was working on the fringes of this scene in a way that anticipated some of the amateur printing in the Netherlands in World War II.

By the time Victoria was firmly on the throne, a much saner and more tolerant attitude prevailed. It is, therefore, somewhat awkward to discuss in the context of *clandestine* presses the work of one that was never subject to prosecution and was conducted quite openly; nevertheless the pronounced republican character of the press operated by W. J. Linton in the Lake District for a while in the early 1850s fits better with these other political amateurs than with any other group of private printers.

The story of Linton's press at Brantwood on Lake Windermere has been told in detail by James S. Dearden. A wood engraver (and a very good one) by trade, Linton was a republican writer by choice, and in the early 1850s he was editing a monthly review, the *English Republic,* which was published by James Watson (who had been Julian Hibbert's printer). It was printed commercially, and the costs of production were borne by a wealthy supporter in Durham, Joseph Cowan. To assist Linton when he moved to Brantwood in 1853 Cowan underwrote the cost of installing a press and equipment, on which from 1854 the *English Republic* and the monthly paper of similar political cast the *Northern Tribune* were printed. Linton, who engraved the blocks and edited the *Republic,* was assisted in a sort of workers' cooperative by a number of young men, including Thomas Hailing (later publisher of *Hailing's Circular* and English agent for a number of American typefoundries). Through 1854 and early 1855 they toiled at their task, sharing Linton's meagre earnings from engraving when he had some, going without when there was no money, and producing regular publications of respectable quality many miles from the nearest railway, with all materials being carted in over the hills and the publications being carted out in the same way.

The formal part of Linton's venture came to an end in 1855, when the abolition of stamp duty on newspapers made it easier to produce journals that would reach the intended audience. The *Tribune* was absorbed into a London paper, and the *Republic* was discontinued. The equipment at Brantwood was still used from time to time; sometimes for less serious work such as the *Brantwood Miscellany* in May 1856, a family paper very much like the other hobby journals produced by Victorian amateur printers. A number of broadside editions were printed of some of Linton's poems and finally some *Occasional Tracts* in 1866, shortly before Linton finally emigrated to the United States. Later at Appledore Farm near New Haven, Connecticut, Linton was again to set up a private press and there to continue writing, engraving, and printing until shortly before his death in 1897. The fate of his Brantwood press is not known; it was still there when John Ruskin purchased the house from him in 1871. Ruskin as printer is one of the more interesting might-have-beens of the private press.

Although Britain had many surreptitious printers, there have been even more on the Continent. At one extreme there have been the relatively public presses set up by those powerful enough to defy government censorship. For example, Jan Potocki, the author of *The Saragossa Manuscript* and one of the founders of Slavic archaeology, quarreled with the government of Poland over the freedom of the press and in 1789 set up a free printing press in his castle from which numerous books were issued. These "Wolna Drukarnia" publications were scarcely seditious—*A Chronological Atlas of European Russia, An Essay on Universal History,* and *A Description of the New Machine for Coining Money* are typical titles—and although the authorities may have been annoyed at the flouting of their authority, the work of the press can not have caused them much worry. At the other extreme there was at about the same time as Count Potocki's press a surreptitious undertaking operating in Brabant. The police of the Austrian Netherlands were seriously concerned by the appearance of the revolutionary writings of the Abbé François Xavier de Feller and spared no efforts in their search for the abbé and his press. To escape from their pursuit he is said to have set up a press at the bottom of a coal mine near Liège, from which his seditious sheets were, with impunity, produced and distributed throughout the whole of the Austrian Netherlands.

Presses of this kind were to be found frequently in the nineteenth century and later. In Russia there were very many underground presses before 1917, in occupied Belgium during the First World War the Abbé de Feller provided the example for many ventures of the same kind, and in occupied Europe during the Second World War clandestine printing was by no means the least important aspect of the various Resistance movements. It is safe to say that every occupied country developed this means of countering German control. In Czechoslovakia, for example, Joseph Skalda edited the first such underground paper *V Boj* for two years until caught by the Nazis in the fall of 1941; but Skalda's execution did not mean the end of the Czech underground press by any means.

In Vichy France the difficulties of organizing clandestine presses were considerable. France was split into the occupied and unoccupied zones; the French divided into the supporters of Vichy, who were prepared to collaborate with the Germans, and their opponents who were by no means prepared to do so. This situation, like the religious dissensions of the sixteenth century, made it difficult to recognize who could be trusted and who not. The vast majority of publishing houses, and many individual writers, gave in to *force majeure.* Many were willing to collaborate. Many of the editors and printers of the first Resistance presses and newspapers—of *Pantagruel,* of *La Pensée Libre*—were caught and shot. But out of the failure of *La Pensée Libre* came a development that was to lead to the establishment of the most successful of all presses of the Resistance: Les Editions de Minuit.

Jean Bruller, an engraver, illustrator, and journalist, had at the invitation of Pierre de Lescure

ILLUS. 31. The cellar under Comte's Paris workshop where he printed the *Temoignage Chrétien* as part of the French Resistance, 1941–1942.

written a story called *Le Silence de la Mer,* which was to have appeared in the next issue of *La Pensée Libre* under the pseudonym of Vercors. Suddenly he was left, an author without a publisher. But before the war Bruller had been his own publisher for various books: Why should he not now publish his story in the same way?

In his autobiography *The Battle of Silence* (1967) Vercors records that he was influenced to a very slight degree by a story he had heard about some rebels against Napoleon III. At a dinner party they were startled by their host's putting a bust of the hated emperor in the place of honor in the center of the table, but at the end of the meal the host struck the bust in the face with a hammer and out tumbled dozens of copies of Victor Hugo's incendiary poem *Les Châtiments*. It was no mere adolescent romanticism that spurred Vercors in his venture. If he could set up the organization needed for his book, it could serve to produce other books. The propaganda that the Resistance movements would produce would not be enough, he reasoned; there was also a need for a clandestine press which, by producing books of a high intellectual content, would demonstrate that French literary life still survived in defiance of Nazi domination and would provide a rallying point for intellectual resistance.

Jean Bruller found a jobbing printer, Georges Oudeville, who was willing to run the risks that would be involved in the undertaking from a tiny printing office near the Pitié hospital, which had been taken over by the Germans as a military hospital. Oudeville had just enough type to set and print an eight-page form, which had to be distributed before he could set the type for the next eight pages. For three months, with German troops constantly passing and repassing his open door Oudeville printed *Le Silence de la Mer* in whatever time he could take from his legitimate work of producing wedding and funeral announcements. Then the printed sections were taken in small batches to the apartment of a friend, Yvonne Paraf, who organized a team of helpers to sew the sections and to glue them into covers.

Le Silence de la Mer appeared in an edition of 350 copies in February 1942. The secret of the authorship was well kept; of the team of workers only Pierre de Lescure knew who Vercors was. His true identity was not revealed until the liberation. But Vercors became very well known. Copies of the book found their way into the unoccupied zone of France and were taken to England and reprinted extensively—in London, in New York, Dakar, Quebec, Beirut. At the orders of General de Gaulle it was reprinted by the Free French in London, and tens of thousands of miniature copies on India paper were dropped over France by the Royal Air Force. An English version by Cyril Connolly sold 15,000 copies; one of these was taken to Tunis where the novelist Pierre Moinot retranslated it into French in order to circulate it further.

With loans of 3,000 and later 5,000 francs from a close friend Bruller was able to continue with his publishing. By the time of the liberation in 1944 he and his assistants had managed the remarkable feat of publishing 25 books, nearly one a month. Far from depending on help from Resistance funds, they sold the books so successfully that they realized a total profit of 300,000 francs, a sum that was later distributed through the Comité National des Écrivains to the families of those printers who had died for their country in the Resistance.

Although the printers had many anxious moments, neither the Vichy authorities nor the Gestapo succeeded in stopping the production of the Editions de Minuit. In fact, near the end they despaired of doing so and instead conceived the idea of producing spurious editions of its books themselves, which, because of the veiled propaganda they would contain, would bring the real books into discredit.

ILLUS. 32. The Resistance Press in Paris. The artists Pontremoli and Philibert, and Mme. Pontremoli printing anti-Hitler leaflets, c.1941.

ILLUS. 33. Bicycle-powered press used for the production of clandestine printing in Nazi-occupied Europe.

Although the idea was excellent, its successful execution eluded the Germans. Eighty thousand copies of the first of these false editions were printed and delivered to Hachette, the official distribution agency. So they should appear clandestine, the *justification du tirage* carried an obviously false censorship permit, No. 00002. Immediately Hachette seized on this: If they distributed the books, they would be liable to prosecution for illegal distribution, so they demanded a written order to protect themselves. If the Germans were to issue the written order, however, the books would be clandestine no longer, and the "cat would be out of the bag." It was too difficult a problem for the Teutonic mind. At the liberation the 80,000 copies were still in Hachette's basement!

In all occupied countries the range of clandestine printing was remarkable. Much of it was concerned simply with forgery (of ration cards, identity documents, and the like) or with the production of newssheets, the number and range of which were astonishing. It was claimed that one or two copies of every issue of *V Boj* reached every Czech village, while in the Netherlands it has been estimated that well over a million copies of their various newssheets were distributed, despite all setbacks, and well over 100 Dutch writers and printers died for their work in the Resistance.

Dutch underground printing is of particular interest, because it went well beyond the production of such "routine" Resistance material in whatever form could be achieved in the circumstances; indeed it included the deliberate production of work in the finest typographical style possible, which in the country of S. H. de Roos and Jan van Krimpen is saying a great deal.

Much of the Resistance work in the Netherlands was, of course, undistinguished typographically. The typographer S. H. Hartz spent much of his time underground in forging the documents needed for the members of the Resistance movement. But he also engraved a plate to illustrate a Dutch edition of Vercors's *Le Silence de la Mer* in an edition that never appeared because its printers were found by the security police while it was still being printed.

Of the clandestine fine presses one of the first was that of the Amsterdam bookseller and publisher A. A. Balkema. His "Five pound press," so-named for a loophole (quickly stopped) in the early occupation regulations allowing the production of books using no more than five pounds of paper, together with the other imprints he employed produced about 50 slim books in all, often in collaboration with Jan van Krimpen as designer. Although slim, some were large, like the selection of Baudelaire published under the title of *Le Vin* in 1943, with etchings by Jeanne Bieruma Oosting, or the calligraphic rendering in English and German of *Ten Poems by Emily Dickinson* (1943). Each book in the series has its own individual style, and all were beautifully produced.

In contrast, the 27 books published in the *Schildpadreeks* or "Tortoise Series," by Jac Romijn were of uniform size and shared other common design features. They were all new unpublished works by Dutch writers who were named; prose works each had a frontispiece, and poetry a specially designed cover. The designers included Charles Nypels and A. A. M. Stols, who was also active in producing fine editions, mainly of French texts. Stols often printed them under his own name but with the precaution of dating the edition before the German occupation.

One of the most substantial of the clandestine presses was De Bezige Bij ("The Busy Bee"), which, like Vercors's Editions de Minuit, was to survive the war and become a regular publishing house. Its editions included a translation into Dutch of Fitzgerald's version of Omar Khayyam (1944), for which photogravure reproductions of John Buckland-Wright's engravings for his Golden Cockerel edition were employed. This was in its *Quousque tandem* series, which included many other translations. The most important of the press's publications were its *rijmprents,* illustrated broadsides of poems of a sort that had been in vogue in Holland since the 1920s and lent themselves well to the mood of the war. These were distributed for sale widely throughout the country, and proved a great success from the start of the series, Jan Campert's *De Achttien Dooden* (1943). The original intention has been to raise funds for the support of Jewish children saved from Amsterdam, but so successful was the undertaking that it brought in far more money than was needed for this purpose alone. In the end over $300,000 was contributed to the general Resistance fund.

One of the many printers who perished for his work was the Groningen artist and printer Hendrik Nicolaas Werkman. Between the wars, Werkman had been closely associated with the art group De Ploeg, a Groningen group much influenced by German expressionism. Although some of his earlier work such as *Het Boek van Trijntje Soldaats* (1928) had been widely praised, his amazing *druksels,* pamphlets and prints produced by a mixture of various printing techniques, were of a kind that flouted all conventions of classical typography. In 1940 he became the printer to *De Blaue Schuit* ("The Blue Ship"), a group consisting otherwise of a chemist, a schoolmistress, and a clergyman. The group was named for Erasmus's blue ship of fools, or those belonging to no guild, by inference those Dutch writers who refused to join the German-dominated Kultuurkamer. Its first publication was a *rijmprent* of Martinus Nijhoff's poem *Het Jaar 1572* produced for Christmas 1940. It was to be followed by 40 other publications; some (like *Die Houtdiefstal* by Simon Vestdijk and F. R. A. Henkels, 1944) texts written and smuggled out by those already interned by the occupying power. Werkman was eventually arrested by the Nazis in March 1945, and was shot on April 10, three days before Groningen was liberated by the Allied advance.

Werkman's printing, which employed such techniques as stencils, hand-stamped wood type, and other devices, has had considerable influence on later Dutch graphic work. During the war he was closely associated with W. Sandberg, whose own *experimenta typographica* had been worked out while he was in hiding, and soon after Sandberg became Director of the Stedelijk Museum in Amsterdam, he devoted an exhibition to Werkman's graphics.

It might be thought that in contemporary Britain or America clandestine presses of this sort have disappeared completely. In general, there is little need for them, although in Britain in the late 1960s there were police attempts to suppress some anti-Vietnam War and pro-Rhodesian pieces. No doubt there are groups on the extreme right wing who find the race relations legislation compels some degree of clandestine work for their lunatic outpourings, but there is certainly nothing to correspond with the *samizdat* work produced in Soviet Russia. We are fortunate that the amateur printer can concern himself with other things, but it is worth remembering Beatrice Warde's splendid words:

> Any private press has fearsome claws sheathed in its velvet pads. What keeps them sheathed is not *force majeur* but free will. . . . Every private press is in some sense a Press of the Resistance. In its ancestry is the blood of martyrs who crept by night to secret cellars with forbidden texts; its heroes of our own century are the men who risked their lives to purloin handfuls of precious type from Nazi-guarded composing rooms. And if you see anything in this modern world that makes you cry "No, I resist," you need not try to capture the nearest radio station. Goliath has a more insidious enemy. He can keep a sharp eye on the millionfold instruments of communication and yet never see what doom is awaiting him from the perfidious Albion.

Chapter 9

CLANDESTINE PRESSES II: IMMORAL

IT IS NOT ONLY to avoid religious or political oppression that presses may prefer to operate in secret. An author may have excellent reasons for wishing a purely private circulation for books he does not want attributed to him or he does not want regarded as in the main current of his work. There are contemporary examples of private presses operated under a pseudonym because the owner feels that his identity as a printer should not be confused with his identity in his real profession. To avoid public censure was perhaps the reason for the privacy with which Jacob Ilive, a printer and type-founder, printed a famous literary forgery, *The Book of Jasher*, in 1751. Ilive was a man of very odd beliefs. In 1733 he published the text of an oration he had delivered a few years earlier, in which he attempted to prove the plurality of worlds, that this earth is hell, that men's souls are apostate angels, and similar fancies. *The Book of Jasher* was a pretended translation from the Hebrew, supposedly made by "Alcuin of Britain," and is a text of which modern editions have been made for use by the Rosicrucians.

> The account given of the translation [wrote Edward Rowe Mores in his *Dissertation Upon English Typographical Founders,* 1778], is full of glaring absurdities: but of the publication this we can say from the information of the Only-One who is capable of informing us, because the business was a secret between the Two: *Mr. Ilive* in the night-time had constantly an *Hebr.* bible before him . . . and cases in his closet. he produced the copy for *Jasher,* and it was composed in private, and the forms worked off in the night-time in a private press-room by these Two after the men of the Printing-house had left their work.—*Mr. Ilive* was an expeditious compositor though he worked in a night-gown and swept his case *to pye* with the sleeves.

The normal reason for most printers' wishing to avoid public censure is much more straightforward than this: It is the printing of pornography. One of the most interesting of these pornographic presses—most of them are very dull indeed—was the one maintained by the Duc d'Aiguillon on his estate at Verets in Touraine. On this press a small edition (perhaps of 12 copies) of erotic Italian and French poetry was printed in 1735. Edited by Paradis de Moncrif and the Abbé Grécourt (who was connected also with the Imprimerie du Vourst and its tasteless *Maranzakiniana*), the volume bore the title *Recueil de Pièces Choisies: Rassemblées par les Soins du Cosmopolite* and was published with the punning imprint of "A Ànconne, chez Uriel Bandant, à l'enseigne de la liberté."

According to Gustave Werdet, writing in the prudish 1860s, this was the most licentious book ever printed. It certainly had close competition from another book that came from the same press in 1742, the bawdy songbook *Les Muses en Belle Humeur* issued from "Ville Franche" and probably also edited by Moncrif and Grécourt. Gershon Legman, whose *The Horn Book* (1964) is packed with curious learning, has suggested that the "Cosmopolite" for whom the books were printed was not the pseudonym of a single person, but instead of an orgiastic group of noblemen and noblewomen who met under the Duc d'Aiguillon's protection to engage in what was then called devil worship. Legman quotes a magnificent story from a suppressed page in the Pixerécourt catalogue; the young Duchesse d'Aiguillon, put to setting type for the *Recueil des Pièces Choisies,* asked her husband if there should be two R's (a pun on *heures,* "hours") in *foutre.* "Indeed there should," replied the Duke gravely, "but one normally gives it only one."

In England the most famous of all clandestine presses of this kind was that of John Wilkes. Following the publication in April 1763 of the famous "number 45" of the *North Briton,* the sluggish government was stirred into the ill-considered action of issuing a general warrant against its un-named authors, printers, and publishers; this action was eventually to lead to the recognition of the illegality of such warrants. Wilkes was then unable to find any commercial printer willing to take the risk of working for him. He, therefore, had two presses installed in his house in Great George Street in Westminster, and engaged two journeymen printers to work them. Originally his idea seems to have been to publish an account of his own persecution, but the idea was not received well by his friends. The two printers were therefore set to printing a number of relevant items, such as Lord Temple's *A Letter to Lords Halifax and Egremont,* which dealt with the seizure of Wilkes's papers by government agents. An edition of the 45 numbers of the *North Briton* was also put in hand. In a foolish moment in May 1763 Wilkes instructed his printer Michael Curry to set to work on an indecent parody of Pope, the *Essay on Woman.* Some years earlier Wilkes had become a member of the notorious Hell Fire Club, a society whose members—Sir Francis Dashwood, Lord Sandwich, Bubb Dodington, and others—engaged in extravagant ceremonies and orgiastic rites similar to those practiced by the Duc d'Aiguillon's group at Verets. The *Essay on Woman,* probably written by Thomas Potter, the libertine son of a former Archbishop of Canterbury, had circulated in manu-script among the members of the Hell Fire Club. Despite a good opening it is (like most similar pieces) remarkably tedious; but in the printed version the facetious and scandalous notes (wickedly ascribed to Dr. Warburton, Pope's editor, but probably written by Wilkes himself) give the *Essay* considerably more sparkle.

Wilkes cannot have considered how dangerous the *Essay* could prove to him when he ordered the edition of 12 copies to be printed for presentation to his intimates. It was not long before he found out. The government spies who were sniffing around his press got wind of the *Essay* and by insinuating themselves into the confidence of one of the workmen they managed to obtain a copy of it while Wilkes was abroad. The government made the best use they could of the *Essay* to support their general case against the *North Briton.* In the House of Lords the attack was led by Lord Sandwich, Wilkes's erstwhile companion in Hell Fire meetings.

Sandwich had good reason for disliking Wilkes. At a meeting of the Hell Fire Club at Medmen-ham Wilkes secretly introduced a baboon into the company. The frightened beast leaped onto Sandwich's back and clung there while Sandwich fell on his knees crying "Spare me, gracious Devil. I am as yet but half a sinner. I have never been half as wicked as I have pretended." His humiliation when he realized that he was not in Satan's clutches was acute. At another well-known encounter with Wilkes he also came off badly. When he observed that Wilkes would die of a pox or on the gallows, he was shattered by the retort that it depended on whether Wilkes embraced his Lordship's mistress or his principles. Sandwich's attack was therefore a ferocious one, and he was strongly supported by Warburton, who was Bishop of Gloucester, and solemnly protested against the attribution of the notes in the *Essay* to him. The result was a resolution of the House of Lords condemning the publication as "a most scandalous, obscene and impious libel."

For once the public was less susceptible than Parliament to this mass hypocrisy. During a current performance of the *Beggar's Opera,* at MacHeath's line "that Jemmy Twitcher should peach I own surprises me," the whole theater collapsed in laughter; Lord Sandwich remained "Jemmy Twitcher" to the end of his life. Nevertheless, because of the *Essay,* Wilkes had become a political liability and was thrown over by the ailing Pitt.

Wilkes's press was by no means the only private press that was set up for a more serious purpose but dabbled in the production of erotica. In 1783 a volume bearing the imprint of *Londres* was published under the title of *Amusemens, Gayetés et Frivolités Poetiques, pour un Bon Picard.* This very rare book was written by Pierre-Antoine de la Place and contains a selection of songs, stories, and epigrams of a decidedly free nature. La Place recorded in one copy that the book was printed by the Prince de Ligne and his son, using a manuscript pilfered from the author as "copy," and that a few copies of the small edition were stolen by a valet who took them to Paris, and where at the author's request they were seized and destroyed.

Many amateurs of all periods have indulged themselves by printing little pieces of this nature. Whether Isaiah Thomas did or did not print an edition of *Fanny Hill* need not detain us, nor need we pay much attention to the many who have printed Mark Twain's *1601,* variorum editions of *Eskimo Nell,* and the like. The traditional handpress has long ceased to be a tool for the hard-core pornographer, and in contemporary society commercial publishers can issue erotic books with little fear of prosecution. But during those periods in which the risk of censorship lies heavily upon the literary world, private presses have often succeeded in publishing questionable material when other more commercial undertakings would almost certainly have been prosecuted. There has always, at any rate in this century, been a market for expensively produced and lusciously illustrated editions of the more lubricious classics. Some of the private and quasi-private presses of the 1920s and 1930s jumped in to supply this market, confident that prosecution was unlikely. The authorities in England seem to have worked on the assumption that the expensive book would not corrupt its purchasers, whereas cheaper editions would. This taste for printing and reprinting the more erotic classics *ad nauseam* has almost disappeared among today's private presses—and what need for it in a permissive society?—but in its day it certainly made the idea of "private presses" or "fine editions" suspect to many.

Some of the private presses were not above a little baiting of the censors. The Nonesuch Press was by no means one of the publishers of erotica, but they pretended to feel in danger in their 1929 catalogue.

> In these days of literary censorship exercised by Sir Archibald Bodkin (of Savidge case fame), Sir William Joynson-Hicks and a Detective-Inspector of Scotland Yard, no publisher can be positive in his announcement that he will issue such and such a book. Chaucer? Fie, his language is coarse. Plato? The less said about Socrates and his young friends, *if* you please, the better. Shakespeare? He will perhaps pass unchallenged, for Lamb's Tales doubtless exhausted the censors' interest in this prurient author. Farquhar, Don Quixote even—these too may corrupt the corrupt, which is the current legal test of obscenity. With a propitiatory bow to Sir Archibald and to the potent and anonymous

Detective-Inspector (the unlamented Home Secretary gets no more than a distant nod) we therefore give to this list of announcements the precautionary title, "Bodkin Permitting."

Despite the fact that his publications were produced in very limited and expensive editions, Ralph Chubb put himself at some risk for the homosexual nature of his work, as noted in Chapter 7. There is one private printer who suffered considerably under the British obscenity laws in the 1930s, Count Potocki of Montalk.

Geoffrey Wladislas Vaile Potocki is one of the most extraordinary and interesting figures of the literary world, in interest far surpassing Baron Corvo, with whom he bears several points of resemblance, and is on his way to becoming a similar cult figure. Of Polish descent, he was born in New Zealand in 1903 and published his first poems there in such pioneer papers as the *Mangaweka Settler*. He also had a slim volume of his verse printed locally.

Like many others who saw their future in the world of literature, in 1928 he went to London to seek his fortune. Others from the Antipodes sought a new and better world that rejected bourgeois ideals by moving politically to the far left: as a descendant of Polish kings (among other illustrious forebears) Potocki's rejection of the bourgeoisie involved a movement to the extreme right wing. At first he was content to proclaim himself simply as Count Potocki de Montalk and a poet by divine right. It was not until December 1939 that he laid claim to the Kingdom of Poland as Wladislaw V, a claim that, though fantastic, does not lack all foundation. Potocki, in fact, was a man born out of his time; he would fit in perfectly in Casanova's *Memoirs*.

While a theological student in New Zealand, Potocki had seen some of the early mission printing undertaken there and claims that this was the foundation for his move into printing himself: "If some stupid missionary could do this, why not I?" Initially, however, he contented himself with seeking commercial printing of this work. This led to his first brush with the law. Early in 1932 he and a friend, the photographer Douglas Glass, accosted a policeman on duty outside the Old Bailey. They wished, they said, to have some poems containing the words and ideas then taboo set up in type so that they could print them on a handpress for private distribution to friends. The constable, no doubt suspecting a joke, responded in kind and directed them to the nearby printing house of the *Methodist Recorder*, emphatically not one prepared to set lubricious verse! Eventually the two found a firm of Linotype setters who expressed willingness to set the text if Potocki could not get the poems set elsewhere more cheaply. The manuscript was left in the manager's hands, and Potocki and Glass soon found themselves in Brixton charged with publishing obscene verse. "Publication" was their showing the manuscript to the printer! In the Magistrate's Court Potocki demanded trial by jury; the wiser Glass, who did not, was discharged. When the case came up before Sir Ernest Wild at the Old Bailey, Potocki received a sentence of six months' imprisonment, as much for his conduct in court as for his offense, one suspects. But it was a "criminally brutal sentence," as W. B. Yeats described it, and the affair produced a host of supporters including Aldous Huxley, Leonard Woolf, H. G. Wells, Walter de la Mare, and T. S. Eliot. Their support was more for the principle than the man, no doubt (Kingsley Martin has recorded how bitterly he offended Potocki by calling him "Mr. Montalk"), and proved in vain; Potocki's appeal was rejected.

After his release, Potocki published his *Prison Poems* from "the Montalk Press for the Divine Right of Kings," but then moved to Provence and later to Poland, returning from Warsaw only in 1935. On his return with modest financial assistance from Aldous Huxley and Brian Guinness he purchased a small proofing press and started publication of the ultra-monarchist journal the *Right Review*. The first number he had set on the Linotype, but thereafter he had the copy set on a Monotype machine so that he could distribute and reuse his type. By the time number 6 of the *Right Review* was prepared, all the matter was hand set. He had then been given another press, perhaps an

ILLUS. 34. Count Potocki, London. *Whited Sepulchres,* 1936. Front cover, with linocut Tiki by the count (a rare reference back to his New Zealand origins).

early Adana hand platen, which he described as "the invention of a third-rate English engineering genius." Meanwhile he had another brush with the law. As a result of his pamphlet *The Unconstitutional Crisis,* published on the day of King Edward VIII's abdication, the count found himself once more briefly in jail.

At the beginning of World War II Potocki continued initially with his printing of the *Review,* and in December 1939 (issue number 8) he made his formal claim to the thrones of Poland and of Hungary. By July 1940 he was again in jail. He had intended to print the poems of Maurras, but, as he put it:

> We were prevented not merely by the Fall of France . . . and by the ghoulists
> [the Gaullists] having control of all French matters here, but also by the
> circumstances that the British Authorities [M.I.5, the secret service, he claimed]
> with the sneaking brutality that characterizes them, caused Our printing plant
> and all Our paper supplies to be stolen . . . and saw to it that We were unable
> to obtain any real redress.

Released again, Potocki was able to purchase a new Harrild platen press and was soon at work printing pamphlets for the British Union of Fascists disguised as the 18B Dependents' Fund. After quarreling with them, he then espoused the cause of the Poles against their British allies. He was rightly proud of his manifesto on the Katyn massacre ("the *only* statement of the truth in English about this matter till well after the war"), but it is scarcely surprising that in a country at war he once more fell afoul of the authorities: "as a result of which We were involved in further illegal

FOREFATHERS

BY
ADAM
MICKIEWICZ
TRANSLATED FROM THE POLISH
BY COUNT POTOCKI OF MONTALK

Part III
Booklet 3.

PART 3 WILL BE COMPLETE
IN 4 BOOKLETS AT 2s 6d each

2/6

ILLUS. 35. Count Potocki, London.
Forefathers, 1946. Front cover.

persecution and were gaoled by unlawful means, exiled in a forced labour camp in the British Soviet 'punishment republic' of Northumberland, and were cut off from access to Our printing press."

Potocki secured his release, and moved his equipment to Islington, resuming work on such pieces as his *Partition of England,* a satire on the Yalta pact, and others of the same kind (Illus. 35). In 1949 he left England to live in the south of France, and for seven or eight years he did no further printing. Then in 1956 or 1957 he started production of his annual "Poems for the Feast of Saturn," using the crudest of improvised printing methods until in 1959 Richard Aldington and other friends bought him an old Marinoni Platen, on which he started printing once more under the Mélissa Press imprint. A few years later he moved back to England, installing a press in his home in the Dorset countryside. Here he produced a few more characteristic pieces: for example, his views on apartheid in *Two Blacks Don't Make a White* and *One More Folly,* some observations on the Hinton St. Mary Mosaic, which were found sufficiently offensive for an injunction to be obtained against their sale. These and other pieces have continued to infuriate his enemies and divert his friends. The terms of sale for Mélissa Press publications, like everything else about the count's life, are unusual; for *YTT YZZ czycli,* "the first surrealist poem to be issued by this anti surrealist press," he advertised it post free "to Japanese 3d, to Hungarians, Balts, Germans, 18Bs, and sexy women 6d, otherwise 1s6d."

About 1969 Potocki left England to live again in the south of France, and the Marinoni Press saw more service in the production of pamphlets and his poems for the feast of Saturn. Despite the output of his own press and a number of private presses in Britain and New Zealand that have printed some of his poetry, Potocki claimed, in a rather sad account entitled *Myself as Printer,* which he wrote in 1970, that only about 1 percent of his writings had ever been printed. He indicated some

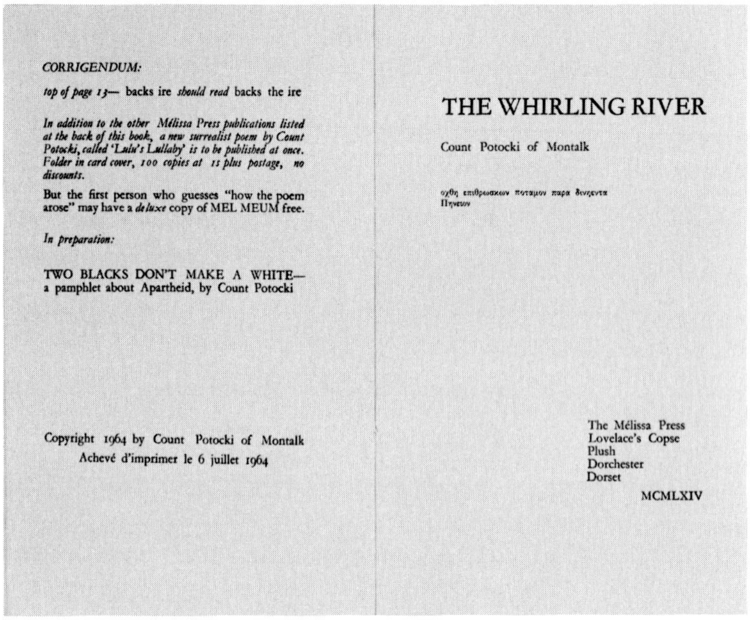

CORRIGENDUM:

top of page 13— backs ire *should read* backs the ire

In addition to the other Mélissa Press publications listed at the back of this book, a new surrealist poem by Count Potocki, called 'Lulu's Lullaby' is to be published at once. Folder in card cover, 100 copies at 11 plus postage, no discounts.

But the first person who guesses "how the poem arose" may have a *deluxe* copy of MEL MEUM free.

In preparation:

TWO BLACKS DON'T MAKE A WHITE— a pamphlet about Apartheid, by Count Potocki

Copyright 1964 by Count Potocki of Montalk
Achevé d'imprimer le 6 juillet 1964

THE WHIRLING RIVER

Count Potocki of Montalk

ηχθη επιβρωσκων ποταμον παρα θενχεντα
Πηγεων

The Mélissa Press
Lovelace's Copse
Plush
Dorchester
Dorset
MCMLXIV

ILLUS. 36. Count Potocki, Dorset. A characteristic late example of the count's work.

of the great difficulties he had always had with his printing through sheer shortage of equipment. To the small band of collectors of Potockiana his work is a delight, but to the count himself "the course of my life is an Indictment of the whole dishonest Racket which calls itself Democracy."

There remains one variety of clandestine press still undescribed: the printers who work in secret because they are engaged in forgery. Not all fraudulent printing is undertaken in secret. The forgeries of T. J. Wise, perhaps the most famous of modern times, were openly and innocently printed for Wise by the firm of Richard Clay & Sons. It is obviously more usual for such fraudulent activities to be undertaken in secret using private equipment.

Presses of this nature are by no means new. Paper currency was in use in Britain's American colonies from 1690 onwards and, whether printed by letterpress or from engraved copper plates, was widely and successfully counterfeited. It was in an attempt to render such imitation more difficult that many of the more interesting developments in the printer's craft have taken place: in such instances as Benjamin Franklin's nature printing (he appears to have successfully used a method of making metal castings from leaves, which he could use as a printing surface that was almost impossible to copy) or in Congreve's compound plate printing. Such counterfeiting is too remote from normal private press activity to warrant detailed discussion here.

Legitimate private presses have often suffered from their association with the illegitimate in the mind of authority. Sir Francis Meynell has recorded that a Scotland Yard detective in pursuit of the printer of some subversive pamphlets arrived at the Nonesuch Press, an obviously suspect concern. It is, however, the manufacturers of presses who really suffer. At one time the office staff of the Kelsey Company, which specializes in making small presses for the amateur market in the United States, lost a great deal of time in attending court hearings at which they had to give evidence against customers who had interpreted their "Print—make money" advertising too literally.

In Eastern Europe, it is naturally assumed that any private press must be clandestine. In an article about his Keepsake Press, Roy Lewis has described that while he was on a visit to one of the Russian satellite countries he mentioned casually that he owned a private press. There was instant attention: What subversive revolutionary things did he produce? and equally instant disillusion: Small books of poetry printed *for pleasure*—that is the effete bourgeois for you!

Chapter *10*

——

PRINTING FOR PLEASURE: THE GROWTH OF A MIDDLE-CLASS HOBBY

UNTIL THE SECOND HALF of the eighteenth century private presses seldom existed as a hobby for personal operation by their owners. The well-to-do could install a printing office complete with workmen, but the equipment of, for example, the Strawberry Hill Press differed very little from that to be found in a commercial printing house of the time and demanded a permanent commitment of space as well as money that only the most determined hobbyist could achieve.

Although the old common-press was cumbersome, and there is no evidence that the press builders regularly made smaller versions, a number of scaled-down wooden presses survive in France that are beautiful examples of the smith's and joiner's crafts. It is very likely that some of the presses that Madame de Pompadour and others had at Versailles were like these, and one now in the Musée de l'Imprimerie et de la Banque at Lyons is traditionally said to have belonged to Fénélon. The "toy press used by Charles I," which was shown at the Caxton Celebration in 1877, whether genuine or not, was probably a scale model of the same kind.

At the other extreme from the wealthy enthusiast who might set up his own printing office, there were those who could experiment in printing without the use of a press at all. One of these, Passmore Stevens, has gained a certain degree of immortality from a footnote in Edward Rowe Mores's *Dissertation on English Typographical Founders and Founderies* (1778):

> *Mr Stevens* was a gentleman of a typographical turn, but no great adept. he
> purchased some letter at *The Hague,* and when he came home he printed for his
> recreation, he used wooden chases nailed upon planks: no composing stick: no
> head-sticks, foot-sticks, side-sticks, gutter-sticks, quoins, or other furniture, but
> nails only with which he pegged his matter together: his balls were a bunch of
> waste paper: his tympans and frisket a dirty handkerchief: his press for small

work the ball of his thumb; for larger a rolling-pin and old rags. he was an antient bachelor of odd humour and of *Dutch* taste, in his garb and gesture antique indeed, and the furniture of his house was of the reign of *Qu. Eliz.* the work in which he delighted was below the degree of *Drops* or *Patters* or *Chaunts* or *Runs.* he devised and printed *title-pages* of strange and ludicrous books *speedily to be published* which were never to be published, nor indeed had any existence; and these title pages he dabbed up in the cool of the evening at the corners of the public streets to stir up the expectations of those who stopped there—this was *his* amusement, and harmless enough.—he printed likewise the epitaphs of his friends richly bedizened with

"The sun, the moon, and all the stars."

the greatest of his performances was the epitaph of *Dr. Holmes* late Pres. of *S. John*'s *coll. Oxon.* which he conceived himself in honour bound to print (and we have it in *black* letter and *red* ink) for some favour shewn by the coll. in the renewal of a lease. it makes a *whole*-half-sheet, and for work of this bulk wooden chases may suffice.—*Sutter*'s portables are little more.—*Mr. S.* was an honest inoffensive and a good natured gent.

Many amateurs have experimented in a similar way with rollers to get an impression, and the crudest galley presses (like that used by Potocki for his earliest work) are but variations of the principle. "Sutter's portables," however, were a break with the tradition of the screw press, and presented an alternative more suitable for the amateur. In the larger form, which J. Sutter of St. Martin's Churchyard announced in October 1769 in an advertisement directed to "Noblemen, gentlemen and ladies curious in printing," it was claimed that two folio pages could be printed at a time, suggesting that the presses were more than the simple bellows press that was used by commercial printers for small cards and labels. The bellows press was essentially two thick rectangular boards (one recessed to hold the type) hinged at one end, with two handles at the other end, which, when grasped together, gave the pressure needed to print. For more than a very few lines some additional method of leverage was needed to produce the requisite power. Unless a surviving press of unknown date and origin now in the Salford Art Gallery and Museum is one of Sutter's portables, as has been surmised, we have no knowledge of the precise method by which his presses functioned. But function they did, and Sutter's skillful advertising ensured a modest success:

The young Nobility and Gentry, by means of this excellent invention, may be easily brought acquainted with the Poets and other Authors, by reprinting the beauties of each and thereby strengthen the memory and early improve the understanding.—Types, and the rest of the Printing Material with proper instructions and examples, how to compose the types, and cast off the Copies, may be had at a small expence, on the shortest notice.—Small Printing Presses, the size of a pocket volume, are just now invented, by which Cards, &c. may be printed.

Sutter's advertisement, not just for his press but for all requisite printing equipment and instructions, struck just the right note. None of his instructions is known to exist, but in the Deutsches Buch- und Schriftmuseum in Leipzig is a copy of a pamphlet by F. C. Ritter of Hamburg, *Nachricht von zweyerley Arten neu erfundenen Taschen-Buchdruckereyen sowol mit als auch ohne Buchdrucker-Presse nebst hinlänglichen Unterricht von deren Gebrauch,* printed in 1772 on one of the "pocket printing offices" it describes. The idea of the small portable printery soon caught on, and on the continent the Breitkopf Typefoundry in Leipzig was in the 1780s advertising little English printing offices from 5 thalers (in the size suitable for marking linen) through to sets suitable for the studies of *grosse Herren* at 80 thalers. The latter included cases, enough type for four octavo pages each of roman and black letter, stands, and a press. Perhaps a wooden press now in the museum at Hamm in Westphalia, which can be closed away in a box, is a survivor of this concentration on an amateur market.

Among the amateurs we know who used such equipment were George Allan at the Grange Press, who bought his press in 1769, and the Greenland missionary Jesper Broderson who had acquired his "Handbuchdruckerey" while on leave in Germany, about 1790. In 1776 Boswell and Johnson visited the museum of Richard Green, an apothecary of Lichfield, which Boswell described as "a wonderful collection. . . . He has all the articles accurately arranged, with their names upon labels, printed at his own little press." This could have been a simple bellows press, or one of Sutter's, or one of the other refinements like the "Leaver printing press" patented by Isaac Moore and William Pine in 1770. I suspect that a book published from the press of the Reverend Henry Burrough, vicar of Wisbech, his own *Sermons on Several Subjects and Occasions* (1770), may also have been printed on one of Sutter's presses. An octavo of 364 pages, the signatures extend to Zzzz, and it is hard to see why the vicar should have resorted to such small gatherings unless his press could take no more than four octavo pages at a time. A note on the verso of the title page hopes that "the reader will be candid enough to excuse many errors in the following work as it issues from his private press, and is the first of his Typographical Attempts"; as far as I have been able to trace it had no successors.

The "*petites imprimeries anglaises,*" which the friends of the Marquis de Bercy were given as New Year's gifts in 1790 were almost certainly of the kind marketed by Breitkopf. Such small amateur printing offices were to be found in many parts of Europe. To quote one further example, in 1786 the poet Alfieri wrote to a friend enclosing a sonnet that, he explained, he had printed on a little portable press just large enough to handle the fourteen lines.

At times the determined amateur used such presses for work much more extensive than these primitive devices were really suited for. Gabriel Peignot wrote slightingly of the three volumes of his *Théâtre* that Jean Castaing printed on such a press in 1791–1792—volumes in which the text and presswork were equally abominable, he stated. In fact, the only thing about the work he praised was Castaing's sense in limiting the edition to 30 copies, thus ensuring a limit to the number who could be bored by his work! These were not the only products of Castaing's little press, although they may represent the culmination of his efforts as author and printer. The catalogue of the Bibliothèque Nationale also records two other works, which had run to a second edition: *Opuscules de J. Castaing, Revus, Corrigés et Augmentés* and his *Distiques et Pensées Morales et Philosophiques,* printed by him in 1790.

Some amateurs were not content with the presses on the market. William Davy's press at Lustleigh, which he built "on a principle very different from those in general use," must have answered well enough, as it served for the production of the whole of his *System of Divinity,* but Davy was a skillful carpenter and mechanic, to whom the devising of a suitable press would have given added pleasure. Yet he was by no means the only amateur to build a press of his own design. Peter Buchan, the author-printer of Peterhead, in 1819 "constructed a new press on an original plan, to work with the feet instead of with the hands, and which printed equally well from stone, copper and wood, and would have been as suitable for printing on cloth." Buchan used this press (nothing further is known about its design) to print his *Annals of Peterhead* and other books that he issued from his Auchmedden Press.

On a very much slighter scale than this was a printing press operated by a 15-year-old boy named Howard Dudley at Midhurst in Sussex in the middle 1830s. Dudley's press was a very small one, on which he could print no more than a page at a time (and his pages were no more than 4½ by 3½ inches). The press was of his own design and substantial enough for him to be able to print his 140-page *Juvenile Researches, or a Description of Some of the Principal Towns in the West of Sussex and the Borders of Hants,* which he wrote, printed, and illustrated with his own wood engravings in 1835 (Illus. 37). Despite the crudity of the work, the small edition was much sought after and a second edition of 50 copies was printed in the same year. In 1836, having moved to London where he adopted the trade of wood engraver, he issued a much larger book, *The History and Antiquities of Horsham.* This was illustrated with wood engravings and lithographs, and it seems probable that it was printed on a more amenable press than his homemade effort. It was the last book from Dudley's private press. Some years later he issued a prospectus for a book on the history of Midhurst, but it was never published.

In Ireland, in Ladiston, County Westmeath, there was an unusual instance of an amateur printer abandoning a purchased press for one he built himself. John Lyons, a member of the vanished race of Anglo-Irish gentry and "a gentleman of varied attainments, and a most ingenious mechanic," in 1820 bought a small press in Edinburgh. It was probably one of Ruthven's presses, of the same sort used by Sir Alexander Boswell, but Lyons did not find it satisfactory. After a few years he replaced it with a much larger machine that he constructed on a plan of his own, and with this he printed the results of his own antiquarian and horticultural research for the next 30 years. His *Remarks on the Management of Orchidaceous Plants* (1843) was of considerable importance in its time as the first manual on orchid growing, and he received the gold medal of the Horticultural Society of Dublin for the second edition that was printed commercially in 1845. Among his many other works from his press was *A Book of Surveys and Distributions of the Estates Forfeited in the County of Westmeath in the Rebellion of 1641,* which has the unusual feature of possessing two prefaces: one written from the Catholic and the other from the Protestant point of view, and printed in parallel text—a good Irish solution to a difficult problem! Lyons's press remained at his home Ledeston House until 1964, when it was taken to Longford-Westmeath County Library at Mullingar and restored. It is now displayed there together with some of the books printed on it between 1827 and 1853.

These men were all unusual amateurs in their determination to print, and they took considerable pains to overcome the difficulties that lay in their way. For the average man looking for a recreation, the lack of a really satisfactory simple and portable press was enough to prevent him from taking up printing at all. Sutter's presses met the need in a small way, but the fact that real enthusiasts like George Allan abandoned them for the common press indicates that they were considerably less than perfect for serious work.

All this was to change in the early nineteenth century. The development of the iron press in England—the Stanhope, the Albion, the Ruthven, and others—meant that far more consistently reliable presses became readily available in various sizes. In the United States there was the Columbian, and the work of Adam Ramage in producing easily transportable wooden presses, and the Wells, Smith, Stansbury, and Washington presses, while on the Continent many manufacturers marketed their own versions of presses incorporating these presses' advances.

A number of early nineteenth-century amateurs used these full-scale presses. At Great Totham Hall near Maldon in Essex an unusual gentleman-farmer named Charles Clark operated a press from 1831 until the late 1840s or perhaps even as late as 1862. Some of his work followed the fairly standard pattern of the antiquary's press, with a substantial *History of the Parish of Great Totham* and a number of reprints of local interest, such as Tusser's *Hundreth Good Poyntes of Husbandrie* (1834) or *Pleasant Quippes for Upstart Newfangled Gentlewomen* (1847). Clark also amused himself by producing a long series of single sheets of songs and parodies—work that much later the *Dictionary of National*

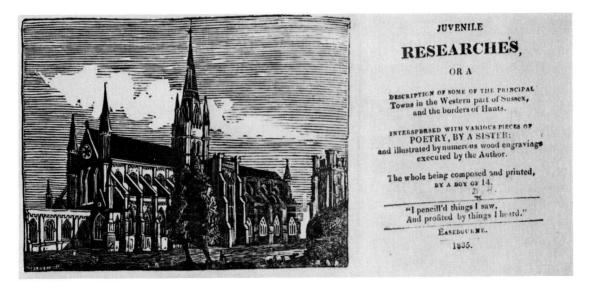

ILLUS. 37. Howard Dudley, Sussex. Title opening of Dudley's first book, printed on a press of his own design, 1835.

Biography was to characterize as "exceedingly silly and indecent," and of interest only to the printer's cronies, the neighboring farmers, and tavernkeepers! Nonetheless, Clark's contribution to the preservation of much local history material was not slight.

Another "local history" press was that of the Reverend George Wilson Bridges, already mentioned as Rector of St. Ann's, Jamaica. His press is worth noting for two reasons. First, he was the first amateur in the West Indies, and second, he combined his interest in letterpress printing (used for his *Statistical History of the Parish of Manchester in the Island of Jamaica,* 1824) with experiments in lithographic printing, for which he had presumably purchased one of the small lithographic presses being marketed by Ruthven and Taylor & Martineau in the 1820s. Although lithographic printing is outside the scope of this book, it should be mentioned that the nineteenth-century amateur was as active in the field of lithography as in letterpress work. There are several other interesting colonial presses of this kind, such as the Behar Amateur Press at Patna, India, from which in the late 1820s Sir Charles D'Oyly issued a number of albums with lithographic illustrations of costume and other subjects for circulation to friends and colleagues.

By the 1830s the social climate in Britain was right for an expansion of amateur printing. The increase in population and the growing prosperity of the middle classes meant that in country rectories or in the thousands of suburban villas springing up over the country many with sufficient time, money, and education would find printing an amusing pastime if it was presented to them in the right way. Sutter's advertising had indicated its educational value; 60 years after he had pointed the way, a number of firms were producing equipment aimed directly at the amateur market, and in their advertising attempting to show that it was useful, elegant, and foolproof.

As early as 1834 Messrs. Holtzapffel & Co., "Engineer, lathe and tool manufacturers" of Long Acre, were advertising printing presses "on the Stanhope and other principles, in small sizes," and over the following decade they appear to have built up a good business selling presses and printing equipment to amateurs. By 1839, the firm appears to have been producing "Mr. Cowper's Parlour Printing Press" and marketing it together with all requisite equipment and a set of complete instructions for its use. Copies of this instruction book or of the second edition cannot now be traced, but of the third edition, 1846, *Printing Apparatus for the Use of Amateurs, Containing Full and Practical*

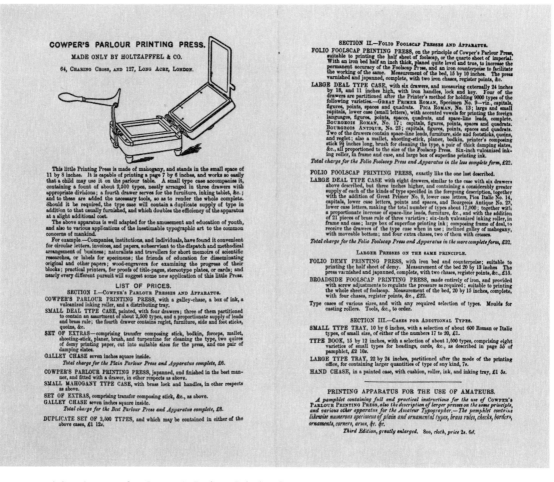

ILLUS. 38. Advertisement for Cowper's Parlour Printing Press, c. 1873.

Instructions for the Use of Cowper's Parlour Printing Press . . . and Various Other Apparatus for the Amateur Typographer there is an offset litho reprint with valuable notes by James Mosley and David Chambers published by the Private Libraries Association in 1971.

Edward Cowper, who was a partner with August Applegath in building cylinder presses for the *Times* newspaper, had devised this press, so the manual declares, "for the amusement and education of youth, by enabling them to print any little subject they had previously written." His press design was derived from the old bellows press, but with the incorporation of an impression level incorporating a knuckle joint at the opposite end of the platen from the hinges. (For simplicity of operation it could scarcely be bettered. Although rather slower than the modern Adana flatbed press, it is in fact superior in power to today's press.)

The press was strongly made, and available in two forms: plain at £1 14s., or "japanned and finished in the best manner and fitted with a drawer" for 2 guineas. The price list at the end of the useful little instruction book included details of the other equipment offered: For £5 6s. one could buy the plain press, a case of painted deal containing four drawers of type, galley chases, and other impedimenta. For an extra £1 16s. the better quality press, and mahogany type case with brass lock and handles were supplied. Larger presses, music type cases, and "type books" (ingenious little cases made to look like books, which could hold eight card fonts of display faces) were also offered. A

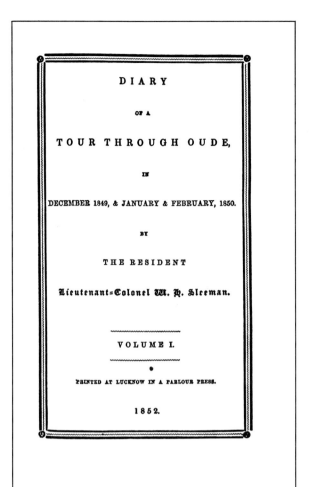

ILLUS. 39. Sir William Sleeman, Lucknow, India. *Diary of a Tour through Oude,* printed on a Parlour Press, 1852.

range of text and display types (from the Caslon foundry) were also offered at prices ranging from three pence per dozen sorts upwards.

The effectiveness of Cowper's press can be seen from the work that was printed on it. Mosley and Chambers, in their edition of the manual, describe and illustrate work undertaken by three amateurs, one—that of Lieutenant Colonel Sir William Sleeman—as far away as Lucknow, India, where Sleeman had 18 copies of his *Diary of a Tour through Oude* printed in 1852 (Illus. 39). (It is interesting that Holtzapffel was listing "printing presses for regimental and parlour use" in 1865, and indeed as late as 1927.) Of the other known owners of Parlour Presses, Godfrey Levinge used one in London and Ireland for his *The Traveller in the East,* started in 1839 and completed in 1846, and also for work done for the Westmeath Protestant Orphan Society from 1841 to 1846. (While at Cullean, in County Westmeath, Levinge must have known John Lyons as another amateur.) The other Parlour Press owner known to Mosley and Chambers, Nathaniel Brown Engleheart of Blackheath, produced his first book in 1840 but was still using his press as late as 1864 when he printed *Omnium Gatherum . . . A Selection of Odds and Ends from an Old Portfolio.*

Another tribute to the worth of Cowper's press was paid in *Notes & Queries* in December 1862. In response to an inquiry from a writer signing himself Γ asking what sort of press he should use for printing a duodecimo half-sheet, there were two replies both recommending Holtzapffel's equipment. The second correspondent said he had used it successfully for octavo half-sheets; should Γ wish to print larger sizes, he recommended a regular Albion press at a cost of £15 to £20, a pretty considerable increase in cost for the amateur.

Although the manufacturers made much of the virtues of Cowper's press "for the amusement and education of youth," they were by no means slow to point out its advantages for other less high-minded purposes: "Companies, institutions and individuals, have found it convenient for circular letters, invoices, and papers subservient to the despatch and methodical arrangement of business; naturalists and travellers, for short memoirs of scientific researches, or labels of specimens." Schoolmasters and clergymen are among the others whom they suggest could find "some new application of this useful little apparatus." By implication, the purchaser of one of these presses could save himself money that otherwise might have to be paid out to commercial printers.

Later nineteenth-century manufacturers of small presses in England were to strike a similar note in their advertising. D. G. Berri's *The Art of Printing* (third edition 1871) speaks of the advantages to owners of his "People's Printing Press" in very explicit terms: "Men in business could print more rapidly than can be done by any other press or hand machine now in use, *and at a tithe of a printer's charges,* their circulars, cards, handbills, invoices.... Many persons also, not in business, frequently wish to have printed notes, ... catalogues of their libraries ... but are deterred by the price charged by printers for doing what would be to themselves a very instructive and agreeable employment." But it remained for American enterprise to develop and publicize the idea of amateur printing as a means of making money in one's spare time.

In the United States, portable presses of the Ramage type, or the iron Washington, Columbian, and Ruthven presses were commonplace in commercial printing shops, but there was nothing designed specifically for the use of amateurs for over 15 years after the debut of the Parlour Press in England. For some reason Holtzapffel's press does not seem to have been imitated in the United States, although it was not exclusive to England; a version was being marketed in Paris by Berthier et Cie in 1876. However at the Fair of the American Institute held at the Crystal Palace, New York, in 1857, Samuel W. Lowe exhibited a press that was an attempt to provide for amateur needs. Patented the previous year, it had a heavy conical roller, which moved in an arc backwards and forwards, pressing the tympan down on to the type. It was awarded a silver medal, the highest prize awarded any press, "it being the cheapest, simplest and best press exhibited." Its price certainly recommended it (from $5 for one 5 by 6 inches to $50 for one 19 by 23 inches) and it was claimed that not only was it simple enough for an eight-year-old to manage, but also that one person could print from 300 to 500 sheets an hour. In practice, however, it did not prove so satisfactory (although Ben Grauer has used a surviving Lowe Press with considerable success at his Between-Hours Press). Two other small presses that were developed in the early 1860s and used extensively in the field throughout the campaigns of the Civil War—Adam's Cottage Press and its close relation the Army Press—were very much simpler and more efficient. They were essentially a modification of the traditional copper plate or etching press, with the pressure applied by means of a cylinder moving across the tympan.

By 1869 another sort of press designed for amateur use was in production; a machine that, like the Parlour Press, was to have a long line of descendents, right down to the present day. This was an adaptation of the commercial printers' treadle platen presses, of which the first models had appeared in 1851. In these presses the chase was held not on a flatbed, but vertically (which frequently caused disaster for the amateur printer who had not locked his type up tightly enough) in a bed to which the platen was hinged. In principle, a bellows press stood on end. The first platen press to be made for amateurs was the Novelty, made by B. O. Woods & Company of Boston. With modifications this press continued to be manufactured until 1883 when the firm was taken over by its great rival, the Kelsey Company of Meriden, Connecticut.

The career of William A. Kelsey, the founder of the firm, was in many respects an epitome of the American dream. While still in his teens he had run a stamp business, worked for the Parker Gun Company, and, by the age of 20, become editor of their magazine (which was to become *Forest and Stream*); not only this, but he had tried out all the amateur presses on the market and come to the conclusion that he could make one that would be better and cheaper. In his spare time from working for the Parker Company he tried to design a press that could sell at a price he thought the average boy would pay. On December 19, 1872, he advertised his first press in the *Youth's Companion:*

> $5 Printing Press! A *perfect* Press at the right price. Business Men save expense
> and increase business by doing their own printing and advertising. For BOYS
> delightful, *money-making* amusement.

Unfortunately for Kelsey, his press (which like the Novelty Press was a hand platen) had not been sufficiently tested, and would not work. He was left with a host of orders, and no means of filling them. After much burning of midnight oil he devised a new press, the Excelsior, which *would* work and which he patented in the spring of 1873. He was not at all abashed by his previous blunder: "Great changes have been made from the original plan of our Press," he boldly advertised, "till we have reached what we firmly believe perfection." His confidence in the new press was not misplaced; it was a thoroughly satisfactory machine. By dint of advertising in all the leading American journals of the day, such as *Harper's Weekly,* and in practically everything else available, from Southern revivalist magazines to Barnum & Bailey's Circus program, a large mail-order business was built up. At the Philadelphia Centennial Exhibition of 1876 an improved version of the press with automatic inking received a medal. The Kelsey Company was firmly established.

The Excelsior was not the only press made for the amateur market in the United States. The Kelsey Company did most of its business through mail order, and, in its early days, a number of publishing firms were used as sale agents. One of these, realizing the market potential, decided to go into business themselves, and produced the Model Press, another excellent hand press, which continued to be manufactured until well into this century. Many Model presses survive and are still used by amateurs.

Other rivals to the Kelsey Company were also dangerous. Curtis & Mitchell made the Caxton Press and the very good Columbian Press until the 1890s; in Boston, Golding's Pearl and Official Presses (two more sound machines that are still often used by pastime printers) were made until the 1920s. Golding, which had attempted to move into a larger scale of business by building presses for commercial use, was then absorbed by the mammoth American Type Founders Company, for whom the amateur market was of little interest.

Most other attempts to siphon off potential Kelsey customers failed. The firm of J. Cook & Company, in whose Meriden workshops the first Kelsey presses were made until Kelsey built his own factory, made the Victor and Enterprise Presses. They were good machines, but Cook could not rival Kelsey's masterly advertising and ferocious price cutting. In 1883 the Kelsey *Catalog* contained this obituary notice:

> DEAD. Competitors of this establishment do not seem to prosper. We have
> bought out B. O. Woods & Co., Novelty Presses, started in Boston in 1864.
> J. Cook & Co., after spending $20,000 in attempting to compete with our
> excellent presses, have sold out to us at a great sacrifice. Our machines are too
> good to allow much chance for competition. We shall meet all rivals with cut
> prices!

Another rival to be absorbed by Kelsey was Joseph Watson, who as the manufacturer of Lowe and Adam's Cottage presses had been in the business much longer than Kelsey. He manufactured a range of hand platens that gave the Excelsior more competition than these earlier lines could, but in 1896 his firm finally succumbed.

In England, too, the 1870s saw the introduction of new presses for the amateur market, many of them derived from American machines. Berri's "People's Printing Press" was based upon the conventional copper plate press, and seems to have been inspired by the American Army Press, although unlike that it had a bed moving by means of a gear wheel under a fixed cylinder instead of a fixed bed and moving cylinder as in the Army Press. Berri claimed that because the pressure of the cylinder could be adjusted on his press, it could be used for printing letterpress, lithographically, or from copper plates. It seems doubtful that the construction of his press was rigid enough for copper plate printing; several satisfied customers vouched for its efficiency in lithographic and letterpress work in the testimonials printed at the end of his handbook on *The Art of Printing*, but there is no reference to its use for intaglio work.

The great advantage of Berri's press was that its use of a cylinder meant that a large surface could be printed without the need for a massive platen. It was relatively cheap (the smallest size, to print an area of 5⅛ by 4⅜ inches, cost two guineas; the largest, 22 by 15½ inches, was eight guineas) and it was simple to operate. Berri, although pointing out the advantage of his press for business use, was also confident of its value to amateurs. "It may be suggested that this machine might be made the means of great and pleasing amusement among residents in the country, in issuing gazettes for circulation among their friends," he suggested. In a fine expansionist vein he continued, "for those pioneers who daily leave our shores to establish a home midst the pathless forests and the rolling prairies, and to perpetuate our industry with our language on the continents of Asia and Africa, and the distant islands of Polynesia," it would also be useful. There was nothing of the brash Yankee commercialism of Kelsey's "Print—make money" about this.

One of Berri's closest competitors for the growing amateur market was Jabez Francis of Rochford, Essex. Francis's press was a cast-iron variation on the theme of the wooden Parlour Press, and rather cheaper than Berri's presses (25 shillings for the smallest, printing an area 6 by 4 inches, to 3 guineas for a larger, 9½ inch model). His pamphlet *Printing at Home* was aimed almost entirely at the amateur. "Printing may be made to afford a profitable amusement for many," he wrote. "Either parent may write an essay, poem, or a note to friends at a distance, a young lady daughter may 'compose' it . . . the proofs may be read by all and corrected, it is then 'made ready,' and one rolls the 'forme' or type, while another prints at the press." To reinforce the appeal of a hobby for all the family he included a wood engraving of such printing in the parlor (Illus. 40).

Francis was wise to concentrate his attentions on the purely amateur market. Both his and Berri's presses were designed for hand inking, and must have been very slow in operation. Competition from the newer and faster self-inking American platens must have hurt their sales to those wishing to make money by their printing. For the pure amateur, the older presses were simpler to use, and, in a veiled attack upon the newer platens, Francis claimed that his presses could not go wrong and would last a lifetime.

Of the American presses introduced into England, the Model Press, developed by Kelsey's rival, was the most successful. Originally manufactured and sold in England by C. Squintani & Company of Liverpool Street, it was taken over in the late 1880s by the Model Printing Press Company of Ludgate Circus, and finally by the Excelsior Printers Supply Company of Farringdon Street, a firm that had originally been organized for the distribution of Kelsey's Excelsior presses in England, which continued to manufacture the press until World War II. The Excelsior Printers Supply Company still deals in secondhand Model presses as part of its general trade in printers' sundries.

ILLUS. 40. "For the amusement and education of youth"; hobby printing as portrayed in Jabez Francis's *Printing at Home,* 1870.

The Model Press was (as in America) advertised in a much more aggressive way than its earlier rivals had been. Much less emphasis was placed on its value for the amusement and education of youth and much more on its advantages in business practice. It cost less than a commercial printer in the use of office labor to print labels, letterheads, invoices, and the like. Squintani advertised complete printing outfits at prices ranging from 5 to 100 guineas.

There were native English presses able to compete with the Model and Excelsior. As well as the larger Albions, which continued to be made into the 1930s, there were many firms of printers' engineers who developed their own lines of small platen presses. One such was the Simplissimus Press, a lighter and cheaper variation of the platen principle manufactured by the Birmingham Machinists Company and advertised by them in their *Eclectic Handbook of Printing* of about 1875. It was highly regarded by professionals, who used it for small jobbing work, as well as amateurs. There were other presses aimed more exclusively at the hobby printer. One was manufactured by C. Morton of City Road. In his *The Art of Printing Simplified for Amateurs* (1875), he made large claims: "An uncontracted experience of the requirements of an Amateur Printer has enabled me to thoroughly comprehend the difficulties he has to contend with. As a Typefounder and Press Manufacturer, I, in a business way, continually make the acquaintance of 'distressed' Amateur Printers, to whom I have had, as it were, to be a physician." His own press was distantly related to the Albion in design, but was suspiciously cheap: The physician seems in fact to have been something of a quack.

By no means all printing firms had welcomed the expanding amateur market with enthusiasm. The printers themselves were, scarcely surprisingly, unhappy at the growth in the numbers of what they derisively called back-bedroom printers, who worked at cut rates; some suppliers were also distinctly uncooperative. In July 1879 the Caslon Foundry, finding that they had been included in a list of suppliers printed in a handbook for amateurs announced in their *Circular* that:

> We cannot undertake to supply founts of type smaller in quantity or assortment
> than are required by regular professional printers. . . . We are not among those
> who are alarmed at the increase in amateur printing in this country, though we
> will not encourage it. In the majority of cases amateur dabblers in a handicraft
> about which they know nothing, discover sooner or later that they have spent
> all their money to no purpose, and return to the professional printer with a
> higher and more professional appreciation of his services.

A RYGHTE
Goodlie Lyttle Booke
OF

Frisket Fancies

SET FORTH FOR

BIBLIOMANIACS !

BY

Edwin Roffe.

PRIVATELY PRINTED.

ROCHESTER PRESS.

TWELVE COPIES.

LONDON:
Set up, and Im **I** *printed, in Leisure-time, by*
EDWIN ROFFE:
At his Birth-place, 48, Ossulston Street,
SOMERS' TOWN. MDCCCLXI.

ILLUS. 41. Rochester Press, London. Title page of a characteristic piece of spare-time printing by Edwin Roffe, 1861.

It is to the credit of the Caslons' sense of ethics, if not their business acumen, that they did not resort to selling small fonts of type to amateurs at prices far higher than those charged the trade, as many suppliers did.

What sort of work was produced by the amateur purchasers of all these different presses, and who were the purchasers? Among those who played with printing at one time or another were such men as Thomas Edison, Rudyard Kipling, Lord Northcliffe, and, unlikely picture, the son of Mrs. Hodgson Burnett, "Little Lord Fauntleroy" himself, who printed a little magazine and two small books in 1891–1892. At one extreme of the craze there was the appeal of Yankee entrepreneurism at its most highly developed, as we have seen. At the other extreme there was the quintessence of Victorian high-mindedness: At the 1862 Exhibition Mrs. Daniel Jones exhibited a miniature Albion Press (Illus. 42) together with a prayer for peace printed in 46 languages which she had produced on it. In the words of *Cassell's Illustrated Exhibitor,* her entry was:

> An appeal to ladies to turn their attention to a private study to produce gems of thought, in elegancies of well-assorted type, and clever arrangement, so as to relieve the fingers from the ornamental intricate worsted work and crochet labyrinthal pattern, and to exert the same perseverance in leisure hours to the cultivation of private circulation of new ideas, which would soon grow into a pleasure in the doing and a necessity for fireside entertainment.
>
> In speaking of the merits of this undertaking [continued the *Exhibitor*] we see a useful, neat, powerful printing press, suited to the library . . . and the

ILLUS. 42. Mrs. Daniel Jones demonstrating printing as an occupation for ladies at the 1862 Exhibition, London.

boudoir of the lady, whose ingenuity and reflective habits would be greatly assisted could she, in her leisure hours, be enabled to print many beautiful passing thoughts, which would otherwise float away, and have no means of being retained in the private manner which her judgment and sympathies would suggest.

The *Exhibitor* advised ladies that Mrs. Jones was willing to give lessons to those who wished to try printing for themselves, an interesting parallel with other contemporary attempts to introduce women into a male preserve, like those of Emily Faithfull or the Devonport Sisterhood. It remained unusual, however, for the Victorian lady to attempt printing entirely without masculine assistance. One suspects that the writer in the *Exhibitor* let his enthusiasm run away with him: A Cowper press in the parlor is one thing; an Albion in the boudoir quite another!

An interesting example of a feminine press is that owned by the young Jane Bickersteth at Roehampton from 1848 to 1851. The press she owned (probably a Parlour Press) was used to print a number of magazines, each consisting of a single page only, "price one farthing." For these, *The Elf, The Fairy,* and *The Mite,* her assistant was Anthony Panizzi, the greatest of the librarians of the British Museum. The unkind could see the explanation for his adoption of this unfamiliar role in that Jane's father, Lord Langdale, was one of the museum trustees and, therefore, a useful man for Panizzi to cultivate (as indeed he was when Panizzi's appointment as Principal Librarian was considered in 1856), but there seems no doubt that there was genuine kindliness and affection in the help he gave to the young printer.

Panizzi was by no means the only man of eminence to play with printing in this manner, nor was it anything new at the time. Davies Gilbert, who was President of the Royal Society from 1828 to 1831, set up a small press in his house at Eastbourne in 1825 for the amusement of his family circle. Type and probably the other equipment was obtained from B. Nichols of Parliament Street. Most of the work of the press seems to have been done by Gilbert's eldest daughter Catherine, and for 14 years (until his death in 1839 called a halt to the hobby) a large number of single sheets of poems and ephemera were printed. No serious or extensive work was undertaken; it was purely printing for pleasure.

An interesting press of the 1840s was that owned by Gaetano Polidori at Park Village East, Regents Park. Polidori had formerly been the head of a London firm of printers and publishers, and when in his mid-70s he once more felt an urge for his old craft he set up a press in his own home. It cannot have been a small affair, and without doubt Polidori had the assistance of workmen in its operation, for in 1840 he issued a three-volume edition of Milton's works in Italian, translated by himself. Two years later he followed this with some of his own dramas and, then, in 1843, with the first of two books that were of real importance. Polidori's daughter was mother of Dante Gabriel and Christina Rossetti, and their grandfather printed a small edition of *Sir Hugh the Heron,* which Dante Gabriel had written at the age of 13. Four years later, in 1847, he printed a duodecimo volume of *Verses* by Christina, with a note recording that the poems had been written while she was still of tender age and that it was only with difficulty that he had persuaded her to allow him to print them. The last book from this press was an unfinished Italian poem by an ancestor, *Il Losario* by Francesco Polidori, and this is also of considerable interest as it included a conclusion composed by Dante Gabriel Rossetti.

Another early Victorian private press that is remarkably little known (considering the high standards of workmanship its work displayed) was the Duncairn Press, near Belfast. It was operated from 1850 onwards by Edmund MacRory, a Bencher of the Middle Temple, who used to while away the long vacations he spent in his father's Irish home by printing. The press was set up in a very workmanlike manner. A small foolscap folio Albion Press was first purchased, to be joined by a larger Columbian in 1852. Type was obtained from Robert Bensley and from H. W. Caslon, ornaments from Paris typefounders, and wood engravings were commissioned from Robert Branston and from H. Swain in London. Although the press lay idle for more than 10 months in every year, during the 10 years or so that the equipment was in use a respectable number of very substantial books were produced. The largest was a 247-page octavo edition of *The Private Diary of Elizabeth Viscountess Mordaunt AD 1657–68* of which 100 copies were completed in 1856 (Illus. 43). Other works included a catalogue of pictures in Duncairn House, *Notes on the Temple Organ* (later reissued commercially), and the usual offering of poetry written by the friends of the printer.

It is now impossible to estimate the number of amateur printers who were at work in Victorian times, but from the 1840s until the 1880s there were many more who could be named, ranging widely in purpose and achievement. At Canford Manor in Dorset, for instance, there was a variation to the usual Victorian house party during which Lady Layard, Lord Wimborne, Lady C. Schreiber, and other guests of the Honorable Ivor Bertie Guest in 1867 printed small editions of two pieces by Tennyson. In Leamington Spa a solicitor named Charles Griffin bought a press in 1848 to print various posters in connection with a claim to the Leigh barony, while at the same time Nathaniel Merridew, a bank clerk in the same town, amused himself from 1845 to about 1865 with work for which he enjoyed a high reputation locally. No doubt a similar range of amateur work was to be found on the Continent. I shall mention only one, that of the Abbé Pierre Poucher, who from about 1880 until the early 1900s produced a long list of books from the remote village of S. Martin de

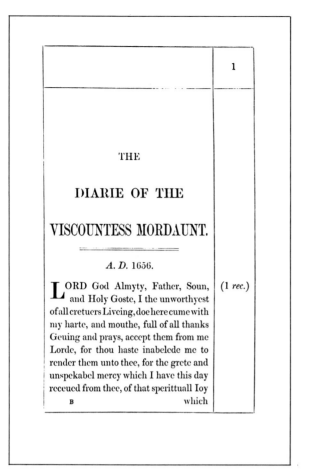

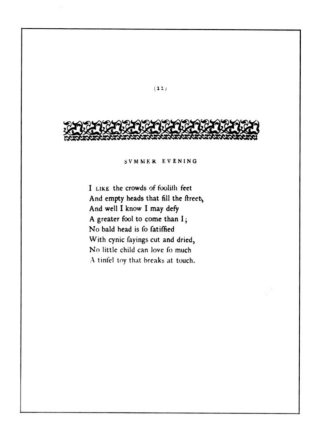

ILLUS. 43. Duncairn Press, Belfast.
Page from one of the books printed
by Edmund MacRory, 1856.

ILLUS. 44. Daniel Press, Oxford.
Henry Patmore *Poems,* 1884. Good use of
Fell ornaments, but poor page design.

Bonbaux (Gévaudan). The most substantial was his *Histoire de la Bête du Gévaudan* (1889), some 1,040 pages in all; Poucher, in fact, may be regarded as the French William Davy.

The majority of amateur printers did not, then as now, go in for book work, contenting themselves instead with ephemera and the production of amateur journals. In the United States these were even more common. The earliest journal I have traced is the *Village Post* of Gill, Massachusetts, of which the *Boston Traveller* (1832) reported:

> It is the production of a lad of the name of Cannan, ten years of age . . . But the typography of this *petite Post* (2½ × 2 inches) is not the most remarkable fruit of the boy's ingenuity. There is no printing office in the town where he lives, and we have it from one who knows the young Franklin well, that the types, of lead, and the press, of wood, are entirely of his own manufacture, and the chief tool used in their construction was a common penknife. The press is large enough to receive an ordinary duodecimo page. Besides his weekly issue, little Cannan has printed and published *A Treatise on the Dog* 27 pp., ornamented with a large cut, which he carved out without any instructions, with the same instrument of all work mentioned above.

Not many amateur journalists revealed this degree of ingenuity, but from the 1860s to 1880s there were hundreds of little newspapers produced throughout the country by teenage boys (and sometimes girls) who used Kelsey, Novelty, or other small platen presses bought by mail order. Once they had taught themselves the rudiments of their craft, their work often performed a useful function in the absence of a local paper. The *Willow Dale Press* of which the 13-year-old Florence Carter and her 10-year-old brother Arthur produced 12 monthly issues in San Gabriel Valley, California, in 1879 is an excellent example of the best of such work.

By far the most important of all these Victorian printers for pleasure was the Reverend C. H. O. Daniel (1836–1919). He started his printing activities in a commonplace way. While a child at Frome in Somerset, where his father was vicar, he and his brother George were given some type to play with in 1845. With this they laboriously printed a number of small pieces, inking them with their thumbs and impressing the type by hand in the manner of Mores's Passmore Stevens. One of the earliest surviving pieces of their printing, produced in the summer or autumn of 1846, recorded a great advance in their resources. The vicar, well pleased with his sons' interest in the craft, had given them a small press (almost certainly one of Holtzapffel's Parlour Presses). Charles printed a letter of thanks to his father, promising good conduct and pathetically asking "qlease do not mind my very bad printing, for when any one looks on any part of it, it is really immensely, terribly, and dreadfully horrible"—which was no exaggeration. Then Charles went away to boarding school for a year, and when he returned home in 1848 he did not resume his pastime. But in the spring of 1850 he turned again to his hobby, and when in July of that year he was given a miniature Albion he continued still more enthusiastically, producing texts for his father's sermons, invitation cards, small pamphlets of verse, amateur magazines, and the like. From 1853 to 1854 he was again away at boarding school, so the press at Frome languished, and it might have gone the way of most childhood hobbies had not Charles's two youngest brothers taken it over and continued to print until the 1860s. Charles Daniel himself had gone on from school to Worcester College, Oxford, in 1854, and after graduating taught in London for a few years before returning to Oxford to take up a fellowship at his old college in 1863.

Were this the whole history of the Daniel Press, it would be no more interesting or remarkable than that of dozens of other parlor printers in mid-Victorian England. Where it was to differ was in its revival and triumphant growth. By the early 1890s the bookseller Bertram Dobell was predicting that future collectors would eagerly seek Daniel's books "since they have not only their intrinsic merits to recommend them, but also their comely apparel." By luck, and a typographic eye informed by his taste for seventeenth century literature, Daniel was able to transform his press from that of the printer for pleasure into one close to those that flourished at the end of Victoria's reign and were concerned with printing as a fine art.

In 1874 Daniel, after a visit home, took back the miniature Albion and the store of type with him to Oxford, and set to work on printing some *Notes from a Catalogue of Pamphlets* in Worcester College Library. He printed some 25 copies, which he circulated to friends towards the end of the year. It was not in itself a pretty piece of printing. In the long period since he had last used the press the printer had evidently lost much of his cunning. He was himself well aware of its shortcomings; he improved the layout and arrangement of a continuation of the same work, but abandoned the project before completion, and most copies were destroyed. Then came the turning point in the career of the Daniel Press, with the revival of the Fell types. Dr. John Fell had lavishly endowed the Oxford University Press with these types nearly two centuries earlier, but they had fallen almost entirely into disuse during the eighteenth century, and by the 1870s were virtually forgotten.

The tradition of Daniel's revival of these types is a romantic one. According to the *Memoir* by Sir Herbert Warren in *The Daniel Press: Memorials of C. H. O. Daniel with a Bibliography of the Press 1845–1919* (Oxford, 1921) Dr. Daniel "had recourse to the Clarendon Press for type, and as he turned over their old stocks his artistic eye lit on a broken and imperfect fount, a dusty, disused legacy left by 'the unreasonably hated' Dean Fell, and called after his name. He divined the possibilities, and spurred by its charm . . . went on to new elaborations." In fact, the credit for Daniel's adoption of this type must rest equally with Professor Bartholomew Price, who had for many years been Secretary to the Delegates of the Press. Stanley Morison in his splendid study of *John Fell: The University Press and the "Fell" Types* (Oxford, 1967) suggested that during Price's discussions with Daniel of the latter's printing problems it must have become apparent to Daniel that to use Victorian black letter or roman type for reprinting seventeenth-century material using the old spelling was a typographical crime. Obviously the best way to avoid the crime would be for the University Press to supply Daniel with a font of the Fell types. Whether the suggestion came from Price or Daniel is unimportant; what is interesting is that early in 1876 Dr. Daniel purchased some of the Fell type and ornaments, to which he was to remain faithful as long as he printed. It was partly as an indirect result of Daniel's use of the types that the University Press itself came to revive them in its own splendid typographical renaissance at the beginning of this century.

The first use at the Daniel Press of its new types was in *A New Sermon of the Newest Fashion* (1877), printed from manuscript and originally written about 1643. This was followed by Erasmus's *Colloquia* (1880) of which Walter Pater wrote that "it is, I suppose, the most exquisite specimen of printing that I have ever seen"; this was, from him, remarkable praise, indicating how much improvement there had been in the work of the press since Daniel had resumed his hobby six years earlier. But the most celebrated of all his books was still to come. Some time in 1880 Thomas Humphry Ward suggested to Daniel that the first birthday of Daniel's infant daughter Rachel should be celebrated with special poems written by his friends at the press, after the mode of the famous *Guirlande de Julie*. Enough of Daniel's friends responded for *The Garland of Rachel* to be a success when it appeared in October 1881, with contributions from Austin Dobson, Andrew Lang, Edmund Gosse, James Addington Symonds, Lewis Carroll, Robert Bridges, and a host of others. It was not only successful from a textual point of view; the design and execution of the book (set in the Fell types, with woodcuts by Alfred Parsons and miniated by Mrs. Daniel) was in a Victorian way quite charming. In effect the book was as successful a cradle-crowning of the Daniel Press as it was of Rachel. Each of the 17 contributors was presented with a copy of the book containing a special title page naming it as by him "and divers kindly hands." Only 36 copies in all were printed; these have always commanded a high price on the antiquarian market. The book had the distinction (if that is the right word) of being pirated in a sort of type facsimile by Thomas Bird Mosher at Portland, Maine, in 1902.

The very favorable reception that *The Garland* received inspired Daniel to continue with his hobby, and in the winter of 1881–1882 he purchased his first press that was more than a toy for amateur use: an Albion Press that had been made by J. & J. Barrett in 1835. His first experiment on this, *Hymni Ecclesiae,* proving satisfactory, he set to work on an Elizabethan translation of Theocritus's *Six Idillia,* which was published in 1883. This was the first book he had offered for sale. From then until 1903 the Albion was seldom idle, another 52 substantial books of considerable literary interest being produced in the time that Daniel could spare from his work as Bursar of his College and his many appointments in the university and city. It was not that he was without assistance; just as the press at Frome had been operated jointly with his brothers, so at Oxford Mrs. Daniel and his two daughters, Rachel and Ruth, when old enough, assisted with the composition and presswork, in some instances producing whole books by themselves.

In 1903 Dr. Daniel was elected Provost of Worcester College, and he decided that the press should be discontinued. Despite the pleas and protests of his many friends, he would not move from this decision. He relented only once, in 1906, when his daughters printed a form of prayers used in the college for the gaudy. One more book was to be printed on the press: the *Memorials* and bibliography of its work, which were printed in the Bodleian Library to which the press was presented on Dr. Daniel's death in 1919.

The Daniel Press is significant for two reasons: the excellence of the texts selected for printing (they included more than a few first printings of the work of Robert Bridges) allied to the charm of the production. Daniel Press books were quite unlike other private press books produced at the turn of the century. There is nothing of the pseudogothic or would-be renaissance spirit about them. Although they are unmistakably of their time, Daniel's deep interest in seventeenth-century literature together with his use of the Fell types and ornaments made him produce a series of books that hark back to the printing of the period in a very refreshing manner.

Although in the nineteenth century presses developed that were designed specially for amateur use, there remained—as there still remains—a small number of individuals who found part of their pleasure in building their own presses. One such press was at work between 1871 and 1892 in the Old Vicarage, Grantchester, an address more commonly associated with Rupert Brooke. Its owner, Samuel Page Widnall, was decidedly an original: a retired farmer, who built a pseudomedieval folly, "Burgherst Tower" at the bottom of his garden and occupied his leisure time with stone and wood carving, photography, making architectural models, and with inventions of one sort or another. That such a man, seized of the idea of printing, should construct his own press was scarcely surprising. Whatever the form of his press, it worked well enough for him to be able to print four pages at a time upon it, and with it he printed some seven books between 1871 and 1892. The first book, *The Millar's Daughter: A Legend of the Granta,* was illustrated with lithographs that were his first attempt in the medium. With the exception of the third book from his press, a very substantial volume of records of *The Smith-Carrington family,* which he printed to oblige his brother-in-law in 1884 (and the only one of his books which is at all common), all his publications were written as well as illustrated and printed by himself. They are interesting examples of substantial amateur work, but in layout, ornament, and type little different from the work of any small jobbing printer of the time. In Professor Bruce Dickinson's words, "it would be idle to claim for him distinction as a printer."

By the time that Widnall's last book had appeared, the boom in amateur printing was past. A writer in *The British and Colonial Printer* for 1902 recalled "the period between 1875 and 1885, when amateur printing was at its zenith and numbered its votaries by thousands," and discussed some of the presses that had been produced.

> What brought about the decadence of amateur printing as a hobby? is a question that has often been asked, but never satisfactorily answered. Certain it is, that after 1886 the number of amateurs became fewer, and continued to dwindle until now their ranks are very much thinned, and instead of being—as at one time they threatened to be—a menace to the professional, they are now only to be found in rare and isolated instances.

His own opinion was that the reason for the decline of interest in printing for pleasure was that the development of the dry plate had made photography so much more straightforward that many amateurs abandoned their presses for the quicker rewards of the camera.

There were other hobbies as well. For the teenage amateur journalists of the United States, Carey S. Bliss suggests that the bicycle began to capture the time and money of those who a few years earlier would have turned to printing. Whatever the cause, by the end of the nineteenth century amateur printing had dwindled to such an extent that the writer in *The British and Colonial Printer* predicted that "we are not likely ever again to have a recrudescence of the hobby"!

Chapter II

———

PRINTING AS ONE OF THE FINE ARTS: WILLIAM MORRIS AND THE KELMSCOTT PRESS

IF ONE WERE SEEKING A DATE for the foundation of the Private Press Movement, that date would be November 15, 1888, when a lecture on printing was given at the first exhibition of the Arts and Crafts Exhibition Society. The speaker was Emery Walker, whose influence on fine printing in both Britain and the continent would be hard to overestimate, but there is no doubt that this was its first public manifestation.

Emery Walker was a self-made man who had been engaged in process engraving since 1873, and in the course of his work had added to a thorough understanding of the practical aspects of the printing trade a considerable knowledge of good printing of earlier centuries. From 1884 he had been a friend and neighbor of William Morris at Hammersmith and spent much of his spare time with Morris at Kelmscott House discussing the work of early printers. A shy man without experience in public speaking, Walker had been reluctant to accept Thomas James Cobden-Sanderson's invitation to speak at the exhibition and decided not to rely on his own expository skills but to use photographic lantern-slides to demonstrate graphically the points he wished to make. In selecting the exemplars for the slides to be made at his own firm, he turned to Morris's library, and the two men spent long hours discussing the merits of various incunabula, on what constituted effective design, and the like.

William Morris had been interested in book production long before this. As early as 1865 he had been planning an edition of *The Earthly Paradise* with lavish illustration by Edward Burne-Jones, but after some trial settings in both Caslon and Basle Roman types at the Chiswick Press, the project was put aside. The same had happened with trial pages for a decorated edition of *Love Is Enough* in 1872. Though still untutored in typography, Morris seemed to have recognized the lack of balance between type and woodcuts in both these ventures. But by the summer of 1888, inspired by Walker, his fascination with typography was growing, and growing in an informed way. In the fall of that year he had an edition of *A Tale of the House of the Wolfings* printed to his specification, at Walker's suggestion using the Basle Roman type for the text.

The effect of Walker's lecture was quite remarkable. In a warm notice in the *Pall Mall Gazette,* Oscar Wilde declared that nothing could have been better, and noted that the slide from Arrighi's writing book "was greeted with a spontaneous round of applause." But of all the audience, none became so excited by the greatly enlarged examples of fifteenth-century type projected on the screen than the already half-converted Morris. "Let's make a new fount of type," he proposed to Walker as they strolled away from Bloomsbury after the lecture was over. It was from this stimulus that Morris's "endeavour . . . to re-attain a long-lost standard of craftsmanship of book printing" was to grow.

At first it was by no means clear in Morris's mind that he wanted a press of his own. With help from Walker, he embarked on designing a type font, but while that was still in progress, he was continuing experiments with C. T. Jacobi of the Chiswick Press, producing *The Roots of the Mountains* in 1889. In this, Morris again used Basle Roman type (with a modified sort for the "e"), and attempted one or two changes in treatment of the title page and chapter titles, which produced an improvement in layout over the earlier book, although the characteristic wide setting of the Victorian compositors that he had noticed had "managed to knock the guts out of [the type] somehow," was not made visibly more compact in this second experiment. Nevertheless, Morris declared he was well pleased with "the best-looking book issued since the seventeenth century." Soon after its publication he wrote, "I am so pleased with my book . . . that I am any day to be seen huggling it up, and am become a spectacle to Gods and men because of it." For a time it seemed possible that he would continue to satisfy his typographic interests by commissioning the Chiswick Press to produce his books, in much the way that a few years later Robert Bridges was to have his splendid *Yattendon Hymnal* printed by Oxford University Press. But, as Morris was to write to F. S. Ellis, in November 1889, about *The Roots of the Mountains:*

> The difficulty of getting [the presswork] really well done shows us the old story
> again. It seems it is no easy matter to get good hand-press men, so little work is
> done by the hand-press: that accounts for some defects in the book, caused by
> want of care in distributing the ink. I really am thinking of turning printer
> myself in a small way.

A last experiment, *The Story of Gunnlaug Wormtongue,* which Morris had the Chiswick Press set in William Howard's facsimile recutting of one of Caxton's types, was printed in 1890 but never published. By that time, assured by detailed estimates prepared by Walker that for the cost of buying one of the finer incunabula he could expect to be able to get out a few copies of a "decent-seeming" book for distribution to a few friends, Morris had finally decided to set up his own press. He invited Emery Walker to go into partnership with him: "Mind you, I shall want my own way!" he is reputed to have said. Walker refused the offer, "having some sense of proportion" (as he later somewhat cryptically put it) but, nevertheless, he remained an éminence grise. In Sir Sydney Cockerell's words, "no important step was taken without his advice and approval."

What were Morris's aims in setting up the Kelmscott Press? He had been struck, while he was selecting examples of the best commercial printing of the time for the Arts and Crafts Exhibition, by the fact that not one of his own many books was of such a standard as to merit inclusion, and undoubtedly he was equally struck by the inferiority of contemporary books to the incunabula that he and Walker had been examining. He would not have been Morris had this not been enough to make him determine to try his own hand at achieving the standards of the fifteenth century, and he would not have been true to himself had he not made an intensive study of all the various technical aspects of printing. As W. R. Lethaby wrote, these studies by Morris were:

not of the superficial look of things, but of their very elements and essence. When . . . first producing textiles, Morris was a practical dyer; when it was tapestry, he wove the first pieces with his own hand; when he did illumination, he had to find a special vellum in Rome and have a special gold beaten; when he did printing, he had to explore papermaking, inkmaking, type cutting, and other dozen branches of the trade. His ornaments and the treatment of Burne-Jones's illustrations were based on his personal practice as a woodcutter. Morris was no mere "designer" of type and ornaments for books, but probably the most competent book-maker ever known. Indeed, it is a mistake to get into the habit of thinking of him as a "designer"; he was a work-master.

This is a very generous assessment of Morris's importance, but Lethaby's description of his methods clearly indicates that Morris did not ignorantly attempt to clear typography of the mess of centuries. Before the Kelmscott Press started work he made a thorough investigation into the various materials and processes that go into a book, individually and in relation to one another. Then, and only then, he "began printing books with the hope of producing some which would have a definite claim to beauty, while at the same time they should be easy to read and should not dazzle the eye, or trouble the intellect of the reader by eccentricity of form in the letters." This was the opening statement in his *Note . . . On His Aims in Founding the Kelmscott Press.*

The production of the new type (of which fuller details are given in Chapter 25) was under way. The selection of the right paper was another problem. After some searching, Morris decided that a Bolognese paper of about 1473 (a "neat, subtle and courtlike" paper, as Thomas Fuller had described such papers in the seventeenth century) was the best. He had some little difficulty in getting paper of this quality made—"we can do nothing with Whatman but take what he has on the shelves"—until he went with Emery Walker to visit Joseph Batchelor's mill at Little Chart, Ashford, in the autumn of 1890. While there, he tried his own hand at papermaking (doing very creditably, according to J. W. Mackail), but finding Batchelor as enthusiastic as himself he was content to let the latter experiment in producing the right paper. By February 1891 Batchelor had produced one that was satisfactory, and he continued to make all the paper ever used for Kelmscott Press books.

As well as paper, vellum was thought to be necessary for "superior" editions. A small stock of vellum, which he had obtained years before from Rome for illumination remained unused, but when Morris tried to purchase a further supply he found that all the vellum had been promised to the Vatican. In desperation he was contemplating a direct appeal to the Pope (on the grounds that *The Golden Legend,* which he intended to print, was a book in which the Pope should be interested!) when a friend suggested that Henry Band, who made binding vellums at Brentford, might, like Batchelor, be willing to try to produce the right kind of surface. It was a happy suggestion. Though Band's experiments took too long for vellum copies of *The Golden Legend* to be printed, by 1892 satisfactory skins were being produced in England.

Ink was to present another problem, "as one might have known, seeing that those damned chemists have a freer hand with it!" Morris commented bitterly. After many trials he found English and American inks which, with a little modification to eliminate their blue or red undertones, would have been satisfactory, but their makers adopted a take-it-or-leave-it attitude. Eventually he found an ink said to be made from the old-fashioned pure ingredients by Jaenecke of Hanover. With this, unwilling to turn inkmaker himself, although he often spoke of it, Morris was content. Morris's satisfaction with the ink was not shared by the pressmen. According to a letter written by Emery Walker many years later, they found Jaenecke's ink so stiff and difficult to work that its introduction nearly caused a strike, only thwarted by Morris's threat to close the press altogether.

For a press, he found the Albion perfectly satisfactory. As his printing activities grew, he added two more Albions and a proofing press. For printing with the sort of ink and paper that he intended to use, these were far better than powered presses and for the short runs that he was to print they were far more economical. At times Morris has mistakenly been accused simply of wishing to put the clock back, but that he was content with nineteenth-century cast-iron presses and with having the ink distributed by rollers is sufficient proof that Kelmscott was not a medievalist's hobby. It would have been perfectly simple for him to have had common-presses built of wood and to have distributed the ink using the age-old method of ink balls. Had he merely wished to print in the fifteenth-century manner this is what he would have done, but this would have been less satisfactory technically; Morris unhesitatingly turned to nineteenth-century equipment and methods when they could do the work better. Nevertheless, as a medievalist in spirit he was not altogether without regrets. "Pleased as I am with my printing," he was to write in May 1891, "when I saw my two men at work on the press yesterday with their sticky printers' ink, I couldn't help lamenting the simplicity of the scribe and his desk, and his black ink and blue and red ink, and I felt almost ashamed of my press after all."

By January 1891, with type and paper nearly ready, premises were taken at 16 Upper Mall, Hammersmith, and a compositor and pressman appointed—W. H. Bowden, who was later to be joined by his daughter and his son. The Kelmscott Press was born. Bowden later told a splendid story of its christening:

> When the type came in from the founders, he [Morris] was very anxious to help
> lay it in the cases; but not having served his time to the business, more often
> than not put the type into the wrong box. It was very amusing to hear him
> saying to himself "There, bother it; wrong box again!" But he was perfectly
> good humoured, and presently ran off and came back, bustling up the path . . .
> without a hat, and with a bottle of wine under each arm, with which to drink
> the health of the Kelmscott Press.

Bowden's story is sufficient indication of the good state of working relations at the Kelmscott Press, despite the affair of Jaenecke's ink. Morris enjoyed talking with and observing his employees at their work until his theoretical knowledge of the niceties of composition and of presswork were very good, although, strangely enough, he seems never to have tried his own hand at the press.

Was the Kelmscott Press then a *private* press at all? Morris's "little typographical adventure," as he had described it to Bowden when offering him a post, and which in the seven years of its existence was to have a turnover of more than £50,000, was obviously on a very different scale from even so esteemed and successful a private press as that of Dr. Daniel. Many have regarded Kelmscott as too commercial to warrant the name of private press, yet undoubtedly in its infancy it *was* private in the strictest definition of the term. Morris set it up for his own interest, to see what could be done in the way of producing a good book at his own expense, and his original intention was to print only 20 copies of its first publication, *The Story of the Glittering Plain,* for distribution to personal friends. Only when news of the forthcoming book had leaked out to the press, and Morris was being badgered to make copies available for purchase did he decide with some misgivings to print extra copies for sale. He was no remote aesthete but a practical man, and if the public was prepared to give financial support to his experiments in printing what he wanted and in the manner he wanted, he was happy to let them do so. That the Kelmscott Press was successful enough to cover the very heavy production costs of its books was no slur on its amateur status.

ILLUS. 45A. Printing the Kelmscott *Chaucer.*
Photograph: Courtesy of St. Bride
Printing Library.

ILLUS. 45B. Binding of the Kelmscott *Chaucer.*
Photograph: Courtesy of the Trustees
of The Pierpont Morgan Library.

The Golden Legend had been intended as the first book from the press, but because the first sizes of paper supplied by Batchelor were wrong for the work *The Story of the Glittering Plain* was printed instead. Work on *The Golden Legend* started as soon as it was completed, but because of its length five other books had been issued before it was finished in November 1892. By that time the style of the Kelmscott books had become clear—volumes carefully designed; with wide and well-proportioned margins; magnificently decorated with borders designed by Morris and illustrations by Burne-Jones engraved on wood, usually by W. H. Hooper, one of the old master engravers; splendidly printed on the best materials available.

Up to and including *The Golden Legend* all the books were printed in Morris's "Golden" type, based upon Jenson's roman letter of 1470. But already Morris's appetite had been whetted, and in June 1891 he had started on the designs for a black letter that was cut and cast at the end of the year. In the same month, realizing that the single press and the existing premises were inadequate, he moved the press to a new home next to Sussex House, in which Emery Walker's process-engraving business was already situated, and added a second press so that the output of work could be increased.

The first book to be printed in the larger size of the black letter (the "Troy" type) was Caxton's translation of *The Recuyell of the Historyes of Troye,* the first book printed in English and long one of Morris's favorites, which was published through Bernard Quaritch in November 1892. Quaritch had also published *The Golden Legend* (earlier books had been handled by Morris's old publishers Reeves and Turner), but so many inquiries were received at the Kelmscott Press that a book list had to be prepared. From July 1892, Halliday Sparling was named as Secretary of the press—a position to which Sydney Cockerell was to succeed in 1894, becoming Morris's right-hand man, after Sparling's marriage with Morris's daughter May had broken up. A few more books were published through

HERE BEGYNNETH THE PROLOGE OF SYR JOHAN FROISSART OF THE CHRONICLES OF FRAUNCE, INGLANDE, AND OTHER PLACES ADJOYNYNGE

The first Chaptre

THAT the honorable and noble aventures of featis of armes, done & achyued by the warres of Fraunce and Inglande, shulde notably be inregistered, and put in perpetuall memory, whereby the prewe & hardy may haue ensample to incourage them in theyr well doyng, I, syr Johan froissart, wyll treat and recorde an hystory of great louage and preyse: but, or I begyn, I require the sauyour of all the worlde, who of nothyng created al thynges, that he wyll gyue me suche grace and vnderstandyng, that I may continue and perseuer in suche wyse, that who so this proces redeth or hereth, may take pastaunce, pleasure, and ensaumple It is said of trouth, that al buyldynges are masoned & wroughte of dyuerse stones, and all great ryuers are gurged and assemblede of divers surges and sprynges of water: in lyke wyse all sciences are extraught & compiled of diuerse clerkes, of that one wryteth, another parauenture is ignorant; but by the famous wrytyng of auncient auctours, all thyng is ben known in one place or other.

WHAN to attaygne to the mater that I haue entreprised, I wyll begyn, fyrst, by the grace of God and the blessed Virgyn our Lady Saynt Mary, from whom all comfort and consolation procedeth, and wyll take my foundation out of the true cronicles somtyme compyled by the right reuerend, discrete and sage maister Johan la Bele, somtyme chanon in Saint Lambartis of Liege, who with good herte & due diligence dyd his true deuoure in wrytyng this noble cronicle, and dyd contynue it all his lyfes days, in folowyng the trouth as nere as he myght, to his great charge and coste in sekyng to procure and to haue the perfight knowledge thereof. He was also in his lyfes days welbeloued, and of the secret counsayle with the lorde sir Johan of Haynaulte, who is often remembred, as reason requyreth, here after in this boke; for of many fayre & noble auentures he was chiefe causer, & to the kyng right nigh, & by whose meanes the said syr Johan la Bele myght well knowe and here of many dyuers noble dedes. The whiche here after shal be declared.

TROUTH it is, that I who have entreprised this boke to ordeyne for pleasure and pastaunce, to the whiche always I have been inclyned, & for that intent I haue folowed and frequented the company of dyuerse noble & great lordes, as well in fraunce, Inglande, and Scotlande, as in diuerse other countries, and have had knowledge by them, and alwayes to my power iustly haue inquired for the trouth of the dedis of warre and auentures that haue fallen, and specially syth the great batell of Poytyers, where as the noble kynge Johan of france was takyn prisoner, as before that tyme I was but of a yonge age or vnderstandyng Howe be it I toke it on me assoone as I come from scole, to wryte and recite the sayd boke, & bare the same compyled into Ingland, and presented the volume thereof to my Lady Phelyppe of Heynaulte, noble quene of Inglande, who right amyably receyued it to my great profite & auauncement.

AND it may be so, that the same boke is nat as yet examyned nor corrected so iustely as suche a case requyreth: for featis of armes derely bought & achyued, the honor therof ought to be gyuen & truly deuided to them that by prowes & hard trauayle haue deserued it Therfore to acquyte me in that bihalfe, & in folowyng the trouth as near as I can, I Johan froissart haue entreprysed this hystory on the forsaid ordynaunce & true fundacion, at the instaunce and request of a dere lorde of myn, Robert of Namure, knight, lorde of Bewfort, to whom entierly I owe loue and obeysaunce, & God graunt me to do that thyng that may be to his pleasure. Amen.

Here spekethe the auctour of suche as were most valiant knyghtis to be made mencion of in this boke. Capitulo II.

ALL noble hertis, to encorage & to shewe them ensample and mater of honour, I Syr Johann froissart begynne to speke after the true report and relation of my master Johan la Bele, somtyme Chanon of Saynte Lambertis of these firms, but from *The History of Godefrey of Boloyne* (1893) on it became normal practice for the press to publish directly. This is a course much more usual with private presses, and it had the advantage of saving bookkeeping, giving Morris information on sales, placing him in a position to guard against overprinting, and enabling him to give preference to purchasers of individual copies over booksellers laying in stock against an anticipated rise in price. A few more books were commissioned by publishers or booksellers, and in the case of one, Tennyson's *Maud* published by Macmillan in 1893, there was an apparent case of overprinting. Three hundred copies were sold at once, but the other 200 hanging fire, Macmillan announced that they would be sold as a remainder. And sold they were, by noon on the day following the announcement!

Undoubtedly the most important of the Kelmscott publications was the *Chaucer,* hailed by the editor of the *Nineteenth Century* as "the greatest triumph of English typography." Work on this started in the summer of 1896, although Morris had been talking of it a year earlier, but it was not until June 1896 that the book was ready to be issued. By the time it appeared, Morris, whose health had been visibly failing since 1894, was a very sick man. He knew that he was dying, and in August 1896 asked Sydney Cockerell whether he and Walker would be prepared to carry on the press after his death. Cockerell was in favor of its ceasing, lest it should fizzle out by degrees. After Morris's death on October 3, 1896, Cockerell continued to run the press with Walker and F. S. Ellis for another 18 months in order to complete work already in hand. Much of the work was abandoned as being in too early a stage of preparation to be carried through, including a splendid *Froissart* (Illus. 46). In the seven years of its life the press published 52 books in 66 volumes—no small achievement for the "little typographical adventure" of an elderly man.

Nobody can judge the printing of the Kelmscott Press without handling the books themselves; no reproduction, however good, can convey the color of the ink, the feel of the paper, and the impression of the types on the page, which is why Morris refused to allow Edward F. Strange to reproduce Kelmscott work in his *Alphabets* published in 1895. The books were unlike any the late Victorian public had ever seen before. There were many critics. Walter Crane was probably the first to comment unfavorably that Morris's first type was more Gothic-looking than its model, a criticism with which even the most ardent supporter of Morris would today agree. Morris himself was unrepentent: "this is a fact, and a cheerful one to me," he wrote. Others objected to the presswork of the books, his *imprinting* of the type into the dampened paper instead of giving the kiss impression of a machine press.

> Witness has been born against Morris [wrote Frank Colebrook in the *Printing Times*] in regard to what is called the embossing of the back of the page, an evidence that the other side of the page we are reading is also printed upon. The effect is displeasing to most eyes, and it detracts from the vividness of the letter which is being read, to the degree to which it detracts from the whiteness of the intervening space between the words. I don't think this concomitant of the hand-press, with its enormous vertical pressure, is really gratifying to Morris, however indulgently he may look upon it for its reminiscences of old-world books. It is simply the lesser of two evils. If a perfect, dense, deep

---

ILLUS. 46. Kelmscott Press, London. Proof page from the never-completed *Froissart,* work on which was abandoned after Morris's death.

black is not to be obtained without the drawbacks of the embossing of the back
of the page, well, on the balancing of advantages, he chooses to have the more
legible letter. He, indeed, procures so deep a black it can afford the sacrifice of
a little white in the contrasting spacing.

Despite Colebrook's comment, Morris certainly did look indulgently on this fault. Bodoni had dried his printed sheets under pressure between heated copper sheets in order to remove the indentations left by the type, and so painstaking a craftsman as Morris would certainly have resorted to a similar method (just as the more fastidious of today's private printers borrow their wives' irons for the purpose!) had he felt the indentation to be a blemish. Very probably he regarded it as an essential part and evidence of handwork, and as such not to be concealed.

At times there were protests that too many of the books he printed were written by himself—a foolish argument to advance against a *private* press. For the politically minded attacks that he was "preaching socialism and going away to prepare books that none but the rich could buy," there was little to be said. Many of his prices were certainly high (the velum *Chaucer* cost 120 guineas), but others were low. His own lecture *Gothic Architecture,* printed at the Arts and Crafts Exhibition in 1893, cost half a crown. Again, in Frank Colebrook's words:

> He sets up his press, not really to make money, whether out of the rich or the
> poor, but to produce a book as beautiful as he can make it. When he has paid a
> high price for his paper . . . When he has used black ink about 10s. a pound,
> when he has designed his three types and had them cut; when he has paid fair
> wages to his workmen . . . he is not able to sell the product of all this for a less
> sum.

But Morris's quest for perfection was beyond the comprehension of some. In *The Kelmscott Press and William Morris, Master Craftsman* (1924) Halliday Sparling tells how Morris once took:

> the head of a large commercial printing works, with some pretensions to artistic
> leanings, over the Press. The visitor watched the careful setting and justifying of
> the compositors, watched the pressmen examining each sheet as it was pulled
> and commented "That's all very well for Mr. Morris, but there isn't a man here
> that would be worth a penny an hour to me after he'd been here a week!"

The commercial printer might grumble that it was "all very well for Mr. Morris," but the books sold very well indeed. One writer who made good use of the fashion for Kelmscott books was Thorstein Veblen, who saw it as an example of his theory of conspicuous consumption:

> Here we have a somewhat cruder type, printed on hand-laid deckle-edged
> paper, with excessive margins and uncut leaves, with bindings of a painstaking
> crudeness and elaborate ineptitude. The Kelmscott Press reduced the matter to
> an absurdity—as seen from the point of view of brute serviceability alone—by
> issuing books for modern use, edited with obsolete spelling, printed in
> black-letter, and bound in limp vellum fitted with thongs. As a further
> characteristic feature which fixes the economic place of artistic book-making,
> there is the fact that these more elegant books are, at their best, printed in
> limited editions. A limited edition is in effect a guarantee—somewhat crude, it
> is true—that this book is scarce and that it therefore is costly and lends
> pecuniary distinction to its consumer.

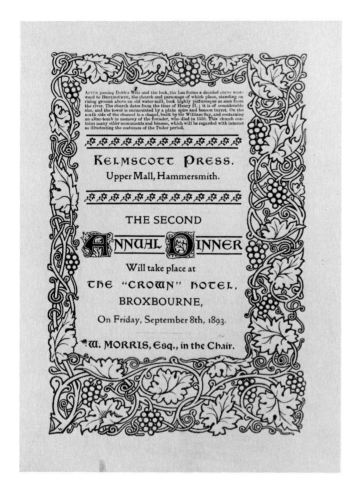

ILLUS. 47. Kelmscott Press, London.
Wayzgoose, Menu, second dinner.
Photograph: Courtesy of the Trustees
of The Pierpont Morgan Library.

Most other contemporary criticisms of the Kelmscott Press were unimportant and based on misunderstanding. In the 90-odd years since it was closed, opinion has fluctuated considerably, with an initial and inevitable reaction against what had been so highly admired and imitated. Daniel Berkeley Updike was carefully ambiguous in his statement that Morris "was a great printer because he was a great man who printed greatly." By the time of the William Morris Centenary Dinner held at the Double Crown Club in 1934, Holbrook Jackson was prepared to be considerably more outspoken. In a deliberately provocative address (later printed in his *The Printing of Books*, 1938) Jackson declared that the Kelmscott Press books were:

> typographical curiosities from birth, and so far removed from the common way of readers that they have become models of what a book should not be. . . . His typefaces became picturesque, his margins inclined to pomposity, and his paper was pretentious. The Kelmscott books are overdressed. They ask you to look at them rather than to read them. You can't get away from their overwhelming typography.

Jackson was laying it on rather thickly for his audience, particularly in his conclusion that the books were "museum pieces, typographical monuments—beautiful and ineffectual angels beating in the void their luminous wings in vain," but his statements were more than just a witty after-dinner speech. His ideas have been echoed by John Russell Taylor in his thoughtful study of *The Art Nouveau Book in Britain* (1966), which stated: "Any opening of a Morris book . . . is probably splendid: it is only when one comes to leaf through an entire volume, or worse still tries to read one, that aesthetic indigestion sets in." Many aspects of the Kelmscott Press books put them at the rich princely end of the whole Arts and Crafts aesthetic. Burne-Jones described the Kelmscott *Chaucer* as "a pocket cathedral—it is so full of design," and it has such total coherence of design and such individuality that cathedral is the right architectural description for this work, which remains the most frequently reproduced of all private press books. But the man building a cathedral does not think that the only kind of building; as Morris stated in an address to the Bibliographical Society:

> A book quite unornamented can look actually and positively beautiful, and not
> merely un-ugly, if it be, so as to say, architecturally good. . . . Now, then, let us
> see what this architectural arrangement claims of us. First, the pages must be
> clear and easy to read; which they can hardly be unless, secondly, the type is
> well designed; and thirdly, whether the margins be small or big, they must be
> in due proportion to the page of the letter.

In working at Kelmscott, Morris was not aiming at the production of such plain work of a kind suitable for reading on a train. In exploring the full possibilities of rich design, in most Kelmscott books in any case much more limited than the ornate pages that dominate the public mind, Morris preferred the stately and formal large volume, the "big folio [which] lies quiet and majestic on the table, waiting kindly till you please to come to it, so that your mind is free to enjoy the literature which its beauty enshrines."

The Kelmscott Press works are magnificent, and as revolutionary manifestos in the cause of better printing they were of real importance. Cost prevents many of us from forming our own opinions on whether they are in fact books *to be read*; their reputation and value have themselves ensured that save for the lucky few they have become museum pieces, typographical monuments.

Chapter 12

AFTER KELMSCOTT: THE FINE PRESS IN BRITAIN

WILLIAM MORRIS'S TYPOGRAPHICAL ADVENTURE WAS by no means the only essay in printing as an art in England in the 1890s. But it was the first manifestation of the Arts and Crafts Movement in book work, and its influence for good or bad on the work of succeeding private presses was considerable. Needless to say, not all amateur printers who set up a few years after Kelmscott were under Morris's spell. There is, in fact, no evidence of an awareness of Kelmscott at all in the books Sir George Sitwell had printed under his supervision at Scarborough, or in the long series of genealogical publications issued from the private press of Frederick Arthur Crisp, Grove Park Press, or in the Gaelic dictionary and other work emanating from E. Dwelly's press at Herne Bay. These presses were late examples of an earlier variety of private press, in the tradition of Prince Louis-Lucien Bonaparte or the Middle Hill Press.

Other yeasts besides Kelmscott were working in the ferment of the nineties. One of the most interesting, and relatively undervalued, designers of the time was Charles Ricketts. Born in 1866, he was orphaned in 1882 at the age of 16 and then, through the indulgence of his grandfather, he was allowed to follow his inclination to a career in art and was apprenticed to a wood engraver. In the same year he and his fellow-apprentice Charles Shannon formed an alliance that was to last until Ricketts's death in 1931. Having completed their apprenticeships, Ricketts and Shannon set up house together in London in 1887 and adopted an extraordinary artistic program whereby Ricketts worked as designer and illustrator to earn their livelihood while Shannon perfected his technique as a painter. However, the very pressure of the hackwork Ricketts undertook for such magazines as *Black and White* and *Magazine of Art* and in commercial book production enabled him to develop as an artist far more thoroughly than Shannon, who worked at a more relaxed pace.

For their London base, they took over the lease of a house in Chelsea, The Vale, from James McNeil Whistler. Whistler's taste in typographic design, shown perhaps at its best in *The Gentle Art of Making Enemies* (1890), was in its own way extremely influential, although few of us would go all the way with A. J. A. Symons in his claim that it was Whistler's "personal example, more than any other, that influenced later comers in typography." There can, however, be no doubt of his influence on Ricketts and Shannon; their occasional literary/artistic journal the *Dial,* which first appeared in 1889, uses many of Whistler's methods and materials and, like his work, was printed commercially by the Ballantyne Press. The first number so impressed Oscar Wilde that he came to The Vale to meet the two and is said to have begged them not to bring out a second number, as "all perfect things should be unique" (in fact, four more successful issues of the *Dial* were to appear irregularly from 1892 to 1897). Wilde commissioned Ricketts to design his books (with the sole exception of *Salomé*), which were published by Osgood McIlvaine & Co.; and Ricketts was to design several other books for that firm and later for Elkin Mathews and John Lane at the Bodley Head. Several of them like John Gray's *Silverpoints* (1893) or Wilde's own *The Sphinx* (1894) are now regarded as among the finest books of the period.

In addition to this work in commercial publishing, in which he had steadily moved toward total control of the materials used and the coordinated design of all elements in the book, Ricketts was engaged in more private plans for book production. At the time he knew nothing of Morris's pre-Kelmscott experiments, and his first impression on seeing *The Story of the Glittering Plain* was one of disappointment. It was by a totally independent and parallel process that he repeated Morris's moves in creating his own private press. First, in conscious emulation of the *Hypnerotomachia Poliphili,* Shannon and Ricketts together worked on wood-engraved illustrations and initials for a lavish edition of *Daphnis and Chloe,* which was printed under Ricketts's supervision at the Ballantyne Press, and after two years' work eventually completed in 1893.

Daphnis and Chloe was a considerable success, and far more than a pastiche, although in his *Modern Illustration* (London, 1895) Joseph Pennell dismissed it as necessarily serving "to perpetuate the imperfections of the Middle-Age woodcutter," and to modern eyes its use of Old Style type weakens the effect. Ricketts was not altogether satisfied with it, particularly with the degree of imbalance between illustrations and text created by the initials and lines set in capitals, and for his next private venture selected the smaller-scale *Hero and Leander* so that closer attention to detail would be practicable. Completed in 1894, it shows significant advances: Caslon Old Face replaced Old Style, and the balance in weight between text and illustration was very good. The quality of the presswork, on paper specially made for Ricketts by the papermakers, Arnolds, was distinctly better.

By this time, in effect and almost in name (since the paper was watermarked VP, and the Vale Press monogram appears on the spine of the copies in vellum binding), the Vale Press was created. It was originally intended that the printing should be done at The Vale, but planning regulations forbade the establishment of what was technically a workshop in a residential district. The work method adopted was, therefore, still to use the resources of the Ballantyne Press, where a handpress and pressman were reserved exclusively for Ricketts's use under his own personal supervision.

One last step remained. Ricketts felt that "whatever the effort made in design and ornament, the poverty of the founts I had used was a thing not to be discounted." Like Morris before him, and many other private printers later, he felt the need for his own individual typefaces, yet lacked the capital to underwrite these and the production costs of the books he wished to make. A legacy of £500, and a lucky introduction by William Rothenstein to Llewellyn Hacon, a wealthy lawyer whose taste for the arts was such that he was willing to put £1,000 into the Vale Press in return for a "vague understanding" about a half-share in any profits, were sufficient to launch the enterprise.

Purists who objected that Kelmscott was not truly a private press have found the Vale Press still more questionable, partly because of the technicality that Ricketts did not own his printing equipment, but even more because its books were advertised and marketed with considerable efficiency. Premises were taken in Warwick Street, off Regent Street; C. J. Holmes (much later to become Director of the National Gallery when Ricketts himself refused this politically demanding post) was general factotum, and distribution of the books was organized through John Lane. This left Ricketts free to concentrate on the design of the books, following his own carefully thought-out aesthetic, which was applied with fastidious care.

There were to be 46 different works issued under the Vale Press imprint, including a Shakespeare in 39 volumes, designed throughout by Ricketts, from the watermark through the typeface, decoration, wood engravings, *mise-en-page,* and bindings. The results are quite different from those obtained by Morris at the Kelmscott Press, and in many ways superior.

In some respects the differences are those between the philosophies of Arts and Crafts and those of Art Nouveau. In methods and in design Morris was direct, consistent, unaffected, and robust, and he revealed the almost revivalist fervor of the true Arts and Crafts man. Ricketts, however, reveals the sophistication, eclecticism, and very highly mannered qualities of the best British Art Nouveau work. The differences were not so great that Ricketts could not admire Kelmscott work, while according to Sturge Moore, Morris on his deathbed was reduced to tears of admiration when shown the early Vale Press work.

It would be an exaggeration to say that when you have seen one Kelmscott book you have seen them all, but Morris's own manly ideas on typography and decoration are imprinted firmly on their pages, and the family resemblance of the various books tends to conceal from us their individual characteristics. The books are heady, romantic, emotional typography; one almost feels that the type and ornament have grown together and could continue growing like some monstrous hothouse plant, or, as one critic has wittily but unkindly put it, the Kelmscott Press books were the continuation of wallpaper by other means. The Vale Press books on the other hand were individually designed, with much closer attention given to each of the volumes in a style that accorded with the needs of the individual texts being printed, and with total control of all features of the books' design in Ricketts's own hands. To be sure the individual literary tastes of Morris show clearly in most Kelmscott work, and the ungenerous critic in pointing to the rather miscellaneous "Eng. Lit." nature of the Vale Press list may say that selection was perhaps based more on marketability than on an underlying literary taste. But whether individual design of each book was forced on Ricketts or not, his practice of thinking each work out afresh was a valuable lesson for later book designers, and most noticeable perhaps in Meynell's work at the Nonesuch Press.

Unfortunately, the design of Vale Press books is a little too intellectual. Ricketts's appreciation of the Italian book of the renaissance certainly enabled him at times to achieve the same effect of pages full of light (against his definition of Kelmscott pages "full of wine"), which he so admired. But there is the feeling of overmuch thought, of pages and borders that have not grown naturally but have been trained and clipped to fit into a deliberately planned arrangement (Illus. 48). Their self-conscious good taste is a little too obvious. "The aim of the revival of printing [Ricketts wrote] is to give a permanent and beautiful form to that portion of our literature which is secure of permanence. . . . I mean permanent in the sense that the work reflects that conscious aim towards beauty and order which are ever interesting elements in themselves." His "conscious aim towards beauty and order" was carried out by trying to make every part of the Vale Press books exquisite; the result too often was to make them merely mannered and precious.

By the start of the twentieth century Ricketts felt the time was coming for him to close the Vale Press, because it had completed nearly all the work he had set out to produce. A disastrous fire at the Ballantyne Press in 1899, in which most of his engraved blocks and other materials were consumed, had the immediate effect of making his later books more austere in execution and provided a sound reason for calling a halt to his typographic work. In 1903, "as it is undesirable that these founts should drift into hands other than their designer's and become stale by unthinking use," he consigned his punches and matrices to the bed of the river Thames, retaining only enough type to

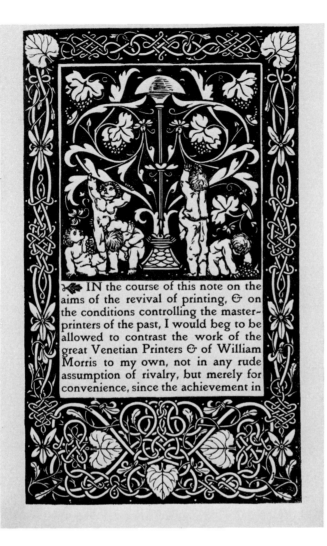

IN the course of this note on the aims of the revival of printing, & on the conditions controlling the master-printers of the past, I would beg to be allowed to contrast the work of the great Venetian Printers & of William Morris to my own, not in any rude assumption of rivalry, but merely for convenience, since the achievement in

ILLUS. 48. Vale Press, London. *A Defence of the Revival of Printing,* 1899. Decoration by Charles Ricketts.

produce a final *Bibliography of Books Printed by Hacon and Ricketts* (1904). Running the press had been a happy undertaking, and Ricketts recorded his emotion on shaking hands with the pressmen after the last sheets of the *Bibliography* had been printed, realizing "that I was bidding good-bye to a portion of my life." Only in his last years did he return to the book arts. It was not as a private printer himself, but his illustrations and binding designs in a few books for Nonesuch and others published in the late twenties and early thirties confirmed his mastery.

For some years the Vale Press was very closely associated with the Eragny Press, which was run by the artist Lucien Pissarro. Ricketts and his lifelong companion Charles Shannon had befriended the young Lucien soon after he came to London from France and had encouraged him to contribute to their publication the *Dial.* In 1894, Pissarro had purchased a handpress and laboriously printed *The Queen of Fishes,* the text of which was reproduced by process engraving from hand lettering, with colored wood engravings. As neither Pissarro nor his wife knew anything of printing, the work gave endless trouble, but the results were sufficiently good for John Lane to agree to market the book, for Pissarro to decide to continue with printing, and for Ricketts to offer Pissarro the use of his Vale type for subsequent publications. The next 15 books printed at the Eragny Press between 1896 and 1903 were accordingly all in Ricketts's type and published through the Vale Press. But though Pissarro had learned much of typography from Ricketts they were by no means imitations of

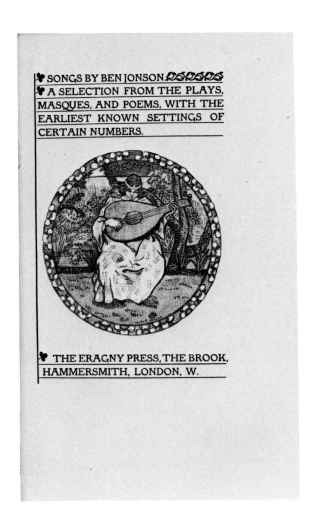

ILLUS. 49. An Eragny Press
title page in the Brook type.

the Vale manner; Eragny books had a charm and freshness quite unlike anything to be found in the work of any other private press, and in the printing of colored wood engravings in particular the press excelled (Illus. 49). Not a small part of their charm came from the gaily patterned paper over boards used in their bindings, and in this respect at least Ricketts seems to have come under Pissarro's influence; the cheaper Vale Press books employed similar colored patterned papers that Ricketts designed to fit in with the mood of the book. Time has wrought such destruction that we can seldom see either the Vale or Eragny bindings in pristine condition.

After 1903, when the Vale Press types were no longer available, Pissarro continued to print, using his own font of type for a further 16 books. The greater part of the work of producing these was done by himself and his wife, Esther, who engraved his blocks, but when funds permitted, a local printer, Thomas Taylor, was employed to assist with the presswork. *When funds permitted:* unlike the Vale Press that repaid the original investment more than eight times over, the Eragny Press was no money-spinner, and Pissarro was not sufficiently businesslike to price his books highly enough to compensate for the time and work he lavished on each book in an attempt to make it perfect. Although Pissarro's books were highly praised, and he had the distinction of being commissioned by the Société des Cent Bibliophiles and by the Société du Livre Contemporain to produce books for them (and magnificent books they were!) World War I and the consequent loss of Continental subscribers hit him too hard for the press to be able to continue. Although he did not dispose of the press until after the war, *Whym Chow,* privately printed in 1914 for two friends of Ricketts, was to be the last book from the Eragny Press. Posterity was the poorer.

In point of time, one of the earliest followers of Kelmscott was the Ashendene Press, which was started by C. H. St. John Hornby in 1894 and survived until 1935. Hornby was a director of W. H. Smith & Son, and named his press from the family estate in Hertfordshire, where it was set up originally in a little summer house. In its original form the press was not unlike some of the earlier Victorian amateur affairs, at first being operated by Hornby and his sisters without outside help. But there was an important difference from most of the parlor printers. Hornby was a warm admirer of Morris's work at Kelmscott, and while a student at Oxford he had become acquainted with the work of the Daniel Press. At first the Daniel influence was the stronger. After printing three books in Caslon type Hornby managed to obtain the loan of various fonts of Fell types from Oxford University Press, and he used these to print 10 more books. In 1900 he moved his press to Shelley House in Chelsea, which remained its home until it closed.

Although Dr. Daniel's work strongly influenced the outward appearance of these early books, its influence did not last.

> How well I remember that afternoon in March 1895 when I came to Kelmscott House [Hornby wrote to Sir Sydney Cockerell in 1940]. It was shortly after I started the Ashendene Press, and I was brimful of enthusiasm for Morris and all his works. I remember my talk with him in his book-lined room, and going with him to see the sheets of the *Chaucer* on the Press . . . all as if it were yesterday.

Probably much more important than the example of Kelmscott, which was an inspiration rather than a direct influence, was the friendship Hornby struck with Cockerell and through him with Emery Walker.

> From these two [he wrote in the Foreword to the *Ashendene Press Bibliography* in 1935] . . . I received inspiration and encouragement in my venture, and unstinted help and advice. The friendship then formed has lasted unbroken for more than thirty years, and has been a source of much happiness in my life. Cockerell was an unsparing and outspoken but withal kindly critic, and Walker a mine from which to draw a wealth of counsel ever at the free disposal of any struggling beginner. I owe them a debt which can never be repaid.

The earliest substantial effect that Walker and Cockerell had on Hornby's books was that of persuading him to have his own proprietary typeface cut. In 1900 his "Subiaco" type, originally projected by Morris for Kelmscott use, was cut, and for the next quarter century the Ashendene Press used it exclusively (Illus. 50). Based on the type that Sweynheym and Pannartz, the first printers in Italy, had used at Subiaco, the design had a sturdy elegance, which suited Hornby's typographical style admirably. From the first book in which it was used, *Lo Inferno di Dante* (1902), the style of the Ashendene Press was to develop and be refined but never to change considerably. It was a more restrained style than that of Kelmscott, with much more of renaissance subtlety replacing Gothic exuberance, and there was no self-conscious proclamation of intent or object. Hornby was content to produce books as well as could be done, admittedly in circumstances of complete economic freedom, and let them stand as a statement of his aims. He was not above being chaffed about his hobby. "If you want to satisfy yourself that I really *do* do my own printing," he wrote to Cockerell in 1902, "look in here tomorrow about teatime and stay to dinner. . . . Bring Walker with

SICCOME DICE IL FILOSOFO NEL PRINCIPIO della Prima Filosofia 'tutti gli uomini naturalmente desiderano di sapere.' La ragione di che puote essere, che ciascuna cosa, da provvidenza di propria natura impinta, è inclinabile alla sua perfezione. Onde, acciocchè la scienza è l'ultima perfezione della nostra anima, nella quale sta la nostra ultima felicità, tutti naturalmente al suo desiderio siamo soggetti. Veramente da questa nobilissima perfezione molti sono privati per diverse cagioni che dentro dall'uomo, e di fuori da esso, lui rimuovono dall'abito di scienza. ❡Dentro dall'uomo possono essere due difetti e impedimenti : l'uno dalla parte del corpo, l'altro dalla parte dell'anima. Dalla parte del corpo è, quando le parti sono indebitamente disposte, sicchè nulla ricevere può ; siccome sono sordi & muti, e loro simili. Dalla parte dell'anima è, quando la malizia vince in essa, sicchè si fa seguitatrice di viziose dilettazioni, nelle quali riceve tanto inganno, che per quelle ogni cosa tiene a vile. Di fuori dall'uomo possono essere similmente due cagioni intese, l'una delle quali è induttrice di necessità, l'altra di pigrizia. La prima è la cura famigliare & civile, la quale convenevolmente a sè tiene degli uomini il maggior numero, sicchè in ozio di speculazione essere non possono. L'altra è il difetto del luogo ove la persona è nata e nudrita, che talora sarà da ogni studio non solamente privato, ma da gente studiosa lontano. ❡Le due prime di queste cagioni, cioè la prima dalla parte di dentro & la prima dalla parte di fuori, non sono da vituperare, ma da scusare & di perdono degne; le due altre, avvegnachè l'una più, sono degne di biasimo e d'abominazione. Manifestamente adunq; può vedere chi bene considera, che pochi rimangono quelli che all'abito da tutti desiderato possano pervenire, & innumerabili quasi sono gl'impediti, che di questo cibo da tutti sempre vivono affamati. O beati que' pochi che seggono a quella mensa ove il pane degli Angeli si mangia, e miseri quelli che colle pecore hanno comune cibo!

ILLUS. 50. Ashendene Press, London. The Subiaco type.

you, so that I may convince both the unbelievers of my *bona fides*." There were to be many such little dinners over the next 30 years, as the friendship became closer.

The Ashendene Press was to publish many books in the Subiaco type. A good many were enriched with woodcut initials designed by Eric Gill, Graily Hewitt, and Louise Powell—all early pupils of Edward Johnston in the calligraphic revival of the beginning of the century. Cockerell was instrumental in introducing Hornby to their work. In some cases the initials were not printed, but instead spaces were left for the scribe to add them by hand afterwards. In one case, *The Song of Songs* (1902), the initials were illuminated exquisitely by Florence Kingsford, who was to become Cockerell's wife a few years later.

In 1925 Hornby added a second proprietary typeface to his repertoire, a recutting of a face first used by Holle at Ulm for the first edition of Ptolemy's *Cosmographia* in 1482. As a design it lacked the virtues of the Subiaco face, but was used with great success in a number of books, notably in a fine *Don Quixote* published in 1927. Long before this the press had grown beyond its original humble form, and Hornby employed a craftsman printer to help with the work. Although Hornby still did much of the composition himself, the presswork was normally left for his assistants to carry out, just as Morris had done. The high quality of the work of many of the private presses of the late Victorian and Edwardian periods is due in no small measure to these underpraised men. Finally, in 1935, Hornby decided that he should call a halt to his press and concluded his work with a splendid *Bibliography*, copiously illustrated with specimen pages from the books he had produced. "Perfect . . . as an example of printing and as a compilation," was how Cockerell, who was not given to fulsome praise, described it. Hornby's own pressman had died before it was produced, and the presswork was carried out by H. Gage-Cole, who at that time was working at the Stourton Press for

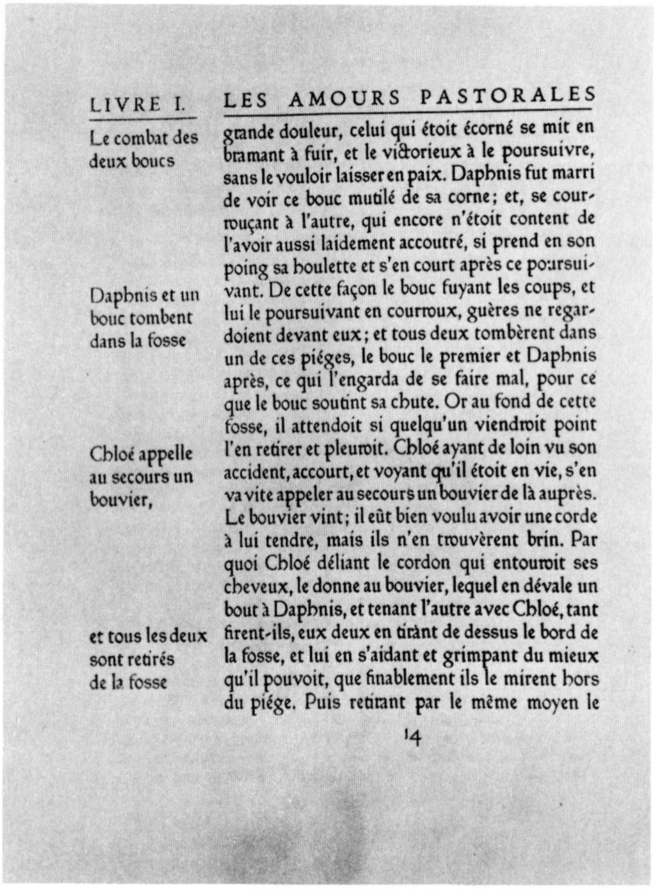

LIVRE I. LES AMOURS PASTORALES

Le combat des deux boucs

grande douleur, celui qui étoit écorné se mit en bramant à fuir, et le victorieux à le poursuivre, sans le vouloir laisser en paix. Daphnis fut marri de voir ce bouc mutilé de sa corne; et, se courrouçant à l'autre, qui encore n'étoit content de l'avoir aussi laidement accoutré, si prend en son poing sa houlette et s'en court après ce poursuivant. De cette façon le bouc fuyant les coups, et lui le poursuivant en courroux, guères ne regardoient devant eux; et tous deux tombèrent dans un de ces piéges, le bouc le premier et Daphnis après, ce qui l'engarda de se faire mal, pour ce que le bouc soutint sa chute. Or au fond de cette fosse, il attendoit si quelqu'un viendroit point l'en retirer et pleuroit. Chloé ayant de loin vu son accident, accourt, et voyant qu'il étoit en vie, s'en va vite appeler au secours un bouvier de là auprès. Le bouvier vint; il eût bien voulu avoir une corde à lui tendre, mais ils n'en trouvèrent brin. Par quoi Chloé déliant le cordon qui entouroit ses cheveux, le donne au bouvier, lequel en dévale un bout à Daphnis, et tenant l'autre avec Chloé, tant firent-ils, eux deux en tirant de dessus le bord de la fosse, et lui en s'aidant et grimpant du mieux qu'il pouvoit, que finablement ils le mirent hors du piége. Puis retirant par le même moyen le

Daphnis et un bouc tombent dans la fosse

Chloé appelle au secours un bouvier,

et tous les deux sont retirés de la fosse

14

ILLUS. 51. Ashendene Press, London. The Ptolemy type as used in *Daphnis et Chloe,* 1933.

B. Fairfax Hall. He was a handpress craftsman of the old school, having worked at Kelmscott and later at the Doves Press.

St. John Hornby's influence on commercial printing was considerable. This influence came largely through his professional work, not his hobby, through his employment of such men as Eric Gill, Joseph Thorp, and Bernard Newdigate on work for W. H. Smith & Son. The Ashendene Press itself was of only minor importance in this respect, though in the 40-odd years of its life it had established and maintained a standard of production quite as high as that of Kelmscott, and it fully deserves its place as one of the trinity of great English private presses.

The third member of this trinity was the Doves Press, which was established by Thomas James Cobden-Sanderson and Emery Walker in 1900. Cobden-Sanderson was a strange figure. The son of a senior civil servant, in his youth he was apprenticed to a shipbuilder; abandoning that to read for holy orders at Cambridge, he left without a degree after a breakdown, and for eight years went through a period of mental anguish. In 1871 he was called to the bar, but after some time spent in codifying the London & Northwestern Railway's various acts his health once more collapsed. While recuperating in Italy, he met Annie Cobden (the daughter of Richard Cobden, the great "Free Trader"), who later became his wife. At a suggestion from William Morris's wife, and with encouragement from his own wife, he found an answer to his search for "something which should give me means to live upon simply and in independence, and at the same time something beautiful, and, as far as human things may be, permanent" in bookbinding. Although his wife and the Morrises encouraged him, most other members of his circle were appalled:

> I heard of your book binding, but I own with regret [wrote Lady Russell in
> 1884]. With an education such as yours I should like better to hear that you
> were employing your mind on something which others of less cultivated
> interests could not do. I can, however, well understand the interest of being
> brought into contact with a class of human beings of whom we know little
> except by the articles they produce.

Others were to hear of Cobden-Sanderson's bookbinding with less regret. After learning his craft under Roger de Coverley, he rapidly acquired a high reputation for the beauty of the bindings, and today is generally regarded as one of the leading figures in the revival of fine binding at the end of the nineteenth century.

From the establishment of the Arts and Crafts Exhibition Society (the phrase "Arts and Crafts" was of his invention), Cobden-Sanderson was closely associated with William Morris, and followed the fortunes of the Kelmscott Press closely—so closely, in fact, that in 1894 he set up the Doves Bindery close to Morris's press in Hammersmith with the initial aim of:

> Beginning a tradition in association with the Kelmscott Press. . . . The idea of a
> workshop; a young, active, imaginative printing press to feed the Bindery; a
> house to let immediately opposite to that printing press; the first link in the
> formation of a Tradition, and an apprentice ready to hand!

As it turned out, the Doves Bindery was never to work in collaboration with Kelmscott; but in any case Cobden-Sanderson found that bookbinding alone was not enough to satisfy his search for "man's ultimate and infinite ideal."

Toward the end of 1898 he wrote in his *Journals,* "I must, before I die, create the type for today of 'the Book Beautiful' and actualise it—paper, ink, writing, ornament and binding. I will learn to write, to print and to decorate." A catalytic role was now played by Sydney Cockerell, when he remarked that it was strange that nobody had yet revived Jenson's roman in its pure form—*here* was Cobden-Sanderson's model for his ideal type! By 1900 his resolutions were being carried out. With his son and daughter he enrolled in classes in lettering taught by Edward Johnston at the Central School of Arts and Crafts. Despite his aside that watching a demonstration by Johnston "is like watching some strange bird," he and Johnston soon became firm friends, and were discussing plans for a scriptorium to be associated with the Doves Bindery and with Cobden-Sanderson's new press. His decision to print was also no longer passive: work on the typeface was already progressing. In his *Journals* for April 29, 1900, he recorded:

> I have in hand now 1) *Organisation of printing press.* We are now in treaty for
> No.1 in the Terrace, and propose to install our printing press there. . . . We
> have taken No.1 Hammersmith Terrace, and it is now whitewashed throughout,
> and is sweetly clean. . . . And we have engaged a compositor, J. H. Mason. . . .
> He began work last Monday week on *Agricola* at the Bindery, in the attic over
> my room. This has at last set us in Motion; we have ordered "oddments" of all
> "sorts," and an additional fount to keep him going, and finally a press and
> paper. . . . Proofs have been taken at the Bindery presses and have been sent to
> Mackail for revision.

What Cobden-Sanderson did not record in his *Journals,* unless the references were removed through filial piety when his son published them in 1926, is that the Doves Press was not a solitary adventure on his part but had been started in partnership with Emery Walker. They were a peculiarly ill-assorted pair; Cobden-Sanderson the enthusiastic, idealistic, and obstinate visionary, and Walker the sober prosaic partner whose technical knowledge was sorely necessary to make the enterprise a success. But a success it was, from the publication of the *Agricola* in January 1901 on. As Ruari MacLean has remarked, the pages of the Doves Press books were the most devastating criticism ever made of Morris's work at the Kelmscott Press. Completely without ornament or illustration, they depended for their beauty almost entirely on the clarity of the type, the excellence of the layout, and the perfection of the presswork. They were, in fact, the ruthlessly simple application of Cobden-Sanderson's dictum that "the whole duty of typography . . . is to communicate, without loss by the way, the thought or image intended to be communicated by the author." It was this restraint, and not Morris's lavish romanticism, that was to point the way for printing in the first half of the twentieth century (a way that in many respects has already been forgotten). Beatrice Warde's statement that "printing should be invisible" is another way of saying the same thing that the Doves books were trying to express. Though it seems obvious enough to those of us whose typographic taste was formed in the school of Stanley Morison, it was by no means plain in the aftermath of Kelmscott, as the sub-Morrisian extravagances of the endpapers and title pages of the early volumes in the Everyman's Library bear witness. The simplicity of the Doves pages was, of course, deceptive. Johnston's masterly calligraphic initials, like the unforgettable opening to Genesis, in the *Bible* (1903–1905) were a perfect example of how to marry calligraphy and typography, and J. H. Mason's setting was full of those almost invisible refinements that only another printer can

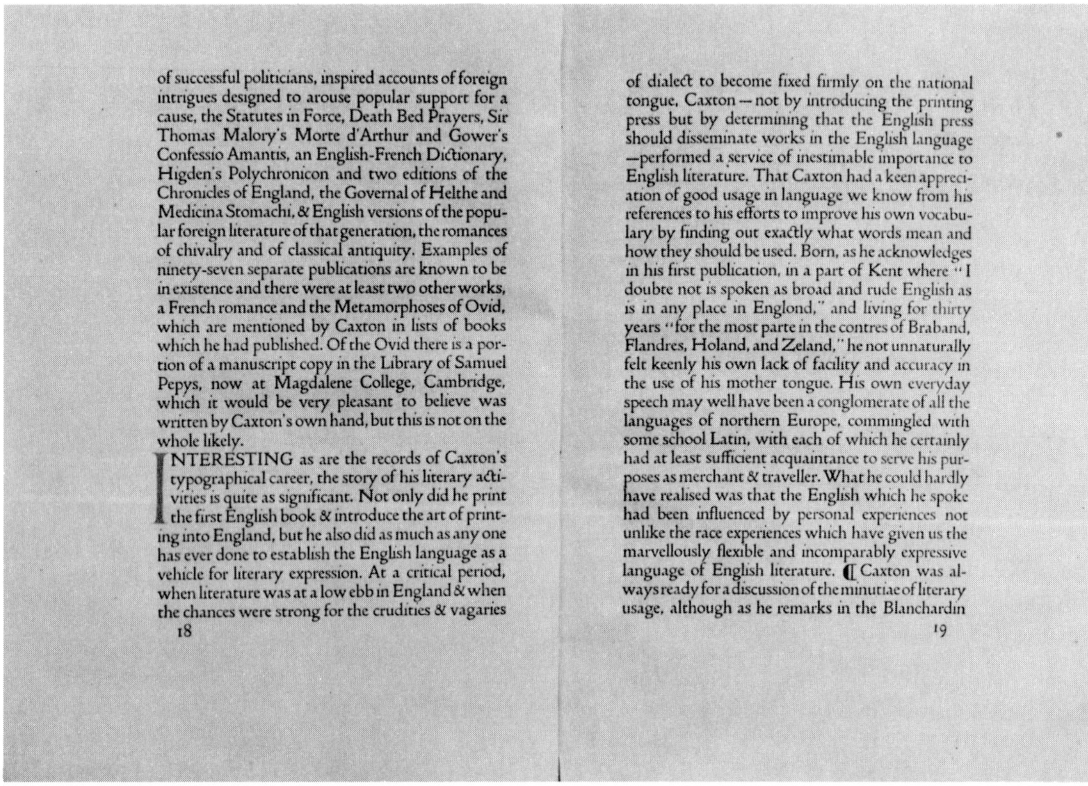

of successful politicians, inspired accounts of foreign intrigues designed to arouse popular support for a cause, the Statutes in Force, Death Bed Prayers, Sir Thomas Malory's Morte d'Arthur and Gower's Confessio Amantis, an English-French Dictionary, Higden's Polychronicon and two editions of the Chronicles of England, the Governal of Helthe and Medicina Stomachi, & English versions of the popular foreign literature of that generation, the romances of chivalry and of classical antiquity. Examples of ninety-seven separate publications are known to be in existence and there were at least two other works, a French romance and the Metamorphoses of Ovid, which are mentioned by Caxton in lists of books which he had published. Of the Ovid there is a portion of a manuscript copy in the Library of Samuel Pepys, now at Magdalene College, Cambridge, which it would be very pleasant to believe was written by Caxton's own hand, but this is not on the whole likely.

INTERESTING as are the records of Caxton's typographical career, the story of his literary activities is quite as significant. Not only did he print the first English book & introduce the art of printing into England, but he also did as much as any one has ever done to establish the English language as a vehicle for literary expression. At a critical period, when literature was at a low ebb in England & when the chances were strong for the crudities & vagaries

18

of dialect to become fixed firmly on the national tongue, Caxton — not by introducing the printing press but by determining that the English press should disseminate works in the English language —performed a service of inestimable importance to English literature. That Caxton had a keen appreciation of good usage in language we know from his references to his efforts to improve his own vocabulary by finding out exactly what words mean and how they should be used. Born, as he acknowledges in his first publication, in a part of Kent where "I doubte not is spoken as broad and rude English as is in any place in Englond," and living for thirty years "for the most parte in the contres of Braband, Flandres, Holand, and Zeland," he not unnaturally felt keenly his own lack of facility and accuracy in the use of his mother tongue. His own everyday speech may well have been a conglomerate of all the languages of northern Europe, commingled with some school Latin, with each of which he certainly had at least sufficient acquaintance to serve his purposes as merchant & traveller. What he could hardly have realised was that the English which he spoke had been influenced by personal experiences not unlike the race experiences which have given us the marvellously flexible and incomparably expressive language of English literature. ¶ Caxton was always ready for a discussion of the minutiae of literary usage, although as he remarks in the Blanchardin

19

ILLUS. 52. Doves Press, London. Opening from G. P. Winship's *William Caxton*, 1909.

recognize. It is worth noting that J. H. Mason had served his apprenticeship at the Ballantyne Press from 1891–1898. Although I have not traced any evidence to confirm that he worked on any of the books produced at the press for Whistler or was involved in the setting of any of the Vale Press books, there can be no doubt that Mason absorbed much of the atmosphere of fine printing in the Ballantyne works. The 1899 fire at the press threw him out of work just at the time that Walker and Cobden-Sanderson were starting to look around for a compositor for their venture.

With most of the other "fine art" presses one can trace a development in style; in the Doves books there was little change from first to last because Cobden-Sanderson's "ideal book" was realized almost from the start. We can recognize, as Charles Ricketts had already demonstrated, that a single formula for the ideal book is doomed to failure, however good the formula may be. Sir Francis Meynell was to write of Cobden-Sanderson's books:

> They are lovely, impeccable, taut and silky like young muscles in play; but they
> are in series a little automatic, a little boring; typographical Tiller girls.

In some ways it isn't a bad definition of what was wrong with the Doves Press work, but to my mind his imagery of chorus girls gives an entirely false picture. Kelmscott books were undoubtedly virile and masculine; Ricketts's work gay. But Cobden-Sanderson's creations are cold and sterile in their perfection; automata of the book world. Such life as they possess is derived from Johnston's initials. We cannot but admire, but it is impossible to love.

After some 20 volumes had been produced at the press, the Walker and Cobden-Sanderson partnership broke up in 1909, and at much the same time Mason left. The reason for the rupture was not hard to find: Cobden-Sanderson was a man who found collaboration with others very difficult, seeming to regard it almost as an attack on his own identity. Although he had set up the Doves Bindery with the avowed aim of working in conjunction with Kelmscott, when it came to the point Cobden-Sanderson felt that "we had in the first place to establish ourselves—to be independent. I therefore fought shy of Morris and his ideas. I had first to develop my own." The result was that the Doves Bindery never worked on Kelmscott books. Although Walker was by no means as dominating a personality as Morris, he believed strongly that the Doves type should be made available for general, commercial use. Cobden-Sanderson, on the other hand, "regarded it as a consecrated instrument, and shrank away from what he regarded as desecration," as Mason put it. No reconciliation of views was possible, so Walker withdrew from the press, and Cobden-Sanderson continued to direct it alone. In 1911 he made "the last will and testament of the Doves Press":

> To the Bed of the River Thames, the river on whose banks I have printed all
> my printed books, I bequeath The Doves Press Fount of Type—the punches,
> the matrices and the type in use at the time of my death, and may the river in
> its tides and flow pass over them to and from the great sea for ever and for
> ever, or until its tides and flow for ever cease; then may they share the fate of
> all the world, and pass from change to change for ever upon the Tides of Time,
> untouched of other use and all else.

In various places in his *Journals* he recorded his growing resolve to close the press, and in 1916 he finally did so with a last *Catalogue Raisonné,* having previously thrown the punches and matrices and ultimately the types themselves into the Thames at Hammersmith Bridge.

> I stood upon the bridge, and I walked to and fro and bethought me of the time
> when I had crossed and recrossed it in winter time, in the darkness, and as the
> buses brought protection threw the type from the bridge into the river. Then I

lifted my thoughts to the wonder of the scene before me, full of awful beauty,
God's universe and man's—joint creators. How wonderful! And my Type, the
Doves type was part of it.

In bequeathing the type to the Thames, Cobden-Sanderson was following Ricketts's act in destroying the Vale Press types, and for similar reasons. It was a sincere gesture, but its nobility was tarnished by the fact that he was throwing away another man's property. When his partnership with Walker had finally collapsed, Cobden-Sanderson refused to allow Walker any of the Doves type unless hedged around with so many limitations as to make it useless to him. With his patience worn out, for the disagreement had built up over several years, Walker had commenced a legal action against his partner. To Sydney Cockerell, who had for some time been trying to repair the breach between his two friends, Cobden-Sanderson wrote:

> To implore you, as you at the outset implored me, to make an end of these
> disgraceful "proceedings." And this I ask not for my own sake but for E.W.'s
> own. His "proceedings" at the utmost can only result in "damages" or in
> imprisonment: and think of that! for nothing on earth will now induce me to
> part with the Type. I have "devoted" it to the Press and I have full power to do
> so. I have the will, and I have in my actual possession the punches and the
> matrices without which it is impossible to have a Fount of Type. . . . I am, what
> he does not appear to realise, a Visionary and a Fanatic, and against a Visionary
> and a Fanatic he will beat himself in vain.

Cockerell found a formula that seemed satisfactory. Cobden-Sanderson (by far the older man) should have the sole use of the type for his life, and that if Walker survived him it should then pass into his possession. Walker agreed to this, but with misgivings: "If I tell you I agree to the suggestion . . . he may by some means circumvent me. I can't trust him after what he has done," he confided to Cockerell. And how right he was! After Cobden-Sanderson's destruction of the types, Walker did not attempt to obtain legal redress, which would have been poor compensation indeed for his loss. "Of unswerving rectitude of thought and deed," as Cockerell described him in the *Times* obituary, he must have realized that Cobden-Sanderson was hardly answerable for his actions and forebore to press the old man. The last words must be Cobden-Sanderson's own, written to Cockerell in 1917:

> If you, and the other old friends who lament my action and the shipwreck of
> my reputation, cannot enter into my feelings [in committing the types to the
> Thames] I may indeed weep, but I cannot help it. All things I was prepared to
> sacrifice for that one action and the dedication of the type, as I had dedicated all
> that I had done by its means, to the symbolism of life, as I had dreamed it
> among the stars, my witnesses.

After Kelmscott had closed, several of the workmen employed there moved to the Essex House Press, started by C. R. Ashbee in 1898 as an addition to the several crafts practiced at his 10-year-old Guild of Handicrafts, originally at Essex House in Mile End Road, London. It was different from the other private affairs of the time in that it was deliberately conceived as a part of a larger whole. Ashbee wrote that it:

> was but one of a group of workshops . . . working with such machinery as
> could be controlled in the interests of the corporate life, working with a

common purpose in which the life was the first consideration. . . . In a mechanical age that had destroyed the crafts, the unit was not the individual designer, as Morris and some of the older men had at first supposed, but the small workshop group.

The Essex House Press was then an Arts and Crafts press *par excellence*; no doubt as a result of Ashbee's work in other crafts, such as jewelry and metalwork, it reveals more of Art Nouveau in many of its books than one would have expected from so devoted a follower of Morris (Illus. 53). And the place of the Essex House Press as one craft in an artistic community as the guild virtually was (and became even more completely with a move from London to Chipping Camden in the Cotswolds in 1902) not a source of strength but of weakness, and it was contaminated by "articrafti- ness" of the worst kind. Under the Kelmscott influence a number of books printed in Caslon type with Art Nouveau woodcut initials by Ashbee and Richard Savage were not without charm (al- though, strangely enough, the presswork was far from perfect in the early volumes, as though the Kelmscott craftsmen had lost their skill). Some of its publications were of real importance, like its surveys of historic buildings in London, but no consistent literary program emerged, and more than a few projected books—a Froissart, *Piers Ploughman*, the *Poems of Burns*, and above all a lectern *Bible*—had to be abandoned for lack of support. The types Ashbee himself designed were alarmingly mannered, and although in the Essex House *Psalter* (1902) the effect is not without a somewhat

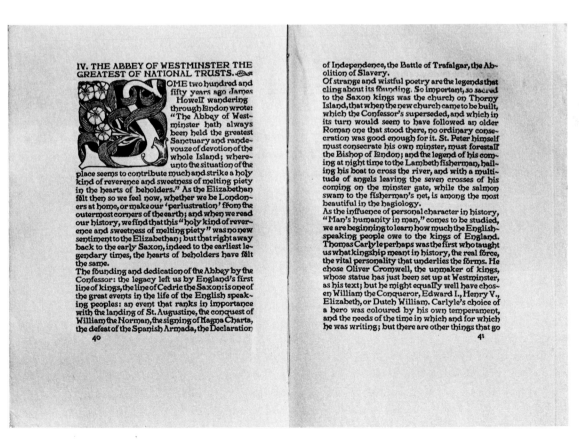

ILLUS. 53. Essex House Press, Gloucestershire. Opening from *American Sheaves*, 1901.

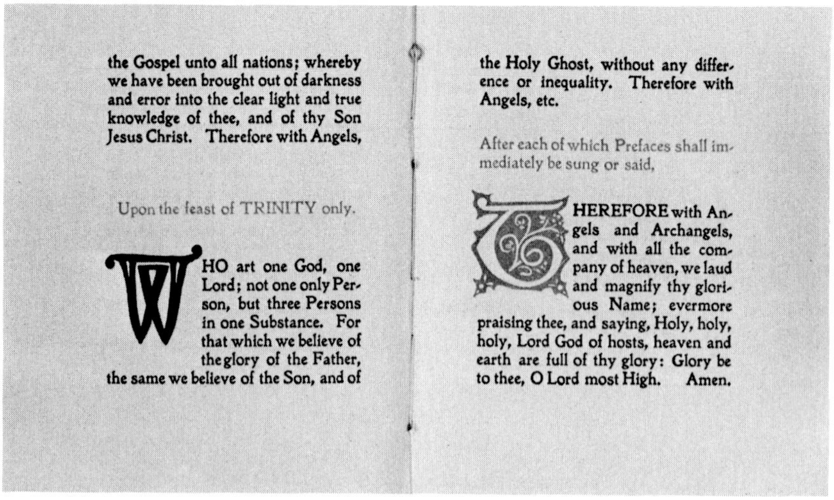

the Gospel unto all nations; whereby we have been brought out of darkness and error into the clear light and true knowledge of thee, and of thy Son Jesus Christ. Therefore with Angels,

Upon the feast of TRINITY only.

WHO art one God, one Lord; not one only Person, but three Persons in one Substance. For that which we believe of the glory of the Father, the same we believe of the Son, and of

the Holy Ghost, without any difference or inequality. Therefore with Angels, etc.

After each of which Prefaces shall immediately be sung or said,

THEREFORE with Angels and Archangels, and with all the company of heaven, we laud and magnify thy glorious Name; evermore praising thee, and saying, Holy, holy, holy, Lord God of hosts, heaven and earth are full of thy glory: Glory be to thee, O Lord most High. Amen.

ILLUS. 54. Caradoc Press, London. Opening from *Holy Communion*, 1903.

cloying charm, in continuous prose and formats like *The Last Records of a Cotswold Community* (1904) the results are dismal and oppressive.

Ashbee's direct involvement in the press diminished after 1907 and most later work was directed by Ananda Coomaraswamy. The press, like the Guild of Handicrafts itself, was falling into difficulties. Without Coomaraswamy's contribution or the strong American support the Essex House imprint would have disappeared earlier. As it was, Ashbee's swan song, *The Private Press: A Study in Idealism, to Which Is Added, a Bibliography of the Essex House Press* (1909), was only produced "by the courtesy and at the charges of the Club of Odd Volumes of Boston," and in 1910 printing work was discontinued by the guild.

Although it is hard to be enthusiastic about the Essex House Press, it was an honest if misguided enterprise and by no means the worst in its misconception of what Morris's "little typographical adventure" had been about. Comparison with another post-Morris press, the Caradoc Press of Chiswick from which H. G. Webb set, illustrated, and printed some 20 books between 1899 and 1909, makes the worst Essex House work look brilliant (Illus. 54). The real standard of comparison should not, however, be with such tawdry efforts, but with the work of Ashendene or Vale, Doves or Eragny. Compared with these, Essex House books appear vain things indeed, fondly invented.

Chapter 13

———

MORRIS IN AMERICA

LONG BEFORE THE ARTS AND CRAFTS MOVEMENT in England at the end of the nineteenth century was to produce its crop of private printers concerned with printing as an art, there had been private presses in America. In the Dunkers community at Ephrata, near Lancaster, Pennsylvania, there was a late example of the sort of religious press that had been common in Europe in the fifteenth and sixteenth centuries (and, indeed, later, with some of the printing needs of nonconformists in eighteenth-century Britain, like that of the Countess of Huntingdon's Connection at Trevecka in South Wales). At Ephrata, settled in 1732, a printing house was set up with press and types and workmen sent out by the Brethren in Germany to provide free religious texts for the poor German settlers. In all, they produced over 40 publications, the most remarkable being a Mennonite martyrology, *Der Blutige Schau-Platz*, completed in 1748. For this massive folio of more than 1,500 pages (the largest book ever printed in colonial America) the paper was made in a mill built by the Brethren.

In so young a country there was no wealthy leisured class among whom the plaything presses so common in Europe could flourish, no country houses and rectories in which gentlemen would dabble in antiquarian printing. Nevertheless, from the early nineteenth century when in 1812 Thomas G. Cundie, Jr., published the *Juvenile Portfolio* in Philadelphia, there was amateur interest and activity. Most of such amateur enterprise took the form of journalism, like the examples given in Chapter 10. This sort of work was particularly common in the last 30 years of the nineteenth century; the National Amateur Press Association was founded in Philadelphia in 1876, and such was the activity of Kelsey and his rivals that it almost seems every boy had his own press as a necessary part of growing up. But however enjoyable or profitable for the hobbyists, such presses had nothing to do with the arts of the book.

One early press does deserve notice, the Appledore Press at Hamden, Connecticut, which issued some 41 publications between 1875 and 1897. It was virtually an English press in exile, having been set up by the wood engraver W. J. Linton after he had settled in the United States. Its work is a good deal more interesting than his previous private printing in England and is seen at its best in *The Golden Apples of Hesperus: Poems Not in the Collections*, which was completed in an edition of 225 copies in 1882. In the Introduction, Linton asked the reader's consideration for any defects in the book, as "the whole of it—drawing, engraving, composition and printing (the printing my first attempt), being the work of my own hands, at odd times, with long intervals, and many hindrances." The charm of the book comes from Linton's sure hand as engraver of the many cuts scattered throughout the book, much less from the typography in which his hand was much less sure.

Just as in some of the events in English bookmaking of the 1880s one can discern a coming together of the various factors that would make William Morris's "little typographical adventure" of such importance, so in the United States the time was ripe for a major change in book production. As Susan O. Thompson shows so well in her *American Book Design and William Morris* (New York, 1977) there was considerable interest in bibliophile editions. Through such journals as *Art Age,* printed at the Gillis Press, whose owner Walter Gillis had earlier been one of the myriad boy printers who earned pocket money with a Novelty Press, and *American Bookmaker,* readers were kept closely in touch with developments in Britain. As early as 1887 a writer for the *American Bookmaker* had drawn attention to the work of Walter Crane and Morris in book design; by 1890 Emery Walker's lectures on printing were noticed, and news of Kelmscott was reported well before its first book appeared.

A bare six months after the publication of the first Kelmscott book, *The Story of the Glittering Plain,* a photographic facsimile of it was published in Boston by Roberts Brothers, the regular American publishers of Morris's works. Kelmscott design without Kelmscott materials and press-work provided a poor basis for judgment, and one critic (in the *Nation,* December 18, 1891) was scathing: "In default of any other *raison d'être,* we imagine that this artistic combination of imitation vellum, parchment, and antique lettering may be intended to take a place with other bric à brac on a drawing-room table." Plenty of copies of original Kelmscott volumes were to reach America very quickly, and Rossetti's *Hand and Soul* (1895) was published in an American edition commissioned from Morris by Way & Williams. These were to exert very considerable influence. But for many Americans, the concepts of "the book beautiful" were not received directly but at secondhand and through a curious interpretation. The interpreter was Elbert Hubbard.

Hubbard (1856–1915) is a figure who for many years was derided, even more in England than in the United States. May Morris's disdainful dismissal of him as "that obnoxious imitator of my dear father" only voiced a fairly general opinion. Having made a modest fortune as a soap salesman, in 1892 he abandoned commerce. After a visit to Morris and the Kelmscott Press in 1894 he was filled with enthusiasm not only for printing but for Arts and Crafts generally. He was not by any means the only pioneer for spreading the Arts and Crafts message in the United States, but he was by far the most successful. On his return he set up the Roycroft Shop at East Aurora, New York. In some ways not unlike the Essex House community, the shop grew into a vast pseudomedieval combination of inn, printing shop, smithy, furniture and other craft factories, which at its height was to employ some 500 men and spread its products into many American homes.

Hubbard was a natural salesman, and his journal, the *Philistine,* which was written almost entirely by himself, achieved a circulation of nearly a quarter of a million. In the Roycroft interpretation of the Kelmscott style, in fact, Morris's manner became far more widely known in the United States than in England.

The Roycroft interpretation, however, was poles apart from Morris's little typographical adventure and its overriding concern with good materials and handcraftsmanship whatever the cost. Hubbard had abandoned business but not the business approach, and the Roycroft Shop was not really a private press at all. True, the first books were hand printed and he used handmade paper, but hand-setting and handpresses were soon abandoned for the greater ease of the machine, often with very poor presswork. The close setting and unleaded lines of Morris's work were ignored; it was the flashy decoration of Kelmscott books that was imitated. Above all, the personal attention that characterizes the work of Morris and his English followers was absent: Hubbard had little to do with the making of the Roycrofters' books, leaving their design to a number of assistants, most notably W. W. Denslow, Samuel Warner, and later Dard Hunter.

From such men effective design could and did come, and the work of the Roycroft Shop is

GREAT REFORMERS—Henry George

"PROGRESS & POVERTY," like every other great book (or great man) was an accident—a providential accident ❧ The book was ten years in the incubation ❧ It began with a newspaper editorial in 1869, and found form in a volume of five hundred pages in 1879 ❧ The editorial merely called attention to the fact that California in spite of her vast wealth was peopled, for the most part, with people desperately poor; and that ground in the vicinity of any city, town or place of enterprise was held at so exorbitant a figure that the poor were actually enslaved by the men who owned the land. That is to say, the men who owned the land, controlled the people who had to live on it, for man is a land animal, and can not live apart from land any more than fishes can live at a distance from water. And moreover we tax for the improvements on land, thus really placing a penalty on enterprise.
The article attracted attention, and opened the eyes of one man at least—and that was the man who wrote it ❧ He had written better than he knew; and any writer who does not occasionally surprise himself does not write well.
60

GREAT REFORMERS—Henry George

Henry George had surprised himself, and he wrote another editorial to explain the first. These editorials extended themselves into a series, and hand-polished and sand-papered were reprinted in pamphlet form in 1871, under the title of "Our Land Policy." The temerity which prompted the printing of this pamphlet was evolved through a letter from John Stuart Mill. Henry George knew he was right in his conclusions, but he felt that he needed the corroboration of a great mind that had grappled with abstruse problems; so he sent one of his editorials to Mill, the greatest living intellect of his time.
Mill showed his interest by replying in a long letter, wherein he addressed George as a man with a mind equal to his own, not a sophomore trying his wings. ℚ The letter from Mill was to him a white mile-post. The corroboration gave him courage, confidence, poise ❧
The thousand copies of the pamphlet cost Henry George seventy-five dollars ❧ The retail price was twenty-five cents each. Twenty-one copies were sold. The rest were given away to good people who promised to read them. Pamphlets are for the pamphleteer, but let the fact here be recorded that new ideas have always been issued at the author's expense—and also risk. Martin Luther, Dean Swift, John Milton, Paine, Voltaire, Sam Adams were all pamphleteers ❧ The early colonial "broadsides" were pamphlets issued
61

ILLUS. 55. Roycroft Press, New York. A restrained example of Roycroft work.

eagerly sought today by collectors. Even the worst of its books, with their wretchedly inappropriate and derivative design, poor presswork on unsuitable paper, and cheap suede bindings, known appropriately in the trade as "limp ooze," command high prices. Collectors have swung away from the judgments made at the time of the Morris centenary in 1934, when Holbrook Jackson commented that Kelmscott "found its nemesis in Elbert Hubbard's Roycroft Books," and Carl P. Rollins wrote of:

> Hubbard's printing [which] was unbelievably bad: it was bad in itself, it was ludicrous as a copy of Kelmscott work. As a follower of the Arts and Crafts movement, he was beneath contempt, both artistically and ethically.

If one takes seriously Oscar Wilde's paradox "If a thing is worth doing, it is worth doing badly," Roycroft provides the perfect illustration. And yet with all its faults Hubbard's work did help to foster the idea that there could be something better than mass production and awakened thousands of Americans to ideals of craftsmanship.

Chicago was an important center for fine printing, and in the 1890s supported a literary and book-collecting life of considerable proportions. McClurg's bookshop on Wabash Avenue provided a center at which many saw the work of the English private presses for the first time. In 1895 W. Irving Way, a partner in the newly established house of Way & Williams, arranged for the American edition of the Kelmscott *Hand and Soul*. In the same year his wealthy partner Chauncey L. Williams set up an amateur press, together with a neighbor William H. Winslow, in the attic of his house. At this Auvergne Press they printed Keats's *Eve of St. Agnes* with the help of Frank Lloyd Wright who had designed Williams's house. The following winter (1896–1897) Wright and Winslow together printed William C. Gannet's *The House Beautiful* to a lavish design by Wright.

Perhaps the earliest on the fine printing scene in Chicago, and certainly the most important, was Frederic W. Goudy (1865–1947), who in 1890 had moved to Chicago to become a bookkeeper. From childhood he had been interested in illustration and design, and without any formal training he gradually moved into commercial art. With financial backing from a friend he started the Camelot Press, a small commercial printing shop for which he designed his first typeface and printed a number of books for Stone and Kimball. The press was not a success, and Goudy had to retire to the security of bookkeeping. He continued designing type, producing a number of advertising types, until, encouraged by his wife, he turned to full-time commercial art.

Among those who were influenced most strongly by Elbert Hubbard had been a young man in Snohomish, Washington, Will Ransom. Even as a child he had been fascinated by the idea of producing books, an idea that influenced his decision to take a job with the local newspaper when he left high school. With the financial assistance of a friend, in the autumn of 1901 he produced his first book, "after the dainty style set by the Roycrofts," using the newspaper equipment but rubricating and binding the volumes at home. Another book followed in 1902. Encouraged by the mild success that they had, Ransom decided to go east to Chicago, where he had been told prospects were good for a young man interested in fine printing and where he could enroll at the Art Institute of Chicago. In Chicago he soon became a friend of the Goudys.

In 1903 Goudy decided to start his own private press and invited Ransom to join him in the undertaking. Undoubtedly spurred by the English work he had seen, and probably also by the private printing a number of his Chicago friends were beginning to produce, Goudy found the reason for setting up his press in a wish to make his "Village" type known to the printing world. This face had originally been designed as an advertising type for the exclusive use of the Kuppenheimer clothing firm, but the clients had balked at the cost of having the type cut and cast. Ransom managed to persuade a friend to advance the $250 needed, and the new type was ordered from Robert Wiebking. By the end of July 1903 the Village Press had been set up in the Goudys' home in the Chicago suburb of Park Ridge and had issued its first piece, which was, appropriately, a quotation from Cobden-Sanderson's *The Ideal Book.* By September 1903 the press's first book was completed: a reprint of the essay on printing that William Morris and Emery Walker had contributed to *Arts and Crafts Essays.* In its appearance just as much as in its content this book showed the Kelmscott influence very strongly, as did much more of the Village Press work for a considerable time afterwards. But from 1904 on the press was run by the Goudys (Bertha Goudy was always a very active partner in its work) without outside help. Ransom withdrew when the Goudys decided to move from Chicago to Hingham, Massachusetts. He issued one more volume, including both *A Vision* and *The Dream of Petrarca,* under the Handcraft Shop imprint, but he found his interest in private printing was waning rapidly. For some years he had to abandon his dreams of book building and, like Goudy, he found employment as a bookkeeper. In 1921 Ransom again set up a private press, publishing some 10 volumes of contemporary verse and entering into a cooperative arrangement with the Golden Cockerel Press described in Chapter 15. Again the public response was insufficiently encouraging for him to be able to continue beyond 1923, but he kept up his interest in private printing, and his *Private Presses and Their Books* (1929) and *Selective Check Lists of Press Books* (1945–1950) remain standard reference works in the field. To the many amateur printers in the 1930s and later who turned to him for advice, he was extraordinarily generous and encouraging. In his very different way he was perhaps as significant a figure as Emery Walker had been in the English private press movement.

The Goudys' Village Press had only a short stay at Hingham, issuing a few more books including William Morris's *The Hollow Land,* which had been designed by Ransom, in 1905, before moving to New York in 1906. Goudy eked out a living as a free-lance designer while continuing to run the press, until a studio fire in 1908 destroyed his press, types, books—in fact almost all his possessions. The Village Press was restarted in 1911, producing a few more books, but by now Goudy had built up a connection with the Lanston Monotype Corporation, a connection that was to last into the 1940s. There was no need for him to use the Village Press as a means of publicizing his types any more. His interest in private printing continued—in 1924, following a move to Marlborough-on-Hudson, New York, he purchased one of the Albions used to print the Kelmscott

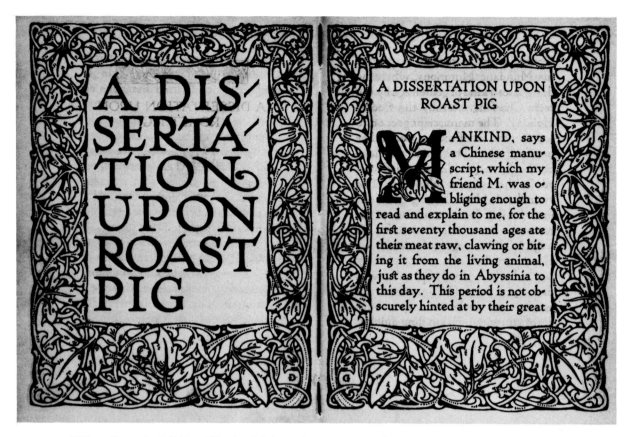

ILLUS. 56. Village Press, Park Ridge, Illinois. *A Dissertation upon Roast Pig,* 1904. Photograph: Courtesy of the Rare Books and Manuscripts Division, The New York Public Library, Astor, Lenox, Tilden Foundations.

Chaucer—but by now the press was far more a hobby than anything else, and not much more work of real substance was printed.

Goudy's influence on American printing, which was considerable though not entirely beneficial, stemmed almost entirely from his very large number of type designs. With one or two exceptions these have never been admired extensively in the Old World, and most of them have dated very badly.

Among Goudy's circle in Chicago had been Frank Holme, the newspaper artist, with whom Goudy worked at Holme's School of Illustration—a short-lived affair, but one that turned out some very competent lettering artists, including Oswald Cooper and W. A. Dwiggins. In 1895 Holme printed 74 copies of a little book called *Just for Fun,* which included a selection of verses such as *Casey at the Bat.* The imprint used, The Bandarlog Press, came from the *Jungle Book* nicknames given to Holme and his wife by friends who accused them of "always pecking at new things." It was a lighthearted effort, typical of much work produced by printers for pleasure, and little more might have come from the press had Holme not been compelled by tuberculosis to give up his newspaper work. While he was in a sanatorium in Asheville, North Carolina, he produced a second book, *Swanson, Able Seaman,* of which 174 copies were printed for presentation to friends. In a vain search for health Holme decided in 1902 to go to Arizona, and in order to help him the Bandarlog Press was incorporated, with many of his friends including Booth Tarkington, George Ade, and later Mark Twain, buying shares in the company at $25 each. The control of the press remained entirely in Holme's hands, and before he died in 1904, at the age of 36, he managed to produce seven more

ILLUS. 57. Bandarlog Press, Arizona. Title page of one of Holme's pastiches of the dime novel.

books. Some of these had a serious artistic intent, like *Her Navajo Lover* (1903), but others were very lighthearted. There were three burlesques by George Ade of the dime novels then popular, published in a series called the "Strenuous Lad's Library," which Holme illustrated in an appropriate style. The titles give some idea of these splendid stories: *Rollo Johnson the Boy Inventor, or the Demon Bicycle and Its Daring Rider* (Illus. 57); *Handsome Cyril, or the Messenger Boy with the Warm Feet;* and *Clarence Allen, the Hypnotic Boy Journalist.* They were by no means well printed, but were deliberately produced as "a bum job" to be in keeping with their models. Though Holme was certainly in sympathy with the aims of the Arts and Crafts Movement, he had a sense of proportion and an ability to laugh at his own beliefs, which were unusual traits among private printers at that time. Private printing was regarded with an almost religious devotion by Cobden-Sanderson and a good many others. After reading through some of the pompous credos they solemnly issued, Holme's *All About the Bandarlog Press* comes as a very refreshing change:

> In every article relating to printing that you pick up nowadays you are bound to run across the words "dignity" and "simplicity" and "legitimate use of materials."
>
> Now "dignity" being a sort of extraneous husk or shell rather than an inherent quality, it is sometimes liable to stand in the way of one's having a good time. It is all right for those who like it and who have the patience to keep it up—besides it's largely a matter of opinion anyhow, so the Bandarlog Press will have to pass it up as a steady thing and let the other Presses corner it if they choose. . . . But when it comes to "legitimate use of materials," that's the Bandarlog Press's long suit.
>
> That's where it shines.

In the revolt against machinery it accompanies the pendulum to the limit of its swing.

Precisely what Holme meant by this can be seen in some of his colophons:

> This rare and limited edition was done into type and the refined and elegant illustrations were done into wood cuts on best grade North Carolina yaller poplar timber with an IXL jackknife (two blades), and the whole business was done into its present shape in the month of December. AD 1901, by F. Holme, who at that time had nothing else to do, and the whole job was done in Asheville, North Carolina, and at the Bandar Log Press. But 174 copies have been printed, after which the type were put back where they belonged and the refined and elegant wood blocks were done into kindling wood.

Some other presses from this Chicago group are also of interest. *By the Candelabra's Glare,* which Frank Baum printed in his own workshop in 1898 in an edition of 99 copies, was an essay in bookmaking in the Morris style, very different from *Father Goose* or *The Wizard of Oz* for which the author is better known. Also heavily under the Arts and Crafts influence was the Blue Sky Press. From 1899 until 1906 this press produced competent if not especially distinguished work by contemporary writers as well as a number of standard texts, at a time when so many private printers' imagination stretched no further than another version of *Sonnets from the Portuguese.* Typographical and business direction of the press was undertaken by Alfred G. Langworthy, while the literature and art were controlled by his partners Thomas Wood Stevens and, until 1902, Alden Charles Noble. In some respects the Blue Sky books reflect the work put out by the aesthetic publishers like the Bodley Head no less than Kelmscott work. Although undoubtedly derivative, their design was not slavish in its following of a particular style, and the books they published remain charming examples of the taste of the period. Their version of Robert Browning's *In a Balcony,* 1902 (Illus. 58), unlike a lot of their other work, is most obviously derived from Kelmscott; for it, designs by Frederic Goudy and W. A. Dwiggins were used.

Rather more imitative and less successful was Ralph Fletcher Seymour's Alderbrink Press. Seymour's introduction to fine printing had been something like that of Will Ransom. As a schoolboy in Cincinnati, Ohio, Seymour had been inspired by seeing reproductions of old block books in the museum library, and tried his hand at hand-lettered pages in the same manner. Soon after he had come to Chicago, where he obtained employment as a commercial artist with the Manz Engraving Company, he decided to have line blocks made of one of these, Keats's *Ode to Melancholy.* An edition of six copies of this was printed on one of his employer's proofing presses in 1897. Pleased with the effect, he produced another hand-lettered book, *Three Merry Old Tales,* by the same method. A copy of this fell by chance into the hands of the Reverend F. W. Gunsaulus, a well-known Chicago book collector. Gunsaulus encouraged Seymour to continue this work and, by persuading many of his friends to subscribe to his next book, enabled Seymour to set up business for himself. Seymour was one of the artists employed by Frank Baum for *Father Goose* and for *By the Candelabra's Glare,* and he built up a commercial art practice alongside his own press. He progressed from hand lettering through the use of Caslon type to his own font, the Alderbrink type. In its design he had considerable help from Goudy, and in 1902 he had his first book, Morris's *The Art of the People* (Illus. 59), printed in Alderbrink by a friend. Produced on handmade paper using imported German ink, it was a very successful exercise in the Kelmscott manner and one indicating the future of the Alderbrink Press. Some other fine work was produced, like the edition of James Westfall Thompson's *The*

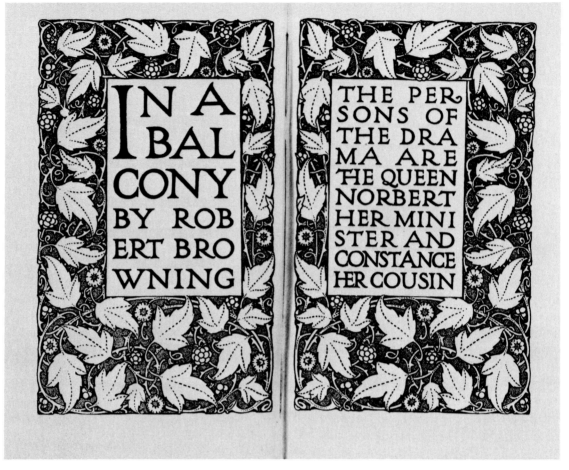

ILLUS. 58. Blue Sky Press, Chicago. *In a Balcony,* 1902.
Photograph: Courtesy of Susan O. Thompson.

Frankfurt Book Fair commissioned by the Caxton Club, but the press soon moved into a purely commercial sphere. Although Seymour continued to produce books in a workmanlike manner for many more years, the elements of complete personal selection and control—the real criteria of a *private* press—had gone.

Chicago was by no means the only American city in which private presses were established as a result of Morris's influence. At the opposite extreme from Elbert Hubbard's commercialized Roycroft work was the Cranbrook Press, which the manager of the *Detroit Evening News,* George Booth, ran from 1900 until pressure of business compelled him to call a halt in 1902. Booth was familiar with the work of the Kelmscott Press and had traveled to East Aurora, New York, to examine the work of the Roycrofters at firsthand. He had enough taste to decide which was the better model for his own press, and the design of his books was to be closer to Kelmscott than those of any other private printer, not only the design, in fact, but also the execution. Booth worked hard to emulate the craftsmanship of Morris. His reasons for beginning his press were irreproachable: having seen thousands of rare books in the Lenox Library in New York he had concluded that to print more was "excusable only if the printer chose such works as his best judgement told him were worthy of preservation." He tempered this by adding, "I conceive it also to be the sphere of good books to entertain, if devised only to amuse, providing the influence is good"; the Cranbrook Press books

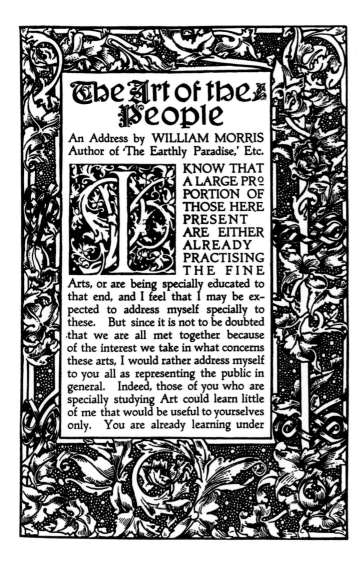

ILLUS. 59. Alderbrink Press, Chicago.
The Art of the People, 1902.
Photograph: Courtesy of
Susan O. Thompson.

maintained a high seriousness of intent, and none was devised only to amuse. They were such books as *The Dictes and Sayings of the Philosophers, The Revelation of St. John the Divine* (Illus. 60), and *Utopia.*

In starting his own press, Booth did it in style. A room in the top floor of his office building was altered to resemble a medieval workshop and filled with furniture in the same style; a handpress was purchased, and a printer engaged "who had learned his trade before the days of Linotype." Paper was specially made, and type copied from the Kelmscott designs by American founders was purchased. Nearly all the work of the press was performed by his workmen but under Booth's close and careful supervision. Like Morris before him, Booth designed many of the elaborate strapwork borders used in the books.

Almost as imitative of Kelmscott in its earliest years was Clarke Conwell's Elston Press, set up in New York City in 1900 and moved to the suburb of New Rochelle in 1902. Conwell's literary taste was limited to the dreary, predictable classics, but, aided by the brilliant designs of his wife Helen Marguerite O'Kane, he managed to produce some powerful volumes, beginning with *Sonnets from the Portuguese* in 1900 (Illus. 61). After *The Tale of Gamelyn* in 1901 Conwell discontinued the use of fonts imitative of the Kelmscott faces and turned to the use of Caslon Old Face, as Essex House and

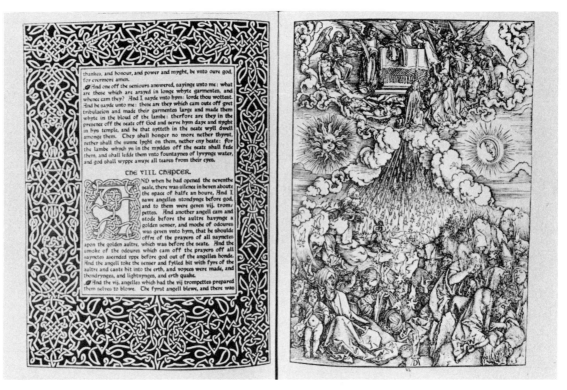

ILLUS. 60. Cranbrook Press, Detroit, Michigan. *The Revelation of St. John the Divine*, 1901. Photograph: Philip Grushkin.

ILLUS. 61. Elston Press, New York. *Sonnets from the Portuguese*, 1900. The first book of the press. Photograph: The Library of Philip Sperling.

The Rape of
The Lock
Canto IV

Wrapt in a gown, for sickness, and for show.
The fair ones feel such maladies as these,
When each new night-dress gives a new disease.
         A constant Vapour o'er the palace flies:
Strange phantoms rising as the mists arise;
Dreadful, as hermit's dreams in haunted shades,
Or bright, as visions of expiring maids.
Now glaring fiends, and snakes on rolling spires,
Pale spectres, gaping tombs, and purple fires:
Now lakes of liquid gold, Elysian scenes,
And crystal domes, and angels in machines.
         Unnumber'd throngs on every side are seen,
Of bodies chang'd to various forms by Spleen.
Here living Tea-pots stand, one arm held out,
One bent; the handle this, and that the spout:
A Pipkin there, like Homer's Tripod walks;
Here sighs a Jar, and there a Goose-pie talks;
Men prove with child, as pow'rful fancy works,
And maids turn'd bottles, call aloud for corks.
         Safe past the Gnome thro' this fantastic band,
A branch of healing Spleenwort in his hand.
Then thus address'd the pow'r: "Hail, wayward Queen!
Who rule the sex to fifty from fifteen:
Parent of vapours and of female wit,
Who give th' hysteric, or poetic fit,
On various tempers act by various ways,
Make some take physic, others scribble plays;
Who cause the proud their visits to delay,
And send the godly in a pet to pray.
A nymph there is, that all thy pow'r disdains,
And thousands more in equal mirth maintains.
But oh! if e'er thy Gnome could spoil a grace,
Or raise a pimple on a beauteous face,
Like Citron-waters matrons cheeks inflame,
Or change complexions at a losing game;
If e'er with airy horns I planted heads,
Or rumpled petticoats, or tumbled beds,
Or caus'd suspicion when no soul was rude,

16

Or discompos'd the head-dress of a Prude,
Or e'er to costive lap-dog gave disease,
Which not the tears of brightest eyes could ease:
Hear me, and touch Belinda with chagrin,
That single act gives half the world the spleen."
         The Goddess with a discontented air
Seems to reject him, tho' she grants his pray'r.
A wond'rous Bag with both her hands she binds,
Like that where once Ulysses held the winds;
There she collects the force of female lungs,
Sighs, sobs, and passions, and the war of tongues.
A Vial next she fills with fainting fears,
Soft sorrows, melting griefs, and flowing tears.
The Gnome rejoicing bears her gifts away,
Spreads his black wings, and slowly mounts to day.
         Sunk in Thalestris' arms the nymph he found,
Her eyes dejected and her hair unbound.
Full o'er their heads the swelling bag he rent,
And all the Furies issu'd at the vent.
Belinda burns with more than mortal ire,
And fierce Thalestris fans the rising fire.
"O wretched maid!" she spread her hands, and cry'd,
(While Hampton's echoes, "Wretched maid!" reply'd)
"Was it for this you took such constant care
The bodkin, comb, and essence to prepare?
For this your locks in paper durance bound,
For this with tort'ring irons wreath'd around?
For this with fillets strain'd your tender head,
And bravely bore the double loads of lead?
Gods! shall the ravisher display your hair,
While the Fops envy, and the Ladies stare!
Honour forbid! at whose unrivall'd shrine
Ease, pleasure, virtue, all our sex resign.
Methinks already I your tears survey,
Already hear the horrid things they say,
Already see you a degraded toast,
And all your honour in a whisper lost!
How shall I, then, your helpless fame defend?

17

The Rape of
The Lock
Canto IV

ILLUS. 62. Elston Press, New York. Opening from *The Rape of the Lock*, 1902.

other private presses had done before him. At the same time he adopted a simpler decorative style for the other books produced before the Elston Press closed in 1904 (Illus. 62).

Also in New York, Frank Hopkins had installed a handpress in the attic of his home in Jamaica, as early as 1896 "as a relief from ordinary suburban amusements." He was no stranger to printing, having grown up in a printing office and at the time being employed by Theodore Low DeVinne. Hopkins in fact was the designer of some of the more important books to come from DeVinne's shop. At his own press, named the Marion Press after his daughter, he started to produce a number of books that were well executed and, for their time, unusually restrained in their design; undoubtedly Hopkins was influenced by the Aesthetic and Arts and Crafts schools, but he was no unthinking admirer and imitator of Morris. In 1898, however, his employer presented him with an ultimatum. DeVinne had old-fashioned ideas about employees' spare-time activities and insisted that either Hopkins gave up his hobby printing or he would have to leave. Hopkins chose to do the latter, and turned the Marion Press into a full commercial venture, undertaking many commissions for the Caxton Club, the Rowfant Club, and other bibliophile groups.

In other smaller centers there were other private presses through which the Kelmscott style ran its course. Two of the longer-lived presses, the Clerk's Press of the Reverend Charles C. Bubb and William Lewis Washburn's Palmetto Press, are discussed in Chapter 17, as most of their work was done at a later date. Between 1900 and 1902 the Alwil Shop in Ridgewood, New Jersey, produced some eight slim books that are splendid examples not so much of the Morris style but of a blend of this and American Art Nouveau. There was a close relationship between the Alwil Shop and the Blue Sky Press in Chicago. The Alwil designer and leading spirit, Frank B. Rae, Jr., designed some

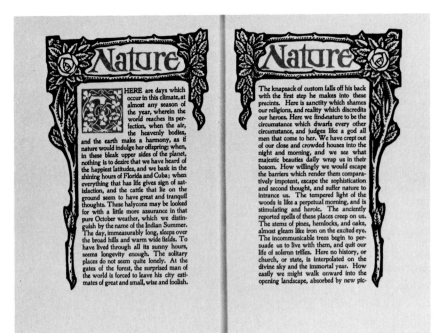

ILLUS. 63. Alwil Shop, Ridgewood, New Jersey. *The Essay on Nature,* by Ralph Waldo Emerson, 1902. Photograph: Courtesy of Susan O. Thompson.

of the better Blue Sky books, while Alwil published some titles by the literary directors of Blue Sky, Thomas Wood Stevens and Alden Charles Noble. Inbreeding among private presses is no new thing!

Another New Jersey press was at Englewood, where Frederic M. Burr ran his Hillside Press in the Morris tradition from 1906 to 1915. Some of his work is of considerable interest, like Burr's *A Criminal in Stone* (1908) or his wife's *The Sleep of Beppo* (1909), both of which were designed by Frederic Goudy working in his Kelmscott manner, but the design and presswork of the Hillside books were not of high quality.

At Wausau, Wisconsin, Philip Van Vechten and William H. Ellis took time off from running their newspaper and jobbing business to produce a substantial list of books and a magazine under the imprint of the Philosopher Press from 1896 to 1904. Some of these, like Emerson's *Self-Reliance* (1901) were heavily Morrisian in design, but their style varied considerably. Unlike the books of the Hillside Press, their presswork was excellent, thanks to the skill of Helen Bruneau Van Vechten who was the press hand for most Philosopher Press books.

Although the output of the Philosopher Press was not limited to the usual classics with which so many amateurs thought to make the art of the book more appetizing to a sated world, their list was heavily loaded with the *Rubaiyat*, Tennyson, Emerson, and others whose work dominates the private presses of the time. The Kirgate Press, which Lewis Buddy ran from Canton, Pennsylvania, during the first five years of this century, seems all the more attractive for being cast in a different literary mold. Named after Horace Walpole's printer, the press was largely concerned with reprinting various pieces of Walpoliana, but it also put out some other very interesting literary and bibliographical work. Its most ambitious undertaking was a type-facsimile of Emerson's quarterly the *Dial*, which was reprinted with painstaking care in the same style and types as the original.

The influence of the English private presses in the Arts and Crafts Movement was considerable in the United States, but it was not through private presswork that the movement flowered most luxuriantly. It was through the designers and printers in the commercial field—through such men as Will Bradley, D. B. Updike, Bruce Rogers, Carl Rollins, and T. M. Cleland—that Morris's ideas were spread most effectively across the Atlantic. These were men with the ability and the under-standing to abandon mere facile imitations of the Kelmscott style very early. One or two of them had toyed with private presses; Cleland at the turn of the century ran the Cornhill Press whose books, as he said, "were printed in black letter types and were very hard to read, and I had a notion at that time that being so made them especially romantic and beautiful." Such notions were general then; their replacement in good commercial work by such firms as the Merrymount Press and the Riverside Press has been well recorded elsewhere.

Chapter 14

FINE PRINTING ON
THE CONTINENT

IN THE EIGHTEENTH CENTURY and earlier, private presses had flourished on the continent to a far greater extent than in England. It might, therefore, have been anticipated that England's nearest neighbor, France, would have had at the end of the nineteenth century a similar flowering of presses that regarded printing as an art. France certainly had its share of parlor printers earlier in the century; it had those in the field of typography who turned back to an earlier period for inspiration; and, in the person of Anatole Claudin, it had a director of the Imprimerie Nationale with taste and learning who could have provided the same sort of service that Emery Walker did to the English private press.

A few years before Walker's 1888 lecture, Octave Uzanne had written in a splendidly chauvinistic vein:

> The art of printing beautiful books is the only one that foreigners have been
> unable to imitate. Essentially, it is a purely French art. . . . Printing, illustration,
> sewing, binding, make us the absolute superior of all others in Europe and
> America, and this is true not only of our artists' talents, but of the perfect taste
> of our principal publishers.

In the smug self-satisfaction of the Third Republic, which this passage evokes so clearly—and to be fair, it was not without justification so far as nineteenth-century conventions of fine printing were concerned—there was little chance for Morris's notions to catch root. France was the one country in western Europe in which his ideas on book design had no influence then or since; hence, the development of their separate tradition of the *livre d'artiste,* so different from Britain's own "fine books."

It is sad that French private presses did not develop. In his novel *A Rebours,* J. K. Huysmans had in 1883 suggested how magnificent such a French press could be. We read how the novel's hero, Des Esseintes:

> had in the past had certain books set up just for himself and printed on
> hand-presses by workmen specially hired for the job. Sometimes he would
> commission Perrin of Lyons, whose thin clear types were well suited for

antiquarian reprints of old texts; sometimes he would send to England or to America for new founts to print modern works; sometimes he would apply to a Lille printing house which for centuries had possessed a complete fount of black letter; sometimes again he would employ the old Enschedé foundry at Haarlem, which had preserved the punches of the civilité types.

For the paper of his books he had done the same. Deciding that he was bored with the usual expensive papers—silver from China, pearly gold from Japan, white from Whatman's, grey-brown from Holland, buff from Turkey and the Seychel Mills—and disgusted by machine-made papers, he had ordered special papers to be made by hand for him at the old papermills at Vire, where they still used pestles once employed on crushing hempseed. In order to introduce a little variety into his collections, he had on several occasions imported flock papers, linen woves and the like from London; while to show his contempt for other book collectors he had a Lübeck merchant supply him with an improved greaseproof paper of a bluish tint, crackly and brittle to the touch, in which instead of straw fibres there were flecks of gold like those in Dantziger Goldwasser.

In this way he had made some books which were unique, and for which he always chose unusual formats; having them bound by Lortic, by Trautz-Bauzonnet, by Chambolle, or by Cape's successors; irreproachable bindings of old silk, of embossed oxhide, of Cape morocco—all full-bindings, tooled and inlaid, with endpapers of watered silk; enriched in ecclesiastical fashion with metal clasps and corners, sometimes even decorated by Gruel-Engelmann in oxidized silver and gleaming enamel.

Thus he had commissioned Baudelaire's works to be printed in the admirable episcopal type of the old firm of Le Clerc, using a large format similar to that of a missal, on very light Japanese paper; a porous paper as soft as elder-pith, its milky whiteness tinged faintly with pink. This edition, limited to the single copy and printed in a rich velvety black, had been bound in a wonderful flesh-coloured pigskin—one in a thousand—dotted all over where the bristles had been, and tooled in black with marvellously apt designs by a great artist.

What books these would have been! Had they existed in fact, the simpler volumes would have demonstrated many of the features with which Francis Meynell was to delight purchasers of Nonesuch Press books half a century later, and we would be obliged to accept Uzanne's claim as no more than the truth.

Outside France, Morris has been universally recognized as *the* pioneer in typographic reform and revival. In the establishment of private presses, his influence was to show itself first in Belgium, where it coincided with the renaissance of Flemish literature that was a feature of the 1890s. As far as French language printing in Belgium was concerned, he had no influence, but as early as 1889, before Morris started work at the Kelmscott Press, the artist Henry van der Velde had made his work in other arts and crafts the theme of lectures he gave at Antwerp.

It was natural that van der Velde should follow the work of the Kelmscott Press closely, and, in fact, his wife Maria visited the press while in England to find out more about it for him. When his friend Auguste Vermeylen, who was planning to publish a literary magazine called *Van Nu en Straks* asked him to take charge of its layout and design in 1892, van der Velde explored the possibilities of having a special typeface cut for the magazine but unfortunately had to reject the idea. For his own short-lived little private press, La Joyeuse, he used Caslon type in the *Six Chansons* (1895) written by his partner in the venture, Max Elskamp. Van der Velde's most important contribution to the fine press movement before 1914, however, was not in his homeland but in Germany, where he had moved before the turn of the century. Another amateur Flemish press that operated in the 1890s indirectly under the Kelmscott influence was that of Julius de Praetere. At Laethem St. Martin he printed a number of exquisite little volumes of poetry by H. Tierlinck and others, illustrated with his own woodcuts. But for de Praetere, as for van der Velde, Belgium did not prove a satisfactory environment in which to work, and he moved to Zurich where he became the first director of the Kunstgewerbeschule.

In Germany, where Morris's influence was to be strongest, it did not sweep triumphantly into a vacuum. In 1887 Ludwig Meper, Director of the Leipzig Akademie der Graphischen Künste, had said that "printing, even in the edition de luxe, is *not* an art"; nevertheless, there had been a restlessness, a dissatisfaction with the traditional development in the arts in Germany just as much as elsewhere. One result had been the growth of *Jugendstil*. It was not with the old dreary tradition of bad design (or more often than not, no design at all) that Morris's teaching had to compete, but rather with the freedom, the anarchy of Art Nouveau's tangled ribbons and tendrils, which were overpowering the German book.

In *The Art Nouveau Book in Britain* John Russell Taylor makes some useful generalizations about the differences between British and Continental Art Nouveau. He points out that the British form was a reaction against earlier intricacy in favor of simplicity and spareness, concerned largely with the arrangement of empty spaces, whereas on the continent Art Nouveau appears as further elaboration and a concern with filling spaces in a way that was almost a reaction against form itself. As far as the art of the book is concerned, it is worth nothing that the Arts and Crafts Movement and the Kelmscott influence came early in the emergence of Art Nouveau in Britain; on the continent their influence was not felt until the *Jugendstil* was well established.

In Henry van der Velde's work in Germany, Morris's teaching was transmuted into Art Nouveau forms—van der Velde would have denied that his work was Art Nouveau at all, having rejected the plant patterns used by Otto Eckmann in his book design and instead using more abstract patterns. In van der Velde's work for the Insel Verlag, in *Ecce Homo* and *Also Sprach Zarathustra* (not, of course, private press work, but in the direct tradition) there was an application of the Morris principles allied to a completely modern system of decoration. But, by this time the reaction against the nightmare foliage of Eckmann and his school had set in; as early as 1901 a working group of young graphic artists, the Steglitzer Werkstatt, had called for a stand against exaggerated decorative trends in book design.

The influences from England were not restricted to the work of William Morris. Of even more importance in the spread of the private press movement in Germany were the books of the Doves Press and the calligraphic teaching of Edward Johnston, which had been taken back to Germany by his pupil Anna Simons, who was to translate his seminal *Writing and Illuminating and Lettering* a few years later in 1910.

An important figure in this work was Count Harry Kessler (1868–1937). Kessler, the son of a Hamburg banker whose death in 1895 gave him a substantial private income, had his schooling in France and England before attending universities in Bonn and Leipzig. Free to do what he wanted, he devoted himself to the service of art. Appointed Director of the Weimar Art Museum, he came heavily under the influence of Henry van der Velde. As early as 1900 he had encouraged the designing of a new type by the Belgian artist George Lemmen (the face used later in van der Velde's books for the Insel Verlag). Then, following a visit to England in 1904, during which he met

Edward Johnston, Eric Gill, and others, he invited Emery Walker to design a series of German classics, the *Grossherzog Wilhelm Ernst* series, for the Insel Verlag. This series, with its calligraphic title pages designed by Johnston and Gill, was to have a marked effect on German book design—not least of which from its use of roman type in place of black letter.

August Kippenberg, who at that time was jointly responsible with Kessler for the work of the Insel Verlag, had a large degree of responsibility for the establishment of one of the first truly private German presses of this period: the Ernst-Ludwig-Presse at Darmstadt, which was started under the patronage of the Grand Duke of Hesse, for whom it was named, in 1907. This press was under the artistic direction of the brothers Friedrich Wilhelm and Christian Heinrich Kleukens. Friedrich Wilhelm, who had been a member of the Steglitzer Werkstatt from 1901 to 1903, remained at the Ernst-Ludwig-Presse only until 1914; his brother continued to direct its work until 1937. Beginning in 1918 the work of the press was expanded, and only occasionally did it produce work for the Grand-ducal house. The style of the press was relatively severe; all illustration was eschewed, the only decoration being in title pages and initials and in the types used. To a considerable degree the press was a vehicle for experiment with the typefaces designed by the Kleukens brothers; this practice was followed by several other German private presses, most of which went far beyond the one or two proprietary faces used by the English Arts and Crafts printers. The result was that many of their volumes look mannered and intentional. In Daniel Berkeley Updike's words, "they produce a certain sensation, but not that of pleasure; they astonish rather than charm."

Very closely modeled on the work of the Doves Press was the Janus-Presse, founded in 1907 in Leipzig by Walter Tiemann and C. E. Poeschel. Poeschel was a printer, and for some years Kippenberg's partner in the Insel Verlag; Tiemann a typographic designer and lecturer at the Akademie der Graphischen Künste in Leipzig. The press was a sort of busman's holiday at which the two of them carried out the operations of presswork and composition themselves as a change from directing the operations of others. Tiemann designed the press's special typeface, a forerunner of his well-known "Mediaeval" type, and cut the titles and initials in wood. Strictly a spare-time occupation, in the 16 years of its life, the press published only five books, two in 1907 and 1910, and three more after the end of the war; but what they lacked in number they made up for in quality. The books were superbly produced and the texts selected were of real worth.

There were more than a few other private presses in Germany in the years before World War I. The Officina Serpentis, founded by E. W. Tieffenbach in 1911, was based closely on the English private presses in its operation but adopted a much more decorative manner in its work than was usual (Illus. 64). Less influenced by non-German sources than almost any other press was the Rupprecht-Presse. Founded in Munich in 1913 by the typographer F. H. Ehmcke, and named for the popular crown prince of Bavaria (who acted as godfather at its christening), in the 20 years of its life the press produced some 57 books, mostly German literature. All were printed in Ehmcke's own typefaces—roman, fraktur, schwabacher—and they convey the German tradition in typography with splendid effect. Even more steeped in the Teutonic past were the "Rudolfinische Drucke," occasional pieces of printing issued between 1911 and 1924 by Rudolf Koch and Rudolf Gerstung. Koch was the German equivalent of William Morris and Edward Johnston rolled into one. A craftsman of very great talent, Koch was responsible for the splendid flowering of black letter in the first third of this century, a flowering that was at its best in the block books *Elia* and *Jesaia* produced at his private press. Although William Morris would have relished his work, it is far too Germanic for most English tastes, and I have found few who share my own enthusiasm for Koch's achievements.

Much more closely in the traditions of the typographic work of Emery Walker and Cobden-Sanderson and, therefore, more admired in the English-speaking world, was the Bremer-Presse. Founded in 1911 by a group of whom Willy Wiegand was the chief, the press was very much in the

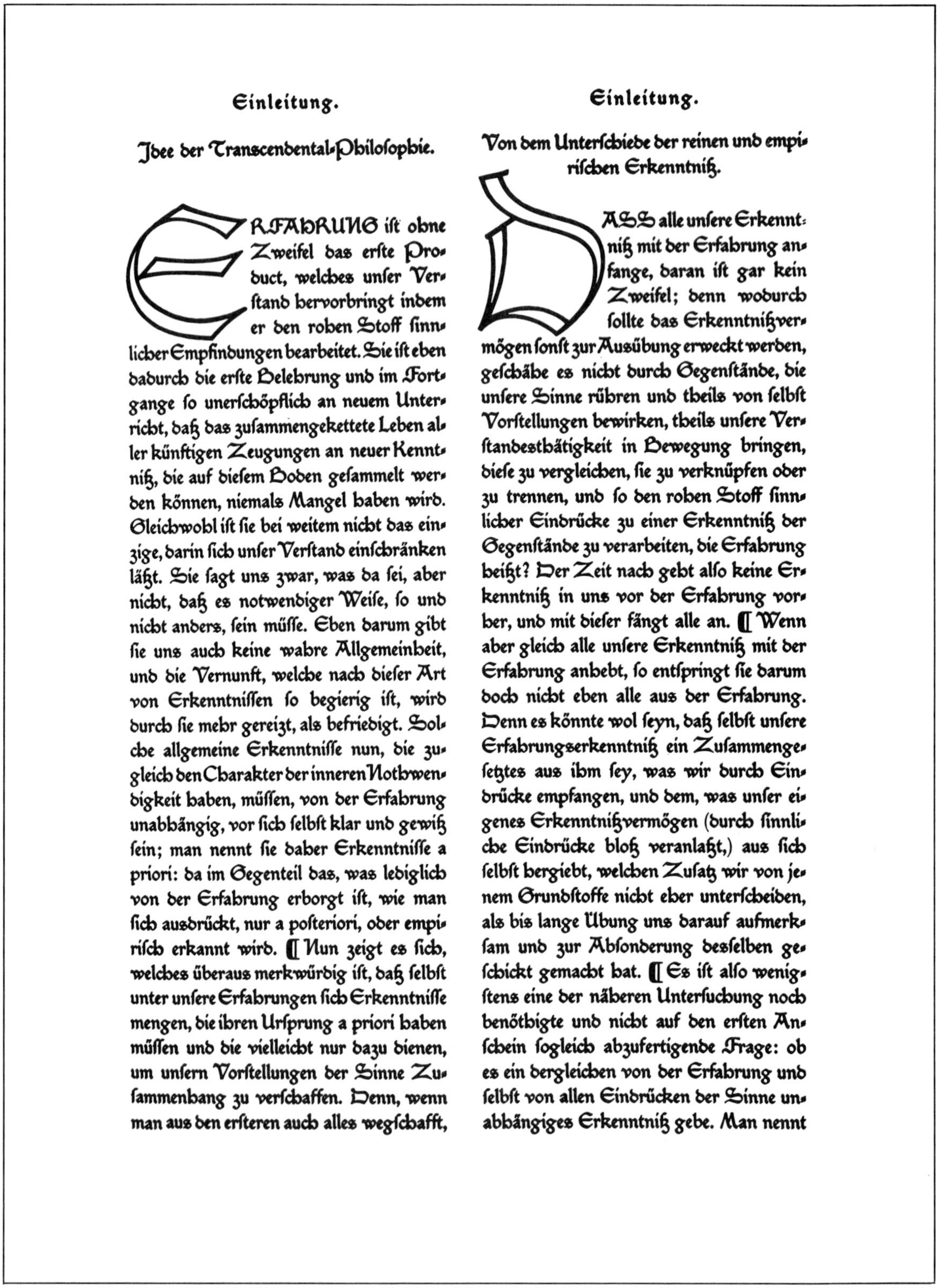

Idee der Transcendental-Philosophie.

ERFAHRUNG ist ohne Zweifel das erste Pro- duct, welches unser Ver- stand hervorbringt indem er den roben Stoff sinn- licher Empfindungen bearbeitet. Sie ist eben dadurch die erste Belehrung und im Fort- gange so unerschöpflich an neuem Unter- richt, daß das zusammengekettete Leben al- ler künftigen Zeugungen an neuer Kennt- niß, die auf diesem Boden gesammelt wer- den können, niemals Mangel haben wird. Gleichwohl ist sie bei weitem nicht das ein- zige, darin sich unser Verstand einschränken läßt. Sie sagt uns zwar, was da sei, aber nicht, daß es notwendiger Weise, so und nicht anders, sein müsse. Eben darum gibt sie uns auch keine wahre Allgemeinheit, und die Vernunft, welche nach dieser Art von Erkenntnissen so begierig ist, wird durch sie mehr gereizt, als befriedigt. Sol- che allgemeine Erkenntnisse nun, die zu- gleich den Charakter der inneren Nothwen- digkeit haben, müssen, von der Erfahrung unabhängig, vor sich selbst klar und gewiß sein; man nennt sie daher Erkenntnisse a priori: da im Gegenteil das, was lediglich von der Erfahrung erborgt ist, wie man sich ausdrückt, nur a posteriori, oder empi- risch erkannt wird. ¶ Nun zeigt es sich, welches überaus merkwürdig ist, daß selbst unter unsere Erfahrungen sich Erkenntnisse mengen, die ihren Ursprung a priori haben müssen und die vielleicht nur dazu dienen, um unsern Vorstellungen der Sinne Zu- sammenhang zu verschaffen. Denn, wenn man aus den ersteren auch alles wegschafft,

Einleitung.

Von dem Unterschiede der reinen und empi- rischen Erkenntniß.

DASS alle unsere Erkennt- niß mit der Erfahrung an- fange, daran ist gar kein Zweifel; denn woduch sollte das Erkenntnißver- mögen sonst zur Ausübung erweckt werden, geschähe es nicht durch Gegenstände, die unsere Sinne rühren und theils von selbst Vorstellungen bewirken, theils unsere Ver- standesthätigkeit in Bewegung bringen, diese zu vergleichen, sie zu verknüpfen oder zu trennen, und so den roben Stoff sinn- licher Eindrücke zu einer Erkenntniß der Gegenstände zu verarbeiten, die Erfahrung heißt? Der Zeit nach geht also keine Er- kenntniß in uns vor der Erfahrung vor- her, und mit dieser fängt alle an. ¶ Wenn aber gleich alle unsere Erkenntniß mit der Erfahrung anhebt, so entspringt sie darum doch nicht eben alle aus der Erfahrung. Denn es könnte wol seyn, daß selbst unsere Erfahrungserkenntniß ein Zusammenge- setztes aus ihm sey, was wir durch Ein- drücke empfangen, und dem, was unser ei- genes Erkenntnißvermögen (durch sinnli- che Eindrücke bloß veranlaßt,) aus sich selbst hergiebt, welchen Zusatz wir von je- nem Grundstoffe nicht eher unterscheiden, als bis lange Übung uns darauf aufmerk- sam und zur Absonderung desselben ge- schickt gemacht hat. ¶ Es ist also wenig- stens eine der näheren Untersuchung noch benöthigte und nicht auf den ersten An- schein sogleich abzufertigende Frage: ob es ein dergleichen von der Erfahrung und selbst von allen Eindrücken der Sinne un- abhängiges Erkenntniß gebe. Man nennt

ILLUS. 64. Officina Serpentis, Berlin. Specimen sheet, 1928.

grand tradition; a few good, special typefaces were cut and used with magnificent effect in large-format editions of Homer, Dante, Tacitus, the Luther Bible, and similar books. Apart from splendid initials drawn by Johnston's pupil, Anna Simons, the books were entirely without ornament, and only one—*Vesalius,* printed for an American medical society—was illustrated. In 1922 the press expanded and produced a number of educational books, such as Hofmannthal's *Deutsches Lesebuch,* which were printed on powered presses, an example of the extension of private press ideals into the commercial field. For some years the handpress tradition and good commercial printing were carried on side by side. After the Nazis came to power, economic and political difficulties killed the Bremer-Presse, but in its long life its influence on German printing was probably greater and longer lasting than that of any of the other fine presses.

The "Rudolfinische Drucke" were the most purely Germanic private printing. In contrast, when Count Kessler set up his own private press in 1913 it was the most international in spirit. It had high

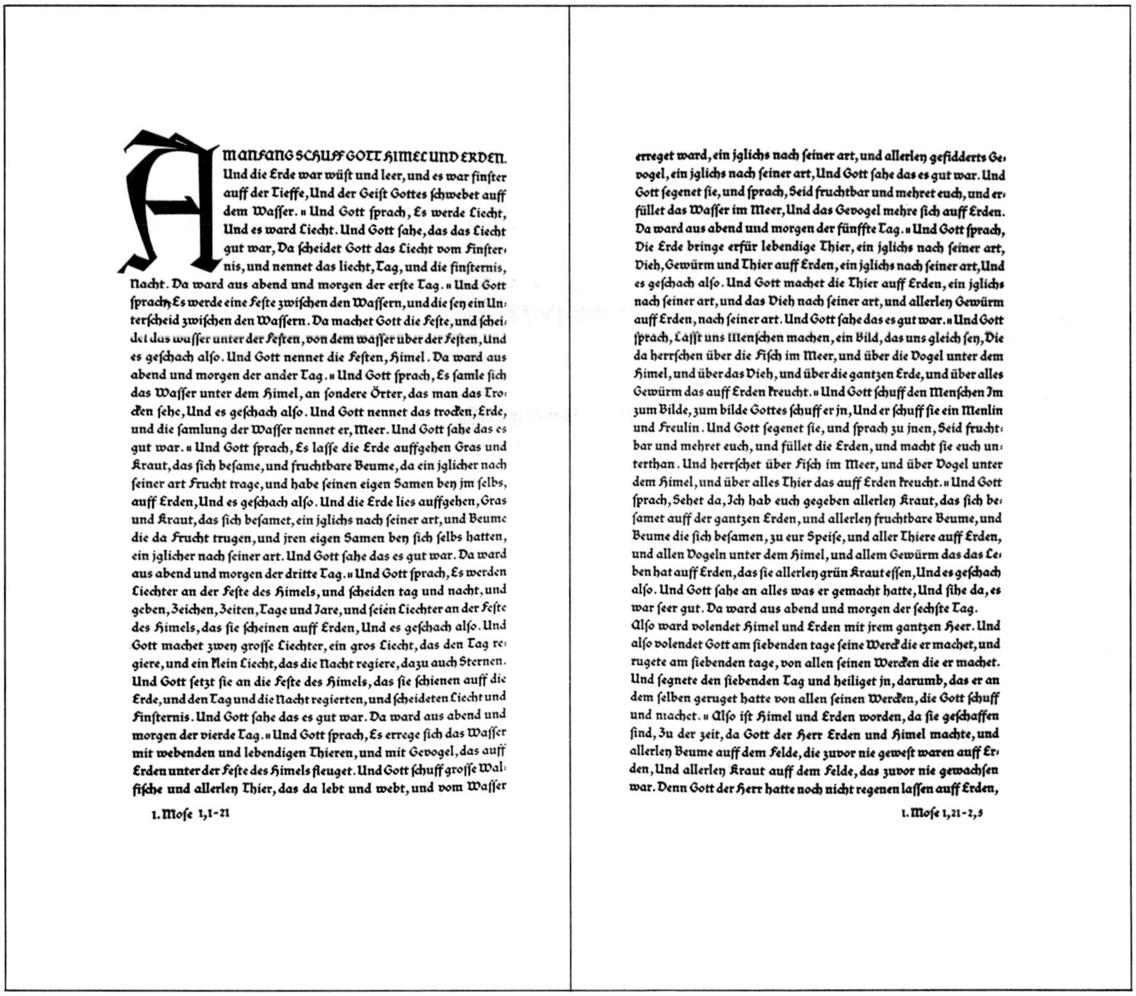
AM ANFANG SCHUFF GOTT HIMEL UND ERDEN. Und die Erde war wüſt und leer, und es war finſter auff der Tieffe, Und der Geiſt Gottes ſchwebet auff dem Waſſer. ‖ Und Gott ſprach, Es werde Liecht, Und es ward Liecht. Und Gott ſahe, das das Liecht gut war, Da ſcheidet Gott das Liecht vom Finſternis, und nennet das liecht, Tag, und die finſternis, Nacht. Da ward aus abend und morgen der erſte Tag. ‖ Und Gott ſprach, Es werde eine Feſte zwiſchen den Waſſern, und die ſey ein Unterſcheid zwiſchen den Waſſern. Da machet Gott die Feſte, und ſcheidet das waſſer unter der Feſten, von dem waſſer uber der Feſten, Und es geſchach alſo. Und Gott nennet die Feſten, Himel. Da ward aus abend und morgen der ander Tag. ‖ Und Gott ſprach, Es ſamle ſich das Waſſer unter dem Himel, an ſondere Örter, das man das Trocken ſehe, Und es geſchach alſo. Und Gott nennet das trocken, Erde, und die ſamlung der Waſſer nennet er, Meer. Und Gott ſahe das es gut war. ‖ Und Gott ſprach, Es laſſe die Erde auffgehen Gras und Kraut, das ſich beſame, und fruchtbare Beume, da ein jglicher nach ſeiner art Frucht trage, und habe ſeinen eigen Samen bey jm ſelbs, auff Erden, Und es geſchach alſo. Und die Erde lies auffgehen, Gras und Kraut, das ſich beſamet, ein jglichs nach ſeiner art, und Beume die da Frucht trugen, und jren eigen Samen bey ſich ſelbs hatten, ein jglicher nach ſeiner art. Und Gott ſahe das es gut war. Da ward aus abend und morgen der dritte Tag. ‖ Und Gott ſprach, Es werden Liechter an der Feſte des Himels, und ſcheiden tag und nacht, und geben, Zeichen, Zeiten, Tage und Jare, und ſeien Liechter an der Feſte des Himels, das ſie ſcheinen auff Erden, Und es geſchach alſo. Und Gott machet zwey groſſe Liechter, ein gros Liecht, das den Tag regiere, und ein klein Liecht, das die Nacht regiere, dazu auch Sternen. Und Gott ſetzt ſie an die Feſte des Himels, das ſie ſchienen auff die Erde, und den Tag und die Nacht regierten, und ſcheideten Liecht und Finſternis. Und Gott ſahe das es gut war. Da ward aus abend und morgen der vierde Tag. ‖ Und Gott ſprach, Es errege ſich das Waſſer mit webenden und lebendigen Thieren, und mit Gevogel, das auff Erden unter der Feſte des Himels fleuget. Und Gott ſchuff groſſe Walfiſche und allerley Thier, das da lebt und webt, und vom Waſſer

1. Moſe 1,1–21

erreget ward, ein jglichs nach ſeiner art, und allerley gefidderts Gevogel, ein jglichs nach ſeiner art, Und Gott ſahe das es gut war. Und Gott ſegenet ſie, und ſprach, Seid fruchtbar und mehret euch, und erfüllet das Waſſer im Meer, Und das Gevogel mehre ſich auff Erden. Da ward aus abend und morgen der fünffte Tag. ‖ Und Gott ſprach, Die Erde bringe erfür lebendige Thier, ein jglichs nach ſeiner art, Vieh, Gewürm und Thier auff Erden, ein jglichs nach ſeiner art, Und es geſchach alſo. Und Gott machet die Thier auff Erden, ein jglichs nach ſeiner art, und das Vieh nach ſeiner art, und allerley Gewürm auff Erden, nach ſeiner art. Und Gott ſahe das es gut war. ‖ Und Gott ſprach, Laſſt uns Menſchen machen, ein Bild, das uns gleich ſey, Die da herrſchen über die Fiſch im Meer, und über die Vogel unter dem Himel, und über das Vieh, und über die gantzen Erde, und über alles Gewürm das auff Erden kreucht. ‖ Und Gott ſchuff den Menſchen Im zum Bilde, zum bilde Gottes ſchuff er jn, Und er ſchuff ſie ein Menlin und Freulin. Und Gott ſegenet ſie, und ſprach zu jnen, Seid fruchtbar und mehret euch, und füllet die Erden, und macht ſie euch unterthan. Und herrſchet über Fiſch im Meer, und über Vogel unter dem Himel, und über alles Thier das auff Erden kreucht. ‖ Und Gott ſprach, Sehet da, Ich hab euch gegeben allerley Kraut, das ſich beſamet auff der gantzen Erden, und allerley fruchtbare Beume, und Beume die ſich beſamen, zu eur Speiſe, und aller Thiere auff Erden, und allen Vogeln unter dem Himel, und allem Gewürm das das Leben hat auff Erden, das ſie allerley grün Kraut eſſen, Und es geſchach alſo. Und Gott ſahe an alles was er gemacht hatte, Und ſihe da, es war ſeer gut. Da ward aus abend und morgen der ſechſte Tag.
Alſo ward volendet Himel und Erden mit jrem gantzen Heer. Und alſo volendet Gott am ſiebenden tage ſeine Werck die er machet, und rugete am ſiebenden tage, von allen ſeinen Wercken die er machet. Und ſegnete den ſiebenden Tag und heiliget jn, darumb, das er an dem ſelben geruget hatte von allen ſeinen Wercken, die Gott ſchuff und machet. ‖ Alſo iſt Himel und Erden worden, da ſie geſchaffen ſind, Zu der zeit, da Gott der Herr Erden und Himel machte, und allerley Beume auff dem Felde, die zuvor nie geweſt waren auff Erden, Und allerley Kraut auff dem Felde, das zuvor nie gewachſen war. Denn Gott der Herr hatte noch nicht regenen laſſen auff Erden,

1. Moſe 1,21–2,5

ILLUS. 65. Bremer-Presse, Germany. Opening from the Luther *Bible,* 1926–1928.

aims: To publish only masterpieces of literature that were superbly translated, superbly illustrated, and superbly printed.

Kessler himself was equally at home in Paris or London as in Berlin or Weimar. He was to become an international diplomatist, but still devoted a good deal of his time and wealth to intelligent patronage of ballet, music, and the fine arts; as *animateur,* he played an important part. As has already been said, Kessler obtained the services of Emery Walker, Johnston, and Gill for the Insel Verlag in 1904. When he decided to set up the Cranach-Presse, named from his house on the Cranach Strasse in Weimar, in 1910 or 1911 he naturally turned to Walker for advice and assistance. Edward Johnston was engaged to advise on type designs, and when in 1913 the type was ready J. H. Mason, the former Doves Press compositor, went to Weimar for a few months to supervise the installation of the handpresses and assist in engaging compositors and pressmen. Finding that it was far from easy to get workmen skilled in handpress work in Germany, Mason arranged for H. Gage-Cole, also from the Doves, to go to Weimar. Work was proceeding apace; Kessler had persuaded Aristide Maillol to try his hand at woodcuts for a projected edition of Virgil's *Eclogues,* and Gordon Craig to prepare woodcuts for *Hamlet.* Caspard Maillol, Aristide's nephew, was making special paper for the exclusive use of the press. By the summer of 1914 the *Eclogues* were well advanced—despite the fact that there were to be three different editions (with translations in English, German, and French as parallel texts to the Latin) and despite the delays caused by Kessler's many other engagements (his collaborating with Richard Strauss on *Der Rosenkavalier* at Munich or helping with the production of Diaghilev's ballets at Covent Garden). The war stopped all these preparations.

Although one or two very minor pieces seem to have been produced during the war years, and there were a few more publications of a private nature during the early 1920s—such as the volume *In Memoriam Walter Rathenau* in 1922—Kessler's preoccupation with international diplomacy in the aftermath of the war prevented him from resuming work on his half-completed projects until the mid-1920s. In 1926 the German edition of the *Eclogues* appeared, to be followed by the English version the following year (Illus. 66).

In view of the part played by Emery Walker in advising Kessler and in suggesting the design of the roman type, the similarity of these to the best work of the Doves Press was not surprising. The *Hamlet,* however, when it eventually appeared in 1930, was completely individual in style. Shakespeare's text was set in a large black letter face designed by Johnston; the text of the sources (Saxo-Grammaticus and Belleforest) was printed in a smaller size around the text; and the most marvelously conceived woodcuts were perfectly printed as illustration (Illus. 67). Gage-Cole's skill in printing these showed the ability of the pressman at its best: Of all private presswork in the Kelmscott tradition, the Cranach *Hamlet* is the greatest.

A few more books from the press were to appear: a very attractive *Canticum Canticorum* with wood engravings by Eric Gill (Illus. 68) and Rilke's *Duineser Elegien,* both published in 1931. Several other substantial works were planned at this time, which suggest the wide-ranging tastes of its owner: Gerhart Hauptmann's *Till Eulenspiegel,* a Petronius with woodcuts by Marcus Behmer, a Horace with woodcuts by Maillol, Valéry's complete works with engravings by Eric Gill, to name only some of them. But they were doomed never to appear. When Hitler came to power in 1933 Kessler's position in Germany was no longer secure. As a left-wing statesman and as the friend and biographer of Walther Rathenau, whose race and politics were equally detested by the Nazis, Kessler had to abandon his home and possessions at a moment's notice, and the Cranach-Presse produced nothing more.

Because of the international nature of its work, the employment of British and French as well as German artists, and the production of several of its books in French and English editions, the

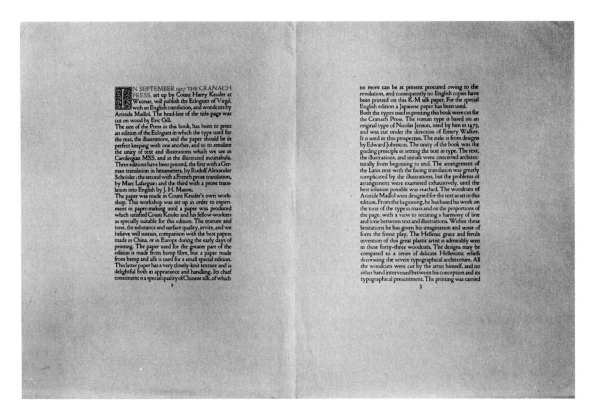

ILLUS. 66. Cranach-Presse, Germany. Prospectus for Virgil's *Eclogues*, 1927.
Set in the Cranach roman cut by E. P. Prince.

Cranach-Presse has received more attention in the English speaking world than any other German private press. Compared with Kelmscott, Doves, or the Bremer-Presse its output was small, and with the exception of *Eclogues, Hamlet,* and *Canticum Canticorum* its work was not altogether satisfactory. Yet, these three books were superb. No greater compliment could have been paid *Hamlet* than C. E. Poeschl's statement to Kessler that he had a sleepless night over it, so excited had he been by the work. For the fruits of over 20 years' work three books may seem a poor showing, but this is to judge the press in terms that are not really valid; Kessler's undertaking was in the grand tradition in which neither time nor cost was important.

In the Netherlands the influence of William Morris and of Cobden-Sanderson was slower to penetrate than it had been in neighboring Belgium, although from the early 1890s the work of Kelmscott had been studied with interest. It was an interest mixed with caution. There was a feeling that the Belgians in such publications as *Van Nu en Straks* had been taking things too easily—that their principles of design were illogical and impure and lacked the earnestness of English work—and neither the Belgians nor the English were by any means eagerly copied. The revival of fine printing in Holland came through the book trade; through the influence of such men as Jan Kalf, J. W. Enschedé, and S. H. de Roos (whose first commission was to design a translation of some of Morris's essays under the title of *Kunst en Maatschappij* in 1903) rather than through indigenous private presswork.

The first true private press in the Netherlands was De Zilverdistel, operated by Dr. J. F. van Royen (1878–1942). After studying law at Leyden, van Royen had entered the Dutch postal service. During the early years of this century he became a member of the circle of the three poets Jan Greshoff, Jacques Bloem, and P. N. van Eyck and the architect K. P. C. de Bazel, all of whom were

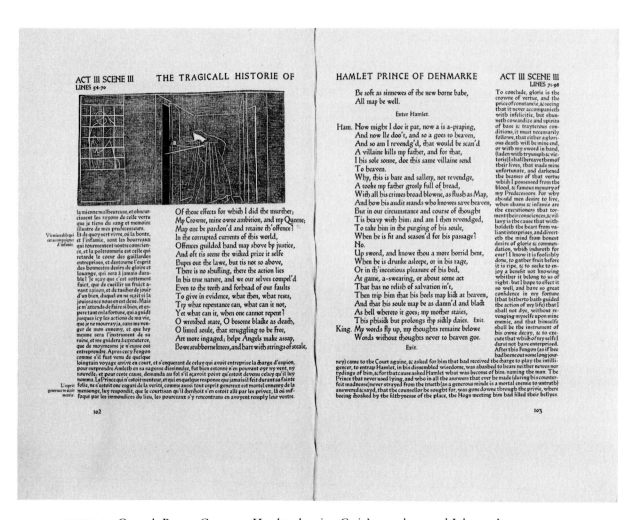

ILLUS. 67. Cranach-Presse, Germany. *Hamlet,* showing Craig's woodcuts and Johnston's types. Photograph: Birmingham City Libraries.

strongly interested in typographic design. Van Royen's own practically applied interest in the subject, as well as in the improvement of standards, was shown in 1912 when (although still in a relatively subordinate position in the postal service) he was instrumental in having de Bazel commissioned to design a new series of postage stamps. In the same year he was to publish a vehement attack on the low standards of official printing in the first issue of a book collectors' magazine called *De Witte Meier.* The improvement of government printing in the Netherlands was to be largely his doing; over the next 30 years, during which he was to rise to the influential position of Secretary General of the Post Office, he influenced standards as thoroughly as Francis Meynell was later to effect improvements at His Majesty's Stationery Office.

In 1910 Greshoff and the other two poets had started De Zilverdistel, a bibliophile series of books of a sort to become much more common in the 1920s, in which the design of the books was undertaken by the partners, but the printers (Enschedé at Haarlem or van der Wiel of Arnhem) were responsible for interpretation and execution of the designs. The program of the press was well within the Kelmscott-Doves tradition; they aimed at "pure, non-ornamental book typography." Their editions were both expensive and limited in size, but this was intended to be only a temporary factor: "a luxury of beauty, not of rarity, is what we need." They were well aware of the dangers that

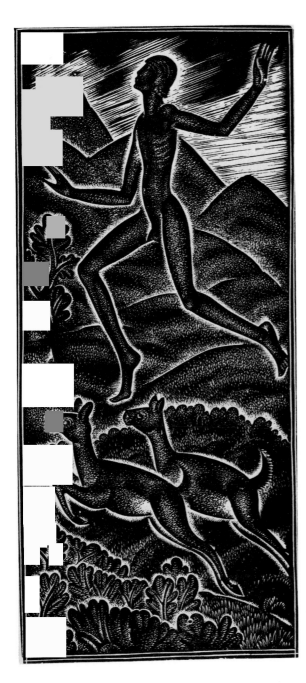

ILLUS. 68. Cranach-Presse, Germany.
The Song of Songs, 1931.
Wood engraving by Eric Gill.

afflicted private presses, as well as of their ideals: "There is one aim, inwardly and outwardly a perfect harmony. There is one risk: snobbery, dilletantism, affectation combining to produce preciousness." On their models (if this was not already clear) they were quite frank: "They would be less German and more English, and among these less the books of the Kelmscott or Vale Presses than the work of the Doves Press."

After the production of three of these semiprivate press books between 1910 and 1912, Greshoff and Bloem withdrew from the undertaking, leaving van Eyck to carry on alone. Van Royen joined him in 1913, but following a trip to England in 1914, during which he visited Cobden-Sanderson, St. John Hornby, and Pissarro, he determined to return to the purer private press tradition by doing his own printing. Van Eyck was not altogether willing, and a few more books were printed commercially; but when in 1915 van Eyck left Holland to become a newspaper correspondent in Italy, he had to leave van Royen to produce the books he thought best. As it was to turn out, De Zilverdistel was to become more like St. John Hornby's Ashendene Press than like its former model Doves, and it is perhaps the only example of a semicommercial press that became truly private. Two special type designs were commissioned; one to be used for contemporary work, which was designed by S. H. de Roos; and one for the printing of older texts, which was the work of Lucien Pissarro. Pissarro was also instrumental in the purchase of an Albion press, which was soon installed in van Royen's home in The Hague.

The first book to be printed on the handpress and in de Roos's new Zilvertype was a joint statement by van Royen and van Eyck of their aims, *Over Boekkunst en De Zilverdistel* (1916) (Illus. 69). For this de Roos also designed the initials. Van Royen printed the next two books in the same type, Jan Hendrik Leopold's *Cheops* (1916) and Shelley's *Prometheus Unbound* (1918); the first use of Pissarro's Disteltype was in a late medieval Dutch text, *Een Boecxken gemaket van Suster Bertken,* printed in 1918. There was to be one more book from De Zilverdistel in the following year, but after that for some years there was a pause in van Royen's printing; the collaboration with van Eyck did not work as happily as it might, and van Royen wanted to be completely his own master.

In 1923 he resumed his hobby under the new name of the Kunera Pers, starting with an edition of Leopold's *Oosterch,* for which he designed and cut the title and initials himself, as he was to do for all the other books from his press. There were to be very few of them, for van Royen's philosophy did not allow him to employ others for the composition or presswork as most of these other private presses did; except for the binding all the work in the production of his books was done by himself, and his official duties at the Post Office left him little time. There was a *Villon* in 1926 (with splendid red and blue initials, the printing of which was very highly praised by St. John Hornby), Arthur van Schenel's *Maneschijn* in 1927, Péguy's *La Tapisserie de Notre Dame* in 1929 (Illus. 70), and then no more until the early 1940s. Under the German occupation, he printed a few small pieces (such as the Ninety-third Psalm) for circulation to friends, and a book, P. C. Boutens's *In den Keerking,* which he completed on March 1, 1942. Four days later van Royen was arrested by the Germans; he died in the concentration camp at Amersfoort three months later. His press and equipment were hidden by friends and colleagues to prevent confiscation. After remaining in storage for some 20 years, in 1964 van Royen's workshop was carefully reconstructed in the former coach house of the Rijksmuseum Meermanno-Westreenianum (that most attractive of all "museums of the book" in The Hague).

The work of De Zilverdistel and of the Kunera Pers, although exquisite of its kind and very highly praised abroad, has never met with unanimous approval in its native land. Jan van Krimpen, a purist among typographers if ever there was one, and whose criticism was as frankly expressed as it was without malice, described its work as "bibelot" books, and van Royen as a printer of "modern incunabula." S. H. de Roos was more complimentary. The books, he believed, were among the finest made either in the Netherlands or abroad; but de Roos shared some of van Royen's romanticism, and between 1926 and 1935 he ran the second Dutch press in the Kelmscott-Doves tradition, the Heuvelpers. He designed a special type (the Meidoorn type) for the press in 1928 (Illus. 71) and printed several books, such as Spinoza's *Tractatus Politicus* and Fromentin's *Les Maîtres d'Autrefois,* which were closely in the old tradition. He did all the setting and printing himself. The economic crisis of the early thirties, which killed so many private presses in England and the United States, compelled de Roos to end his work, and in 1935 he disposed of the type to J. F. Duwaer en Zonen of Amsterdam. He was in fact to use it once more after his retirement from the Typefoundry Amsterdam in 1941, in Jacques Perk's *Eene Helle- und Hemelvaart,* published as one of the clandestine

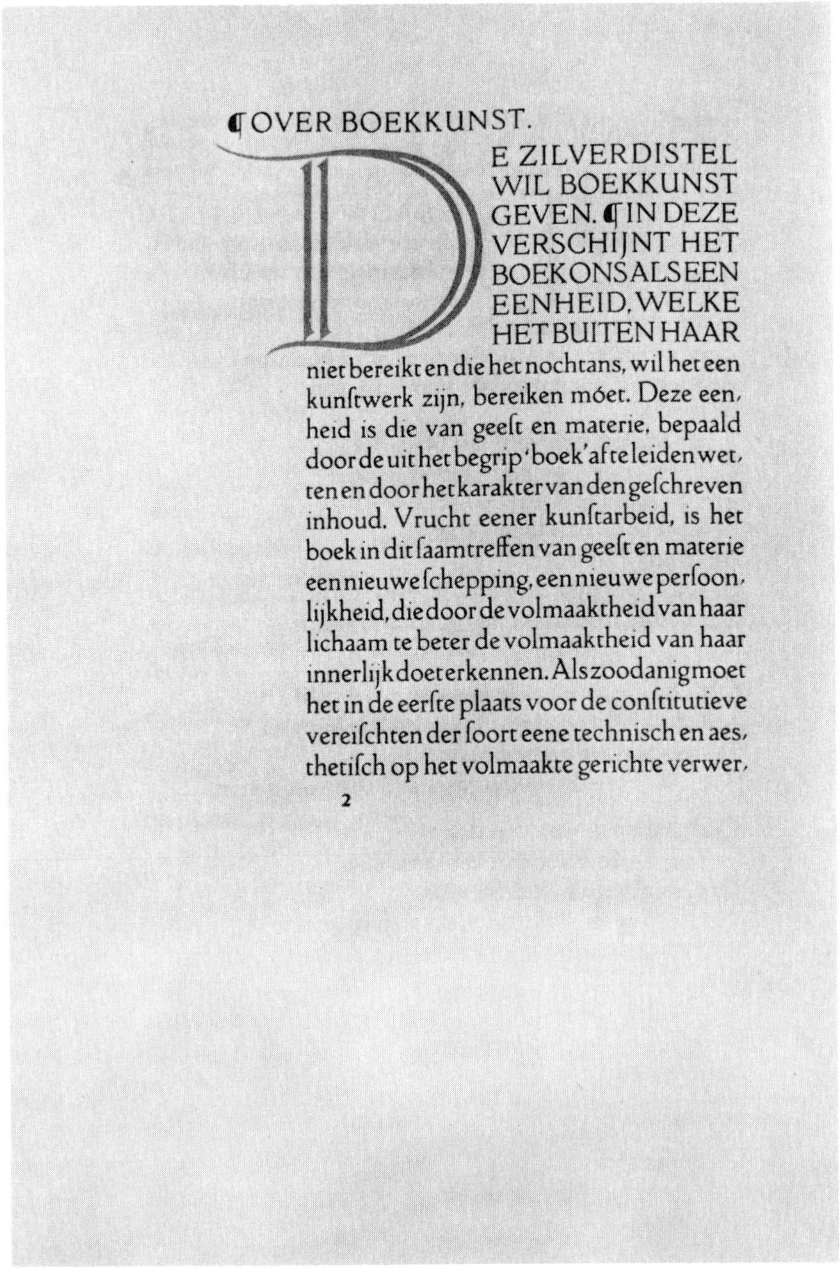

¶OVER BOEKKUNST.

DE ZILVERDISTEL
WIL BOEKKUNST
GEVEN. ¶IN DEZE
VERSCHIJNT HET
BOEKONSALSEEN
EENHEID, WELKE
HET BUITEN HAAR
niet bereikt en die het nochtans, wil het een
kunſtwerk zijn, bereiken móet. Deze een,
heid is die van geeſt en materie, bepaald
door de uit het begrip 'boek' af te leiden wet,
ten en door het karakter van den geſchreven
inhoud. Vrucht eener kunſtarbeid, is het
boek in dit ſaamtreffen van geeſt en materie
een nieuwe ſchepping, een nieuwe perſoon,
lijkheid, die door de volmaaktheid van haar
lichaam te beter de volmaaktheid van haar
innerlijk doet erkennen. Als zoodanig moet
het in de eerſte plaats voor de conſtitutieve
vereiſchten der ſoort eene technisch en aes,
thetiſch op het volmaakte gerichte verwer,

2

ILLUS. 69. De Zilverdistel, Netherlands. Opening from *Over Boekkunst*, 1916, showing S. H. de Roos's version of Jenson's roman in the Zilvertype.

editions of A. A. Balkema's Five Pound Press in 1943. G. W. Ovink wrote of the work of van Royen and de Roos:

> As books they had sometimes many, sometimes few merits. As models in a period when one has to produce with machine paper and machine composition on cylinder presses with automatic feeding, they were valueless. . . . Only as examples of striving after beauty without compromise could they inspire those who . . . hoped to raise the standards of the commercial book.

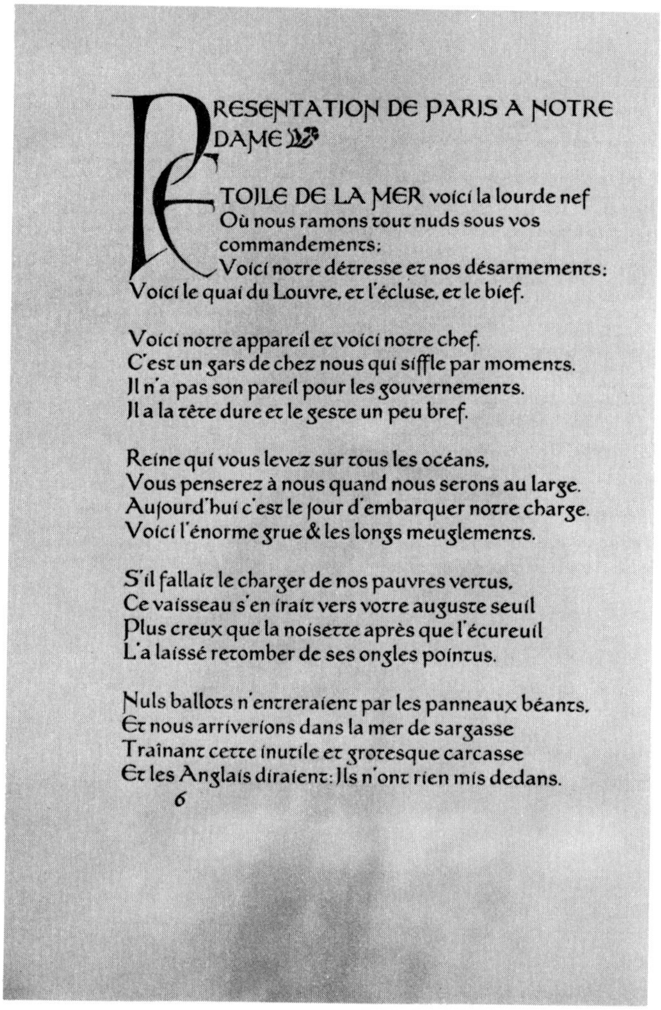

PRESENTATION DE PARIS A NOTRE
DAME ⸎

ETOILE DE LA MER voici la lourde nef
Où nous ramons tout nuds sous vos
commandements;
Voici notre détresse et nos désarmements;
Voici le quai du Louvre, et l'écluse, et le bief.

Voici notre appareil et voici notre chef.
C'est un gars de chez nous qui siffle par moments.
Il n'a pas son pareil pour les gouvernements.
Il a la tête dure et le geste un peu bref.

Reine qui vous levez sur tous les océans,
Vous penserez à nous quand nous serons au large.
Aujourd'hui c'est le jour d'embarquer notre charge.
Voici l'énorme grue & les longs meuglements.

S'il fallait le charger de nos pauvres vertus,
Ce vaisseau s'en irait vers votre auguste seuil
Plus creux que la noisette après que l'écureuil
L'a laissé retomber de ses ongles pointus.

Nuls ballots n'entreraient par les panneaux béants,
Et nous arriverions dans la mer de sargasse
Trainant cette inutile et grotesque carcasse
Et les Anglais diraient: Ils n'ont rien mis dedans.
6

ILLUS. 70. Kunera Pers, Netherlands. Page from *La Tapisserie de Notre Dame*, 1929, set in the Distel type designed by Lucien Pissarro for De Zilverdistel.

As examples, their work was indeed far less valuable than the work of those who followed the original Zilverdistel pattern of commissioning good commercial printers: Jan van Krimpen with his Palladium Editions, or A. A. M. Stols's Trajectum ad Mosam series, for instance. But these are beyond our scope.

Of all the private presses set up on the continent between the wars the greatest, as well as the longest lived, has undoubtedly been the Officina Bodoni. Named for Giambattista Bodoni, the great eighteenth-century Parma printer, it was founded in Rome in 1922 by Hans Mardersteig (1892–1977).

Mardersteig came of a well-to-do family with a background in the fine arts in Weimar. Among the many distinguished visitors at his home Count Kessler must be singled out as a significant influence. His parents' ideas on education were advanced: as well as formal university study in law and art history he was encouraged to develop manual skills by working with carpenters, printers, and other skilled craftsmen. A few months' voluntary "apprenticeship" at the Officina Serpentis formed Mardersteig's only formal introduction to the craft of printing, but its style, methods, and typefaces were not to his taste and had no influence on his work.

Compelled by tuberculosis to move to Switzerland, Mardersteig's first interest was in the fine arts. In 1917 he organized an exhibition of the German Expressionists in Zurich, and then returning

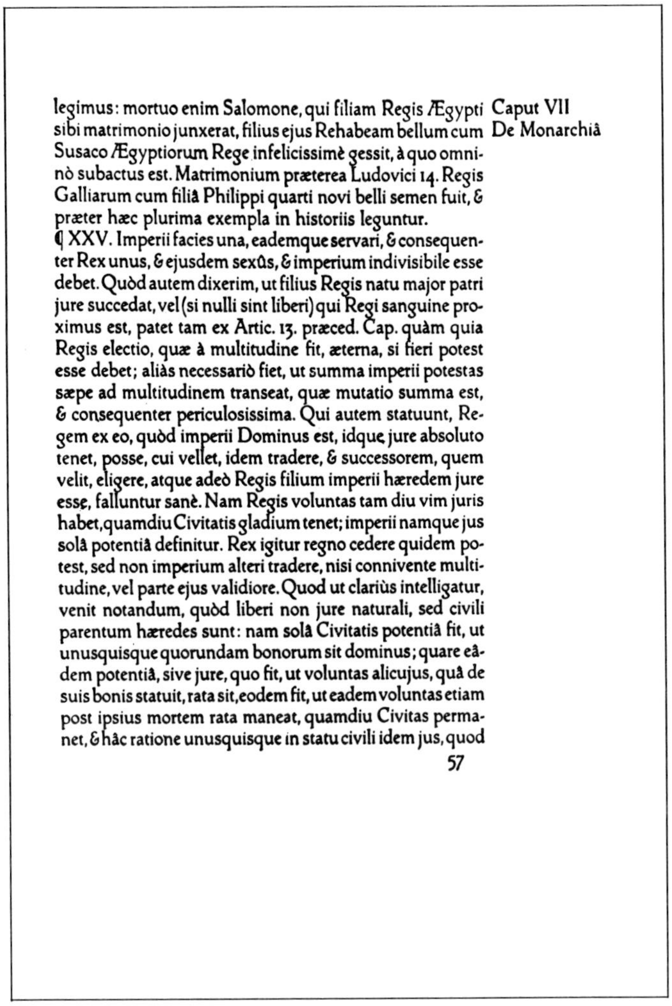

legimus: mortuo enim Salomone, qui filiam Regis Ægypti Caput VII
sibi matrimonio junxerat, filius ejus Rehabeam bellum cum De Monarchiâ
Susaco Ægyptiorum Rege infelicissimè gessit, à quo omni-
nò subactus est. Matrimonium præterea Ludovici 14. Regis
Galliarum cum filiâ Philippi quarti novi belli semen fuit, &
præter hæc plurima exempla in historiis leguntur.
¶ XXV. Imperii facies una, eademque servari, & consequenter Rex unus, & ejusdem sexûs, & imperium indivisibile esse
debet. Quòd autem dixerim, ut filius Regis natu major patri
jure succedat, vel (si nulli sint liberi) qui Regi sanguine pro-
ximus est, patet tam ex Artic. 13. præced. Cap. quàm quia
Regis electio, quæ à multitudine fit, æterna, si fieri potest
esse debet; aliàs necessariò fiet, ut summa imperii potestas
sæpe ad multitudinem transeat, quæ mutatio summa est,
& consequenter periculosissima. Qui autem statuunt, Re-
gem ex eo, quòd imperii Dominus est, idque jure absoluto
tenet, posse, cui vellet, idem tradere, & successorem, quem
velit, eligere, atque adeò Regis filium imperii hæredem jure
esse, falluntur sanè. Nam Regis voluntas tam diu vim juris
habet, quamdiu Civitatis gladium tenet; imperii namque jus
solâ potentiâ definitur. Rex igitur regno cedere quidem potest, sed non imperium alteri tradere, nisi connivente multitudine, vel parte ejus validiore. Quod ut clariùs intelligatur,
venit notandum, quòd liberi non jure naturali, sed civili
parentum hæredes sunt: nam solâ Civitatis potentiâ fit, ut
unusquisque quorundam bonorum sit dominus; quare eâ-
dem potentiâ, sive jure, quo fit, ut voluntas alicujus, quâ de
suis bonis statuit, rata sit, eodem fit, ut eadem voluntas etiam
post ipsius mortem rata maneat, quamdiu Civitas perma-
net, & hâc ratione unusquisque in statu civili idem jus, quod
57

ILLUS. 71. Heuvelpers, Netherlands.
Page set in S. H. de Roos's
Meidoorn type, 1929.

to Germany he became one of the editors and the typographic designer of an art journal, *Genius*, which was published by the Kurt Wolff Verlag in Leipzig. At the end of World War I good materials and workmanship were hard to find, and Mardersteig's experience with *Genius* led him steadily in the direction of a private press of his own, as he concluded that the best work could be achieved only when editing, design, printing, and binding were under the control and close supervision of a single person. Among those who worked with him in Leipzig was a bookbinder named Demeter who had previously worked for Cobden-Sanderson, and this further exposure to the Doves Press influence was significant. When Mardersteig's health compelled him to move south in 1922, Demeter was of great help to him in setting up his own private press at Montagnola near Lugano.

Mardersteig's press had another source of inspiration, Giambattista Bodoni, the great eighteenth-century printer and punch cutter of Parma. Mardersteig had become acquainted with Bodoni's work as a student while browsing through an antiquarian bookseller's stock, and he acquired a small collection of Bodoni's books. Subsequently, when at Leipzig, he came across Walbaum's types and traced their descent from those of Bodoni. This discovery strengthened his growing belief that Bodoni's modern face types, rather than the somewhat archaic and anachronistic faces cut for the English private presses, were those he should use. With the help of an Italian friend who shared his enthusiasm for Bodoni he obtained permission from the Italian government to make fresh castings for some of Bodoni's faces from the original matrices that survived in the Biblioteca Palatina at Parma.

A taste for neoclassical typography rather than quattrocento printing might seem to have put Mardersteig as far from the ideas of the Arts and Crafts Movement as it was possible to get: Had not William Morris written of "the sweltering hideousness of the Bodoni letter, the most illegible type that was ever cut?" Nevertheless, Mardersteig's view of the printer's task reveals that there was not so much distance from them. In *Ein Leben den Büchern Gewidmet,* an address given at the first award of the Gutenberg Prize in Mainz in 1968, he defined these tasks as: (1) service to the author, by seeking out the form best suited to his subject; (2) service to the reader, by making reading as pleasant and easy as possible; and (3) giving the whole book an attractive appearance, without obtruding the printer's own personality or idiosyncrasies. The interpretation of these tasks through the medium of the handpress (through which alone, Mardersteig believed, the greater subtlety of impression and closest attention to detail could be obtained), meant that the work of the Officina Bodoni represented an important development from the printers of the Private Press Movement.

Mardersteig's typographic adventure lasted a lifetime rather than the few years of Kelmscott or Doves, or the spare-time activity of Ashendene; and he was to be not just artist-printer but also scholar-printer. Although he shared the spirit of handicraft that drove Morris, it was not marred by quasi-medieval romanticism; his quest for perfection was as earnest as Cobden-Sanderson's, but he was not obsessed by a vision of "the ideal book," recognizing that different forms and styles of presentation are necessary.

For the first few years of the Officina Bodoni's work at Montagnola, Mardersteig used only Bodoni types. From the start the Officina Bodoni books were "of impeccable quality—there were no preliminary falterings," as John Dreyfus observed; this success did not come without trouble. To satisfy himself that the work was of satisfactory quality 4 small books were printed in editions of 5 to 25 copies before any were prepared for public consumption. It was a wise precaution; for the first of these proofs, Goethe's *Urworte Orphisch,* printed on dampened paper produced a dot in the counter of the lowercase "e" caused by a defect in the casting that dry printing did not reveal.

Mardersteig's perfectionism paid off. The publications of the Officina Bodoni—with faultless presswork on papers from France, Italy, Germany, and Holland, and with a few copies on vellum obtained from Henry Band of Brentford (Morris's old suppliers)—attracted favorable attention throughout Europe. When only four books had been published the novelist Hermann Hesse wrote a rave review (if that is an apt description of a very perceptive account) in the *Neue Zürcher Zeitung,* and very soon afterwards Stanley Morison paid a first visit to the press. From this contact, which was to ripen into a close friendship, came one development at the Officina Bodoni: the production of several books employing Frederic Warde's reinterpretation of Lodovico degli Arrighi's superb chancery italic faces, in the first of the books on calligraphy and typography that were to form a small but significant part of the press's output.

In collaboration with Frederic Warde, Mardersteig contemplated a move to Florence and in 1926 had got as far as proofing a prospectus for an "Academia Typographica" they planned to set up there. When he moved to Italy in 1927, however, it was to Verona and for a very different purpose. He had won a limited competition organized by the Italian government for producing the national edition of the works of Gabriel d'Annunzio, and it was stipulated that it must be printed on Italian soil.

With this move, the first phase of the Officina Bodoni came to an end. In the five years it had been publishing it had produced 10 books under its own imprint, and a further 11 commissioned by other publishers—John Holroyd Reece's Pegasus Press and Frederic Warde in Paris, Elkin Mathews

& Marrot in London, and Mondadori in Verona. The books had ranged widely in nature and language, from Michelangelo's *Poesie* (1923) to Walpole's *Hieroglyphic Tales* (1926); works appeared in Latin, French, German, Italian, and English. The designs and formats varied considerably, and although in Goethe's *Das Römische Carneval* (1924) Mardersteig had skated perilously close to "period typography," his skill then (and subsequently) was such that the design never degenerated into pastiche.

The purist could argue that with more than half of its output being for other publishers the Officina Bodoni was from the start not a private press but a commercial undertaking, yet a less appropriate description for Mardersteig's undertaking would be hard to find. Typographically the work was up to Bodoni's original standards, and textually it was far superior, for much of Bodoni's textual work had been as poor as the calligraphic masterpieces of the fifteenth century. Mardersteig's care with his texts ensured that his reputation was not derived only from the excellence of his printing.

Production of d'Annunzio's *Opere* was no slight undertaking. There were to be 49 quarto volumes, many of 500 pages or more, all hand set in the Bodoni types. They presented many difficult

---

ALFRED DE MUSSET · LES NUITS

ORIGINAL FRENCH TEXT. FIVE COPIES ON VELLUM, 225 ON HAND-MADE WOVE PAPER FROM THE DU MARAIS PAPER-MILLS. TYPE, BODONI, 16 AND 20 PT ITALIC. QUARTO, PP. 56. SEPTEMBER 1924.

    A. On vellum, bound in red morocco.
    B. On paper, bound in red oasis morocco.
    C. On paper, bound in vellum.
    D. On paper, linen binding, uncut.

Alfred de Musset's love affair with George Sand left a deep impression on his life. He never quite recovered from the breach with this woman once so passionately loved. From the bitterness of his complete disillusion there resulted a series of poems, written at long intervals, but forming a complete cycle: Les Nuits. De Musset's brother was able to give the following account of the inner circumstances in which the first poem of the cycle was written.

Un soir de printemps, en revenant d'une promenade à pied, Alfred me récita les deux premiers couplets du dialogue entre la muse et le poète, qu'il venait de composer sous les marronniers des Tuileries. Il travailla sans interruption jusqu'au matin. Lorsqu'il parut à déjeuner, je ne remarquai sur son visage aucun signe de fatigue. Il avait comme Fantasio le mois de mai sur les joues. La muse le possédait. Pendant la journée, il mena de front la conversation et le travail, comme ces joueurs d'échecs qui jouent deux parties à la fois. Par moments, il nous quittait pour aller écrire une dizaine de vers et revenait causer encore. Mais le soir il retourna au travail comme à un rendez-vous d'amour. Il se fit servir un petit souper dans sa chambre. Volontiers, il aurait demandé deux couverts afin que la muse y eût sa place marquée. Tous les flambeaux furent mis à contribution; il alluma douze bougies. Les gens de la maison, voyant cette illumination, durent penser qu'il donnait un

56

La Muse

Poète, prends ton luth, et me donne un baiser;
La fleur de l'églantier sent ses bourgeons éclore.
Le printemps naît ce soir; les vents vont s'embraser;
Et la bergeronnette, en attendant l'aurore,
Aux premiers buissons verts commence à se poser.
Poète, prends ton luth, et me donne un baiser.

Le Poète

Comme il fait noir dans la vallée!
J'ai cru qu'une forme voilée
Flottait là-bas sur la forêt.
Elle sortait de la prairie;
Son pied rasait l'herbe fleurie;
C'est une étrange rêverie;
Elle s'efface et disparaît.

La Muse

Poète, prends ton luth; la nuit, sur la pelouse,
Balance le zéphyr dans son voile odorant.
La rose, vierge encor, se referme jalouse
Sur le frelon nacré qu'elle enivre en mourant.
Écoute! tout se tait; songe à ta bien-aimée.
Ce soir, sous les tilleuls, à la sombre ramée

ILLUS. 72. Officina Bodoni, Italy. Opening from Mardersteig's *The Officina Bodoni*, 1929, showing his use of Bodoni types in de Musset's *Les Nuits*.

problems in the layout of the verse, but in one respect Mardersteig gained what every typographer hopes for—the confidence of the poet, who responded to all his typographic suggestions:

> I once showed him the first page of one of his texts on which an abundance of commas created a confusing effect, and I asked him to eliminate some. He looked at the sheet, paused for a moment, and agreed—"Via con questi vermicelli!" [Away with these worms!] It was difficult to prevent him from removing every comma.

For the National Edition, 218 copies were printed on Japanese vellum and 9 on vellum on the handpress; 2,501 more were printed by machine on handmade Fabriano paper. For this mammoth undertaking the handpress was installed in special premises in Arnaldo Mondadori's printing house (echoing the procedures of the Vale Press) and there the volumes were worked off under the constant care of Mardersteig and Remo Mondadori. Use of Bodoni's faces on the powered presses was difficult because of the wear on the sharp serifs, and it proved necessary to stop the presses every few hundred copies to change the worn sorts. For some particularly fragile letters Mardersteig had more resistant recuttings undertaken by the Paris punch cutter Charles Malin—a real test of his skill, which he passed with flying colors, as even Mardersteig could not distinguish between his sorts and Bodoni's originals when printed.

Scarcely surprisingly, the edition of d'Annunzio occupied the Officina Bodoni pretty fully until it was completed in 1936. From 1930 to 1932 only four other books were printed, and none from 1933 to 1935. But Mardersteig was not standing still. He was experimenting with the use of other faces that had become available from founders or Monotype—Poliphilus, Baskerville, Garamond, Janson—had designed the Fontana face that Monotype cut for the Collins Cleartype Press in Glasgow (where he spent a year in 1935–1936), and, in conjunction with Charles Malin, was working on the first of his own proprietary types to be used. At the same time, he expanded the scope of his printing house considerably by adding handpresses for intaglio and lithographic work, so that when the Officina Bodoni resumed its production of hand-printed books in 1936 many were illustrated by modern artists of the caliber of Franz Masereel, Fritz Kredel, Gunter Böhmer, and Francesco Messina.

As before, many of its books were commissioned by discerning clients; a number for sale but a good many being private editions that were never put on the market. For all these, as for those it published itself, the Officina Bodoni remained true to its own ideals and standards. To be sure, one or two of the private commissions took the concept of the limited edition to the lengths dreamed of by Des Esseintes in *A Rebours:* Berto Barbarini's *San Zen che ride* (1938) and Kenneth Graham's *The Reluctant Dragon* (1941) were limited to a single copy of each. In countenancing this mad logic Mardersteig was at fault; the deliberate manufacture of rarities, the misuse of the printing press in what should be the sphere of the calligrapher, is strangely in contradiction of the main thrust of his work.

Handsome though the books printed on commission were, those published by the Officina Bodoni itself frequently surpassed them. In particular the press's texts with "early illustrations" are important. They had their origin in a visit Fritz Kredel paid to Verona in 1938 shortly before he emigrated to America. Together they discussed the woodcuts used in some fifteenth-century books and embarked on experiments in which Kredel recut blocks following the original designs closely. The results were so successful, so very much better than photoengraved copies can ever be, that they embarked on a recutting of Bartolommeo di Giovanni's fifteenth-century cuts that had survived only in inferior sixteenth-century reprints. Kredel's recutting for Boccaccio's *Il Ninfale Fiesolano,* which

second of the three miracles. The third was
the healing of Gallienus' daughter, whose
body the demon vacated amidst much clam-
our at the Saint's command. When the
grateful Gallienus presented San Zeno with
a valuable crown, the Saint at once broke
it into small pieces which he distributed
among the poor. Nevertheless, a demon who
had twice offered resistance could not be
allowed to go unpunished; San Zeno therefore compelled him to carry from Rome to
Verona a large porphyry basin, another gift
of the Emperor. This task the demon accomplished in an instant, but in his fury
he scratched the surface of the stone; the

11

ILLUS. 73. Officina Bodoni,
Italy. The Zeno type.

was published in an Italian edition in 1940, was as successful as it was ambitious. An edition of an
Elizabethan translation, *The Nymphs of Fiesole*, appeared in 1952.

Still more ambitious was the edition of Terence's play *Andria* for which Mardersteig and Kredel
started planning in 1939. With this they were to work from the Basle Kunstmuseum's set of Albrecht
Dürer's drawings on wood, which were made about 1492 for an edition planned by the Basle printer
Johann Amerbach, but never published. Although a few of these had then been cut, most of them
remained as Dürer had left them. World War II prevented early realization of their plans, and it was
not until 1971 that the Officina Bodoni editions of the play appeared. There were three versions: an
Elizabethan English translation, the Italian version of Macchiavelli, and a German text by Felix
Mendelssohn.

This practice of issuing Officina Bodoni books in a number of different language editions was
employed for some of the press's other work in which early woodcuts were recut by contemporary
artists, notably in *The Holy Gospels* (English 1962; Latin and Italian 1963). Parallel editions were also

published of some other works, including Felice Feliciano's *Alphabetum Romanum* (Illus. 74) in English, German, and Italian (1960), Sophocles' *King Oedipus* in English and Italian (1968)—incidentally one of the press's books with fine original illustrations by a contemporary artist, Giacomo Manzù—and Cardinal Bembo's *De Aetna* in English, German, and Italian, with the original Latin (1969). To celebrate the fiftieth anniversary of the establishment of his press, in 1973 Mardersteig published a very fine *Aesop,* with Latin, Italian, and English versions of the fables within the single edition. For this reinterpretation of the Veronese edition of 1479, the woodcuts were recut by Anna Bramanti and printed in two forms in different volumes, in black and white and, in the other, hand-colored after the excellent copy of the original in the British Museum—a copy that Mardersteig believed was colored by the original designer of the cuts.

To mention all the important or attractive Officina Bodoni editions would demand a catalogue of all its works. As has been indicated above, not only did the press weather the difficult war years (thanks in part to the commissions of I Cento Amici del Libro in Florence, all of whose work was

Suole l'usanza antiqua cauare la littera di tondo e quadro, la summa de le qual forme ascende al n. lij, del qual si caua il numero perfecto che è X. E cossì uol esser la tua littera grossa la X^a. parte de l'alteza et per questo modo hauerà tanto del tondo quanto del quadro; et uolsi causare la soprascripta littera doue si tagliano le linie .x. con la circonferentia. Et questo è quanto per misura io, Felice Feliciano, habia nelle antique caractere ritrouato per molte pietre marmoree, cossì ne l'alma Roma quanto negli altri [luoghi].

ILLUS. 74. Officina Bodoni, Italy. Page from Felice Feliciano, 1960, showing use of Mardersteig's Dante type.

ILLUS. 75A. Mimmo Guelfi, Genoa, Italy. *Pervigilium Veneris,* 1972. Fine work from a contemporary Italian private press.

ILLUS. 75B. Mimmo Guelfi, Genoa, Italy. *Pervigilium Veneris,* 1972. Binding.

printed by Mardersteig from 1939 to 1974), it went on to produce far finer works, and its most successful and productive years came at a time when most men have retired. Mardersteig's work at the Officina Bodoni was, as Will Carter has said, that of "probably the finest pressman the world has ever seen or is ever likely to see." But his influence was not simply through the handpress; in 1948 he founded the Stamperia Valdonega alongside the Officina Bodoni in order to make finely printed editions available to a larger number of readers at a lower price. Working closely in collaboration with the Officina, its bread-and-butter has been the excellent series of Ricciardi classics, which (as might be expected from Mardersteig) are as distinguished for the quality of their texts as their printing. Fine examples of the work of the Stamperia (now under the direction of Mardersteig's son Martino) can be seen in the catalogues of the Officina Bodoni exhibitions held in the British Museum in 1954 and 10 years later in the Royal Libraries in Brussels and The Hague.

Chapter 15

BETWEEN THE WARS IN BRITAIN I: THE GREAT PRESSES

WORLD WAR I PROVIDES a traditional and fairly convenient division between the first generation of English private presses in the Arts and Crafts Movement and the rather different style of fine printing that flourished in the twenties and thirties. Most of the major presses had come to a halt before 1914, and when the war came, Eragny was killed and work at Ashendene was suspended; only at the Doves Press did work continue.

Other newer promising ventures were stopped by the outbreak of hostilities; the most promising was Flying Fame, the publishing title chosen in 1912 by Claud Lovat Fraser, Ralph Hodgson, and Holbrook Jackson for a series of broadsheets and chapbooks that rapidly won a high reputation (Illus. 76). As John Russell Taylor has so aptly put it, Lovat Fraser's work had "a style which is somehow none the less charming for all its evident determination to charm," and his private press ventures had an informal gaiety that contrasted with the high seriousness of Doves or Ashendene.

The changes between these generations of private printers did not coincide with the war. In the 1890s the Dutch writers Jan Kalf and L. Simons had objected that the archaic and slow Kelmscott methods could not be a guide to the everyday production of printed matter of good quality. Before the twentieth century was into its teens a period of development and consolidation in printing methods (especially in process engraving and in machine composition) was over, and there was emerging a generation of printers and typographers who were considerably less under the glamor of the Private Press Movement than those of a few years earlier. The lamentably short-lived journal, *The Imprint,* in 1913, was intended primarily to interpret the private press gospel in practical terms for the commercial printer. To have a special type cut was within the tradition, but *The Imprint* type was a reformed and regularized version of the Caslon design undertaken by J. H. Mason and Gerard Meynell to suit the needs of mechanical setting and of printing on machine-made papers on powered presses. By making the face generally available for Monotype composition, *The Imprint* group was taking an important first step in this interpretation. The coming of the war delayed further moves of this kind.

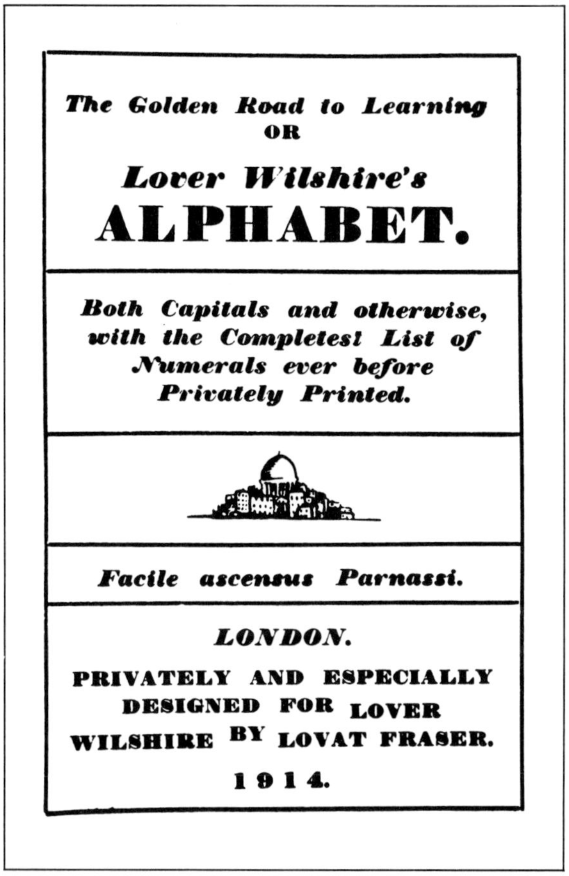

The Golden Road to Learning
OR
Lover Wilshire's
ALPHABET.

Both Capitals and otherwise,
with the Completest List of
Numerals ever before
Privately Printed.

Facile ascensus Parnassi.

LONDON.
PRIVATELY AND ESPECIALLY
DESIGNED FOR LOVER
WILSHIRE BY LOVAT FRASER.
1914.

ILLUS. 76. An example of Lovat Fraser's work; remarkably early use of modern-face types.

There were, of course, to be a few ventures in the private press field between 1914 and 1918. One that is of interest is the Mall Press, operated by Emery Walker and Bruce Rogers, who in 1916 came to London from America to work at it. Only one book was produced, an English translation of Albrecht Dürer's *Of the Just Shaping of Letters,* of which 315 copies on paper and 3 on vellum were printed for the Grolier Club in 1917. Set in Centaur, the version of Jenson's roman types which Rogers had designed and Robert Wiebking cut two years earlier, the book was to prove rather a labor for Rogers and to demonstrate how difficult the times were for these ventures. Rogers professed "a lack of enthusiasm for the printer's craft *as* a craft, a distaste for printer's ink"; but when the Mall Press's one workman was conscripted into the army, Rogers had to make ready and print the book himself. Being a thoroughgoing Yankee he succeeded splendidly, but continuation beyond one book was not practicable. When the syndics of Cambridge University Press invited him to become the press's typographic adviser, at the instigation of Sydney Cockerell (then director of the Fitzwilliam Museum), Rogers quickly agreed. A second book was to result from his collaboration with Emery Walker many years afterwards, T. E. Lawrence's translation of the *Odyssey* published in 1932.

The first fruit of what was to be a very much richer harvest than this had come from the Romney Street Press in 1915. Francis Meynell (1891–1975) was from a family that had many links with the newer movements in printing. His cousin Gerard Meynell has already been mentioned; his mother was the poet Alice Meynell, his father Wilfred, the managing director of the Catholic publishers Burns & Oates, which produced work of distinctive quality; and his brother Everard was to publish some of Lovat Fraser's work during the war years. Having grown up in an atmosphere in which literature and the practicalities of printing were entwined, in 1913 Francis started his career at Burns & Oates, where he was soon joined by the young Stanley Morison who had earlier abandoned work as a bank clerk to join Gerard Meynell on *The Imprint.*

In 1914 Francis Meynell had purchased a handpress as a personal venture, distinct from his regular work; he kept it in his dining room in Romney Street. Like C. H. O. Daniel and St. John Hornby before him, he negotiated with the Delegates of Oxford University Press for some of the Fell types, which were released to him on condition that the type could be recalled if they felt he was misusing it. In 1915 he issued a prospectus; years later he said he regarded it "with mixed feelings of shame and admiration at my audacity; for if ever there was a goldbrick prospectus this was one." This was how it read:

> The Romney Street Press at 67 Romney Street, Westminster, has been set up
> for the better and unaffected production of Books, & Pamphlets, & single
> sheets of poetry. The type of the Press (used for this Prospectus) is the finest of
> the series imported from Holland in about 1660 by Bishop Fell for the Oxford
> University Press, by whose courtesy it is now used. The editions of the Romney
> Street Press will be limited to a maximum of fifty copies. The preliminary costs
> of equipment amount to £40, & Francis Meynell, the Director of the Press,
> invites subscriptions to cover this amount.
>
> Subscribers will have first call upon the publications of the Press at cost
> price up to the amount of their subscriptions.
>
> The first publications will be seven poems by Alice Meynell, written since
> the issue of the Collected Poems. There will follow Mary Cary [sic], the
> meditations, occasional poems and spiritual diary of the wife of a Cromwellian
> captain, now first published, from her Ms. Note-book; & Love in Dian's Lap,
> by Francis Thompson. But the process of production will be but slow.
> Suggestions for other books, particularly of seventeenth century reference, will
> be welcome.

Although three books were announced, only two were produced—*Ten Poems* by Alice Meynell in December 1915 (for which Edward Johnston wrote in the initials in each poem) and Mary Carey's *Meditations,* which were printed on Japanese vellum and issued in 1918 (an earlier impression of this, which Meynell had printed on handmade paper in 1917, was never issued because the presswork proved unsatisfactory). Despite the persuasiveness of the prospectus, there were no general subscriptions to the press, and the 50 copies of the two books published were sold only with great difficulty. Disheartened with this reception and finding the single-handed production of the books irksome, Meynell discontinued his private printing and instead concentrated his attention on building up the Pelican Press, which, with the help of George Lansbury, he had started in 1916 as an offshoot of the Victoria House Publishing Company.

Even with the new movement in presses, William Morris's influence could still make itself felt. The distinguished typographer Oliver Simon wrote, years later, that soon after his demobilization in 1919 it was the chance sight of the Kelmscott Chaucer in a bookseller's window that persuaded him to abandon his vague plans of entering the cotton trade or of taking up forestry: "It was plain to me that I *must* become a printer." He was very fortunate in his employer, the Curwen Press, at which Harold Curwen was commencing the transformation of a small family printing business into the distinguished house it so soon became. Also at Curwen was Bernard Newdigate, himself freshly demobilized. By 1922 Newdigate, Holbrook Jackson, Morison, Meynell, and Simon had formed the

Fleuron Society, which Simon suggested should produce one book a year to demonstrate to collectors and others that books set by machine could be quite as successful aesthetically as the work of the prewar private presses.

The society did not flourish; indeed, it lasted for only two stormy meetings. In view of the praise later heaped on Mardersteig's work at the Officina Bodoni it is somewhat ironic that it was Newdigate's firm belief in the superiority of the handpress that prevented any progress! But from these first discussions came *The Fleuron,* the greatest of all English typographical journals, which Simon and Morison produced together from 1923 to 1930. Newdigate was to follow his own line at the Shakespeare Head Press (discussed in Chapter 16), but it was Francis Meynell who was to follow the Fleuron Society's first ideas at his own press.

Soon after the war had ended he had tried without success to persuade publishers to allow the Pelican Press to print fine editions for them; with the collapse of the Fleuron Society he persuaded David Garnett (at that time a partner in the bookselling firm of Birrell and Garnett) and Vera Mendel to join him in making books "for those among collectors who also use books for reading." The Nonesuch Press was born.

The propriety of their use of the word *press* was questioned by Arnold Bennett and others; for those who attempt to define the term *private press,* Nonesuch remains a stumbling block. It was not a press in the Arts and Crafts tradition of Kelmscott or Doves, with all the work being done by hand under the direct personal supervision of the owner. It was not even to make special use of the

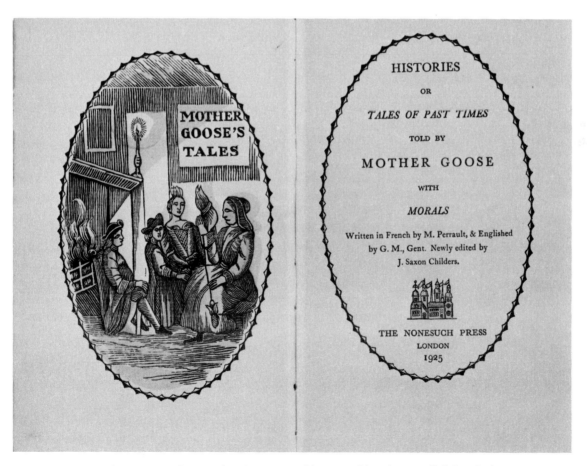

ILLUS. 77. Nonesuch Press, London. *Mother Goose,* 1925. Title page with color-stenciled frontispiece.

resources of a single commercial printer, as Ricketts had used the Ballantyne Press for the Vale books, or Robert Bridges had employed Oxford University Press for the *Yattendon Hymnal*. Instead, as Meynell wrote in *The Nonesuch Century* (1936), its stock in trade was "the theory that mechanical means could be made to serve fine ends; that the machine in printing was a controllable tool. Therefore we set out to be mobilisers of other people's resources; to be designers, specifiers, rather than manufacturers; architects of books rather than builders." Accordingly books were printed for Nonesuch by good commercial printers—by the Kynoch Press, the Curwen Press, by T. & A. Constable, by the two university presses, by Joh. Enschedé en Zonen and others—in order to exploit the various skills and the wide range of excellent typographical material that was becoming available and that no single printing house could possess no matter its size. In this Nonesuch was doing no more than any commercial publisher might. Where it differed from the commercial publishers of the time (apart from doing it better than they) was in its possession of a small printing plant of its own, on which experimental pages for the press's books were printed as a part of the process of designing them before the production was finally handed over to a commercial firm. Whole books were composed on the premises in Janson types, of which Nonesuch was then the only English possessor, and on occasion the press printed its books as well, in the delightful volume of Thomas Beedome's *Select Poems* (1928) for example (Illus. 78 and 79).

In such works as this, Nonesuch was adhering strictly to the tradition of Doves or Ashendene. In the books commissioned from commercial firms the perfectionism of the private press spirit was certainly predominant; for one book printed by R. & R. Clark 37 different title pages were set up before Meynell was satisfied. William Maxwell, the manager of R. & R. Clark, commented that he didn't mind "losing" money on the text of Nonesuch books because he always recovered it on the title page! But none of the printers employed by Meynell minded "losing" in this way; the challenge presented by the work, and the prestige and sense of achievement obtained from producing books that undoubtedly equaled the work of the prewar private presses fully compensated for the technical difficulties they encountered.

At first the Nonesuch Press operated on a very small scale. Garnett was working full time in his bookshop and Meynell at the Pelican Press; the routine work, from editing texts to sticking stamps on letters, was done by Vera Mendel, who had provided the press's small capital. Nonesuch could very easily have become one of the many short-lived amateur publishing ventures that appeared and rapidly disappeared in the 1920s. That it did not do so was due in part to the skill with which Meynell designed the books; in part to sheer hard work (enlivened by occasional "invoice bees" at which friends were enlisted to write invoices, statements, and the like between drinks), but most of all to the policy of the press in aiming at collectors "who also use books for reading." Unlike so many private and quasi-private presses whose owners had (sometimes) more typographic imagination than literary taste, Nonesuch books were books that had a very good reason for being put into print. They were books that had not previously been published, or of which no editions were in print, or of which the existing editions were inadequate. And though an extraordinary amount of care was lavished on the physical production of Nonesuch editions, no less attention was paid to the editing of the texts. Meynell was not a scholar-printer like Mardersteig or even Newdigate, but in such books as the collected editions of the works of Congreve (1923), Wycherley (1924), and of the other restoration dramatists, in Geoffrey Keynes's editions of Donne and of Blake, the press was to perform a very useful service to the cause of literature.

There were, of course, failures, such as *The Book of Ruth* and Apuleius's *Cupid and Psyche* (both of which Meynell later condemned as being "toy" books in the bad private press tradition). There were frivolities, like Amanda Ros's *Irene Iddesleigh*, printed with a suitable solemn gravity in 1926; or James Laver's splendid mock eighteenth-century verses in *A Stitch in Time* and other slim volumes.

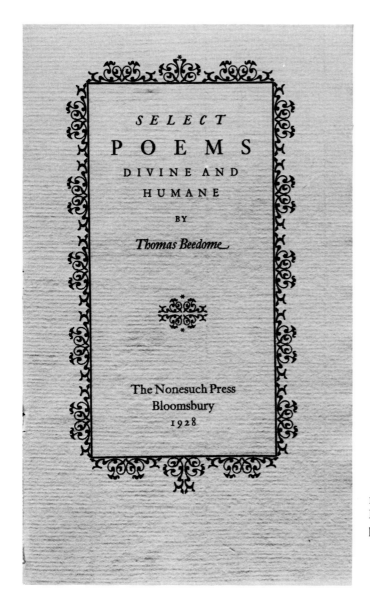

ILLUS. 78. Nonesuch Press, London.
Beedome's *Select Poems*, 1928. Title
page.

The Nonesuch Press never took itself too seriously (as the splendid ebullience of the long series of prospectuses shows), and it is evident that the producers of the books had as much pleasure in their work as the readers were later to receive. One instance of this was related by Sir Francis Meynell at an address he delivered at the opening of the Times Bookshop's exhibition of private press books in 1961–the Reverend Montague Summers, who had edited several of the seventeenth-century dramatists for the press, arriving with his typescript of Rochester's poems:

> I have discovered some hitherto unknown couplets, which are, regrettably, very
> indecent (he announced cheerfully). Fortunately in the original text the most
> opprobrious words are replaced by dashes, but (very cheerfully) I regret
> infinitely to report that these words almost always came at the end of lines and
> therefore (with a joyous chuckle) the rhymes unfortunately indicate the missing
> word!

Although the Nonesuch Press started in such a humble way, the excellence of its work became known, and instead of having to boost sales the partners found themselves in the pleasant position of

EPITAPHS

Epitaphium Regis Swedorum.

Here sleepes hee who was and is
The subject of eternall blisse.

Religion, and no other end,
Caus'd him his blood and means to spend.

He conquer'd all, onely his breath,
He lost, by which he conquer'd death.

Now would'st thou know whom we deplore
'Tis Sweaden, Reader; hush, no more:

Lest while thou read, thou and this stone
Be both alike, by death made one.

For death and griefe are neare of kinne,
So thou might'st die, being griev'd for him.

Cujus memoria sacrata hæc pie flevit:

Tho. Beedome.

30

Epitaphs

An Elegy on the death of the renowned
& victorious *Gustavus Adolphus*,
King of Sweathland.

Can the dry sound, Hee's dead, no more affright
The world with terrour, than had some meane knight,
Languish't to death in downe? or can the sound
That Sweaden hath received a fatall wound
Passe by, and like the bullet, hurt no more
Than his stout brest, that felt the mortall sore?
Oh no! it rankles in each weak'ned part,
And strikes a chill amazement to the heart
Of feeble Christendome, that by his losse,
Puts on it's titles badge, The Christian Crosse:
And 'twas a great one too, yet let none wonder
That heaven forebore to ring his knell in thunder;
Or that some angry Meteor did not stare,
And to the world their publique losse declare.
No, no, some such Ambassador as this
Had beene too mercifull! and made us misse
Our just deserved punishment, for wee
Knowing our sinne begot this misery,
Might by a faign'd repentance have procur'd
A pardon for the Prince: but now assur'd
Of our owne weaknesse, we with teares may say,
We are losers, though our army wonne the day.
His death begot his conquest, and his foes
Mourn'd at his fate, witnesse those death wing'd blows

31

ILLUS. 79. Nonesuch Press, London. Beedome's *Select Poems*, 1928. Double spread.

having to ration orders. In 1925 they moved from their cellar under Birrell and Garnett's shop to new premises in Great James Street, and incorporated the firm legally. Thanks to the quality of their work they were able to continue operations right through the years of the Great Depression, when other presses that seemed equally secure died.

It is almost impossible to give any idea of the richness and variety of the Nonesuch books by word or by illustrations. Almost all were different, for it was Meynell's deliberate policy to avoid anything like a house style (Illus. 81): "I did not want people to be able to say at the first sight of our books 'Oh yes, that must be a Nonesuch book.' I wanted them to say 'That's not a bad-looking book' and then to find it was ours."

The Nonesuch Press was to survive many more years, but its history after it passed into the ownership of George Macy in 1936 belongs to later chapters. For its golden age from 1923 until 1936, *The Nonesuch Century,* published in 1936 as an account of the press's first 100 books, remained until recently the best substitute for handling and reading the books themselves. But it has become a rare book itself, and we are fortunate now to have John Dreyfus's *History of the Nonesuch Press* (1981) as a further memorial to this unique enterprise.

ILLUS. 80. Nonesuch Press, London. Slipcase and title page of *The Courtier's Library*, 1930.

That the Nonesuch Press should prove as important and influential as it did was remarkable. But it is far more remarkable that after Nonesuch the most important English press to grow up in the twenties was the Golden Cockerel Press, for its beginnings were anything but propitious.

Golden Cockerel was founded in 1920 to be a small cooperative venture at which the partners would themselves print new books of literary merit by young authors. There were four partners to start with; the moving spirit being Harold Midgely Taylor, a young man on the fringes of the literary world who provided the premises and capital for the venture. The others were his wife Gay and two other women, Barbara Blackburn and Pran Pyper who had been London flatmates with Gay before her marriage, and who were inspired by Hal Taylor's talk of a literary venture that would allow young writers a chance denied them by the conventional publishing world. There was no thought initially of fine printing: indeed at the time none of the four knew how to print, although Hal Taylor had made the acquaintance of Bruce Rogers at Cambridge and was not without some typographic taste. To learn printing, Hal and Gay spent some months in 1920 working with Hilary Pepler at the St. Dominic's Press in Sussex, so that they would in turn be able to teach the other two, when their venture got under way at the fruit farm Taylor owned at Waltham St. Lawrence in Berkshire. Everything went wrong: under the tenancy laws operating in Britain after the war Taylor could not get possession of his house from the sitting tenants, and the wooden hut in its grounds, which was intended to house the printing plant (a Wharfedale press, binding, and other equipment were installed) had also to house the partners! Neither Barbara nor Pran found the realities of waking at dawn to light the stove (their only source of heat through the bitterly cold winter of 1920–1921) and then setting type with numbed hands to be the exciting creative companionable time they had looked forward to, and they soon dropped out. Fortunately Hal Taylor's contacts had produced some commissions for work for others: the first production being an issue of the literary magazine *Voices* in January 1921 (Illus. 82). He also persuaded a number of new writers of real worth to allow Golden Cockerel to produce their work. In his autobiography *It's Me, O Lord*, A. E. Coppard was later to describe how Taylor bicycled 25 miles across the Berkshire Downs to invite him to join the venture and how his *Adam and Eve and Pinch Me* became the press's first book, eventually completed on All Fool's Day 1921. Coppard helped with the work, "doing some of the printing, folding, pasting, binding and labelling. In the end my eyes were so bedazed by the

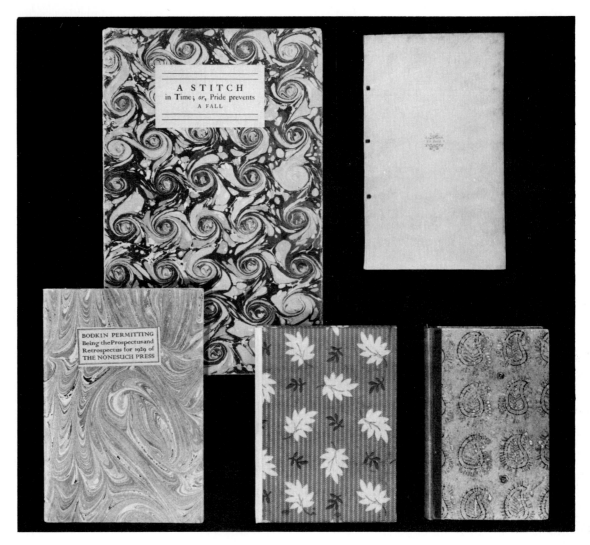

ILLUS. 81. A range of Nonesuch Press bindings.

titlepage that they were blind to the inadequacies of the rest; the type was poor, the paper bad, the leaves fell out, the cover collapsed." Coppard was exaggerating; the book was not as bad as that (although it was anything but fine printing); the standards of the press improved as the printers gained experience. The earliest Golden Cockerel books have importance for their texts, not their production. There was an interesting attempt at an alliance with Will Ransom (who in Chicago printed a fine edition of Golden Cockerel's eighth book, Richard Hughes's *Gipsy Night*), but the alliance could not continue as planned for other titles because neither Ransom nor Taylor had capital to develop in this way. Taylor's tuberculosis, for which he had been released from the army, compelled his return to a sanitorium, and a new direction for the press was vital. The original plans were put aside; pressmen and compositors were engaged and the concentration thereafter was on the production of "fine editions of books of established worth" of which several were to be produced in 1923: *Daphnis and Chloe, The Golden Ass,* and several books by Sir Thomas Browne. A number of others were planned that never appeared, for Hal Taylor's health was rapidly failing; Gay and Coppard maintained a degree of control, but the operation of the press was complicated by the fact that they had embarked on a disastrous love affair. However, the new program of work had proved

10 STORM JAMESON

THE GENIUS OF KATHERINE MANSFIELD*

THERE is none so dull and blind but knows that this world is a Janus-faced spirit. There is none of you but has seen the one face slip aside as a mask slips —suddenly, at a secret touch. You have held a flower in your hand and felt that its life throbbed in your grasp. It answered your heart-beats and joined itself with you in the rhythmic pulse of the universe. And even while it thus became for you the body of the Created, you saw it also as a single flower, with fine tracery of purple veins and secret glowing heart. For one moment you 'held infinity in the palm of your hand.' The moment passed and the mask slipped back, but you did not altogether forget that other face. Thenceforth for you the weakest created thing was a-glow with the power that makes worlds. You stood forever on the verge of that discovery.

For the true artist, as for the true mystic, the mask-like face of creation is always transparent. The eternal mother is revealed through her many coloured garments. It is the artist's privilege that he is able, even though imperfectly, to show us the vision his eyes have seen. He can so draw a blade of grass that it appears a symbol of the universe, and tell the story of an obscure life so that through it humanity is revealed in the immortal aspect of its mortality. He is able to do this because for him the two faces are one: beneath the body that changes and dies he discerns the deathless spirit. He is an accredited citizen of two worlds, and he walks in the world of the spirit with as sure a tread as in the world of material appearances. If he cannot do this he is no true mystic just as he is no true artist.

Neither is he a true and faithful artist if in his efforts to reveal the undying spirit he offers to us a blurred and dishonest picture of the body that perishes. Life is the only vehicle of spirit, and to present a distorted and untruthful picture of life is to destroy its spiritual significance, and to take away from us our only key to the door that opens outwards from the things of time onto the things of eternity. It is therefore a double service that we, in the name of life, ask of the artist: that he should, observing life delicately, present it truthfully; and not truthfully only, but significantly, so that seen through his eyes, the meanest life glows with a sacred fire and we understand that a divine sympathy unites all created things.

The touchstone of genius is then just this power it has of seeing life self-revealed through the inward eye of art, *and of communicating to us the thrill of that revelation.* Mastery over the means of communication—the power to share with us his inspired knowledge—is the unique possession of the artist. Without it, the sensitive gift which he shares with the mystic lacks hand and tongue. He can thrill to his vision of reality but the vision remains his incommunicable experience; he cannot make of himself a channel for the spirit, and the thrill does not pass to us.

The more penetrating an artist's observation of life the finer must be his technique,

Bliss & Other Stories. Constable, 9s. net.
In a German Pension. Constable.

STORM JAMESON 11

lest the music should be marred by his faulty playing. Miss Katherine Mansfield has a technique at once so just and so supple that it responds to every movement of her questing imagination. She plays upon it as a master upon a perfect instrument. No change of mood is lost or blurred. From this subtle instrument she draws a music of terrible poignancy. The listener is compelled to hold his breath lest one of the flawless notes should be missed. So in the story named *Bliss*, Bertha's happiness fills us with a monstrous foreboding. It shines before our eyes like a sharp flame. Its sharpness stabs us as it stabbed Bertha. The moods of her diverse guests are transmitted with the same fine precision: as they reach us through Bertha's quivering apprehension they merge into a harmony through which her secret ecstasy throbs, falling and rising, to its final shattering note.

Beauty, the mortal beauty that passes, unfolds itself at Miss Mansfield's touch. Smiling, it utters the secret at its heart. It shines through her words, forever elusive, escaping the breath of decay. She writes in *The Escape* of a tree, and the tree reveals its singing spirit:

"It was then that he saw the tree, that he was conscious of its presence just inside a garden gate. It was an immense tree with a round, thick silver stem and a great arc of copper leaves that gave back the light and yet were sombre. There was something beyond the tree—a whiteness, a softness, an opaque mass, half-hidden—with delicate pillars. As he looked at the tree he felt his breathing die away and he became part of the silence. It seemed to glow, it seemed to expand in the quivering heat until the great carved leaves hid the sky, and yet it was motionless. . . . Deep, deep, he sank into the silence, staring at the tree and waiting for the voice that came floating, falling, until he felt himself enfolded."

And in *Bliss* there is 'a tall slender pear tree. . . . becalmed against the jade green sky'.

Miss Mansfield's rare technique serves her genius well, and not her genius alone. The gift of art to life is the divine gift of self-awareness. Through art life is made to reveal herself and the completeness of this revelation is the measure of an artist's power. For this service to life, Miss Mansfield's superb technique is perfectly adapted. She tells the story of 'a stout lady in blue serge, with a bunch of artificial "parmas" at her bosom, a black hat covered with purple pansies, white gloves, boots with white uppers and a vanity bag containing one and three,' and out of it draws a vision of the human spirit, with its fierce pitiful pretences and its incredible courage. But do not imagine that Miss Ada Moss is in the least aware that she is a symbol. She smiled jauntily when we met yesterday. Oh, how are you, Miss Moss, anything special on? Miss Moss is very cheery, searching in her bag for her 'old dead powder puff.' She just missed a splendid job yesterday but with her education and West End training she is sure to fall into something tomorrow or the next day. Poor Miss Moss: with what an odd pain at the heart we turn away from you. There is only the Café de Madrid and the stout gentleman with the sausage fingers for you now.

The wry irony which touches all Miss Mansfield's stories has its root in a profound pity. It is indeed the other face of pity. She shares with the world's supreme artists

ILLUS. 82. Golden Cockerel Press, Berkshire. *Voices,* January 1921. Double spread.

C A S A N O V A' S

came a perfume at once kindred to that of the thousand flowers of the garden, and yet unique.

The Abbess, still without a word, conducted the visitors between the flower-beds upon narrow, winding paths which traversed the garden like a lovely labyrinth. The graceful ease of her gait showed that she was enjoying the chance of showing others the motley splendours of her garden. As if she had determined to make her guests giddy, she moved on faster and ever faster like the leader of a lively folk-dance. Then, quite suddenly, so that Casanova seemed to awaken from a confusing dream, they all found themselves in the parlour once more. On the other side of the grating, dim figures were moving. It was impossible to distinguish whether, behind the thick bars, three or twenty veiled women were flitting to and fro like startled ghosts. Indeed, none but Casanova, with eyes preternaturally acute to pierce the darkness, could discern that they were human outlines at all.

The Abbess attended the visitors to the door, mutely gave them a sign of farewell, and vanished before they had found time to express their thanks for her courtesy.

Suddenly, just as they were about to leave the parlour, a woman's voice near the grating breathed the word 'Casanova.' Nothing but his name, in a tone that seemed to him quite unfamiliar. From whom came this breach of a sacred vow? Was it a woman he had once loved, or a woman he had never seen before? Did the syllables convey the ecstasy

100

H O M E C O M I N G

of an unexpected re-encounter, or the pain of something irrecoverably lost; or did it convey the lamentation that an ardent wish of earlier days had been so late and so fruitlessly fulfilled? Casanova could not tell. All that he knew was that his name, which had so often voiced the whispers of tender affection, the stammerings of passion, the acclamations of happiness, had to-day for the first time pierced his heart with the full resonance of love. But, for this very reason, to probe the matter curiously would have seemed to him ignoble and foolish. The door closed behind the party, shutting in a secret which he was never to unriddle. Were it not that the expression on each face had shown timidly and fugitively that the call to Casanova had reached the ears of all, each might have fancied himself or herself a prey to illusion. No one uttered a word as they walked through the cloisters to the great doors. Casanova brought up the rear, with bowed head, as if on the occasion of some profoundly affecting farewell.

The porter was waiting. He received his alms. The visitors stepped into the carriage, and started on the homeward road. Olivo seemed perplexed; Amalia was distrait. Marcolina, however, was quite unmoved. Too pointedly, in Casanova's estimation, she attempted to engage Amalia in a discussion of household affairs, a topic upon which Olivo was compelled to come to his wife's assistance. Casanova soon joined in the discussion, which turned upon matters relating to kitchen and cellar. An expert on these

101

ILLUS. 83. Golden Cockerel Press, Berkshire. *Casanova's Homecoming,* 1922. Double spread typical of Hal Taylor's plain style as applied to a commissioned work.

sufficiently successful for it to be possible to advertise Golden Cockerel for sale as a going concern, and early in 1924 it was bought by Robert Gibbings.

Gibbings was a founder-member of the Society of Wood Engravers, and under his direction the Golden Cockerel Press was to be transformed into the principal vehicle for the renaissance of wood-engraved book illustration that took place in the years between the wars. Before he took the press over, little use had been made of illustration in its books. Apart from a litho portrait of the author in *Gipsy Night* and the process blocks used for Peter Quennell's decorations to his *Masques and Poems* (1922), only *The Wedding Songs of Edmund Spenser* (1923) had been illustrated, and in that Ethelbert White's wood engravings did not accord well with the Caslon type. Another book that was in progress when the press was sold was Brantôme's *Lives of Gallant Ladies,* which had been announced with engravings by White, but, not surprisingly, when the two volumes were published in July 1924, the engravings were by Gibbings instead.

Although there was a period of apprenticeship in which the color of the Caslon type and of the engravings did not harmonize with complete success, or in which the paper chosen proved less than perfect as a vehicle, Gibbings possessed considerable typographic skill as well as consummate ability as an engraver, and, in general, succeeded in producing books that showed how well the wood engraving can be integrated into the printed page. For the first few books produced under his direction at the Golden Cockerel Press, he was its only illustrator, and four of the five books published in 1924 had engravings by him. From the beginning of 1925 he also used other engravers, starting with John Nash in Swift's *Directions to Servants,* and following these with books illustrated by such engravers as Eric Gill, John Farleigh, Noel Rooke, David Jones, and Eric Ravilious as well as himself—in fact one can scarcely think of an important English wood engraver of the time who was not represented in the Cockerel series. Although wood engraving formed the major illustration method used, from 1926 a number were produced with copper engravings by such artists as Eric Gill, J. E. Laboureur, and Denis Tegetmeier, and these (despite the much greater difficulty of marrying text to illustrations) are scarcely less good than their wood-engraved companions (Illus. 85).

For a considerable period Gibbings's policy at the Golden Cockerel paid off handsomely in financial as well as aesthetic terms. An extra platen press (as well as a Columbian, which was used extensively for proofing the engravings) was installed, and in the late twenties two more pressmen were employed to work on the books; but the depression hit the Golden Cockerel hard, much harder than it had the Nonesuch. Although in artistic terms the press's work in the early thirties was even better than before—the *Four Gospels,* printed in 1931 with engravings by Eric Gill and set in a new proprietary typeface that Gill had designed, is arguably the finest of all private press books printed between the wars—it did not pay its way. The press was no rich man's plaything; Gibbings had to make his living from its work. In 1933 he felt compelled to call an end to his bookmaking, and the press was taken over by Christopher Sandford, Francis Newbery, and Owen Rutter. Under their regime the Cockerel took on a new lease of life.

Sandford was not new to fine press work when he took over the Golden Cockerel. While still an undergraduate at Cambridge he had come under what he described as the "fascinating influence" of William Morris, and after some years abroad he joined the Chiswick Press of which he subsequently became a director. In 1930 he started the Boar's Head Press at Manaton in Devon, from which until 1936 he issued a number of books, mainly by contemporary authors and many of them with wood engravings by his wife, Lettice. For the first few of these he set the type himself, but all were printed at the Chiswick Press under his supervision—a reversion to Charles Ricketts's method with the Vale Press books. In 1932, together with Francis Newbery, he succeeded in persuading the Chiswick Press to back a larger publishing enterprise, the Golden Hours Press, which was intended to produce an edition of the works of Christopher Marlowe in nine volumes. The press died after

ILLUS. 84. Golden Cockerel Press, Berkshire. *Pelagea*, 1926. Double spread. Wood engraving by Robert Gibbings.

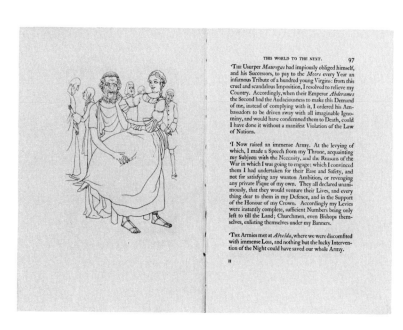

ILLUS. 85. Golden Cockerel Press, Berkshire. *Journey from This World to the Next*, 1930. Double spread. Etching by Denis Tegetmeier.

only three volumes of Marlowe (Illus. 87) and one other book had appeared. They were very well produced, Eric Ravilious's illustrations for *The Jew of Malta* and Blair Hughes-Stanton's for *Faustus* being particularly good, but the market for fine printing had contracted and they did not sell. (Indeed, even though the unsold copies were remaindered and sold off in a cheaper binding it took a very long time for the stocks to be cleared; the volumes can still be bought much more cheaply than much inferior private press work of the time.) Whether Newbery and Sandford would have found a way of continuing the Golden Hours Press after 1933 had they not purchased the Golden Cockerel is a matter for conjecture; with an ailing Cockerel to care for, it was an obvious impossibility.

Sandford's partners left the active direction of their press in his hands, and his solution to the economic problems of its survival was the obvious one for a man with his background. The

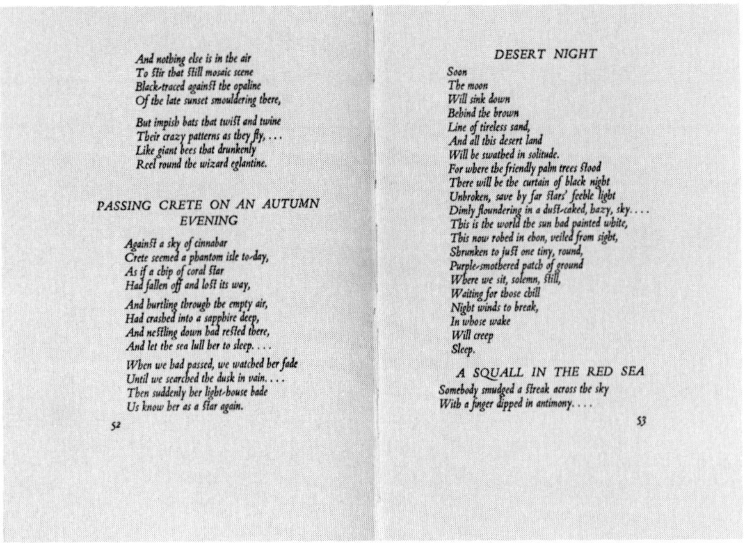

And nothing else is in the air
To stir that still mosaic scene
Black-traced against the opaline
Of the late sunset smouldering there,

But impish bats that twist and twine
Their crazy patterns as they fly, . . .
Like giant bees that drunkenly
Reel round the wizard eglantine.

PASSING CRETE ON AN AUTUMN
EVENING

Against a sky of cinnabar
Crete seemed a phantom isle to-day,
As if a chip of coral star
Had fallen off and lost its way,

And hurtling through the empty air,
Had crashed into a sapphire deep,
And nestling down had rested there,
And let the sea lull her to sleep. . . .

When we had passed, we watched her fade
Until we searched the dusk in vain. . . .
Then suddenly her light-house bade
Us know her as a star again.

52

DESERT NIGHT

Soon
The moon
Will sink down
Behind the brown
Line of tireless sand,
And all this desert land
Will be swathed in solitude.
For where the friendly palm trees stood
There will be the curtain of black night
Unbroken, save by far stars' feeble light
Dimly floundering in a dust-caked, hazy, sky. . . .
This is the world the sun had painted white,
This now robed in ebon, veiled from sight,
Shrunken to just one tiny, round,
Purple-smothered patch of ground
Where we sit, solemn, still,
Waiting for those chill
Night winds to break,
In whose wake
Will creep
Sleep.

A SQUALL IN THE RED SEA

Somebody smudged a streak across the sky
With a finger dipped in antimony. . . .

53

ILLUS. 86. Boar's Head Press,
Devon. *East & West*, 1932.
Interesting verse layout.

MARLOWE'S TWO LYRICS

The passionate Sheepheard to his loue.

Come liue with mee, and be my loue,
And we will all the pleasures proue,
That Vallies, groues, hills and fieldes,
Woods, or steepie mountaine yeeldes.

And wee will sit vpon the Rocks,
Seeing the Sheepheards feede theyr flocks
By shallow Riuers, to whose falls
Melodious byrds sings Madrigalls.

And I will make thee beds of Roses,
And a thousand fragrant poesies,
A cap of flowers, and a kirtle,
Imbroydred all with leaues of Mirtle.

A gowne made of the finest wooll,
Which from our pretty Lambes we pull,
Fayre lined slippers for the cold,
With buckles of the purest gold.

A belt of straw and Iuie buds,
With Corall clasps and Amber studs,
And if these pleasures may thee moue,
Come liue with mee, and be my loue.

The Sheepheards Swaines shall daunce & sing
For thy delight each May-morning.
If these delights thy minde may moue,
Then liue with mee, and be my loue.

Finis

ILLUS. 87. Golden Hours Press, London. Marlowe's *Hero and Leander*, 1933.
Wood engraving by Lettice Sandford.

maintenance of their own equipment and skilled labor at Waltham St. Lawrence was abandoned, and an arrangement was made with the Chiswick Press so that they were able to use its plant and men when needed; in other words, to the purist the Cockerel became, like Vale or Nonesuch, no more than an imprint. It was a drastic remedy but it worked, and for the remainder of the 1930s the Golden Cockerel Press continued to produce books finely illustrated with wood engravings. For some of these the proprietary Golden Cockerel type was used, but not by any means for all; the press made use of several of the many good faces available for Monotype composition, an indication of Nonesuch influence. To improve the justification of the lines, Monotype-set matter was normally "put through the stick" by hand afterwards, a practice still followed by several private presses, but the machine had conquered. As Sandford freely admitted, it could produce work equal or superior to setting by hand, at considerably less cost.

The third of the triumvirate of private presses established in the early 1920s was not English, but Welsh. In 1919 the great country house of Gregynog, near Newtown in Montgomeryshire, had been purchased by two wealthy sisters, the Misses Gwendoline and Margaret (Daisy) Davies. Deeply interested in music and the fine arts, they formed a magnificent collection of paintings, and had dreams of making Gregynog a center for the encouragement of many crafts: pottery, weaving, furniture design, and fine printing. Behind the sisters' concern lay considerable unease at the source of their wealth (derived from the South Wales coalfields), and their aim was philanthropic. Daisy devoted much energy to attempts to promote social welfare through the development of convalescent homes and the like; the Gregynog venture was undertaken more from Gwen's wish to bring color and meaning into lives from which they were otherwise absent. But like many wealthy people their genuine wish to extend patronage was flawed by a fear of being exploited. To safeguard themselves they leaned very heavily on a number of advisers, particularly the art critic Hugh Blaker, brother of their erstwhile governess, and Dr. Thomas Jones, then Assistant Secretary to the Cabinet in London and an old friend, known always as T.J.

ILLUS. 88. Golden Cockerel Press, London. *The Hansom Cab and the Pigeons*, 1935. Wood engraving by Eric Ravilious; set in Gill's Golden Cockerel type.

To run a crafts center of the kind being considered clearly needed a competent controller. On Blaker's recommendation (and despite the misgivings of T.J. who wanted a Welshman) the ladies appointed Robert Ashwin Maynard, a painter for whom Blaker had sought the sisters' patronage as early as 1913. In February 1921 Maynard started on an 18-month program of work in London to learn as much as possible about the various crafts. Much of his time was spent studying printing under J. H. Mason, and wood engraving in which he was largely self-taught.

While Maynard was away, there were fruitless negotiations to buy the Shakespeare Head Press at Stratford-on-Avon, and it was not until Maynard took up residence at Gregynog in June 1922 that printing equipment was ordered. By that time alterations to Gregynog's stable block and coach house (including rooms for a print shop and bindery) had been completed; but disheartened by their architect's slow progress with the conversion and by Maynard's evident lack of enthusiasm for other crafts, the Davies sisters abandoned their plans for pottery and weaving. The concentration was to be on printing alone.

By mid-December an Albion press had been installed and a supply of Kennerley type obtained, and on December 27, Maynard printed a season's greeting card, the first of many to be produced at Gregynog. But surprisingly, a program of work for the press had not yet been decided. In discussions over the Christmas season for future work at Gregynog, at which ideas for music-making, art exhibitions, summer schools, and the like were flown, it was suggested that the press might produce books on art for use by schoolchildren. In the end a move toward their eventual program was made by Gwen Davies. They must start in a small way, limiting themselves to small editions of books that were of literary worth as well as examples of fine workmanship: "What worries me is that we are weak on the literary side, and I fear this is going to hamper us in the printing. Of Welsh stuff I have no doubt we can get plenty, but we must print English as well."

The first book in the press's series for sale was not to be published until December 1923, a year after the Albion was installed. In the meantime, Maynard had been very busy. A Victoria platen press had been installed; John Mason (J. H. Mason's son) recruited as binder; an Anglesea lad, John Hughes Jones, taken as apprentice; and several slighter pieces printed, *The Annual Goodwill Message to the Children of Wales,* a catalogue of an art exhibition, a pamphlet for the Geographical Association, concert programs, posters, and Christmas cards. Such ephemera (of which well over 200 are listed in Dorothy Harrop's definitive *History of the Gregynog Press,* 1980) were to be a constant product of the press throughout its life.

The first book, *The Poems of George Herbert,* selected by Sir Walford Davies, was a happy choice reflecting the press's dual English-Welsh interests. Three hundred copies were printed on the Albion on undamped paper (astonishingly it was not until 1927 that Maynard learned of the virtues of dampening handmade papers, from a chance remark of Bernard Newdigate) and most copies were quarterbound by Mason. As was to become usual with Gregynog books, some copies were specially bound in full morocco and a few copies kept in sheets and bound much later in a variety of materials. It was a chaste, unassuming little book whose virtues contain little foretaste of the excellent work to follow.

Typographically, the books published over the next two years showed only modest advance. But *Poems by Henry Vaughan,* selected by Ernest Rhys (1924), and their first book in Welsh, *Caneuon Ceiriog,* edited by J. Lloyd Jones (1925), revealed in their illustrations the increasing mastery of Maynard and of Horace Walter Bray, an old friend of Maynard's who had joined the staff as resident artist in 1924. The Maynard-Bray partnership was to flower and bring forth some exquisite work in the remaining years of the twenties.

There were to be changes in the staff of the press: Idris Jones had joined as printing assistant at the same time as Bray, and John Mason left in the summer of 1925 to take up a post at the

Shakespeare Head Press. For a while, the press was without a binder, but after a temporary appointment of Sydney Cockerell (son of Douglas, and later famous as a binder in his own right and particularly for his marbled paper) the post was taken by one of Douglas Cockerell's ex-pupils, George Fisher. Fisher was to remain at the press for 20 years, and through his special bindings contribute in no small way to the fame of Gregynog. Other appointments included the skilled compositor Richard Owen Jones, and more importantly Dora Herbert-Jones, an old friend of the Davies sisters who was to act as secretary to the press and look after its business affairs. As a sort of intermediary between the owners and the artists and craftsmen, hers was a very difficult task, and it was due in no small part to her efforts that the press was to continue successfully through some difficult times under its various controllers. A few weeks after her appointment, it acquired a pressman of consummate skill, Herbert John Hodgson.

The limitations of Kennerley type as the press's only face had become apparent. In 1924 there was an attempt to persuade Edward Johnston to design a face for Gregynog, but the great calligrapher was not to be tempted. Not for another 10 years did the press have a proprietary type, but in 1925 a Monotype caster was purchased so that the press could make use of some of the revived faces being produced for that machine. By that time the Press Board (on which T.J. and Gwen Davies were initially the key figures, and later W. J. Burdon Evans was to dominate) had arrived at a much firmer understanding of the kind of work to be produced, although their program was to change from time to time, and several works—*The Book of Job,* White's *Natural History of Selbourne,* Glyn Davies's translation of poems by the Dane Jeppe Aakjaer—were to be abandoned when production was already far advanced.

Some splendid work was still to come from Maynard and Bray. The high point of Gregynog under their direction came in 1928 with *The Autobiography of Edward Lord Herbert of Cherbury* (Illus. 89) and Peacock's *Misfortunes of Elphin* with superb wood engravings by Bray. Maynard was scarcely less successful for *Penillion Omar Khayyâm,* a translation of the *Rubaiyat* in which Maynard had to contend with a translator (Sir John Morris-Jones) who had forthright views on typography and illustration, which he argued at such length that Maynard feared the book would never be finished.

Some of their later work was to achieve equal excellence. In 1930 Wilfred Scawen Blunt's *The Stealing of the Mare* with masterly hand-colored engravings by Maynard, and Lamb's *Elia* for which Bray engraved illustrations of great delicacy and charm, were books that rank with the greatest work from private presses. But in that year they resigned from Gregynog: the artistic isolation of Montgomeryshire had taken its toll on them, and the ill health of one of Bray's children required a move. The two were to continue in partnership at the Raven Press whose work is discussed in Chapter 16.

In searching for replacements, the Press Board had some fascinating possibilities. One great might-have-been was the partnership of Douglas Percy Bliss and Edward Bawden, recommended by Joseph Thorp, but in the end it was again Hugh Blaker's candidate who was appointed: Blair Hughes-Stanton. On Hughes-Stanton's suggestion the Scottish painter and sculptor William McCance was appointed Controller, while he himself was engaged as resident artist.

There was a significant advantage in these two appointments, quite apart from the artistic caliber of the two men. Their wives, Gertrude Hermes, and Agnes Miller Parker, were also well known as wood engravers, and, for a modest retainer to each, Gregynog had four distinguished artists' services available. But there was also a significant disadvantage. Like Maynard and Bray before them, neither man had any printing experience. Despite "crash courses," for which the two were attached briefly to good English commercial firms, the Gregynog was undoubtedly weaker typographically for the first part of the Hughes-Stanton/McCance regime.

Fortunately it now had highly skilled compositors, pressmen, and binders, and in Dora Herbert-Jones, a person of much typographic taste, but her relations with the two men were never easy.

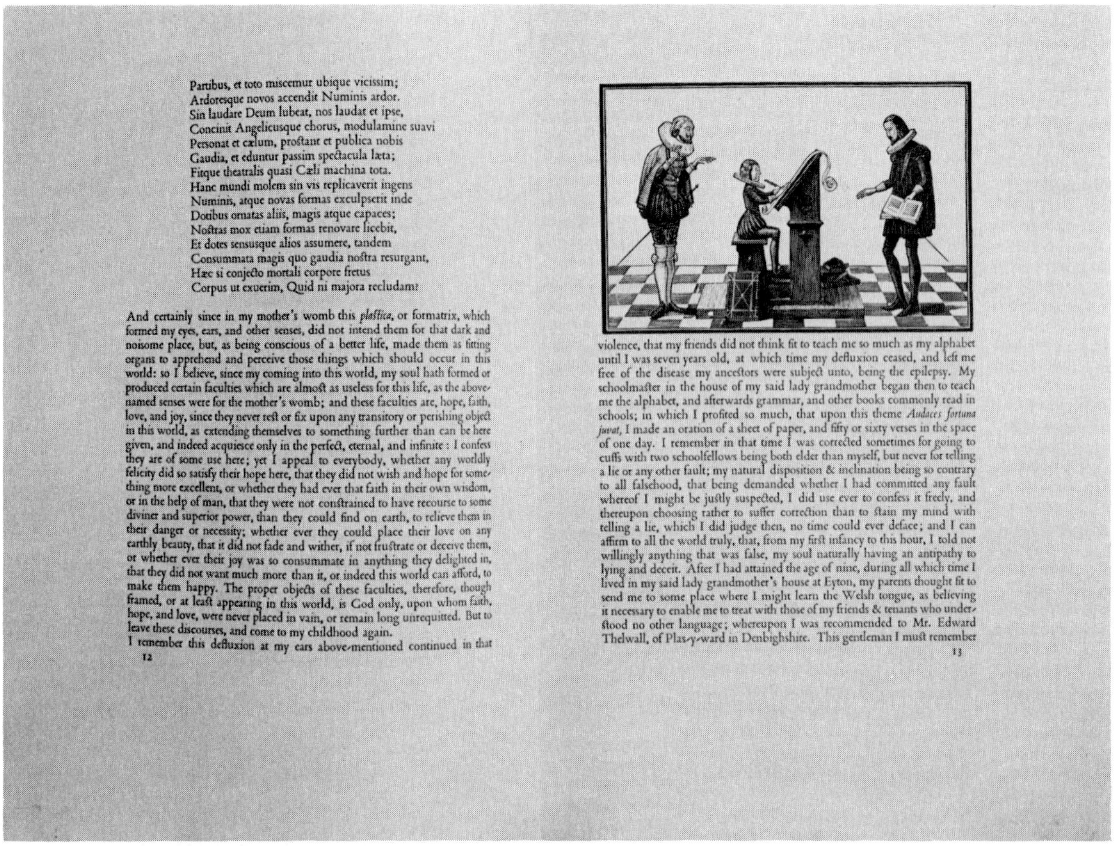

Partibus, et toto miscemur ubique vicissim;
Ardoresque novos accendit Numinis ardor.
Sin laudare Deum lubeat, nos laudat et ipse,
Concinit Angelicusque chorus, modulamine suavi
Personat et cælum, prostant et publica nobis
Gaudia, et eduntur passim spectacula læta;
Fitque theatralis quasi Cæli machina tota.
Hanc mundi molem sin vis replicaverit ingens
Numinis, atque novas formas exculpserit inde
Dotibus ornatas aliis, magis atque capaces;
Nostras mox etiam formas renovare licebit,
Et dotes sensusque alios assumere, tandem
Consummata magis quo gaudia nostra resurgant,
Hæc si conjecto mortali corpore fretus
Corpus ut exuerim, Quid ni majora recludam?

And certainly since in my mother's womb this *plastica*, or formatrix, which formed my eyes, ears, and other senses, did not intend them for that dark and noisome place, but, as being conscious of a better life, made them as fitting organs to apprehend and perceive those things which should occur in this world: so I believe, since my coming into this world, my soul hath formed or produced certain faculties which are almost as useless for this life, as the above-named senses were for the mother's womb; and these faculties are, hope, faith, love, and joy, since they never rest or fix upon any transitory or perishing object in this world, as extending themselves to something further than can be here given, and indeed acquiesce only in the perfect, eternal, and infinite: I confess they are of some use here; yet I appeal to everybody, whether any worldly felicity did so satisfy their hope here, that they did not wish and hope for something more excellent, or whether they had ever that faith in their own wisdom, or in the help of man, that they were not constrained to have recourse to some diviner and superior power, than they could find on earth, to relieve them in their danger or necessity; whether ever they could place their love on any earthly beauty, that it did not fade and wither, if not frustrate or deceive them, or whether ever their joy was so consummate in anything they delighted in, that they did not want much more than it, or indeed this world can afford, to make them happy. The proper objects of these faculties, therefore, though framed, or at least appearing in this world, is God only, upon whom faith, hope, and love, were never placed in vain, or remain long unrequitted. But to leave these discourses, and come to my childhood again.
I remember this defluxion at my ears above-mentioned continued in that

12

violence, that my friends did not think fit to teach me so much as my alphabet until I was seven years old, at which time my defluxion ceased, and left me free of the disease my ancestors were subject unto, being the epilepsy. My schoolmaster in the house of my said lady grandmother began then to teach me the alphabet, and afterwards grammar, and other books commonly read in schools; in which I profited so much, that upon this theme *Audaces fortuna juvat*, I made an oration of a sheet of paper, and fifty or sixty verses in the space of one day. I remember in that time I was corrected sometimes for going to cuffs with two schoolfellows being both elder than myself, but never for telling a lie or any other fault; my natural disposition & inclination being so contrary to all falsehood, that being demanded whether I had committed any fault whereof I might be justly suspected, I did use ever to confess it freely, and thereupon choosing rather to suffer correction than to stain my mind with telling a lie, which I did judge then, no time could ever deface; and I can affirm to all the world truly, that, from my first infancy to this hour, I told not willingly anything that was false, my soul naturally having an antipathy to lying and deceit. After I had attained the age of nine, during all which time I lived in my said lady grandmother's house at Eyton, my parents thought fit to send me to some place where I might learn the Welsh tongue, as believing it necessary to enable me to treat with those of my friends & tenants who understood no other language; whereupon I was recommended to Mr. Edward Thelwall, of Plas-y-ward in Denbighshire. This gentleman I must remember

13

ILLUS. 89. Gregynog Press, Wales. Opening from *The Autobiography of Edward Lord Herbert of Cherbury,* 1928. Wood engraving by H. W. Bray.

A rift in the Hughes-Stanton household caused such misery to Gertrude Hermes that her creative ability was stultified, and an unsympathetic attitude from her employers when she left early in 1932 killed the projected *Natural History of Selbourne* on which she had been working. They disapproved as strongly of her husband's personal life and were tempted to terminate his contract, although in the end he stayed until the following year. Relations between the board and the McCances were also strained, which makes it the more remarkable that such masterly work as *The Fables of Esope* (Agnes Miller Parker, 1931), *The Revelation of St. John the Divine* (Blair Hughes-Stanton, 1932), and *The Singing Caravan* (William McCance, 1932) could appear.

In the *Revelation* and even more in his superb *Lamentations of Jeremiah* (1933) Hughes-Stanton gave full play to his virtuosity as a wood engraver, and their success was confirmed by Herbert Hodgson's incomparable presswork. The *Revelation* and *Jeremiah* deservedly received high acclaim, although it is worth noting that Bernard Newdigate's judgment was that however much the skill of the engraver was to be admired, the books were not completely satisfactory: *Revelation* because of the break with the traditions of Christian iconography and *Jeremiah* because "neither these nor any other engraved pictures can convey the sense of utter desolation born by the bible text." Unadorned typography, he seemed to suggest, was superior for the second book, but this stern approach was not the Gregynog way.

In 1933 Hughes-Stanton and the McCances left. Once more, the Press Board had some attractive possibilities in recruitment: Vivian Ridler and David Bland of the Perpetua Press (rejected as too young), Vincent Stuart of the Tintern Press, Harry Carter, and Reynolds Stone among others. In the end, having rejected those recommended by Brooke Crutchley, Stanley Morison, and others, they settled for the candidate put forward by John Johnson, the Printer to Oxford University Press. His recommendation was for Loyd Haberly.

Haberly was a young American Rhodes Scholar, who after completing a law degree at Oxford had settled in Long Crendon, Buckinghamshire, where he had built and set up his own private press, the Seven Acres Press. So impressed were the board by Johnson's recommendation and their own judgment of Haberly when he visited Gregynog, that they acquiesced in a part-time appointment as he was unwilling to settle in Wales.

Perhaps because of the personal difficulties that there had been under the previous regime, or perhaps as a result of his absentee status, Haberly at first enjoyed considerable freedom in directing the press's activities. He persuaded the Press Board to accept a volume of his own verse, *Anne Boleyn and Other Poems,* to mark "the beginning of the third dynasty," as he put it. For Robert Bridges's *Eros and Psyche* (to be illustrated with engravings after Burne-Jones's designs for William Morris's abortive edition of *The Earthly Paradise*) he obtained their agreement for a new typeface to be cut. This was to be based on the face used by Johann Neumeister for Dante's *Divine Comedy* printed at Foligno in 1472 and Haberly suggested that it would harmonize well with the illustrations.

Nevertheless, when the book was eventually printed in October 1935 it was far from a complete success. Despite Bernard Newdigate's enthusiasm for the face, the general critical opinion was that it was a failure; there is no doubt that it was much too heavy for the illustrations, which while faithful enough to Burne-Jones's drawings were sadly emasculated when compared with the original wood engravings made by Morris. Nor did the choice of color and decoration for *Anne Boleyn* (November 1934) succeed; in Dorothy Harrop's words "the book has a precious air about it, and an amateurish one at that." There was one major disaster for which the Press Board and Haberly must share the blame. So angry was Glyn Davies at the treatment he received over his translation of Aakjaer's poems that he withdrew permission for Gregynog to print them, saying, in a letter that pulled no punches:

> I would not consider the preposterous pretences and make-believe of your
> Board for a moment. There is a touch of arrogance, petty meanness, small-
> mindedness and ill-breeding about its views that settled the question for me at
> once. I am not giving any press the right to play the fool at its own discretion
> with any work of mine, not even a university press, much less a board of
> unskilled outsiders. Your Board was stupid to imagine that I would submit to
> the humiliation of having to subordinate my judgment to the vulgar whims of a
> young novice playing with his first big toy, who did not know the language of
> half the poems he was supposed to put into typography appropriate to the
> matter, and whose performance on some of the English texts I shall be glad to
> show anyone who wants to see what can be done in flamboyant bad taste.

Only one real success came from Haberly's control at Gregynog: Philemon Holland's transla- tion of Xenophon's *Cyrupaedia* (1936), for which Haberly's hand-colored floriated initials match the Poliphilus text perfectly.

The next and last appointment of a Controller was not of an artist or a typographer, but it was an inspired one: James Wardrop. A distinguished authority on calligraphy, Wardrop was on the staff of the Victoria and Albert Museum, and so could assume only a part-time position when he joined Gregynog in June 1936. Under his care five more books were published. The most sumptuous—and arguably the best book to appear over the Gregynog imprint—was the Sieur de Joinville's *History of St. Louis* (1937), a large folio with initials and special openings designed by Alfred Fairbank, with

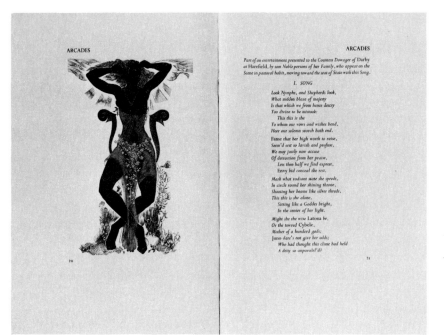

ILLUS. 90. Gregynog Press, Wales. Opening from *Four Poems by Milton,* 1933. Wood engraving by Blair Hughes-Stanton.

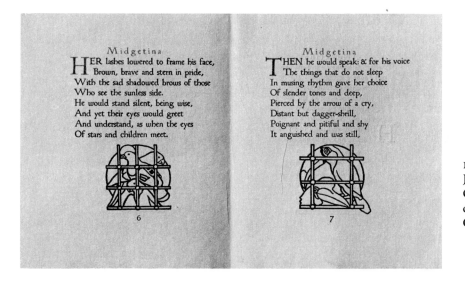

ILLUS. 91. Loyd Haberly, New Jersey. The Paradiso or Gwendolin typefaces originally designed and cut for the Gregynog Press.

maps by Berthold Wolpe and armorial engravings by Reynolds Stone. Stone was also the illustrator for the press's smallest book, Henry Vaughan's translation of Antonio de Guevara's *The Praise and Happinesse of the Countrie-Life* (1938) in which the simplicity of the design and illustrations were perfect for the text. By October 1939 Wardrop had been called for war service, and his post at Gregynog was terminated from the following February. Two books then in progress were completed in 1940 and George Fisher continued with binding special copies until 1945, but no further work appeared from the press.

During its life, Gregynog published some noble books: how many of which were completely successful is remarkable when one considers some of the difficulties. Its controllers had all been compelled to fit into a mold predetermined by the nature of the press and the character of its owners; and they were further limited by the decisions of a press board, not all of whose members were sympathetic to fine printing, let alone the artistic temperament. As T.J. put it in a letter to Gwen Davies when Wardrop's appointment was terminated, "so rarely are we able to part with any Press employee in a quite unclouded atmosphere," and it is a sobering fact that of all the senior staff employed, only George Fisher left without rancor.

The contrast with Count Kessler's Cranach-Presse—the best parallel with Gregynog among twentieth-century private presses in the Old World—is very striking. Both Kessler and the Davies sisters endowed the search for the perfect book on a scale that recalled the aristocratic presses of the eighteenth century. Admittedly Gordon Craig recalled a visit to Weimar during the production of his father's illustrations to *Hamlet* and said that the printers "were all very much like soldiers in front of the general when Kessler was present," but he also noted that it seemed like "a happy family affair." Kessler respected and could relate to those he employed, from Gage-Cole to Aristide Maillol, and from his own enthusiasm could enlarge the capabilities of his artists and craftsmen. The Davies sisters could not, and the success of the Gregynog Press was thereby diminished. Despite this, some splendid work was produced, and the standard by which we judge their press's books is a very high one. Many other private printers would be happy to achieve standards as high as in the Gregynog Press books we regard as failures.

Chapter 16

BETWEEN THE WARS IN BRITAIN II: BACKWATERS AND TRIBUTARIES

ALTHOUGH NONESUCH, GOLDEN COCKEREL, AND GREGYNOG are conventionally regarded as the triumvirate that ruled the private press scene in Britain between the wars, there were many other presses of interest that produced work of much merit. Only one can be said to challenge their dominance: the Shakespeare Head Press at Stratford-on-Avon.

In its origins Shakespeare Head was different from these just as it was older. It was the dream child of the distinguished scholar and editor A. H. Bullen, who was anxious to produce a good edition of Shakespeare's works that was set up, printed, and bound in Shakespeare's home town. Starting in 1904, Bullen completed his "Stratford Town Shakespeare" in ten volumes in 1907, and followed it with a number of other well-printed works, for example, Yeats's *Collected Works* in eight volumes (1908) and Buckingham's *The Rehearsal* (1914). For those wanting good "library editions" Shakespeare Head offered good value, yet its purpose and method were not of the Private Press Movement, but more those of a discriminating publisher with a captive plant.

In 1921 Bullen died, and the future of the Shakespeare Head Press seemed uncertain. As a business venture it was not flourishing, and there was an attempt by the Gregynog ladies to purchase the equipment for their new press, but this came to nothing as Bullen's will required that the press be kept in Stratford. Instead, the plant and goodwill were purchased by a partnership set up by Basil Blackwell, the Oxford bookseller, Sir Adrian Mott, Benjamin Chandler, and Bernard Newdigate. With Newdigate's aesthetic and technical control, the business acumen of the other partners, and a sound program ensured by the appointment of H. F. B. Brett-Smith as literary adviser, the revitalized Shakespeare Head was in a strong position.

Purists have argued that Shakespeare Head was not a private press at all, but simply a good commercial printing plant that produced some books under its own imprint as well as undertaking work for others. In this strictest sense it was no more private than Nonesuch or Golden Cockerel or Vale, but that is really to miss the point: Under Newdigate's control it worked within the tradition set by Morris and Cobden-Sanderson, and Newdigate was fortunate in having partners who respected his quest for excellence and did not demand that profit dictate design and methods.

When Newdigate came to Shakespeare Head he was already in his fifties. In a number of ways he is comparable to the great American printer Daniel Berkeley Updike with whom he shared both an unintentional move into printing and success that came more through application than inspiration. Like Updike he had considerable scholarship that was reinforced by firm religious faith, though, like so many of those concerned with fine printing in Britain, it was based on the Catholic rather than the Episcopalian church. In 1890 he joined his father in the Art & Book Company, a small firm of Catholic printer-publishers at Leamington. In 1904 the printing side was separated under the name Arden Press, and became well known for the quality of its work for Burns & Oates and other publishers. Its progress was hampered by lack of capital, however, and in 1908 it was taken over by W. H. Smith & Son and moved to new premises in Letchworth Garden City, where it was to print, among other work, the first eleven books for Philip Lee Warner's Florence Press.

Newdigate accompanied the press on its move in the post of "adviser," but, although St. John Hornby at the top of W. H. Smith was sympathetic to Newdigate's ideals of workmanship, the middle management with whom he had to deal day to day was unperceptive and unsympathetic, if not overtly hostile. It was not the happiest time for him. Away from work he gained from greater acquaintance with Emery Walker and Father Adrian Fortescue, a fine calligrapher who was his parish priest. On a small Albion press he had put in his cottage, in 1913, Newdigate and his sister Mary set and printed a volume of *Latin Hymns* with English translations by Fortescue.

When the war came in 1914, Newdigate, well over age, applied for a commission in the Warwickshire Regiment. Had it not been for a bad motorcycle accident that rendered him unfit for active service, he would no doubt have gone the way of so many of his battalion in France, but instead, Newdigate had to be content to act as musketry instructor until the war's end.

His career had not so far had the success that his scholarship and industry merited. After a year with the Curwen Press (1919–1920), however, and despite the disappointment of the Fleuron Society, his fortune changed. In 1920 he started to contribute his "Book Production Notes" to the *London Mercury,* which were to be for 18 years a significant contribution to public awareness and appreciation of the book arts. Then there was the start of his reign at the Shakespeare Head Press.

Throughout its life, the press was to produce handsome workaday library editions of the English classics at modest prices—13 volumes of Smollett in 1925–1926, Richardson in 11 volumes in 1929–1930, 19 volumes of the Brontës in 1932–1936, and so on. The press used good, solid, masculine typography, having taken the lessons of the private presses into the marketplace. But, parallel with this series, some much finer work was also undertaken.

Some of this was for other publishers, like *England's Helicon* (1925) (Illus. 93) and a number of others for the "Haslewood Books" series published by Etchells & MacDonald. They were unassuming but very competent books with a strong feel for the period in their design. Other more ambitious commissions, like the edition of Bacon's *Essayes* for the Cresset Press (1927), were closer to the fine editions issued directly by the press. Of these, Froissart's *Chronycles* (1927–1928) and the Chaucer (1928–1929) were outstanding examples of the way in which Newdigate could use Caslon Old Face with better effect than almost any other printer—and this was a minor part of their success. The hand coloring of the arms and devices in the Froissart provides an interesting comparison with the much later Gregynog *History of St. Louis.* For the Chaucer, Hugh Chesterman redrew the figures of the pilgrims from the Ellesmere manuscript, and Lynton Lamb the miniatures from an early French manuscript, which were again hand colored with delightful effect. For the vellum

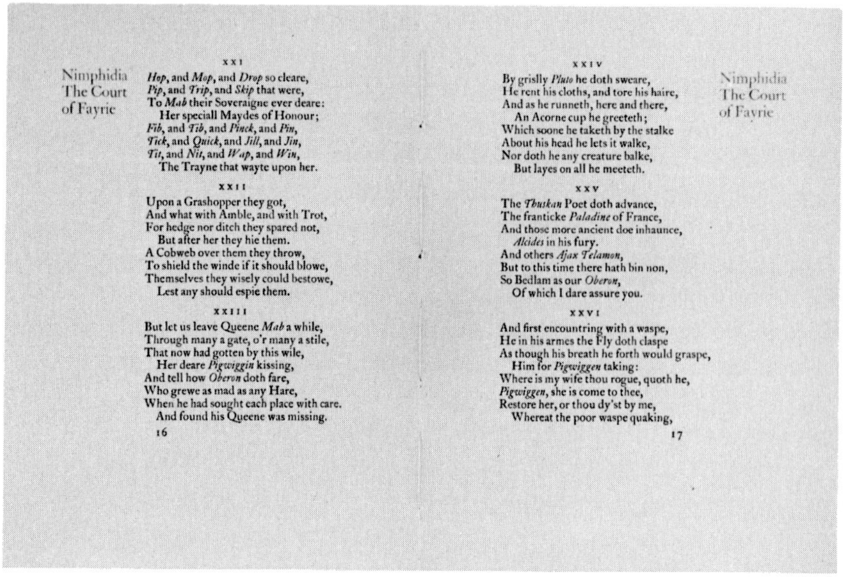

ILLUS. 92. Shakespeare Head Press, Warwickshire. Drayton's *Nimphidia*, 1924. Newdigate's plain use of Caslon types.

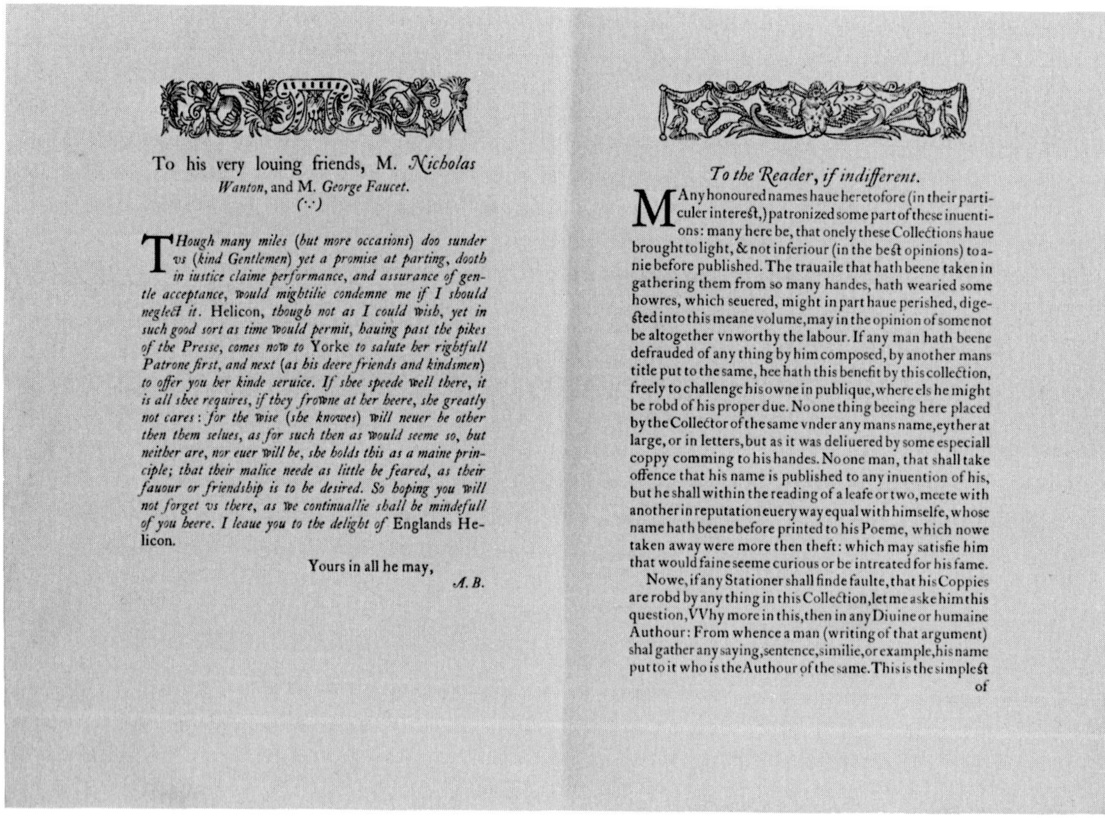

ILLUS. 93. Shakespeare Head Press, Warwickshire. *England's Helicon*, 1925. Double spread.

copies, for which burnished gold as well as color was used, the work was especially fine, and unequaled by anything else in the private press field.

It is fair to characterize Newdigate as a Caslon man, but that was not the only face he used with distinction. His use of Centaur in Chapman's *Homer* (1930–1931) or Cloister in the Bacon or Loyd Haberly's *Mediaeval English Paving Tiles* (1937) showed in these fine editions his more general mastery to which the library editions also bore witness.

Shakespeare Head Press books were to range widely in period and subject: from the Greek and Latin classics through to works on modern craftsmen like Ernest Gimson. Some, like its *Rubaiyat* (1927) or Sheridan's *School for Scandal* (1930), both with decorations by Thomas Lowinsky, come as close as Newdigate could to the Nonesuch manner, but his real interest lay elsewhere, in the long series of editions of the Elizabethans and of Elizabethan translations that appropriately formed the core of Shakespeare Head work. As Colin Franklin has so well put it in a phrase in which he linked Morris, Cobden-Sanderson, Hornby, and Newdigate, the books appear as if the literary works were privately digested as well as printed, and presented in the form proper to them.

For one or two of its works, it is interesting to observe that Newdigate anticipated Mardersteig in his use of recut woodcuts from early editions to illustrate the texts. Thus for Bede's *History of the Church of Englande* (1929), he had cuts by John Farleigh after the originals of the 1565 Antwerp edition, and followed a similar practice for his *Decameron* (1934–1935). My own favorites among the Shakespeare Head volumes are of a slightly different kind: the two volumes of Pindar's *Odes* (1928 and 1930) for which Scholderer's New Hellenic and Poliphilus were used on facing pages for the Greek and English texts, and for which Farleigh furnished wood engravings inspired by Greek vase painting.

In 1930, the press moved from Stratford to premises in Oxford, where Newdigate continued work until 1941, when the plant was requisitioned for war purposes. When Newdigate died in 1944, Stanley Morison, in a warm obituary notice, commented that he had "succeeded in . . . conferring the greatest measure of distinction upon plain contemporary material," a judgment of which Newdigate would have been proud indeed.

Of very much less importance in purely typographical terms was another long-lived press, originally set up in 1902 by Elizabeth and Lily Yeats, the sisters of the poet William Butler Yeats. Started at Dundrum in County Dublin, it was initially part of a larger enterprise that was intended to stimulate Irish industry and to give training and employment to Irish girls by the production of such things as rugs and embroidery. The press was named the Dun Emer Press after the Lady Emer, famous in early Irish history for her embroidery.

The printing and publishing side of the enterprise was under the direction of Elizabeth Yeats, who had studied the craft at the Women's Printing Society in London and had, like so many others, received advice from Emery Walker. Equipped with an Albion press and Caslon type, and using paper specially made at the nearby Saggert Mills, the press set to work producing new works by modern Irish writers and new editions or translations of classical Irish works. This plan was obviously made an easier one to follow through the association of W. B. Yeats with the press; a very distinguished list of books by such writers as Lady Gregory, Synge, and Gogarty was to be produced. Compared with the finest work of the Private Press Movement, the books issued by the sisters' press were not fine; although the composition and layouts were workmanlike, their press-work was often defective. But to be fair, the enterprise did not aim at "fine printing," and the merits of the books lay in their content, not their presentation.

In 1908 the press was moved and the name changed to the Cuala Press, under which style it continued to work through the troubled period of the war and the twenties, and indeed until the late 1940s. As well as books, Cuala produced calendars, greeting cards, and other small pieces, of which the colored broadsheets are the most interesting. The attraction of the broadsheets is closer to the naive charm of the chapbook than of fine printing, and they fell well below the inspiration of Lovat Fraser's "Flying Fame" sheets (Illus. 94A and 94B). An uncommon series of these was commissioned by Dora Herbert-Jones, who persuaded Miss Yeats to print for her some small broadsheets of Welsh songs in the early 1920s. They were a valiant attempt, attractively presented, to promote interest among the Welsh in their own poetry, but they did not arouse much interest among the audience at whom they were aimed, and the difficulties of production were considerable. After a final broadsheet of a poem "Cymru fach i mi" in which Mrs. Herbert-Jones found to her horror that the Cuala printers had, as she put it, left enough room for a coach-and-four to drive through the space between the initial C and the rest of the word, she abandoned the experiment in disgust.

Another press of at least equal importance in literary terms was to be started in a very different way in 1917—Leonard and Virginia Woolf's Hogarth Press. This was originally intended purely as a hobby. Leonard Woolf was anxious to find a manual occupation that would interest his wife, in an attempt to reduce her intense and exhausting absorption in her writing, which had on previous occasions caused her collapse and ultimately was to lead to her suicide in 1941. During 1916 they had decided that they would learn to print, but attempts to enroll in classes at St. Bride's met with a rebuff: the trade had no welcome for amateurs. It seemed that some other means of relaxation would have to be found; then in March 1917 they found themselves by chance passing the Excelsior Printing

ILLUS. 94A. Cuala Press, Ireland. *Broadside*, no. 1, 1908.

ILLUS. 94B. Cuala Press, Ireland. *Broadside*, no. 10, 1909.

Supply Company's shop, that haven for the earlier spare-time printers. They went in and explained their predicament. There was no need for training or apprenticeships, the shopman said; with the aid of his 16-page pamphlet they would soon find themselves to be competent printers.

Half an hour later when they left the shop they had purchased a small handplaten, type, and other equipment. In all this, the episode was typical of thousands of the same sort since the introduction of Cowper's Parlour Printing Press three-quarters of a century earlier; where it differed from these was in the growth of the hobby into a distinguished publishing house.

When the press and the other materials were supplied to their home, Hogarth House at Richmond, they installed it in their dining room and started to experiment. The man at the suppliers had been quite right; with the aid of his booklet they were soon able to set the type and print a page, and after a month's practice they felt sufficiently competent to start work on a pamphlet. They decided to produce a paper-covered booklet containing one story by each of them, which they would sell on subscription; if it were a success they could proceed further with the printing and publishing of short works that would be of no interest to the commercial publisher.

Considering the printers' lack of experience, the production of *Two Stories,* the first publication of the "Hogarth Press," was very fair. Some features betrayed their inexperience (the backing-up in particular was poor) but they had gone to a good deal of trouble to make the pamphlet attractive, binding it in a gay Japanese paper, a practice which at that time was very uncommon. This use of unusual and attractive cover papers was to become a feature of the Hogarth Press, for later they imported some brilliant patterned papers from Prague, from Roger Fry's daughter in Paris, and from other sources; to some degree they may have been responsible for starting the fashion in the 1920s for such cover papers (Illus. 95). They tried to produce their books well, but they were not in the least interested in producing fine books as such; their concern was with the text above all.

The reception given to *Two Stories* was excellent; it was published in July 1917 and by the end of the month almost all the edition had been sold. Encouraged by this, the Woolfs went ahead with something more ambitious, Katherine Mansfield's *Prelude.* This was a substantial undertaking, a 68-page book—too substantial for them to print a page at a time on their handpress, so Leonard Woolf machined it on a larger press belonging to a nearby jobbing printer with whom they had become friendly.

The story of the Hogarth Press from its very modest beginnings to a full-scale publishing house has been told by Leonard Woolf in two volumes of his autobiography, *Beginning Again* (1964) and *Downhill All the Way* (1967). The success of the first books printed at the press between 1917 and 1920 was so great that they were unable to cope with the orders they received for them. (When one considers that these books were by the Woolfs, Katherine Mansfield, and T. S. Eliot, and that the editions were of fewer than 300 copies, it does not today seem so surprising.) They were compelled to fall back on the services of commercial printers to reprint the books, and gradually a steadily increasing number of Hogarth Press books were produced through normal trade channels. For many years, however, a number of the press's books continued to be printed on the premises at Hogarth House or later from the Woolfs' new home at 52 Tavistock Square, where the printing press was installed in an old scullery. Here, until well into the 1930s, some of the Hogarth Press books were printed, although the majority of the books appearing on its lists, such as Freud's *Collected Works,* or the novels of V. Sackville-West, were printed by commercial firms. By this time, the Hogarth Press had become a business, and staff had been engaged to take over many of the tasks concerned with its operation. Leonard Woolf's own rather cold, bare-bones account can be fleshed out by Richard Kennedy's reminiscences of the period he spent working as a gauche office boy in Tavistock Square in 1928. Described by John Lehmann, who also worked at the Hogarth Press, as "absolutely accurate," *A Boy at the Hogarth Press* (1972) is a minor classic in its own right.

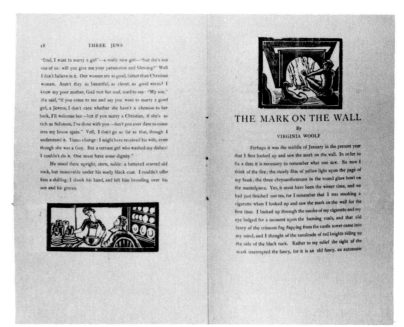

Among the many amateurs of fine printing who had considered setting up a private press was T. E. Lawrence. As early as 1906 he and a fellow undergraduate at Jesus College Oxford, Vyvyan Richards, had discovered a mutual enthusiasm for the work of Kelmscott and its followers. For many years they planned the private press that they would establish together; in the middle of World War I, for example, Lawrence wrote from Cairo, "Shall we begin by printing Apuleius' *The Golden Ass,* my present stand-by?" After the war, their press came near to being set up at Pole Hill in Epping Forest; but as Richards was later to write, "there was much planning about it, but it never came off." In the end, Richards started a press of his own in St. Johns Wood, but only one book (of no special typographic merit), Caxton's *Prologues and Epilogues* (1927), was to appear from it.

Even though so little came directly from Lawrence or Richards, their influence was by no means absent from one of the most interesting and important of the literary private presses, that of Laura Riding and Robert Graves. Both these writers knew of the Woolfs' work at the Hogarth Press: Graves's *The Feather Bed* had been printed by them in 1923; Laura Riding's *The Close Chaplet* and *Voltaire,* in 1924 and 1927. Graves had known Lawrence at Oxford, and through him had met Richards. Yet the idea of setting up a press of their own did not occur to the two poets until Richards made a friendly visit to their home in St. Peter's Square, Hammersmith. At the time Richards's conversation was full of his own press, and in Laura Riding's words:

> His talk about the possibility of doing one's own printing fired thoughts in us
> of publishing possibilities outside the regular-publisher channels. . . . Poems are
> difficult commodities to market; publishers tend to accept them in the sense of
> doing a favour. The idea of a press, and publishing one's own poems, seemed to
> spell freedom; it intrigued us, then excited us.

The press was quickly to develop from an idea into reality. An old Albion press was procured. According to some accounts Richards's own press was transferred from St. Johns Wood to Hammersmith, but Laura Riding's recollection is of purchasing a press from a printer's supplier to whom Richards directed them. Richards helped the two collaborators in learning how to handle it. A few lessons were sufficient; Riding and Graves were not interested in producing "fine books" any more than the Woolfs had been. Riding soon found a name for their undertaking. The idea of ownership,

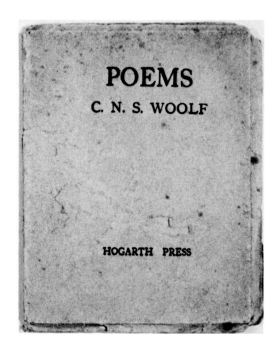

ILLUS. 95. Hogarth Press, Richmond. *Opposite page: Kew Gardens,* 1919; and the first book of the press, *Two Stories,* 1917, by Leonard and Virginia Woolf with woodcuts by Dora Carrington. *This page:* C. N. S. Woolf's *Poems,* 1918.

"of possession of ground of life for making the Good come into words" was in her imagination; Roget yielded "Seizin." It seemed right, and they sought no other.

The first book from the Seizin Press ("Seizin One") was a slim demy octavo, Laura Riding's *Love as Love, Death as Death* (1928). It was laboriously printed on Batchelor handmade paper from type that had been Monotype-set and put through the stick by hand. Plainly bound in a pleasant linen canvas, its only decoration was a design on the title page by Len Lye. He had recently made what is sometimes described as the first abstract film, *Tusalava,* and was to become very closely associated with the press, designing the very gay bindings that were a feature of the later Seizin books. For "Seizin Two," Gertrude Stein's *An Acquaintance with Description* and "Seizin Three," Graves's *Poems* (both published in 1929), the same methods of production were employed.

Printing at Hammersmith ceased in 1929. For personal reasons (touched on briefly in Graves's *Goodbye to All That*) the two poets wished to leave England and find a new home from which to continue their work, and the printing equipment was put into storage. After spending a while in France with Gertrude Stein, near whom they almost decided to settle, they moved briefly to Germany and from there to Majorca. Finding a village they liked, they settled in Deyá and had the press and the other printing equipment shipped out to them from England.

A good deal more printing was to be produced from the press's new home despite the difficulties of obtaining type and paper. Four more books and a number of slighter pieces were to be printed by hand: Len Lye's *No Trouble* (1930), Laura Riding's *Though Gently* (1930) and *Laura and Francisca* (1931), and Graves's *To Whom Else?* (1931). Something of the difficulties that the printers encountered in their work can be seen in these volumes—change in size, change in paper used, italic type that does not always match the roman with which it was used—but the work was by no means bad for two amateurs less interested in the medium than in the message.

In *Laura and Francisca* there is a passage on the work of the Seizin Press:

> How's that? How's anything you know or don't?
> You can't believe . . . on ordinary paper . . .
> Printed by myself, and Robert . . .
> He's human, by every imperfection

> He's made a dogged art of . . .
> Yes, I ink, he pulls, we patch a greyness
> Or clean the thickened letters out

As time went on, Laura Riding's part in the physical production of the hand-printed volumes grew smaller as she concentrated more on the editorial side of the press's work. The handpress was proving inadequate as a vehicle for the public expression of the Seizin program, and she negotiated an agreement with Constable, the London publishers, whereby they published books sponsored by Graves and herself. Several books of importance were published under the imprint "Seizin Press—Constable," including the critical volumes *Epilogue* (1935–1937), Laura Riding's *A Trojan Ending,* Honor Wyatt's *The Heathen,* and Graves's *Antigua Penny Puce.* With the outbreak of the Spanish civil war, their use of the handpress in Majorca was brought to an abrupt and forced halt. It was not to be revived; when Laura Riding and Graves parted company in 1939, the life of the press was over. The printing equipment and the premises were by arrangement put into Graves's exclusive ownership, but the Seizin identity had been extinguished. On his return to Majorca in 1946, Graves sold the printing press; he applied the Seizin imprint on at least one pamphlet, Jay MacPherson's *Nine Poems,* which he had printed commercially in Palma in 1955.

Hogarth and Seizin followed a not uncommon pattern in changing from being purely private presses into commercial (albeit highly individual) publishing concerns. In the Netherlands De Zilverdistel had followed the opposite pattern as van Royen's influence became stronger.

One of the most private, but at the same time commercial (and certainly individual) of English private presses was the St. Dominic's Press of Hilary Pepler. Originally a Quaker, Pepler had in the early years of the century been engaged in social work, running Hampshire House (a working men's club) in Hammersmith for the London County Council. While in Hammersmith, he had become close friends with two of his neighbors in Hammersmith Terrace, Eric Gill and Edward Johnston. Emery Walker and Cobden-Sanderson were also nearby, and it was almost inevitable that he should become interested in printing. His own emotional involvement in the Arts and Crafts Movement could not have been greater, and after Gill and Johnston had both moved to Ditchling in Sussex he felt that he

> wanted to escape from the town and earn my living in the country. . . .
> Moreover, in my ignorance, I thought any fool could print. And there were
> books I wanted to print—books about crafts which machinery threatened with
> extinction. I felt that the Press, which had destroyed the kind of civilisation I
> loved, should be used to restore it, or at least help in preserving such records of
> it as came my way.

So in 1916, as a convert to Catholicism, he also moved to Ditchling to set up his press.

The St. Dominic's Press was not a private press in the sense that, say, the Doves had been. Pepler did not establish the press in order to produce the Book Beautiful. He did not think very much of the more fanciful claims of the private presses. In his fascinating essay on *The Hand Press* (originally printed by him for the Society of Typographic Arts, Chicago, in 1934, and reprinted by the Ditchling Press in 1952) he quoted from a claim made by the Bremer-Presse that the real aim of the book "should be to act as mediator between the artistic creation of genius and the mind of the reader . . . the printed page should reflect the sound and rhythm of the language and the character and form of the work itself." God help us, he commented; "it would be an impertinent and grotesque performance because the function of the printer is no more (and no less) than that of the pump which conveys water from the well to the bucket." He was a *craftsman,* with the craftsman's wholesome contempt for the more absurd fancies of those who would like to be thought artists. As such, he did not consider commercial commissions for books or for jobbing printing beneath him; his first printing, in fact, was a beer bottle label for a Ditchling publican. His press was, then, not a private press at all in the "art" sense; its privacy consisted in the honest production by hand of books that the printer thought deserved to be printed, books he printed as well as he was able.

There is, no doubt, a rather alarming air about all this. In rejecting the aesthetic ideals of the presses he thought pretentious, there was a danger that Pepler's work would be at the other extreme of the Arts and Crafts Movement: a bibliographical equivalent of the terrible hairy tweeds and heavy uncomfortable furniture that an obsession with craft so often produced. In practice his achievement was nothing like that. Perhaps as a result of his close association with Johnston and with Gill (both of whom left their mark on the St. Dominic's Press), Pepler's work from the start had a simple grace that was particularly attractive. Among its earliest publications the press issued a little periodical called *The Game*. It was produced by Johnston, Pepler, and Gill, because they had decided "to print our views about things in general which we regarded, as all men regard games, as of supreme importance." For the Christmas number in 1916 Johnston wrote out in each copy a full page *Gloria in Altissimis Deo*. The price? Half-a-crown.

By 1920 the press had established itself sufficiently well to have been chosen by Harold Midgely Taylor as his own training ground for his Golden Cockerel Press, as described in Chapter 15. Throughout the 1920s Pepler produced a long series of books, posters, rhyme sheets, penny tracts, calendars, and the like, which are at once the delight and despair of collectors. Their bibliography is, to say the least, confused. One instance will suffice: For the first poster printed by the press, Pepler used a block of a basket of flowers for decoration. This was worked with four inkers, one for the black and one each for the three colors, with the blocks being lifted and the ink dabbed on the flowers between each impression. In this way they were able to achieve four-color printing with a single impression, but to make the work more interesting, more of a game, they did not stick to the same colors for the same flowers or to replacing the flowers always in the same position, but instead made many changes during the course of the printing. The result of such experiments has been that for a good many of St. Dominic's productions, each copy has an individuality rare indeed among printed books.

The venture was completely successful; by 1934, when so many private presses were dead or dying, it had six men working full time with as much work as they cared to undertake. But in 1937, when the press attained its majority, there was a change of pace with the installation of a Linotype machine. At about the same time Pepler's own involvement with the day-to-day work of the press became less, because after G. K. Chesterton's death Pepler had become manager of *G. K.'s Weekly* and Secretary of the Distributist League: he was later to become editor of the *Weekly Review*. The St. Dominic's Press was no longer private in any sense of the word, and in 1940 when it came under new management it was renamed the Ditchling Press, a commercial firm producing good work in a way Pepler would have approved.

Another press, which combined the elements of commercial printing and of privacy, the Walpole Press of Norwich, remains remarkably little known. Martin Kinder set up his press in 1913, inspired by a visit he had paid to the Cuala Press while on a tour to Dublin with Nugent Monck, founder of the Norwich Players, who was then producing a play at the Abbey Theatre. Encouraged by Monck, he bought an Albion press and some Caslon type, and having taught himself to print, he set to work on producing material for Monck's productions with the Norwich Players—playbills, tickets, programs, and the like. One book was also produced, an edition of Monck's *The Interlude of Holly and Ivy*, which had been performed in 1911. After the interruption of World War I, his printing activity was resumed with the production of similar theatrical ephemera; with the acquisition of a treadle press and an increasing repertoire of types, he branched out into jobbing work of good quality, producing concert programs, wedding services, Christmas cards, and similar work for friends and acquaintances in the Norwich area. He was, in fact, considering giving up his work in insurance and devoting himself to a career as a jobbing printer, rather in the way that later Will Carter was to do so successfully, but because of ill health he never took the plunge, and remained always a spare-time printer.

Some of his personal ephemera produced between the wars has a very real charm; like, for example, the invitations (individually addressed in type) to a fancy-dress party:

> Will you help us celebrate
> This (for us) auspicious date
> By coming here on Satur*dy*
> The 27th of July
> Punctually at half past eight,
> Disguised as beggar, sans-culotte,
> Ragamuffin, tramp, or what
> You like?

But the real interest of the press lies in the books it produced. These included an edition of Sir Thomas Browne *On Dreams,* and two volumes of "Songs from the Dramatists"; *Thomas Nashe* in 1929 (Illus. 96), and *Thomas Dekker* in 1931. There were to have been two more volumes in the series, containing the songs of Lyly and of Peele, but the inhibiting effects of the depression on the sales of the volumes already published prevented their appearance. Had Kinder's work become well known outside the Norwich area there is no doubt that they would have sold readily, for at three shillings and sixpence each they were remarkably good value. This was no amateur printer battening on the collectors' market to sell his books at high prices; in fact, had Kinder been less modest in his

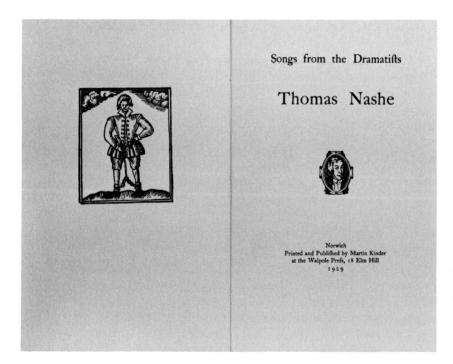

ILLUS. 96. Walpole Press, Norfolk. *Thomas Nashe,* 1929. Title-page opening.

pretensions he would probably have sold his work far more readily, but as it was, stocks of the books remained unsold until well into the 1960s.

There were a few more pamphlets published by the Walpole Press between the wars; in 1945 an edition of *The Book of Tobit* with gravure reproductions of paintings by old masters, and right up until his death in 1967 Kinder continued with his jobbing printing. He was not a great printer, but he was a good one; his books were not "fine books," but they are honest workmanlike editions of worthwhile texts, pleasant to handle and to read. It is surprising that collectors of private press work have paid so little attention to his work, for the Walpole Press was a link between the great presses of the Edwardian era and the amateurs of today.

Another venture whose promise was betrayed by the difficult years of the thirties was the Raven Press at Harrow Weald, Middlesex. This was set up in September 1930 by Robert Ashton Maynard and Horace Walter Bray on their departure from the Gregynog Press in Wales. They had acquired a considerable reputation as well as experience in their years at Gregynog and had high hopes that at their new press they would be able to continue in the same way, but without the frustrations of the Gregynog Press Board.

They could not have chosen a worse time. Although in 1931 they produced under the Raven imprint some books that were little less successful than their Gregynog work—*Venus and Adonis* and *The Book of Tobit* with engravings by Bray, and a rather less successful *Samson Agonistes* with Maynard's engravings—and an edition of Tusser's *Five Hundred Points of Good Husbandry* for another publisher (Illus. 97), the depression meant that the books did not sell. Several other works that had figured in their first announcement had to be abandoned altogether.

For awhile, the Raven Press was saved by two developments. The first was an arrangement with Constable & Company, a firm of publishers with a good eye to book design, who undertook publication of a series of limited editions, the "Raven Miscellany" to be printed and illustrated by the partnership. It was a brave effort, but only two volumes were issued before economics forced Constable to abandon the venture. The second was a move into the production of greeting cards, initially with wood engravings by Maynard or Bray, but later with work by many other designers as well.

By this time, the Raven Press was not really a private press any more. In 1934, Bray had a breakdown brought on by worry over disputes that had developed with Maynard, and the partnership was dissolved at the end of that year. It is sad to recall that Bray (who returned to his old pre-Gregynog occupation of scene painting for the theater), was so disheartened by events that he never made another wood engraving. Indeed 20 years later, he still looked back on his time at the Raven Press with such dislike that he burned most of his own unsold stock of Raven Press books. Maynard continued alone until 1937, when, with the assistance of H. J. Hodgson (the Gregynog pressman), he produced at least one fine edition, Gray's *Elegy*, undertaken for the Limited Editions Club (1938). However, the mainstay of the firm until Maynard closed it in 1965 was the greeting card business.

Of the many other private presses that grew up in the hectic atmosphere of the 1920s, few were more successful than the Raven Press in surviving the depression if the sale of the books that they printed was a matter of real importance to their owners. Many of those that died were of little importance, and their demise scarcely a matter of regret. One notable exception was the Beaumont Press, which the bookseller Cyril W. Beaumont had started from his Charing Cross Road bookshop in 1917. Beaumont had considerable interest in fine printing as well as in the dance and ballet (for which he is better known) and had for some time toyed with the notion of his own press, which, to distinguish it from Eragny, Doves, and the others, should concentrate on new work by distinguished contemporary writers. To supplement his theoretical knowledge of printing gained from

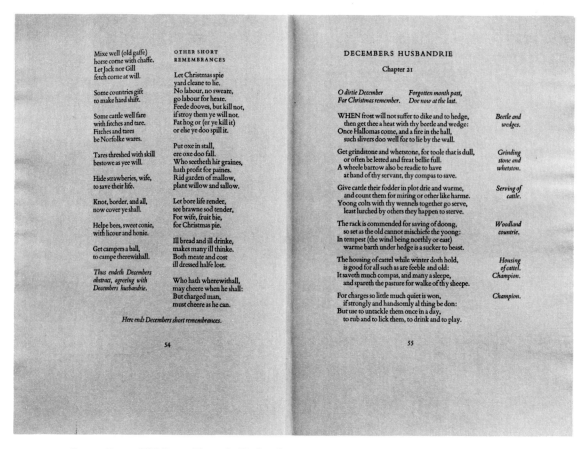

Mixe well (old gaffe)
horse corne with chaffe.
Let Jack nor Gill
fetch corne at will.

Some countries gift
to make hard shift.

Some cattle well fare
with fitches and tare.
Fitches and tares
be Norfolke wares.

Tares threshed with skill
bestowe as yee will.

Hide strawberies, wife,
to save their life.

Knot, border, and all,
now cover ye shall.

Helpe bees, sweet conie,
with licour and honie.

Get campers a ball,
to campe therewithall.

*Thus endeth Decembers
abstract, agreeing with
Decembers husbandrie.*

OTHER SHORT
REMEMBRANCES

Let Christmas spie
yard cleane to lie.
No labour, no sweate,
go labour for heate.
Feede dooves, but kill not,
if stroy them ye will not.
Fat hog or (er ye kill it)
or else ye doo spill it.

Put oxe in stall,
ere oxe doo fall.
Who seetheth hir graines,
hath profit for paines.
Rid garden of mallow,
plant willow and sallow.

Let bore life render,
see brawne sod tender,
For wife, fruit bie,
for Christmas pie.

Ill bread and ill drinke,
makes many ill thinke.
Both meate and cost
ill dressed halfe lost.

Who hath wherewithall,
may cheere when he shall:
But charged man,
must cheere as he can.

Here ends Decembers short remembrances.

54

DECEMBERS HUSBANDRIE

Chapter 21

*O dirtie December   Forgotten month past,
For Christmas remember.   Doe now at the last.*

WHEN frost will not suffer to dike and to hedge,   *Beetle and*
  then get thee a heat with thy beetle and wedge: *wedges.*
Once Hallomas come, and a fire in the hall,
  such slivers doo well for to lie by the wall.

Get grindstone and whetstone, for toole that is dull,   *Grinding*
  or often be letted and freat bellie full.   *stone and*
A wheele barrow also be readie to have   *whetston.*
  at hand of thy servant, thy compas to save.

Give cattle their fodder in plot drie and warme,   *Serving of*
  and count them for miring or other like harme.   *cattle.*
Yoong colts with thy wennels together go serve,
  least lurched by others they happen to sterve.

The rack is commended for saving of doong,   *Woodland*
  so set as the old cannot mischiefe the yoong: *countrie.*
In tempest (the wind being northly or east)
  warme barth under hedge is a sucker to beast.

The housing of cattel while winter doth hold,   *Housing*
  is good for all such as are feeble and old: *of cattel.*
It saveth much compas, and many a sleepe,   *Champion.*
  and spareth the pasture for walke of thy sheepe.

For charges so little much quiet is won,   *Champion.*
  if strongly and handsomly al thing be don:
But use to untackle them once in a day,
  to rub and to lick them, to drink and to play.

55

ILLUS. 97. Raven Press, Middlesex. Tusser's *Husbandry*, 1931.

The Imprint and elsewhere, Beaumont learned typesetting and presswork from a friend who was a commercial printer, Bertram Bell. The first three books issued in 1917 and 1918 (of verse by John Drinkwater, Walter de la Mare, and W. H. Davies) were printed on Bell's equipment, but in 1918 Beaumont installed an Albion press in the basement of his shop, which was thereafter used for Beaumont Press work.

Though he did not remain entirely faithful to his original notion of work by contemporaries—two of his most successful volumes were Goldoni's *The Good Humoured Ladies* (1922) and John Clare's *Madrigals and Chronicles* (1924)—he had good taste in the selection of artists commissioned to illustrate or decorate the books. The bindings, in quarter buckram with patterned paper boards, were particularly well chosen for his books and in general the work of the Beaumont Press showed an attractive light touch that is refreshing indeed compared with some of the more pompous and pretentious press books of the period. Twenty-six books in all were published, the last in 1931, before economic conditions forced Beaumont to close his press.

Others who tried in the same sort of way to further the production of well-printed editions of modern authors were less successful. John Rodker started the Ovid Press in Hampstead in 1919 intending "to bring before the public work that was then considered advanced," and produced a few volumes of poetry by Ezra Pound and T. S. Eliot, and a number of volumes of drawings by Wyndham Lewis and Gaudier-Brzeska. But the public response was cool, and at the end of 1920, Rodker abandoned his private press to continue his missionary activities through more conventional publishing channels.

Another short-lived press, which has close affinities with the Seizin Press, was that operated from La Chapelle-Réanville, Eure, in Normandy, by Nancy Cunard. She had bought a little peasant house named "Le Puits Carré" there in the spring of 1928, and wanted to try printing for herself. Various friends tried to put her off—Virginia Woolf, who had hand set her long poem *Parallax* for the Hogarth Press in 1925 pointed out what a messy business it could be, while John Rodker, with memories of his lack of success at the Ovid Press, was most discouraging. But she was not deterred, and when William Bird (whose "Three Mountains Press" in Paris had been one of the ornaments of expatriate America) offered to sell her his equipment at a bargain price she accepted without hesitation. Bird came down from Paris to supervise the installation of the old Mathieu press and was instrumental in obtaining for her the assistance of a first-rate printer, Maurice Levy.

The success of the Hours Press (as she named her venture) was never in doubt except at the very beginning, when Nancy Cunard had only vague ideas of producing contemporary poetry—for George Moore offered to send her something "to start off your press with a good bang," and very soon other friends like Norman Douglas, Arthur Symons, and Richard Aldington offered her work of theirs to print. Of the first eight books printed at the Hours Press, six were by these authors. (The first, Norman Douglas's *Report on the Pumice-Stone Industry of the Lipari Islands,* which he had written as a report for the Foreign Office in 1895, was produced as a present for the author. It must have been an abominably difficult book on which to learn typesetting and printing.) In Moore's *Peronnik the Fool,* the first book offered for sale, the work was much better. Caslon type on Rives paper was used, as in most of the later books. Its binding was relatively plain, unlike later Hours Press books in which much use was to be made of bindings decorated with photomontages by Len Lye, Man Ray, and others.

One book of remarkable interest was produced in Normandy in 1929, Aragon's *La Chasse au Snark,* a tour-de-force of translation (Aragon regarded Lewis Carroll as well within the realm of surrealism), and the only Hours Press book not in English. But in the winter of 1929–1930, after many a 16-hour day at the press, Nancy Cunard decided to move back to Paris. George Sadoul found her a little shop on the Left Bank, the equipment was brought from Normandy, another press purchased, and the Hours Press resumed work. There was to be much more contemporary poetry produced—by Roy Campbell, Laura Riding, Robert Graves, and others as well as *Whoroscope,* Samuel Beckett's first separately published work. But the management of the press took up far too much of Nancy Cunard's time—and she wanted to be printing herself, not to employ others to do the work for her. One or two books were farmed out to commercial printers: Ezra Pound's *A Draft of XXX Cantos* to Bernouard of Paris, and John Rodker's *Collected Poems* to the Curwen Press in England. Two works were to be produced at the Hours Press by a temporary manager working without supervision—indeed one of them, Havelock Ellis's *The Revaluation of Obscenity,* was printed without Cunard's knowledge. There was no pleasure in this for the owner, so at the height of its literary success in 1931 the press was closed. One of its presses was sold to Guy Lévis-Mano, the other taken back to Réanville. This, and the African sculpture and other possessions that Nancy Cunard had there, was to be destroyed by German and French looters during the war; the remaining stock of books was trodden into the mud and destroyed. In its three years, the Hours Press was typographically insignificant (despite its exciting bindings), but in literary terms it was one of the most important of all the private presses.

With so many private and quasi-private presses on the fringe of the literary world, one might have expected them to figure occasionally in contemporary novels. But the fictional private presses of the period between the wars are no more typical of their time than Des Esseintes's had been in *A Rebours*—and they are a good deal less interesting. Henry Wimbush's *History of Crome,* written over a period of a quarter of a century, and then occupying four years in the printing, was clearly a delightful book, as the excerpts from the life of Sir Ferdinando Lapith in Huxley's *Crome Yellow*

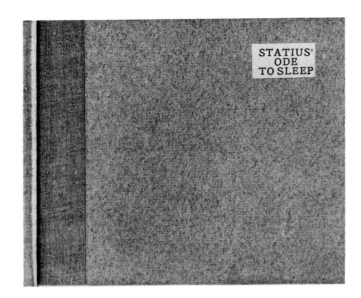

ILLUS. 98. *Left:* Stanton Press, Middlesex. *Ode to Sleep,* 1923. Binding. *Bottom:* Title page.

show. But one suspects that the printing was only pedestrian; it was a press in the tradition of Sir George Sitwell rather than of St. John Hornby. Jasper Shoon's press was a much more ambitious affair, and the idea of having a press in a Gothic cellar equipped with clanking chains and gesticulating skeletons would have amused other amateur printers as well as the author of *The Castle of Otranto.* But they would have been doubtful about the use of a powered press, and would have wanted to know more about the work of the Shoon Abbey Press besides its complimentary verses before giving their approval. The plot of Michael Innes's *Stop Press* does not give it.

Among the private presses that safely survived the depression, there were some more in the tradition of the Victorian parlor printers or of the Daniel Press than of Kelmscott and the Arts and Crafts Movement. The earliest of these to be established was the handpress of E. H. Blakeney, who started printing for his own diversion at Ely in 1908. Some 10 booklets, mostly of poetry, were printed in small editions before 1918, when the printer (who for some years was Secretary of the Amateur Printers' Association) moved to Winchester to become a master at the college. For a while he ceased printing, but in 1925 he resumed his hobby, and continued to produce respectable and collectible little books from his press until the early 1950s. Most of these were intended purely for private circulation to friends, though a few copies were occasionally sold for a shilling or two.

The High House Press, which was run as a hobby by another schoolmaster, John Masters of Shaftesbury, was a very much more ambitious affair than Blakeney's had been. It was set up, like most such presses, purely for the pleasure the owner found in printing texts that interested him. All the work of composition, presswork, and binding was carried out by Masters and his wife, and the many books they produced show very clearly the mastery they had gained in the craft. They were handsomely produced books, all of considerable literary interest; some reprints of classical works, but others editions of contemporary verse. It was a long-lived press; after his retirement to Westbury-on-Trym, Masters continued with his printing until his death in 1943. Other purely amateur presses producing work of a high standard in the 1920s were seldom so long lived; at the Priory Press in Tynemouth Robert King printed a number of books of north-country interest, such as his *Old Tyneside Street Cries* (1924); at Wembley Hill, Richard Stanton Lambert and his wife produced a few books of some merit, of which their edition of Walafrid Strabo's *Hortulus* (1924) was perhaps the most attractive. This press was, however, something of a throwback to an earlier period. Although Lambert was later aware of the work of Morison, Simon, and others in improving typographic standards, his own taste (or that of his wife Elinor who provided the woodcut illustrations) was very much closer to the earliest followers of William Morris. Seeing some of their books, like Hieronymus Vida's *Game of Chess* (1921) or Laurence Binyon's *The Sirens* (1924), one can scarcely believe that the books were not printed in the nineties. At the short-lived Azania Press at Medstead (Hampshire) some work of African interest was produced, most unusual for a private press (Illus. 99).

At a much lower standard of technical accomplishment, Giles Dixey's press at Oxford is interesting. From 1919 to 1945 he was a master at the Dragon School, and started printing at the school with an Adana flatbed press about 1922, producing school programs, Christmas cards, and such pieces as a part of the work of a handicrafts hut under his charge. When he handed over his

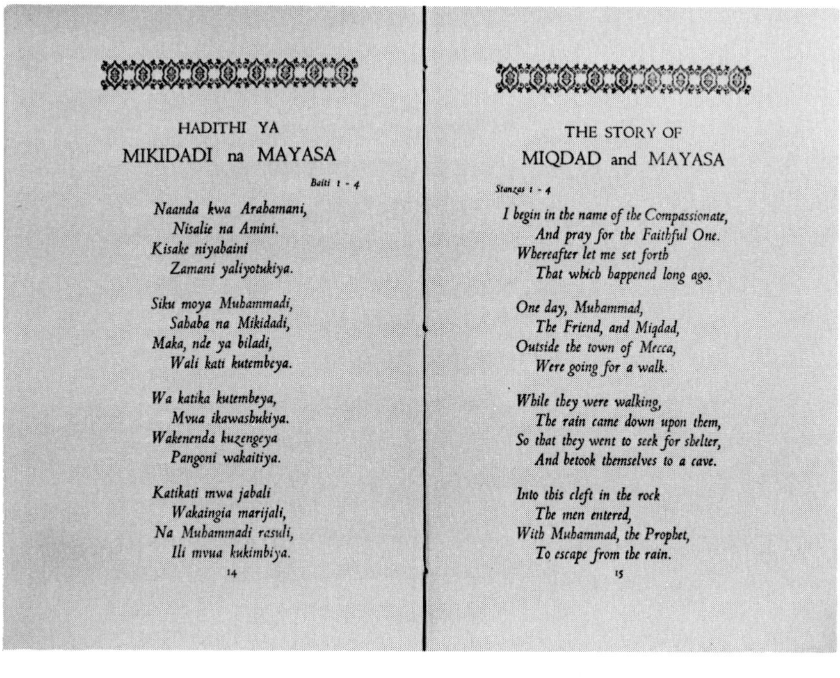

HADITHI YA
MIKIDADI na MAYASA

Baiti 1 - 4

Naanda kwa Arabamani,
Nisalie na Amini.
Kisake niyabaini
Zamani yaliyotukiya.

Siku moya Muhammadi,
Sababa na Mikidadi,
Maka, nde ya biladi,
Wali kati kutembeya.

Wa katika kutembeya,
Mvua ikawashukiya.
Wakenenda kuzengeya
Pangoni wakaitiya.

Katikati mwa jabali
Wakaingia marijali,
Na Muhammadi resuli,
Ili mvua kukimbiya.

14

THE STORY OF
MIQDAD and MAYASA

Stanzas 1 - 4

I begin in the name of the Compassionate,
And pray for the Faithful One.
Whereafter let me set forth
That which happened long ago.

One day, Muhammad,
The Friend, and Miqdad,
Outside the town of Mecca,
Were going for a walk.

While they were walking,
The rain came down upon them,
So that they went to seek for shelter,
And betook themselves to a cave.

Into this cleft in the rock
The men entered,
With Muhammad, the Prophet,
To escape from the rain.

15

ILLUS. 99. Azania Press, Hampshire. *Miqdad and Mayasa*, 1932. Double spread from a press specializing in Africana.

responsibilities for handicrafts to another master he took his press home and used it for printing verses, producing a little volume every two or three years. After his retirement in 1945 his rate of production increased, and little pamphlets still appeared occasionally from his press for another 20 years. They were not great printing and did not contain great poetry, but they are interesting examples of the work of the most genuine of all private printers, those whose owners would say with Walpole that "present amusement is all my object," and leave theorizing about the Book Beautiful strictly alone.

Chapter 17

—

BETWEEN THE WARS
IN THE U.S.A.

ALTHOUGH A NUMBER OF INTERESTING and important presses in Britain and Europe were started in the period 1914–1918, World War I interrupted work there to a far greater extent than in the United States. In part, this resulted from America's lesser and later involvement in the hostilities, and to some degree from the different form taken by the revival of interest in fine printing that grew out of William Morris's "little typographical adventure." In the United States, the role of some of the better commercial printing houses and of such typographers and book designers as Daniel Berkeley Updike, Bruce Rogers, and Will Bradley had earlier tended to relegate private presses to a less significant position.

One private press started during the war years was Dard Hunter's Mountain House Press. Hunter had grown up with a familiarity with printing through his family's newspaper printing business in Chillicothe, Ohio. Before going to the university, he had been fascinated by his father's purchase of one of Morris's Kelmscott books, and while at Ohio State University he saw more Kelmscott and Doves work. In 1903, Hunter joined the Roycrofters in East Aurora, New York, and contributed to their publishing and crafts program. In 1905–1907, in particular, he designed some of the better Roycroft volumes, though later in life he wrote slightingly of his accomplishments there.

In 1909, Hunter went to Europe to study and work. He was admitted to the Austrian Imperial Printing School (on the basis of a forged diploma, as he wrote in his autobiography *My Life with Paper*), and studied under Rudolph von Larisch, who ranked with Edward Johnston as the most significant figure in calligraphy at the time. In 1911, he moved to London, where he earned his living by commercial design work and also broadened his knowledge of the English private presses. He visited the Doves Press and formed a friendship with Lucien Pissarro at the Eragny Press. At the same time, through study at the Science Museum, he had become fascinated by the exhibits on papermaking and typefounding by hand. Gradually these various influences produced in him a determination to set up his own private press—but one with a difference. In his own words, "I wanted my work to be individual and personal, without reliance upon outside help from the typefounder or papermaker. I would return to America and attempt to make books by hand completely by my own labor—paper, type, printing."

Hunter spent the next three years at an old fruit farm he purchased at Marlborough-on-

Hudson, building a small paper mill and making paper. In summer, when the water level was too low to drive the mill, and in winter, when the millstream was frozen, he busied himself with cutting his font of type (on which he had started work in London in 1912) following the instructions in Joseph Moxon's *Mechanick Exercises* (1683). Hunter's determination to make books entirely by his own labor was to demand from him far more than Morris or any other private printer of the time put into their own enterprises.

After two years of papermaking and work on the type, he was ready to print a book. In 1915, he printed W. A. Bradley's *The Etching of Figures* and in 1917, Frank Weitenkampf's *The Etching of Contemporary Life,* two small books that were commissioned by the Chicago Society of Etchers. Perhaps it is not strange that Hunter's enthusiasm for doing things the hard way should have waned, and that instead of following Moxon's instructions to build a common-press, he purchased an old Washington handpress to print the two! The books were by no means without merit, but Hunter was deeply disappointed by the results of all his efforts and nearly abandoned his private press altogether.

But he did not; instead, the press took a new direction. Hunter pursued his studies of paper-making methods and history, and thereafter, following a move from Marlborough-on-Hudson to his home town of Chillicothe in 1917, all his own books were to be devoted to different aspects of this subject. He rapidly became renowned as an expert. The first of these to be issued by his "Mountain House Press" (named for his home in Chillicothe) was, in 1923, *Old Papermaking* (Illus. 100), to be followed in 1925 by *The Literature of Papermaking 1390–1800, Primitive Papermaking* (1927), and *Old Papermaking in China and Japan* (1932) in all of which Hunter's own type was used. Meanwhile, in the intervals from his world travels to collect the materials for his books, he had established the Lime Rock Mill in Connecticut to make handmade paper by traditional methods, using equipment and craftsmen brought over from Britain. It was a gallant venture, but it came too late, and near the end of 1931, he was forced into receivership: "The revival of the craft of making paper by hand had cost more than sixty thousand dollars. All I received from the venture was experience, not all of it in the field of papermaking." From the Lime Rock Mill, Hunter had obtained enough paper for his 1932 book, and a sufficient amount remained for the fifth of his own private press books. (Some of his researches were published elsewhere by the Pynson Printers, but, handsome as bookmaking though these were, they were not private press publications.) This fifth book was *Papermaking in Southern Siam* (1936). Set in Caslon type, the edition was much smaller. In the colophon of the book it was bluntly stated: "Due to my strong aversion to the monotony of press-work only 115 copies of this book have been made." The actual printing on the hand press was always burdensome; this part of the work was never a pleasure. For the next book, *Chinese Ceremonial Paper* (1937), Caslon type was again used for the small edition, which was printed on handmade Chinese paper with the illustrations on Hunter's own paper made at Lime Rock or at Marlborough-on-Hudson.

World War II caused a delay in the production of his next book, *Papermaking in Indo-China* (1947). For this, Hunter had the assistance of his son Dard Hunter, Jr., who acted as pressman and also cut the ornaments used in the book. Dard, Jr., was only a little less accomplished a craftsman than his father. In the late 1930s he had also cut his own typeface for hand casting, first shown in a specimen on Lime Rock paper printed in the Paper Museum at the Massachusetts Institute of Technology in 1940 (to which his father had moved in 1939). Toward the end of 1950 this new typeface was used to very good effect in a limited edition of *Papermaking by Hand in America,* a massive volume of research for which Dard, Sr., set his text and his son printed it off two pages at a time (Illus. 101). It was to be a fitting finale to the work of one of the most remarkable private presses there has been.

Dard Hunter's was not the only long-lived private press. Of the older presses, the Palmetto

OLD
PAPERMAKING

BY
DARD HUNTER

MCMXXIII

PAPERMAKING
BY HAND
IN
AMERICA

DARD HUNTER

CHILLICOTHE, OHIO
UNITED STATES OF AMERICA
MOUNTAIN HOUSE PRESS
Anno Domini 1950

ILLUS. 100. Mountain House
Press, Ohio. Dard Hunter, *Old
Papermaking*. Title page.
Photograph: Courtesy of the
Trustees of The Pierpont
Morgan Library.

ILLUS. 101. Mountain House
Press, Ohio. Dard Hunter,
*Papermaking by Hand in
America*, 1950. Title page.
Photograph: Courtesy of the
Trustees of The Pierpont
Morgan Library.

Press had the earliest origins, its owner William Lewis Washburn having played with a toy press and published a miniature newspaper while a small boy in Connecticut in the 1870s. The hobby languished, but in 1900 when Washburn had become associated with a newspaper in South Carolina the "typus fever" again attacked him, and during a long and peripatetic career, the Palmetto imprint was to be used on many books. In its earliest form, his work had a distinctly Arts and Crafts air about it, in such books as *Svend and His Brethren* (1901), but Palmetto work changed considerably in style, and in the 1930s Washburn attracted attention for his miniature books.

A far more solid program of work was undertaken by the Reverend Charles C. Bubb at his press, which he set up in his Rectory at Fremont, Ohio, in 1908. Most of its work (originally issued under the imprint of the Grace Church Press, but from 1909 on from the Clerk's Press) was connected with the church, such as his excellent *Eight Greater Antiphons for Advent* (1917), which he printed complete with the music, black notes on red staves in the good old manner. Most of it was in the form of small pamphlets, produced in small editions, and in his earlier work at least he showed a sober interpretation of the Kelmscott style. A small handpress operated in spare moments does not readily lend itself to the production of lengthy books, and few amateurs would attempt anything more than booklets, but at least one publication of the Clerk's Press—Thomas Stanley's 1655 translation of *The Clouds of Aristophanes* with parallel Greek text (1916)—ran to well over 200 pages. To look through a list of his publications is to see something of the taste of the printer who was a scholar with a catholic choice of texts to be printed. As well as the many works of piety were translations or texts of literary works from Greek, Latin, Italian, French, and other sources, including an interesting *Ten Poetical Versions of the XXXIst Ode of Anacreon* (1914), in which the Greek text was accompanied by the versions of such writers as Herrick and Byron. There was a much lighter side to the Clerk's Press, too, shown by such volumes as *Selections from "The Forget-Me-Not," a Jest in Sober Earnest* (1915) in which the printer amused himself at the expense of the wretched woman versifier. Unfortunately, Clerk's Press editions were so small—frequently no more than 32 copies— that Bubb's work is much less well known than it deserves to be.

At the other extreme from Dr. Bubb's press were Frank Holme's Bandarlog frivolities, at the beginning of the century (see Chapter 13). While Holme had still been a newspaper artist in Chicago, one of his friends had been a young Detroit journalist named Edwin Hill. Hill had gone through the common boyhood stage of hobby printing before becoming a journalist; but unlike most boys he retained his enthusiasm for the craft and continued to print throughout his life. His earliest work was in the form of small amateur journals, which were circulated to like-minded fellow members of the National Amateur Press Association, but he also produced a number of small poetry booklets and one very substantial book. This was an anthology of 10 articles on the work of Thoreau, which he printed a page at a time between 1900 and 1901. All this was in addition to his long hours as News Editor of the *Detroit Journal,* and this heavy work load ruined his health. In 1901 he was compelled to abandon journalism and to adopt an outdoor life. After seven years in the Michigan woods, he entered the U.S. Reclamation Service, and moved to Mesa, Arizona, and subsequently to a small Mexican-Indian township, Ysleta, near El Paso, Texas. He remained there until his retirement many years later, all the time printing occasional pamphlets and broadsheets. He was particularly active in his hobby from about 1920 on, and his years at Ysleta saw the circle of his literary correspondence broaden to include E. V. Lucas, Vincent Starrett, Herbert F. West, Frank Dobie, and many others. Hill was no ordinary man; in circumstances that could scarcely have been less propitious he became a Lamb scholar and an authority on Thoreau (many of his more than 200 pamphlets are devoted to these two authors) and an expert on the bibliography of the American Southwest. For some years he was President of the Frank Holme Memorial Group in Tucson, and several of his booklets were devoted to the work of his old friend.

In 1945, some years after his retirement, Hill moved to Tempe, Arizona. Before his printing equipment could be moved to its new home the warehouse in which it was stored was destroyed by fire. There are not many men of 78 who would attempt to start again, but Hill did so. Will Washburn presented him with an old Columbian and with other equipment he had used at the Palmetto Press, and Hill printed another 16 pamphlets before his death in 1949. He was by no means a great printer, but his work was in the best traditions of those amateurs who print mainly for their own pleasure and almost incidentally publish material of value to others. None of his publications paid for the paper on which they were printed, and he made no attempt to profit from his work. His was a very honest private press, far preferable to many more pretentious undertakings that sprang up in the United States, just as they did in England, in the 1920s.

Another newspaperman who had a long-lived press was Hal Trovillion, owner and editor of the *Herrin News* in the coal-mining area of southern Illinois. Inspired in part by the little bibelot editions of Thomas Bird Mosher, and in part by some keepsakes he had received from a paper importer, in 1908 he decided to produce a booklet for circulation to friends at Christmas. The booklet, *Thoughts from R. L. Stevenson,* was by no means a piece of beautiful typography, and no wonder; it was printed "in between issues of a small weekly paper in a wild booming mining town, with a cursing foreman and a periodically drunken printer who was always getting his long, unanchored, grease-spotted necktie mixed in the fountain of dabby black ink." A far cry indeed from the serenity of the Doves Press.

For many years the only private productions of Trovillion's press were these annual Christmas booklets, in which the standard of printing steadily improved. But as his printing business grew larger, so did his resources for this private printing, and several books of considerable interest were produced "At the Sign of the Silver Horse"—anthologies of garden lore and a number of reprints of rare gardening books. The *First Garden Book,* an edition of Thomas Hyll's *A Most Brief and Pleasant Treatyse, Teachynge How to Dress, Sowe and Set a Garden,* the earliest book on gardening in English, had never been reprinted before the Trovillions issued it in 1938. There was an immediate demand for the book, and it was partly as a result of this demand that in the same year the Trovillion Press first offered its books for sale; they could no longer afford to give copies to all who requested them. The *First Garden Book* was reissued in a new edition, as were several of their other books for which there was a steady demand. Of these perhaps the most important was *Delightes for Ladies,* a reprint of a recipe book by Sir Hugh Plat originally published in 1602.

Beginning in 1940 an annual prospectus-retrospectus entitled "At the Sign of the Silver Horse" gave news of the work of the press, which ceased only with the death of the owner in the early 1960s. In its last years much play was made in its advertising of its position as "America's oldest private press" (a position to which it had succeeded on Edwin Hill's death in 1949), but in fact it had become more of a publishing concern than a private press. Undoubtedly it was still conducted with little idea of making a profit; for some time it used the normal resources of Trovillion's newspaper office, the work being done entirely by his employees. The last two books were produced elsewhere, one in London by the John Roberts Press, the other a photolithographic reprint of an earlier edition. Many of the books were printed in objectionably small sizes of newspaper typefaces, and in many of the books there was a want of taste in the binding materials used and in other details of production. These faults, together with a sort of smug coziness that pervades a good deal of its editorial work, did not prevent the Trovillion Press from having a good deal of success. Herman Schauinger's fulsomely written *Bibliography* of the press (1943) shows this clearly enough; and in its physical production, reveals the lack of distinction all too common in the press's work. This is a severe judgment on a press whose work gave pleasure to many readers, but I would not recommend any collector to specialize in its work.

A very much more inspired and inspiring press was that of Joseph Ishill. Of Roumanian descent, Ishill was a printer by trade, and originally turned to printing for pleasure while living in Stelton, New Jersey, in 1916. The hobby rapidly grew to be his real life's work. Working in New York City, and with four hours spent commuting each day, he somehow managed to find the time to print a considerable number of very substantial books, as well as a flood of slighter pieces. Plenty of amateurs have done as much, and the results of their labors have often been abominable. Ishill's work was very different indeed: He was in the good old tradition of American radicalism and the texts he printed were often of considerable importance—works by Stephan Zweig, Elie Faure, Havelock Ellis, Anne Cobden-Sanderson, Peter Kropotkin, and others. It was not only in the choice of his texts that Ishill was outstanding, but typographically his work was also exciting—"sufficiently unusual and unusually efficient," as Will Ransom put it. In layout, in choice of paper, type, color of ink, and illustrations the Oriole Press (as Ishill named it in 1926) revealed its owner's very individual ability. In some of his smaller pieces there is a charm and delicacy in the conception that is reminiscent of Pissarro's work at the Eragny Press, but he was no mere imitator, nor did his work depend purely on his layout for its success; his illustrators included Franz Masereel, Louis Moreau, and John Buckland-Wright.

All the Oriole Press books were printed on a handpress from hand-set type. Few of them were placed on sale; instead they were distributed free of charge despite the financial hardships that this decision caused Ishill. It was not a decision forced on him by circumstances; by the mid-1930s his work was widely known and admired, and he could have sold it with ease had he not believed it would better support his aims to give his books away.

Probably the most important of Ishill's publications, in representing his own philosophy as well as his typography, are the two volumes of *Free Vistas: An Anthology of Life and Letters,* which he published in 1933 and 1937. But his later books, like the *Collected Works* of his wife Rose Freeman-Ishill (10 pamphlets, each of 20 to 50 pages, enclosed in a slipcase), which he published in 1962, show his consistency and his application equally well. At the time of his death in the spring of 1966 he was at work on *A Calendar for Dinah* by Marney Pomeroy, and the book was completed by another New Jersey amateur, Ralph Babcock. With the passing of the Oriole Press went one of the finest of all amateur printers; in the modesty and probity of its work, the press is unlikely to be equaled.

Another private press that flourished in the early 1920s was that operated by the scholar and librarian George Parker Winship, working "At the Sign of the George." From the 1890s on, Winship had from time to time produced small limited editions of books of historical, literary, or bibliographical interest. He did this in the belief (so he said) that since his professional life was devoted to removing rare books from the market, it was his duty to replace them by others "which might not be just as good, but which might supply future collectors with something to talk about." In this he certainly succeeded, and many of his private publications—more than a few printed for him by Daniel Berkeley Updike at the Merrymount Press—have become very much sought after. It was not until 1920, however, that Winship turned printer himself. A friend had given his young son a handpress and some type (with the result that when the son went to school, he had never heard of "capital letters" but knew all about "upper case") and with this press Winship produced some pieces to demonstrate deceptive cataloguing and the dangers inherent in manufactured rarities to the class he was teaching at Harvard. Several pieces of a sort to appeal to collectors were produced, the largest being Robert Louis Stevenson's *Confessions of a Unionist,* which had not previously been published. Indeed, in order to test his own mastery of the tricks of the trade, Winship issued two versions of this, one on handmade paper at $10, and another very much smaller impression on ordinary paper, which he offered at $1.50 "for libraries . . . of no collector's value." The ten dollar issue sold very well; of the latter only two or three copies were sold.

Though a few pieces were printed on the premises, it was not Winship's usual practice. His children were so much better at distributing the ink on their clothes than on the forms of type that he decided it was wiser to limit their work to composition. The presswork was normally farmed out to a commercial printer in Cambridge.

Winship's press was deliberately lighthearted in its approach to books for collectors and the mystique of fine printing. There were several other private presses in the United States in the 1920s that had a similarly lighthearted approach and a disregard for whether their work sold or not. Some of these ventures were busman's holidays; amateur printing by professional printers or typographers. Carl Purington Rollins's printing at "The Sign of the Chorobates," L. A. Braverman's Fleuron Press in Cincinnati, and the Holiday Press (a private press within the works of the giant Lakeside Press of R. R. Donnelly & Sons, which was set up "to promote more virile and original expression of design and craftsmanship in American printing") were examples of the zest for their craft that more than a few printers retained after their day's work was done. Some of these amateur affairs were amusing in their irreverence, like Earl H. Emmons's long-lived Maverick Press, which published such pieces as *The Saga of BRnacle BRuce the Sailor* and the *Ballad of Mae West's Bust,* many of them with very skillfully executed type pictures.

Probably the finest of these presses was Arthur K. Rushmore's Golden Hind Press, originally set up in 1927 as an aid in producing experimental layouts for books published by Harper & Brothers, where Rushmore was in charge of production. This was by no means an uncommon practice; even today when Letraset and other modern aids make it easier to produce lifelike mock-ups of pages, many typographers still turn occasionally to a small handpress for such work. But in Rushmore's case, the pleasure of printing took over and turned the Golden Hind into far more than an experimental proofing press. Early in its career a chance came to print a definitive edition of a well-known poet's works. It was to be a massive undertaking; seven folio volumes printed on handmade paper, with no expense spared to make it right. Type was ordered from Enschedé in Holland, some trial pages were set and printed, and then the project fell through—perhaps fortunately, since so huge a task would have weighed heavily indeed on part-time printers. But the type was to prove useful on many occasions, for the Golden Hind Press composed (although it did not itself print) many of the volumes of poetry of Edna St. Vincent Millay, which were published by Harper. Although private, the Rushmores did accept commissions if the books concerned were books they wanted to produce, and if they were allowed to take whatever time they found necessary to do the work properly. Their printing was always interesting, but it is those books they published themselves that have most appeal. Some of these were placed on sale, although the majority were given away.

One of the most intriguing was a book they produced for presentation to friends at Christmas 1940. In that year there was a rash of exhibitions, lectures, pamphlets, and articles about Gutenberg to celebrate the five-hundredth anniversary of printing. Rushmore was something of a skeptic about this; therefore, as his own contribution to the celebrations, he "discovered" in a Mainz garret the private diary of Gutenberg's wife, which established conclusively that the real credit for the invention of printing belonged to her. *The Mainz Diary: New Light on the Invention of Printing* was published with reproductions of the bindings and of a page of the manuscript of the diary. There were plenty of people in the joke; the librarian who had supplied suitable bindings, Otto Fuhrmann, who had translated the text into German and written out the page of manuscript, W. A. Dwiggins who, as Dr. Herman Püterschein, wrote the Foreword. But when the 200 copies were sent out, letters began to pour in that showed the joke was being taken at face value. Rushmore had a difficult time for a while, although his comment that his story had as much truth in it as most of the stuff he had been forced to listen to during the year, was not unjustified.

After his retirement in 1950 Rushmore was able to devote himself entirely to the press ("Being in business always was a nuisance") and by 1955, when work ceased, the Golden Hind Press had produced nearly 200 books and pamphlets, many of which had been included in the American Institute of Graphic Arts' (AIGA) "Fifty Books of the Year" shows. On the lighter side, the press had produced a lot of interesting ephemera (including some fine nature prints made in the 1940s), and the Rushmore children and grandchildren had enjoyed many hours of playing with type.

Another even longer-lived printer's press was the Stratford Press of Elmer F. Gleason. On a much humbler scale than the Golden Hind, it had its origins in the demise of Gleason's commercial printing firm of the same name in Worcester, Massachusetts, in 1913. For a few years he printed only amateur journals and ephemera; but from 1922 (when it was reestablished in Cincinnati) until the mid-1960s Gleason produced a considerable number of books, of which the most important was probably his *The Rowfant Club: A History,* published in 1955. Without the panache of the Rushmores, the Stratford Press was nevertheless an excellent example of the sound work of which the amateur is capable.

Just as in the years after William Morris's typographical adventure it was the commercial printers in America who really comprehended his purpose and were to follow his teaching, so in the 1920s the production of fine books was to be dominated by the commercially run presses. As reference to Will Ransom's *Private Presses and Their Books* or his *Selective Lists of Press Books* shows very clearly, far better and more substantial work was being done by many commercial undertakings—firms like Pynson Printers, W. E. Rudge, C. P. Rollins, or the Spiral Press—than was being produced by any amateur.

The line dividing the commercial press producing fine printing, and the private press, which sells its books successfully and produces some work commissioned by others, is a very fine one. There were several presses operating in the twenties and thirties that had aims and methods very close to the private press in spirit, even though the purist could argue that they, like Nonesuch, were not private at all.

Of these, the outstanding success story is that of Edna and Peter Beilenson. Forsaking his father's diamond business for the greater attraction of a printing career, in 1926 Beilenson started on a two-year period of apprenticeship: with W. E. Rudge in Mount Vernon, with Frederic Goudy at Marlborough-on-Hudson, and finally at Melbert Cary's Press of the Woolly Whale in New York City. Then, with a small font of Oxford and Original Old Style faces and a Golding Pearl press, which he installed in his father's basement, he set to work on his own. It says much for the quality of his work that with his first book, *With Petrarch: Twelve Sonnets* (1928), he made the AIGA "Fifty Books" selection for the year.

From that time Beilenson never faltered. His publications (mostly issued under the imprint the Peter Pauper Press, though a few of the more risqué volumes appeared "At the Sign of the Blue-Behinded Ape") were to be delightful, exuberant, decorative books. Usually sold at prices of no more than two or three dollars apiece, in their own very different way these books brought into thousands of homes examples of good bookmaking that did much to carry the message of the Private Press Movement far beyond those homes reached by Nonesuch and others.

ILLUS. 102. Peter Pauper Press, New York. *The Pilgrim's Progress*. A characteristic example of the press's less expensive work.

In 1929, in collaboration with Edmund B. Thompson, Beilenson set up the Walpole Printing Office at New Rochelle. For the next three years, they produced excellent work commissioned by others as well as continuing with the Peter Pauper books for which Edna Beilenson had been acting as compositor. But in 1932 Thompson (who had found the Beilensons' hectic pace more than he could take) withdrew from the partnership and Edna became her husband's partner in a growing publishing venture; they produced 10 or 12 new Peter Pauper volumes every year until Beilenson's early death in 1962 and, thereafter, the press operated under the direction of Edna Beilenson alone.

After withdrawing from his partnership in the Walpole Printing Office, Edmund Thompson moved to rural Connecticut. In his home at Windham he installed a small printing shop from which, at their own gentler pace, he and his wife set up by hand and printed a number of very attractive works. Many of these were commissions for collectors like Wilmarth S. Lewis or for collectors' societies like the Grolier and Columbiad Clubs, but a good proportion were published by Thompson under the "Hawthorn House" imprint. These reflected Thompson's wish to "work new ground, with the feeling that reprints of the classics are being excellently (and adequately) done by others." Among their own publications were several concerned with cartography and the history of mapping, reflecting another of Thompson's interests, and one that was ultimately to prevail over printing; soon after Pearl Harbor, he joined the Army Map Service in Washington and never returned again to printing.

Peter Pauper and Hawthorn House were excellent enterprises whose modification of private press methods was justified. But there was also a host of quasi-private presses and publishing imprints that emerged in America as in Britain to feed on the book-collecting boom of the twenties about which little is worth saying. With the depression the bubble burst; the pity is that several of the more honest workmanlike ventures were to disappear with their imitators.

The American private and semi-private presses in Paris were a microcosm (if an unusually literary one) of the whole fine book production scene. Among the "pure" private presses was William Bird's Three Mountains Press. Bird had been told by another expatriate American writer in Paris of a handpress that was being sold cheaply; he purchased it, installed it in a diminutive shop on the Ile St. Louis, and used it to produce small editions of work by Ezra Pound, Ernest Hemingway, Ford Madox Ford, and others, all printed by Bird himself. So small were his premises, in fact, that Sylvia Beach has recorded that when she went to call on him they had to converse on the pavement outside; there was no room for more than one in the printing office. When Bird eventually lost interest in his press, the equipment was sold to Nancy Cunard, who used it at her Hours Press in Normandy.

Bird was a partner with Robert McAlmon in Contact Editions, a publishing imprint used on small editions of avant-garde works by James Joyce, William Carlos Williams, Hemingway, and other writers. These were printed commercially, but had much of the spirit of private presses about them.

> Contact Editions [the partners wrote] are not concerned with what the "public"
> wants. There are commercial publishers who *know* the public and its tastes. If
> books seem to us to have something of individuality, intelligence, talent, a live
> sense of literature, and a quality which had the odour and timbre of
> authenticity, we publish them.

Other expatriate printers were less single minded in their devotion to literature and wanted to make fine books. At the Black Sun Press, which they set up in 1927, Harry and Caresse Crosby produced some fine volumes with the help of a master printer, Roger Lescaret. Their books included Archibald MacLeish's *Einstein* and Joyce's *Tales Told of Shem and Shaun* as well as some of the more usual standbys of the printers of fine books: Poe, Oscar Wilde, Sterne. After Harry Crosby's death in 1929, his widow carried on the press, but it became far less private and more of a publishing imprint. At "Harrison of Paris" Monroe Wheeler, financed by Barbara Harrison, designed a series of 13 books that were (in the Nonesuch manner) printed elsewhere by such firms as Enschedé. Many of them were in the usual range of classics of which there were already more than enough satisfactory editions (Aesop, Merimée's *Carmen,* Shakespeare's *Sonnets*), but there were also titles by a sprinkling of young contemporary authors; and in their *Typographical Commonplace Book* (1932), they created a splendid display of fireworks. Harrison of Paris was, in fact, a very good press of the sort producing deluxe editions, but the 1930s did not provide a place for such presses as the 1920s had done.

Only in California, it seemed, was it possible for excellent work in the private press tradition to continue, even to flourish. It is the only one of the states to have developed a strong regional character in its printing. Perhaps because of its relative lack of large printing houses that dominate the trade in other parts of the country, perhaps because of its distance from the traditional publishing centers of Boston and New York, or perhaps because of the presence of wealthy patrons, societies, and bookshops who commission local work—or probably as a result of all these factors—California has proved an ideal locale for many small and highly individual presses working in the private press tradition.

The earliest of these was John Henry Nash, who, starting in 1916, produced many books of merit (if rather heavily influenced by William Morris) for the Book Club of California, for William Andrews Clark, and for other clients as well as many produced on his own account. But infinitely more attractive and original was the work of the Grabhorns. Born in Indiana, the two brothers, Edwin and Robert, set up their press in San Francisco in 1919; two years later they started on book work with Emma Frances Dawson's *A Gracious Visitation,* which was commissioned by the Book Club of California. Their lively and virile work, in the best traditions of the private press movement (and very far removed from the pseudopresses with their cult of the deckle edge and the like) quickly earned them a high reputation. Like every other printer, they were hit badly by the depression, but they weathered it successfully and continued until 1965 to produce books of the highest quality.

Many Grabhorn books were produced on commission, but a good many were purely private publications. Some of their most successful work was for the Book Club of California, work such as *The Letter of Amerigo Vespucci* (1926), in folio, with initials and woodcuts by Valenti Angelo. Angelo (who was later to produce distinguished work in collaboration with the Walpole Printing Office and Hawthorn House under the Golden Cross Press imprint, and in the late forties started his own Press) collaborated closely with the Grabhorns over a six-year period, and shares the credit for some of their finest work, of which *Leaves of Grass* (1930) is often accounted their greatest (Illus. 103). Another artist who worked closely with the Grabhorns was Mallette Dean, who was to contribute to some 30 of the press's books. In its later period from 1951 on, the most important work undertaken by the Grabhorns was their series of Shakespeare's plays, for which Edwin's gifted daughter, Mary Grabhorn, furnished skillful colored woodcuts. Series is perhaps the wrong way to describe these volumes; apart from Mary's illustrations and the pervasive Grabhorn gusto they all share, they were anything but uniform in format, design, or choice of typeface.

Jane Grabhorn (Robert's wife) produced in addition to the books printed under the family imprint, some splendid pieces from her Jumbo Press and Colt Press; and some of the later private printers—Adrian Wilson, Sherwood Grover, Jack W. Stauffacher, Andrew Hoyem—received more than a little inspiration and encouragement from their association with the Grabhorns. *Life & Hard Times, or Sherwood Grover's Twenty-Five Years with the Grabhorn Press,* produced by the Roxburghe and Zamorano Clubs in 1968, was an excellent brief account of their working methods. A comprehensive record of the Grabhorns' work was published by the press: Volume 1 compiled by Elinor

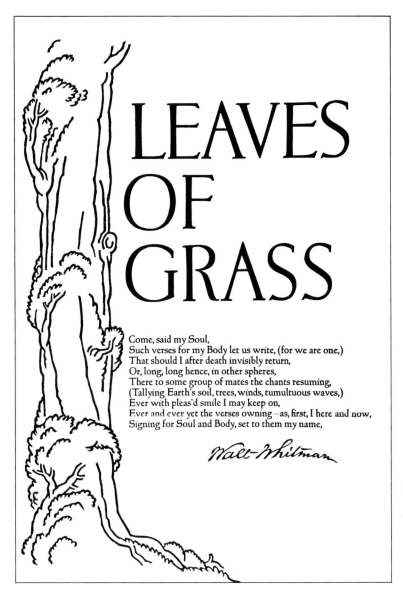

Come, said my Soul,
Such verses for my Body let us write, (for we are one,)
That should I after death invisibly return,
Or, long, long hence, in other spheres,
There to some group of mates the chants resuming,
(Tallying Earth's soil, trees, winds, tumultuous waves,)
Ever with pleas'd smile I may keep on,
Ever and ever yet the verses owning—as, first, I here and now,
Signing for Soul and Body, set to them my name,

Walt Whitman

ILLUS. 103. Grabhorn Press, San Francisco. *Leaves of Grass,* 1930. Photograph: Courtesy of the Rare Books and Manuscripts Division, The New York Public Library, Astor, Lenox, Tilden Foundations.

Heller and David Magee (1940) covered its earliest years; Volume 2 by Dorothy and David Magee carried the story forward to 1956. A third volume covering the last years of the press continued the record with the work of Andrew Hoyem, who worked in partnership with Robert Grabhorn until the latter's death in 1973. Altogether, these volumes cover a remarkable family enterprise and a press that produced some extremely handsome books. Strangely enough, although the Grabhorn Press was early esteemed not only in its home state but throughout America, its work has never enjoyed the same esteem in Britain. An easy explanation is in the brother's fondness for Goudy's types, which were less highly regarded in the Old World; but this is an insufficient reason, since the press also made extensive use of Lutetia, Janson, Centaur, and other faces against which British typographers and typophiles have no such objection. I believe their hesitation has come much more from the vigor and innovation that marked Edward Grabhorn's typographic design. As Joseph Blumenthal has observed, "his large and lavish and, occasionally, flamboyant style can be readily recognised as typically Grabhorn. It could have been born and matured only in the American Far West." William Morris would have relished much in the Grabhorn Press's work and would have recognized the hard work and love that was put into even those volumes he disliked. But Cobden-Sanderson would have been appalled and frightened by the exuberance, and I suspect that much later English opinion has seen only the surface foreign nature of their work.

Fine printing in the Kelmscott-Doves tradition was not to flourish only in the San Francisco Bay area. In Los Angeles, Saul and Lillian Marks's Plantin Press, established in 1931, produced some of the best and most classical printing in the United States. The firm was deliberately kept small in order to retain personal control of quality, and work of a very high standard indeed has been printed for such clients as the Huntington Library and Dawson's Bookshop.

Another equally fine, though more prolific and bolder undertaking, was the Ward Ritchie Press. While Ward Ritchie was reading law without much enjoyment at college, he came across a copy of T. J. Cobden-Sanderson's *Journals,* and was filled with enthusiasm for printing. He went to San Francisco to ask advice of the Grabhorns and of Nash, and in 1928 entered a trade school in order to learn the rudiments of the craft. There followed a period in which he worked during the day in Vroman's bookstore in Pasadena, and spent the evenings with Lawrence Clark Powell (later to become Librarian of the University of California, Los Angeles) printing in the Abbey of San Encino. They produced a good number of small pamphlets of poetry by such writers as Archibald MacLeish and Robinson Jeffers, which they gave away to any friends who seemed interested. In 1930 Ritchie took himself to Paris to work in the atelier of François-Louis Schmied, who had written in the *Fleuron* on the books of the future. While in Paris, Ritchie printed a small edition of Jeffers's *Apology for Bad Dreams,* and after his return to California in the following year continued with some other privately printed pieces. But in 1932, when the Ward Ritchie Press really started, the emphasis moved steadily toward more commissioned work. From 1935 on—especially when Gregg Anderson (who had previously operated the Grey Bow Press with Roland Baughman) joined up with him—the press grew apace, producing some very powerful typographic work for the Huntington Library, the Limited Editions Club, and other outside publishers. Like the Grabhorn Press, the Ward Ritchie Press continued to publish many books in its own right; some of these, like *XV Poems for the Heath Broom* by "Peter Lum Quince" (Ritchie himself) of which 50 copies were printed in 1934, were without doubt private press work. During the difficult years of World War II the press contracted; with Ritchie working for the Douglas Aircraft Company and Gregg Anderson in the army (he was killed in Normandy in 1944), operation of the press was continued by Joe Simon, brother of Lillian Marks of the Plantin Press. After the war, under the style of Anderson Ritchie and Simon, the press grew considerably, adding lithographic and bindery sections. The survey of its work, *The Ward Ritchie Press and Anderson Ritchie & Simon,* published in 1961, gave an excellent picture of the vigor of good Californian printing, too little of which finds its way to England. Ritchie himself retired from the firm in 1974 and resumed personal printing on an Albion press under the style Laguna Verde Imprenta.

In the completely private field, much of the most interesting printing of the 1930s was also produced in California. Wilder Bentley, who had worked for three years with Porter Garnett at the Laboratory Press at Carnegie Institute of Technology in Pittsburgh, printed a range of handsome pamphlets and books (some commissioned by the Book Club of California) on his handpress in Berkeley. Another was Thomas Perry Stricker, a self-taught printer in Los Angeles who between 1930 and 1940 produced some interesting books with meticulous craftsmanship. Some of his contributions to the Typophiles' keepsakes are particularly successful.

One very interesting and little-known press was that of Tuley Francis Huntington at Palo Alto. His output was small: "The Master writes the books he prints, he sets up each letter of the text and each type-ornament, he oils and inks the press, and he turns and holds the wheel to gather the lingering pressure that produces the black type-block of the page perpetual." Huntington printed three books, starting with *The Acre of the Earth Turner* (1929) and three issues of *The Lagday Letter* in editions of 50 copies or less. The literary style can be gathered from the passage quoted, but he was right in saying "Quite unique are the color-effects, and designs modernistic, many in two or three colors, that adorn these books"—books that are charming examples of the taste of the period, and deserve to be better known.

It was not in California, however, but on the eastern seaboard that the greatest of all private presses of the 1930s was to be established: the Overbrook Press of Stamford, Connecticut. In the scale of its work, and in its record of many volumes given away and few sold, it is not unlike Strawberry Hill; in its quest for technical excellence regardless of cost, the work of Count Kessler at the Cranach-Presse is a truer parallel.

Frank Altschul, its wealthy owner, had been tempted as a child by printing. He has recorded how he was given a press one Christmas, but that it did not remain in his possession for long. When his mother found smears of ink all over the house, it was soon confiscated. After his marriage in 1913 Altschul set up a small press in his New York apartment, printing a few pieces of ephemera on it until the demands of a growing family requisitioned his printing room. Once more his interest in printing had to be suppressed, and it was not until 1934 that it was revived in practical form. About that time August Heckscher, who had been running the Ashlar Press as a hobby, decided to bring its activities to an end. (Heckscher, too, was to find the love of printing too much to resist; small pieces from his Uphill Press continued to appear occasionally for many years.) Margaret B. Evans, who had been the guiding spirit of the Ashlar Press, approached Altschul to find out whether he would be interested in continuing the venture. He responded enthusiastically: Some outbuildings at his home, Overbrook Farm, in Stamford were adapted, a secondhand Colt's Armory Press and other necessary equipment installed, and Evans was engaged to act as designer and compositor. The pressman was John MacNamara. Altschul was a good deal more successful in the staff he engaged than many owners of private presses; Evans remained at the press until 1944, when John Logan succeeded her as designer; MacNamara continued as pressman until his early death in 1955, after which the printing was done by Frederick Warns.

The lavish scale on which the Overbrook Press was set up was fully equaled by the ambitious books it produced. But not only books; during the more than 30 years that the Overbrook Press was active, it printed a considerable number of ephemeral pieces—awards, certificates, programs, and the like—for many organizations such as the English-speaking Union, the Woodrow Wilson Foundation, the Committee for the Marshall Plan, and the American Institute of Graphic Arts, organizations in which Altschul was interested. Many of its pamphlets and smaller books had a seriousness of purpose not frequently encountered in the work of private presses, and an excellence of typography and presentation not often to be seen in political or social publications. Such productions as the *Adverse Report of the [Senate]Committee on the Judiciary on a Bill to Reorganise the Judicial Branch of the Government* (1937) or Senator J. William Fulbright's *Towards a More Creative Foreign Policy* (1959) are not the sort in which one would expect to find much typographic merit, but the Overbrook Press's care and success in the printing of works of this sort was far better than that of the majority of private presses working in far easier fields. On the many occasions that Overbrook itself produced books in the more conventional areas for a private press, its work was of a quality that placed it in the very highest class of those concerned with the art of the book. Many artists were commissioned to work for the press: Valenti Angelo, Anna Simons, Bruce Rogers, W. A. Dwiggins, Rudolph Ruzicka, and others produced decorations for many books. Of the early work of the press the most ambitious book was the edition of Robert Louis Stevenson's *An Inland Voyage* published in 1938 (Illus. 104). For this the French artist Jean Hugo was engaged to follow Stevenson's route along the canals of France and the Low Countries, the gouaches he produced being printed in Paris by the firm of Jean Saudé, using the pochoir process, while the text was printed at Overbrook.

ILLUS. 104. Overbrook Press, Connecticut. Page from *An Inland Voyage*, 1938. Gouache illustration by Jean Hugo.

One area of book production in which the Overbrook Press published some outstandingly well-designed books during the 1940s was that of books on chess. As a devotee of the two-move chess problem, Altschul had noticed how poorly produced were most of the books on the subject. Starting with *A Century of Two-Movers* (1941) the press produced a series of half a dozen books of chess problems, demonstrating superbly how attractively such work could be presented, using the ordinary chess type in conjunction with good type and superlative presswork (Illus. 105).

In these volumes, in the political pamphlets, and in the fine books, the design and the choice of types (mainly hand-set Caslon, Centaur, and Lutetia, although machine setting in such faces as Electra, Bembo, and Janson has also been used) without exception produced books one feels impelled to read. Even the largest and most sumptuous of Overbrook volumes were books designed for reading; one never has the impression that they are museum pieces to be looked at and admired but not read.

Without doubt much of the credit for this must go to Margaret Evans, who masterminded the production of most of them. But besides hers, the name with which some of the best of the Overbrook books were most closely associated was that of the artist T. M. Cleland. Starting with Richard Aldington's *A Dream in the Luxembourg* (1935), Cleland later illustrated Sterne's *Sentimental Journey* (1936) and some minor pieces for the press. In the 1950s he was responsible for the production of the press's most ambitious book, Prévost's *Manon Lescaut*. Published in 1958, the volume had

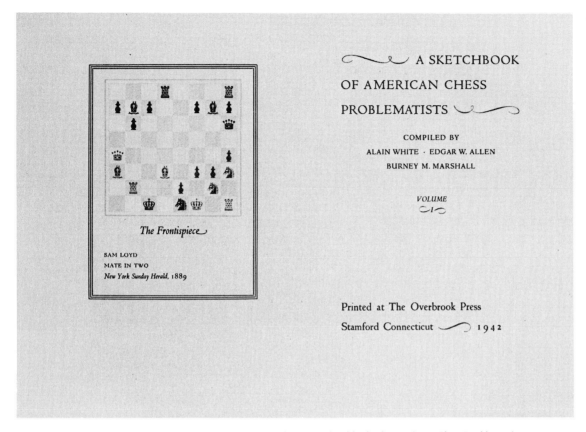

ILLUS. 105. Overbrook Press, Connecticut. Opening from *A Sketchbook of American Chess Problematists,* 1942.

been six years in the making. The many illustrations were produced by the artist using the silk-screen process, himself printing every sheet (and many of the illustrations called for 8 or 10 different workings) before returning them to the press for the text to be printed in conformity with a layout he had previously designed. The expense of the production was enormous, but the delicacy of coloring could not have been achieved by any commercially viable process. As an example of the luxurious book at its most magnificent and at its furthest remove from commercial printing, the Overbrook *Manon Lescaut* was unequaled among postwar private press books and had few peers among the books of earlier presses.

Chapter 18

—

WORLD WAR II AND THE AFTERMATH IN BRITAIN

LOOKING BACK AT THE PRIVATE PRESS scene in Britain in the mid-1930s, one can with hindsight clearly discern that the main presses of the Private Press Movement were running out of steam. Some magnificent books were still being made and these continued even into the postwar period, but the old force was declining.

There were many reasons for this. In some cases, the slowing pace was a natural consequence of the printers' own age, as with St. John Hornby or Bernard Newdigate. For others, the difficult economic climate created problems, as with Nonesuch and Golden Cockerel. To be sure, little private printing of the late 1930s would have the charm of novelty. Those who come late in any tradition are not to be condemned for lack of novelty. One cannot complain that books of the period made less attractive use of wood-engraved illustrations than those of 10 years earlier, nor that their printers made no better use of the range of new typefaces or materials. The established presses continued to produce excellent work. However, among the newer presses that were set up in the mainstream of fine printing, there was no sureness of touch. Exciting and innovative though they no doubt seemed to their owners, they seldom brought anything fresh to the art of the book, and in some respects there was a falling-off in standards.

One difficulty was in the lack of trade printers skilled in working with fine materials on the handpress. William Morris had complained of the difficulty of finding good handpress men 50 years earlier, and time had meant that apart from the few who worked within the private press field there were almost none to be found. At the Ashendene Press, St. John Hornby had great trouble with his last books when his pressman, Faulkner, fell ill.

Fortunately for Hornby, he was able to get help from H. Gage-Cole, the old Doves and Cranach pressman, who at that time was working for B. Fairfax Hall. Inspired by Nonesuch and Ashendene books, Hall had set up the Stourton Press in London in 1930. Having asked advice of the wrong people, he had acquired some Caslon type and a Cropper treadle press and was feeling thoroughly discouraged by the poor quality of his work when an opportunity came to employ

Gage-Cole. His printing room was revolutionized: The Cropper was replaced by an Albion and the other equipment Gage-Cole thought necessary. For a young man on a junior employee's salary to engage a skilled craftsman was rather adventurous—and very alarming for Hall when he realized what thorough but unhurried work was needed. Hall learned much from Gage-Cole, but the latter's strong pro-union attitude was a barrier between them. Also, although in 1931 Gage-Cole completed Dryden's *All for Love* for the Stourton Press, it was hard for Hall to find work for him, as well as money for his wages, and it was something of a relief to allow him to go to work for Hornby.

In one other respect the Stourton Press was much closer to the great private presses of an earlier period than to its contemporaries: It had its own proprietary typeface. This face, designed by Eric Gill, was provided at the expense of Sir Percival David, who had commissioned Hall to print what was originally planned as a small catalogue of his collection of Chinese ceramics and gradually grew into a huge complex folio. For this catalogue, published in 1935, and for a few smaller pieces set in the same Aries type, Gage-Cole came back to the Stourton Press, returning finally to Hornby to print the *Bibliography of the Ashendene Press* before retiring.

No further books were produced by the Stourton Press until 1947, when P. D. Ouspensky's *Strange Life of Ivan Osokin* was printed by Hall alone. In 1949 he moved to South Africa, and in the next 12 years issued some 14 other books, mainly by Ouspensky. These were far removed from the fine press tradition, most of them being lithographed on a Rotaprint machine, sometimes from IBM text, sometimes using the larger Aries type to provide repro-pulls from which Hall made litho plates. After his return to London in 1961, he resumed fine printing, this time using a Vandercook proofing press and his proprietary typeface to produce such books as *Passing Scene,* with multicolor linocuts by Rupert Shephard (1966) and Hugh Ross Williamson's *Letter to Julia* (1974).

Another interesting and ambitious undertaking was the Guyon House Press set up by Theodore Besterman. Though much better known for his work as a bibliographer or for his postwar direction of the Institut et Musée Voltaire at Geneva, Besterman was a man with a good typographic eye. It is, therefore, all the more surprising that the edition of *Magna Carta and Other Charters of English Liberties,* which was issued in 1938, should be so disappointing (Illus. 106). Its presswork, though good, was not of the same standard achieved by Gregynog or Ashendene; the headpieces by Berthold Wolpe were overpowering, although his tailpieces were charming; and there were some irritating defects (no folios, no running heads), which flaw a fine conception. But the war prevented any further work.

Another press ultimately killed by the war was the Corvinus Press, which was set up by Viscount Carlow in 1935. Named for Matthias Corvinus, the great bibliophile king of Hungary, Carlow's press reflected a number of earlier traditions among amateurs of fine printing, most notably in the wide variety of papers that would be used for a few copies of Corvinus Press books. Distinctly experimental in character, the press used many different typefaces as well as the Corvinus design, ranging from Graily Hewitt's unhappy calligraphic Treyford type through some of the Monotype revivals to contemporary faces from German founders.

Most of the books printed at the press were small, although a number of more substantial volumes were commissioned from trade houses in the Nonesuch manner, as well as being issued in very small editions. Perhaps because of the range of papers used, the presswork was often uneven in quality; nevertheless, in such books as *Poems by Walter de la Mare* (1937) or Ouida's *Tale of a Toad* (1939), the results could be very pleasing. Work continued during the war years (indeed Carlow's enthusiasm was such that while on a diplomatic mission to Finland in 1940–1941, he had a limited edition printed to his specifications by a Helsinki firm), but a good deal of the press's output was uncompleted in 1944 when he was killed en route to Yugoslavia. Among this unfinished work was Norman Douglas's *Summer Islands*; although the 45 copies (on six different papers) were printed in

ILLUS. 106. Guyon House Press, London. Opening from *Magna Carta and Other Charters of English Liberties*, 1938. Decorations by Berthold Wolpe.

1942, they were not bound until after Carlow's death. Perhaps because much of the best Corvinus Press work was produced in the war years, Lord Carlow's press has never received the attention it deserves.

In 1945, a year after Carlow's death, Lord Kemsley took over the plant and equipment and set up the Dropmore Press, which was put under the direction of Edward Shanks. Dropmore was not Lord Kemsley's only venture in the private press field; he also controlled the Queen Anne Press, which was under Robert Harling's artistic direction. Neither Harling nor Shanks was ignorant of earlier fine printing, but the lesson of Nonesuch was clearly lost on the owner of the two presses. By endeavoring to go back to the sumptuous work of an earlier generation in the difficult time of postwar reconstruction, Kemsley's presses were attempting the impossible. The dearth of handpress skills is evident in the inferior presswork that mars so many Dropmore books, and the critical climate of the time was not welcoming. In some Dropmore books, like *The Revolt of the Tartars* by De Quincey (1948) or the selections from Landor published as *The Sculptured Garland* in the same year, there was an inept pretentiousness allied to an ultraconservative view of what merited fine printing (Illus. 108). Despite its printing of one or two good books, there were not many who grieved when the Dropmore Press ceased operations in 1955.

Alone among the well-established presses, the Golden Cockerel was to continue right through the war years. That the Cockerel should have been able to survive the bombing of its premises and that it should have been able to continue operations throughout the blitz, with both its owners away on active service, seems remarkable; but it was a form of defiance, of a determination to carry on business as usual despite the difficulties, not altogether unlike the spirit that drove the Dutch in the

IMAGES

FROM THE PROGRESS

OF THE SEASONS

BY

Edward Shanks

WITH DECORATIONS BY

Charles Berry

LONDON

THE DROPMORE PRESS

1947

ILLUS. 107. Dropmore Press, London.
Images, 1947. Title page and (*below*) double spread.

Now, where the sunshine falls
Along the woodland's edge,
Beneath the primrose hedge,
While the carefree cuckoo calls,
The palsied rabbit, with dry throat,
Watches the dancing of the stoat.

Through waving grass and flowers
And the bird-harbouring tree,
The nectarous breath of spring
Goes witless on its way.
It is but atoms of the sun
And by the same compulsion moves,
To move again unwittingly
Everything that strives and loves.

Now on the eyes and lips of man
It wafts a double influence,
Soothing and firing every sense
—What then, O man? what then, O man?
Life answers, while the sages ask,
With fierce desire and heavy task,
The far-horizon-passing dream
Or with the easier plan,
To sit beside the running stream,
To handle the wild flowers
And watch the dragon-flies,
To spend the simple hours,
Sunrise and noon and moonrise.

All these things we have done,
Under compulsion of the sun.

IMAGE

NUMBER FOUR

clandestine production of finely printed books. The difficulties were considerable indeed, but perhaps less so than for a press working at a less exalted level. For the ordinary commercial publisher, materials were strictly rationed and the "authorised war economy standards" imposed on book production had a marked (although not altogether deleterious) effect on book design. But the very small quantities of paper needed for private press work—for example, the pure rag papers needed for printing the engravings that were a feature of Golden Cockerel books—could be obtained at a price. Similarly, for a small volume of work, good leather for binding and real gold for blocking could still be found.

War conditions undoubtedly affected the quality of production adversely. Supervision of the printers was not easy, and Christopher Sandford has recorded some unsatisfactory features in the design of the first volume of Napoleon's *Memoirs* (1945) resulting from misinterpretation of instructions sent while he was in army service. In more than a few cases—for instance in the second volume of the press bibliography *Pertelote* (1943) or in *Together and Alone* (1945)—the Chiswick Press was unable to print the engravings to prewar standards. Nevertheless, the press survived, and after the death in 1944 of one partner, Owen Rutter, it was continued alone by Sandford who had by that time been invalided out of the army. During his convalescence, he reconsidered his work as a book designer and, inspired by the work of Meynell, produced a number of books that were considerably more experimental than his earlier work.

The books produced by the Golden Cockerel Press during the late 1930s and the 1940s have not received nearly as much praise as its earlier publications. In part this was because the press was not breaking new ground, but just carrying on Robert Gibbings's policy of publishing books finely illustrated with wood engravings; and in part it was because in the war years there was not a public with leisure to discuss and admire the latest Cockerels—any more than did the volumes produced by the Corvinus Press receive the attention they deserved. And yet, many of the Golden Cockerel books produced during this period were as fine as anything the press ever published, and many of the texts had a genuine importance. *The Log of the Bounty* (1937), *The Voyage of the Challenger* (1938), which had the author's colored sketches copied by hand in each copy, and such other volumes as *A Voyage Round the World with Captain James Cook* (1944), published in the press's "Sea Series," *The Travels and Sufferings of Father Jean de Brebeuf* (1938), and *The First Crusade* (1945) were all splendid books.

In the austere years of the postwar world, Sandford continued producing books in his old fashion. Some of these, like Keats's *Endymion* (1947), perhaps the finest of all the books illustrated by John Buckland-Wright, or John Barclay's *Euphormio's Satyricon* (1954), were fine essays in the traditional Cockerel manner. During the 1950s, some attractive books less obviously Cockerels were also produced; such books as *The Ephesian Story* by Xenophon of Ephesus (1957), with collotypes of linoleum paintings by Eric Fraser (Illus. 109), or Shelley's undergraduate extravaganza *Zastrozzi* (1955), for which Cecil Keeling provided some splendid gothic wood engravings (Illus. 110). There were also a few late essays in the grand manner, like the folio *Songs and Sonnets of John Dryden*, the last book to be set in the Golden Cockerel type, with highly mannered illustrations by "Lavinia Blythe." But the market for expensive books of this sort had been declining for years. In the 1940s Sandford had said that "half a dozen such books was as much as the market could absorb," and by the late 1950s the market had shrunk too far for Sandford to feel it was worth continuing. In 1959 he sold the press to Thomas Yoseloff, the New York publisher, and although three books already in production were completed under the new ownership, no new work was undertaken. After nearly 40 years, and the production of some 200 books containing some of the best wood engraving of the century, the Golden Cockerel ceased crowing.

By the time Sandford sold his press to Yoseloff, a new movement in private printing was beginning to make itself felt. This was almost a recrudescence of the Victorian parlor printers—

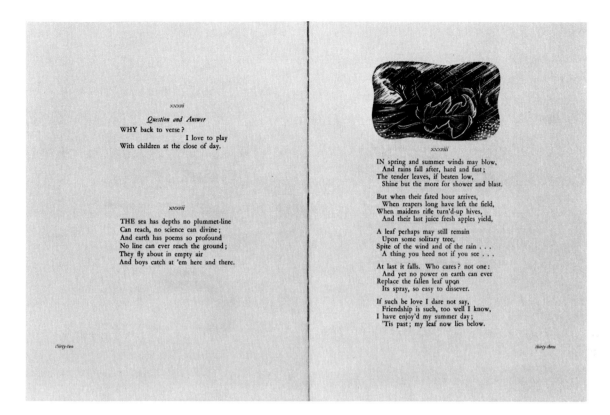

ILLUS. 108. Dropmore Press, London. *The Sculptured Garland*, 1948.

amateurs with modest means, equipment, and time determined to try their hand at the art of printing. But these men and women had one significant difference from their Victorian forebears: they were typographically informed by the work of printers of the period between the wars—commercial as well as fine printers—and by intelligent reading of the work of Stanley Morison, Beatrice Warde, and others. The publication of John Ryder's *Printing for Pleasure* in 1955 marks this new movement.

There had of course been earlier presses of this kind. At Bristol in the early 1930s Vivian Ridler and David Bland had started experimenting with an Adana press at their Perpetua Press. The Adana was soon replaced by a powered platen, and later the young men added a secondhand Miehle cylinder press—for their enterprise was not just a hobby. They did a good deal of jobbing work, from advertising leaflets and parish magazines to wallpaper, operating from the basement in the vicarage, which was Bland's family home. The press was a leisure activity and not a business, however, and the profits from their jobbing work were put into little books they published themselves or through local booksellers. These included the lively *Fifteen Old Nursery Rhymes,* with hand-colored linocuts by Biddy Darlow, which was selected as one of the "Fifty Books of the Year" in 1935, and *The Little Chimney Sweep* (1936), which was illustrated with silhouettes from the film by Lotte Reininger. Then in 1937 both Ridler and Bland left Bristol: Ridler to go to Oxford University Press (and later to become university printer); Bland to join Faber & Faber in London. A little work was done on occasional visits to Bristol, but at the beginning of the war they decided to sell the plant. The Perpetua Press imprint still was used occasionally by Vivian Ridler for the pieces printed on a platen press at his Oxford home. This sort of occasional leisure printing by professional printers was to be characteristic of one group of John Ryder's "Printers for Pleasure" in postwar years.

Another private or semiprivate press from the 1930s that had Bristol connections was the Latin Press of Guido Morris, which started inauspiciously enough with the production of *The Bristol Zoo*

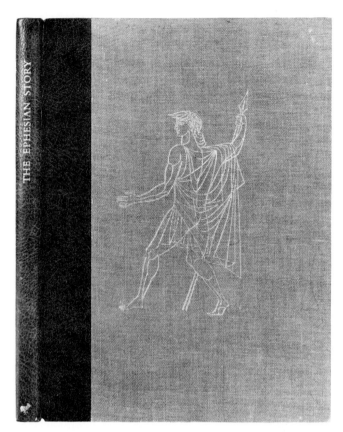

ILLUS. 109. Golden Cockerel Press, London. *The Ephesian Story,* 1957. Binding. *Opposite page:* Double spread. Illus. by Eric Fraser.

Broadsheet in 1935. Like his one-time friend Count Potocki, Guido Morris became something of a cult figure to several British private press enthusiasts a few years ago, but much earlier such people as Beatrice Warde, John Johnson, Gordon Craig, and John Farleigh had given him support and encouragement, seeing in this laboratory-technician-turned-printer some very real promise.

Promise there was. Morris was capable of superb work and revealed his ability in such pieces as the magazine *Loquela Mirabilis* or the printed letters sent to friends or potential patrons. But of the books announced in the Latin Press's "First Announcement" (March 1936)—*Ecclesiastes* in the Latin of the Vulgate, Bernard Silvestris's *De Mundi Universitate,* Peter Abelard's *Sic et Non* —none was to appear, and this pattern was to be typical. Although he could be very businesslike at times, there was a very unworldly quality to Morris, typified by the (perhaps apocryphal) story that once having been commissioned to print a wedding service he became so fascinated by the text of the service for the burial of the dead that he set that up instead! There were many moves for the Latin Press; much good ephemera was printed, as were a few books, such as the seven pamphlets in the "Crescendo Poetry" series (1951–1952) or Baron Corvo's *Letters to Grant Richards* (1952), but in 1953 Morris abandoned printing and, to everyone's amazement, became a guard on the London Underground.

In the first edition of this book, I wrote that it seemed unlikely that Morris would return to printing again. However, contrary to my expectations, in 1970, he set up a small printshop in London from which under the imprint Officina Mauritiana Londini, he once more embarked on jobbing work (Illus. 112). Writing to me at the end of 1971, he described himself as the "last of the Mohicanic printers—those who without regard to personal [or others'] cost, print for the still greater glory of an unknown God." Nevertheless, limited funds and inadequate equipment restricted output, and when he died a few years later no more books had appeared from his press.

had a lot of valuable slaves and money on board his ship, they decided to attack it and seize the cargo, killing all who tried to resist and carrying off the rest to be sold as slaves in Phoenicia—for they did not expect them to put up much of a fight. The pirates were led by a young man called Corymbus, who was very tall, with flashing eyes and long shaggy hair.

When the ship left harbour, the pirates had followed at a discreet distance, and now about midday, when everyone on board was lying either dead drunk or fast asleep, Corymbus and his men suddenly rowed their galley at full speed towards them. As soon as they got close enough, they leapt on to the ship fully armed, brandishing naked swords. Some of the crew jumped overboard in their panic and were drowned, and many others were cut down while trying to defend themselves. But Habrocomes and Anthia ran up to Corymbus and fell on their knees at his feet.

'Take all our money,' they cried, 'and make us your slaves—but please spare our lives! In the name of all that you hold sacred don't kill us now we've surrendered! Take us wherever you like and sell us as slaves—only for pity's sake sell us both to the same master!'

As soon as they said this, Corymbus gave an order for the killing to stop; but when he had transferred everything of value to his own boat, including Habrocomes and Anthia and a few of their slaves, he set fire to the ship and everyone else was burnt to death, for he decided it would not be safe to take them all. It was a dreadful scene as the galley began to move away with the prisoners and the others were left on the burning ship, stretching out their hands in agony towards their master and mistress.

'Oh, where in the world are they taking you?' they cried.

'You're lucky!' one of the captured slaves shouted back. 'You'll never know what it's like to be put in chains and ordered about by pirates!'

All this time the prisoners were being carried further and further away and the others were dying in the flames. At the last moment Habrocomes' poor old tutor felt he could not bear to be parted from his

19

Of the new presses that started in the 1950s, one of the most ambitious was the Vine Press, set up in 1956 in the village of Hemingford Grey, Huntingdonshire. It was owned by Peter Foster, an architect with a great interest in fine printing, and his close neighbor John Peters, a typographic designer at Cambridge University Press and designer of the elegant Castellar titling type. Both men had noticed the inferiority of postwar presswork and gradually developed the wish to see whether they could themselves achieve the skills of an earlier generation. Having obtained the loan of a Cope & Sherwin Imperial press from the university press, they set it up in an outbuilding of Peters's house and put their ideas into practice.

Almost a year later, in August 1957, their first work was completed. It was a leisurely beginning to what was always strictly a spare-time venture. At first, they had little idea of the style of type they should use and explored the possibility of obtaining some of Graily Hewitt's Treyford type from Oxford University Press; those who care about fine printing and admire the work of the Vine Press are glad that their efforts came to nothing. Into the first book they built as many of the problems of composition and presswork as they thought might have to be faced. Unlike their prewar models, they had no intention of employing professional pressmen. They were to do all the work themselves in their spare time, using skills acquired by reading printers' grammars, from friends in the trade, and most of all by trial and error. No trouble was spared in their quest for perfection; like Morris before them they imported ink from Jänecke Schneemann (though for later books they used English ink), and all except one of their books was printed on paper made by hand.

The first book, *Vitis Vera,* an anthology of passages on the vine taken from the Bible, was set by hand, with the Latin text from the Vulgate in 12-point Perpetua Titling and the parallel English of the Authorised Version in 18-point Perpetua. One hundred copies were planned, but in the course of printing they discovered some of the unforeseen eccentricities of their century-old press, some of

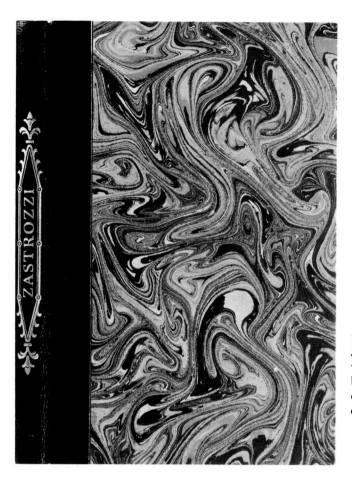

ILLUS. 110. Golden Cockerel Press, London. *Zastrozzi,* 1955. Binding. Black morocco with black and red marbled paper over boards. *Opposite page:* Cecil Keeling's wood engravings match the Gothic extravagance of the text superbly.

which they were able to resolve in later books, but others they had to accept as a natural hazard. In the end, 40 copies were completed to their satisfaction and distributed to friends, but they had discovered that if they were to manage to produce one book a year handsetting would have to be abandoned.

For their second book, the first to be offered for sale, they secured a short story by Marjorie Sisson, *The Cave,* which they thought would respond to lively illustration. Frank Martin was commissioned to provide wood engravings, the text was machine set in Perpetua at the Shenval Press, where Peters had worked for some years, and work was begun. The presswork still gave some problems, however. Despite excellently printed blocks, in some cases the type was somewhat patchy in appearance. The results, although highly satisfactory to most purchasers, were rather disappointing to the printers (Illus. 113). Their third book, Constantine Fitzgibbon's *Watcher in Florence* (1959), was more satisfactory and, in fact, presented less trouble than any of their other books. In format, it was a charming little sextodecimo, and the type (Blado italic, with a special alternative sort cut for the *z*) was again set at the Shenval Press.

Inspired by the success of *Watcher in Florence,* Peters and Foster embarked on the production of their most ambitious book, Sir Herbert Read's play *The Parliament of Women.* The idea that they should publish this and three of Read's plays written for radio had been suggested to Peters by Philip Ward, founding secretary of the Private Libraries Association, in summer 1958, and plans for the production of the single play they decided to print started then. Experiments with the design of the book began early in 1959, but the book was not completed until the end of the following year. The text was set in Monotype Centaur at Cambridge University Press, and Reg Boulton, who had

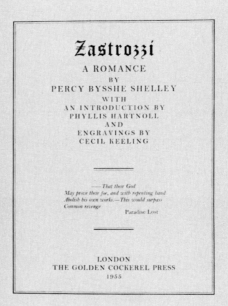

provided a wood engraving for the title page of *Watcher in Florence,* executed the large three-color illustrations, which were produced by a combination of relief-etched plate, linocut, and wood engraving. As each of the sheets containing an illustration also carried at least two pages of backed text and a heading in red, several printings were required, and the paper had to be dampened twice, with consequent risk that the sheets would stretch different amounts. It is a tribute to their increased skill that there was not much wastage. There was one near disaster with the black printing of the final sheet: For some reason the ink would not take properly on the second color. It took a considerable time before they found a solution—sponging the image with a weak solution of household detergent. The book, quarter-bound by Gray of Cambridge in saffron morocco, with the boards covered in marbled paper especially made by Cockerell, was extremely successful, although the printers expressed themselves only "reasonably satisfied with the presswork . . . the text lacked something in tonal quality."

The next large work from the Vine Press was also by Sir Herbert Read; his oration to the Society of Industrial Artists on the subject of *Design and Tradition* (1962). At the time, Octavian, the new typeface designed for the Monotype Corporation by Will Carter and David Kindersley, was being used in a series of experimental settings at Cambridge University Press. Peters and Foster took the opportunity to employ this typeface for Read's book as an extension of the experiments, using generous leading and printing on a coarse moldmade paper. The coarseness of the paper caused considerable trouble in the printing of the fine-line engraving by Peter Reddick; this was resolved by plate sinking the paper before printing the engraving. Several American private presses later used the Octavian face.

ILLUS. III. Miniature Press, London. Some contributions to John Ryder's
Miniature Folio, 1960, showing a range of small press work.

There was to be one more book from the press: *Twenty-five Poems* by Evelyn Ansell, with wood engravings by Diana Bloomfield. Set in Monotype Centaur at the University Press, it was printed on some Kelmscott paper Batchelors had made 60 years earlier, which had come into the possession of Cambridge University Press through the good offices of Sir Sydney Cockerell. The preparation and printing went smoothly, but the book was nearly ruined in the binding. Despite instructions on this vital point, the trade binder put the sheets into a hydraulic press with obvious and disastrous results. Fortunately, Gray and Sons, who had been entrusted with the binding of 10 "special" copies, were able to restore the damaged sheets to near pristine condition, and most of the other 90 copies were retrieved, although a few of them still showed slight traces of setoff. The 10 special copies represented what the two printers, at last satisfied, regarded as "the limit in presswork of what we felt we could achieve with our archaic equipment." Having achieved this, they called a halt to their printing venture. They had demonstrated to their own satisfaction that the self-taught amateur could attain standards of presswork comparable to those earlier private presses whose owners had the means to employ skilled pressmen, and that the operation of a press in the grand tradition did not necessarily demand a substantial private income. The sales of Vine Press books adequately covered the payments to artists, authors, and suppliers, with sufficient money left over for the two printers to enjoy a bottle of claret with each shift at the press—a very appropriate reward.

The experiments in printing on dampened handmade paper at the Vine Press were to provide a model for other English private presses. One that benefited most from the Vine example was by no

OFFICINA MAURITI
ANA LONDINI
BCM-PRINTER LONDON WC1

THE PRINTER GUIDO MORRIS quietly announces that thirty-five years after the founding of The Latin Press and seventeen years after its eclipse, he has been enabled to equip a small Printing Office, and is again at work in London.

The scale of work can only be small; the standard of the printing he hopes will be high. For the time being he has set aside his beloved Aldine 'Bembo' and has chosen instead to work with types closely modelled upon those of Christoffel Van Dijck van Amsterdam (c. 1660).

In the Springtime of the coming year the Printer will put out a Type Specimen showing available sizes of roman and italic. (The largest size of roman Capitals is shown overleaf.) Meanwhile he solicits small orders such as noteheadings, trade cards and invitations.

Floreat Typographia

And the rain came down and the floods came and the storms blew
and they fell against that house
and it fell not
for it was built upon the rock

SPRINGTIME 1971

ILLUS. 112. Late ephemera from Guido Morris, c.1971.

means a new press. At Stanbrook Abbey, a Benedictine house near Worcester, a printing press had been installed as early as 1876, at the initiative of Fr. Laurence Shepherd, its chaplain. Father Shepherd was himself an enthusiastic amateur printer, with a table Albion press of his own, and he took personal direction of the Stanbrook Abbey Press. The press had not been set up to provide the nuns with an artistic hobby; its purpose was to serve the needs of the English Benedictine Congregation, and it was to become an integral part of the nuns' life of dedication and prayer.

In this it was not particularly unusual; there have been many such monastic presses, and they have produced work of a respectable mediocrity. Stanbrook was to be very different. The technical excellence and artistic mastery revealed in its books have been due not only to the devotion of its printers but also to their talent for knowing when and from whom to seek advice and how to follow it. Sir Sydney Cockerell, a close friend of Dame Laurentia McLachlan, for many years was to play no small part in the affairs of the press, giving advice, recruiting expert help from his friends (both Emery Walker and St. John Hornby were to visit Stanbrook Abbey at his request), and providing commissions for work to be done. Nor was his influence to be exercised only in the field of printing; the high standards in calligraphy that had been set by Edward Johnston were to grow in the abbey and to flourish with visits from Katherine Adams and Madelyn Walker. The books from the press

included several of considerable importance: Abbot Gasquet's *Bosworth Psalter,* the *Reguli Sancti Benedicti,* and the standard English text of St. Teresa of Avila.

During World War II, the quantity and the quality of the abbey's printing declined considerably, but in the 1950s a remarkable revival took place. Robert Gibbings, the former owner of the Golden Cockerel Press, recommended the purchase of Eric Gill's Perpetua type, to replace the press's stock of worn-out Caslon and Dolphin types, and suggested that John Dreyfus might be able to give technical advice. Dreyfus and later John Peters of the Vine Press were to give considerable help in improving standards. Through Dreyfus, a long correspondence began between Dame Hildelith Cumming at Stanbrook and the eminent Dutch typographer Jan van Krimpen, who through his work at Enschedé had come to know many Benedictine houses in France and North Africa. Several of his own type designs—Spectrum, Romanée, Romulus, and Cancellaresca Bastarda—were to be installed at Stanbrook, but van Krimpen's death in 1958 came too soon for him to see the magnificent way in which the press was to use them, often in conjunction with calligraphic initials by Wendy Westover and Margaret Adams.

The first of the new Stanbrook works was *Christmas Lyrics,* a collection of twelfth-century Christmas poems, of which two (slightly different) editions were printed in 1956 and 1957. Although it was a handsome volume, it was to be dwarfed by the splendor of such books as *Magi Venerunt* by St. Ambrose of Milan (1959), Siegfried Sassoon's *The Path to Peace* (1960), and *Rituale Abbatum,* printed for the use of the English Benedictine Congregation in 1963. Nor is the work of Stanbrook any less assured in its smaller books. In such publications as *St Leo on the Birthday of Our Lord Jesus Christ* issued in 1958 (Illus. 114), or Guigo's *The Solitary Life,* translated by Thomas Merton (1964), or *The Pelican* by Philippe de Thuan, printed for Philip Hofer in 1963, their touch was exquisite.

As the press drew near to completing its first century, its pace did not falter. The outsider's view of the work of an enclosed order of nuns is likely to be one of peace and tranquility, and certainly not one of gaiety and lightheartedness. That such lightheartedness is possible was shown by a delightful spoof produced by Dame Hildelith Cumming's assistants, to honor her Silver Jubilee in 1967. *Stanbrook Abbey Press: A Tribute to Its Work and Spirit* contained every imaginable error in setting, design,

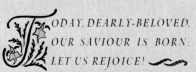

TODAY, DEARLY-BELOVED, OUR SAVIOUR IS BORN: LET US REJOICE! Surely there is no place for mourning on the birthday of Very Life, who has swallowed up mortality with all its fear, and brought us the joyful promise of life everlasting. No one is excluded from taking part in our jubilation. All have the same cause for gladness, for as our blessed Lord, slayer of sin and death, found none free from guilt, so has He come to set us all alike at liberty.

Let the saint exult, since he is soon to receive his recompense; let the sinner give praise, since he is welcomed to forgiveness; let the pagan take

ILLUS. 114. Stanbrook Abbey Press, Worcestershire. *St Leo on the Birthday of Our Lord Jesus Christ,* 1958.

and execution. Dame Hildelith must have been delighted by this token of affection produced "by the MIniOns of the stanqrook Abbeyp Ress," as they styled themselves in the colophon.

In 1970, the press published *Stanbrook Abbey Press: Ninety-Two Years of Its History,* a fascinating account of its work, which in the special edition of 50 copies had the text volume supplemented by a second volume of specimens of its work from the period 1878–1970. For its centenary in 1976, it produced *The Mother's Birds: Imagery for a Death and a Birth,* haiku written by Meinrad Craighead and accompanied by a suite of her charcoal drawings lithographed at Skelton's Press, Wellingborough.

Cooperation with other printers has been a feature of a good number of the press's more recent books: in its simplest form, having the text trade-set on Monotype machines for subsequent rejustification by hand, or having colored illustrations printed outside the abbey, as for Alec Robertson's *Contrasts: The Arts and Religion* (1980). Sometimes outside cooperation has taken a different form, as with *Earnest-Pennies: An Anthology of Prayers and Meditations on the Holy Eucharist* (1973), for which the type used for the ordinary edition commissioned by A. R. Mowbray & Co. was reimposed and printed in a special edition on Green's handmade papers with a hand-gilded initial by Margaret Adams. The special edition was finely bound by George Percival of Leicester, whose work on Stanbrook books is of very high quality. His bindings not infrequently use Japanese papers for endpapers or boards, and the press had occasionally but effectively used Japanese papers in combination with van Krimpen's Cancellaresca Bastarda type for the text, as in A. Samaan-Hanna's poems *Moods That Endure* printed in 1979 (Illus. 115).

The book that is Dame Hildelith's own favorite is different from all these: Alberic Stacpoole's meditation in poetic idiom *The Seven Words from the Cross* (1974). For this slim single-section book, bound by Percival (with three copies bound by Ivor Robinson), there was unusual use of color: the

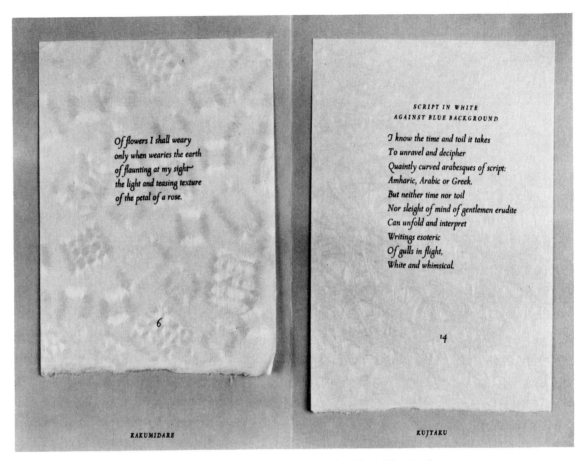

Of flowers I shall weary
only when wearies the earth
of flaunting at my sight
the light and teasing texture
of the petal of a rose.

6

KAKUMIDARE

SCRIPT IN WHITE
AGAINST BLUE BACKGROUND

I know the time and toil it takes
To unravel and decipher
Quaintly curved arabesques of script:
Amharic, Arabic or Greek.
But neither time nor toil
Nor sleight of mind of gentlemen erudite
Can unfold and interpret
Writings esoteric
Of gulls in flight,
White and whimsical.

14

KUJYAKU

ILLUS. 115. Stanbrook Abbey Press, Worcestershire. Prospectus for *Moods That Endure* showing van Krimpen's Cancellaresca Bastarda type on two different Japanese papers.

words in Romulus Open Capitals printed in a smoke blue, and the commentaries on the facing pages in Spectrum printed in burgundy, with the two colors picked up in the bindings.

It was not only in the completely noncommercial field of fine printing, in which both Stanbrook Abbey and the Vine Press operated, that the apparently inhospitable postwar world could be overcome. As a jobbing printer and private press owner, Guido Morris failed, but the causes of his failure cannot be put down to an unwillingness on the part of the public to support a small jobbing printer doing fine work. In Cambridge, the Rampant Lions Press, which was to do precisely this, was launched successfully in 1949 by Will Carter. Carter had been active as an amateur printer ever since 1924, when at the age of twelve he visited Oxford University Press. His interest in printing was sustained throughout his school days, and on leaving school he went to work in the printing firm of Unwin Brothers. Later he moved to Cambridge where for many years he worked for Heffers.

In 1930, he bought a wooden flatbed press, and in 1936 he replaced it with an Albion, two years later adding a treadle platen press. For in addition to his full-time employment at Heffers, Carter was a spare-time printer of the sort so disliked by the trade, one who produced a good deal of jobbing work for friends and associates as well as a number of small books on his own account. But he was a "back-bedroom printer" with a difference; his skill and taste were remarkable and were to be reinforced by a visit to the workshop of Rudolf Koch in Frankfurt in 1938.

After the war, which Carter spent in the Royal Navy, he returned to his former employers and also resumed his spare-time printing activities. But after three years, the call of printing on his own account became so strong that he decided to set up in business. "I was convinced," he wrote in *The First Ten,* an anniversary publication that he issued in 1959, "that there was a market for fine jobbing printing of the sort that was too small to be handled by the big printing houses and yet was beyond the scope of the small jobbing firm. Being blessed with a useful pair of hands I was by now a fair compositor and pressman and had acquired some ideas of simple typography. With these skills and a small printing plant and any amount of encouragement from wife and friends the wind seemed set fair." And certainly the wind was set fair; by 1959 the pressure of commissions was such that one pair of hands could not cope with the demand, and much of the bread-and-butter jobbing work was relinquished to allow him to concentrate on printing books.

Many of the books and pamphlets printed at the Rampant Lions Press (the first, Robert Nichols's *A Spanish Triptych,* had been published as early as 1936 when Carter was working the press part-time) were printed for publication by others, like the splendid version of *The Rime of the Ancient Mariner,* with David Jones's copper engravings, printed for the Chilmark Press of New York in 1963–1964. But like the Officina Bodoni, which it resembles in being closer to an early printing shop than the "normal" firm, the press has produced many small books on its own account, like Christopher Smart's *A Song to David* (1960), or John Farrow's *Seven Poems in Pattern* (1955), or William Johnson Cory's *Lucretilis.* Not the least interesting of the work to be printed on the Rampant Lions equipment was in fact the work of a press within a press.

Will Carter's own enthusiasm and skill in printing was inherited by his son Sebastian, who started issuing his own books "from the Junior Branch of the Rampant Lions Press" at the age of thirteen. Later, in vacations from school and university, he produced several books of considerable interest and distinction, such as *Poems from Panmure House,* printed for "The Ninth of May" in 1960, or Sir William Jones's *Poems* (1961). Since 1966, when Sebastian Carter joined his father as a full partner in Rampant Lions, the press has gone from strength to strength. Perhaps the most ambitious undertaking was their edition of William Morris's *Cupid & Psyche* (1974) done for Clover Hill Editions using the Troy type (freshly cast at Oxford University Press from the original matrices preserved at Cambridge University Press, a rare instance of cooperation between two old rivals) in an unjustified setting, which complements the original wood engravings in a way none but the bravest would have attempted, and with delightful results.

Other work undertaken for Clover Hill has included several volumes showing the work of David Jones. In *The Chester Play of the Deluge* (1977), the press for the first time printed Jones's wood engravings with the care they should have received (and did not) in the Golden Cockerel edition of 50 years earlier. For this they selected the 18-point Golden Cockerel type, which had been borrowed from Cockerel's owner Thomas Yoseloff. He later agreed to sell them the type, which also was chosen for their new edition of *The Book of Jonah* (1979), again using Jones's blocks from the Cockerel edition of 1926.

Work for publication by others has included a good many well-printed volumes for the Rainbow Press of Ted and Olwyn Hughes, starting with Sylvia Plath's poems *Lyonesse* (1971). With the artist Michael Rothenstein, the Carters have cooperated on three portfolios using Rothenstein's powerful woodcuts: *Suns and Moons* (1972), *Seven Colours,* poems by Edward Lucie-Smith (1974), and *The Song of Songs* (1979). For these very large (Imperial Folio) works, the text was set in 24-point Albertus Light, a rare use of this face.

Besides the Golden Cockerel roman, Rampant Lions now holds several other distinguished and distinctive faces. Frederic Warde's two versions of the Arrighi italic Vicenza and Vicentino (freshly cast for the press from the matrices held by the Metropolitan Museum of Art) were used in *The Elegies of a Glass Adonis* (1973), and Hermann Zapf's Hunt Roman type, of which the press first

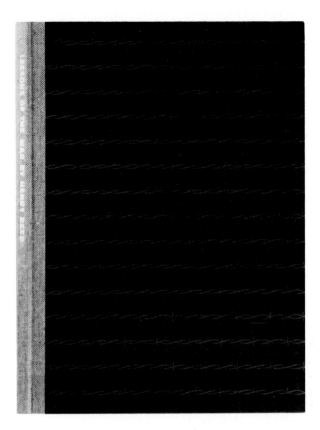

ILLUS. 116. Rampant Lions Press, Cambridge. *Lessons of the War,* 1970. Binding. Effective use of barbed-wire patterned paper over boards. *Opposite page:* Double spread. Barbed-wire motif of binding repeated.

showed its fonts (cast by Stempel) in *The Rampant Lions Press: A Printing Workshop through Five Decades* (1982). This splendid catalogue of the exhibition of the Carters's work held at the Fitzwilliam Museum supplements some other guides to their work: *Portfolio One* (1967) (Illus. 117), *Portfolio Two* (1974), and *Portfolio Three* (1982). Among them, they provide an excellent guide to the work of this distinguished printing house.

A much more modest affair than Rampant Lions was the private press of Thomas Rae at Greenock in Scotland. Rae, the junior partner in an old-established family firm of jobbing printers was becoming interested in book design at about the time that John Ryder's *Printing for Pleasure* was starting to attract a new generation of amateurs. In the mid-1950s, for his own satisfaction he produced a slim pamphlet containing part of *Pickwick Papers* as an experiment in printing Dickens in a more readable form than most editions of Dickens' works. In 1956 he printed a little book on *Thomas Bewick, Wood Engraver* to aid the St. Bride Printing Library, and so successful was this first product of what Rae named the Signet Press that the edition soon sold out and he was able to present a substantial sum to the library.

There was some fumbling with Rae's next books. *Wordsworth in Scotland* (1957) was a typographic experiment that greatly disappointed him. His own *Andrew Myllar: A Short Study of Scotland's First Printer,* which he published for the four-hundred-fiftieth anniversary of the introduction of printing into Scotland (1958), was typographically far more satisfying (it made very effective use of Myllar's device, blind-blocked on the cover) but received such a mauling from a reviewer in the *Scottish Historical Review* that he decided "to end my brief essay into the realms of scholarship." Nevertheless, he did not cease production of books concerned with printing history: In 1962 he published *Some Notes on Wood Engraving,* selected from Bewick's *Memoir* and illustrated with several of Bewick's cuts printed from the original blocks. In 1963 he published an edition of James Watson's

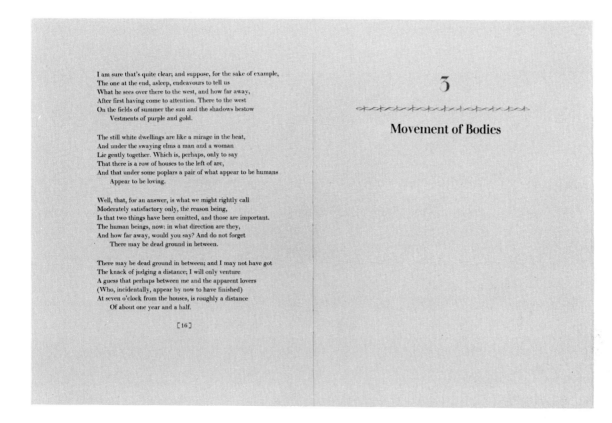

Preface to the History of Printing, 1713. The *Preface* contained the first account ever published of Scottish printing, and Rae's attractive little edition edited by "James Munro" was a very appropriate way to mark the two-hundred-fiftieth anniversary of the text in which Watson appealed to his fellow Scottish printers for an improvement in their work.

Before this, in 1958, Rae had published *The Book of the Private Press,* a very useful directory of more than 240 private printers at work in the English-speaking world. It was largely because this provided so solid a foundation that in 1959 the Private Libraries Association was able to start publication of its annual checklist *Private Press Books,* and for the first four issues Rae was its joint editor, as well as its printer. Pressure of business commitments thereafter compelled him to give up his share in the work, and at the same time to cut back on his avocational production of Signet Press books, although several others appeared during the 1960s.

In 1967 he was compelled to change the name of his press: It was too close to that of a paperback series, and he had to bow to legal pressure. Under the new name of Grian-Aig Press (taken from the Gaelic form of its hometown), he did work for other publishers: *Anaglyptography* for the Plough Press of Loughborough and *The Private Press: Handbook to an Exhibition* for Loughborough School of Librarianship (1968), but his own output became very much less.

The work of Rae's Signet and Grian-Aig Presses was usually solidly traditional, depending for its effect on the plain unaffected manly qualities obtained with the use of handset Caslon and Perpetua types, on good-quality machine-made papers on powered presses. Only once did he attempt a more florid style, in *The Death of Mary Queen of Scots* (1960), in which his use of American Uncial types on Zerkall moldmade papers shows how successfully he could undertake work of a different kind.

The wood-engraved frontispiece portrait of Mary Queen of Scots came from the hand of David

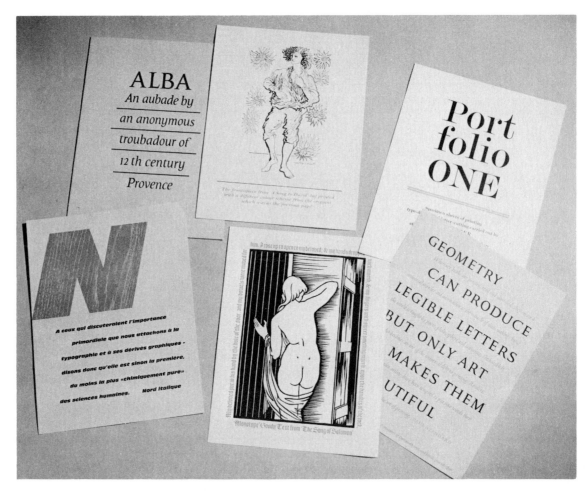

ILLUS. 117. Rampant Lions Press, Cambridge. Leaves from *Portfolio One,* 1967.

Chambers, who was to be Rae's successor as the principal editor of *Private Press Books* and designer of most of the Private Libraries Association's publications. At his Cuckoo Hill Press at Pinner in Middlesex, Chambers has represented another aspect of private press endeavor for many years. His involvement with printing goes back to 1950 when, irritated by the poor quality of mass-produced greeting cards, he decided to try his hand at printing his own wood engravings. Using a heavily modified office copying press and an assortment of secondhand type and equipment, he and his father over the next five or six years produced a substantial quantity of ephemera (including handbills, letterheads, and dance tickets) of a kind typical of many amateur printers.

Chambers, however, was to be drawn in a quite different direction from those who sacrifice quality for quantity: He prints little, but very well. Purchasing boxwood blocks at T. N. Lawrence's shop, he was brought into contact with some of the best European and Japanese papers as vehicles for blocks or type; through his work on *Private Press Books* and his own collecting he became unusually well-informed about the work done by other private presses of the past and present. In working out the role for his Cuckoo Hill Press he has never been concerned to publish much, or widely; his pleasure has been in tackling various technical printing problems: "Although I find perfection in printing well-nigh unattainable there is a lot of satisfaction to be had in the attempt."

Himself a wood engraver, Chambers gained much of his satisfaction from printing engravings; for instance, his edition of *The Apostle's Creed* (1965) has finely executed and powerful engravings by

Philip Ross. More recently, following a joint purchase with Iain Bain (whose own Laverock Press has produced an interesting series of small books) of a series of blocks by Thomas Bewick and his school, Chambers has concentrated on the problems of taking fine-quality impressions from the work of past masters, with 16 sets of the Bewick engravings (1969–1971), 5 sets of engravings by T. Sturge Moore (1970), and *The Wood-Engravings of William Blake for Thornton's Virgil, 1821* (1977), for which (as the original blocks cannot leave the British Museum) the Cuckoo Hill Press's Alexandra press had to be taken to the museum.

ILLUS. 118. Signet Press, Greenock, Scotland. A range of Thomas Rae's work.

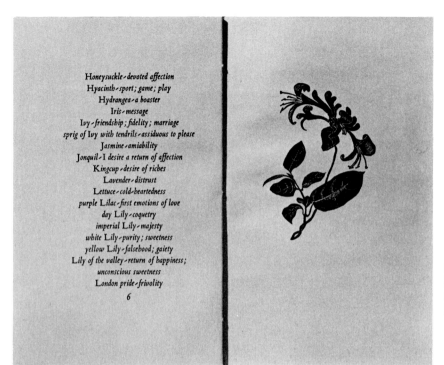

Honeysuckle - devoted affection
Hyacinth - sport; game; play
Hydrangea - a boaster
Iris - message
Ivy - friendship; fidelity; marriage
sprig of Ivy with tendrils - assiduous to please
Jasmine - amiability
Jonquil - I desire a return of affection
Kingcup - desire of riches
Lavender - distrust
Lettuce - cold-heartedness
purple Lilac - first emotions of love
day Lily - coquetry
imperial Lily - majesty
white Lily - purity; sweetness
yellow Lily - falsehood; gaiety
Lily of the valley - return of happiness;
unconscious sweetness
London pride - frivolity
6

ILLUS. 119. Cuckoo Hill Press, Middlesex. *Here's Rosemary*, 1959. Wood engraving by David Chambers.

Other Cuckoo Hill Press work has often reflected Chambers's deep involvement with the contemporary British private press and printing history scene. Examples are his edition of some of Count Potocki's poems *Meillerie* (1973); *Autumn Leaves,* two fragments by Ralph Chubb (1975); and a facsimile undertaken for the Printing Historical Society, *Caractères de l'Imprimerie Nouvellement Gravés par S. P. Fournier le Jeune* (1975). With his many other commitments, it is no wonder that Chambers has been unable to produce more work from his private press. Those who care for fine printing must regret its small output, since his taste and execution are far in advance of most other British private printers of recent years.

Chapter 19

THE CONTEMPORARY SCENE IN BRITAIN

BY ITS NATURE, the private press has never been tied to a particular center or group of centers. Nevertheless, at times an individual's enthusiasm for the arts of the book will be persuasive: personal endeavor leads to "a movement." Twenty-five years ago, when amateur interest in printing in Britain was beginning to grow again, the focus of activity was not in London, Oxford, or any of the other obvious centers, but in Leicester, and concentrated on the city's college of art.

Before World War II there was at least one Leicester private press, the Garswood Press, from which Falconer Scott and A. Christopherson printed an attractive edition of *The Wisdom of Andrew Boorde* in 1936 (Illus. 120). But the real growth of the Leicestershire presses came later, through the student work in printing at the college and through John Mason's experiments with papermaking.

Because Mason had been a compositor and binder at the Gregynog Press and was the son of J. H. Mason, the former Doves Press compositor, the threads linking the Leicester group to the earlier Private Press Movement were clear. In 1954, when Mason started papermaking, he was head of the Bookbinding Department in the college, and at the invitation of the principal he transferred his papermaking activities, hitherto carried on at home with improvised equipment, to the College of Art. Gradually his "Twelve by Eight" paper became known to those interested in the book crafts, and following the publication of his *Papermaking as an Artistic Craft* (1959), his papers became widely sought. And deservedly so; they were full of variety in color and texture, and in publications such as the Private Libraries Association's edition of Mason's address to the Double Crown Club, *Twelve by Eight* (1959), its charm can be seen very clearly. Since then, Mason published a number of specimen books of his papers and other books like Oliver Bayldon's *The Papermaker's Craft*, a free translation from the seventeenth-century Latin poem *Papyrus* by Father Imberdis, which was printed for him by Will Carter in 1964. But Mason's activities were purely those of a papermaker and publisher; unlike Dard Hunter before him, or later Henry Morris or Walter Hamady and their followers, he did not himself attempt to use his paper for printing.

Among the most enthusiastic of John Mason's assistants in papermaking was Rigby Graham. Some of the most interesting of Mason's experimental papers were those with thread pictures in them, which were executed by Graham. So great was the latter's enthusiasm for the craft that he set up his own paper mill, the Holt Mill. Graham was later to become the central figure among the

THE WISDOM OF
ANDREW BOORDE

EDITED WITH AN INTRODUCTION
AND NOTES BY H. EDMUND POOLE
ILLUSTRATED BY
A. E. CHRISTOPHERSON

PRINTED BY FALCONER SCOTT AT THE
GARSWOOD PRESS AND PUBLISHED BY
EDGAR BACKUS FORTY-FOUR CANK ST
LEICESTER MCMXXXVI

ILLUS. 120. Garswood Press,
Leicester. *The Wisdom of
Andrew Boorde,* 1936. Title-
page opening.

Leicestershire presses, with an influence extending far beyond the confines of the county, but in the late 1950s he was not himself the owner of a private press. His earliest work in this field, apart from his illustrations for *The Private Press at Gregynog* (which was printed at Leicester College of Art) was as a contributor to the Orpheus Press. Set up in 1958 by Douglas Martin, this "fugitive private press," as it so aptly described itself, worked at first without premises or equipment of its own, producing occasional pamphlets on borrowed presses. Its first booklet was a preliminary essay on *Papermaking* by John Mason, of which a very small number of copies was printed on Mason's paper in 1958. The next publication undertaken, by far the finest produced by Orpheus, was Rilke's *Die Sonette an Orpheus* (1959), again printed on Mason's paper and with twelve three-colored lithographs by Graham. Binding took a considerable time, and before the 25 copies were published (from Munich, where Martin had moved with the intention of restarting the press in a more lavish way), three other pamphlets had been published: *Chidiocke Tichbourne* and Clare's *Lines Written in North-ampton County Asylum,* both illustrated by Graham, and Rimbaud's *Les Corbeaux,* with woodcuts by Robert Blythe. The first two were printed in two editions, one on Graham's Holt Mill paper and the other on good-quality machine-made paper. Both editions are now distinctly uncommon: of the Clare, Graham has recorded that "scores were offered for next to nothing in pubs, used as beer mats, and eventually hurled at sneering crowds in the Market Place one Sunday evening." An experiment in taking poetry to the people had failed dismally.

After Martin's return from Germany, the press resumed activity. A backer and premises were found, and many ambitious projects were planned, such as Herrick's *Hesperides,* Shakespeare's fragment *Sir Thomas More,* Lorca's *Llanto por Ignacio Sanchez Mejias,* and a *Life* of the composer Bellini. Little ever came of these plans; the only book to be completed as designed was John Best's *Poems and Drawings in Mud Time* (1960), and this was only because the book was printed commercially at the Curwen Press. The Herrick was scrapped when half-printed; the type for *Sir Thomas More* was accidentally pied and Rigby Graham's illustrations for it used instead in *Kirby Hall: An Uninforma-tive Guide* (of which 50 copies were printed in an afternoon and then circulated in the way that had become normal for the press—in the pubs). So chaotic an undertaking could not long survive, and despite the very real promise of its early work, the Orpheus Press disappeared from the Leicester scene.

The imprint was revived once, by Rigby Graham, Patricia Green, and Toni Savage (who had also assisted with Orpheus Press work) on Thomas Churchyard's *Lovesong to an Inconstant Lady* in 1961. Once was enough; they found that the name had too many unfortunate associations, and for subsequent books they adopted the name of the Pandora Press. Considering the partners' lack of printing experience and the equipment at their disposal (an Adana flatbed press and two cases of worn and battered type), they managed to produce a considerable number of books rapidly. Most of their publications have been small; such things as Swinburne's *Garden of Proserpine,* Byron's *When We Two Parted,* Marvell's *Thoughts in a Garden,* or *Poems and Translations* by Count Potocki. These were produced only because they wanted to print them, regardless of how well they would sell, and the size of the edition was normally "decided by an aching arm or blistered palm or both." Only once have they printed for outsiders: a booklet entitled *The Living Theatre,* which was printed and sold to aid a little professional theater in Leicester that was threatened with closure for lack of financial support.

Nearly all the books produced had the illustrations in color, calling for two or three impressions. In the most substantial book of the Pandora Press, Thea Scott's *Fingal's Cave* (1961), the 52 pages went through the press 80 times, a total of well over 20,000 impressions in all, as the edition was intended to consist of 250 copies. Disaster struck the project after the seventy-sixth printing. At the time the Pandora Press was operating from the attic of an old rectory at Aylestone, and the sheets had been spread out over the floor to dry. A sudden spell of sunshine hatched out woodworm in the floor, and overnight more than 100 sheets were peppered with holes. As the sheet had a five-color progressive linocut on it, reprinting was impossible, and the edition was reduced by nearly half in consequence.

As well as being a partner in the activities of the Pandora Press, Rigby Graham was also involved in the production of three ambitious books printed by the monks of Mount St. Bernard's Abbey in Charnwood Forest. Two of these were produced jointly with George Percival, the binder of many Stanbrook Abbey publications and John Mason's successor as head of the bookbinding department at Leicester College of Art. The first of these, *Vale,* printed as a farewell to John Mason on his retirement, consisted of a humorous account of his career generously sprinkled with wrong fonts, phrases upside down, and similar tricks printed on Twelve by Eight paper purloined (so they claimed) from Mason. The Chinese-style binding was a real tour de force. The binding of the second book, Wilde's *The Nightingale and the Rose,* was equally exciting with its use of green metallic boards and·pink metallic doublures blocked in gold. From the point of view of owners of the book, it is one of the most difficult of bindings to preserve from damage, but a splendid experiment in the use of unusual binding materials.

Graham also played a considerable part in the work of the Brewhouse Press at Wymondham, run by the bookbinder Trevor Hickman. Hickman had originally been drawn into private press work through his binding of Pandora's *Fingal's Cave* and *Sicilian Memory;* as a binder, he has been less interested in typography than many other private printers, and several of the Brewhouse books have been printed by others (*An Autumn Anthology,* 1964, was printed at Mount St. Bernard). Still others have been produced on equipment no more sophisticated than a binder's nipping press, and not the least successful books by any means. *The Pickworth Fragment,* which was selected for exhibition at Frankfurt in 1966, was a highly successful and original variation on the Japanese "whirlwind binding"—leaves joined at the fore-edges to make a panorama of text, colored linocut, and "action tooled" illustration nearly 14 feet long. The whole was contained in a quarter-binding of brown suede, with gold-tooled and colored linocuts on the brown paper boards. Other Brewhouse publications have been less startlingly unusual, though nearly all have been original in design and embodying worthwhile texts. Several have been concerned with aspects of printing history, like

Typographia Naturalis (1968), a history of nature printing illustrated with original nineteenth-century nature prints of seaweeds and ferns and modern essays in the fascinating technique by Rigby Graham and Morris Cox, or the series of 13 "Brewhouse Broadsheets" issued between 1966 and 1974, which dealt individually with topics such as Count Potocki, Gauguin as printer, and early printing in Guernsey (Illus. 121).

Other Brewhouse books have been concerned with aspects of local history, such as David Tew's large 1968 folio *The Oakham Canal* (Illus. 122), Dennis Prestidge's *Tom Cribb at Thistleton Gap* (1971), or *Country Cooking* (1978), a collection of local recipes. Brewhouse does not exist only to provide a vehicle for Graham's work, but in such books as his *The Casquets . . . The Most Dangerous Channel Islands* (1972), *Deserted Cornish Tin Mines* (1976), or *Seriatim* (1978), Hickman allowed his gifted (and prolific) colleague an excellent showing.

Most artists and printers would be hard pressed to find the time for all these activities. But Graham also had his own Cog Press, from which he produced the splendid little *Cogs in Transition* (1963), as well as work of a less traditional and purely letterpress kind, exhibition catalogues, and little magazines printed partly letterpress and partly by office offset from typewriting.

In a long series of broadsheets issued between 1973 and 1975 as Cog Press broadsheets and thereafter as "Barwell Broadsides," Graham returned to something rather like the early Orpheus poetry for the people, printing these for distribution to the Ampersand Folk Club, which met at The Three Crowns at Barwell. (Much of Graham's work, like that of some of the other Leicestershire printers, is deliberately closer to street literature than to the more rarified fine printing.) And if this were not enough, he has inspired the work of the Threotheotha Press, the "Wind Tunnel Irregulars," and many others. Whoever attempts to prepare a comprehensive bibliography/iconography of his work will have a difficult task indeed. Even with the little review *Fishpaste* printed on his Adana press (Illus. 123), the production of issues numbered "four and a half," "7A," and the like—to say nothing of the bogus issues circulated by friends—was enough to give acquisitions librarians apoplexy! For Graham and his group, printing is to be enjoyed. The fact that they allow themselves jokes does not mean that their work is not to be taken seriously.

ILLUS. 121. Brewhouse Press, Leicestershire. Some of the "Brewhouse Broadsheets."

ILLUS. 122. Brewhouse Press, Leicestershire. Opening from *The Oakham Canal*, 1968. Colored lithography by Rigby Graham.

Of other presses in Leicestershire, Toni Savage's New Broom Press, Duine Campbell's Black Knight Press, the Offcut Press (run jointly by Savage and Campbell), and Savage's series of "Phoenix Broadsheets" produced in the mid-seventies have been closest to the Graham work already described—not least in the complexity of their output. Since 1974, from his Ashby Lane Press at Bitteswell, B. K. Foster has produced a number of interesting and modestly priced small books, such as G. H. Godbert's *Ides of March* (1976). Though an entirely independent venture, Foster's books with their bold vigorous linocuts have the same chapbook air about them that characterizes much of the Leicestershire work.

The best general guide to these presses is Ann Morris's *The Private Press in Leicestershire* (1976). This was published by Geoffrey Wakeman from his Plough Press at Loughborough, one of the few local presses not at all under the Graham influence. In its origins, the Plough Press did not promise more highly than many other amateur ventures started by those interested in printing and with access to printing equipment. It took its name from an idea that Wakeman had as a result of my passing on to him some electrotypes of agricultural implements, which he used to illustrate some suitable quotations he printed (on the press of the School of Librarianship where we were both then lecturers) as *A Share of Ploughs* (1968). But after some "prentice work" with a Golding Pearl press, which he set up in his garage, he turned to the production of volumes about printing and the book, in particular drawing on his expertise in Victorian illustration processes. Starting with *XIX Century Illustration: Some Methods Used in English Books* (begun in 1968 and completed in 1971), he commenced production of books in which the illustrations were originals taken from broken copies, in the sound

FISHPASTE *Four & a half*

A letter from PINLEG

Produced by
Rigby Graham, Peter Hoy, & Toni Savage
Published from 32 West Avenue Leicester

FISHPASTE *THREE*

Produced by
Rigby Graham, Peter Hoy, & Toni Savage
Published from 32 West Avenue Leicester

postcard review
of Art & Letters

Fishpaste

Fishpaste Twenty
Rigby Graham, Peter Hoy & Toni Savage
97 Holywell Street Oxford

Dancing Caryatid by Rigby Graham

March 1968

```
        r
       ar
      lar
     ular
    gular
   ngular
  angular
 iangular
riangular
triangulareflection
    reflectio
    reflecti
    reflect
    reflec
    refle
    refl
    ref
    re
    r
```

PASTE HAS MOVED
to 97 HOLYWELL ROAD OXFORD

FISHPASTE EIGHT
28 June 1967

On the Heights

Wait until I come
To cleave the cold which holds us back.

Cloud, as menaced in your life as I in mine.

(There was a cliff in our house.
Which is why we left and set up here.)

Translated from Char by Peter Hoy

Produced by
Rigby Graham, Peter Hoy, & Toni Savage
Published from 32 West Avenue Leicester

ILLUS. 123. Cog Press, Leicester. A range of issues of *Fishpaste*,
printed on an Adana flatbed press by Rigby Graham and Toni Savage.

belief that only the original prints—such as anastatic printing, medal engraving, and autotypes—have the qualities needed for effective illustration of the text. Other Plough Press books of this kind have included such volumes as *Printing Relief Illustrations: Kirkall to the Line Block* (1977), *XIX Century Colour Illustrations* (1976), and *Victorian Colour Printing* (1981). Wakeman's interest is not limited to illustration: Like Henry Morris at Bird & Bull, he has produced several volumes on aspects of papermaking, such as *English Marbled Papers: A Documentary History* (1978) and *XX Century English Vat Paper Mills* (1980), or more lightheartedly *Loughborough Marble* (1971), a specimen book of various marbled designs—"Rutland Shell" and "Widmerpool Spot" among them—produced by this imaginary local industry.

Wakeman is not a private press purist who insists on doing all his work himself. Although some of his work is printed on dampened handmade paper on the Albion he acquired in 1975, he is not averse to using other printers (such as Skelton's Press) or resorting to offset lithography when it seems advantageous. He uses his press and equipment as a publisher and seeks the best means to that end. A press in an unheated garage was not the best means in wintertime, but following a recent move to Kidlington, near Oxford (and warmer premises for the press), more good work can be expected. *The Plough Press, 1967–1981: Fifteen Years Printing in a Loughborough Garage* (1981) provides a good guide to the Plough Press in Leicestershire.

This bibliography was published at almost the same time as *The Whittington Press: A Bibliography, 1971–1981* (1982). Compiled by another library school lecturer, David Butcher (whose own Cherub Press at Solihull has produced some promising small pieces), it provides a superb record of the most substantial and prolific private press set up in Britain in the past 15 years.

Whittington's owner, John Randle, was infected by printing while a pupil at Marlborough College, where he worked on the College Press's edition of a selection of Siegfried Sassoon's *Poems* (1958). After some years in publishing in London, Randle and his wife, Rosalind, decided to find somewhere they could print in peace on the weekends and were lucky enough to find a derelict cottage in the Cotswold village of Whittington, Gloucestershire, that was suitable. They were even more fortunate in their choice of the first book to print, Richard Kennedy's *A Boy at the Hogarth Press* (1972), which took them a year of weekends to print on their Columbian press (Illus. 124).

ILLUS. 124. Whittington Press, Gloucestershire. Title opening of *A Boy at the Hogarth Press,* 1972.

There was an element of luck about it, but the Randles's choice of their subsequent books, *To the War with Waugh* (1973) and *A Folding Screen: Selected Chinese Lyrics* (1974), and the fine production they gave them, were so successful that in 1974 they decided to make the Whittington Press a full-time business. In the eyes of some purists they have "a small publishing firm that happens to have its own presses," but in fact the Whittington Press is no less devoted to printing than to publishing. Rather than follow the traditional pattern of editions of classical works, they have sought original work worthy of careful loving production. There is a recognizable "Whittington style," not in the sense that there was an Eragny or Doves style, but that comes from the Randles's involvement in all stages of book design and production. It includes preference for Caslon (and the press is now equipped for Monotype as well as handsetting). The wood engravings of Miriam Macgregor and the late Hellmuth Weissenborn have been frequently used, and the press's own marbled paper (made for it by Jane Lyons) often appears in its bindings.

Of the books published under the Whittington imprint, *The Diary of Edward Thomas 1 January– 8 April 1917* (1977) with engravings by Weissenborn (who by coincidence had been serving in the same sector on the Western front—but in the German trenches—and could therefore produce particularly apposite illustrations), James Reeves's *Arcadian Ballads,* with drawings by Ardizzone (1977), and the several small volumes of Jim Turner's poems, *Cotswold Days* (1977), *Other Days* (1979), and *Lost Days* (1981) with Miriam Macgregor's engravings, are to my mind the most attractive.

Several of the books printed at the press have been for other publishers, ranging from the absurdly cheap (and very successful) *Some Observations on the Diseases of Brunus Edwardii* produced for Heals, the furniture store, to the very expensive edition of *Shakespeare's Sonnets,* with wood engravings by John Lawrence (1978) commissioned by the exclusive store Aspreys and published by them in a lavish binding by Sangorski & Sutcliffe. Particularly valuable joint ventures with Simon Lawrence have been the volumes *S. T. E. Lawrence: Boxwood Blockmaker* (1980) and *Fortyfive Wood-Engravers* (1982), which have presented superb examples of the work of established and newer wood engravers; the first volume as an eightieth birthday tribute to the supplier of their blocks. And in the journal *Matrix,* of which the first issue appeared in November 1981 and the second a year later, the Randles have provided all enthusiasts for fine press work with a journal of great importance.

Also in Gloucestershire, at Nailsworth, is Thomas A. Clark's Moschatel Press. Moschatel is at the other extreme from Whittington and the professionalism of the Randles's work, although they share a sincerity and concern for the book as expressive form. Limited to a small Adana press on which he prints his own poetry, Clark's little pamphlets seldom extend beyond a few pages or cost more than a few pence, but his output since 1973 has been substantial. Being generally too slight for listing in *Private Press Books* and too cheap for individual record in the Basilisk Catalogues, his work has received less attention than it deserves.

Across the Severn in Herefordshire, there are two presses that have produced substantial and attractive work. The wood engraver Kenneth Lindley originally set up his Pointing Finger Press in Hereford to demonstrate the printing arts to students, but it has grown into a more substantial affair at which Lindley (using a proofing press) designs, prints, and illustrates all the work. Some of the most successful have also been written by him, such as *Herefordshire: Late Autumn* (1977), in which he used some nature-printed illustrations as well as his own full-page engravings. In others, such as David Burnett's poems *Shimbara* (1972) and *Figures and Spaces* (1978), he has combined wood engraving with relief prints and linocuts. Glenn Storhaug's Five Seasons Press at Madley has for several years been producing small volumes of poetry printed on a hand-fed power press. His most substantial book has been *The Kilpeck Anthology* (1981), in which the design problems of a book incorporating letterpress, line drawings, wood engravings, and silk-screened illustrations have been well and sensitively handled. Storhaug also printed the text for the volume *Protest: A Poem by D. M.*

Thomas after a Medieval Armenian Poem by Frik (1980), which was published by the Hereford artist Reg Boulton, who cut the 12 full-page engravings on Perspex. Printed in color, heightened by the use of watercolor and gold, the book catches the mood of the Byzantine empire very successfully indeed.

At Burford, Simon Rendall's Cygnet Press is something of a weekend diversion from his working week (at the Curwen Press in London), at which he has printed a number of stylish little books such as William Blake's *Auguries of Innocence* (1975) and *Rupert Brooke* (1978). For more substantial work produced under the Cygnet imprint, Rendall has understandably used the resources of the John Roberts Press and of Curwen in such volumes as *Temples of Power* (1979) and Joyce Nankivell Loch's *Collected Poems* (1980).

The Perdix Press at Sutton Mandeville near Salisbury is the retirement activity of Walter Partridge, taken up when he left Fleet Street and newspaper design. Working in the traditional way using handset types and an Albion press, Partridge has produced several attractive small books, such as Jeni Couzyn's *Thirteen Spells* (1978) and *Selected Poems from William Barnes* (1981). Also in Wiltshire, from his Libanus Press at Marlborough, Michael Mitchell set himself a high standard with his first book, *Azrael and Other Poems* by Sylvia Townsend Warner (1978). He has maintained the standard in the volume he printed for Anthony Baker's Gruffyground Press, *Buzz Buzz: Ten Insect Poems* by John Heath-Stubbs (1981), which has a superb title-page engraving by Richard Shirley Smith. For his own press's *Twelve Months of a Year,* poems by Joy Finzi (1981), Mitchell used the wood engravings of Simon Brett to equally good effect.

Even newer is D. R. Wakefield's Chevington Press in Devon. Wakefield studied with Leonard Baskin, which no doubt assisted in making his first book, *The Diary and Observations of a Tench Fisher* (1981), as successful as it was. The text and etchings were both by the printer, who stayed with the subject for his second book, the smaller but equally accomplished *Trout Fishing on Rapid Streams* by H. C. Cutcliffe (1982). Wakefield's illustrations—in the second book combining colored woodcut with etching—show how well the traditions of the private press and of natural history illustration can blend together.

In Shropshire, at their Tern Press, Nicholas and Mary Parry have since 1974 been printing many books as vehicles for Nicholas Parry's illustrations (Illus. 125). Their choice of texts has been interesting and unusual, including several by the Hungarian poet Thomas Orszag-Land, such as his translation of Miklós Radnóti's *The Witness* (1977); a series of Early English texts and translations, including the very successful *Sir Orfeo* (1980); and the first printing of *The Gospel According to St Mark*, as translated into English in 1380 by John Purvey, completed in 1981. For some special copies of this, as of *Sir Orfeo,* Parry substituted original watercolors for the bright wood engravings used in the bulk of the edition.

A third group of the Tern Press's books is of Anglo-Welsh material, appropriate in a Shropshire press, from *The Poems of Llywarch Hen* in a new version by Bill Griffiths (1976), to Peter Abbs's *Songs of a New Taliesin* (1979). In the latter, as in Orszag-Land's *The Seasons* (1980), some of the verses were written to illustrate the already-cut blocks, rather than the more usual procedure.

Although one must admire the Parrys's energy and devotion, there is a "handcrafted" air about some features of their production—uneven presswork and a number of disappointing bindings—that prevents it from being completely successful. No doubt their primary concern with illustration accounts for this. Nevertheless, the very roughness I dislike has its attractions for some purchasers. Like the Randles before them, the Parrys intend to make the Tern Press a full-time venture, and some of their plans for future work (such as a suite of 150 wood engravings to illustrate the Psalms) show high promise.

In Wales itself, Ivor Waters's Moss Rose Press at Chepstow has for several years used an Adana

ILLUS. 125. Tern Press, Shropshire. Wood engraving by Nicholas Parry.

treadle press to produce small books devoted to local history and archaeology, such as his series of fascicules on *The Town of Chepstow* for the Chepstow Society (1974–1975) or *Mounton Valley Paper Mills* (1978), unassuming and ridiculously underpriced little books that continue in the old manner of the private press, quite independent of the Morris/Cobden-Sanderson tradition. Within this tradition, however, by far the most important development in Wales was the decision of the University of Wales to revive the Gregynog imprint on finely printed books—an institutionalized revival rather like the reopening of the Cuala Press in the home of Ann Yeats in 1969.

The moving force in recreating Gwasg Gregynog was Glyn Tegai Hughes, the university's warden of Gregynog. In 1969, with encouragement from the Welsh Arts Council, a Gregynog Fellowship was established. The first recipient was the gifted novelist B. S. Johnson (who wrote amusingly of his attempts to print while at Gregynog in the spring 1973 *Private Library*); not until 1974 was the first printing fellowship awarded, to Michael Hutchins, who taught at Camberwell School of Art.

Hutchins's time at Gregynog was spent working on a collection of poems by R. S. Thomas, *Laboratories of the Spirit.* It was decided that the book should be unillustrated, depending for its effect on pure typography, with the 16-point Janson supplemented by special lettering based on Roman inscriptions. As the tradition of Gregynog was for fine binding, even the ordinary copies were quarter-bound in morocco by Sangorski & Sutcliffe, with "specials" in full blue levant with various onlays, by Sally Lou Smith. The book, eventually completed in November 1976, lived up to the great traditions of the Gregynog Press. Subsequent Gwasg Gregynog books, produced under the direction of Eric Gee, with assistance from David Vickers, have also included attractive work, whether in very slight pieces, such as Loyd Haberly's poem *The Wild Cherry of Gregynog,* produced as a french-fold in 1979, or Kate Robert's *Two Old Men and Other Stories,* with colored linocuts by Kyffin Williams (1981), although the tight binding and some design features of the latter prevent the volume from being the complete success one expects from Gregynog.

After his Gregynog Fellowship and his return to teaching in London, Hutchins set up his own press, the Chimaera Press at Beckenham in Kent. In the two books so far produced, *Landscapes: A Sequence of Songs* by Emyr Humphreys, illustrated by Keith Holmes (1979), and John Wain's *Thinking about Mr. Person,* with colored etchings by Bartholomeu dos Santos (1980), Hutchins demonstrated his own skill as printer, and his wife, Helen, demonstrated hers as marbler and binder—a combination of talents within the family that many private printers would envy!

Keith Holmes's own private printing shows a very individual approach to bookmaking. For another book by Emyr Humphreys, for which the illustrations are close to those used in *Landscapes,* he cut the whole of the text on lino. *The Kingdom of Bran* (1979) and its sequel *Pwyll a Riannon* (1980) are powerful books—not to my personal taste, but indicating clearly how in competent hands the book without type can be very successful.

Much more traditional has been the work of Michael Gullick at his Red Gull Press at Hitchin. While still a final-year student at Camberwell in 1968, he produced a very attractive edition of *The Life and Work of Wolfgang Fugger* by Fritz Funke, which showed an appreciation of the traditional techniques (being sewn on vellum tapes laced into the covers) all too rarely encountered (Illus. 126A and 126B). In *A Working Alphabet of Initial Letters from Twelfth Century Tuscany* (1979), a facsimile of a manuscript in the Fitzwilliam Museum, Gullick's scholarly predilections as well as his practical skills as printer were also shown, and his volume of verse by Peter Scupham, *Transformation Scenes* (1982), is remarkable for its very low price.

Peter Scupham is the owner of the Mandeville Press (also at Hitchin), which since 1974 has produced many similar small books of contemporary poetry, handset and printed on a Model Three hand-platen, and also sold at modest prices. With his partner John Mole, Scupham has provided a service of real significance to modern English poetry. A similar philosophy and approach underlies several other "poetic" presses in the London area, such as John Cotton's Priapus Press at Berkhamsted and Alan Tarling's Poet & Printer now at Pinner. The inspiration for all these was probably Oscar Mellor's Fantasy Press at Oxford, which between 1951 and 1962 produced the early work of many new poets.

Among the older private presses in the London area, one of the most visually exuberant is Ben Sands's Shoestring Press. Established in London in 1958, and moved to Whitstable in 1960, the press has had a relatively small output, but in such books as *The Walrus and the Carpenter, The Tragical Death of a Apple Pie* (Illus. 127), or Lamb's *A Dissertation upon Roast Pig* (1975), he has produced some of the most lively linocuts to be found in modern British work. Another long-established press to make extensive use of linocuts has been the Taurus Press of Willow Dene, at which Paul Peter Piech

ILLUS. 126A. Michael Gullick. Hertfordshire. Binding of *The Life and Work of Wolfgang Fugger,* produced in 1968, while Gullick was still a student at Camberwell.

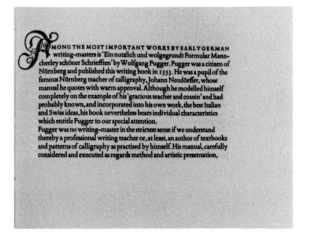

ILLUS. 126B. Michael Gullick. Hertfordshire. Text opening of *The Life and Work of Wolfgang Fugger.*

ILLUS. 127. Playing with the alphabet. Top: *a.apple pie,* printed at the Shoestring
Press, Kent, 1966, with colored linocuts by Ben Sands. Bottom: Gus Rueter's
Character & Symbol, 1972, printed at the Aliquando Press, Toronto.

has since 1959 produced a long series of booklets, prints, and posters. Much of Piech's work is
startling and disturbing, and deliberately so: His aim is social and political. Even in such "neutral"
work as William Blake's *London* (1976) or Hugo Manning's *The Daughter* (1975), the strength of
Piech's feeling comes through.

Other presses in the London area are poles apart from Piech's political and social concerns. In
1969, Ian Mortimer set up his press, I M Imprimit, initially to print his own engravings and
woodcuts (Illus. 128), issuing such volumes as *From a Satyric Country* (1971) and *Legendary Towers*
(1977), both by Anthony Richards. Gradually, Mortimer has built up his equipment so that he is
now much more in the position of a specialist printer to whom publishers of fine editions turn when
they need the care he gives his work—for example, James Kirkup's *Scenes from Sesshu* (1977), printed
for Birgit Skiöld's Pimlico Press, or Pauline Sitwell's *Green Song,* printed for the Opal Press in 1979.
Presses such as these are closer to the French tradition of *livres d'artiste* than to the English private
presses. Although Great Britain now has several such artist's presses—the most important perhaps
being those of Natalie d' Arbeloff and the World's End Press run by Ann Brunskill—to extend this
chapter to discuss them would be to distort it.

Within the private press tradition in the London area are several other presses producing

ILLUS. 128. I M Imprimit, London.
Woodcut by Ian Mortimer from
From a Satyric Country.

notable work, which fit into the private press categories already discussed. At the Glade Press in Surrey, for more than 12 years A. S. Osley has printed small editions in good classical style, usually on matters concerned with calligraphy or printing, such as *Scalzini on Handwriting* (1971) or Thiboust's *Printing's Excellencie* (1978), books that are valuable contributions to their subject as well as attractive in themselves. Nearby, the retired printer Edward Burrett set up his Penmiel Press in 1974 and has produced a wide range of small books, of which his *Full Point—A Typographer Remembers*, printed for the Caxton celebrations in 1976, is particularly attractive.

At Blackheath, since 1979 Nicolas McDowell has been printing on a Columbian press. He uses two imprints: Old Stile for such work as Robert Buchanan's *The Ballad of Judas Iscariot* (1981), with strong linocuts by J. Martin Pitts, and the Kouros Press, under which he has produced several small volumes as well as the more ambitious (and successful) *No Other Gods,* poems by Mario Stefani translated by Anthony Reid (1982). For some copies of this, he used paper made by his wife Frances McDowell: it is a paper of good texture that McDowell marries well with Pitts's linocuts.

At his Florin Press near Tonbridge, Graham Williams, formerly a designer with the Folio Society, has set up as a specialist printer in much the way that the Carters and Randles or Ian Mortimer have done. In addition to his work for other publishers, such as the edition of Jane

Kanalia lud zwycięża,
kanalia krwią się karmi:
generałowie, księża,
bankierzy i żandarmi!

Po zemstę nad Paryżem
już ciągnie zgraja katów
z bagnetem, złotem, krzyżem
przez pierś proletariatu.

Lecz Paryż umie zginąć,
Komuna się nie podda!
Wolności! Tobie płynąć,
czerwona twoja woda . . .

II

ILLUS. 129. Oficyna Stanislawa Gliwy, London. Page from *Komuna Paryska*, 1975. Wood engraving by K. M. Sopócko.

Austen's *Sir Charles Grandison* for David Astor's Jubilee Books at Burford (1981), Williams has published a number of well-presented books under his own imprint. The most important of these has been Thomas Bewick's *Fables of Aesop and Others* (1980), for which superb prints from the original blocks were made by R. Hunter Middleton at his Cherryburn Press in Chicago, with accompanying text written by Iain Bain, the foremost Bewick scholar.

The skills needed to print from blocks engraved a century or more ago, for which printers like Hunter Middleton and David Chambers are well known, are shared also by David Esslemont, who works in Newcastle-upon-Tyne—a most appropriate base because it had been the home of Thomas Bewick. Himself an engraver, Esslemont printed *Sixteen Contemporary Wood Engravers* (1982) to accompany an exhibition of some of the fine work being done in Great Britain today. His *Luke Clennell: Bewick Apprentice* (1982) was a superbly printed showing of Clennell's work, which not only revealed Esslemont's skills as a printer but also as a bookbinder. Also in northeastern England, at his Septentrio Press at Hexham, E. D. Jordan is following a pattern of producing finely printed small editions of books with his own illustrations cut in lino or engraved in transparent thermoplastic (called Plexiglas in the United States and Perspex in Great Britain).

North of the border in Scotland, private press work tends to be more purely tied to literature, conventionally presented. This impression is true of two of the most prolific presses, both owned by booksellers. In Edinburgh at his Tragara Press, Alan Anderson has since 1954 printed many small books of literary interest on his treadle press, ranging from the simple *Selected Poems of Alexander Robertson of Struan* (1971) to collections of letters by such writers as Baron Corvo (*Aberdeen Interval*, 1975). Anderson has produced a good record of his substantial and valuable output in his *Tragara Press, 1954–1979: A Bibliography* (1979). In Peeblesshire, Alex Frizzell's Castlelaw Press has followed a similar pattern since he first bought a treadle press from Anderson in 1969. His small books have included a good range of Scottish subjects, such as *Poetical Descriptions of Orkney* (1971), originally written in 1652, and also work by contemporary poets.

To round out this brief survey by region, it is appropriate to return to the London area for one long-established, important, and successful press that does not fit in with any of those described above, yet typifies the private press in more general terms. This is the Oficyna Stanislawa Gliwy, which has been at work since 1953. As the name of his press suggests, Stanislaw Gliwa mainly prints books in Polish intended for the Polish community in Great Britain. Because of the textual inaccessibility of many of these books and pamphlets they have received much less attention from typophiles than if Gliwa's printing was in English. His work has included some books in other languages, such as the edition of Sylvia Plath's *Three Women* (1968), which was published by Turret Books, and W. J. Stankiewicz's *Guide to Democratic Jargon* (1976). Operating in isolation from the mainstream of private presses, and for many years with very little recognition outside his own community for the quality of his work, Gliwa has provided the Poles in Great Britain with more than a few well-designed and handsomely illustrated books.

Chapter 20

THE UNITED STATES TODAY

WORLD WAR II AND ITS AFTERMATH were to be far less decisive factors in changing the face of the private press in the United States than in the Old World. Frank Altschul's Overbrook Press was by no means the only press of major importance set up in the 1930s that was to continue work in very much the old spirit, right up to the 1960s or even later.

The world of fine and amateur printing was larger in America, and the expansion of interest and activity to be seen there within the past 20–30 years has been even more extensive than in the other English-speaking countries. In a *Newsweek* article for August 16, 1982—the publication of which in itself marks a heightened awareness of the private press in wider circles—it was estimated there are now about 300 private print shops in America. This is to say nothing of the many hundreds of other amateurs who, continuing the traditions of the Victorian parlor printers, use the presses they have in their basements or attics for the production of greeting cards, letterheads, and amateur journals. With such a plethora of presses, this chapter can only survey briefly the work being done and the printers' methods and purposes. No attempt is made to name every private press printing good work.

Though private presses of many kinds (including those set up for publishing verse, typographic experimentation, and scholarly publishing) exist throughout the United States, there are some areas in which activity is particularly intense. Frequently the reason is to be found in the presence of a particular printer or school whose teachers have inspired others to print, and to print well. Just as it was hard to find an English private press of the Arts and Crafts Movement that did not owe a debt to Emery Walker or, more recently in Leicestershire, to the catalytic role of Rigby Graham, so there have also been influential figures in the United States.

In the Northeast, the workshop and lecture series on the history and art of the book conducted by Professor Ray Nash at Dartmouth College from 1937 to 1970 was important as such an influence, but less perhaps on private presses than on those concerned to produce well-designed books in the wider commercial field, through such men as Alvin Eisenman, Roderick Stinehour, and David R. Godine. The latter's publishing house in Boston was in its earlier days close to the private press tradition.

Another significant New England influence was Leonard Baskin's Gehenna Press at Northampton, Massachusetts. A sculptor, printmaker, and wood engraver, with what he described as "a secondary passion for printing," Baskin's first essay in printing was undertaken on a student press in Jonathan Edwards College at Yale, at which he printed some youthful verse, *On a Pyre of Withered Roses* (1942). His next books, the first with the Gehenna imprint, produced while he was an instructor in printmaking at Worcester (Massachusetts) Art Museum in the early 1950s, were somewhat crude as examples of book production, although they were good vehicles for Baskin's prints. However, from publication of *Blake and the Youthful Ancients* (1956), with Baskin's own superb engravings, and *Thirteen Poems by Wilfred Owen* (1956), with powerful drawings by Ben Shahn, typography and binding were well-handled. These were the first books produced by the press following Baskin's move to Northampton; the improvement came partly from Baskin's alliance with Richard Warren of the Metcalf Printing Company; thereafter the Gehenna Press was able to use the company's plant and craftsmen much in the way that Charles Ricketts had depended on the Ballantyne Press. No believer in handwork for its own sake, Baskin has been happy to resort to Monotype composition and the use of powered presses for Gehenna books.

For their success—whether in such splendid illustrated books as Baskin's own *Horned Beetles*

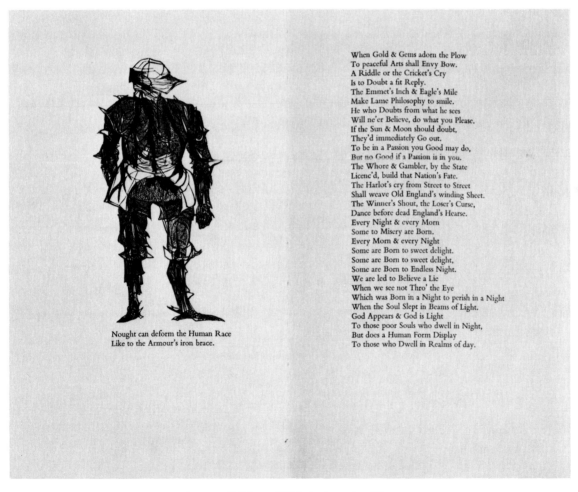

Nought can deform the Human Race
Like to the Armour's iron brace.

When Gold & Gems adorn the Plow
To peaceful Arts shall Envy Bow.
A Riddle or the Cricket's Cry
Is to Doubt a fit Reply.
The Emmet's Inch & Eagle's Mile
Make Lame Philosophy to smile.
He who Doubts from what he sees
Will ne'er Believe, do what you Please.
If the Sun & Moon should doubt,
They'd immediately Go out.
To be in a Passion you Good may do,
But no Good if a Passion is in you.
The Whore & Gambler, by the State
Licenc'd, build that Nation's Fate.
The Harlot's cry from Street to Street
Shall weave Old England's winding Sheet.
The Winner's Shout, the Loser's Curse,
Dance before dead England's Hearse.
Every Night & every Morn
Some to Misery are Born.
Every Morn & every Night
Some are Born to sweet delight.
Some are Born to sweet delight,
Some are Born to Endless Night.
We are led to Believe a Lie
When we see not Thro' the Eye
Which was Born in a Night to perish in a Night
When the Soul Slept in Beams of Light.
God Appears & God is Light
To those poor Souls who dwell in Night,
But does a Human Form Display
To those who Dwell in Realms of day.

ILLUS. 130. Gehenna Press, Massachusetts. Edition of Blake's *Auguries of Innocence* with wood engravings by Leonard Baskin, 1968.

(1958), or *The Defense of Gracchus Babeuf* (1964) with etchings by Thomas Cornell, or the purely typographic *Cancellaresca Bastarda Displayed* (1965)—the credit was due not only to Baskin as designer and *animateur* of the projects, but also to the other craftsmen involved in the books' production. Bindings by such master binders as Gray Parrot and Arno Werner and the use of a variety of splendid handmade papers were also important; but above all it was due to the skills of Harold McGrath, Gehenna's full-time pressman since the late 1950s, that the books worked so well.

In returning to a paid pressman in the manner of William Morris, Baskin took a step unusual in one whose prime interest was in printmaking. At Gehenna's near-contemporary Eden Hill Press in Connecticut, Joseph Low set up his private press for the sound reason that only the artist himself can print his work with the care necessary in such press considerations as make-ready and ink density; if the artist hands his work to another, even to a pressman as skilled as McGrath, he also hands to him some of the responsibility for the work in its finished form. Like many other artists, Low did not wish to share responsibility for the execution, and his delightful exuberant work shown in such publications as *Ten Proverbs* (1959) and *The Wren Boys' Rhyme* (1961) (Illus. 131) revealed his mastery of the coarse-textured cut, sometimes etched or scraped or sanded down to change the texture.

After Baskin left Northampton in the mid-1970s for England (where his influence is to be seen in such books as H. C. Cutcliffe's *The Art of Trout Fishing on the Rapid Streams,* illustrated and printed by D. R. Wakefield at his Chevington Press in Devonshire, 1982), the Gehenna personnel split up. At the Hampshire Typothetae, McGrath has continued to print in a masterful way, particularly for the Pennyroyal Press in Easthampton. Owned by the distinguished wood engraver Barry Moser (whose work has been seen in books from presses across the United States), Pennyroyal has produced a number of books that are primarily vehicles for Moser's superb work, such as his *Fifty Wood Engravings* (1981), *Wood Engraving: Notes on the Craft* (1979), and *Men of Printing: Anglo-American Profiles* (1976), in which the text to support Moser's portrait engravings was culled from obituary notices in *The Times* and the *New York Times.* Pennyroyal has also produced some contemporary poetry, such as Paul Mariani's *Timing Devices* (1978) and Allen Mandelbaum's *A Lied of Letterpress* (1981), but its most substantial and important work so far is the 1981 edition of *Alice's Adventures in Wonderland.* It is a finely annotated reader's version edited by Selwyn Goodacre, with annotations by James Kincaid, and printed on paper especially made for the press; the Pennyroyal *Alice* is one of the most important and successful fine editions of recent years. Like all Pennyroyal books, it was a cooperative effort: Monotype setting by Michael and Winifred Bixler in Boston, with hand composition at the press by Arthur Larsen; calligraphic titling and initial by G. G. Laurens; engravings by Moser; superlative presswork by McGrath; binding by Gray Parrot. The price of $1,000 on publication put it beyond the range of most of us, but the trade edition published by the University of California Press a year later permits all to enjoy the Pennyroyal text and illustrations at a more modest price and to look forward to a similar edition of the companion *Through the Looking Glass.*

At the Cheloniidae Press, Alan James Robinson is developing a similar project, intended "to tie together the talents of individual craftsmen from this area and to produce unique and finely crafted limited edition books." Himself a printmaker, Robinson provided powerful etchings and wood engravings for the first book, Poe's *The Raven* (1980). With presswork by McGrath and a binding by David Bourbeau, which made effective use of black marbled papers (by Stephen Auger) resembling folded wings on the boards, it was one of the most accomplished first books to have appeared for a long time.

A much more modest press with links to Gehenna is the Warwick Press of Easthampton, Massachusetts, at which Carol Blinn has been working independently since 1975. Like many of the

The rann, the rann, the King of all birds,
St. Stephen's Day she was caught in the furze;
Though she is little, her family's great,
O Luck for me lady, and give us a treat.
Me boots is worn, me clothes is torn,
Following the rann three miles or more,
So up with the kettle and down with the pan,
Give us an answer before we go on;
Put your hand in your pocket,
From that to your purse,
If ye don't give us money, we'll give ye our curse,
If ye don't give us money, if ye don't give us meat,
We'll bury the rann at the pier of the gate;
Up with your kettle, down with your pan,
A penny or tuppence to bury the rann.

THE WREN-BOYS' RHYME is still sung in Ireland on St. Stephen's Day, December 26th, by boys who carry a live wren from door to door — unaware that their chant is the survival of an ancient, ritual king-killing at the winter solstice, meant to ensure the return of the sun and the beginning of a new year. It is sent to you now with the latter intention by JOSEPH LOW and the EDEN HILL PRESS in Newtown, Connecticut.

ILLUS. 131. Eden Hill Press, Connecticut. *The Wren Boys' Rhyme*, 1961, with spirited rubbercut by Joseph Low.

smaller presses set up in recent years, Warwick is not exclusively a private press. It is a small letterpress printing house that depends on commissioned work (such as a catalogue for the Ashendene Press collection at Trinity College, Hartford) to underpin the work it publishes itself. Starting modestly with *A Poem* (on papermaking) by Richard Frame (1976), the press's work has included *One Man's Work* (1982), a study of the binder Arno Werner from whom Carol Blinn learned her skills for making the paste papers that are often used in binding Warwick Press books.

The work of Pennyroyal and of Cheloniidae is relatively expensive. At the Penmaen Press in Lincoln, Massachusetts, Michael McCurdy has adopted a different approach to making books with his strong wood engravings widely available. McCurdy's usual practice is to print large editions of 1,000 or more copies of which 200 or 300 are signed, numbered, and handbound, with the balance of the edition being published casebound or in paperback at low prices. Occasionally, as with

Banquet, Five Short Stories (1978), he produces a small letterpress edition with a larger and cheaper offset litho reprint.

Textually, Penmaen has been quite adventurous, with a series of modern fiction, including such titles as Robert Coover's *Charlie in the House of Rue* (1980), Brian Swann's *Elizabeth* (1981), and Paulé Bartón's Haitian stories *The Woe Shirt* (1980), in addition to a range of contemporary verse and some classical texts. Although McCurdy's own engravings have been used on the majority of Penmaen books, they have also used the work of others such as Lynd Ward in Voltaire's *Poem upon the Lisbon Disaster* (1977) or Jerome Kaplan's relief-etchings in *To Eberhart from Ginsberg* (1976).

Kaplan was also illustrator to two of the most effective books—Kafka's *Der Kübelreiter/The Bucket Rider* (1972) and Lorca's *Ballad of the Spanish Civil Guard* (1963)—issued by the Janus Press of Claire Van Vliet (Illus. 132). Based since 1966 in West Burke, Vermont, Claire Van Vliet first used her imprint in 1955 for John Theobald's poem *An Oxford Odyssey,* for which she used equipment at San Diego State College. Borrowed equipment in Philadelphia, Wisconsin, Germany, and New

ILLUS. 132. Janus Press, Vermont. Lorca's *Romance de la Guardia Civil Espanola,* 1974. Double spread. Woodcut by Jerome Kaplan; interlinear English translation in silver.

Jersey was to underpin the press's work for the next 11 years. A particularly important influence on her technical skills as printer was an apprenticeship (1958–1960) to John Anderson of the Pickering Press (himself an apprentice from 1936 to 1938 to Peter Beilenson at the Walpole Printing Office); also significant was an association at the Janus Press with James McWilliams in the early sixties, when McWilliams used the imprint for a number of original and McLuhan-inspired publications, such as *Four Letter Word Book* (1964) and *Polyurethane Antibook* (1965).

In contrast with McWilliams's experimental work, Janus books designed and executed by Van Vliet at this time showed appreciation and respect for the traditions of book design, seen most delightfully in the series of books illustrated by Helen Siegl (Illus. 133), such as *A Felicity of Carols* (1970) and *Mother Goose* (1972), and in the work she illustrated herself, for example, her relief-etchings in Kafka's *A Country Doctor* (1962).

There is also an experimental side to Van Vliet's work, particularly successful (to my mind) in her willingness to accept new illustration techniques, as with Ray Metzker's electrostatic prints in Estelle Leontief's *Razerol* (1973) and his color xerographic print used in Margo Lockwood's *Bare Elegy* (1980). I am less enthusiastic about some other Janus experiments, such as the nontextual responses to nature found in *Sun, Sky, and Earth* (1964) or *Sky and Earth: Variable Landscape* (1973), or the picture books produced in collaboration with Peter Schumann's Bread and Puppet Theatre— *White Horse Butcher* (1977), *St Francis Preaches to the Birds* (1978), and *Dream of the Dirty Women* (1980).

Dream of the Dirty Women was a project undertaken jointly with Kathryn and Howard Clark of the Twinrocker Handmade Paper Mill at Brookston, Indiana, which for the past 10 years has been producing fine papers for limited edition work. Janus/Twinrocker cooperation started in 1976 with the production of a special "paperwork" landscape of different colored pulps, used in the 50 copies of Hayden Carruth's *Aura* (1977). A similar "paperwork" was used in Leconte de Lisle's poem *Midi/Noon* (1977). *Dream of the Dirty Women* also used different colored pulp within the same sheet, which combined with the text and illustrations with remarkably good effect. In such books, how-

ILLUS. 133. Janus Press, Vermont. *A New Herball*, 1968. Double spread, with two-color block print by Helen Siegl.

ever, the modest prices normally placed on Janus work were necessarily higher, and in less skilled hands than Van Vliet's, the use of paper as a positive element in printmaking has real danger if one regards the book as vehicle for text.

Elsewhere in New England there are other private presses of a much more traditional kind. The Printing Office at High Loft, "a summer venture at Seal Harbor, Maine" is the holiday press of August Heckscher at which he has printed several agreeable pieces such as Adin Ballou's *After Reading Thoreau: Sonnets* (1978). At their Cat Island Press in Salem, Massachusetts, Winifred and Michael Bixler, who monotype-set much work for other fine printers, produce some small elegant books like Gerry Williams's *The Skate and Other Poems* (1981). At Amherst, from his Swamp Press Ed Rayher is producing sound work, such as the haiku *Dusk Lingers* (1981), while under the imprint of the Nocturnal Canary Press his wife is also producing good work of which Steven Ruhl's *No Bread Without the Dance* (1979) is representative. Sylvia and Robert Gutchen's Biscuit City Press in Rhode Island has produced a wide range of small books printed on their Albion press, from *The Act of Renunciation of Allegiance* for the bicentennial in 1976, to Samuel Butler's *Dildoides* (1980). At Typographeum in New Hampshire, since 1977, R. T. Risk has produced several modest but interesting books, including his life of Count Potocki, *It Is the Choice of the Gods* (1978). Claude Fredericks's Banyan Press at Pawlet, Vermont, dates back to 1946 when it was set up in New York, and in its long life has produced a number of valuable books, such as Gertrude Stein's *Things as They Are* (1950) or Bernard Malamud's *Two Fables* (1978).

To a considerable extent, the renaissance of fine printing in the Midwest had its roots in New England, through the Cummington Press (whose work is described below). The first significant press, however, was Carroll Coleman's Prairie Press in Iowa. This had its origins as a youthful hobby in the 1920s, when Coleman produced *The Golden Quill,* a magazine of the kind so often produced by amateur printers. After some time working in newspapers and commercial printing plants, he set up his own press in 1935. Allowing for the time spent teaching typographic design at the University of Iowa (where he established the Typographical Laboratory in 1945) and as director of the university's publications, it is astonishing how much good work the Prairie Press was able to produce. It was a private press very far removed from the amateur undertaking at which the owner could print a few books regardless of expense. Coleman's press had to pay its way and in many instances it printed books for publication by others, as did Saul Marks at the Plantin Press, or the Carters at Rampant Lions. For the Prairie Press's own publications, almost entirely work by contemporary writers, prices were kept low by printing somewhat larger editions (500 or 600 copies) and using good quality machine-made paper, although almost always the traditions of handsetting and superlative presswork were maintained. Whether in early books such as Althea Bass's *Young Enquirer* (1937), or in later ones like Ethan Ayer's *The Beneficiary and Other Poems* (1967), Coleman's work was of a solid, unpretentious kind that struck a responsive chord among many.

Carrying on and diversifying his work, Harry Duncan has been a seminal figure. Duncan began printing while on a teaching scholarship at the Cummington (Massachusetts) School of the Arts. The first book to appear under the Cummington Press imprint was *Incident on the Bark Columbia* (1941). Finding printing to be at the core of his interests, but dissatisfied with the extent of his skills, he took a brief apprenticeship with Edmund Thompson at Hawthorn House and also gained much from the advice and help of Victor Hammer (then at Wells College, New York), with whom he jointly published an edition of William Carlos Williams's *The Clouds* in 1948. After the death of Duncan's partner Wightman Williams in an automobile accident, Duncan accepted an invitation to teach typography at the University of Iowa, taking over direction of the Typographical Laboratory from Coleman. Using his own Cummington Press imprint (and the Washington press he had removed from Massachusetts), he concentrated on printing good editions of modern American

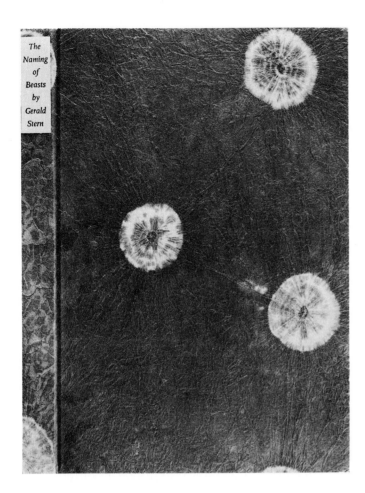

The Naming of Beasts by Gerald Stern

ILLUS. 134. Cummington Press, Iowa. *The Naming of Beasts*, 1974. Binding in Japanese tie-died paper over boards; the label, like the text of the book, in Octavian type.

literature in a severe, restrained classical style that, in such books as Stephen Berg's *Bearing Weapons* (1963), shows clearly the line of descent from presses like the Doves Press. Not all Cummington books were so traditional in approach: James Agee's *Four Early Stories* of the same year experimented with unjustified text in double column (Illus. 135), which to my mind was not completely successful, but the execution was again superb.

In 1972 Duncan moved again, this time to Omaha where he teaches at the University of Nebraska and conducts a printing and publishing program under the imprint Abattoir Editions. At Omaha, Duncan has continued to print, in a similar manner, distinguished and unaffected books of similar textual importance. Whether in such "slight" pieces of classical bookmaking as the 1974 *Selected Poems of S. Foster Damon* (Illus. 136), or the more ambitious *Thistles and Thorns* by Paul Smyth (1977), which is powerfully illustrated by Barry Moser's wood engravings, there is a grace and skill to Duncan's work too rarely to be found. Only in his choice of papers, which seem occasionally to be too heavy in weight for the size of book printed, as in S. J. Marks's *Lines* (1972), or John Logan's *The House That Jack Built* (1974), does Duncan's ability ever seem to falter, and at the extraordinarily modest prices set on Abattoir Editions one can scarcely complain that the texts chosen for publication are at times opaque and difficult for the general reader.

The influence of Harry Duncan has been profound, both locally and elsewhere in the United States and abroad. Perhaps the most distinguished of his pupils has been Kim Merker, who starting as a graduate student in the poetry workshop in the university in 1956, soon "without much considered thought, found myself to be a printer/publisher." From Duncan he gained a love of the Washington handpress and a penchant for Jan van Krimpen's type designs, which he has put to

ILLUS. 135. Cummington Press, Iowa. Opening from *Four Early Stories by James Agee,* 1964.

distinguished use at his own Stone Wall Press, in such books as Donald Justice's *A Local Storm* or Thom Gunn's *A Geography* (1966), using a severely classical typographic style of a kind van Krimpen would certainly have approved. His editorial policy, never to reprint work but to accept only original manuscript, and his own sound editorial taste, have made Stone Wall books textually, as well as visually, particularly attractive.

Going beyond his own private press, in the mid-1960s Merker persuaded the University of Iowa to set up its own press, the Windhover Press. Under his direction, the same clean, uncluttered style, sound execution, and low prices for superb craftsmanship have typified its work in such books as Philip Levine's *The Names of the Lost* (1976) and Peter Scupham's *Natura* (1978). Unlike Stone Wall, at which Merker has remained faithful to his Washington press, Windhover uses a proofing press and often its own special paper.

Harry Duncan's successor as director of the Typographical Laboratory was Kay Amert, whose own Seamark Press has produced excellent work in the Cummington tradition in such books as Donald Justice's *From a Notebook* (1972) and Scott Wright's *Odd Weather* (1976). In West Branch, another press owing its inspiration directly to the Typographical Laboratory is the Toothpaste Press of Allan and Cinda Kornblum, which has built up a strong list of contemporary poetry since its first letterpress production, Paul Violi's *Waterworks* (1973). As the Kornblums have developed, their style has also grown more independent of the Duncan style, although the success of such books as the translations of Antonio Machado by Robert Bly, *I Never Wanted Fame* (1979) and *Canciones* (1980),

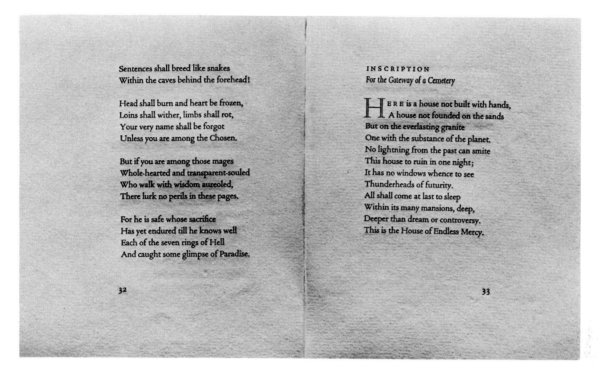

ILLUS. 136. Abattoir Editions, Nebraska. *Selected Poems of S. Foster Damon,* 1974.
On Wookey Hole paper, showing unusual and effective combination of Cloister Old Style,
Joanna italic, and Romulus Open types.

or of Jim Hanson's *Reasons for the Sky* (1979), is due in no small part to the foundation laid by Duncan.

Further afield, in Mixcoac, a suburb of Mexico City, Juan Pascoe's Taller Martín Pescador is another press at which Duncan's training has been put to excellent use since the press was set up in 1975. With its first book, Cristina de la Peña's *Eólicas* (1975), through such later work as Tomás Segovia's *Cuaderno del Nomada,* the restrained taste in design and materials and the choice of original work by contemporary writers showed the sound Cummington influence strongly. Nearly a quarter of a century ago, a sojourn in Mexico and Guatemala by the Dutch typographer A. A. M. Stols was influential in raising standards of local book production; one hopes that through Pascoe's work the Duncan influence will be equally beneficial.

At Lisbon, Iowa, Bonnie O'Connell's Penumbra Press is another small concern set up to produce modestly priced but finely printed editions of poetry by new writers. Remarkably, it is not one of the offspring of Cummington or the Typographical Laboratory (although O'Connell did work with Kim Merker for a time), but of the other great influence in the Midwest, Walter Hamady and the Perishable Press. In such books as Tess Gallagher's *Stepping Outside* (1975) or Rita Dover's *Ten Poems* (1977), O'Connell has produced excellent work with subtle use of color.

The Perishable Press of Mount Horeb, Wisconsin, is undoubtedly one of the most interesting and important presses to have developed in the United States in the past generation. Since 1964, Hamady (a professor of art at the University of Wisconsin) has distinguished himself as papermaker as well as printer, and much of his work has used the excellent Shadwell paper made at his own mill. One of the earlier private printers to prefer a Vandercook proofing press to the traditional Albion or Washington, Hamady approaches printing with a fresh, exuberant, playful style. Although undoubtedly aware of the tenets of classical typography, he is not bound by them in the way that somebody coming out of a printing background would have been. He has, not infrequently, broken the rules,

ILLUS. 137. Perishable Press, Wisconsin. *In Sight of Blue Mounds*, 1972. Two leaves from the portfolio.

sometimes with conspicuous success, as in his unusual use of color. The title page to his own *The Plumfoot Poems* (1967), for instance, is all in black except for a single hyphen in violet. Many other Perishable Press books (largely of modern poetry) have been marked by similar subtleties, and all by consummate craftsmanship in the overall production.

One feature of Hamady's work (which is in marked and very refreshing contrast to the high seriousness with which some other private press owners treat their work) is his lighthearted informality. Particularly noticeable in his ephemera and in his colophons (from which we learn his opinion of local politics and whether the dogwood is in flower, as well as the information normally conveyed in a colophon) it has been built up into a witty and entertaining minor art in the series of *Interminable Gabberjabs* (Illus. 139), of which *Gabberjab Number Four* (the hundredth book of the press) was published in 1981.

This is the positive side to Hamady's undoubted achievement: some remarkable, vital work with unique solutions to design problems. There are some negative aspects to his work. Quite apart from the selection of texts to be printed in the superb Perishable style, with which a number of critics would quarrel (as they would with the work of Abattoir, Windhover, and several of the other contemporary poetry presses), some questions surface about the manner and methods of the press. As Kathy Walkup put it in a perceptive review of the 1978 Perishable output:

> One is *conscious* of their art, beyond their existence as books. With more exposure to the books, one begins to ask questions about them. Are they the issue of a private press, in the limited sense of that phrase, or do they seek a wider audience? Are they more eccentric than innovative? Are they enduring, or merely endearing? Is Walter Hamady a contemporary genius, or the Elbert Hubbard of our day?

Walkup's conclusion that Hamady and Hubbard were very different was one with which few would disagree, and her judgment was sound in pinpointing one defect in Perishable books, the constant repetition of some innovations in small volumes, rather than their development in larger works or books intended for circulation to a wider group. My own main reservation about the Perishable Press is of a different kind: its influence on other printers.

Like Harry Duncan before him, Walter Hamady has gathered a large number of pupils, apprentices, and disciples about him at different times, to whom he has been able to convey his own enthusiasm for printing with great success. Besides Bonnie O'Connell's Penumbra Press, there is a large group of others whose owners have learned from Hamady the superb work possible with a Vandercook press: Bieler, Black Mesa, Blue Moon, Crepuscular, Iguana, Penstemon, Red Ozier, Salient Seedling, Triangular. These and other presses have learned much from Walter Hamady.

It is what they have learned that gives me most concern. For disciples to work closely in the manner of their masters for awhile may be no bad thing, and in the case of Harry Duncan's pupils it has certainly resulted in some excellent work. One of the disasters of Kelmscott, however, was the number of persons so bewitched by the Kelmscott manner that they could not interpret the Morris message. There are more than a few indications that some of Hamady's pupils have been so glamorized by the way in which he tackles certain problems that they simply copy the Hamady manner without the Hamady skill. Hamady's way with paper in some of the collage constructions and his way with words in the colophons and Gabberjabs are fine, the imitations and derivations of his work by some of his pupils jejune and pathetic.

What makes their derivative work particularly depressing is that the technical printing skills they have gained from Hamady are of a very high order indeed. For some of them, the pleasures of papermaking by hand have led them to produce books as art objects rather than vehicles for literature: the Triangular Press's *Sequential Picture Plane* (1980), for instance, although not unpleasing in its way is not a *book*; too often one has the feeling that printers (and not only Hamady's followers) have forgotten the purpose of typography.

Among those who have studied with Hamady, particularly successful work has come from Gerald Lange's Bieler Press in Madison. Since setting up his press in 1975, Lange has produced an interesting and attractive series of well-produced small books, such as Gayle Feyrer's *Demon Letting* (1976) or Gerald Williams's *Common Ground* (1980). Also in Madison, Jim Lee, from his Blue Moon Press, produced two attractive books with his own linocuts, *The Illustrated Goose* (1979) and *The Deadly Sins* (1980), before moving to the University of Manitoba where he is now teaching graphic arts. Steve Miller also started his Red Ozier Press in Wisconsin in 1976, but has since moved the press to New York. With his partner, Ken Botnick, he also runs the Tidepool Paper Mill, whose paper is often used for the bindings (sometimes for the texts) of Red Ozier books. Their output has included some accomplished work, such as Robert Bly's *Mirabai Versions* (1980), in which the Perishable influence is still clear, although in other books like Galway Kinnell's *The Last Hiding Places of Snow* (1981), with wood engravings by Barry Moser, a more independent approach was shown. In their superb edition of Isaac Bashevis Singer's story *One Day of Happiness* (1982), with color lithographs by Richard Callner, they have produced a book of real artistic success and importance.

Also in New York, Nadja, the press of Carol Sturm and Douglas Wolf, has produced some distinguished small editions, usually of contemporary poetry, with great technical skill. For their earlier work, such as W. D. Snodgrass's *If Birds Build with Your Hair* (1978), they used Univers, Helvetica, and other sans-serif faces, although for more recent books, like Richard Eberhart's *Chocorua* (1981), they have turned to the old-face romans more often found in fine press work.

Ron Keller's Red Angel Press in New York City is a relaxation from commercial book design; he undertakes all the work—setting, illustration, presswork, binding—by himself. Several of Keller's most interesting and attractive books—examples being Longfellow's *The Birds of Killingworth* (1974) and two based on selections from Melville: *Cetology* (1973) and *Rock Redondo* (1981)—have grown from his interest in nineteenth-century literature. *Rock Redondo* is one of the rare instances in which the use of a paper-cast strengthens a book rather than weakens it.

At Tannersville in New York State, Leonard Seastone has been running his Tideline Press since 1972. Largely self-taught, Seastone's early work, like *The Island Hunter* by Peter Wild (1976), was printed on a Washington handpress, but for more recent books, such as Thomas Johnson's *The*

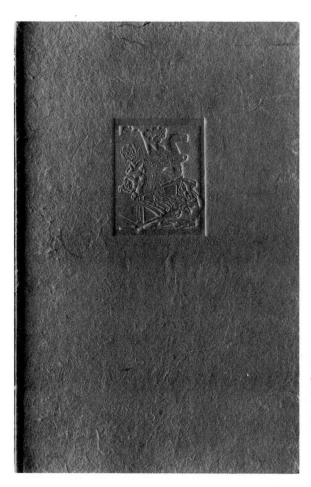

ILLUS. 138. Perishable Press, Wisconsin. *Left: Two Stories,* by Kenneth Bernard, 1973. Blind-blocked binding, paper over boards. *Opposite page:* Title-page spread printed on Hosho paper.

Noctambulist Papers (1980), he has turned to a Vandercook proofing press, as have so many other small printers. In his work, he has made subtle use of blind-blocking, and in some books, such as Amiri Baraka's *Spring Song* (1979), interesting and effective use of monoprint illustrations. Like the majority of small printers, his own publication program has to be supported by jobbing and commissioned work, like the attractive *John Anderson and the Pickering Press* for Fairleigh Dickinson University (1980); under the "mild guidance" of Anderson and Seastone, students at Fairleigh Dickinson's Arthur W. Rushmore Laboratory Press are learning the skills and joys of handprinting.

Strangely enough, Pennsylvania is not a state with substantial private press activity. In Pittsburgh a few years ago, the late Norton Peterson's Fragment Press produced some attractive books illustrated with his own strong woodcuts (Illus. 140), of which Mary Pardo's *A Bestiary of Sorts* (1972) was characteristic. Charles Ingerman's Quixott Press at Doylestown shows the continued health of another kind of private press whose interest is in producing work of local interest or by local authors in a no-nonsense way but with no pretensions of being fine printing, in such useful books as Joseph Clark's *Travels among the Indians, 1797* (1968) or *Edward Hucks: Friends' Minister* (1974) by George Emerson Haynes.

The relative lack of local work is the more surprising in that the state is the home of the Bird & Bull Press, at which for many years Henry Morris has been making his own paper and printing books with real value on the history of the craft. These have ranged from his first, Father Imberdis's *Papyrus* (1961), through such volumes as *Five on Paper* (1963), *Omnibus* (1967), a very useful volume for the amateur papermaker, to Timothy Barrett's *Nagashizuki* (1979) and Richard J. Wolfe's translation of Franz Weisse's *The Art of Marbling* (1980).

Two Stories by Kenneth Bernard
the magic illustration by Ellen Lanyon
The Perishable Press Limited, Mt Horeb
copyright, January 1973 by Kenneth Bernard

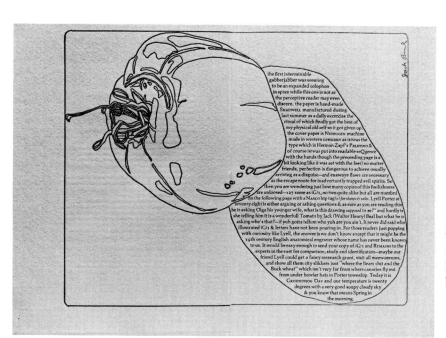

the first interminable
gabberjabber was seeming
to be an expanded colophon
in space while this one is not as
the perceptive reader may even
discern. the paper is hand-made
SHADWELL manufactured during
last summer as a daily excercise the
ritual of which finally got the best of
my physical old self so it got given up.
the cover paper is NIDEGGEN machine
made in western GERMANY as is/was the
type which is Herman Zapf's PALATINO &
of course is/was put into readable seQuence
with the hands though the preceding page is a
bit looking like it was set with the feet) no matter
friends, perfection is dangerous to achieve usually
arriving as a disguise—and enaways flaws are necessary
as the escape route for inadvertantly trapped evil spirits. So
then you are wondering just how many copies of this foolishness
are unloosed—125 same as iG/1, no two quite alike but all are numbrd
on the following page with a Nasco hip tag(s) *for shows & sales.* Lyell Porter at
seventy eight is either arguing or asking questions & as sure as you are reading this
he is asking Olga his younger wife, what is this drawing *supposed to be?*" and hardly is
she telling him it is a wonderfull Tomato by Jack (Walter Henry) Beal but what he is
asking who's that?—if yuh gotta tellum who yuh are you ain't. It never did said who
illustrated iG/1 & letters have not been pouring in. For those readers just popping
with curiosity like Lyell, the answer is we don't know except that it might be the
19th century English anatomical engraver whose name has never been known
to us. It would be easy enough to send your copy of iG/1 and REMAINS to the
experts in the east for comparison, study and identification—maybe our
friend Lyell could get a fancy research grant, visit all them meewzeeums,
and show all them city slickers just "where the Bears shit and the
Buck wheat" which isn't very far from where canaries fly out
from under bowler hats in Porter township. Today it is
GROUNDHOG DAY and our temperature is twenty
degrees with a very good soupy cloudy sky
& you know that means Spring in
the morning.

ILLUS. 139. Perishable Press, Wisconsin. *ig²: Hunkering in Wisconsin,* 1974. A characteristic Hamady colophon; illustration by Jack Beale in red and black.

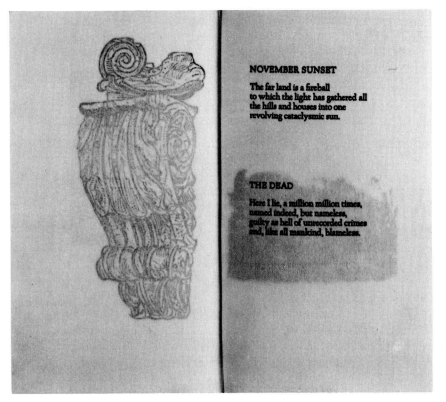

NOVEMBER SUNSET

The far land is a fireball
to which the light has gathered all
the hills and houses into one
revolving cataclysmic sun.

THE DEAD

Here I lie, a million million times,
named indeed, but nameless,
guilty as hell of unrecorded crimes
and, like all mankind, blameless.

ILLUS. 140. Fragment Press, Pennsylvania. *Verse,* by Walter Leuba, 1969, with woodcuts by Norton Peterson. Deliberate use of thin Japanese paper so that the images carry through several leaves.

There is a lighter side to Bird & Bull, characterized by such books as *The Private Presses of San Seriffe* by "Theodore Bachaus, issued by the Miracle Book Division of San Serriffe Publishing Co." (1980). My own favorite remains one of his earliest books, *Three Erfurt Tales* (1962), which is an exceptionally attractive little exercise in the manner of the fifteenth-century book. *Twenty-One Years of Bird & Bull,* a bibliography compiled by W. Thomas Taylor and Henry Morris (1980), provides an excellent overview of its work so far.

A very different spirit prevailed in the work of Victor Hammer (1882–1967), whose long career in the fine arts and in the printing of books goes back to renaissance roots. Viennese by birth, and trained as an architect, Hammer was very much in the renaissance tradition of artist-craftsman: musician, painter, sculptor, goldsmith, printer, calligrapher, and carpenter—he managed to unify all these crafts and to reduce complexity to simplicity in a life devoted *ad maiorem Dei gloriam.* His interest in calligraphy dated from Anna Simons's German translation of Edward Johnston's *Writing and Illuminating and Lettering* published in 1910; he started printing while living in Florence in the early 1920s. As he was a believer in the workshop tradition, he attracted talented apprentices, and it was with the help of Fritz Kredel and Paul Koch that a wooden press was built, punches cut, type cast, and printing started at his "Stamperia del Santuccio," so named for a Florentine saint of little interceding power.

The first publication, *Samson Agonistes,* was published in Florence in 1931. Other works appeared slowly from the Stamperia's later homes of Alsace and Austria until the Nazi occupation of Austria. In 1939 Hammer abandoned all his possessions and with his family attempted a fresh start in the United States. At Aurora, New York, he worked on private printing at the Wells College Press (1941–1947), where Harry Duncan among others learned from him, and with his son Jacob at the Hammer Press. But it was not until he moved to Lexington, Kentucky, at the invitation of the president of Transylvania University, that Hammer revived his Stamperia del Santuccio.

Lexington already had those interested in the arts of printing, including Joseph Graves, a local businessman whose Gravesend Press produced some distinguished work in the 1950s, ranging from an edition of *Aucassin and Nicolette* (1957) with engravings by Kredel, to Judge Soule Smith's recipe for *The Mint Julep* (1959). Graves was not always printer of Gravesend books but sometimes discriminating patron, commissioning work from the Hammers, Kredel, and others; but in what was probably the most successful book, Boccaccio's *The Three Admirable Accidents of Andrea del Piero* (1954), all the work was executed in the Gravesend stable.

Another very significant figure was Carolyn Reading, owner of the Bur Press, a librarian on the staff of the University of Kentucky who in 1955 was to become Hammer's wife and coworker. In 1952 Graves, Carolyn Reading, and several others joined to establish the Anvil Press, another private press for which Victor Hammer would design the books to be printed by Jacob Hammer. This arrangement continued until Jacob's departure from Lexington and Graves's death, producing some noble volumes, such as Pico della Mirandola's *Oration on the Dignity of Man* (1953); thereafter the imprint was continued by Carolyn Reading Hammer and two others.

The books designed or printed by Hammer, regardless of the imprint under which they were published, had a unity rare indeed in private printing: Absolutely uncompromising in design and execution, they represented admirably the superb instrument a private press can be in the hands of an individual intent on perfection, or in the hands of his followers. Carolyn Hammer's later work, such as *Notes on the Two-Color Initial of Victor Hammer,* printed as a keepsake for Gallery 303 in 1966, continued the Hammer tradition well. A good study of *Victor Hammer: Artist and Printer* was published under the Anvil Press imprint in 1981, in a handsome volume printed by Martino Mardersteig at the Stamperia Valdonega.

From 1956, members of the university's King Library staff, under the influence of Mrs. Hammer, have produced books under the imprint of the King Library Press. This press grew gradually from a lunch-time hobby to a full-scale teaching and publishing press of a kind to be found now at several universities. At the King Library Press, Victor Hammer's influence is naturally still strong, but in such powerful books as *The Rabbinal* (1977), with superb illustrations by Christopher Meatyard, or the edition of Swinburne's *On the Cliffs* (1980), printed under the direction of W. Gay Reading, there is evidence that Lexington's vitality in the book arts is not due solely to the remarkable figure of Victor Hammer.

Elsewhere in the South, private printing is pursued less single-mindedly than in the Lexington area. One small press in Darien, Georgia, William G. Haynes's Ashantilly Press, has produced a good range of attractively printed books on topics of local history, such as *Johnny Leber and the Confederate Major* (Illus. 141), published in 1962, and *The Field Diary of a Confederate Soldier* (1963); in Atlanta, Charles F. Robertson's Tinhorn Press produced some very attractive small pieces. Now based in Athens, Georgia, Dwight Agner's Press of the Nightowl has printed Martha Lacy Hall's *Call It Living: Three Stories* (1981); from its previous address in Baton Rouge, Louisiana, the Nightowl imprint also appeared on some other interesting books, including Agner's important *The Books of WAD* (1974), a bibliography of the books designed by Dwiggins (Illus. 142A and 142B). In Missouri, there is Kay Michael Kramer's The Printery at Kirkwood (like the Nightowl, this press owes much to the influence of Alexander Lawson at Rochester Institute of Technology). The Printery has published relatively little, but books like *You Are Now My Enemy* (1972) and *By a Vote of Congress* (1976) reveal a considerable talent.

In Kansas, there has been vigorous work in the past. In Coffeyville, Don Drenner's Zauberberg Press produced a number of successful volumes of poetry in the 1950s and early 1960s, such as Joseph Stanley Pennell's *Darksome House* (1959), or his own *The Graphics of Love* (1961), whose superb craftsmanship shows what can be achieved by the self-taught printer remote from centers of advice

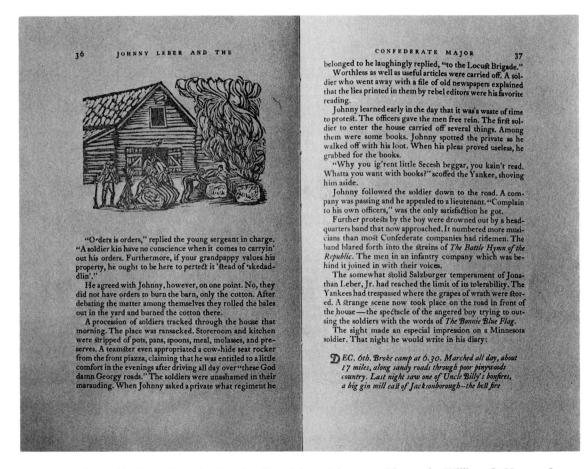

ILLUS. 141. Ashantilly Press, Georgia. Opening from *Johnny Leber,* 1962. Linocut by William G. Haynes, Jr.

and encouragement. In Wichita, Bill Jackson's "Printing House at the Sign of the Four Ducks" was notable for the exuberant linocuts with which Jackson enlivened his work, particularly in the *Four Ducks Annual Reports,* a variation on the Christmas booklets produced by many small printers.

The late Philip Metzger's Crabgrass Press in Prairie Village, Kansas, is likely to be remembered as a one-book press, for the superb collection of Hermann Zapf, *Orbis Typographicus: Thoughts, Words and Phrases on the Arts and Sciences,* which Metzger published in 1980. A sort of final volume for Zapf's *Manuale Typographicum,* the Zapf/Metzger collaboration on this splendid collection was spread over many years, but while it was being planned, or was in production, Metzger took time off to produce a number of very attractive small books, ranging from Raymond DaBoll's *Regarding Calligraphy* (1974), to Metzger's own *Words on Paper,* printed in 1978 for the fourth exchange of the PLA Society of Private Printers, issued as *An Infant's Library* in 1980.

Another private printer whose debt to Zapf is very clear is Leonard Bahr at the Adagio Press near Detroit. Bahr has been a printer since his college days in 1956, but printing has always been strictly a spare-time activity pursued during evenings and weekends. Relatively few substantial books have been printed because of the time one particular job takes—for the most substantial, the important study *C-S the Master Craftsman* by Norman H. Strouse and John Dreyfus (1969), production was to occupy 14 strenuous months. Bahr has therefore concentrated on the production of collections of matter of typographic interest for which design and execution of a particular piece can be completed in a short period, such as *Experiments with the Bradley Combination Ornaments* (1966) or *A Manner of Printing* (1974).

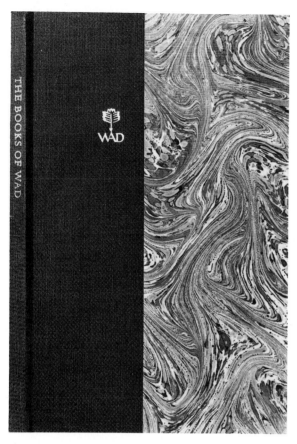

The Books of WAD

A Bibliography of the Books

Designed by *W. A. Dwiggins*

Compiled by Dwight Agner

with a Foreword by Alexander Lawson

and printed and published at

THE PRESS OF THE NIGHTOWL

Baton Rouge, Louisiana 1974

ILLUS. 142A. Press of the Nightowl,
Louisiana. *The Books of WAD*, 1974.
Binding case.

ILLUS. 142B. Press of the Nightowl,
Louisiana. *The Books of WAD*, 1974.
Title page.

Paul Hayden Duensing's work at his Private Press and Typefoundry (also in Michigan) represents the same high technical quality. Most of Duensing's output is limited to work on aspects of type design and typefounding such as Phil Nuernberger's *Electrolytic Matrices,* or Rudolf Koch's *Buchstabenfreude* (1976) issued jointly with William Rueter of the Aliquando Press. A good proportion of his work is not published but prepared for distribution at the annual meetings of The Typecrafters; one example is *25: a Quarter-Century of Triumphs and Disasters in the Microcosm of the Private Press and Typefoundry of Paul Hayden Duensing* (1976). As a result, the work of this talented printer is less widely known than it should be.

Another long-established Michigan private press, the Press of John Cumming at Mount Pleasant, is one of the private presses established to publish historical matter of local importance. Growing from his work as a librarian at Central Michigan University, Cumming has selected, edited, printed, and published a substantial volume of material, ranging from George Burges's *Journal of a Surveying Trip into Western Pennsylvania in the Year 1795* (1965), to the lengthy series of reports on *The Gold Rush* reprinted from nineteenth-century Michigan papers.

Just as those who set out from Michigan to California in 1849 found a very different world waiting across the Rockies, so today the West Coast presents many different features and levels of activity from the rest of the United States.

In the Bay Area, the influence of the Book Club of California, founded in 1912, and of the other

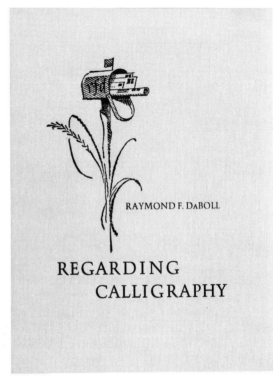

RAYMOND F. DaBOLL

REGARDING
CALLIGRAPHY

ILLUS. 143. Crabgrass Press, Kansas. Two booklets, *Regarding Calligraphy*. Left: By Egdon Margo, 1972. Right: By Raymond F. DaBoll, 1974. Calligraphy by Rick Cusack, in brown and red.

societies of collectors and typophiles that have since sprung up (Roxburghe in 1928; in Los Angeles, Zamorano in 1928 and Rounce and Coffin in 1931) has been very strong indeed. It is partly the influence of these groups that at an early stage led to a difference between California and most of the other states: The enouragement and commissions given by these clubs and their members to promising local printers have enabled many to devote time to fine typographic work in a semi- or fully commercial way rarely to be found elsewhere until much later. For an outsider like myself to visit California and its printers requires the abandonment of much mental baggage: The distinction between the private press and the commercial printer cannot clearly be drawn. Sandra Kirshenbaum and her associates were wise when, in establishing their review for the arts of the book, they avoided these somewhat artificial distinctions and simply called their invaluable journal *Fine Print*.

There are, of course, amateur printers in the Bay Area who are carrying on a different tradition of the amateur bookmaker, with no pretensions of printing as an art form. The Rather Press in Oakland, for example, has since 1968 produced a considerable number of books and pamphlets, many written by Lois Rather, such as her *Women as Printers* (1970) or *Henry George—Printer to Author* (1978).

In complete contrast to this cheerful and lighthearted press whose interest is in writing and publishing, the Allen Press has since 1939 been producing carefully wrought books intended as a contribution to the book arts. Until 1950, Lewis and Dorothy Allen's printing was a part-time activity (but never merely a pastime; their philosophy was that of the creative craftsman), but thereafter they were able to devote themselves full time to printing, with some 46 books completed by 1980 and recorded in the sumptuous *Allen Press Bibliography MCMLXXXI*.

Eclectic in their choice of texts and of designs for their books, the Allens's approach has in many ways been closer to the French publishers of *livres d'artiste* than to the traditional English private presses in their quest for that very different thing, The Book Beautiful. Interesting and accomplished work was undertaken during the forties, including a number of commissions for the Book Club of California, such as *Heraldry of New Helvetia* (1945), but a year spent in France in 1951–1952 (during which time they printed Stevenson's *La Porte de Maletroit*) strengthened their interest in French fine printing. In their own words they were

> lured from the strict and all-too-narrow path of straight book-making. It
> seemed to us that it was about time for American collectors to be exposed to a
> *livre de peintres*. And so, with high enthusiasm, we cast about for a text which
> would be in English, and which would be illustrated by one or more of the
> great artists of our day.

The first Allen Press essay in this manner was a very successful example of the genre: Yvan Goll's *Four Poems of the Occult* (1962), illustrated (by line-block and collotype reproductions) with drawings by Fernand Léger, lithographs by Picasso, etchings by Yves Tanguy, and wood engravings by Jean Arp—the illustrations that had been used by the French publishers of the original separate editions of each poem. To bring some order and consistency into the design, border decorations and initials were commissioned from Mallette Dean (who has printed some handsome books on his own account, as well as contributing to the success of other Allen Press books). The book was not bound; instead the unsewn sections were in the French manner enclosed in a portfolio that was in turn enclosed in a hinged box.

Subsequent Allen Press books have sometimes adopted a similar alternative to binding, for example Basil Hall's *The Great Polyglot Bibles* (1966) or Nikos Kazantzakis's play *Christopher Columbus* (1972). Generally, however, they have reverted to conventional binding for their books—very much to be preferred, in my opinion, if the printer is putting the reader's convenience first.

In setting by hand, and printing by hand on dampened handmade paper, the Allens have achieved a regular standard of work that is the envy of most other fine printers. Lewis Allen's *Printing with the Handpress* (1969) is one of the outstanding texts for those who aspire to high standards of craftsmanship.

With 46 books produced, and individually designed, it is natural that there should be failures as well as successes. It is in the selection of illustrations that things seem to have gone awry more than with any other aspect of their books' design: Against the undoubted successes as Poe's *Murders in the Rue Morgue* (1958) or *The Splendid Idle Forties* (1960), there have been less successful books, like *The Book of Genesis* (1970). Usually the Allens's own estimation (in the *Bibliography*) of their more successful volumes accords with one's own judgment, but I was surprised to find the Dryden *All for Love* (1976) among them: The idea of having a frontispiece portrait of Cleopatra painted by contemporary Egyptian artists was undoubtedly attractive, but not successful in its execution.

Almost as old as the Allen Press, but much less ambitious is the Hart Press in Berkeley from which since 1940 James D. Hart has annually printed a small book for Christmas distribution to friends. These books have a strong family likeness—always the same format, the same handset Caslon, the illustrations by Victor Anderson—and make one regret that the owner does not print other books as well. At the Grace Hoper Press, Katherine and Sherwood Grover (for many years a compositor with the Grabhorns) produced a series of *Typographical Commonplace Books,* in which quotations were set with amazing virtuosity in a style and typeface suited to the passage (Illus. 145).

Of a new generation of printers growing up at the end of World War II, three are of particular importance, William Everson, Adrian Wilson, and Jack Stauffacher.

Although printing was in his family background, Everson's first significant association with printing came during the war, in a conscientious objectors' camp at Waldport, Oregon. In reaction

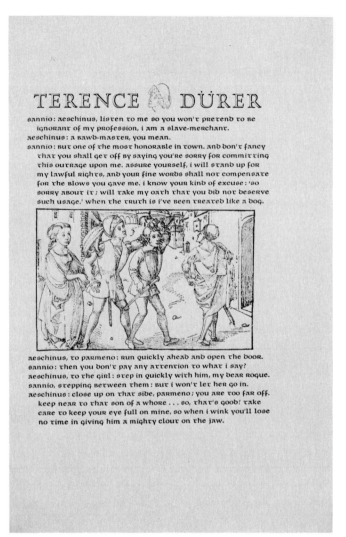

ILLUS. 144. Allen Press,
California. Page from
Terence, 1968.

to the official camp paper *The Tide,* Everson and others produced their own "underground" paper, *The Untide.* After the war, Everson moved to San Francisco, where in association with the artist Mary Fabilli he produced his own first books of poetry, *A Privacy of Speech* (1949) and *Triptych for the Living* (1951).

These were well-executed, but slight compared with his next, unfinished, book. He had entered the Dominican Order and, as Brother Antoninus, he worked on a large folio, *Novum Psalterium Pii XII,* as an entirely voluntary undertaking, handsetting in Goudy Newstyle and printing on dampened handmade paper. After three years' work the project was abandoned, but the incomplete work was purchased by Mrs. Estelle Doheny who commissioned Saul Marks of the Plantin Press to print a title page and Everson's introduction so that the book could be published. It is a remarkable volume, showing the contrast between dampened handpress work and dry powered printing, both at their best in the two parts of the book.

Subsequently Everson returned to secular life, and at the Lime Kiln Press (the teaching press set up at the University of California at Santa Cruz, with an Acorn handpress donated by the Allens) produced two books of considerable importance in influencing ideas about fine printing for the future. The first was Robinson Jeffers's *Granite & Cypress* (1975). Immaculately produced, it received enthusiastic notices on publication. Only Abe Lerner, in his valuable talk to the Double Crown Club

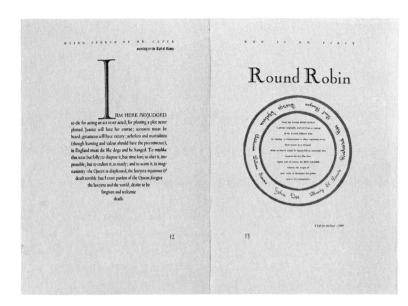

ILLUS. 145. Grace Hoper Press, California. Opening from one of its *Typographical Commonplace Books.*

"Assault on the Book," voiced reservations after claiming it as "one of the finest books given us by the American private press movement." His first hesitation was about the slipcase, fashioned of Monterey cypress with an inset of granite from Jeffers's own quarry, which he regarded as a cerebral choice out of tune with the typography and binding. His second reservation was about a feature for which most who have seen the book had nothing but praise: the printing of the text *in reverse* on versos to balance the poems which were printed only on rectos. It was an interesting aesthetic solution, one which in Everson's hands worked (although I must confess to sharing Lerner's psychological unease in reading the rectos). The danger however is clear: Walter Hamady's tricks and stratagems work well—for him; in a teaching press like Lime Kiln, there is a strong risk that students may adopt similar methods without Everson's sureness of touch.

Lime Kiln's next book, Walt Whitman's *American Bard* (1981), had fewer unusual features in its design, although there were many difficulties with the casting of type, the provision of paper from the Imago Papermill, and other aspects of the production. It was, however, an extremely satisfying book when eventually completed, of which a reduced offset lithographic trade edition has been published by Viking. In itself a successful and handsome book, the Viking *American Bard* can however give only a faint flavor of Everson's original.

Adrian Wilson, the second of the group to emerge at the end of the war, had also been at the Waldport Camp and had work with Everson. In the late 1940s, together with Jack Stauffacher, he worked on an edition of Eric Gill's *And Who Wants Peace?* with engravings by Mary Fabilli. Setting up as a small jobbing printer, together with his wife (the actress Joyce Lancaster), he started the Interplayers, and much of his jobbing work was for theatrical purposes. *Printing for Theater* (1957) was a major work that he wrote, designed, printed, and published himself. Although most of his work as book designer has been for printing at other plants, his Press in Tuscany Alley has produced a number of special limited editions, particularly of the children's books written and illustrated by his wife, such as *The Swing* (1981). Recently awarded a MacArthur Prize Fellowship, Wilson's current project for his press is a retrospective view of *The Work and Play of Adrian Wilson,* expected to appear in the fall 1983.

Jack Stauffacher, the third of the trio, now runs the distinguished Greenwood Press. From 1958 to 1963 he was director of the New Laboratory Press at Pittsburgh, after which he spent some time as typographic director of Stanford University Press. Although his own private publications have been small in number, his *Janson: A Definitive Collection* and *Phaedrus: A Dialogue by Plato* (1976) are remarkable, thoughtful volumes that have had considerable influence.

One press that attracted considerable attention in the early 1960s was the Peregrine Press, the imprint chosen by Henry Evans for the books he printed and published from his Porpoise Bookshop in San Francisco. Relatively little appeared from the press—Patricia Evans's *A Modern Herbal* (1961) and Kenneth M. Johnson's *Champagne and Shoes* (1962)—before the artist in Evans won the struggle with the printer (indeed to examine these two side by side is almost to be able to see the struggle taking place), and he abandoned printing books to concentrate on his flower prints as his means of expression.

About the same time, Dave Haselwood was at work at the Auerhahn Press, one of the imprints most closely associated with the poets of the Beat generation. Haselwood had his first book printed for him, but thereafter printed Auerhahn books himself, being joined in the venture by Andrew Hoyem in 1961. *A Bibliography of the Auerhahn Press & Its Successor Dave Haselwood Books* was compiled and printed by Alastair Johnston from his Poltroon Press in 1977.

Andrew Hoyem, the one-time partner in Auerhahn, spent some time working at the Grabhorn Press and set up his own printing house (as Andrew Hoyem/Printer) in 1965. Robert Grabborn joined him in a harmonious partnership until his death in 1973. Hoyem's shop took over all the Grabhorn plant, with its extensive range of types, and under the imprint Arion Press, Hoyem commenced his own fine-printing publishing program with his own *Picture/Poems* (1975).

Among the eight or nine books published since then, there have been considerable successes. *The Psalms of David and Others* (1977) was a handsome book in the Grabhorn tradition. The interesting *A Travel Book* by Fred Martin (1976) was perhaps over-ambitious in its attempt to catch the savor of Bernard von Breydenbach, the *Nuremberg Chronicle,* and other works; Edwin Abbott's *Flatland* (1980) was a remarkable and successful attempt at an appropriate physical presentation of Abbott's two-dimensional world, in an accordion-fold extending to 33 feet, enclosed in an anodized aluminum box—what might be called the bullet-proof edition!

By contrast with the experimentation of *Flatland,* later to be carried further in *Shaped Poetry* (1981), the Arion Press edition of Melville's *Moby-Dick* (1979), with wood engravings by Barry Moser, was a magnificent traditional example of bookmaking. Handset in Goudy Modern, with a special titling letter (aptly named Leviathan) designed by Charles Bigelow and Kris Holmes, the book was printed on a dampened blue-gray paper handmade for the book by Barcham Green. In contrast to the over-dramatic illustrations provided by Rockwell Kent for the 1930 Lakeside Press edition of *Moby-Dick,* Hoyem and Moser decided that strictly factual illustrations—of species of whales, of whaling gear, and views of the whaling ports, for example—should be used. The result was a superbly understated version, supremely readable.

Only one other press has attempted work on the same grand scale as Lime Kiln or Arion: Richard Bigus's Labyrinth Editions, formerly of California and now based in Athens, Ohio. A pupil of Everson's at Lime Kiln who also worked with Jack Stauffacher, for his first book, Pablo Neruda's *Ode to Typography* (1977), Bigus produced a tour de force of the typographer as artist, rather than as servant to writer. In his shrewd commentary on contemporary press books "Assault on the Book," Abe Lerner termed the Neruda "expressionist typography" and Bigus's second book, Whitman's *Out of the Cradle Endlessly Rocking* (1978), "abstract typography." I find it no more to my taste than to Lerner's, however much I admire the imagination, skill, and superb craftsmanship involved. As Lerner put it, "Art it may be; reading it ain't." For his third book, an edition of Everson's wartime poetry *Eastward the Armies* (1980), Bigus returned to a more conventional book, with much promise fulfilled by a later volume, Kenneth Rexroth's *Between Two Wars* (1982).

For *Eastward the Armies,* Bigus commissioned fine linocut illustrations from the California artist

Tom Killion. At his own Quail Press at Santa Cruz, Killion has published an impressive series of landscape books, starting with *The Coast of California: Point Reyes to Point Sur* (1979).

Other presses in the Bay Area have been equally inventive and experimental, if working on a smaller scale. In Berkeley, Wesley Tanner's Arif Press has produced some effective work, often centered on calligraphic or typographic themes, such as Rimbaud's *Voyelles* (1980) or Cobden-Sanderson's *The Ideal Book or Book Beautiful* (1981). His modest edition of Voltaire's *Memnon* (1981) was a most attractive example of allusive typography; *Sappho: Fragmenta Nova* (1981), a successful collaboration with the Twinrocker Paper Mill. At the Rebis Press, Mimi Pond and Betsy Davis have produced interesting experimental work; at Poltroon Press—one of those small publishing houses that uses filmsetting, serigraphy, and offset litho as well as conventional letterpress—Frances Butler and Alastair Johnston have printed and published a range of books that dance between classical typography and concrete poetry in an altogether delightful way. Tom Clark's *The Mutabilitic of the Englishe Lyrick* (1978) is a good introduction to Poltroon work.

Clifford Burke's Cranium Press produced many typographically successful volumes of poetry, such as Denise Levertov's *Summer Poems/1969* (1970) or Burke's own *Griffin Creek* (1972). His manual on *Printing Poetry* is one of the most useful guides to the amateur in printing.

A press with something of a split personality is the Blackstone Press of Shelley Hoyt-Koch and Peter Koch. Started at Missoula, Montana, in 1975, as a press to print poetry, the Kochs moved to Mecca (as they put it) two years later, and Peter Koch apprenticed himself to Adrian Wilson for awhile. Very attractive small books have been produced by the two partners, Michael Poage's *Handbook of Ornament* (1979) and *Reflections on Color* by Susan Roether (1982) being representative of their later work.

The women's movement in printing has produced some of the most interesting work to come from the Bay Area. Maryann Hayden's Sombre Reptiles (like Poltroon) is not wedded only to traditional letterpress work, but in such books as Jerry Ratch's *Chaucer Marginalia* (1979) or Robert Peters's *Celebrities* (1981) has shown great talent. Originally from Iowa, where her first books were printed, Leigh McLellan at the Meadow Press has produced some accomplished work in books such as Charles Simic's *Shaving at Night* (1981). Robin Heyeck, at the Heyeck Press, in *The Arts of Fire* (1982) by Frances Mayes, made successful use of red marbling at the foot of the title-opening, as one design feature of a very successful book.

The Five Trees Press, formerly run by Kathy Walkup, Cheryl Miller, Jaime Miller, and others, was responsible for several accomplished books, including Susan MacDonald's *Dangerous as Daughters* (1976) and Denise Levertov's *Modulations for Solo Voice*. Cheryl Miller has since continued at the Interval Press with books such as Judith Grahn's *Spider Webster's Declaration* (1983). At the Matrix Press, Kathy Walkup has printed books like Janet Lewis's *The Indian in the Woods*, while also acting as organizer and publisher of *Women Writing Poetry in America* (1982), 15 broadsides printed by 16 women printers in the area. With the work being done by students at Mills College as well, there is no doubt that these presses in the Bay Area will continue to produce work to delight the eye.

In southern California there is a similar diversity of work. One of the most interesting and truly private ventures of the 1940s was the Breakfast Press, an informal group composed of Merry and Paul Landacre, Josephine and Jake Zeitlin, Helen and Grant Dahlstrom, Mildred Maxwell and Preston Tuttle—a constellation of talents. Only two books appear to have been produced: *When Are You Going to Laugh, America?* (1940) and *The Parallelogram, the Amphisbaena, the Crocodile* by A. E. Housman (1941), both illustrated with wood engravings by Paul Landacre and printed by Grant Dahlstrom.

Dahlstrom's Castle Press, like the Plantin Press of Saul and Lillian Marks, was characteristic of the distinguished small printing house that undertakes work for others as well as producing its own publications. Two recent books are of particular interest: *Grant Dahlstrom and the First Fifty Years of the Castle Press* (1980), edited by D. W. Davies, and Davies's *Clyde Browne: His Abbey & His Press* (1982), a fascinating study of the man whose Abbey of San Encino was a late West-Coast attempt in the Roycroft tradition and whose equipment had been used by Ward Ritchie for his first faltering steps in printing.

The University of California at Los Angeles has been among the most active patrons of Dahlstrom and the Marks, particularly through the university library, the William Andrews Clark Memorial Library, and the library school. Staff members of all three have from time to time been active amateur printers themselves. In the early 1960s, Roberta Nixon and Margaret Gustavson Taylor produced a number of small books of severely classical design from their Magpie Press: *What Went on at the Baroness'* by Machado de Assis (1964) and Eleanor Edelstein's *Seven Poems* (1967) being representative. More recently the late Andrew Horn's Battledore Press at Glendale continued this tradition with such books as Sandy Dorbin's *Eleven Poems* (1978) and two studies of whodunnits by another UCLA library staff member: Betty Rosenberg's *Booked for Murder* (1979) and *Bibliomania or Bound to Kill* (1981), both titles subsequently reprinted by Patrick Reagh, another of the small high-quality commercial printing houses of the region.

One of Battledore's books was *The Enchanted Couple* (1979), a charming essay on Daphnis and Chloe by Lawrence Clark Powell, who in his many years at UCLA was responsible for commissioning much of the good work done. In recent years, Powell has had most of his privately printed work done for him by Richard J. Hoffman of Van Nuys, in such books as *My Haydn Commonplace Book* (1983).

A recent book printed by Hoffman was Mary Lutz Jones's *A Los Angeles Typesticker: William M. Cheney* (1981). Cheney was a fabulous figure among Californian printers, whose own *Natural History of the Typestickers of Los Angeles* had appeared in 1960. Long resident at the Gatehouse of the Clark Library, Cheney was an adept at the mock-scholarly and in the production of miniature books, the two talents being well-combined in his treatise *Pocket Knives,* originally printed in 1964 and in a revised reset form in 1968. The closure of the Press in the Gatehouse, following Cheney's retirement from the Clark Library in 1974, was a real loss to the world of private printing.

Many of the miniature books printed by Cheney were published through Dawson's Bookshop in Los Angeles, a shop whose owners' own enthusiasm for printing has frequently led them beyond patronage into actual involvement in the books published through them, for example, Christopher Weimann's charming *Marbling in Miniature* (1980). Carey S. Bliss's *A Bibliography of Cheney Miniatures* (1975) was printed for Dawson's by Vance Gerry whose Weather Bird Press formerly at Pasadena has relocated at Fallbrook. Weather Bird has produced a number of interesting and well-constructed books published on its own behalf, with several on culinary topics, such as Rochelle Lucky's *The Art & Antiquity of Cookery in the Middle Ages* (1978) and Dan and Betty Bailey's *The Everyday Gourmet* (1973). Gerry trained under Grant Dahlstrom; *Some Fond Remembrances of a Boy Printer at the Castle Press* (1968) is precisely what the title suggests.

Another small printer patronized by Dawson's, and also working in collaboration with Carey S. Bliss at the Huntington Library is Pall Bohne at the Bookhaven Press. Bliss's *The Willow Dale Press, 1879,* printed by Bookhaven in 1974 (Illus. 146), was an important contribution to the literature of amateur printing in California.

On a smaller scale, and (like the Magpie Press) more representative of truly amateur work, Frank J. Thomas's Tenfingers Press produced many small attractive books in the 1960s, like *Proverbis on Musyke* (1962) or *Mission Cattle Brands* (1967); several of them combined his professional skills as photographer with his avocational talents as printer, as for instance *Circus Waggons* (1972). On a larger but still modest scale, since 1964 Roy A. Squires in Glendale has been printing small careful

ILLUS. 146. Bookhaven Press, California. *The Willow Dale Press, 1879.* Double spread.

conservative editions of poetry and prose by a few selected writers, particularly Clark Ashton Smith, beginning with his *¿Donde Duermes, Eldorado?* Squires is outside the mainstream of private printers; his self-imposed limitations of matter and manner (so characteristic of one group of handprinters whose interest is in *publishing*) have prevented his work becoming well-known outside a very small group.

None of these presses has shown the extravagance in experimentation that has come from some of those in the Bay Area. At the Paradise Press, Susan King has done good work with such books as her own very attractive *Georgia: A Series of Prose Poems on Georgia O'Keeffe* (1981). Kitty Marryat at the Two Hands Press and Christie Bertelson at Scripps College have also done interesting work. At their Press of the Pegacycle Lady, the booksellers William and Victoria Dailey have since 1972 printed and published some stimulating and important work, such as De Sade's *A Letter from the Bastille* (1975). Their *Specimens of Handmade Botanical Papers* (1979) by Vance Studley, a joint venture with the author/artist/papermaker, was an interesting addition to this growing field; for Robert N. Essick's *William Blake's Relief Inventions* (1979), the text was set and printed by Patrick Reagh, only the illustrations being printed on the Daileys' Asbern proofing press. At Santa Barbara, Harry and Sandra Liddell Reese's Turkey Press is producing adventurous work in such books as *Bozobook* and the suite of poems by Kirk Robertson *West Nevada Waltz* (1981).

In the Pacific Northwest there are several interesting presses at work. In Portland, Oregon, the Chamberlain Press has produced an altogether charming edition of *A Frog He Would a'Wooing Go* (1981), continuing the pattern of children's books illustrated with the superb wood engravings Sarah Chamberlain had started in works by Lear and the brothers Grimm, which were published from the press's former address in Connecticut. In Port Townsend, Washington, Tree Swenson's Copper Canyon Press has issued several handsome volumes of poetry, such as Denise Levertov's *Wanderer's Daysong* (1981); nearby at Graywolf Press, Scott Walker pursues a similar sound policy of publishing important work in well-designed and well-executed volumes, such as Philip Levine's *Ashes* (1980).

One major press remains to be discussed that was undoubtedly American though based in Italy for most of its life: Richard-Gabriel Rummonds's Plain Wrapper Press. Started while Rummonds was in Ecuador in 1966 and, with encouragement from Giovanni Mardersteig, finally established in

Verona in 1971, Plain Wrapper's policy was to produce fine limited editions of new work by contemporary writers, with illustrations by outstanding artists. What should have attracted attention to Plain Wrapper was the success with which these aims were carried out, whether in the slighter publications like Constantine Cavafy's *Three Poems of Passion* (1975) or the grand volumes like Jorge Luis Borges's *Seven Saxon Poems* (1974). Few noted that if ever there was an author for whom fine press work is appropriate it is Borges; what drew attention to the Plain Wrapper edition was the price tag: $1,800 in 1974. Plain Wrapper books have always been very highly priced (even when one takes into account the fine materials of which they are made) and, therefore, particularly open to criticism of the kind given to Anthony Burgess's *Will and Testament* (1978) in the *Fine Print* review by Mark Livingston. In it he described the book as "born into the Imperial Easter Egg succession of the book world" and therefore: "I, hypothetical buyer, take the book's unusual expense [$1,600] as my warrant to be unusually exacting in judging it. This is a hazard with which the makers of courtly volumes must reckon in democratic times." Livingston's review, although critical, was not unfavorable. But for those without much more substantial backing than was available to Rummonds and his partner Alessandro Zanella, the late 1970s were hard times to be producing Imperial Easter Eggs. The Plain Wrapper Press has now closed; Rummonds now teaches at the University of Alabama.

At the other extreme from presses like Plain Wrapper or Lime Kiln, Perishable, or Pennyroyal, are the many hundreds of pastime printers with limited equipment, ambition, and time. For them, printing is a hobby not a way of life, and they find production of extensive work difficult. One way in which many of these amateurs have found it possible to produce more substantial work without their pastime losing its freshness has been through the growth of the Chappel movement.

> Every *Printing-house* is by the Custom of Time out of mind, called a *Chappel*;
> and all the Workmen that belong to it are *Members of the Chappel*.

The term "Chappel" was borrowed from Moxon's *Mechanick Exercises* by Ben Lieberman of the Herity Press as a suitable name for a club of amateur printers living close enough together to meet regularly and to cooperate in printing projects as a group. The advantages were obvious: among them, the companionship of those with like interests, the chance to talk shop, to pool knowledge, and to borrow or buy scarce equipment. The first to be set up was the Moxon Chappel (now 25 years old) on the West Coast, but it was soon followed by others, such as the New York Chappel and the Westchester Chappel in the eastern United States. The rather less clubbable English did not take up the idea to the same extent, generally preferring a different structure for their own cooperation, such as the PLA Society of Private Printers.

Without doubt, the Chappel movement has been helpful in fostering interest in printing and in improving the standards of workmanship of the tyro. Some of the cooperative ventures have been full of verve—the calendars printed by the New York and Westchester Chappels, for example, in which each press had responsibility for producing the leaf for a particular month. The New York Chappel went further than this, printing its *Uncommonplace Books,* the *New York ABC* (1963), and other pieces. In such work, the standard of craftsmanship is obviously variable, and there is clearly a limit to the amount of successful cooperative printing that can be done. The most attractive work often comes in the small books that some Chappel members print separately; in New York, for example, Lili and Erich Wronker produce delightful work at their Ron Press, and in *Nasty Nancy and Her Cat: A Horrid ABC Book* (1962), Fridolf Johnson printed one of the most charming of all miniature books at his Mermaid Press.

Such cooperative work is not limited to the Chappels. The various exchanges of the PLA Society of Private Printers are similar, and there are also ad hoc arrangements. John Ryder assembled his *Miniature Folio of Private Presses* with considerable success some years ago, a success shared by Charles Antin, owner of the Serendipity Press in New York, in the *Folio of Private Presses* he organized in 1978. Antin was earlier responsible for several other keepsakes, for Alfred A. Knopf (1965) and in memory of Paul Bennett (1968), slipcases containing a number of four-page gatherings printed by distinguished printers (public as well as private), which formed collections of contemporary printing as good as one could hope to see. At a rather lower level, the same was done for many years by William F. Haywood with his annual collection of work from many different private printers, *It's a Small World*.

To attempt to describe the work of all, or even a sample, of the pastime printers who produce interesting work in the United States calls for a book in itself. I will close by mentioning only one, Banter University Press, which operated in New York City in the early 1960s, now alas no longer at work.

George Rike's work as "associate director" of this smallest of university presses was distinctly subversive. Far too little Banter work is generally available, although the quotations from it given in Bernard Keelan's *A Bold Face on It* (1964) are very tempting. Consider Banter's application for a grant to the Ford Foundation:

> We are encountering vexing problems in our research in a field that lies largely
> unexplored—Medieval Printing in the United States. Obtaining the necessary
> documents, especially, is proving quite costly since in most cases we must
> manufacture these ourselves. We wish therefore to make application to the Ford
> Foundation for the sum of $584.17. . . . We understand that foundations look
> with horror on such relatively small grants. If, however, you feel that the
> expense of the necessary paperwork would not justify the granting of such a
> tiny sum, we shall be glad to oblige by revising our request upwards to
> $1,647,382.31.

With such presses at work, who can doubt the pleasure and value of amateur printing?

Chapter 21

————

CANADIAN PRIVATE PRESSES

NORTH OF THE FORTY-NINTH PARALLEL, one finds private press activity that is closely related to, but different from, that further south, just as the Canadian provinces are themselves different from the States of the Union. The different cultural heritage of the French and British Canadians, too, has been the cause of a distinctive pattern. Several of the Québecois printers, such as Editions Erta, Hugues de Jouvancourt's Editions La Frégate, Guy Robert's Editions du Songe, and Michel Nantel produce work within the tradition of the French *livres d'artiste* rather than that of the private press. Visually exciting and successful though much of this work is, it has not been included in the brief survey that follows, as it needs to be described and assessed from the point of view of the Gallic tradition of fine bookmaking.

With the exception of some early missionary work, like that of the Reverend James Evans (described in Chapter 24), Canada was relatively late to develop in private press activity. One of the first Canadians to be concerned with matters of book design in the spirit of the private presses was Louis Blake Duff, an historian and bibliophile who owned the Welland *Telegraph* newspaper. From the early twenties he published an occasional series of well-designed books, initially under the imprint of the Tribune-Telegraph Press, and later, after he had sold his newspaper, under the style the Baskerville Press. These were not true private press publications, but intelligent and carefully planned work commissioned from commercial firms, in the spirit (though not the style) of Nonesuch.

A much more ambitious project was undertaken by J. Kemp Waldie of Toronto. Inspired by the superb typefaces being produced by Jan van Krimpen for the Enschedé Typefoundry in Haarlem, Waldie was to pioneer the use of the fine Lutetia type in Canada at his Golden Dog Press, so named for the classic Canadian novel. His work included several pieces concerned with the book arts (among other subjects), his own *The Press That Never Was: A True Story of Two Printers Who Set Out for the New Found Lands During 1517* (1933) and Marie Tremaine's *Early Printing in Canada* (1934)— work that although successfully demonstrating his own skill in applying fine typefaces, was not unfortunately to establish a tradition.

Most Canadian private printers undertake their work as an extension of their professional interests in a book-related field. One who has been very closely concerned with the book over a 30-year period, Lawrence Lande, is a Montreal businessman and lawyer without any professional concern in printing, although his collection of Canadiana (presented to the Redpath Library at McGill) and his many publications on music, literature, and history have demonstrated a personal commitment to the book that few can rival. Lande has been a private publisher rather than printer, commissioning from several different printers and binders work in expressive dress, ranging from *The Story of Stories: The Book of Job* (1946), bound in gray burlap to get the "sackcloth and ashes" effect, to the elaborate dress given to his *L'Accent* (1970), in which the three pamphlets were accompanied by two long-playing records.

Several of Lande's works were printed for him by the Morriss Printing Company of Victoria, British Columbia, a printer's imprint that appears on not a few of the better-designed Canadian books. Charles Morriss opened his printing house in 1950 and since then has produced a good deal of distinctive work, particularly the volumes published by the Vancouver lawyer William McConnell under the Klanak Press imprint, but also a good many other books of verse that Morriss has himself published.

British Columbia is one of the centers of fine printing in Canada: less evidently perhaps in the "pure" private press than in the work of a bibliophile group. The Alcuin Society, founded in 1965, is not just a society of book collectors, but one that has the aim of promoting a wider appreciation of fine printing through its own editions. Its quarterly journal *Amphora* contains much of interest beyond the Canadiana that is naturally at the core of the society's publishing activities.

Several of the books and other publications of the Alcuin Society were printed for it by Wil Hudson, a Californian who set up a press in Vancouver in the early 1960s. The most substantial were *A Theatrical Trip for a Wager!* (1966) and John West's *Substance of a Journal . . . at the Red River Colony* (1967), although some of his slighter pieces were to my mind more successful. In addition to his work for Alcuin, and other commissions for the Vancouver Public Library and the Library of the University of British Columbia, Hudson published some work under his own imprint, the Grouse Mountain Press, including Berthold Brecht's *Posterity* (1964).

Like many such bibliophile groups, the Alcuin Society has had its books and keepsakes printed by several different firms or individuals besides Hudson and the Morriss Company. As its name suggests, the society has a special interest in calligraphy, and several of its most attractive works have been produced as offset-lithographic printings of calligraphic texts. One related work, which was printed by letterpress, was a translation of Trithemius's *De Laude Scriptorum* (in praise of scribes), which was started for the society by Gerald Giampa, who had formerly worked with Wil Hudson before starting his own Cobblestone Press. Much plainer in design than most Cobblestone work—Giampa's liking for the use of printers' flowers using second and third colors is very marked—the Trithemius volume was started in 1975 but not completed until 1977. It was completed by members of the society, a feature of several other Alcuin publications, which transforms the society from being just a club commissioning fine printing: Ebenezer Johnson's *Short Account of a Northwest Voyage Performed in the Years 1796, 1797 and 1798,* printed on a handpress by members of the society in 1974, was another such venture.

Several of the publications made available to Alcuin members have come from school and teaching presses, many from students (and staff) at the Graphic Arts Department of Vancouver Vocational Institute, such as a broadside reprint of Randle Holme's *Customs of the Chappel* (1973) and *The Diary and Narrative of Richard Henry Alexander in a Journey Across the Rocky Mountains* (1973). Several of the other school presses in Canada have produced keepsakes for Alcuin, such as *A Cooke,* from Earle's *Microcosmographie* (1976), which was designed and printed by W. Craig Ferguson at the Basement Cage Press at Queen's University, Kingston, Ontario, a press whose other publications have been bibliographical projects by English classes.

Although based in British Columbia, Alcuin is not in its interests nor in its membership limited

LEAVES ARE FALLING ON THE RIVERS
FRUITS ARE FALLING IN THE GARDEN

poems

DAVID A. DONNELL

THE VILLAGE PRESS / THORNHILL

ILLUS. 147. Village Press,
Ontario. *Poems*, 1961.

to the west coast, as the keepsake from the Basement Cage Press shows. Nor is it indeed exclusively Canadian. In 1977, the late Phil Metzger printed Austin Dobson's *The Passionate Printer to His Love* for members at his Crabgrass Press in Kansas. Most other work has been commissioned from small and private presses in Canada.

Although the vigor of the Alcuin Society tends to dominate one's impression of printing in British Columbia, there have been other important influences. From 1949 until his move to Montreal (to become designer for McGill University Press) in the early 1960s, Robert Reid produced several very attractive small books, such as Alfred Waddington's *The Fraser Mines Vindicated* (1949) and John Newlove's *Grave Sirs* (1962). In the 1950s he was joined by Takao Tanabe, a teacher at Vancouver College of Art. Tanabe's later personal printing from his Periwinkle Press in such books as Anne Margaret Angus's *Where I Have Been* (1963) and Harry Stanbridge's *Mirrored Barriers* (1968) is neat, unobtrusive, and successful.

Many of the small presses in the Vancouver area have the production of volumes of poetry as their main *raison d'être*. Among these, the Blackfish Press at Burnaby and Wendy and Vernon Bender's Fireweed Press at Sooke on Vancouver Island are among the most ambitious in terms of production. The translation of Gongora's *Polifemo*, which Fireweed published in 1977, is perhaps the most successful book from a press that started with offset and has graduated to letterpress printing, the reverse of the usual process! Robert Sward's Soft Press at Victoria, which started with some stylish small editions of modern Canadian poets in 1970, is one that seems to have moved in the opposite direction, its later work showing less preoccupation with format.

Of all Vancouver private presses, the one that achieved the highest reputation was George Kuthan's Honeysuckle Press. A Czech who had studied in Prague and Paris before moving to Canada in 1950, Kuthan's main work was his *Aphrodite's Cup* (1964) with linocuts by himself. A reprint edition was published commercially in 1976, 10 years after his death. Under the imprint of the Nevermore Press, in 1960 Kuthan's *Menagerie of Interesting Zoo Animals* was produced by a team including several others active in the private press field: Gus Rueter, Felicity and Robert Reid, and Fritz Brunn. It is a scarce book—only 70 copies were bound and issued—which has been described

SILENCE

Now it is still –
There is no more singing,
The green wood is still –
Laden the skies
And heavy the hush
Presaging rain;
Dawn will come
And sunrise again,
A slow dawn bringing
Soft bird cries
From mist-hidden trees.
But no more singing
Here on this hill
Where night sighs,
Waiting,
And the dark wood is still.

ILLUS. 148. Aliquando Press, Ontario. *The Shadow of the Year*, 1976. Double spread.
The color of Rosemary Kilbourn's wood engraving well-matched by the Trajanus type.

in very enthusiastic terms ("the most imaginative yet produced in Canada"; "no finer private press book has been produced in North America").

Outside British Columbia, the main center for private printing is in Ontario. In the prairie and mountain provinces, the Four Humours Press in Winnipeg is virtually the only press concerned with fine printing by hand. Run since 1974 by Susan and Myron Turner from the basement of St. Paul's College at the University of Manitoba, with a Chandler & Price Gordon press, the Turners and their friends have produced several attractive volumes, such as Kenneth McRobbie's *What Is on Fire Is Happening* (1975) and Douglas Smith's *Thaw* (1977).

An extremely important influence in the Ontario scene came from the teacher and typographer Carl Dair, whose Cartier-type design is too little-known and used. Dair was the guiding spirit in the early years of the Guild of Hand Printers, an informal group based in Toronto, which since 1960 has sporadically produced *Wrongfount,* a collection of pieces by a variety of Canadian (and occasionally American) private printers.

Among those who worked with Dair was Gus Rueter, whose Village Press at Thornhill was active between 1957 and 1965. A compositor by trade, Rueter produced some very attractive work, such as David Donnell's *Poems* (Illus. 147) in 1961 and *The Ballad of Thrym* (1965), the latter in partnership with Dair. The Rueter fondness for fine printing is shown even more clearly in the work of his son William Rueter, a designer for the University of Toronto Press. At his Aliquando Press,

William Rueter started work in 1962 while he was still an art school student, in order to learn at first hand the basic skills of design, setting, printing, and binding. Having printed one book on a borrowed press and equipment, he moved on in the way suggested by John Ryder in *Printing for Pleasure,* purchasing a secondhand Adana flatbed and a small font of Bembo type, to which he added "a few ornaments scrounged from a hell-box, and a great deal of naive enthusiasm. Only the enthusiasm has remained a constant in the Press's operation." Until 1972, all Aliquando work was printed on the Adana, but then (thanks to help from Leonard Bahr of the Adagio Press in Michigan) it was replaced by a Chandler & Price Pilot press, to which Rueter has since added a Poco proof press. Though in its earliest years the press did not produce much of substance or that Rueter now regards as worthwhile, by 1966 his typographic taste was formed. It was shown to good effect in such books as Jane Austen's *The History of England* (1966) and Barry McKinnon's *The Golden Daybreak Hair* (1967). The use of Bembo was replaced by other faces, sometimes rarely seen designs, often used in unusual and effective combinations. *The History of England* married Poliphilus to Cochin Open Capitals; in James Agee's *Knoxville, Summer 1915* (1970), the manly Octavian type was used with an ornamented Victorian display letter in a daring but totally successful way. Experiment with different types and different combinations of designs has remained a feature of Rueter's work; he notes that his press was the first in Canada to use Eric Gill's Joanna, Victor Hammer's Samson Uncial, and a number of Rudolf Koch's designs, as well as the Octavian.

Several of the most successful Aliquando books have been of contemporary Canadian poetry. In *Seer* (1973), written by Richard Outram and illustrated with offset reproductions of charcoal drawings by Barbara Howard (the two owners of the Gauntlet Press mentioned below), Rueter used a tall duodecimo format that matched the verse and illustrations well. A more ambitious book was Florence Wyle's *The Shadow of the Year* (1976), in which he used the rarely seen Trajanus type in a perfect match with Rosemary Kilbourn's evocative wood engravings (Illus. 148).

Music forms one of the recurring themes in the list of Aliquando Press books, and one in which Rueter's crisp and stylish use of printers' flowers (in the effective use of which he stands beside John Ryder and Leonard Bahr) is seen to excellent effect. These have included Gerard Manley Hopkins's *Henry Purcell* (1974) and a short anthology of seventeenth- and eighteenth-century poems, *Music Divine* (1977), although my own favorite remains the charming small volume in landscape format,

ILLUS. 149. Aliquando Press, Ontario/Paul Hayden Duensing, Michigan. *Buchstabenfreude,* 1976. Title page.

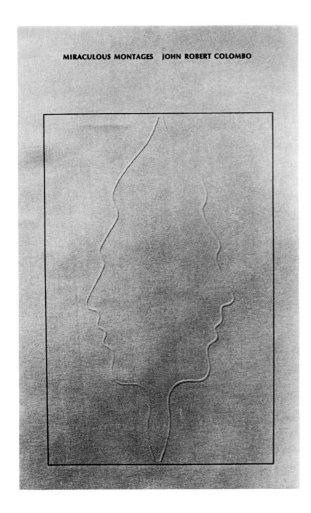

MIRACULOUS MONTAGES   JOHN ROBERT COLOMBO

ILLUS. 150. Heinrich Heine Press, Ontario.
Miraculous Montages, 1966.
Blind-blocked title leaf.

Laurels for the Third Muse (1973). In this selection of devices from early keyboard instruments, Rueter used several of the typefaces cast at the Private Press and Typefoundry of Paul Hayden Duensing in combination with various printers' flowers. Cooperation with Duensing was carried through very well with a joint publication: *Buchstabenfreude; the Delight of Letters* (1976), a collection of quotations from Rudolf Koch, set in a variety of designs by Koch (Illus. 149). Delight also comes in the title of a brief account of the press that Rueter published in 1976, *Order Touched with Delight;* it is a good way of describing the sparkle that characterizes the work of Aliquando.

Much less productive than Rueter has been Peter Dorn, who started his own Heinrich Heine Press while working as a printer at the University of Toronto Press. While in Toronto, Dorn produced some interesting and effective work, such as John Robert Colombo's *Miraculous Montages* (Illus. 150) in 1966 and Aba Bayefsky's *Legends* (1969). This portfolio of colored block-prints was a real tour de force. With text in English, French, and Cree, it employed both Canadian typeface designs, Dair's Cartier and James Evans's Cree syllabic type, the leaves being contained in an unusual and effective box of corrugated cardboard, with the Cree symbols cut by hand through the top layer of the board. Since a move to Kingston as a free-lance designer, Dorn has not managed to produce so much from his private press, although Barker Fairley's *Poems of 1922 or Not Long After* (1972) was an extremely interesting book.

Another long-established press is George McDonagh's Roger Ascham Press, set up in 1965. McDonagh's output is limited by his decision only to produce books of literary merit, of which

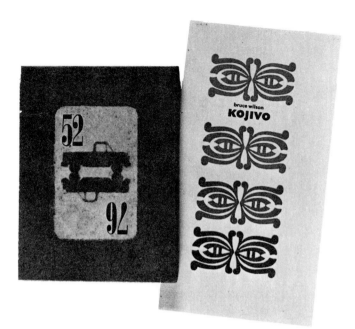

ILLUS. 151. Dreadnaught, Ontario. Covers of *52 Pickup* and *Kojivo*, both 1976.

ILLUS. 152. Mad-Ren Press, Ontario. *Milk Recipes*, 1977. Serigraph by Wendy Cain. Paper made by the printer.

Douglas Lochhead's *Millwood Road Poems* (1970) and Ralph Gustafson's short stories *The Brazen Tower* (1974) are representative.

At the Gauntlet Press in Toronto, Richard Outram and his wife Barbara Howard have operated a press of a very personal kind since 1960, all its work consisting of Outram's poetry with wood-engraved illustrations by his wife. Using only the simplest equipment (an Adana horizontal hand-platen press), they have produced some very attractive work. Much of it is single sheets, or very small booklets using Japanese papers, but in such volumes as *Creatures* (1972), *Locus* (1974), and *Arbor* (1976), full bindings using French marbled papers on the boards complement the skills of the poet and artist very effectively.

Another artist to make extensive use of wood engravings in his work has been G. Brender à Brandis. At his Brandstead Press at Carlisle, the quality of the artist's fine wood engravings and very precise linocuts has been shown in such books as Margaret Lang's *Mingling Uneasy* (1974), a volume in which effective use was made of tie dyed linen for the binding.

In general, Canadian private printers have been content with papers available commercially, whether machine-made or the Barcham Green papers employed in *Mingling Uneasy*. At his Mad-Ren Press, Soren Madsen makes his own paper, on which he then prints in a carefree, exploratory style that has been likened to that of Walter Hamady at the Perishable Press. Madsen's paper is visually and tactually exciting: sometimes too much so, the flecks of the paper in his slim volume of poems by Walter Sawron, *Cloud-drift* (1977) being too pronounced for the convenience of the reader. Nevertheless, in *Milk Recipes* (1977), which has effective silkscreen illustrations by Wendy Cain (Illus. 152), the effect is very successful.

Chapter 22

—

FINE PRINTING DOWN UNDER

HISTORIES OF PRINTING, as of so much else, tend to deal with Great Britain, the Continent, and North America, and to forget the rest of the world. If one is concentrating on the development of new technology, or new schools of design, such preoccupation is natural enough. Nevertheless, there are other parts of the English-speaking world with the same cultural traditions as Great Britain and the United States where one might expect some comparable degree of private press activity.

Although printing developed early in the British settlements in Australia and New Zealand, the pattern of work within the trade was (unsurprisingly) that of pioneer societies rather than of publishing centers. In the nineteenth century (apart from the volume of missionary printing in New Zealand described below), there was a concentration of newspaper and jobbing work of very much the same kind, and produced under the same difficulties, as in the American West. For books, the Australasian market was supplied from Great Britain. The local societies were client societies, closely attached to "home"; not until well into the present century did local publishing gain momentum, and it remains the case today that a much greater proportion of a bookshop's stock will have come from overseas than would be true in either the United States or Great Britain.

The earliest printing in New Zealand was the work of amateurs, through the activities of various missionary groups. In 1830, the Anglican clergyman William Yate purchased a small Albion press and type in Sydney and took them back with him to his Church Missionary Society (CMS) station at Kerikeri, where he laboriously and ineptly printed a six-page Maori catechism. Evidently Yate found the black art too difficult to undertake much more work, and the press lay idle until 1842 when it was purchased by one Benjamin Isaacs, who used it briefly for his paper *The Bay of Islands Advocate* and then took it back across the Tasman Sea to New South Wales. Meanwhile, another CMS missionary, William Colenso, whose work has been described briefly in Chapter 2, had started work at Paihia in 1835 (Illus. 153A). Colenso was by far the most important of the mission printers in New Zealand in the 1830s and 1840s, but there were more than a few others: among them, the Wesleyans under the trained printer William Woon, who had previously operated a mission press in Tonga, were active at Hokianga from 1836 to 1845, and a Roman Catholic press brought in from France at the request of Bishop Pompallier, which was operated at Kororareka by Father Baty and a lay brother, M. Yvert, in the 1840s. But gradually, as the country was settled, the missionary groups tended to pass their printing needs over to the commercial printers who were establishing themselves in Auckland and other centers. One missionary press that lasted longer than most was the St. John's College Press set up by the Anglican Bishop Selwyn, at which a substantial body of work for church purposes was produced through the late 1850s and intermittently thereafter. As its name suggests, St. John's was closer to a school or teaching press than the normal missionary activity.

The first amateur printing not the fruit of missionary zeal came early, with William Golder's *The Philosophy of Love* in 1871, which, as mentioned in Chapter 7, was printed by the author on a press of his own construction at his home in the hills near Wellington. It was very much an oddity; most local authors continued to have their work printed by commercial printers in whatever style the printer could manage—no better (and often no worse) than the sort of commissions given to jobbing printers in Great Britain. But there was at least one other amateur printer in Victorian New Zealand, the horticulturist Henry Budden at Nelson in the South Island. To further his business, Budden acquired a small press in 1884 to print his seed catalogues, billheads, and other items, and most of the printing was done by his teenage son, who eventually became a trade printer. In addition to these commercial uses, the press was also employed for printing verse written by Budden and his wife and for the text accompanying Budden's charming watercolors of *Bulbous Flowers*, completed sometime in the 1880s and recently published in facsimile (Illus. 153B).

The Buddens' work reflected accurately enough the debased typographic style of the period. Through the endeavors of the remarkable trade printer and type reviewer Robert Coupland Harding, the local printing trade was kept closely in touch with design developments of the closing decades of the nineteenth century, but Harding's reaction to some of the American imitations of William Morris's typefaces (quoted in Chapter 25) show how little even he comprehended the effect of the Private Press Movement. In New Zealand, although there was from the first at least one discerning collector of the work of the English private presses (Alexander Turnbull), and a pattern of enthusiasm developed among New Zealand book collectors for the work of these presses, the Private Press Movement had no influence on local printing for many years.

In the early 1930s, however, there were several outside the New Zealand printing trade whose typographic taste and endeavors were, in different ways, to uplift the standard of local book production. One of the most important influences was the Caxton Press in Christchurch. It started inauspiciously enough as the Caxton Club, a group of young men equipped with a Kelsey hand-platen and a case or two of secondhand types that in 1932 were installed in a basement of the university college buildings. The club produced one issue of a student magazine, *Oriflamme,* which today seems innocuous indeed but, in the quiet respectable New Zealand of the time, was denounced from many pulpits. As a result of the fuss, permission to maintain the club in the university buildings was nearly withdrawn, but it managed to survive and went on to produce another magazine, *Sirocco,* and a number of other small booklets. Most of these were set and printed alone by Denis Glover, the club's guiding spirit.

After Glover had graduated from the university, he worked for awhile as a reporter, but having lost his job, with "the field of journalism clearly closed to someone identified [as] a socialist, a pacifist, a red-fed and practically everything but a vegetarian," he returned to printing. With a friend, John Drew, as junior partner, he set up the Caxton Press in a disused stable in Christchurch. It was not by any means a private press: They had to make their living from its work (drawing 15s. and 10s., respectively, as weekly wages), and much of their work was jobbing printing of the dreariest description. Nevertheless, they managed also to publish a number of interesting small books themselves, having the ambition to produce "promising literature written by New Zealanders" in a typographic style that showed steady improvement.

In their earliest work they had fallen into a number of traps familiar to the amateur—using a

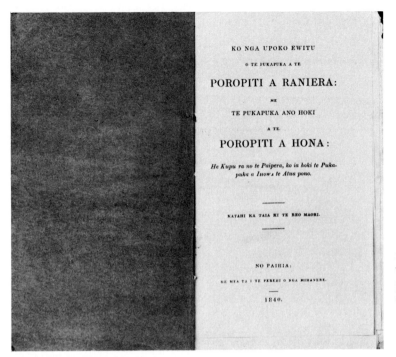

ILLUS. 153A. Early New Zealand work. Bible stories in Maori printed at Paihia by William Colenso, 1840.

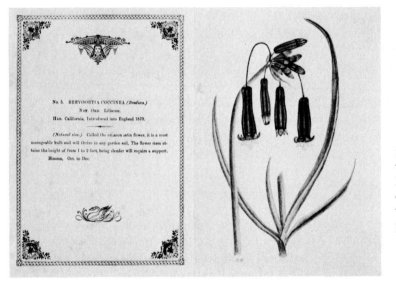

ILLUS. 153B. Early New Zealand work. Opening from Henry Budden's *Bulbous Flowers,* c.1888, for which the text pages were printed on his private press at Nelson.

zero instead of an "O" in the title of one book; stating that another was in a certain face (because that was how the case was labeled!) when in fact it was not—and even when their work was not commercial, it was closer in style to the "little presses" than to the Arts and Crafts Movement. Nevertheless, particularly after Leo Bensemann joined the team in 1937, the partners' interests made them undertake several books characteristic of the private press. These ranged through the 125 copies of a volume of Bensemann's drawings, *Fantastica* (1937), and the 50 copies of *Thirteen Poems* (1939) by Glover, which were "republished as a typographical experiment" in an asymmetric Tschichold-like setting in Gill Sans. In 1940 it was followed by an edition in 25 copies of *Nastagio and the Obdurate Lady,* using handset Caslon on Dene Mill paper.

The partners had from the start "decided to avoid the production of expensive limited editions de luxe," but in this case they deliberately broke their own rule:

> This experiment in fine book production has been made to satisfy a private ambition; we need not therefore detail what labour and expense we have been at to make it a memorable production. A few of the fifteen copies for sale are still available (one guinea) but intending buyers are warned that there is not much of it for the money.

There was not very much of it, nor was the book faultless (the use of red on the title page and running heads having been overdone), but it was a striking book with effective illustrations by Bensemann. There were to be several other books carefully printed in small editions, but during the war years Glover was away in the Royal Navy, and subsequent work from the Caxton Press was much further removed from the private press tradition.

One influential publication from the Caxton Press was a small literary journal, *Book.* In March 1948, it received the distinction of a parody in the form of *Bookie,* a "special horse-followers' number" from the Nag's Head Press. Nag's Head was at that time the alter ego of the Raven Press, a small Christchurch printing firm started by R. S. Gormack and two university friends in emulation of the Caxton Press. Nag's Head remained the imprint used by Gormack for his subsequent private printing, both through his career in the commercial printing trade and subsequently in his retirement (Illus. 154). Some of its work has been as lighthearted in its mockery of aspects of the local publishing and cultural life as *Bookie* was, notably in Gormack's "piecemeal progressive printing" of *The Centennial History of Barnego Flat,* of which the first installment appeared in 1964 and the ninth in 1982. Handset in Caslon, with elegant use of ornament, *Barnego Flat* is typographically far more distinguished than the many local histories it mocks. The same traditional, unassuming but effective typography characterizes other Nag's Head work of a more serious kind, such as the account of a famous cricket match of bygone days, *Great Knock* (1978), or Gormack's own *Diary of One Hundred Days* (1975), as well as work by other contemporary writers, such as Dora Somerville's *Maui's Farewell* (1966). In its quiet way, the Nag's Head Press has provided a good model for other New Zealand amateur printers and has produced some worthwhile books.

Another interesting New Zealand press is that run by D. F. McKenzie, the Wai-te-ata Press. McKenzie (the historian of Cambridge University Press) set this up in 1962 as a bibliographical press for his English students at Victoria University with a Stanhope press on loan from Cambridge, to which he has subsequently added an impressive range of equipment gathered from various New Zealand printing houses. In its early days, Wai-te-ata produced a number of issues of an irregular but substantial literary journal, *Words: Wai-te-Ata Studies in Literature.* For this, trade linotype setting was used, and there was no attempt to produce work that could not have been produced (though more expensively) by employing commercial printers instead of using the press's plant in McKenzie's spare time. Going beyond its purely teaching function, however, the Wai-te-ata Press has printed and published an interesting and useful range of small books by local writers. Mainly poetry, these include James Bertram's *Occasional Verses* (1971), Bill Manhire's *How to Take Off Your Clothes at the Picnic* (1977), and Peter Bland's *Primitives* (1979); they represent the range of Wai-te-ata's textual and typographic styles (Illus. 155). To look at examples of McKenzie's printing is to be reminded of some of the work of the Keepsake Press: Although the styles of the two presses are very different, they share the same literary and typographic life and the same determination to print only work of textual importance, in styles that are appropriate and carefully planned but without much of the affectation of fine printing. Wai-te-ata has set a standard that Victoria University's second bibliographical press (in its Department of Librarianship) will find it hard to rival.

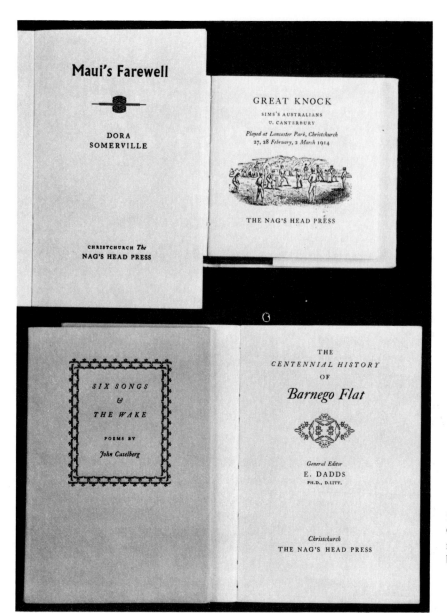

ILLUS. 154. Nag's Head Press, Christchurch, New Zealand. A range of R. S. Gormack's small books.

Parallel with these relatively large-scale ventures have been several smaller-scale amateur printers who have from time to time produced interesting work. From his Colenso Press, Eugene Grayland started in the 1930s with magazine work in Hawke's Bay, and in his spare moments from his job as a reporter occasionally produced a number of small books on local history topics. In Wellington, the civil servant Noel Hoggard used his leisure hours and a treadle platen to publish a literary magazine, *Arena*, and a good many small books from his Handcraft Press. But although both men were enthusiastic printers, their concern with fine printing was slight: As an obituarist of Hoggard shrewdly put it in 1975, "his joy was the Act of Publication." Not until recently did New Zealand have another private printer who would attempt to bring New Zealand up to the standard of the best handpress printing produced overseas.

In its origins, Alan Loney's Hawk Press was no more promising than many another little press devoted to the production of poetry by its owner and other contemporary writers. Work started in winter 1975 in a leaking garage with only oil lamps for lighting, from the delightfully named "Taylor's

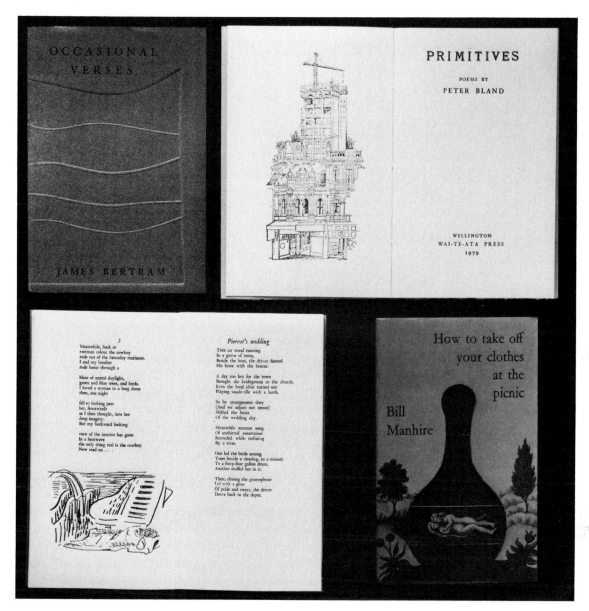

ILLUS. 155. Wai-te-ata Press, New Zealand. Representative work
from D. F. McKenzie's press: *Occasional Verses*, 1971;
Primitives, 1979; *The Back-to-Front Runner Poems*, 1974;
How to Take Off Your Clothes at the Picnic, 1977.

Mistake" near Christchurch. Despite a move to the North Island in 1977, and two subsequent relocations in the Wellington area, the Hawk Press has achieved a creditable publication record, with well over 20 books to its name. When Loney started, he had very little knowledge of presswork; his obsession with Eric Gill's types, however commendable in Denis Glover in the 1930s, was somewhat old-fashioned 40 years later. Many an amateur printer, particularly one whose interests might be assumed to be in "the Act of Publication," would have been quite content with the design and execution of his books. Such volumes as Russell Haley's *On the Fault Line* (1977) or Joanna Paul's *Imogen* (1978) had distinct merit (Illus. 156).

Loney, however, had other goals in mind; that is, fine printing with the handpress in emulation of the best private press work undertaken in Britain and the United States as he makes clear: "One

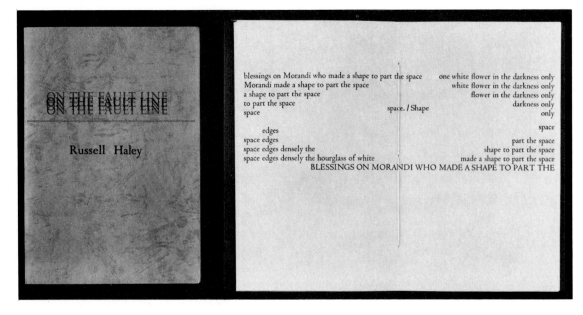

ILLUS. 156. Hawk Press, New Zealand. Left: cover of *On the Fault Line,* 1977.
Right: center opening of *Imogen,* 1978.

chooses either to simply muck about in the shed with an old printing press, or to acquire at considerable labour, cost, and some risk to one's emotional stability, standards of excellence comparable with the finest anywhere in the world." In other crafts such as pottery, New Zealand has despite its remoteness achieved these standards of excellence. With encouragement from groups such as the Alexander Turnbull Library Endowment Trust, which sponsored his first venture of this kind, J. C. Beaglehole's *The Death of Captain Cook* (1979), Loney moved into the big league of private printers.

Because the distinguished scholar J. C. Beaglehole had also been a good typographer of a solidly classical kind (and in his time responsible for revitalizing the design of work from the New Zealand Government Printing Office, as well as one of the shrewdest critics of Caxton Press work), Loney's selection of his first book to be printed on dampened handmade paper on an Albion was a brave one. Locally, his choice of design (in unjustified Poliphilus, with display in Gill Shadow) could be subjected to much criticism for its variance from Beaglehole's own canons; abroad, it would be compared with the work of such printers as Claire van Vliet, Giovanni Mardersteig, and Walter Hamady. *The Death of Captain Cook* was not in its execution of such excellence. To be just, it should be compared rather with the first essays of other self-taught printers who had attempted the same: the Vine Press's *Vitis Vera,* for instance. Loney himself was critical of aspects of his book, its presswork in particular. His latest work using the Albion, Beaglehole's *The New Zealand Scholar* (1982), which was set in Centaur types, shows that he has now satisfactorily mastered the problems of printing in this way.

In addition to the Albion, Loney is now using a Vandercook proofing press, and it is likely that more of the future work from his press will be produced on the Vandercook. But just as many of the British private presses in the past found that they had to look towards sales in the United States to cover the outlay on some of their more expensive books, Loney will need overseas sales to develop his printing program: New Zealand is a perilously small market for work of this kind. His plans for the future include a Greek and English edition of the fragments of the Greek poet Ibykos and a volume of prints by the distinguished local artist and papermaker Kate Coolahan using paper made especially for the project. It is to be hoped that this promising venture receives the support it merits.

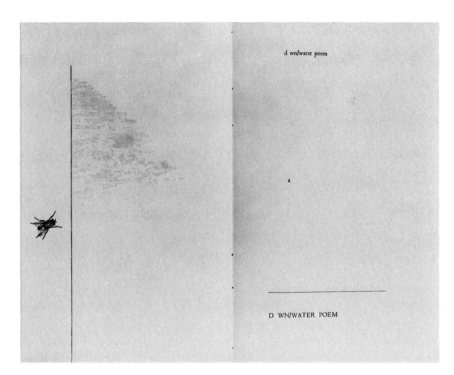

ILLUS. 157. Hawk Press, New Zealand. *Dawn/Water,* 1979. Double spread. "Minimal poetry" in action.

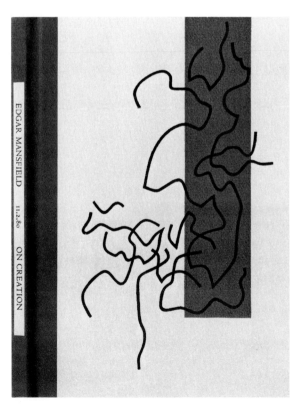

ILLUS. 158. Hawk Press, New Zealand. Binding of Edgar Mansfield, *On Creation,* 1981. Original with red backstrip, boards in yellow.

Across the Tasman in Australia, there has also been considerable private press activity. Toward the end of the nineteenth century, the hobby of amateur journalism had some success, particularly through the efforts of Hal E. Stone, who started with the *Australian Kangaroo* in 1892 and continued with this hobby, using a variety of press and journal names, over half a century.

Some of Stone's pamphlets produced in the early years, such as *Life's Wallaby* (1908), show a very distant Kelmscott influence, but oddly enough this is not to be seen at all in the most accomplished of the early Australian private presses, that run by Sir Edward MacKenzie MacKenzie. For 10 years, from 1898 to 1908, MacKenzie operated a small press from which he produced small editions of verse written by himself and his friends. The presswork on the copies I have seen was immaculate; he ventured into printing on vellum for at least one, *The Ballad of the Broken Heart* (1904), but the design of these is strangely old-fashioned, drawing-room typography of the 1880s.

The other Australian private printers of the earliest period were concerned with the transmission of ideas, and not at all with physical presentation, and it was not until after World War I that one can really identify any influences from the Private Press Movement. In commercial work, Perce Green's design for *The Windsor Book* (1921) may be taken as marking the start of such influence; while the first hand-printed books modeled on the English presses came from the press of John Kirtley a little later.

Kirtley had installed a small Chandler & Price platen press in his apartment in a Sydney suburb, Kirribilli, in late 1922, and was printing in a style derived closely from that of the English presses. His original intention, he recalled later, was to reprint work by Walter de la Mare and Aldous Huxley; but he was instead persuaded that a more adventurous policy of publishing books by Australian writers was appropriate.

At about the same time, two sons of the Australian artist Norman Lindsay (whose work as a book illustrator had on several occasions shown that he had a good eye for the well-produced book), were experimenting on a "broken-down Albion sort of printing-press" they had picked up. These two, Jack and Philip Lindsay, printed one or two small pieces under the imprint of the Panurgean Society—Rabelais was something of a gospel to the whole Lindsay family. Then Philip, who had learned of Kirtley's interest in fine printing, introduced him to his brother, as he tells in his autobiography *I'd Live the Same Life Over*. The Fanfrolico Press was conceived.

Some of the small books printed by the Lindsay brothers, and even the books contemplated in the joint venture, were of a kind that could have attracted unwelcome censorial attention from the police. Titles like *The Pleasante Conceited Narrative of Panurge's Fantastically Brocaded Codpiece* (1924) carried an element of risk in their production that was no doubt part of the attraction for the brothers, but less so for Kirtley. Rather than publish under his own name, or use another imprint closely associated with him, he wished for this distinct and distinctive name, which was taken from Norman Lindsay's unpublished stories about the Duke of Fanfrolico and his court of Micomicon (although no doubt ultimately derived from Rabelais' *fanfreulich/fanfrelucke* in *Gargantua and Pantagruel*).

In Sydney they produced a number of interesting books: Jack Lindsay's *Fauns and Ladies* (1923), with woodcuts by his father, *Seven Poems* by Dora Wilcox (1924), the first book with handcolored illustrations produced in Australia, and *Thief of the Moon*, poems by Kenneth Slessor (1924). Their most substantial production by far was Jack Lindsay's translation of the *Lysistrata* of Aristophanes, printed and published by the press in 1925.

This was to be the last Australian publication from the Fanfrolico Press, although there were several other books printed but not published, of which Jack Lindsay's poems *The Passionate Neat-herd* was the most important. That it was never published was due to a major change in Fanfrolico's affairs: In February 1926, Kirtley and Jack Lindsay moved to London. It was a natural center of gravity for young men with literary ambitions, one in which interest in fine printing was much greater, and also one that (following Norman Lindsay's successful exhibition at the Leicester Galleries in 1924) seemed more fertile ground for the Nietzschean-Dionysian aesthetic of "Norman Lindsayism" that permeated their thinking. The support Norman Lindsay continued to give to the press, through the provision of free illustrations, was extremely important.

In London, the work took a different form. Re-established with offices in Bloomsbury Square, the press was intended to be closer to Nonesuch or some of the other fine publishing houses of the time rather than a private press as such. It was set up with Kirtley as proprietor and business manager and Lindsay as editor. Although it took some time for them to obtain financial backing, in December 1926 they issued a new, large, limited edition of the *Lysistrata* as the first of the London Fanfrolico books. It was followed in 1927 by Kenneth Slessor's *Earth Visitors* and Jack Lindsay's translation of Petronius. But after five books had been completed, Kirtley (whose relations with Lindsay had become strained) withdrew from the press and returned to Australia. In his place another Australian, P. R. Stephensen, who had been a Rhodes Scholar at Oxford, became business manager. Stephensen was a man who made enemies easily: Readers of Aldous Huxley's *Point Counter Point* find Stephensen pilloried as the objectionable Cuthbert Arkwright,

> [who] had an idea that by bawling and behaving offensively he was defending
> art against the Philistines. . . . He made his living, and in the process convinced
> himself he was serving the arts, by printing limited and expensive editions of
> the more scabrous specimens of the native and foreign literature.

An impressive list of books was produced by Fanfrolico, many of them edited by Lindsay. Some were new editions of the books already printed in Australia, but many others were translations of the classics—Petronius, Propertius, Aristophanes, Theocritus, and others. They also printed a number of editions of English literature, which were well worth producing: selections from the works of Robert Eyres Landor (later taken over by Eric Partridge's "Scholartis Press," one of the most interesting semi-private publishing imprints of the time); the works of Tourncur and Beddoes; and a few literary oddities, like the reprint of Sir John Harington's *Metamorphosis of Ajax,* and *Loving Mad Tom,* a splendid anthology of Bedlamite verses of the sixteenth and seventeenth centuries. By no means all were as characterized by Huxley!

The influence of the Nonesuch Press was considerable in Fanfrolico's deliberate adoption of the mode of the sixteenth-century scholar-printers, who themselves edited the texts they published, in the choice of texts for printing and to some degree in their typographic presentation. It can be seen clearly enough from the statement of aims in *Fanfrolicana* (1928) that an attempt was made "adequately to express the individuality of each book" and that "in fine book production the question is not merely *how* to print finely, but *what* to print finely." One difference from Nonesuch was in book illustration, which at Fanfrolico was regarded as "almost the *sine qua non* of a book with character," and for which Norman Lindsay's work was extensively used. The other real difference was the degree of success with which these high ideals were pursued. There are a few aesthetic failures among Nonesuch books; there are many more among those of the Fanfrolico Press—like the monumental *AntiChrist* of Nietzsche, which was set throughout in 16-point capitals Poliphilus and is almost unreadable (Illus. 159), or Byron's *Manfred,* with its illustrations printed in purple—and those books that were successful were less so. Yet, despite these faults, the press enjoyed considerable success.

But Lindsay and Stephensen were drifting apart. In 1929 Stephensen also left Fanfrolico to set up the Mandrake Press (another of the short-lived quasi-private presses, which in the next two years produced a few interesting books), and he eventually returned to Australia. As for Fanfrolico, Jack Lindsay changed the manner of work completely, installing a treadle press in the basement of a

ILLUS. 159. Fanfrolico Press, London. Nietzsche's *AntiChrist*. Illustration by Norman Lindsay.

Hampstead house he had taken. Here, assisted by fellow-Australian Brian Penton and later by his brother Philip Lindsay (recently arrived from down under and yet to make his name as a historical novelist), Fanfrolico became once more a true private press, and a few more books were produced. These were very much simpler and less ambitious than the commercially printed books and very much closer to the Kelmscott tradition. The first of these was the splendid *Mimiambs of Herondas* (1929), with powerful surreal designs by Alan Odle in marked contrast to the predominant Norman Lindsay style of the press's earlier work. My own favorite of this last group is *A Patchwork Quilt*, translations of Ausonius by Lindsay, illustrated with vignettes by the then-unknown Edward Bawden (Illus. 160). Almost as effective was an edition of William Morris's *Guenevere* illustrated with eight of Rossetti's drawings. But despite the success of these volumes the press was doomed; in 1928 it had started publication of *The London Aphrodite*, a deliberately outrageous and iconoclastic "little magazine," whose title was intended to challenge *The London Mercury*. Like most little magazines it was a complete financial failure. Only six numbers were planned, and all were published, but they ruined the press. Although Fanfrolico had been second only to Nonesuch in sales, its financial state had seldom been other than precarious, and in the Lindsay/Stephensen period fiscal control had been lax. In 1930, the stock of unsold books was disposed of to Simpkin Marshall for remaindering; an inglorious end for "fine books," but at least the press's creditors were paid in full. In its brief life, Fanfrolico had published some interesting books, and the 1920s would have been poorer without this "Australian explosion in the English scene," despite the fact that England "politely ignored the noise, held its nose, and went on with its own business."

Of all those who had been concerned with the Fanfrolico Press only Kirtley was to become involved again in private press work in Australia (although Jack Lindsay was later to produce a little interesting work at his Myriad Press in England). It was not until 1943 that Kirtley set up again as a

PERSONAL VERSES
TO HIS WIFE

Dear, let our lives be still the same
as when our love first warmed to life,
and let us each still use the name
whispered when first I called you wife.
Time shall not make us stammer there.
I'll be your *laddie* all my days ;
you are my *young one* I'll declare,
however Time about us greys.
Though Nestor be shortlived to me
and you pass Cumae's Sibyl by,
we shall refuse to Time a sigh,

lifted beyond his hopes and fears.
Better to know Time's worth than be
a careful reckoner of his years,

THE ESTIMATION IN WHICH HIS WIFE HELD HIM

My wife reads through the songs I write
but doesn't ask me : Who are these ?
Lais, Glycera, it's clear,
are girls that men hire by the night,
wicked girls.
She says instead :
These are not infidelities
but just a game with words in bed,
so let him have his fun, poor dear.
There, now you see
what a deep faith she has in me.

ATTUSIA LUCANIA SABINA MY WIFE

In my youth I wept for you,
Early my hopes lay dead ;
for thirtysix whole years
I have refused to wed,
I have thought of you with tears,
I have remembered you.
Age has crept over me ;
still cries the urgent pain,
unceasing, fresh each day—
others find balm again
and laugh their sorrow away.
It is not so with me.
Still I am missing you.

ILLUS. 160. Fanfrolico Press, London. Opening from *A Patchwork Quilt*, 1929. Illustrations by Edward Bawden.

weekend printer with an Albion press installed in a shed in Fern Tree Gully in the hills near Melbourne. Here over the next nine years he produced occasional small quartos of verse in small editions and, despite the fact that his shop was "the haunt of inquisitive possums and roaming bandicoots" managed one important and substantial book, Robert Fitzgerald's *Heemskerck Shoals* (1949), at that time the most lavish (and expensive) essay in private press work seen in Australia. Although Kirtley had plans for a series of other finely printed Australiana, and work was started on several of them, none came to fruition.

Much earlier than this, Ernest Shea, who taught printing at Sydney Technical College, had set up his own private press with an Albion in the cellar of his home at Mosman, near Sydney. Between 1931, when the first of his Sunnybrook Press books appeared, and 1942, he issued small editions of seven books, starting with *Trio*, a book of poems by Kenneth Slessor and two other poets. Shea's eye for book design was good and the quality of his work on the Albion press was excellent. Among the Sunnybrook publications was a study of early Australian printing, *The Howes and Their Press* (1936), by Sir John Ferguson and others, in handset Caslon on Worthy Charta paper. As well as the books Shea published himself, there were some slighter pieces produced for the antiquarian bookseller James Tyrrell; an undated prospectus announced several other Sunnybrook publications including a tempting series of Colonial Reprints "in preparation." But these plans were brought to an end by the war, just as another promising attempt at fine printing, the Australian Limited Editions Society, was brought to a close in 1941 after issuing five books to its members.

Another trade printer who found a similar avocation in private printing in the thirties was John Gartner at the Hawthorn Press in Melbourne. Between 1936 and 1944 he printed many slim unassuming and well-designed octavos from his press, many of them concerned with printing matters, and some undertaken for the Printing Industry Craftsmen of Australia, the Australian Bookplate Club, and other groups. It was strong traditional typography applied to material for which private presses are particularly well-suited: In Britain or the United States there have been many such, but in Australia still too few. After 1945 Gartner's press became a commercial concern.

There were several other private presses operated in different parts of Australia at which authors painfully printed a volume or two of their own work. Since World War II there also have been sporadic bursts of activity, for the most part reflecting the kind of small-scale printing for pleasure so effectively promoted by John Ryder. At the Juniper Press at Burradoo, New South Wales, Mary Quick produced four charming little books on an old Cropper treadle press; from the premises in Fern Tree Gully, which had previously been used by Kirtley, Ron Edwards produced a long series of broadsides, ballads, folksongs and other attractive pieces at his Rams Skull Press. Not all Rams Skull work was as slight in physical extent as suggested; Edwards occasionally ventured into more substantial books with success, such as his edition of *An Epistle from Oberea* in 1955 (Illus. 161).

Much smaller in scale, but with a continuity of effort all too rare among the amateurs of Australian printing, is Gerald Fischer's Pump Press, which has been active since 1956. Using only an Adano quarto flatbed, Fischer has produced a long series of pamphlets of four to eight pages, initially of historical work concerned with South Australia, but since 1963 he also has produced a series of the Pump Press Poets: short verses of historical or literary interest the printer wished to retrieve from oblivion.

One of the most productive and prolific of private presses in Australia was Rolf Hennequel's Wattle Grove Press at Newnham in Tasmania. Hennequel was not a native Australian, and it is perhaps small wonder that his press did not receive much local support, if the statement that he sent me in 1960, that he had "started in 1958, as the only intellectual enterprise of the wonderful Island State of Tasmania. Purpose: to fasten Tasmania down, before it is swept into the void," represented attitudes he expressed locally!

Between 1958 and 1968 Hennequel issued some 25 books, some substantial, in an individual style of typography and binding that challenged all the normal canons. Wattle Grove books were undeniably nasty as examples of printing: verse set in heavily over-inked condensed sans-serif caps, for example. But in their texts, Hennequel's books were rewarding: In some of the verse and prose work of Albin Eiger (*Eastward*, 1959 and 1967, *Red on Purple*, 1962), he produced work that attracted

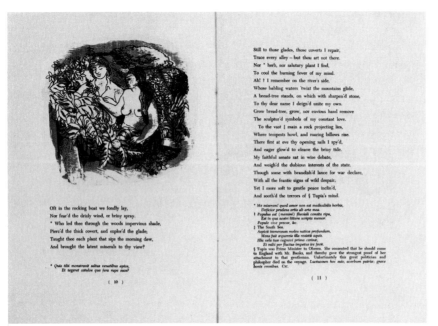

ILLUS. 161. Rams Skull Press, Victoria, Australia. *An Epistle from Oberea*, 1955. Serigraphs by Ray Cooke.

EMPEROR CONSTANTINE PORPHYROGENITOS WAS A
SCHOLAR AND A SCIENTIST IN ADDITION TO BEING A
GREAT SOLDIER. WHEN HE WENT ON VOYAGES OF CON-
QUEST, HE ALWAYS BROUGHT BACK WITH HIM SOMETHING
THAT WOULD BE OF INTEREST AND ENLIGHTENMENT TO THE
POPULACE OF BYZANTIUM. EACH TIME HE ARRIVED HOME
FROM FOREIGN FIELDS, HE HELD TRIUMPHAL PARADES AND
IN THESE PARADES HE WOULD DISPLAY AN INTERESTING
SPECIMEN THAT HE MAY HAVE BROUGHT BACK WITH HIM.
ON THE PARTICULAR OCCASION OF WHICH WE ARE
ABOUT TO TELL, — THE EMPEROR HAD JUST RETURNED
FROM A VOYAGE OF EXPLORATION AND CONQUEST IN THE
MOST DISTANT ISLANDS OF THE BLACK SEA. HE HELD HIS
PARADE ACCORDING TO THE USUAL CUSTOM, BUT IN THIS
PARADE THE CITIZENS OF THE CAPITAL SAW A SIGHT THEY
HAD NEVER SEEN BEFORE: THE EMPEROR HAD CAPTURED
AND BROUGHT BACK A TRIBE OF PEOPLE WHO WALKED

9

ILLUS. 162. Wattle Grove Press, Tasmania, Australia. *Four Tales from Byzantium,* 1964. Double spread showing linocut by the author, Howard Mitcham, and typical Hennequel typography.

considerable interest abroad. It was largely as a result of overseas support that his plans to close down in 1962 were postponed. Though Eiger's work formed the mainstay of Wattle Grove work, in several of his later books Hennequel's contacts with others in the private press field were evident, and in one, *Petra* (1966), he worked with Rigby Graham. Other later books increased the Australian content of his work—in such books as Rodney Hall's *Forty Beads on a Hangman's Rope* (1963) or Dorothy Hewett's *Hidden Journey* (1967)—but Hennequel's unwillingness to change his manner of production alienated him from those groups of potential purchasers vital to such an enterprise.

Several of the small presses working today are spare-time activities of librarians, as is common elsewhere. In Canberra, Alec Bolton's Brindabella Press has, since 1973, produced several volumes of work by major contemporary Australian poets; it handles the problems of printing verse with considerable skill and charm. Also in Canberra, Bill Thorn's Duyfken Press (started in 1975) has produced a reprint of John Dury's *The Reformed Library-Keeper* (1977) which, despite some unevenness in inking, was a satisfactory little book; it promises well for future Duyfken work.

Though Australia now has one small mill making handmade paper, Sonja and Kayes van Bodegraven's The Mould and Deckle at Heathmont, Victoria, there is at present little sign of the successful marriage of papermaking and fine printing that distinguishes several private printers in the United States. The Mould and Deckle's *Futurity* (1978), has been kindly described as "rather like some of the Roycroft books." Nor are Australian little presses in general moving toward finer use of letterpress equipment in the private press manner. Philip Roberts's Island Press, begun in 1970, had excellent promise. After an early childhood fascination with printing and later (through friendship with Robert Graves) exposed to Seizin Press work, Roberts started with an old treadle press and some Garamond type. But Roberts's satisfaction came in the literature he was printing, not in the labor of printing: "I was developing curvature of the spine and varicose veins in the left leg. It was getting to be a drag." When the opportunity came in 1976 to switch to an IBM typesetter and to have his books produced by a sympathetic offset litho printer, he abandoned letterpress with no regrets.

Geoffrey Farmer, the historian of Australian fine, private, and amateur printing, has remarked on the disparity between Australia and New Zealand, pointing out that the (New Zealand) Association of Handcraft Printers had a membership of over 40, at least four times as many amateurs as were active across the Tasman. Amateur printing has never really flourished in Australia, and the private presses mentioned earlier represent occasional "exotic" growth rather than a normal facet of local cultural and craft life. But in one type of private press work both Australia and New Zealand have been active: in the bibliographical presses set up in university libraries, library schools, or departments of English studies. Fourteen or fifteen such presses have been founded on both sides of the Tasman. The amount and kind of work produced is very much dependent on the enthusiasm of staff, and by no means all those established are regularly in use today. None of the others has the sustained and substantial publication record of D. F. McKenzie's Wai-te-ata Press, although in New Zealand, the Mount Pleasant Press in Auckland produced a respectable number of pamphlets on local printing history and literature under the direction of W. J. Cameron from 1958 to 1963, and in Dunedin occasional small books and pamphlets are produced from the Bibliography Room by Keith Maslen and his students. Across the Tasman, the most active of these presses, so far as work other than ephemera is concerned, have been those at Sydney (the Piscator Press, formerly the Fisher Press), in Tasmania (the New Albion Press) and at Monash University. From Monash's Ancora Press, Jean Whyte and Brian McMullin have, since 1978, been producing small books that show an agreeable growth in both ambition and expertise. The latest, Hector Monro's *The Sonneteer's History of Philosophy* (1981) is an excellent example of the good work being done by such presses; perhaps its example will encourage the growth of other private presses in Australia.

Chapter 23

SCHOOL AND TEACHING PRESSES

It was not only among the aristocracy that the virtue of the printing press for teaching purposes was realized. One tends to think of the school press, at which pupils will share in producing a school magazine and sometimes more ambitious work, as being essentially a twentieth-century phenomenon, but in fact it is much older. A good many such presses were established quite early in the nineteenth century by progressive schoolmasters who seized the opportunities offered the amateur by the iron press.

Among such schoolmasters one may include Thomas Wright Hill of Edgbaston, Birmingham, whose pupils at Hazelwood House School produced the *Hazelwood Magazine* from 1822 to 1830. Frequently, parish clergymen with schools would use their presses to serve both parish and educational needs; for example, the Rev. James Young, rector of Whitnash (near Leamington Spa), whose press in the 1850s was employed to print the *Whitnash Parish Magazine* and the recitations of his pupils, who set the type themselves.

The earliest teaching press I have traced, however, was of an earlier period and not in a school or even on dry land. This was on board H.M.S. *Caledonia* while she was blockading Toulon during the Napoleonic wars. Shipboard presses are of course commonplace enough—from the one carried on board the Comte d'Estaing's flagship during the American war of independence through to the specialized print shops used on board liners to print menus, news sheets, and the like. Most of them are really just a nautical variation of the in-house printing department. The *Caledonia*'s press by contrast was supplied by Admiral Pellew for the instruction and amusement of the cadets on board.

It was an inspired provision. The maintenance of the blockade was a wearisome business, and the chance the press gave the cadets to relieve their enforced idleness must have been particularly welcome. On it, two books were printed; the first, a horrifying account of cold-blooded slaughter (first published by Sir Walter Scott in the *Edinburgh Annual Register* for 1810), being *The Bloody Journal Kept by William Davidson on Board a Russian Pirate in the Year 1789*. This 38-page octavo was completed by the cadets in 1812, and the following year they printed a small quarto volume of nearly 100 pages, which contained translations (made on board ship) of the speech by Ruiz de Padron, *The Tribunal of the Inquisition,* and of Jovellanos's *Bread and Bulls*.

The principal purpose of the *Caledonia*'s press was not to teach the cadets the skills of printing but to maintain their morale. A similar purpose underlay the printing presses that accompanied several of the expeditions to the Arctic in the nineteenth century. While the *Hecla* was icebound during Captain Parry's voyage of 1819–1820, a weekly newspaper was printed on board, *The North Georgia Gazette and Winter Chronicle*. Similarly, in the expedition of 1850–1851 in search of Sir John Franklin (who had perished in the search for the Northwest Passage), the officers put the printing press—supplied by the Admiralty for printing balloon papers—to good use in printing songs, playbills, and other trifles. So keen did they become on their hobby that they completely exhausted their stock of paper and had to turn to any other surface that would serve to take an impression: chamois leather, shirts, and blankets, for example. The last playbill produced was printed on a piece of leather:

Royal Arctic Theatre
H.M.S. Assistance
Last Night of the Season
Friday 28th February 1851
Historical Drama in Two Acts of Charles XII
After Which, Grand Phantasmagorical Magic Figures
To Conclude with the New Pantomime of Zero
Doors Open at Six O'clock, Commence at 6.30
Griffiths Island Printing Office

In addition to these Arctic presses, there was to be one in the Antarctic. During the months of April to July 1908, the small Albion press in the winter quarters of the British Antarctic Expedition was used to print *Aurora Australis, 1908–1909* "at the sign of the Penguins." The preface Sir Ernest Shackleton contributed gives an interesting account of the difficulties:

> The reader will understand better the difficulties of producing a book quite up to the mark when he is told that, owing to the low temperature in the hut, the only way to keep the printing-ink in a fit state to use was to have a candle burning under the inking plate; and so, if some pages are printed more lightly than others, it is due to the difficulty of regulating the heat, and, consequently, the thinning or thickening of the ink.
>
> Again, the printing office was only six feet by seven, and had to accommodate a large sewing machine and bunks for two men, so the lack of room was a disadvantage. The printing was done entirely by Joyce and Wilde, the lithography and etchings by Marston, and the covers, made of provision cases, were manufactured by Day.

These expedition presses were exceptional, but like the press on H.M.S. *Caledonia* they seem to have been included with the expeditions' equipment by those who realized that printing could form useful occupational therapy. Although Holtzapffel & Co. and the others who supplied the amateur market in the nineteenth century emphasized printing as a hobby, printing as therapy does not seem to have been mentioned in any of the advertising I have seen. Yet the idea was certainly current in progressive circles. Whether the printing departments set up in many penal institutions in the British colonies can be regarded as therapeutic is debatable (and in any case the kind of work produced on prison presses puts them outside the scope of this book), but there is some evidence that in mental hospitals the press was not neglected.

Evidence for this comes from one of the curious essays that the book collector Octave Delepierre (Belgian consul in London) contributed to the *Miscellanies* of the Philobiblon Society. Writing in 1857, he mentioned two such presses, one at the Royal Edinburgh Asylum for the Insane, where the inmates compiled and printed a monthly journal, the *Morningside Mirror,* which had then been appearing for some 12 years. At another Scottish hospital, the Crichton Royal Institution in Dumfriesshire, the patients were similarly responsible for writing and printing their own monthly magazine which, by an incredible lack of taste on the part of the authorities, was entitled *The New Moon.*

Despite the lack of sensitivity in choosing a title for his patients' magazine, the doctor in charge took considerable trouble to find suitable occupations for them. Music was used extensively, and the press was used for printing programs, among other things. In a letter that Delepierre quotes, the doctor stated:

> Mental occupation has been a marked feature of the establishment from its
> commencement. A monthly journal, composed, published and printed by
> patients, has been in existence for many years. Some years ago, a series of essays
> on our poets, philosophers, &c. were composed and printed also by them. More
> recently a small volume of poems was published by one of our lady patients,
> and we are just now thinking of publishing a selection of poems from our New
> Moon.

In his own collection, Delepierre mentioned that he had several volumes from the series referred to, "Memoirs of Mad Poets, Mad Philosophers, Mad Kings, Mad Churls, by Inmates of the Crichton Institution." He had those on Tasso, Alexander Cruden, Chatterton, and Robert Hall. They have eluded my own search, but for the collector who likes a difficult quarry such private printing has much to offer.

Rather easier as a subject for collection is the work of some other nineteenth-century presses set up with the serious and charitable purpose of teaching a trade to the pupils. One of the earliest of trade schools for printers, the Bonmahon Press, was set up in circumstances that could hardly have been less encouraging; it was a private venture by a Protestant clergyman in rural County Waterford. The Reverend D. A. Doudney had been a printer in London before he felt a call to the church. He entered the Church of Ireland and in 1847 was ordained Curate of Minksland and Vicar of Kilcash, with his parish centered around the little village of Bunmahon on the Waterford coast. It was a wretchedly poor place, just recovering from the horrors of the great famine, and Dr. Doudney set up industrial and agricultural schools with the intention of providing work for the younger generation.

In 1851, inspired by a printing school that had been set up in the East End of London, Doudney decided that printing should be added to the subjects taught at his own school. Through advertisements in the evangelical *Gospel Magazine* Doudney edited, he attracted support for a new edition of Dr. Gill's *Commentary on the Bible* to be printed at Bunmahon. Terms were negotiated with a London publisher for the work, presses, and other equipment, and skilled workmen were obtained. But however encouraging the outside world, in Bunmahon Doudney encountered much opposition. There were very few Protestants in the village, and it is hardly surprising that the Catholic population was less than enthusiastic for a venture of this kind. Nevertheless, Doudney got his press underway, and within two years the boys of the school (who when they started had never seen a press or types) had proved such apt and industrious pupils that they had completed an edition of 2,500 copies of the six stout quarto volumes of Gill's *Exposition.* To be sure, without a providential bequest of £1,000 the venture would have come to grief, for Doudney's outlay included payment of three to twelve shillings per week (according to merit) to each of his pupils after a month of training, but this was the sort of risk on which evangelism flourished.

Much work was subsequently undertaken, including a weekly sheet, *Old Jonathan,* and later the

Gospel Magazine, but the difficulties of running what had become a considerable business from rural County Waterford were great. Only by searching for purchasers for the press's work on his own in England was it possible to continue, Doudney believed, but understandably his bishop was unwilling to allow him to spend much time away from his parish. To avoid running into debt, in 1858 Doudney closed the Bonmahon Press. Soon after, he resigned his living and left Ireland. At Bedminster where he settled, he set up another printing school that had a much longer life. Many of his Bunmahon pupils themselves left and later found employment in printing houses in England and in America.

In 1856 Doudney wrote and published *A Pictorial Outline of the Rise and Progress of the Bonmahon . . . Schools,* which gives a vivid if optimistic account of their work at its height. Visiting Bunmahon myself some years ago, I found that Doudney and his schools were totally forgotten. The Protestant Church was closed, its windows bricked up, the churchyard a wilderness, and the buildings that had housed his printing school and so many hopes were in ruins, silent except for the grunting of a pig rooting in them.

At the other extreme from the Bonmahon Press was another that had a charitable origin, and that was concerned largely with the printing of theological works. This was the Holy Rood Press in Oxford, which operated under the direction of Dr E. B. Pusey. In its origins, the press was neither Pusey's private concern, nor was it at Oxford. It grew from an idea that came to Miss Sellon, the mother superior of the Devonport Society of Sisterhood (a "High Church" organization with which Pusey was closely concerned), that printing was a suitable trade to teach the orphan girls and "fallen women" for whom the Devonport Society had been created. Printing for women was of course very much in the air in the 1850s: Miss Sellon's idea was very much like that of Emily Faithfull and the Victoria Press. Pusey responded with enthusiasm to the idea and assisted in its realization by himself purchasing for the sisterhood the printing equipment owned by his friend the Reverend Charles Marriott, who wished to give up the press he had operated at Littlemore since 1848.

The new printing shop was set up about 1855, initially in Bristol but subsequently at the headquarters of the sisterhood in Plymouth. But Miss Sellon discovered, as Doudney had before her, that it is easier to set up a press as a charitable concern than it is to find work for it to do, and nearly all the printing undertaken was of Pusey's own writing. About 1870, therefore, it was decided that the printing house should be transferred from Plymouth to Oxford, where Pusey would be able to supervise the work personally. Miss Sellon purchased a house named Holy Rood, which was bought by Pusey after her death in 1876.

Thereafter, the Holy Rood Press was in every sense Pusey's private press. It was no slight undertaking: the personnel consisted of Mary Milnes (who had at Pusey's request taken charge of the concern), a housekeeper, a male overseer, and eight orphan girls who were apprenticed personally to Pusey and were housed, clothed, fed, and educated at his expense.

From the time the printing house was moved to Oxford all Pusey's work, every book, sermon, or address he wrote or edited (and they were by no means small in number), was set by his apprentices. The girls had to learn not only how to cope with their benefactor's abominable handwriting but also how to set matter studded with Latin, Greek, and Hebrew. This they managed with surprising skill and neatness: although the books set by the Holy Rood girls are in no sense handsome, they are quite up to the commercial standards of the time.

Most of the work set in type at the Holy Rood Press was not printed there: as in Emily Faithfull's establishment, it was felt that presswork was too arduous for women as a matter of course. It was normal practice, therefore, only to pull proofs at the press (the corrected forms then were sent to the university press for machining), although in a few cases very small editions were printed on the premises. An example is *Eleven Addresses during a Retreat of the Companions of the Love of Jesus,* a duodecimo of 184 pages, of which eight copies were printed in 1882, the year of Pusey's death. With his death, the press also came to an end, and the orphanage was transferred to Ascot Priory.

To the cynic, Holy Rood could seem no more than a vanity press with its total concentration on Dr Pusey's own work. Nonetheless, there can be little doubt that it would in fact have been much simpler, cheaper, and more convenient for him to have his printing done elsewhere by the university press or commercial printers (as other scholars did), and his charitable motives seem impeccable.

One may think of presses of this kind as belonging peculiarly to the nineteenth century. Nevertheless, there was at least one ecclesiastical press that was operated for a quarter of a century, beginning in 1922, from the little Warwickshire village of Long Compton, which bears some resemblance to those of Doudney or Pusey. The King's Stone Press was started by the vicar of Long Compton, the Reverend William Manton, who had previously run a mission press in India. Manton's press was not merely a hobby; he built up a printing business employing three or four men, and during the difficult years of the twenties and thirties a good many young men in the village were trained as compositors or binders. Much of the press's work was of parish magazines and similar church-related books (including a long series on the Cornish Saints), but it also printed several important volumes of local history and archaeology, and during the General Strike of 1926 it produced a news sheet, *The Long Compton Wireless News.* The press was eventually closed in 1949.

Most teaching presses were and are of a very different kind from these undertakings. The commonest of all is the press maintained as an adjunct to the handicrafts room in a school. There are many hundreds of these, varying in their equipment from a flatbed Adana with a few card fonts to well-furnished printing offices in which school magazines and the like are printed with the aid of senior pupils. On occasion these presses have met with an even sourer reception from the trade than did the parlor printers of the late nineteenth century. In the 1920s, for instance, William Williams, headmaster of the Council School at Rhostryfan, Caernarvonshire, obtained a small press and type with the idea of teaching the senior boys the principles of the craft by allowing them to set up some small pieces. There was an immediate outcry among local printers, to such effect that Mr. Williams was prevented from carrying on with his plans. He was allowed to demonstrate how it was done, but no more. As a result, all the work of this press, mostly little booklets on Welsh history, were printed by Mr. Williams alone.

Few of the school presses produce much of any interest to outsiders. One very notable exception is the Art Society Press at King's College School, Wimbledon, which during the fifties and sixties produced a range of books, illustrated with an astonishing number of different processes— wood engraving, linocutting, relief etching, and many more—with splendid results. As anybody who has ever attempted to teach printing to amateurs knows, the difficulties of maintaining the interest of the students throughout the production of a book are considerable, and to maintain a proper continuity in every detail when there may be several dozen people involved in the production is almost impossible. At the Art Society Press, which is far more than an art room frill of interest only to those few enthusiasts "good at art," its production team is always large and includes a good number of sixth-form scientists; they have done things with type and blocks that would make a professional printer's hair go white, but they get away with it. Of all the books from this press, *Victoriana* was probably the most successful and has gone into several editions; to my mind *Graphic Methods,* an anthology of the press's first 10 years published in 1961, is most representative of its enthusiasm.

The trade printing schools have necessarily a less frivolous approach to the book arts: They cannot afford to use methods that would disrupt a normal printing office. They had their roots deep in the Private Press Movement: in 1905 Professor Lethaby, who as principal of the London County

Council Central School was the St. Paul of the Arts and Crafts Movement, invited J. H. Mason to start part-time classes in printing at the school. At the time Mason was still compositor at the Doves Press, but in 1909 he resigned to take a full-time teaching appointment Lethaby offered him. At first in temporary premises over a factory in Union Street, and later in Southampton Row, Mason taught the production methods and the modest, simple typographic style of the Hammersmith crusaders. The specimens of the students' work shows a quest for perfection that was as characteristic of Mason as it was of the Doves Press.

There were critics, of course, who saw in Mason's methods merely a willful defiance of modern industrial methods. What he was doing, in fact, was precisely the same thing Edward Johnston was doing in his classes in lettering at "the Central," returning to first principles, as a strong foundation for his students to build upon in their later work. The result, in Sir Francis Meynell's words, "was to release young minds from those chains of the prison-house with which industrial life too easily shackles those who have been taught *how* to do things before they have any chance to ask why, *why* they are done."

This concentration on "fine edition work" was not of course without its dangers. To return to first principles was all very well, but just as it could be (and was) argued against the private presses of the Arts and Crafts Movement that they were producing books for the wealthy, so Mason's methods were unsuited to improving run-of-the-mill printing. He turned out fine printers when there was a greater need for merely good printers. Meynell at the Nonesuch Press was to grapple with this problem in the field of fine book production and, under Leonard Jay, the Birmingham School of Printing was to demonstrate the virtues possessed by mechanical printing methods.

Jay had been one of Mason's earliest pupils at "the Central," and in 1912 joined him as his assistant. While there, and while Mason was at Weimar advising Count Kessler on the Cranach-Presse, Jay instituted classes in display setting and in advertising design. In 1925, when he was appointed head of the new school of printing in Birmingham, he was able to pursue his ideas about the suitability of powered presses and mechanical setting for good work. Despite opposition within the art school, where some faculty condemned mechanical aids on the grounds that they would promote commercialism and debase standards, Jay persuaded George Davis of Linotype, W. I. Burch of Monotype, and the manufacturers of powered presses to provide equipment as essential training tools. Soon the first in the long series of books and pamphlets that were set up and printed by the students in the printing school were to allay the fears of his opponents. The work of the school's press was to earn an international reputation for excellent work in its charming limited editions, which deservedly have been collected by lovers of fine printing. There was to be no such thing as a "Birmingham style" (any more than there was a "Nonesuch style"); each collector has his own favorites, but the series devoted to Baskerville, and the five volumes set by Jay personally, have particular charm.

As they grew, the other schools of printing in Great Britain were also to produce many handsome and collectible books, although none achieved the output of Birmingham. For the typophile, the work of many of them is far more interesting than that of contemporary amateurs: for example, Leicester College of Art's *Slate Engraving* (1964), an accomplished study of the slate-engraved tombstones of Cornwall and Leicestershire, with lithographs from rubbings of the originals.

Most of these presses moved far from the methods of the Doves Press or of J. H. Mason and followed the Birmingham pattern closely. This was natural enough; the number of printers engaged in book work is limited, and there is far more demand for those with a knowledge of display work, while the trade movement away from letterpress printing reduces the value of training in the traditional skills. One press that is much closer to the tradition of the private presses (although very far from Mason in execution) is the Lion and Unicorn Press, started as a nonprofit-making venture

CHAPTER XII
Why we have caused books of grammar to be so diligently prepared

WHILE WE WERE CONSTANTLY DELIGHT-ing ourselves with the reading of books, which it was our custom to read or have read to us every day, we noticed plainly how much the defective knowledge even of a single word hinders the understanding, as the meaning of no sentence can be apprehended, if any part of it be not understood. Wherefore we ordered the meanings of foreign words to be noted with particular care, and studied the orthography, prosody, etymology, and syntax in ancient grammarians with unrelaxing carefulness, and took pains to elucidate terms that had grown too obscure by age with suitable explanations, in order to make a smooth path for our students.

This is the whole reason why we took care to replace the antiquated volumes of the grammarians by improved codices, that we might make royal roads, by which our scholars in time to come might attain without stumbling to any science.

64

CHAPTER XIII
Who ought to be special lovers of books

ALL THE VARIETIES OF ATTACK DIRECTED against the poets by the lovers of naked truth may be repelled by a two-fold defence: either that even in an unseemly subject-matter we may learn a charming fashion of speech, or that where a fictitious but becoming subject is handled, natural or historical truth is pursued under the guise of allegorical fiction.

Although it is true that all men naturally desire knowledge, yet they do not all take the same pleasure in learning. On the contrary, when they have experienced the labour of study and find their senses wearied, most men inconsiderately fling away the nut, before they have broken the shell and reached the kernel. For man is naturally fond of two things, namely, freedom from control and some pleasure in his activity; for which reason no one without reason submits himself to the control of others, or willingly engages in any tedious task. For pleasure crowns activity, as beauty is a crown to youth, as Aristotle truly asserts in the tenth book of the Ethics. Accordingly the wisdom of the ancients devised a remedy by which to entice the wanton minds of men by a kind of pious fraud, the delicate Minerva secretly lurking beneath the mask of pleasure. We are wont to allure children by rewards, that they may cheerfully learn what we force them to study even though they are unwilling. For our fallen nature does not tend to virtue with the same enthusiasm with which it rushes into vice. Horace has expressed this for us in a brief verse of the *Ars Poetica*, where he says:

All poets sing to profit or delight.

i 65

ILLUS. 163. Birmingham School of Printing. Richard de Bury's *Philobiblon*, 1946, characteristic of Leonard Jay's work.

at the Royal College of Art in 1955, with the aim of giving practical training to the book production students by printing books that would make a serious contribution to design and scholarship. Its work is unlike that of most other schools, in that it is possible for outsiders to subscribe to its books, several of which have been sufficiently successful to be reissued later by commercial publishers. The books have ranged from *The Letters of Gainsborough* to selections from *English as She Is Spoke* and are extremely accomplished examples of bookmaking. For myself, one of the earliest, *The Life of John Wilkes Gentleman* (1955), has most charm, but all are interesting. The Royal College of Art seems to have had little difficulty in obtaining subscribers to its series; it is a pity that other schools of printing have not followed a similar policy.

Looking at some student projects of recent years (and at the work of some presses not discussed in this book), I must confess to a feeling of disquiet at some of the work. To be sure, the traditional graphic crafts play a minor role in the professional life of today's designer. One should perhaps forgive the student who thinks that a relief block enlarged from filmset matter will have the same result as printing from movable type, and forgive the striving for effect in some of the more elaborate bindings. Nevertheless, there is often more ignorance of typographic achievement in the past—whether Arts and Crafts or Bauhaus—than one would expect to find and, in some work innocently enough presented by those who have studied at these schools, the aims of the printers are unsubtle and ill-achieved.

In the United States, as might be expected, there has been a similarly large number of school presses producing fine work. Of these the most famous—and deservedly so—was the Laboratory Press directed by Porter Garnett at Carnegie Institute of Technology in Pittsburgh from 1923 until 1935. The press was planned as a center for the study of fine printing where students "should be encouraged and trained to strive for excellence, dignified originality, and distinction." With its motto *Nil vulgare/ Nil pertriti/ Nil inepti* and Garnett's careful concern with type, paper, and ink used with the handpress, the Laboratory Press was to carry the private press message into the marketplace in very much the same manner that J. H. Mason had done in London. But it was to do so with even more success; less inclined to look back than Mason, Garnett showed a typically American flair in his missionary work, and the effect of the Laboratory Press upon commercial printing was to be

ILLUS. 164. Leicester College of Art. Cover of *The Gregynog Press,* 1964.

considerable. Many projects were produced by the students: books by Paul Valery, Lewis Mumford, Henri Focillon, and others, all of which have become as much collected as the work of the Birmingham school. So successful was the press, in fact, that in 1963 Carnegie Institute revived the venture under the name New Laboratory Press, directed by Jack W. Stauffacher. But the revival was not a success. There was a conflict of policies with the university authorities, and after only a few small books had been produced, Stauffacher returned to his native state of California.

At the Pratt Institute in New York, the Pratt Adlib Press under the direction of Fritz Eichenberg produced a series of annual publications and keepsakes, which were available on subscription. Like the work of the Lion and Unicorn Press, its books, of which *Posada's Dance of Death* and *A Frasconi Family Travelogue* are representative, are splendid displays of virtuosity. The student work produced in the Davison Art Centre of Wesleyan University, on the other hand, was very much closer to the traditional and contemporary ideas of private press work, and some of the experiments Russell T. Limbach's students made in printing Bewick's wood engravings are extremely interesting. The editions are again, however, usually very limited and seldom generally available. The illustrations in *Art Laboratory Impressions* (1960), showing some of the work produced since the press was first set up in 1943, are tantalizing indeed.

One variety of the school press not to be found in England flourishes in the United States in some of the schools of journalism. Students in the Typographical Laboratory at the School of Journalism in the University of Iowa had the benefit of working under Harry Duncan of the

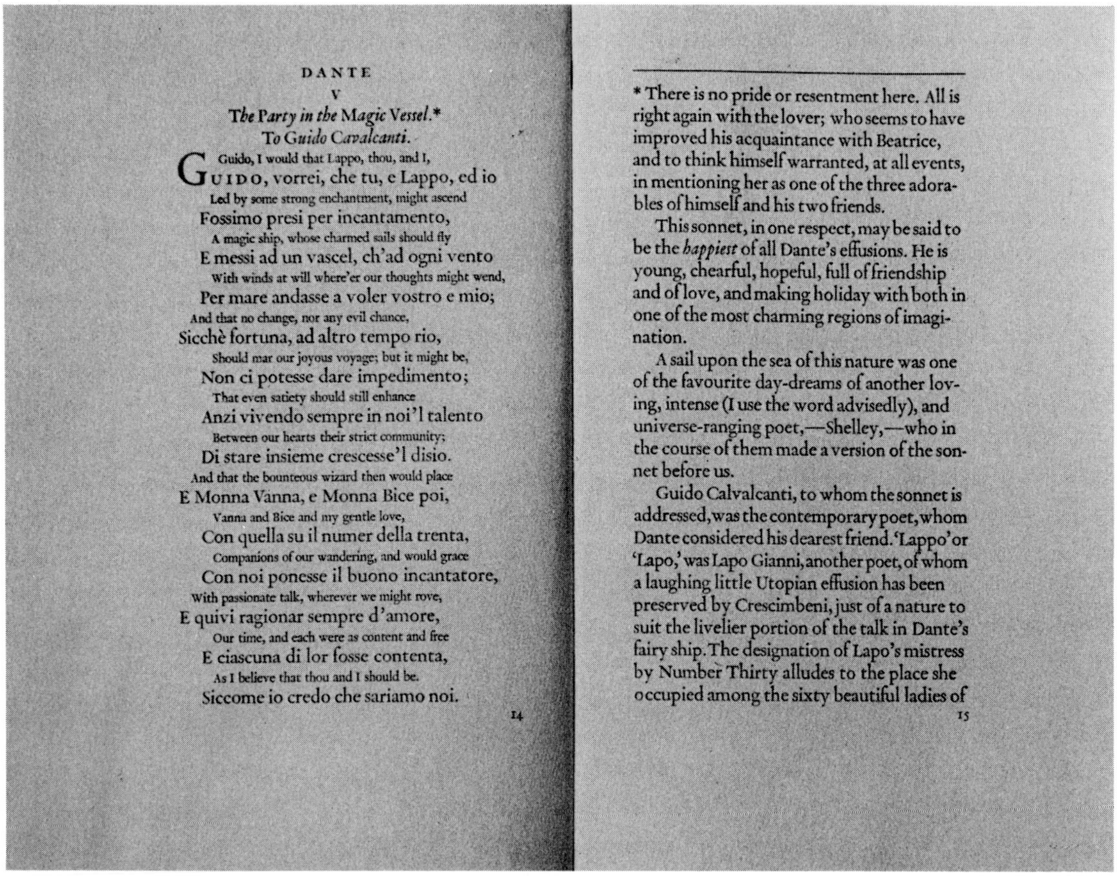

DANTE

V

*The Party in the Magic Vessel.**

To Guido Cavalcanti.

Guido, I would that Lappo, thou, and I,
GUIDO, vorrei, che tu, e Lappo, ed io
Led by some strong enchantment, might ascend
Fossimo presi per incantamento,
A magic ship, whose charmed sails should fly
E messi ad un vascel, ch'ad ogni vento
With winds at will where'er our thoughts might wend,
Per mare andasse a voler vostro e mio;
And that no change, nor any evil chance,
Sicchè fortuna, ad altro tempo rio,
Should mar our joyous voyage; but it might be,
Non ci potesse dare impedimento;
That even satiety should still enhance
Anzi vivendo sempre in noi'l talento
Between our hearts their strict community;
Di stare insieme crescesse'l disio.
And that the bounteous wizard then would place
E Monna Vanna, e Monna Bice poi,
Vanna and Bice and my gentle love,
Con quella su il numer della trenta,
Companions of our wandering, and would grace
Con noi ponesse il buono incantatore,
With passionate talk, wherever we might rove,
E quivi ragionar sempre d'amore,
Our time, and each were as content and free
E ciascuna di lor fosse contenta,
As I believe that thou and I should be.
Siccome io credo che sariamo noi.

14

* There is no pride or resentment here. All is right again with the lover; who seems to have improved his acquaintance with Beatrice, and to think himself warranted, at all events, in mentioning her as one of the three adorables of himself and his two friends.

This sonnet, in one respect, may be said to be the *happiest* of all Dante's effusions. He is young, chearful, hopeful, full of friendship and of love, and making holiday with both in one of the most charming regions of imagination.

A sail upon the sea of this nature was one of the favourite day-dreams of another loving, intense (I use the word advisedly), and universe-ranging poet,—Shelley,—who in the course of them made a version of the sonnet before us.

Guido Calvalcanti, to whom the sonnet is addressed, was the contemporary poet, whom Dante considered his dearest friend. 'Lappo' or 'Lapo,' was Lapo Gianni, another poet, of whom a laughing little Utopian effusion has been preserved by Crescimbeni, just of a nature to suit the livelier portion of the talk in Dante's fairy ship. The designation of Lapo's mistress by Number Thirty alludes to the place she occupied among the sixty beautiful ladies of

15

ILLUS. 165. Typographical Laboratory, Iowa. Opening from *Leigh Hunt on Dante,* 1965.

Cummington Press, and their work, in such books as *Leigh Hunt on Eight Sonnets of Dante* (1965), is distinguished (Illus. 165). And at Syracuse some of the publications of the Castle Room Press, the imprint of students working in the Goudy Typographical Laboratory, are also attractive.

A group of teaching presses that remain faithful to the principles of handsetting and the hand press are the bibliographical presses that have grown up in universities and schools of librarianship in the past 20 or 25 years. Bibliography is by no means a new subject, but the recognition of the importance of bibliography in textual studies is quite recent, despite the fact that R. B. McKerrow presented the case for the establishment of teaching presses as long ago as 1913:

> It would, I think, be an excellent thing if all who propose to edit an Elizabethan work from contemporary printed texts could be set to compose a sheet or two in as exact facsimile as possible of some Elizabethan octavo or quarto, and print it on a press constructed on the Elizabethan model. Elementary instruction in the mechanical details of book production need occupy but a very few hours of a University course of literature. . . . It would teach students not to regard a book as a collection of separate leaves of paper attached in some mysterious manner to a leather back, nor to think that the pages are printed one after another beginning with the first and proceeding regularly to the last. They would have constantly and clearly before their minds all the processes through which the matter of the work before them had passed, from its first being written down by the pen of its author to its appearance in the finished volume,

and would know when and how mistakes are likely to arise; while they would be constantly on the watch for those little pieces of evidence which are supplied by the actual form and "make-up" of a book and which are often of the highest value, in that they can hardly ever be "faked."

The case for practical bibliographical teaching has never been put better than this, and it is in good measure due to the example and teaching of McKerrow that no modern textual scholar would think of the books he examines as being made up of single leaves "attached in some mysterious manner to a leather back." It all seems self-evident now, and the virtues of the hand press in demonstrating such esoteric subjects as skeleton setting or half-sheet imposition need no further justification.

Nevertheless, it was not until 1927 that McKerrow's suggestion was put into practice, when Carl Purington Rollins started the Bibliographic Press in Yale University Library. Others followed slowly: University College London in 1933; Harvard College Library in 1939; Bodley in 1949 (with presses formerly used by Daniel and Ashendene); and King's College Cambridge in 1953. Since the mid-1950s, these presses have multiplied in number considerably. Some are grand affairs, using replicas of the old wooden press built according to Moxon's specifications in *Mechanick Exercises;* most use Albions or Columbians, a few modern platens. Some are for the instruction of small numbers of postgraduate research students, others for demonstration to much larger groups of potential librarians.

Normally the students will use these presses to print small pamphlets of typographic interest, sometimes, as in Bodley's *Dicta Sapientum* (1961), a type facsimile of an early work, in the course of which they will pick up a good general knowledge of printing techniques upon which they may safely build their theories in later research. In particular, they are likely to gain a much truer understanding of the problems of setting and of the textual errors that can result from foul case, pied lines, and the like. Very few of these teaching presses produce substantial books; the difficulty of completing books, when courses generally last only for a term or so, makes most of them limit their output to small pamphlets. Nevertheless, these are often of interest, like *The Glasgow University Printing Office in MDCCCXXVI* (Water Lane Press, Cambridge, 1953), or Dennis Crutch's *Century of Annotations to The Lewis Carroll Handbook,* which was produced by the Northwestern Polytechnic School of Librarianship in 1967. The work of bibliographical presses in New Zealand and Australia has already been mentioned in Chapter 22.

PART TWO

PRIVATE
PRESS
TYPEFACES

Chapter 24

EARLY PRESSES AND THEIR TYPES

IN MOST CASES, THE PRIVATE PRESSES that existed before the nineteenth century used types that were publicly available through the usual trade channels. To distinguish between "public" and "private" presses in the fifteenth and sixteenth centuries is difficult, as we have seen. A number of the early printers worked in a way we may with hindsight regard as being closer in spirit to the private press than to commercial printing, but in most of these cases there is little reason to believe their types were specially designed as part of the aesthetic policy of the printer. No doubt in the fifteenth century, before typefounding had emerged as a separate trade, there was close involvement between the printer and punchcutter and that in the Aldine printing house, for example, Francesco Griffo's introduction of new sorts followed discussion between himself and his master. Deliberate and self-conscious designing of types as one aspect of fine printing certainly came before William Morris and his followers at the end of the nineteenth century, but not typically from private presses.

One possible exception to this general rule is to be found in the work of the Italian writing masters of the early sixteenth century. Lodovico degli Arrighi da Vicenza, a "scrittore de' brevi apostolici," as he described himself, produced at Rome in 1522 the first manual on writing to be published, *La Operina*. The first part of this was printed entirely from wood blocks, but the second part, *Il Modo di Temperare le Penne*, contains several pages printed in a very fine italic typeface modeled on the "cancellaresca formata" hand. The type was fairly obviously derived from the hand used by Arrighi himself; it seems likely that the punches were cut by his partner, who can with reasonable certainty be identified as Lautizio de Bartolomeo dei Rotelli, of whose skill as an engraver of seals Benvenuto Cellini speaks with respect in his *Autobiography*. From 1524 until the sack of Rome in 1527 (in which it is presumed that Arrighi perished), the two partners produced a series of small books printed either in this typeface or in a second chancery italic typeface. If Arrighi's press was not "private" in that he apparently published for profit, nevertheless the style of his production was more that of a man interested in producing a handsome effect than making much money. His types were large (about 16 point) with generous ascenders and descenders; he eschewed all ornamentation and favored a severe style. With the exception of one or two small initials in one of his books, he used no decorative material, but instead affected the manner of the manuscript, with blanks for initials to be filled in later by illuminators.

Arrighi's manner and his type designs were widely imitated in his own day by such printers as Tolomeo Janiculo. Giovanni Antonio Castellione of Milan used a similar, upright, chancery letter; and the same handsome font was employed by Gaudentius Merula at his private press in Bergo Lavezzaro, near Novara, in 1542. In the great revival of classical typefaces in the 1920s, Arrighi was well served: Under the direction of Frederic Warde in 1925, Plumet of Paris recut his faces for a new edition of Arrighi's writing book that was printed by the Officina Bodoni, a press that has made distinguished use of the Arrighi faces in its books. Warde's version of the first Arrighi face needed a good deal of revision for machine composition as a companion face to a roman type, but when issued by the Monotype Corporation married to Bruce Rogers's Centaur type (based upon the Venetian roman used by Jenson in the 1470s), it was an entirely happy union. To accompany the fine recutting of the type used by Aldus Manutius in the *Poliphilus,* which the Monotype Corporation undertook in 1923, Arrighi's second italic was used as a model. Named Monotype Blado, after the printer Antonio Blado who used the type in the 1530s, it is one of the handsomest of italic types. The design of Monotype Bembo italic follows it closely.

During the three centuries that followed the invention of printing, a good number of typefaces were cut for semiprivate use. We can see examples of such in the magnificent Greek face used in printing the New Testament in the Complutensian Polyglot, completed by Arnão Guillen de Brocar in 1514; or in the "Romain du Roi" types cut for the Imprimerie Royale at the turn of the seventeenth and eighteenth centuries. For scholarly printing in particular, it was often necessary or desirable to obtain special typefaces. Thus Sir Henry Savile (1549–1622), the Provost of Eton, having vainly attempted to obtain a font of the French "Grècque du Roi" types for an edition of St. Chrysostom he was interested in producing, eventually imported a special font from the firm of Wechel in Frankfurt am Main. This typeface was based fairly closely on the French Royal Greeks and became known as the "silver type" from the legend that it was cast in silver matrices. The preparation of the Chrysostom cost Savile the enormous sum of £8,000, and the book was completed by John Norton in 1612.

Similarly, when the Anglo-Saxon type used by William Bowyer the elder to print the specimen for Elizabeth Elstob's Anglo-Saxon grammar was destroyed in the disastrous fire that devastated Bowyer's printing house in 1712, Lord Chief Justice Parker undertook to pay the cost of casting a new font of type with which to print her work. This typeface ought to have been a great success, as the drawings for the new design were (at Lord Parker's request) made by the eminent Saxonist Humfrey Wanley. But Robert Andrews, the punchcutter entrusted with the task of translating the designs into type, failed miserably.

> I did what was required [commented Wanley] in the most exact and able
> manner that I could. . . . But it signified little, for when the alphabet came into
> the hands of the workman (who was but a blunderer), he could not imitate the
> fine and regular strokes of the pen; so that the letters are not only clumsy, but
> unlike those I drew. This appears by Mrs Elstob's *Saxon Grammar.*

The verdict of history agrees with Wanley; although the type was used by Bowyer and his son occasionally after the appearance of the *Grammar* in 1715, it was not used at Oxford University Press (into whose possession the punches and matrices eventually passed in 1778) until 1910, when with the addition of some extra sorts it was used as a phonetic script by Robert Bridges in his *Tract on the State of English Pronunciation.*

An outstanding instance of devotion to scholarship can be seen in the punchcutting undertaken by Charles Wilkins, who was in the Civil Service of the East India Company. Early in the 1770s, William Bolts, judge of the Mayor's Court in Calcutta, provided the London founder Joseph Jackson with designs for a Bengali font of type with which the East India Company intended to print a grammar. Only a primary alphabet was completed, as the result was too poor to justify continuing. The project might well have languished, had it not been for the fact that Wilkins, then in his twenties, had been experimenting with the cutting and casting of Bengali type as a hobby. It was to remain a hobby for a very short while only. In the words of the preface to Halhed's *Grammar of the Bengal Language* (1778):

> The advice and even solicitations of the Governor-general prevailed upon Mr Wilkins . . . to undertake a set of Bengal Types. He did, and his success has exceeded every expectation. In a country so remote from all connection with European artists, he has been obliged to charge himself with all the various occupations of the Metallurgist, the Engraver, the Founder, and the Printer. To the merit of invention he was compelled to add the application of personal labour. With a rapidity unknown in Europe, he surmounted all the obstacles which necessarily clog the first rudiments of a difficult art, as well as the disadvantages of solitary experiment.

As the founder of Bengali typefounding, Wilkins was no longer, of course, in the position of an amateur, for typefounding became his chief concern. He trained an Indian assistant, Panchanan Karmakar, as punchcutter and founder, and it seems likely in fact that he was the real craftsman in the enterprise, and that Wilkins's skills were far less than those of his pupil. At any rate, Karmakar continued to run the typefoundry set up in Calcutta after Wilkins returned to England in 1786. Subsequently he entered the service of the Mission Press in Serampore and was responsible for training the other punchcutters whose skill made the work of the Baptist Mission Press so well known in the nineteenth century.

After his return to England, Wilkins continued his linguistic and typographic pursuits, once more at his own initiative and expense.

> At the commencement of the year 1795 [he wrote in the Preface to his *Grammar of the Sanskrita Language*] residing in the country and having much leisure, I began to arrange my materials and prepare them for publication. I cut letters in steel, made matrices and moulds, and cast from them a fount of types of the Deva Nagari character, all with my own hands; and with the assistance of such mechanics as a country village [Midhurst] could afford, I very speedily prepared all the other implements of printing in my own dwelling house; for by the second of May in the same year I had taken proofs of 16 pages. . . . Till two o'clock on that day everything had succeeded to my expectations; when alas the premises were discovered to be in flames, which, spreading too rapidly to be extinguished, the whole building was presently burned to the ground. . . . I happily saved all my books and manuscripts, and the greatest part of the punches and matrices; but the types themselves . . . were either lost or rendered useless.

Subsequently the East India Company directors persuaded Wilkins to resume his efforts, and his work was published in 1808. It was not from his private press (as he had originally intended) but from that of Bulmer. Specimens of Wilkins's types were shown in Johnson's *Typographia*.

Similar special casting of exotic typefaces was probably commoner on the continent than it was in England. In the New World, typefounding was strictly a normal utilitarian trade and was to remain one for very much longer; not until the beginning of the twentieth century were special private press faces cut. But there is some evidence to suggest that long before the first commercial typefounding in Mexico, in 1770, type had been specially cast for the Mission Press operated by the Jesuits in Paraguay.

The Jesuit Republic of Paraguay was one of the most remarkable of all European essays in colonialism, although most of us know little more about it than the distorted picture given in *Candide.* The Paraguayan Indians had extraordinary skill in handicrafts; Francisco Xarque, writing in 1687, commented that they were able to copy a printed missal with the pen so exactly that only the closest examination enabled one to distinguish the written from the printed text; and in 1711 Father Labbé commented on their skill. "I have seen," he wrote, "lovely paintings from their hands, books very correctly printed, others written with much delicacy. . . . " With such assistants available, one wonders less that the Jesuits were able to establish a press that between 1705 and 1727 produced several of the works used in their own Christianization. This printing was carried out "sin gastos, asi de la ejecion, como en los caracteres propios de esta lengua" (without expense in the execution, and in the correct types for the language), and although there is no more than circumstantial evidence to suggest that the type was cast by the Indians, the great Latin American bibliographer, José Toribio Medina, was satisfied that the mission printers were the first typefounders in the Americas.

When Benjamin Franklin was appointed sole minister plenipotentiary of the United States to the King of France in 1776 and set about equipping himself with a printing press, his press was much more than a hobby. It was as much of an official as of a private nature, and it grew to very large proportions. In 1776 he brought a small font of type from Fournier-le-jeune, much larger amounts in 1778 and 1779, and in May 1780 added typefounding equipment at a cost of 5,000 livres. A foreman and three assistants were employed upon this work. Some of the type was cast for American printers cut off from their usual English sources of supply. But it was also employed in casting a special, private, typeface.

In his position as American minister, Franklin was well aware of the danger of having his official documents (such as passports) forged. He was not unfamiliar with the problem. As printer of much of the paper currency used in the American colonies, he had devised an extremely successful method of nature printing to make the forger's task very much harder. In his passports he does not appear to have resorted to this method (which was continued in America right up to the 1780s), but instead to have relied upon typographic ingenuity and upon the use of a distinctive ornamental script type, perhaps designed by himself, for which the matrices were cut by Fournier-le-jeune and cast in 1781 in Franklin's Passy foundry.

In few if any of these private or specially commissioned faces, however, can we sense the particular aesthetic ideals with which the idea of the private press was to become imbued by the end of the nineteenth century. One notable exception is in the Greek typeface used by Julian Hibbert at his private press at No. 1 Fitzroy Place, Kentish Town, in 1827 and 1828. Hibbert is one of the most shadowy and Peacockian figures of the early nineteenth century. Born in 1800 and educated at Eton and Trinity College, Cambridge, he was a member of the wealthy Hibbert family with estates in Agualta Vale, Jamaica. His uncle Robert Hibbert was the founder of the Hibbert Trust, and George Hibbert, the West Indian merchant and book collector, was a cousin. Although Julian read for the law at Lincoln's Inn, he seems never to have practiced, and it is fairly clear from what little we know of him that his main concern throughout his short adult life (he died in 1834, reputedly from shock after being abused by a judge before whom he had refused to swear on the Bible) was to further the cause of free thought and rationalism, in which he was an enthusiastic believer. He did this by lecturing, by generous financial support of Richard Carlile and others when they were imprisoned or otherwise in need, and by his writing and publishing activities. His earliest work was published in Carlile's *Republican,* and we can only guess at his reasons for establishing his own press. He may have had aesthetic reasons, or it may have been pure benevolence. In 1826 one of Carlile's assistants, James Watson, who had received training as a compositor in the *Republican* office, fell ill. In his own words:

> I was attacked by cholera, which terminated in typhus and brain fever. I owe
> my life to the late Julian Hibbert. He took me from my lodgings to his own
> house at Kentish Town, nursed me, and doctored me for eight weeks, and made
> a man of me again. After my recovery, Mr Hibbert got a printing press put up
> in his house, and employed me in composing, *under his directions,* two vol-
> umes. . . . I was thus employed, from the latter part of 1826, to the end of
> March 1828.

The first of the two books on which Watson worked was *ΟΡΦΕΩΣ ΥΜΝΟΙ: The Book of the Orphic Hymns . . . Printed in Uncial Letters as a Typographical Experiment. And Published for the Sum of Three Shillings and Sixpence in the Year 1827*. It is a pleasantly printed octavo of 122 pages. The uncial type so prominently advertised was, according to Hibbert's "Preface addressed by the Printer to Greek Scholars" derived in the first place "from the inspection of inscriptions in the Musaeums of London and Paris, and thus it is no wonder, if it still retains more of a *sculptitory* than of a *scriptitory* appearance." The type was deliberately eclectic (Illus. 166). Having read Montfaucon's *Palaeographia Graeca* and examined facsimiles of the Herculanean manuscripts, he produced his design.

> If I had adopted the alphabet of any one celebrated MS., I should have had
> infinitely less trouble. . . . As it is, I have taken each letter separately from such
> MSS. as I thought best represented the beau ideal of an uncial type; . . . yet
> placed side by side, they look very different from a MS.

Hibbert's aim was twofold: to produce a Greek type that was suitable for ordinary use,

> [and one that] represents with tolerable accuracy the forms of the letters used
> by the Greeks themselves, in the brightest days of their literature. . . . I do not
> mean a type like that used in Bodoni's Callimachus . . . ornamented (or rather
> disfigured) by the addition of what, I believe, typefounders call *syrifs* or *cerefs*.

A second book from Hibbert's press was published in May 1828: *ΠΕΡΙ ΔΕΣΙ-ΔΑΙΜΟΝΙΑΣ: Plutarchus, and Theophrastus, on Superstition*, a 280-page octavo that was priced at one guinea. This strange composite book, which closes with 10 pages of the *principal* addenda and corrigenda (Hibbert was clearly like several other private press owners of the period!), includes an entertaining account of the production of the *Orphic Hymns*. Evidently Hibbert's typographic experiment was undertaken on a modest budget indeed. Only the Greek types had been acquired when he set up, and when he found he needed to print some Latin, for roman type he had "to send to London . . . two or three hours being sometimes lost for a single word." The preface includes an interesting balance sheet for the production of the *Orphic Hymns,* from which we learn that of 258 copies printed, only some 20 seem to have been sold (including "three copies forced upon H. B. Esq."), with an income of £3 9s. 6d. and an outlay of £34 11s. 6d.

Hibbert's experiment was an interesting one, in some respects like Robert Proctor's revival of the Greek used in the Complutensian Polyglot, or perhaps more accurately like recent private press cuttings of Rustic or Uncial forms of the roman alphabet. As a contribution to Greek typography, however, it was a total failure. It received no notice at the time, and later typographic historians have not often shown it much favor. Although Daniel Berkeley Updike allowed that Hibbert's font "had considerable charm" most follow Victor Scholderer, who (in his *Greek Printing Types, 1465–1927*),

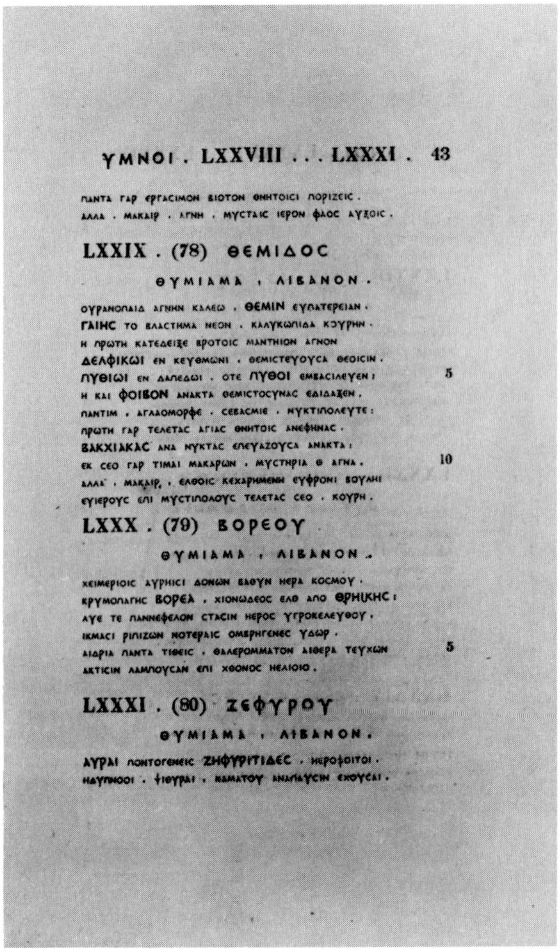

ILLUS. 166. Julian Hibbert, London. Page from *Orphic Hymns,* 1830, showing his Greek type.

while recognizing the possibilities inherent in Hibbert's idea, damns its execution as the work of a man "altogether too much of a dilettante," whose typeface revealed in its design "for the most part mere wilfulness."

Dilettante was certainly the right word for Hibbert, as his two prefaces clearly show. But I believe Scholderer did him an injustice in dismissing the design so scathingly. As shown in the *Orphic Hymns,* the face was in a first experimental form with which Hibbert himself was far from content, hoping it to be "good in theory, altho' I confess the execution of it is detestable." Which typefounder Hibbert employed is unknown, and he had not found the experience a satisfying one:

> I am tired with attempting to produce a better ranging of the characters. I cannot afford to employ the best workmen and the successive changes made by indifferent workmen are not improvements but only expences. . . . It will easily be perceived that the forms of some of the letters slightly vary in almost every different half sheet. The letter Γ, tho' one of the simplest, has given me extraordinary trouble.

Hibbert's offer to attempt improvement if enough interest was shown was not taken up.

Nothing further seems to have come from Hibbert's press after Watson left him in 1828, although it is possible that some more ephemeral pieces were printed. It is evident that Watson and Hibbert parted amicably, for when Watson set up as a printer on his own account in 1831, Hibbert gave him his press and types, and a further legacy of 450 guineas after his death. It is not known whether Hibbert's Greek type was given to Watson with the rest of his equipment; I have not seen any use of it in Watson's later work. Updike said that it was melted down, and from Hibbert's own account this seems likely.

There were other private press typefaces during the first half of the nineteenth century. Cotton, in his *Typographical Gazetteer,* speaks of one Russell who was said to have printed a duodecimo *Natural History of the Bees* in Elgin in 1822, in an edition limited to two copies, using types he had cut himself.

More important were the various exotic faces cut for the Baptist Mission Press in Serampore and for some other missionary activities elsewhere. Most of these faces were produced by regular typefounders in the first instance, although one of the most famous, the Cree Syllabic type had different origins.

A Wesleyan Methodist missionary, the Rev. James Evans, had been at work among the Ojibway Indians in Canada since 1822 and had published a *Speller and Interpreter* in English and Ojibway in New York. Evans, however, like many missionaries, found the roman alphabet less than ideal to represent the sounds of speech in native tongues and eventually (by 1840) perfected a system of 36 syllables he believed would meet all the needs of the Canadian Indian languages.

> Adapted to the Ojibway and all the kindred dialects, to the Assiniboins, the
> Crees, Mushkegoes, the Black Feet near the mountains . . . indeed with some
> slight alterations . . . [it may be used for] writing every language from the
> Atlantic to the Rocky Mountains.

Evans reported that those in his mission at Norway House could read and write it with ease and fluency. At first he copied out his syllabics by hand on pieces of birchbark. These proved so popular that he realized he must resort to printing. But there was a difficulty, quite apart from the lack of type for his syllabary: the Hudson's Bay Company, which controlled all transport, was not in favor of making the Indians literate and refused to bring in a press.

Being a man of much determination, Evans built his own primitive press on the model of the fur presses used at the trading posts. He also overcame the problem of providing type, for which he used musket balls and the linings of tea chests melted down:

> I have got excellent type, considering the country and materials; they make at
> least a tolerably good impression. The letter or character I cut in finely polished
> oak. I filed out of one side of an inch square iron bar the square body of the
> type; after placing the bar with the notch over the letter, I applied another
> polished bar to the face of the mould, and poured in the lead, after it had been
> repeatedly melted in order to harden it. These required a little dressing on the
> face and filing to the uniform square and length, but they answer well.

With some coarse paper and with ink contrived of soot and oil, in 1841 Evans printed 100 copies of a 16-page booklet containing the syllabary and some Bible texts and hymns translated into Cree. This effort was enough to overcome the skepticism of the church authorities about the value of his syllabary. They had a regular font of the type cut in England, and the Hudson's Bay Company withdrew its opposition. With the new type and a small handpress shipped in via Hudson's Bay, Evans and his successors at the mission continued work under rather easier circumstances.

Evans's work is the most famous of this kind. But where missionaries did not abandon the roman alphabet, there was less need for such enterprise. Nevertheless, there were occasions when manual dexterity in such work could be of use. In 1879, while at the court of Mutesa, Kabaka of the

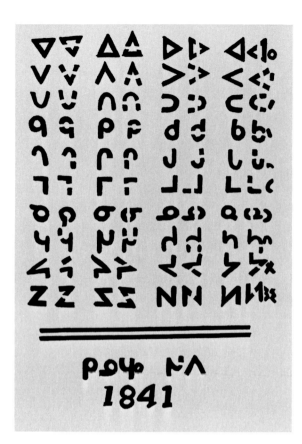

ILLUS. 167. Rev. James Evans, Norway House, Canada. The Cree Syllabary, printed with hand-cut types on his homemade press, 1841.

Baganda, the Anglican missionary Alexander Mackay recorded in his journal how he was printing reading sheets in the Luganda and Swahili languages, using some large wooden types he had cut, and cutting and casting a small font of midsize letters as an intermediate step between the large wooden types and the small-size type supplied with his press. Few of those who undertook missionary work had such skills, however. Even when they had, they resorted to such local production only as a stopgap measure until supplies of superior types became available from Europe.

Chapter 25

MORRIS AND AFTER

THE MANY PRIVATE PRINTERS of the mid-nineteenth century contented themselves with types that were available commercially. Even for commercial printers, with the exception of such isolated instances as William Howard's cutting of the Basle Roman type for the Chiswick Press in 1854, the idea of having one's own proprietary typeface seemed sunk beyond trace. It was not until autumn 1888 that there was to be a revival.

The origins and work of William Morris's Kelmscott Press have already been dealt with in a previous chapter. Morris's earlier experiments with book design in the mid-1860s and again in the early 1870s had been concerned with the book from the point of view of illustration and decoration alone. It did not occur to him, as he later told Sparling, to go beyond what types and other equipment were available. Then, on November 15, 1888, Emery Walker delivered his lecture on printing to the Arts and Crafts Exhibition Society.

> After the lecture, Father was very much excited [wrote May Morris]. The sight of the finely proportioned letters so enormously enlarged, and gaining rather than losing by the process, the enlargement emphasising all the qualities of the type; his feeling, so characteristic of him, that if such a result had been once obtained it could be done again, stirred in him an overwhelming desire to hazard the experiment at least. Talking to Emery Walker on the way home from the lecture, he said to him, "Let's make a new fount of type." And that is the way the Kelmscott Press came into being—the outcome of many talks between the two men which had needed just this impetus, this spur of excitement, to turn the desirable thing into the thing to be done.

It would be idle to regard Morris's impulse to produce his own type as the result of an earlier appeal by Kegan Paul who, writing on "The Production and Life of Books" in 1883, had said that "there could scarcely be a better thing for the artistic future of books than that which might be done by some master of decorative art, like Mr William Morris, and some great firm of typefounders in conjunction, would they design and produce some new types for our choicer printed books," but it is possible that some faint recollection of this suggestion was influential in Morris's decision.

The aims of the Kelmscott Press, so much more than the mere making of a new font of type, have been dealt with in Chapter 11. The design of the press's first typeface, the Golden type, caused Morris a great deal of trouble (Illus. 168). Nothing he had ever done, he told Walker, had caused

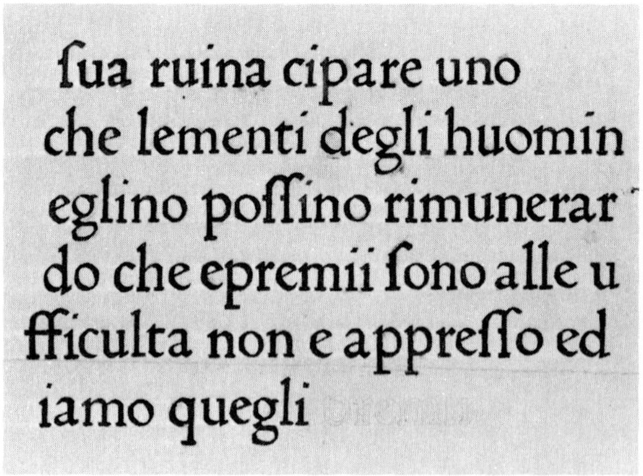

fua ruina cipare uno
che lementi degli huomin
eglino poffino rimunerar
do che epremii fono alle u
fficulta non e appreffo ed
iamo quegli

ILLUS. 168. Drawings for the Kelmscott Golden type. Photograph: Courtesy of the Trustees of The Pierpont Morgan Library.

him so much trouble as the designing of this face. What he wanted, he recorded in his *Note on His Aims in Founding the Kelmscott Press,* was

> letter pure in form; severe, without needless excrescences; solid, without the thickening and thinning of the line, which is the essential fault of the ordinary modern type, and which makes it difficult to read; and not compressed laterally, as all later type has grown to be owing to commercial exigencies. There was only one source from which to take examples of this perfected Roman Type, to wit, the works of the great Venetian printers of the fifteenth century, of whom Nicholas Jenson produced the completest and most Roman characters. . . . This type I studied with much care, getting it photographed to a big scale, and drawing it over many times before I began designing my own letter.

Morris's designs were passed to the free-lance punchcutter Edward Philip Prince in winter 1889–1890. Morris had been introduced to Prince by Emery Walker. It was to be a very successful collaboration between two great craftsmen. Prince's contribution to the type was, however, entirely in the execution of the design; his freedom of action was limited. A trial cutting of a letter in great primer was rejected by Morris as too large, and it was decided to produce the font on an English body (approximately 14 point). During 1890 the punchcutting proceeded rapidly if not always smoothly.

> When the design had passed into the expert and sympathetic hands of Mr. Prince and was cut, the impression—a smoked proof—was again considered, and the letter sometimes recut [May Morris recorded]. My father used to go about with match boxes containing these "smokes" of the types in his pockets, and sometimes, as he sat and talked with us, he would draw out, and thoughtfully eye the small scraps of paper inside. And some of the letters seemed to be diabolically inspired, and would not fall into line for a while.

Surviving smoke proofs and photographic enlargements in the Pierpont Morgan Library and the St. Bride Printing Library show clearly how little latitude was allowed to Prince in his interpretation of the designs. By February 1891 all punches had been cut and the matrices struck; but even at this late stage Morris had second thoughts about the blackness of the "g," and had it recut, before the type was cast at Sir Charles Reed & Son's Fann Street Foundry. The types were cast by machine, which may seem surprising in view of Morris's hostility to machinery as being destructive of the crafts-man's pride and pleasure in his work, but Morris saw no advantage in the older methods of using handmolds. "There wasn't much fun in it for the poor devils who jogged and bumped the mould about," he observed.

To judge the Golden type dispassionately is not easy. Comparison with its model, Jenson's Venetian roman, is difficult as Morris's face was by no means a slavish copy. Emery Walker's comment that it was "less elegant" than the original is a considerable understatement. By his deliberate thickening of the strokes and reduction of the size of the counters (allied to Kelmscott presswork), Morris produced a type far blacker and closer to a *fere-humanistica* than Jenson's pure letter. This worried Morris not a whit; in February 1891 Morris told F. S. Ellis that Walter Crane had seen the type and thought it gothic-looking compared with Jenson's: "This is a fact, and a cheerful one to me." Some contemporaries were full of admiration: Charles Ricketts considered the capitals an improvement on the Italian originals, and the face was paid the rather doubtful compliment of being imitated commercially in several versions in the United States. The first imitation was cut under the direction of Joseph W. Phinney of the Dickinson Type Foundry in Boston in 1895. Phinney applied unsuccessfully to Morris for permission to use his design, but went ahead nevertheless producing the Jenson Old Style type in 14 sizes. It was not a slavish imitation, although far closer to Morris than to the original Jenson types, and achieved rapid popularity—but not with all critics. The New Zealand typographer, R. Coupland Harding, who contributed a regular column to *The Inland Printer,* wrote:

> Eccentricity and quaintness which are quite tolerable, or even admirable, in a
> few display lines or a brief circular, may be quite out of place in a
> body-font. . . . It is here that —with all respect to their artistic taste—I venture
> to join issue with such authorities as Mr Walter Crane and Mr William
> Morris. . . . I confess that I do not like the [Jenson] face at all. This, however, is
> a matter of taste, but I do not think there can be much question as to the
> distressing effect a page or two of this letter would have on the eyes of a
> reader.

Harding was just revealing that he was out of touch with contemporary taste; Jenson was immediately successful and other designs based on the Golden type soon appeared from Barnhart Bros. & Spindler and the Crescent Type Foundry in Chicago, and the Inland Typefoundry, St. Louis. The Dickinson Type Foundry's version retained an important place in the American Type Founders Specimen Books for many years.

Modern opinion would agree with Bernard Newdigate, when he commented in *The Art of the Book* (1914), that the face "lacks the suppleness and grace of the Italian types generally." Despite its deficiencies when compared with Jenson's font, however, the Golden type is not without virtues; its lowercase letters compose excellently together, and some, such as the "h," are if anything an improvement on their originals. Tastes change; the capitals praised by Ricketts have been abused by many other writers, particularly for the treatment of the serifs ("brickbat," "bludgeony," "singularly graceless"). Compared with later interpretations, they certainly do not sit well together, and it is hard now to see why so discerning a critic as Ricketts should have admired them.

Morris had scarcely received his Golden type from the Fann Street Foundry, before he was at work in designing a blackletter face with which to print his Chaucer. The work went very much more easily than had been the case with the Golden type. As May Morris wrote:

> [It] was done with no conscious effort, and with little reference to the models
> by which he was inspired. . . . Emery Walker's vivid remembrance is that with
> practised hand and head full of proportions felt instinctively, he drew the
> alphabet straight away—more or less "out of his head."

Once more the cutting of the punches was entrusted to Prince, who had finished cutting the lowercase by the beginning of August 1891. At the end of the year, the complete font had been cut and cast by Sir Charles Reed & Son on a great primer body.

The type was designed with the avowed intention of redeeming "the Gothic character from the charge of unreadableness which is commonly brought against it." Although inspired by Morris's admiration for the types of Peter Schoeffer, of Gunther Zainer, and of Anton Koberger, the Troy type (as it came to be known) was very far indeed from its fifteenth-century models, much further than was his departure from Jenson in the Golden type. But the nature of gothic is such that variation of this sort can succeed well, and the type was a splendid success. The lowercase type, although not conforming to the characteristics of any group of blackletter types, avoids the "unreadable" nature of the compressed and angular northern European forms by resorting to the rounder, looser-fitting, and less-pointed style of the Italian and Spanish *rotunda* types. As in the Golden type, the capitals are very much less harmonious, some closely resembling Roman inscriptional letters and others being based fairly closely on those used by Koberger about 1480. Although designed with Chaucer in mind, a trial setting in January 1892 persuaded Morris that a great primer font would be too large for a long work, and the type was therefore first used in *The Recuyell of the Historyes of Troye* published in October 1892. For the Chaucer itself, Prince was commissioned to cut the same face on a pica body, and comparison of the Chaucer type with the great primer Troy shows how well Prince cut the smaller version: In the various books printed in both fonts there is a perfect harmony between the two.

Like the Golden type, Morris's blackletter was imitated by ATF with their "Satanick" face, which unlike Jenson Old Style could not claim to be derived from any other source. They advertised it to accompany Jenson Old Style (and the mannered "Jenson Italic" that accompanied it, which of course owed nothing to Morris) and also marketed ornamented initials and decorations derived directly from Kelmscott designs.

No sooner had Prince completed the cutting of the Chaucer type, in June 1892, than Morris informed him that a fourth type was projected, and that sketches would be available "in about three months time." This face was to have been based on the *fere-humanistica* type used by Sweynheym and Pannartz, the first printers in Italy, in Subiaco in 1464. Sydney Cockerell later recollected that the design was never cut, because Morris was not satisfied with his designs. However, a specimen in the Pierpont Morgan Library shows there was a trial cutting of the entire lowercase to the same size as the Troy type (Illus. 169). It was an interesting experiment; the specimen shows clearly that Morris was not striving for a facsimile of the Subiaco design but, besides reducing the descenders, he included several letters (for example "g" and "y") that derived from forms originally considered, but rejected, for the Troy design. Although in some ways it is a pity that Morris did not follow up this experiment, one cannot help feeling glad that the Subiaco design was still free for the Ashendene Press to use a few years later.

Prince also cut the typefaces for Charles Ricketts's Vale Press. The first, the Vale type, was cut in 13 point in 1896, after brush-drawn designs by Ricketts. Although avowedly inspired by William Morris's work, Ricketts was not completely happy with it. "I would define the page of a fine Kelmscott book as full of wine, an Italian book as full of light," he wrote in his strange little *Defence of the Revival of Printing* (1899). The design of the Vale books was very much more Italianate than that of Kelmscott, and his type was obviously intended to be "full of light," as it was designed with a body "slightly larger, more open, and the angle of the serifs different again" from either Morris's or Jenson's types. Nevertheless, the font as cut, based very distantly on the faces of Jenson and of Wendelin of Speyer, was if anything blacker and further from the spirit of the renaissance than the Golden type had been. It had some very affected sorts in the lowercase ("b," "g," "u") and an

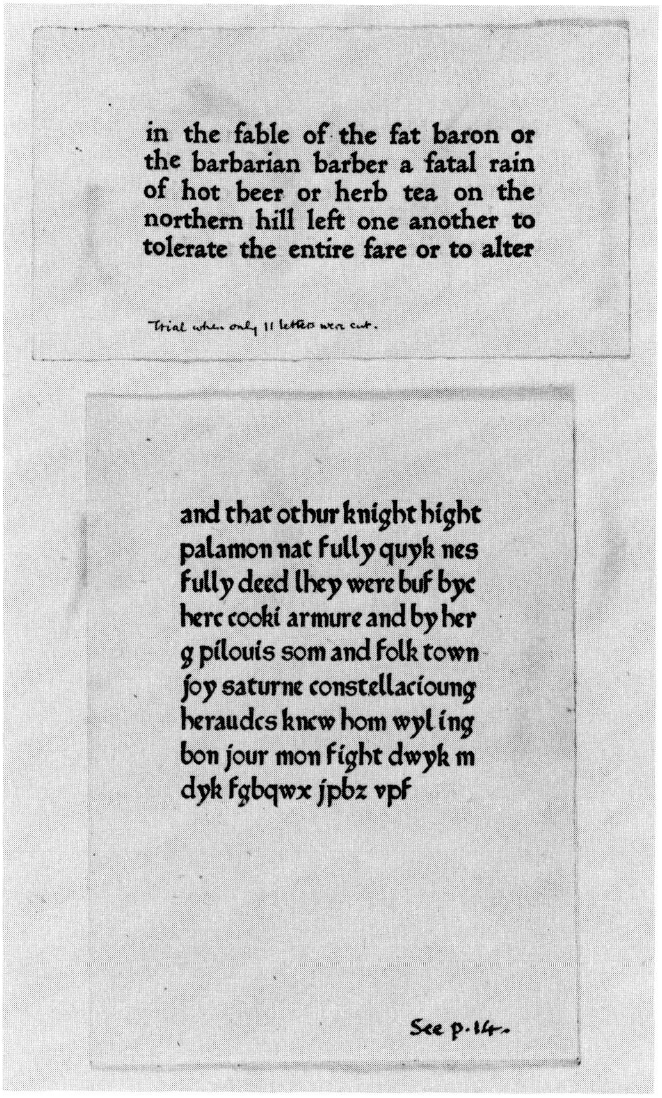

in the fable of the fat baron or
the barbarian barber a fatal rain
of hot beer or herb tea on the
northern hill left one another to
tolerate the entire fare or to alter

Trial when only 11 letters were cut.

and that othur knight hight
palamon nat fully quyk nes
fully deed they were but bye
here cooki armure and by her
g pilouis som and folk town
joy saturne constellacioung
heraudes knew hom wyl ing
bon jour mon fight dwyk m
dyk fgbqwx jpbz vpf

See p. 14.

ILLUS. 169. *Top:* Trials for the Kelmscott Golden type and (*bottom*) for the never used Subiaco type. Photograph: Courtesy of the Trustees of The Pierpont Morgan Library.

unpleasantly obtrusive set of capitals; but books printed in the type, or in the closely related Avon type, cut in 11 point by Prince in 1902, are by no means unpleasant to read (Illus. 170). The same can scarcely be said for the King's Fount, cut by Prince to Ricketts's design for use in *The Kingis Quair* in 1903. Ricketts himself was very pleased with it, thinking it looked "absolutely magnificent in the Latin. It is one of the three founts I like best," but he later admitted that it was "viewed by all with execration." And indeed this type, with its very black and fussy mixture of debased roman and pseudo-uncial, is horrid—one of the worst faces ever designed for private press use. Practically all one can admire about it is the skill of Prince's punchcutting!

Ricketts had generously made the Vale type available to Lucien Pissarro, to use in the books he was printing at his Eragny Press. But in 1901 or 1902, Ricketts warned him of his intention to close the press and destroy his types. So, long before this happened, Pissarro set to work on designing his own typeface. The type, named the Brook type after his home at Stamford Brook, might never have come into being; the chronically poor Pissarro could not afford to have Prince cut the punches until his father, Camille Pissarro, came to his aid. On August 15, 1902, Camille wrote to tell him "You can get your alphabet made. I have swung a little deal which will bring me exactly the necessary money,

In 1894 "Hero and Leander" was printed in a smaller sized Pica than the "Daphnis and Chloe": it is the first Vale book with paper bearing as water mark a V P interlaced with a leaf of wild thyme. An interlaced V P with a rose and initials figures in this edition as an imprint, with a motto since discarded, "The Rose reborn between the leaves," forgotten, shut away in a book. The small leaf in outline is the first paragraph mark used in the Vale press. I engraved it on the wood like some used subsequently and it was cast as type. "The Hero and Leander" is well printed and in margin and proportion of page quite what I would do now. Six copies exist bound as originally intended in blind tooling and gold.

This leads me to that most important question, the proportion of the margins between themselves. Like the writer of the "Contemporary Review," I will quote from William Morris' note on the Kelmscott books.

22

THE position of the printed matter on the page should always leave the inner margin the narrowest, the top "somewhat wider, the outside (fore-"edge) wider still, and the bottom wid-"est of all.... A friend, the librarian "of one of our most important private "libraries, tells me that after careful test-"ing he has come to the conclusion that "the mediæval rule was to make a dif-"ference of 20 per cent...."

From the essentials of this rule I have never departed in the Vale books, though the writer of the "Contemporary" seems to be otherwise informed. The rough and ready rule of thumb that the difference should be 20 per cent. between the margins, should be valuable to those once famous printers north of the Tweed, or in any other provincial towns besides Edinburgh, such as Boston, U.S.A. The mediæval measurement can be applied invariably to prose,

23

ILLUS. 170. Vale Press, London. *A Defence of the Rivival of Printing,* 1899. Double spread showing the Vale type.

two thousand five hundred francs (£100)." The work was put in hand at once. Prince cut the punches, and the type was cast by P. M. Shanks & Co.; its first showing was in T. Sturge Moore's *Brief Account of the Origin of the Eragny Press* in 1903. The type was modeled fairly closely on the Vale type, although with shorter ascenders and descenders as it was cast on a 12-point body. A set of capitals was also cut in 9 point. Thomas Balston, in his study of *The Cambridge University Press Collection of Private Press Types* (1951), considered that the changes Pissarro made in the design were "mostly unimportant, and not very satisfactory," drawing attention to the weak "g," "q," and "K" in particular. Pissarro was not, essentially, a printer; his concern was to produce a typeface whose color would harmonize with that of his wood engravings, and in this he succeeded admirably. Stanley Morison's verdict that the type was "sophisticated, rather than eccentric" was a generous one, but most authorities would concur, as far as Pissarro's own use of the type was concerned. There was to be no other: The Brook type, like the Vale Press fonts, found a watery grave; the punches and matrices and types (other than a few specimen sorts, preserved at Cambridge University Press) were cast into the English Channel by Esther Pissarro in summer 1947, 33 years after the last Eragny Press book had appeared.

These typefaces were by no means the only designs for which E. P. Prince cut the punches in the halcyon years at the turn of the century. Nor were they the most important. In 1900, at age 54, he was at the peak of his powers when he cut the most famous of all private press typefaces, the Doves Press roman.

Just as Emery Walker's 1888 lecture had provided Morris with the urge to design his own typeface, so in 1899 Cobden-Sanderson, inspired by Sydney Cockerell's remark that it was strange that nobody had yet had the good sense to reproduce Jenson's typeface, told Cockerell that he would do so. Although he admired Morris's work at the Kelmscott Press, he did not do so blindly. Some years later, when Cockerell told him plainly that "had there been no Kelmscott Press, there would have been no Doves Press," Cobden-Sanderson was outraged.

> Candidly I do not think that William Morris himself is a great printer. . . . [He] came to printing with a mind set on decoration, and with a mind overscored with tapestry and woven effects, all of which he reproduced where they are not wanted, on the pages of his books. And many of his effects, as I told him at the time, are "typographical impertinences" and utterly destructive of the page as an expression of the author's thought.

In his reply, one can discern behind the shrewd criticism Cobden-Sanderson's pain and anger at Cockerell's comment, arising from his own extraordinary identification of the Doves Press and its types with himself. The story of Cobden-Sanderson's remarkably successful policy of belittling the role of Emery Walker (his partner in the Doves Press), is not a pretty one. In Cobden-Sanderson's opinion:

> All that E. W. did was at my request to photograph that design from a book in my possession, and from that design, so photographed, to draw by the hand of his employee, and under my final directive (for every letter was brought over to me for final selection) the letters of the Doves Press alphabet, and for that alphabet, so drawn, I paid to E. W. what he asked, £6, and I hold the receipt for the same made out to me—not the Press.

No doubt this was true enough as far as it went, but either through ignorance or design, Cobden-Sanderson omitted some important points. The selection of the original pages for enlargement was not only from Jenson's edition of Pliny (which Walker had bought at the sale of Morris's library for Cobden-Sanderson), but also from the Rubeus edition of Aretino's *Historia Florentina*, which had served as the model for Morris's work on the Golden Type. A considerable portion of the Doves font was derived from this source, not the Pliny. Nor did Cobden-Sanderson appreciate the problems in deciding on the true outlines of the original letters to be copied, when these were available only as images corrupted by heavy inking and presswork. As Walker put it, "the most successful of the founts used by the so-called 'private presses' are not exact copies 'stolen' from antiquity, but modifications adapted to modern usage."

The redrawing, which was undertaken by Walker's employee, Percy Tiffin, and only then studied and approved by Cobden-Sanderson, was then cut by Prince. Cast on a two-line brevier body by Millar & Richard, the result was a typeface that "for the first time brought out the full beauty of the Jenson letter," as A. W. Pollard put it.

It was not a type in which Walker had mechanically reproduced Jenson's original design, whatever his partner believed. Among them, Walker, Tiffin, and Prince had removed the accidental irregularities resulting from imperfect cutting, casting, and printing in the original. The design was a typeface perhaps too austere and perfect in its regularity. The Doves type is magnificent, with near perfect proportions for a Venetian letter, but it is cold and formal for extensive reading. The most successful of the Doves books are those in which the monotony is relieved by the extensive use of color, as in the *Pervigilium Veneris* (1911), or by the splendid calligraphic initials of Edward Johnston.

In 1911, Cobden-Sanderson had decided to bequeath the type "to the Bed of the River

Thames . . . untouched of other use and all else." Between 1913 and 1917, the punches and matrices and types were destroyed in this way, according to the story given in Cobden-Sanderson's *Journals* as accepted by Emery Walker, Sydney Cockerell, and others. There is, however, a fascinating alternative story, told by one of Cobden-Sanderson's assistants at the Doves Bindery, that when it came to the point, Cobden-Sanderson could not bear to part with the type and instead buried it in the garden of the Doves buildings at Hammersmith.

Emery Walker had been deprived of his use of the Doves types by Cobden-Sanderson long before they were destroyed, and he never had the satisfaction of working with them. But it must have been some consolation to him to have another chance to work with the Jenson model, and in 1911 he supervised Prince's cutting of yet another version for Count Kessler's Cranach-Presse in Weimar.

Although the Doves and Cranach-Presse types were similar, they were not identical. Ten years' contemplation of the Doves type against the original Venetian designs encouraged Walker to restore to the new face a number of features eliminated from the Doves design. Such changes as the wider "h," the slight lip on the crossbar of the "e," the horizontal ear to the "g," and the thickened terminal of the "y" were all (to my mind) improvements, as were minute alterations in some of the capitals; notably the thinner bar in the "H," which appears overweight in the Doves form. The punches seem to have been completed by Prince toward the end of 1911, and the type was subsequently cast by Shanks. As shown in the Cranach *Eclogues,* it appears a slightly less chilling letter than the Doves roman, although its superiority is not generally recognized.

Already in 1911 Kessler and Walker were discussing the problem of finding a suitable italic face to accompany the roman. Originally they intended to use one of Aldus's italics, but on Walker's advice they changed to a later chancery design by the writing master G. A. Tagliente. Once more Percy Tiffin, under Walker's direction, prepared a clean set of drawings from photographic enlargements for E. P. Prince to use as his model. It was by no means a success: Neither Tiffin nor Prince had appreciated the subtlety of Tagliente's design. As soon as Kessler saw the smoke proofs he saw the type was wrong, that it needed "vivifying, brisking up," as he put it. In the calligrapher Edward Johnston, he thought he knew the man to do it.

In his *Italic Quartet* (privately published, Cambridge University Press, 1966), John Dreyfus has given a full and amusing account of the efforts of Kessler, Walker, Johnston, and Prince in the making of the Cranach italic. It was a splendid example of too many cooks, and when the type was eventually cut and shipped to Kessler in Weimar in December 1913, it was to remain unused for over 10 years; and then it was used only briefly in the prospectus for and the colophon of *The Eclogues of Virgil* (1926). By that time Kessler had come to the conclusion that a new series of small roman capitals was needed for the italic font. Prince was now dead, but another agonizing collaboration was under way. As Johnston wrote to George Friend (who had learned punchcutting from Prince and had been engaged to cut the new punches):

> We are really engaged on an *extraordinarily difficult experiment*. The problem is
> to make an Upper Case Type now to a Lower Case Type made some seventeen
> or eighteen years ago—that is difficult enough in itself, but we have a greater
> difficulty in our modern (at present unavoidable) division and separation of
> labour,
>> 1st *The Designer* (myself) guessing at an Ideal
>> 2nd *The Punch Cutter* (yourself) giving it material shape
>> 3rd *The Type Founder* (Shanks) reproducing them in quantity
>> 4th *The Printer* (Cranach Press) applying the types

Not to mention Assistants, Photographers, etc. We are widely scattered between
London and Weimar, and largely ignorant of each other's work and views.

The new capitals were however cut, but they were used in only one book, Rilke's *Duineser
Elegien* (1931), before Kessler had to abandon his press when the Nazis came to power.

The other typefaces Johnson designed for Kessler were very much more successful. From 1911
or 1912 onward, Johnston was at work on these blackletter faces, said to be based upon the type used
by Fust and Schoeffer in the *Mainz Psalter* of 1457. In fact they bear little resemblance to this, but in
the smaller sizes at least seem to be far closer to Schoeffer's *fere-humanistica* type of 1471. The
punches were cut by Prince in 1913, but the type was not cast before the outbreak of World War I.
When Kessler returned to work on his *Hamlet* (for which the types had been designed), he found
some of the punches rusty or lost, and much of the punchcutting had to be done over again by
Friend. Three sizes were cut, 18 point, 12 point and 10 point, with considerable variation between the
design of individual sorts in the three sizes. Because the overall effect of the type is good in the one
very handsome book in which it was used, the oddities and irregularities of the design have not
received much attention. Critics have drawn attention to the height and obtrusiveness of some of the
capitals, notably the "P," "N," "V" and "W," and to the slight willfulness of the second "H," with its
truncated right stem. The variations in the larger lowercase sorts have not attracted adverse comment, but some sorts are very wide, particularly "h," "v," and the tied sorts "ch" and "th," while
letters like "m," "r," and "w" are compressed so that certain words appear much too narrow
compared with others. But perhaps such variations are unimportant in a blackletter face, and in the
wide 10-point version, the sorts match one another well. They married well together and, as shown
in the *Hamlet,* appeared handsome and readable. The punches and matrices are now in the Cambridge University Press collection.

At about the same time that E. P. Prince was cutting the punches for the Doves roman, he was
commissioned by C. R. Ashbee to cut a face for the Essex House Press, which had taken over the
presses and personnel (but not the types) of the Kelmscott Press in 1898. The first type, the
Endeavour, was cut on a pica body in 1901. Designed by Ashbee himself, the cutting was up to
Prince's usual standard, but the design was without any doubt the worst proprietary type of any cut
for any major private press. Rightly dismissed by Stanley Morison as an "inglorious achievement"
and by Updike as "eccentric, obscure, and dazzling," it added to the woolliness of the Golden or
Vale types a clumsy serif treatment and a willfully abnormal design in many letters. Nor when
Prince recut the design in great primer size, the Prayer Book type, did the design appear any better.
The Essex House typefaces have at best a certain period charm, but they are the least readable one
will encounter.

In 1903, as Sir Sydney Cockerell has recorded, he and St. John Hornby were discussing the
latter's Ashendene Press, which used Caslon and Fell types.

> At the moment of parting I suddenly exclaimed,
> "Why don't you have, like Morris, a special type of your own?"
> "I can't afford such a luxury."
> "It would cost you £100" I hazarded.
> "If that is all" he replied "let us set about it at once."
> Morris had died in 1896. In 1892 he had bought a copy of Augustine's *De
> Civitate Dei* printed in 1467 by Sweynheym and Pannartz in the monastery of
> Subiaco, near Rome. The type, never used elsewhere, is a somewhat compressed
> one, very elegant, neither roman nor gothic. Morris at once decided to have a
> new type based on this model, but it went no further. Recalling this

experiment, I sought out a photograph of Morris's designs. After consultation
with Emery Walker and Robert Proctor, Hornby came to the conclusion that
he could not do better than to take up what Morris had abandoned; so he
instructed the firm of Walker & Cockerell to go ahead. Well, within a year, the
"Subiaco" type was designed and cut. Hornby's bill for it was exactly £100.

This typeface, which was cast on a great primer body by Millar & Richard, is further evidence
of Prince's skill as a punchcutter. The handsome Subiaco design was much closer to Sweynheym and
Pannartz's original face than Morris's experimental version had been. As a result of the elimination
of the long "s" and most of the tied sorts used in the original (and Hornby's more generous spacing
between words), it had a charming open effect and was used in all Ashendene books for the next 23
years. Then, in 1925, Hornby had a new font of type prepared. Once more designed by Emery
Walker, it was an interpretation of another *fere-humanistica* face that was used by Holle in his edition
of Ptolemy's *Cosmographia,* published at Ulm in 1482. They searched for a punchcutter but found
none. E. P. Prince had died in 1923, and there was no other punchcutter in England they could
commission and so they turned to mechanical punchcutting. The type was cast by R. P. Bannerman
and Sons, a firm which a few years later cast Egyptian hieroglyphic type for Dr. Alan H. Gardiner—
an example of a private face for scholarly purposes. The original Ptolemy type had some weak
designs with very uneven set, and it is difficult to understand why Walker and Hornby thought the
face worth reviving; they were neither of them addicted to the quaint. In the recut version, the
capital letters were extensively remodeled, but of the lowercase sorts, apart from being better spaced,
only the "y" was much changed. The overall effect was much grayer than the earlier Subiaco face,
but produced an attractive page particularly in smaller books from the Ashendene Press.

Several more types of considerable interest were cut by Prince for private use, as well as others
that were reserved for the use of individual firms inspired by the Kelmscott-Doves example, such as
the Montallegro type for D. B. Updike's Merrymount Press, or the Riccardi type for the Medici
Society. Of the private faces, by far the most interesting was the Greek font known as the Otter type,
which Prince cut for Robert Proctor in 1903. Proctor was not the dilettante owner of a press with a
taste for Greek, as Hibbert had been 80 years earlier; he was not the owner of a private press at all. A
brilliant incunabulist at the British Museum, he was also a close friend and admirer of William
Morris, having purchased Kelmscott work from the start. Morris's influence, and his own studies of
early printing in Greek, inspired him to attempt an improvement in Greek types. The model he
chose was that used in the New Testament of the Complutensian Polyglot produced for Cardinal
Ximenes in 1514, a face that Proctor regarded as "undoubtedly the finest Greek fount ever cut, and
the only one of which it can be affirmed with certainty that it is based on the writing of a particular
manuscript" (a tenth-century manuscript that had been sent by the Pope to Cardinal Ximenes to help
him in the preparation of his text, and which, it is said, was used in the eighteenth century to make
rockets). Prince's recutting of the lowercase was a skillful reproduction of the Complutensian forms;
for the capitals there were no models from which to work and Proctor supplied him with fresh
designs that match the original lowercase forms admirably. The type was cast by Millar & Richard
early in 1903.

After much deliberation, Proctor asked C. T. Jacobi of the Chiswick Press to be his printer
(much as the Ballantyne Press were the printers of the Vale Press books), and on May 12, 1903, a
four-page specimen was produced. The first work, an edition of Aeschylus, was in proof when
Proctor went on a climbing holiday in the Alps from which he never returned. The Aeschylus was
seen through the press by F. G. Kenyon and was published in 1904. In 1909 an edition of the *Odyssey*
was also printed in the type (Illus. 171). In his *Greek Printing Types* (1927), Victor Scholderer

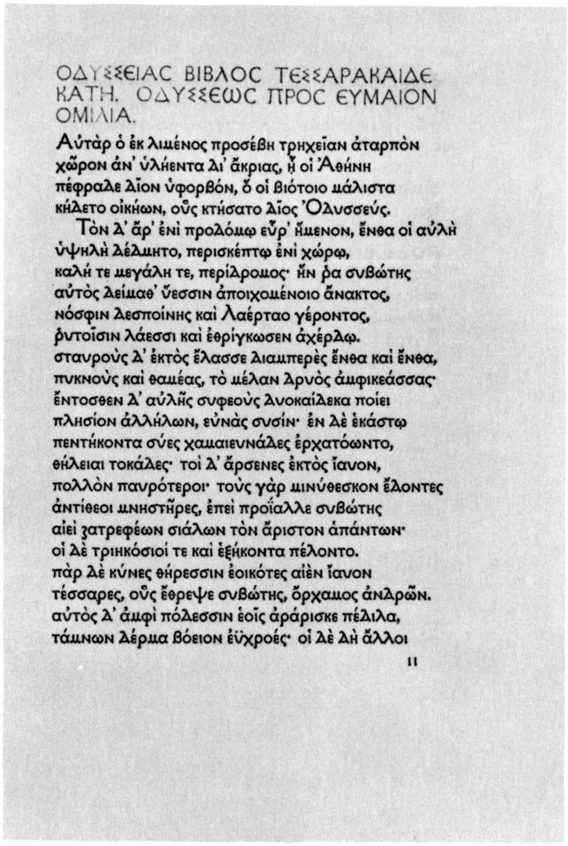

ΟΔΥΣΣΕΙΑΣ ΒΙΒΛΟΣ ΤΕΣΣΑΡΑΚΑΙΔΕ
ΚΑΤΗ. ΟΔΥΣΣΕΩC ΠΡΟC ΕΥΜΑΙΟΝ
ΟΜΙΛΙΑ.

Αὐτὰρ ὁ ἐκ λιμένος προσέβη τρηχεῖαν ἀταρπὸν
χῶρον ἀν᾿ ὑλήεντα Δι᾿ ἄκριας, ᾗ οἱ Ἀθήνη
πέφραδε Δῖον ὑφορβόν, ὅ οἱ βιότοιο μάλιστα
κήδετο οἰκήων, οὓς κτήσατο Δῖος Ὀδυσσεύς.
    Τὸν Δ᾿ ἄρ᾿ ἐνὶ προδόμῳ εὗρ᾿ ἥμενον, ἔνθα οἱ αὐλὴ
ὑψηλὴ Δέδμητο, περισκέπτῳ ἐνὶ χώρῳ,
καλή τε μεγάλη τε, περίδρομος· ἥν ῥα συβώτης
αὐτὸς Δείμαθ᾿ ὕεσσιν ἀποιχομένοιο ἄνακτος,
νόσφιν Δεσποίνης καὶ Λαέρταο γέροντος,
ῥυτοῖσιν λάεσσι καὶ ἐθρίγκωσεν ἀχέρδῳ.
σταυροὺς Δ᾿ ἐκτὸς ἔλασσε Διαμπερὲς ἔνθα καὶ ἔνθα,
πυκνοὺς καὶ θαμέας, τὸ μέλαν Δρυὸς ἀμφικεάσσας·
ἔντοσθεν Δ᾿ αὐλῆς συφεοὺς Δυοκαίδεκα ποίει
πλησίον ἀλλήλων, εὐνὰς συσίν· ἐν Δὲ ἑκάστῳ
πεντήκοντα σύες χαμαιευνάδες ἐρχατόωντο,
θήλειαι τοκάδες· τοὶ Δ᾿ ἄρσενες ἐκτὸς ἴαυον,
πολλὸν παυρότεροι· τοὺς γὰρ μινύθεσκον ἔδοντες
ἀντίθεοι μνηστῆρες, ἐπεὶ προΐαλλε συβώτης
αἰεὶ ζατρεφέων σιάλων τὸν ἄριστον ἁπάντων·
οἱ Δὲ τριηκόσιοί τε καὶ ἑξήκοντα πέλοντο.
πὰρ Δὲ κύνες θήρεσσιν ἐοικότες αἰὲν ἴαυον
τέσσαρες, οὓς ἔθρεψε συβώτης, ὄρχαμος ἀνδρῶν.
αὐτὸς Δ᾿ ἀμφὶ πόδεσσιν ἑοῖς ἀράρισκε πέδιλα,
τάμνων Δέρμα βόειον ἐΰχροές· οἱ Δὲ Δὴ ἄλλοι

11

ILLUS. 171. Robert Proctor's Otter type, based on the Complutensian Polyglot face, as used in *The Odyssey*, 1909.

described the type as "the finest Greek face ever cut," regretting that "it will not bear reduction to a commercial size." In the size available, Scholderer considered it "suitable only for fine printing in the archaistic tradition." It is to be regretted that the type (now in the possession of Oxford University Press) has not been used more extensively.

The example of William Morris, of Cobden-Sanderson, and above all of Edward Johnston was even more considerable on the Continent than in England. In addition to the specifically English contribution to the Cranach-Presse, an English face was produced for the Zilverdistel of Dr. J. F. van Royen in The Hague. In 1914, Prince cut the punches for a face designed by Lucien Pissarro on the basis of the Carolingian minuscule. This type, the Distel, was a deliberately archaistic font, very close to manuscript hands. As used by van Royen, who thought highly of it and "wrote some lyrical passages" in its praise, it could look very fine. But by van Krimpen it was regarded as "an unhappy experiment." The other proprietary typeface of the Zilverdistel, the Zilver type, was cut in 1915 to designs by S. H. de Roos and cast by the Amsterdam Typefoundry. A font that, like the Doves and Cranach romans, was based on Jenson's designs, Zilver was (particularly in the capitals) less true to its model than were the Doves and Cranach romans. The face is a very readable one, with only the serif treatment on some of the capitals standing out at all unpleasantly. Of this face, van Krimpen was less disapproving: "undoubtedly one of the best modern interpretations [of the Venetian letter]. If the detail had been simpler, the Zilver type would be in many respects a perfect letter." These two types are now preserved, like the Zilverdistel's other equipment, in the Museum Meermanno-West-reenianum in The Hague.

In the United States the shadow of Kelmscott also lay heavy. Some private printers, like George Booth at the Cranbrook Press in Detroit or Lewis Buddy at his Kirgate Press in Canton, Pennsylvania, had contented themselves with various commercially available imitations of Morris's faces.

Others with more taste settled for Caslon Old Face. One private printer who showed more initiative was Ralph Fletcher Seymour. The earliest books from his Alderbrink Press in Chicago were written by hand and reproduced by line-block, a thoroughly unsatisfactory method, as anyone who has tried it knows; the books lose the crispness of the manuscript without gaining the satisfying bite of type into the paper. Seymour was dissatisfied with the results, and after a couple of experiments with Caslon had his own special face cut in 1902. The design was by Seymour himself, with considerable advice and help from F. W. Goudy; Robert Wiebking cut matrices for it, and it was cast by Barnhart Bros. & Spindler. The Alderbrink type had considerable merit; a Venetian roman, owing (one would suppose) a good deal to the Doves type, the design of some of the individual letters—the kernless "f," the high-waisted "k"—is not altogether happy, although in other sorts, such as the "y," there is a distinct improvement on the Doves design. The type had excellent composing qualities, and set in mass it reads agreeably.

Much better known than the Alderbrink type was the typeface used by Goudy at the Village Press that, as has already been said in Chapter 13, was intended originally as an advertising face. Will Ransom has recorded that the type was based loosely on fifteenth-century Venetian designs, and that Robert Wiebking was "frankly shocked at some of the 'liberties' Goudy had taken with certain letters." Looking at the Village type through prejudiced English eyes, I can see rather little to recommend it. It is a very wide letter, with some of the sorts, the "e," the "r," and the "y," striking the eye particularly unpleasantly, by comparison, say, with the Doves, Cranach, or Zilver faces, or even the Alderbrink type. Its difference, its eccentricity, was probably useful in its time, just as Morris's distortion of the Jenson roman was in the end justified by the cutting of the Doves type. With Goudy's many later types (he designed over a hundred) we are not here concerned, attractive though many of them are. In their time they received good use from such presses as Grabhorn, and several of his designs are still popular, particularly with amateur printers in the United States. Most of us would however agree with James M. Wells's opinion that the majority of them are "badly dated. Even his book faces often suffer from mannerisms and eccentricity which call attention to the type rather than the text."

The most famous of all American private press types was that of Dard Hunter. Unlike the designs of Ralph Fletcher Seymour or Fred Goudy, which were translated into type through the use of matrix-cutting machines, or the English proprietary designs, which had depended on E. P. Prince's superlative punchcutting skills, the designs of Hunter were done the hard way. As described in Chapter 27, Hunter, determined to produce his face by his own labor, had gone back to Moxon's *Mechanick Exercises* for instruction in building all the tools and equipment he would need to produce type by the methods used before the nineteenth century.

One might well think that a typeface produced in this way, with the punchcutting done over several years in the time he could take from building his papermill at Marlborough-on-Hudson, would be best passed over in silence. As Hunter wrote in *My Life with Paper,* he did not use prepared drawings. Instead, he cut his letters and ornaments directly into the punches without having made any preliminary outlines, merely having fifteenth- and sixteenth-century book pages before him while he worked.

The results were amazingly good. One cannot, of course, judge the font, which was cut in 18 point, by the same standards as the Doves or Cranach romans, or the revived designs intended for general commercial use. Apart from the first two books for the Chicago Society of Etchers, Hunter's type was used only in his own books. It was not a close copy of Jenson's roman, but owed more to some other Venetian printers such as Ratdolt or Miscomini, although clearly the design was eclectic. The usual features of a Venetian roman, with the heavy capitals and somewhat obtrusive serif treatment, are present. The design of many individual sorts can be faulted, and I find the rather

Goudy-like shortness of the descenders a weakness. The relatively slight variation of stress, rounded treatment, and hollowed serifs in some ways anticipate the Old Style designed by Ernst Schneidler cut in the 1930s by the Bauersche Giesserei. Perhaps because of its rounded form, the type is very readable, and the sorts compose well together. As printed—and how magnificently they were printed—in the big Mountain House Press folios, the types have a sparkle and charm that disarms criticism.

These types were used for several of the books on papermaking that Hunter produced at his private press. In the 1930s, he turned to other commercially cast types. But for the last book from his press, *Papermaking by Hand in America* (1950), he used another design produced by his son Dard Hunter, Jr.

This had been cut directly in the punches without any preliminary "designing" (like his father's typeface) in 1938–1940, while Dard, Jr. was working with Otto Egge at Cleveland School of Art. Its first showing was in a specimen printed on the handpress in the Paper Museum at the Massachusetts Institute of Technology in 1940; its second, in a first printing of Robert Frost's *A Considerable Speck* for the Colonial Society in Boston. For both these, the type was cast in the handmold in the traditional way, but for the much larger quantities needed for *Papermaking by Hand in America,* they resorted to mechanical casters. Dard, Jr.'s, is another distinctive and distinguished face, somewhat idiosyncratic but looking well in mass. It is a pity it was so little used.

Chapter 26

———

AFTER 1918

WRITING IN *Modern Book Production* in 1927, Bernard Newdigate recalled that in the special issue of *The Studio* devoted to *The Art of the Book,* which he had edited in 1914, he had "felt it necessary to be a little apologetic for making mention of a machine-set type, however excellent, in an article about fine printing." Most of the typefaces he had discussed in 1914 had been proprietary typefaces for handsetting at private presses or commercial printing houses that emulated the work of the private presses. But in 1927, although he was writing at the height of the twenties' boom in fine printing, Newdigate did not show a single new typeface cut for an English private press.

To be sure, possession of one's own individual reinterpretation of Jenson's roman, in which to print one's own version of *Sonnets from the Portuguese* or the *Rubaiyat,* no longer had the charm for the private printer that it had possessed at the beginning of the century. Some of the reasons for this change in fashion have already been considered in earlier chapters; without any doubt at all the most important reason of all was the existence of the Monotype Corporation's intensive program of commercial revivals of good typefaces. With these available cheaply and in many different sizes, why go to the expense and trouble of having a special face cut that could well be inferior to the Monotype revivals (or the excellent types becoming available from other founders) and would certainly be cut only in a very small range of sizes? Few of the private presses established in the interwar period went so far as to have their own type designs cut, and not one of them used their proprietary face alone, but instead resorted to the Monotype or founder's faces as well. The old Cobden-Sandersonian idea that a press's power or virtue was identifiable with exclusive use of a particular typeface was gone, and only such an old-fashioned press as St. John Hornby's Ashendene Press, with its Ptolemy face cast in 1925, would follow the old pattern.

Whether the Monotype program was a carefully planned policy, as Stanley Morison later claimed, or more accidental in its development (as others have suggested), it was not limited to the revival of good faces of the past. Some of the good contemporary designs from continental founders were also made available on Monotype, and Eric Gill's Perpetua type, cut between 1925 and 1929 and certainly the most important of the new English book faces cut in the 1920s, was to be the parent of the next important design specifically for private press use.

This, the Golden Cockerel type, was commissioned from Eric Gill by Robert Gibbings, and Gill's designs were cut and cast by the Caslon typefoundry in 1929. An italic type to accompany the roman was added two years later. Gill understood the needs of Cockerel, at which the harmonious marriage of wood-engraved illustration to typeface was to count for so much. His method was to take the basic Perpetua design and to make it slightly heavier and more rounded. This produced a design that in its largest sizes succeeded very well indeed; in Robert Harling's words it is a face "lacking perhaps the dignity of the Monotype fount, but equally assured and certainly more robust. . . . [It] is almost without equal in its suitability for use with wood-engravings on a printed page." Anyone who has seen the marvelous Golden Cockerel *Four Gospels* will surely agree (Illus. 172). The accompanying italic was much less satisfactory. Like all Gill's italics, it is far from a scribal chancery hand, being contaminated with his characteristic "sloped roman" features in many letters. As sloping capitals were not cut, but the lowercase was intended to be joined to the roman capitals (in the fashion of the earliest italic faces), the resultant page is uncomfortable and restless.

Golden Cockerel type was wisely restricted in its use to only a score or so of books. During the years of the press's decline after World War II, it was relatively little used, a notable exception being the folio *Songs and Poems of Dryden* (1957). The punches and matrices are now housed in the Cambridge University Printing House, the surviving fonts of the larger sizes held at the Rampant Lions Press, and the 14 point at St. Bride.

The other purely private press typeface designed by Gill was the Aries type—his Joanna and Bunyan were not private in the strictest sense, even though they did not become generally available

ILLUS. 172. Golden Cockerel Press. *The Four Gospels*. Wood engraving by Eric Gill, in perfect harmony with his Golden Cockerel type.

for many years. Designed for the Stourton Press in 1932, Aries was unmistakably a Gill design, but with some features that do not appear in any of his other typefaces. Robert Harling has suggested that Gill may have been influenced in his designs by seeing trial cuttings of Times New Roman; certainly the large x-height of Aries and the design of some of the lowercase sorts—"a," "d," "e," "h," and "m"—are close to some of Morison's work for the Times face. Nevertheless, even when seen at its best, as it was in the book for which it was specifically designed, the *Catalogue of Chinese Pottery and Porcelain in the Collection of Sir Percival David, Bt.* (1934), the Aries roman is less than a complete success (even in the larger 18- and 14-point sizes in which it was cast by the Caslon foundry), largely because its short extenders call for considerable leading (Illus. 173).

The Aries italic type, on the other hand, succeeds better than most of Gill's other italic types, perhaps because it is nearer to a true italic although still full of "sloped roman" features. When set solid, it produces a much stronger and more virile page than is usual with italics, and it lacks the restlessness of Gill's design for the Golden Cockerel Press.

After production of the David *Catalogue,* the Stourton Press was free to use the type for other work. Fairfax Hall held the punches and matrices from which he cast new type as needed, on the press's own pivotal caster, both in England and South Africa. A certain amount of the type is now also owned by the University of Cape Town, to which Mr. Hall presented it before his return to England in 1961.

At the same time that the Golden Cockerel Press was first making use of its new proprietary typeface, the Nonesuch Press also attempted the use of proprietary material. To be sure, the idea of having a specially designed face was hardly compatible with Sir Francis Meynell's aims at the Nonesuch Press, and he never had a special font of type cut for its use, although he did persuade the Monotype Corporation to recut some sorts with longer extenders. Nevertheless, for two books, its editions of the *Iliad* and *Odyssey* (1931), the illustrations were provided by means of figurines designed by Rudolf Koch and cast as type ornaments. Formed into friezes, with the units rearranged in appropriate combinations at the head of each double opening, they made extraordinarily effective decoration. In style, though, such special castings were more like Bruce Rogers's playing with flowers, or W. A. Dwiggins's decorative work, than the normal privately cast fonts.

The last of the triumvirate of presses between the wars, the Gregynog, had toyed with the idea of a proprietary face in its earliest days, and its press board in 1924 had tried in vain to persuade Edward Johnston to design a special face for its exclusive use. It was not, however, until Loyd Haberly's directorship of the press that its own face was cast, in 1934–1935.

Haberly was very much more interested in himself practicing the various crafts than the previous directors had been. There was more of Morris about him, and it was natural enough that Haberly should want to attempt type design himself—although it is difficult to be sure how much

---

Amid accumulated pollen and massed flowers the two phoenixes droop their wings. The colour is confined to that prized by the Yin dynasty (i.e., white, which was the Imperial colour in that dynasty), simple and unadorned. It is not till we come down to the Chu dynasty of Hsüan [Tê] and Ch'êng [Hua]² that we get elaborate painting and the employment of five colours.

Composed by Ch'ien Lung in the spring of the cyclical year *ting yu* (A.D. 1777), and inscribed by Imperial order.

Seal: *t'ai p'o,* 'Great Unpolished-gem'.

ILLUS. 173. Eric Gill's Aries type.

the design was the work of Haberly and how much that of Grailly Hewitt who worked with him on the face.

Based on the type used by Johann Neumeister for the *editio princeps* of Dante's *Divine Comedy* in 1472, the Gregynog face (variously called "Paradiso" or "Gwendolin" at different times) was fairly close to Neumeister's archaic roman face, although Hewitt's influence was unmistakable in letters such as the "w." It was a typeface in very much the same class as the Ashendene Ptolemy type, being deliberately unusual and unsuited for adaptation to ordinary commercial use. In the pages of *Eros and Psyche,* the book for which the type had been designed in the first place and the one Gregynog book in which it was used, the face looked very well.

Archaic faces of this kind had been successful enough in the years before World War I. St. John Hornby's use of Ptolemy, following on the Subiaco face, was acceptable; the position of the Ashendene Press and its work were recognized as belonging to an older style of fine printing. But for typographic pundits of the 1930s, the press's use of the new Gregynog face following its use of Monotype faces, was too retrograde, too much in the direct Morris tradition. Their unfavorable

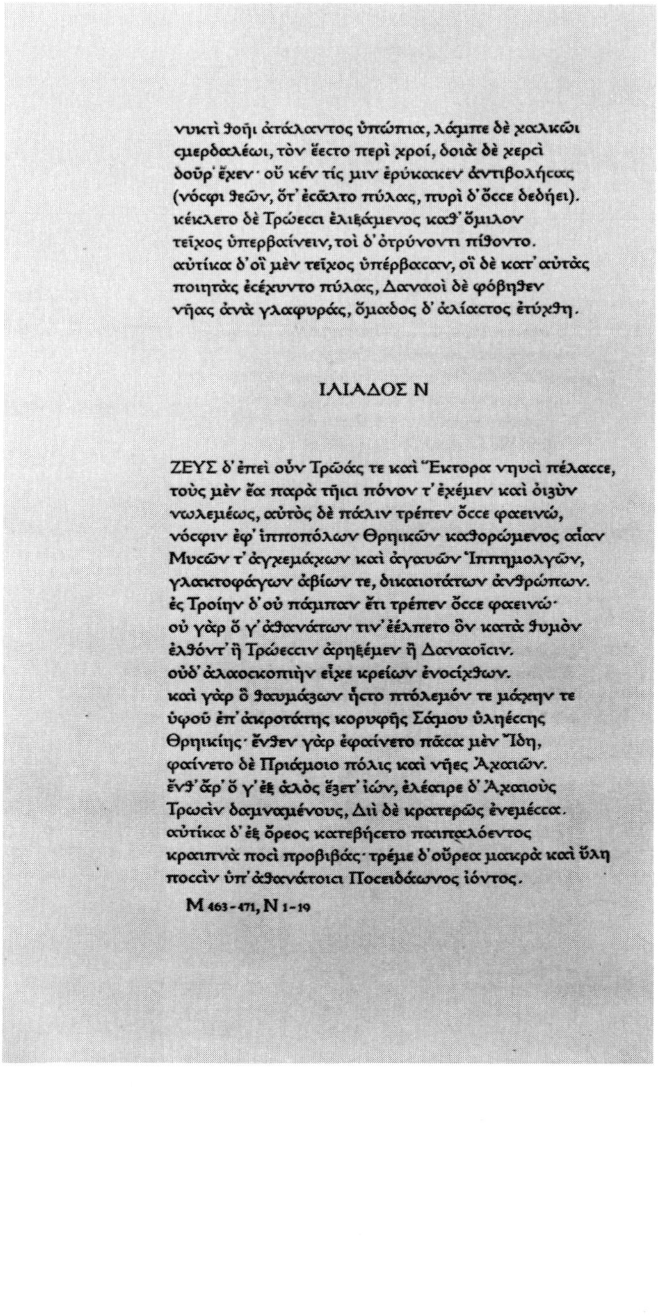
νυκτὶ θοῆι ἀτάλαντος ὑπώπια, λάμπε δὲ χαλκῶι
ϲμερδαλέωι, τὸν ἕεϲτο περὶ χροί, δοιὰ δὲ χερϲὶ
δοῦρ' ἔχεν· οὔ κέν τίς μιν ἐρύκακεν ἀντιβολήϲαϲ
(νόϲφι θεῶν, ὅτ' ἐϲᾶλτο πύλαϲ, πυρὶ δ' ὄϲϲε δεδήει).
κέκλετο δὲ Τρώεϲϲι ἑλιξάμενοϲ καθ' ὅμιλον
τεῖχοϲ ὑπερβαίνειν, τοὶ δ' ὀτρύνοντι πίθοντο.
αὐτίκα δ' οἳ μὲν τεῖχοϲ ὑπέρβαϲαν, οἳ δὲ κατ' αὐτὰϲ
ποιητὰϲ ἐϲέχυντο πύλαϲ, Δαναοὶ δὲ φόβηθεν
νῆαϲ ἀνὰ γλαφυράϲ, ὅμαδοϲ δ' ἀλίαϲτοϲ ἐτύχθη.

ΙΛΙΑΔΟΣ Ν

ΖΕΥΣ δ' ἐπεὶ οὖν Τρῶάϲ τε καὶ Ἕκτορα νηυϲὶ πέλαϲϲε,
τοὺϲ μὲν ἔα παρὰ τῆιϲι πόνον τ' ἐχέμεν καὶ ὀιζὺν
νωλεμέωϲ, αὐτὸϲ δὲ πάλιν τρέπεν ὄϲϲε φαεινώ,
νόϲφιν ἐφ' ἱπποπόλων Θρηικῶν καθορώμενοϲ αἶαν
Μυϲῶν τ' ἀγχεμάχων καὶ ἀγαυῶν Ἱππημολγῶν,
γλακτοφάγων ἀβίων τε, δικαιοτάτων ἀνθρώπων.
ἐϲ Τροίην δ' οὐ πάμπαν ἔτι τρέπεν ὄϲϲε φαεινώ·
οὐ γὰρ ὅ γ' ἀθανάτων τιν' ἐέλπετο ὃν κατὰ θυμὸν
ἐλθόντ' ἢ Τρώεϲϲιν ἀρηξέμεν ἢ Δαναοῖϲιν.
οὐδ' ἀλαοϲκοπιὴν εἶχε κρείων ἐνοϲίχθων.
καὶ γὰρ ὃ θαυμάζων ἧϲτο πτόλεμόν τε μάχην τε
ὑψοῦ ἐπ' ἀκροτάτηϲ κορυφῆϲ Σάμου ὑληέϲϲηϲ
Θρηικίηϲ· ἔνθεν γὰρ ἐφαίνετο πᾶϲα μὲν Ἴδη,
φαίνετο δὲ Πριάμοιο πόλιϲ καὶ νῆεϲ Ἀχαιῶν.
ἔνθ' ἄρ' ὅ γ' ἐξ ἁλὸϲ ἕζετ' ἰών, ἐλέαιρε δ' Ἀχαιοὺϲ
Τρωϲὶν δαμναμένουϲ, Διὶ δὲ κρατερῶϲ ἐνεμέϲϲα.
αὐτίκα δ' ἐξ ὄρεοϲ κατεβήϲετο παιπαλόεντοϲ
κραιπνὰ ποϲὶ προβιβάϲ· τρέμε δ' οὔρεα μακρὰ καὶ ὕλη
ποϲϲὶν ὑπ' ἀθανάτοιϲι Ποϲειδάωνοϲ ἰόντοϲ.
Μ 463–471, Ν 1–19

ILLUS. 174. Bremer-Presse. *Iliad,* 1923, set in the press's calligraphic Greek type.

comments, even those of St. John Hornby, were enough to persuade the Davies sisters not to use the face again. But the face did not remain entirely unused; after Haberly resigned his directorship in 1936, the sisters presented him with a large font of it, and he continued to use it from time to time in the books he printed in Dorset, Massachusetts, Missouri, and New Jersey. The punches and matrices passed to the National Library of Wales at Aberystwyth.

Elsewhere in Europe there was even more activity than in Great Britain. In Germany, in particular, many new typefaces were being produced by such foundries as Stempel, Bauer, and Klingspor, types designed by such men as Rudolf Koch, Walter Tiemann, and E. R. Weiss. Most of the private presses used these commercially available faces (just as the English private printers used the Monotype designs), but several had proprietary designs cut for their own use, of which a number are shown in Rodenberg's *Deutsche Pressen*. Among the more interesting of these were the fine *fere-humanistica* type used at the Officina Serpentis (a design in some ways similar to the Ashendene Press Subiaco font) and the handsome roman and blackletter types used at the Bremer-Presse in Munich. These types bear comparison with the best of the English and Dutch type designs produced under the influence of William Morris.

One Dutch typeface remains to be described. This was the Meidoorn type designed by S. H. de Roos for his own use at his Heuvelpers. Cut for him at the Amsterdam Typefoundry in a single size, 14 point, it is a rather heavily modeled Venetian roman. Jan van Krimpen did not think any more highly of this than of other Dutch private press types:

> This face strikes me as indicating at one and the same time a great admiration
> for the work of Mr St John Hornby, and of certain German experiments,
> leaving me with the impression that the fount was perhaps somewhat hastily
> conceived.

Despite van Krimpen's icy comments, the type could look very well indeed when used in the grand manner for which de Roos had intended it. After de Roos discontinued work at the Heuvelpers, the type passed into the possession of Messrs. J. F. Duwaer en Zonen of Amsterdam.

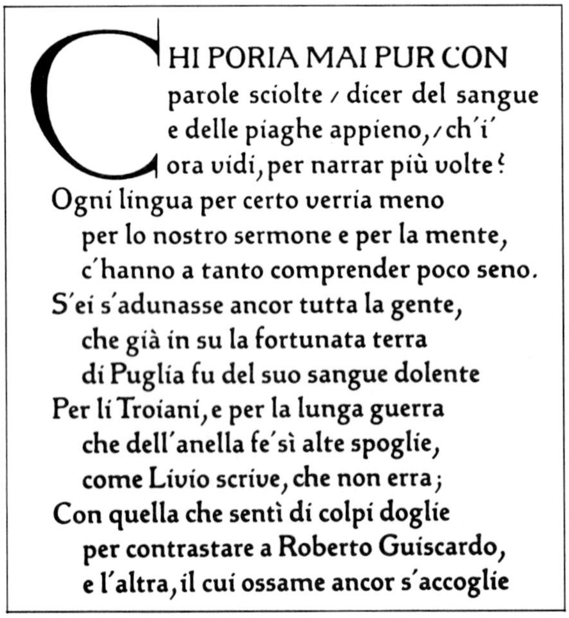

CHI PORIA MAI PUR CON
parole sciolte / dicer del sangue
e delle piaghe appieno, / ch'i'
ora vidi, per narrar più volte?
Ogni lingua per certo verria meno
per lo nostro sermone e per la mente,
c'hanno a tanto comprender poco seno.
S'ei s'adunasse ancor tutta la gente,
che già in su la fortunata terra
di Puglia fu del suo sangue dolente
Per li Troiani, e per la lunga guerra
che dell'anella fe'sì alte spoglie,
come Livio scrive, che non erra;
Con quella che sentì di colpi doglie
per contrastare a Roberto Guiscardo,
e l'altra, il cui ossame ancor s'accoglie

ILLUS. 175. Bremer-Presse. Roman type, with initial by Anna Simons.

It was in Italy that some of the most interesting and beautiful private press typefaces were to be cut. Today, one tends to associate the name of Victor Hammer more with the group of fine printers centered in Lexington, Kentucky, since it was in that city that Hammer's later searches for the perfect uncial form of letter were made. But this was a lifelong preoccupation, which had started while Hammer was running his Stamperia del Santuccio in Florence in the early 1920s.

Hammer's first attempt as a type designer was purely as a designer. About 1924–1925 he supervised the production of an uncial design by the Klingspor Foundry, the Hammer-Unziale, for which the punches were cut by Schuricht. For a generation educated (by Hammer's own work) in the forms of uncial letters, the difficulties of this enterprise are hard to estimate, but it was clear that, in this first attempt, Schuricht's interpretation of the essential form of some letters did not accord with Hammer's own ideas. Although the face was by far the best uncial design that had appeared up to that time, Hammer's own opinion of it is shown by the fact that he never used the type himself.

However, some interesting and effective use was made of this typeface in a semiprivate way by the Irish printer Colm O Lochlainn at his printing house At the Sign of the Three Candles in Dublin. O Lochlainn had met Hammer and the Klingspors while he was himself in Offenbach and persuaded the founders to cast a font for his use in printing texts in Irish. In designing Hammer-Unziale, Hammer had diverged from his Irish models in several letters, and O Lochlainn therefore had his font cast with special sorts that restored the Irish element Hammer or Schuricht had removed. For these special sorts O Lochlainn himself furnished the designs, and in this way the Gaelic version of Hammer's type, Baoithin, was evolved. O Lochlainn subsequently designed another Irish typeface for Monotype, Colum Cille, and made quite frequent use of Baoithin as a display face in conjunction with his other design. It is interesting that Hammer seems to have approved of the changes made by O Lochlainn, and in his subsequent designs he was closer to the Irish forms than he had been in his first typeface.

In 1925 Hammer was joined in Florence by Paul Koch, the son of Rudolf Koch, the great German calligrapher and type designer. Paul Koch taught Hammer the skills of punchcutting, and between 1926 and 1928 they cut and produced a new uncial type, which was used in the Stamperia del Santuccio's edition of *Samson Agonistes* in 1931 (Illus. 176). After this had been published, both Hammer and Koch cut a few experimental letters as improvements on the Samson design. These appeared in a few trial sheets, but were not used extensively since between 1933 and 1935 Hammer himself cut punches for a new uncial, the Pindar-Uncial, which was cast by Klingspor and so called from its first use in Hölderlin's *Fragmente des Pindar* (1935).

More cuttings of trial sorts for individual letters followed as far as Hammer's other artistic activities and commissions permitted. His quest for an ideal type was considerably longer, more laborious, and one might almost say more loving than that of any other designer. But all these plans had to be abandoned after the Nazi takeover in Austria where he was then living. On the advice of friends, he left Europe for the United States in 1939.

An experimental casting of a new uncial design by the American Type Founders Company in 1940 led to nothing, but eventually Hammer's long work as a type designer found its culmination in the American Uncial typeface, which (with financial help from members of the Chicago Society of Typographic Arts) was cast at the Dearborn Typefoundry in Chicago. Eventually, in 1952, it was made generally available in Europe through the Klingspor Foundry again, and it has been seen in several books from private presses, although none to better effect than those printed at Hammer's own Stamperia del Santuccio, in such a book as Hölderlin's *Gedichte* (1949) printed at the press's new home in Lexington, Kentucky.

The type, or more-or-less faithful interpretations of it by other designers, has been widely adopted for display purposes and (even in the more debased versions one often sees) has an

but who are these! for with joint pace J hear
the tread of many feet stearing this way/·
perhaps my enemies who come to stare
at my affliction/and perhaps to insult/
thir daily practice to afflict me more·
chorus
this/this is he/·softly a while/
let us not break in upon him/·
o change beyond report/thought/or belief!
see how he lies at random/carelessly diffus'd/
with languish't head unpropt/
as one past hope/abandon'd
and by himself given over/·

ILLUS. 176. Hammer's Samson-Unziale.

agreeable strength about it. As a face to be used for more than a word or two, opinions vary a great deal. American Uncial is a face that attracts strong opinions, just as the uncial letter itself does. Strong, vigorous, and yet undoubtedly sophisticated, the typeface breaks all the usual rules of legibility derived from roman types. In fine printing of small editions, for which it was designed, it works magnificently.

American Uncial was not Hammer's last exercise in type design. For his own use he cut the punches for a cursive-style uncial, Andromaque, which was cast for him by Deberny et Peignot in Paris. Only a trial casting was made, and the letter has been relatively little used (partly because of difficulties in setting it in its present form), but it illustrated in a fascinating way Hammer's skill in extending the scope of the uncial style into new areas. Rather similar was his use of large two-color initials, cut from brass and printed by a technique like that used by Peter Schoeffer in the Mainz *Psalter* (1457).

Hammer's uncial types have succeeded despite the fact that they challenge normal typographic conventions. The new typefaces designed by Giovanni Mardersteig for use at the Officina Bodoni were even more successful because they did not present the same challenge.

After his earlier use of some of Bodoni's types, and of Frederic Warde's revival of Arrighi's italic faces, Mardersteig's first design for a new typeface was an adaptation of the face cut for Aldus Manutius by Francesco Griffo and used in Cardinal Bembo's *De Aetna* in 1495. This type had been the basis for a new face, which the Monotype Corporation, under the guidance of Stanley Morison, had issued under the name of Bembo in 1929, and which deservedly became the most popular book type in England. In the original Griffo font, perhaps the noblest roman of them all, there was a number of variant sorts for particular letters. In the Monotype adaptation, Mardersteig considered that the selection of particular designs for recutting and regularization had resulted in a typeface markedly inferior to its model.

In his use of Bodoni types for the National Edition of d'Annunzio, Mardersteig had in earlier years turned to the Paris punchcutter Charles Malin to provide stronger but matching sorts that would stand up to the pressure of the powered presses. It was in collaboration with Malin that Mardersteig set about producing his own roman type, which (on Morison's advice) he based on the face of *De Aetna*.

From Mardersteig's own account of the long collaboration with Malin it is clear that it was one of the most harmonious as well as fruitful working relationships. It was to be 10 years before the typeface came into use, being first used in *Due Episodi della Vita di Felice Feliciano* in summer 1939.

montis rupe viatoribus late prospicitur,
unde illud devectum Ovidianum
    Nisiades matres sicelidesque nurus.
Incolae vallem etiam omnem, quae sub-
est, Nisi regionem vocant.
B. P. Erit isto sane modo etiam aliquid
infra Taurominium memorabile. Nam
de hoc poetae versu, si recte memini,

ILLUS. 177. Mardersteig's Griffo type.

Griffo, Mardersteig's face, was cut in 16 point, with capitals also being cut in 14 point. In some individual letters it is almost indistinguishable from Monotype Bembo, but for some other letters it is a much more sympathetic and faithful recutting of the original. The serifs were generally more sharply modeled, the almost imperceptible slope in such letters as the "c," "e," and "s" was retained, and extra terminal sorts were provided for "a," "e," "m," and other letters. The result was a very graceful and sophisticated type, perhaps a little more mannered than Monotype Bembo (perfectly acceptable in a typeface intended for private use only), but with a sparkle that was lacking from the earlier types cut for private use based on Jenson's Venetian types (Illus. 177).

Although at a cursory glance Griffo and Bembo roman can easily be mistaken, they have very different italic fonts to accompany them. *De Aetna* had been printed before the first italic font had been cut. Monotype, having first tried to marry its roman to Alfred Fairbank's Narrow Bembo Italic (and finding his splendid chancery letter too strong for its subordinate role), employed a severely modified version of the italic used by Giovanantonio Tagliente. Mardersteig rather more logically settled for an italic that had been cut by Francesco Griffo as his model. But Griffo's italics were more workaday in design than his face for *De Aetna*, and many critics found the Mardersteig/Malin italic inferior to its mate—"as if a thoroughbred were in harness with a post horse," as Hans Schmoller put it.

The first original design by Mardersteig for the Officina Bodoni was used before Griffo, having been designed soon after work on the Griffo type started, although Malin's cutting of the punches was not completed until 1936. Used first in 1937 in a specimen *San Zeno Vescovo, Patrono di Verona,* and named Zeno after the saint, its design was inspired by a manuscript missal written for Cardinal Giulio de'Medici in 1520. A delicately modeled roman with some Venetian characteristics, as one would expect it is very close to written forms. Cut in 14 and 16 point, and for capitals also in 30 point, it was a face well suited to occasional formal work of the kind for which Mardersteig used it. As became characteristic with all Mardersteig faces, a number of alternative sorts were prepared.

Work on the second of Mardersteig's original designs, first used in 1952 for a *Trattatello in Laude di Dante,* and therefore named Dante started in 1946, but Charles Malin did not complete his punchcutting until 1952. Like Griffo, Dante is a powerful yet delicate old-face design, again married to an italic of an Aldine rather than chancery character, although the match between roman and italic is far closer than for the Griffo face. By the time of his death in October 1955, Malin had cut the 10-, 12-, and 20-point sizes.

For awhile it seemed as if the distinguished Dante face would remain limited to these sizes and would be seen only in the work of its parent press, but in 1957 the Monotype Corporation cut a complete range of sizes from 8 point to 36 point using the foundry specimens as models. Mardersteig sometimes used these, but also had 16- and 20-point sizes cut for him by Ruggero Olivieri in Milan (in the same way that Charles Malin had served him so well). He also employed Olivieri to cut a number of variants for the 14-, 16-, and 20-point sizes, providing the italic face with sorts that made its character closer to that of a chancery italic. These were used in *Songs from Shakespeare's Plays* (1974), but to my mind the attempt was not successful. The rounded forms of the Dante Italic do not compare well with the narrower chancery italic in its pure form, and the mixture merely sacrificed the vigor of the Aldine form without gaining the elegance of the chancery letter (Illus. 178).

While Charles Malin was still cutting the punches for the Dante type, in 1950–1951 he also provided punches for the closely related Pacioli titling type. Based very closely on the capital alphabet constructed by the Franciscan scholar Fra Luca Pacioli, the new font (cut in 14-, 20-, and 24-point sizes) formed one of the most distinguished titling letters to have been cut. It was first shown in Maurice de Guerin's *Poemes en Prose* (1954) and was also used most appropriately in *De Divina Proportione di Luca Pacioli* (1956).

Pacioli and Dante were the last of Mardersteig's own typefaces; indeed, speaking at Mainz in 1968, he said that after the death of his old collaborator Charles Malin, he had lost all desire to produce fresh designs. There had been one fresh typeface, but it was not designed by him. Through a friendship with the Russian graphic designer Vadim Lazursky, which developed after a chance

Now the hungry lion roars,
    And the wolf behowls the moon;
Whilst the heavy ploughman snores,
    All with weary task fordone.
Now the wasted brands do glow,
    Whilst the screech-owl, screeching loud,
Puts the wretch that lies in woe
    In remembrance of a shroud.

ILLUS. 178. Olivieri's cursive characters for Dante Italic.

На берегу пустынных волн
Стоял он, дум великих полн,
И вдаль глядел. Пред ним широко
Река неслася; бедный челн
По ней стремился одиноко.
По мшистым, топким берегам
Чернели избы здесь и там,
Приют убогого чухонца;
И лес, неведомый лучам
В тумане спрятанного солнца,
Кругом шумел.

ILLUS. 179. Officina Bodoni. Lazursky's Pushkin type in its final form.

meeting in 1964, Mardersteig had the chance to produce a new cyrillic type from Lazursky's designs that had appealed to him because of their renaissance qualities.

The new cyrillic type, cut in 14 point by Ruggero Olivieri, was first used in a small trial edition of Pushkin's *Il Cavaliere di Bronzo* in September 1967. However satisfactory the type, and it was an accomplished piece of design and cutting, this first trial edition showed that it had turned out slightly too heavy. The Pushkin type, therefore, was recut and made public in the new edition of *Il Cavaliere* published in January 1968 (Illus. 179). In this edition the Russian text and Italian translation were on facing pages; the Dante type used for the latter matched the new form of Pushkin very well indeed. Pushkin however was the last of the proprietary types cut for the Officina Bodoni. Even ignoring the fine Greek cut to accompany Griffo, Mardersteig had designed or managed to secure five different typefaces, each of which was superior to most other private press designs.

Chapter 27

THE CONTEMPORARY SCENE

THE POSITION OF THE PRIVATE PRESS TODAY is different from that of previous generations. The amateur setting up in the 1890s or in the early years of the twentieth century might well decide to have a font especially prepared. It was relatively cheap—and remained relatively cheap and easy through the middle years of this century. At the end of the eighteenth century, at the time that Wilkins cut his Bengali font, the Caslon Foundry quoted a price of one guinea per punch for similar work. A century later, E. P. Prince's scale of charges to the Kelmscott Press was 10 shillings each for letters, 15 shillings for ligatures and only 5 shillings for punctuation; in other words for £40 to £50 one could have a complete set of punches from the best craftsman. St. John Hornby's outlay of £100 for his Subiaco face at the beginning of this century was in real terms much more than one would have paid as late as 1968, when Messrs. Stephen Austin quoted a price of approximately £240 for furnishing matrices for a complete font.

For the private printer who did not choose or could not afford to have his own face cut, founder's Caslon Old Face was cheaply available in England, and in the United States the various founders' imitations of Kelmscott types could be purchased for a modest outlay. Undoubtedly in the interwar years (and indeed right through to the late 1960s or early 1970s), most private press owners could do far better by purchasing typefaces commercially available, whether ATF, Stephenson Blake, or the various continental typefounders on the one hand, or the Monotype faces on the other, than by limiting themselves to a single proprietary face obtained with more difficulty.

In England, the only new typeface cut in recent years for private use was the Janet face designed by the wood engraver Reynolds Stone, whose engravings had graced so many private press books (High House, Nonesuch, Gregynog, and Officina Bodoni) as well as commercially published work. At Litton Cheney in Dorset he built up a remarkable collection of handpresses (now maintained by Colin Franklin), which he used for pulling proofs of his engravings and occasionally for printing small editions of books. In 1955, Linotype issued his Minerva face to provide display sizes for the recutting of Eric Gill's Pilgrim type (originally, as Bunyan, cut for private use by Hague and Gill). Janet, cut only in 18 point with roman capitals and roman and italic lowercase, was prepared in the mid-1960s and reserved for his personal use. In Kenneth Clark's *The Other Side of the Alde,* which Stone printed in a small edition for Warren Editions in 1968, the type provided a rich accompaniment to his engravings. It was a handsome face, with some family resemblance to the Minerva type and to Stone's wood-engraved letters. The italic, though to my mind spoiled by the "n" and "u," which were too rounded for the narrow chancery form of the other letters, was a particularly subtle and graceful letter. Nevertheless, fine letter though it was, as Ruari MacLean noted in the catalogue of the Victoria and Albert Museum's memorial exhibition held in 1982, the face did not have sufficient advantage over such other calligraphers' types as Joanna, Juliana, or Perpetua to justify cutting in the smaller size that would be required for more routine use.

The changes in the printing trade over the last few years, however, have altered the situation completely. Instead of the array of typefounders and Monotype composition houses serving the commercial trade and from which the private printer could obtain type as and when needed, the number of suppliers has dwindled almost to vanishing point. For a press, set up today to gather together the rich repertoire of type of the Grabhorns, to be able to ring the changes in the way the Grace Hopers did with their *Typographical Commonplace Books* would be nearly impossible.

Although founders still exist, and Monotype composition houses like Mackenzie-Harris in San Francisco or Riscatype in South Wales offer good service to the letterpress printer, private printers today are much more than their predecessors in the position, say, of vintage car enthusiasts seeking spare parts. When castings of particular fonts are offered, through Stephenson Blake or some of the other sources described below, the private printer either purchases at once or relies on the faint chance that he will be able to buy or swap with other letterpress printers at a later date.

Another possibility being explored actively by a number of private printers is to turn to sources of supply that would earlier have been ignored. Berthold Wolpe's splendid and individual Hyperion italic face, originally cut by Paul Koch for the Bauersche Giesserei in Frankfurt, is now marketed (as Homero) only by the Fundicion Tipografica Neufville at Barcelona. In India, where the days of letterpress printing are by no means over, the Gujarati Typefoundry in Bombay still has over 30 pivotal casters in regular use to produce high quality fonts in founders' metal at a very reasonable cost. The range of the foundry's repertoire is remarkable. In addition to its own fonts for Indian languages, it also has many faces that were imported earlier this century from American, British, and continental founders for which electrolytic matrices were made. Many of these faces and ornaments have long disappeared from the catalogues of the original typefoundries, but the typefoundry in Bombay remains a useful source of supply.

The printing trade's move away from letterpress and hot-metal composition has admittedly not been without some short-term benefits for the private printer: Cases of type bought at scrap-metal prices, composing and casting machines sold at ridiculously low prices or even given away—stories of this sort have become commonplace among the private printing fraternity.

Some of those in the private press field have equipped themselves for the future. Harold Berliner's Typefoundry in Nevada City, California, is one instance. Another is at the Whittington Press in Gloucestershire, where John Randle, finding that he could purchase complete Monotype equipment at less cost than having a particular job trade-set, is now able to provide for all his own needs and for those of other printers also. Frequently, although it may be easy enough to get a Monotype, acquiring the expertise to keep it running properly is much harder. Randle has been particularly fortunate in enlisting the help of George Wiggall, who has just retired after 50 years as a caster operator.

By such means, private presses can ensure a continuing supply of type. In addition to this there is another group in the United States particularly: the amateur typefounders. These are not working in the antiquarian tradition of Dard Hunter—cutting punches and casting their type in handmolds—though they have a proper concern that these older skills should not be lost. Rather their interest is to some extent that of the industrial archaeologist, and they have worked to retrieve and preserve the type-casting machines that ousted the handmolds in the nineteenth century and were then made obsolete themselves by the advent of the composing machines. But not many are interested in typefounding without also being interested in printing, and to extend beyond this to a wish to cast type that is not generally available is natural enough.

Sometimes this will be no more than minor modification of existing faces, like, for instance, the rather earlier cutting of a new "z" for the Vine Press edition of *Watcher in Florence,* or the Typographical Laboratory's special casting of Monotype Van Dijck with reduced capitals for *Leigh Hunt on Eight Sonnets of Dante.* Work of this kind, of course, echoes some of the earlier modifications undertaken by Meynell at the Nonesuch Press.

One of the first to be active in having typefaces that had gone out of production reissued was the late Steve Watts of Front Royal, Virginia. His Privateer Press issued one of the most entertaining examples of amateur journalism, *The Pastime Printer.* Watts, for many years sales manager of American Type Founders, was excellently placed for organizing the revival of types of which ATF held the matrices. Two faces he had recut that have been used to good effect by private printers are the handsome Oxford face, in which Updike's monumental *Printing Types* was printed, and Wayside roman. Wayside is a pleasant Scotch roman face, and the reissue had the unusual and useful feature of a set of intermediate capitals, midway between the capitals and small capitals in size. Frederick MacMahon, the "Yankee Ink Dauber" organized the reissue of Hobo, an ugly art nouveau letter better left dead, and more usefully of Worrell Uncial, a type originally available only on Linotype and therefore not a face the amateur, setting type by hand, could have used before.

Another early amateur in typefounding was John S. Carroll, for many years a private printer in Manhattan and a prominent figure in the New York Chappel during its first years. Somehow Carroll managed to pack into his apartment not just three presses and 125 fonts of display typefaces, but also a caster. On this in the 1950s and 1960s Carroll cast several interesting revivals of nineteenth-century decorated types, mainly by means of electrolytic matrices from types in his own collection, using a similar method to that employed by the Gujarati Typefoundry. Other faces that he made available to other private printers included Harlequin, an ornamented titling originally cut by Matthias Rosart for the Enschedé foundry in 1768, and Goudy Medieval (one of Goudy's "lost" typefaces, originally cast in 1930), which was undertaken for the New York Chappel.

Many years ago Bruce Rogers pointed out that although a proprietary typeface might well be beyond their means, even the most modest private presses could afford to have their own individual borders or fleurons. In several instances, Carroll provided the founding facilities for work of this kind. The earliest of these was an experiment undertaken for the present writer in 1960, in which three different versions of a flower were cut by different methods. The first, frankly experimental, was used only in a small leaflet, but the second version was acquired by several members of the Private Libraries Association's Society of Private Printers and has been used occasionally by David Chambers and at Morris Cox's Gogmagog Press as well as in the specimen *Calypso: An Antillean Arabesque* (1962). For Frederick MacMahon, Carroll cut an ink-ball ornament, and for Peter Isaac in Northumberland a "Puffing Billy" in 24 point, which has graced several of the pieces from his Allenholme Press.

The Harlequin type was cast by Carroll for Paul Hayden Duensing in Michigan. Duensing's own Private Press and Typefoundry has since become far more important for its own sensitive and intelligent casting program, which has enriched private and commercial printers well beyond the United States. Duensing's program of work has been rather different from that of such other founders as the Los Angeles Typefoundry or the Out of Sorts Letter Foundry in New York State. These have included type revivals (like the latter's cooperative work with the Smithsonian Institution, using matrices in the institution's collection), but the work undertaken by Duensing has been rather to introduce to the Anglo-American printing world typefaces very rarely seen there earlier. His program of recutting has included, for instance, castings on the Anglo-American point system of some of the splendid typefaces designed by the Czech Oldrich Menhart and a version of Rudolf Koch's Wilhelm-Klingsporschrift. For the latter (a highly sophisticated blackletter type, with both wide and narrow capitals and many variant sorts among the lowercase), Duensing's casting included a recut "k" to render the face more usable for setting matter in English than the original German casting by the Klingspor foundry (Illus. 180).

In addition to these types, Duensing has produced a number of totally original designs. The first of these, XVI Century Roman, cast originally in 1967, was produced through the use of electrolytic matrices made from worn types dating from that century, with freshly engraved characters made to accord with the design for a few letters that were missing. Technically the work was successful, but the effect of the type when printed is of seventeenth-century English printing at its nastiest. For occasional use for ephemera and advertising, the quaintness is acceptable, but for fine printing it is not a type to be recommended.

Duensing's other original designs have a great deal more in their favor. His experiments with a completely new chancery italic type have shown how variations on this form are still possible and desirable. In other faces, he has done for the scribal letters of later Rome rather what Victor Hammer did for the Uncial letter, and Duensing's narrow Rustic and wider Quadrata type provide handsome letters, which genuinely extend the scope of the letterpress printer into new fields (Illus. 181).

In commercial printing, new designs are not being produced as metal types. The letterpress printer may well cast a longing eye at some of the designs available for filmsetting that can be used in offset litho work: for example, Matthew Carter's interpretation of Granjon's designs marketed as ITC Galliard (the face used in this book), or the superb calligraphic ITC Zapf Chancery. Those private presses of the future that use lithography rather than letterpress will be able to explore the possibilities of such designs in much the way that Nonesuch exploited hot-metal composition. The range of letterpress work can still be extended in some ways, of course, by the use of line-blocks reproducing special lettering for particular books as an alternative to new types. One of the most interesting examples of such work came from Michael Hutchins's work as holder of the Gregynog Printing Fellowship, which produced the first of the new Gregynog books, *Laboratories of the Spirit* (1976)—although it is ironic that the effect of the special lettering drawn for the initials and

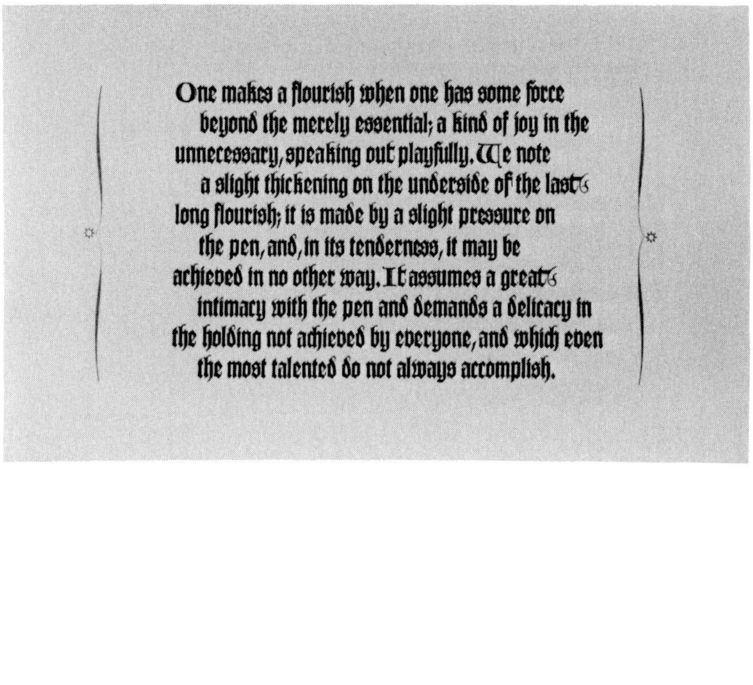

One makes a flourish when one has some force beyond the merely essential; a kind of joy in the unnecessary, speaking out playfully. We note a slight thickening on the underside of the last long flourish; it is made by a slight pressure on the pen, and, in its tenderness, it may be achieved in no other way. It assumes a great intimacy with the pen and demands a delicacy in the holding not achieved by everyone, and which even the most talented do not always accomplish.

ILLUS. 180. Aliquando Press, Ontario/Paul Hayden Duensing, Michigan. *Buchstabenfreude*, 1976. Duensing's cutting of Koch types.

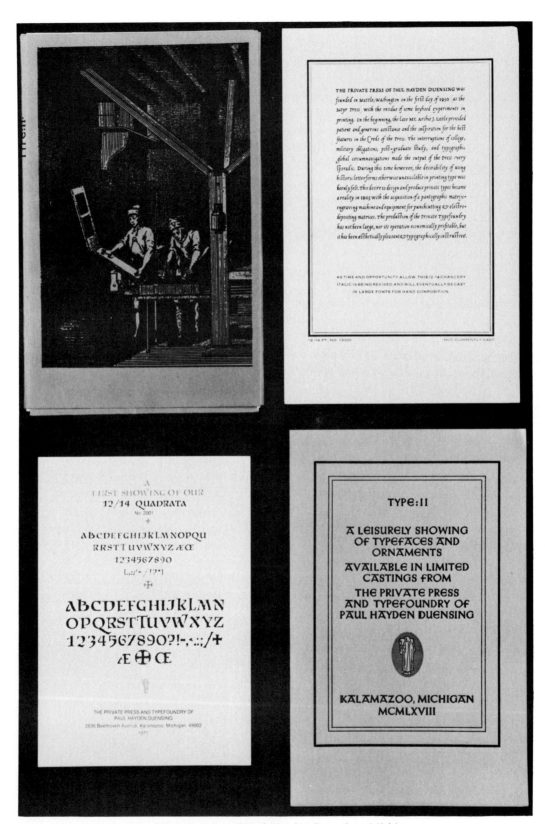

ILLUS. 181. Private Press and Typefoundry of Paul Hayden Duensing, Michigan.
Some of Duensing's type specimens, showing his own Chancery Italic and Quadrata types.

openings in this should have resulted in work reminiscent of Loyd Haberly's special typeface of 40 years earlier. Less-skillful and well-thought-out uses of line-block lettering by other printers, for instance, in the Bracken Press's edition of *Beggars Bridge* (1977), in which the text was printed from an enlargement of Press Roman italic, simply indicate the superiority of printing directly from type.

Printing directly from type is unlikely to remain the mainstay of private presses indefinitely. The wide choice of faces available 40 or 50 years ago is no longer possible, yet typefaces remain but one aspect of the problem to be faced by craftsmen working within an obsolescent technology. What of presses, paper, ink, to say nothing of the other equipment required by the letterpress printer? (In some parts of the world the quest for such basic things as quoin keys or composing sticks presents real difficulty.)

At present, it is still possible to obtain much through printers' suppliers. To purchase an old Albion press at reasonable cost may be hard, but Ullmers are now once more manufacturing these superb machines. For those who do obtain older equipment there are (in Great Britain at any rate) a few specialists who can not only restore a rusty old press to working order but can make it look beautiful at the same time. Christopher Holladay of Modbury Engineering in London is one who has worked effectively with several private printers abroad as well as in Great Britain. The exquisite work done by Tom Craig on the handpresses now owned by Colin Franklin has to be seen to be appreciated fully, but Craig's notes on "The Restoration of Iron Hand-presses" in *Matrix 2* provide useful guidance to those undertaking the work themselves.

With the expansion of interest in papermaking as a craft, the supply of good, although not inexpensive, handmade papers is reasonably well assured. Less expensive machine-made papers designed for letterpress printing rather than offset are becoming more difficult to find anywhere in the world, a problem that will become more severe. Few private printers can afford to order in quantities large enough for the paper mills to make to their specifications. A future function for such groups as the Association of Handcraft Printers or the British Printing Society may be the cooperative purchase of paper designed for letterpress use. The same will no doubt be true of ink: In New Zealand, for example, now one can only purchase offset-litho inks, which although usable for letterpress lack the characteristics of the best letterpress inks. In the long term, perhaps private printers will have to turn ink maker once more, as in the earliest days of printing. But whatever the difficulties, we can be certain that through individual and collective effort, the craft of letterpress printing will survive, and that books to delight the hand and the eye will continue to be made.

BIBLIOGRAPHY

Although relatively few books have been written specifically about private presses, the literature of the subject is extensive. For historical presses in particular much information is to be found only by chance, in books as different as Canon Liddon's *Life of Dr. Pusey* and Casanova's *Memoirs*.

The lack of any generally agreed definition of a private press makes the use of many reference books frustrating, as so many of them do not distinguish between books privately commissioned from a commercial printer and those truly the work of private presses. It is often difficult to discover what definition was applied by the compilers. For some early presses, the only easily accessible information is contained in the Reverend Henry Cotton's *A Typographical Gazetteer* (2nd edition, Oxford, 1831) and its second series (Oxford, 1866), or in the supplement to Jacques-Charles Brunet's *Manuel du Libraire* by Pierre Deschamps, published as a *Dictionnaire du Géographie* (Paris, 1870). Both however are replete with errors and should be used with great caution.

The bibliography that follows does not pretend to be a comprehensive record of the literature of private presses, nor to record every book or article I have read or consulted in the 25 years I have been concerned with the subject. It is rather a record of those publications found useful in writing and revising this book that will assist the reader who wishes to follow up particular aspects of private press history or press book design in more detail. In some cases, photolitho reprints and other editions exist of works listed; I have not attempted to record all these subsidiary editions.

Note: Titles in the bibliography follow the treatment of topics in the individual chapters.

GENERAL

BIBLIOGRAPHIES OF BOOKS AND ARTICLES ABOUT PRIVATE PRESSES

Irvin Haas. *A Bibliography of Materials Relating to Private Presses.* Chicago, 1937.

Private Libraries Association. *Private Press Books 1959– .* Pinner, 1960– . Part III of this annual checklist records "The Literature of Private Printing" and is a good guide to contemporary books and articles.

William Ridler, *British Modern Press Books: A Descriptive Checklist of Unrecorded Items* (London, 1971). Useful supplements to the lists in Tomkinson and Ransom.

BIBLIOGRAPHIES OF BOOKS PRINTED BY PRIVATE PRESSES

P. A. H. Brown, comp. *Modern British and American Private Presses (1850–1965): Holdings of the British Library.* London, 1976.

New York Public Library. *Catalog of Special and Private Presses in the Rare Book Division, the Research Libraries.* Boston, 1978.

John Martin. *A Bibliographical Catalogue of Books Privately Printed.* London, 1834. The British Library possesses Martin's own copy, together with his correspondence relating to the book, which is still of considerable value. The second edition (1854), of which a photolitho edition is available, omitted the lists of private press books and is much less useful.

Henry G. Bohn. *Appendix to the Bibliographer's Manual of English Literature.* By W. T. Lowndes. London, 1864. Includes lists of books printed at British private presses.

Bertram Dobell. *Catalogue of Books Printed for Private Circulation.* London, 1906. Includes useful notes on several early private presses.

Robert Steele. *The Revival of Printing: A Bibliographical Catalogue of Works Issued by the Chief Modern English Presses.* London, 1912.

G. S. Tomkinson. *A Select Bibliography of the Principal Modern Presses, Public and Private, in Great Britain and Ireland.* London, 1928. The standard bibliography for the English private press movement.

Will Ransom. *Private Presses and Their Books.* New York, 1929. Long the standard history. Despite some errors and inaccuracies, this remains the most comprehensive general bibliography of presses in Great Britain and the United States.

————. *Selective Check Lists of Press Books*. Issued irregularly in parts. New York, 1945–1950. Photo-litho reprints of both Ransom titles have been published (New York, 1963).

Julius Rodenberg. *Deutsche Pressen: Eine Bibliographie*. Zurich, 1925. The standard bibliography of German private presses; supplemented by his *Deutsche Pressen, 1925–30* (Berlin, 1930).

HISTORIES OF PRIVATE PRESSES

Adam Lackman. *Annalium typographicorum*. Hamburg, 1740. Chapter 8, pp. 28–87, deals with "Typographea domestica et typi privatorum." The first book to deal at any length with private presses, it contains a lot of information on early private presses not available elsewhere. The author's style is tedious and prolix and his Latin villainous. Recommended only to those who relish the painful acquisition of not very useful knowledge.

Gabriel Peignot. *Recherches Historiques et Bibliographiques sur les Imprimeries Particulières et Clandestines*. Paris, 18—. Peignot's *Répertoire de Bibliographies Spéciales* (Paris, 1810) also contains much of the information in this pamphlet.

Auguste Voisin. *Notice Bibliographique et Litteraire sur Quelques Imprimeries Particulières des Pays-Bas*. 2nd edition. Ghent, 1840.

Philomneste, Jr. [Pierre Gustave Brunet]. *Recherches sur les Imprimeries Imaginaires, Clandestines et Particulières*. Brussels, 1879.

The Times Printing Number (September 10, 1912).

The Studio. *The Art of the Book*, edited by C. G. Holme. London, 1914. The later volumes in this series, *Modern Book Production* (1927) and *The Art of the Book* (1938), both edited by Bernard Newdigate, and *The Art of the Book* (1951), edited by Charles Ede, are also useful.

Daniel Berkeley Updike. *Printing Types: Their History, Forms and Use*. 2nd edition. Cambridge, Mass., 1937. Useful for this as for all typographic studies.

Will Ransom. *Private Presses and Their Books*. New York, 1929. Less useful as a history than for its bibliographies, but still very good.

Paul A. Bennett, ed. *Books and Printing: A Treasury for Typophiles*. New York, 1951. Reprints many articles and excerpts of particular interest. The paperback edition (1963) is particularly good value.

Gilbert Turner. *The Private Press: Its Achievement and Influence*. London, 1954. An excellent brief history of the English presses.

James Moran, "Private Presses and the Printing Industry." *British Printer* (April 1962): 105–120.

Kenneth Day, ed. *Book Typography 1815–1965*. London, 1966. Much wider in scope, but includes a good deal on private and fine presses in several of the chapters.

Loughborough School of Librarianship. *Private Presses: Handbook to an Exhibition*. Loughborough, 1968. A short introductory history.

Colin Franklin. *The Private Presses*. London, 1969. A very readable and thoughtful account of the aims and achievements of the English private press movement.

PRACTICAL MANUALS FOR THE AMATEUR

John Ryder. *Printing for Pleasure*. London, 1955. A very stylish and readable handbook; largely responsible for the increase in amateur printing of good quality in Great Britain in the past quarter-century.

J. Ben Lieberman. *Printing as a Hobby*. New York, 1963. A useful introduction for the novice.

Lewis Allen. *Printing with the Handpress*. New York, 1969. An outstandingly useful manual from one of the foremost contemporary handpress printers.

Frank J. Anderson. *Private Press Work: A Bibliographic Approach to Printing as an Avocation*. South Brunswick, N.J., 1977. A useful introduction to the literature and sources of supply.

Clifford Burke. *Printing Poetry: A Workbook in Typographic Reification*. San Francisco, 1980. As its title suggests, aimed at a very specific audience; an excellent manual combining technical information with the aesthetics of fine printing.

PERIODICALS

The range of journals and magazines that sometimes contain articles on private presses is enormous, as the checklists in *Private Press Books* show. Of journals currently published, *Fine Print* and *The American Book Collector* in the United States, *The Devil's Artisan* in Canada, and *The Private Library* and *Matrix* in Great Britain most frequently include private press studies and reviews. *Antiquarian Book Monthly Review, Quarterly News-Letter of the Book Club of California,* and the German *Philobiblon* often contain material of interest.

PART ONE
THE PRIVATE PRESSES

CHAPTER 2: THE QUASI-OFFICIAL OR PATRON'S PRESS

Anatole Claudin. "Private printing in France during the Fifteenth Century." *Bibliographica* v. 3 (1897): 344–370.

James P. R. Lyell. *Cardinal Ximenes*. London, 1916.

F. J. Norton. *Printing in Spain, 1501–1520*. Cambridge, 1966.

On missionary presses, material is scattered. Geoffrey Moorhouse's otherwise excellent study of *The Missionaries* (London, 1974) is very weak on their printing activities. Several volumes in The Spread of Printing series, edited by Colin Clair, are indicative of missionary work, as well as those listed below (e.g., the volumes on Indonesia, Malta, and South Africa). For mission printing in the South Seas, Richard E. Lingenfelter's *Presses of the Pacific Islands, 1817–1867* (Los Angeles, 1967) is very useful. For the examples given in this chapter, I drew on:

Benedikt S. Benedikz. *The Spread of Printing: Iceland*. Amsterdam, 1969.

Knud Oldenow. *The Spread of Printing: Greenland*. Amsterdam, 1969.

Fiona Macmillan. *The Spread of Printing: New Zealand*. Amsterdam, 1969.

A. G. Bagnall and G. C. Petersen. *William Colenso*. Wellington, 1948.

Alexina Harrison. *A. M. Mackay, Pioneer Missionary . . . to Uganda*. By his sister. Photolitho reprint ed. London, 1970.

Albert J. Schütz, ed. *The Diaries and Correspondence of David Cargill, 1832–1843*. Canberra, 1977.

CHAPTER 3: THE SCHOLARLY PRESS

Sten G. Lindberg. "Mobiles in Books." *Private Library* 3rd series, v. 2, no. 2 (Summer 1979): 49–82.

F. Van Ortroy. "Bibliographie de l'Oeuvre de Pierre Apian." *Le Bibliographie Moderne* (1901): 89–156, 284–333.

E. Zinner. *Leben und Werke des Johann Müller von Königsberg*. Munich, 1938.

John A. Gade. *The Life and Times of Tycho Brahe*. Princeton, 1947.

Lauritz Nielsen. "Tycho Brahes Bogtrykkeri paa Hveen." *Nordisk Tidsscrift for Bog- og Bibliotekswaesen* v. 8 (1946).

Sven Almqvist. *Johann Kankel, Pehr Brahes Bogtryckare på Visingo*. Stockholm, 1965.

Charles Nodier. "De la plus Célèbre des Imprimeries Particulières." In *Mélanges Tirés d'une Petite Bibliothèque*, pp. 173–177. Paris, 1829.

Giulio Natali. "Un Marchese Teologo e Filologo." In *Idee: Costumi, Uomini del Settecento*, pp. 249–254. Turin, 1926.

Edward Rowe Mores. *A Dissertation upon English Typographical Founders and Founderies*. Edited by Harry Carter and Christopher Ricks. Oxford, 1961.

CHAPTER 4: THE PRESS AS AN EDUCATIONAL TOY

Depositio Cornuti Typographici: A Mirthful Play Performed at the Confirmation of a Journeyman. Translated from the German by William Blades. New ed. by James Moran. London, 1962.

G. A. Crapelet. *De la Profession de l'Imprimeur*. Paris, 1840.

"L'Imprimerie du Cabinet du Roi au Château des Tuileries sous Louis XV (1718–1730)." *Bulletin de la Societé de l'Histoire de Paris* v. 18. (1891): 35–45.

Charles Nodier. "La Revolution Prophetisée par Fénelon et par Louis XV." In *Mélanges Tirés d'une Petite Bibliothèque*, pp. 97–100. Paris, 1829.

James Moran. "Printing on the Thames." *The Black Art* v. 2 (1963): 67–70.

Jean Marchand. "L'Imprimerie Particulière du Marquis de Bercy." *Le Livre et l'Estampe* no. 22 (1960): 123–130.

Peter Antrobus. "An Amateur Printer of the French Revolution." *Private Library* 2nd series, v. 1 no. 4 (Winter 1968): 141–144.

CHAPTER 5: THE ARISTOCRATIC PLAYTHING

Wilmarth S. Lewis. *Horace Walpole*. London, 1961.

Horace Walpole. *Journal of the Printing Office at Strawberry Hill*. Edited by Paget Toynbee. London, 1923.

Allen T. Hazen. *A Bibliography of the Strawberry Hill Press*. New Haven, 1942.

Charles Nodier. "De Plus Rare des Ana." In his *Mélanges Tirés d'une Petite Bibliothèque*, pp. 40–43. Paris, 1829.

Luther S. Livingston. *Franklin and His Press at Passy*. New York, 1914.

Randolph G. Adams. *The Passports Printed by Benjamin Franklin at his Passy Press*. Ann Arbor, 1925.

William E. Lingelbach. "B. Franklin, Printer—New Source Materials." *Proceedings of the American Philosophical Society* v. 92 (1948): 79–100.

F. B. Adams, Jr. "Franklin and His Press at Passy." *Yale University Library Gazette* v. 30 (1956): 133–138.

P. Van der Haeghen. "Le Commerce d'Autrefois et l'Imprimerie d'une Duchesse." *Le Livre* (1870): 248–253.

"Imprimerie de Bel-Oeil." *Le Bibliophile Belge* v. 1 (1845): 117–121; v. 9 (1852): 297–300.

Bogdan Krieger. *Friedrich der Grosse und Seine Bucher.* Leipzig, 1914.

Hans Droysen. "Friedrichs des Grossen Druckerei im Berliner Schlosse." *Hohenzollern Jahrbuch.* v. 8 (1904): 83–91.

Paul Seidel. "Georg Friedrich Schmidt, der Erste Illustrator und Drucker Friedrichs des Grossen." *Hohenzollern Jahrbuch* v. 5 (1901): 60–73.

CHAPTER 6: PRIVATE PRINTING
AND THE BIBLIOMANIA

Nicolas Barker. *The Publications of the Roxburghe Club.* Cambridge, 1964.

Robert Henry Allan, ed. *The Life of the Late George Allan . . . to Which Is Added a Catalogue of Books and Tracts Printed at His Private Press. . . .* Sunderland, 1829.

Eiluned Rees and Gwyn Walters. "Thomas Pennant and Paul Panton Jr: Their Printing Contacts with George Allan and Luke Hansard." *Journal of the Printing Historical Society* no. 7 (1971): 54–63.

S. I. Wicklen. "Thomas Johnes and the Hafod House Press." *Book Design and Production* v. 6 (1963): 30–34.

Sir Samuel Egerton Brydges. *The Autobiography, Times, Opinions and Contemporaries of Sir Egerton Brydges.* London, 1834.

Michael Sadleir. *Archdeacon Francis Wrangham, 1769–1842.* London, 1937. Also printed on pp. 201–247 of his *Things Past* (London, 1944), Sadleir's essay includes a good deal that is useful on the Lee Priory Press. This essay appears to be the only publication resulting from a collaboration on a history of the press that he and Stanley Morison embarked upon in the 1930s; a modern study of Brydges's Press is a desideratum.

A. N. L. Munby. *Phillipps Studies.* Cambridge, 1951–1960. Contains much material on the Middle Hill Press, scattered throughout its five volumes. This is more conveniently available to the general reader in Nicolas Barker's abridgment of Munby's work, *Portrait of an Obsession* (London, 1967).

David Chambers. "Sir Thomas Phillipps and the Middle Hill Press." *Private Library* 3rd series, v. 1, no. 1 (Spring 1978): 2–38.

Geoffrey Wakeman. "Anastatic Printing for Sir Thomas Phillipps." *Journal of the Printing Historical Society* no. 5 (1969): 24–40.

Charles Manby Smith. *The Working Man's Way in the World.* With a preface and notes by Ellic Howe. London, 1967.

Simon Nowell-Smith. "Charles Manby Smith: His Family & Friends, His Fantasies & Fabrications." *Journal of the Printing Historical Society* no. 7 (1971): 1–28.

Albert Ehrman. "The Private Press and Publishing Activities of Prince Louis-Lucien Bonaparte." *The Book Collector* v. 9 (1960): 30–37.

CHAPTER 7: THE AUTHOR AS PUBLISHER

Strickland Gibson and Sir William Holdsworth. "Charles Viner's *General Abridgment of Law and Equity.*" Oxford Bibliographical Society Proceedings and Papers v. 2 (1930): 229–243.

A. H. Robb-Smith. "John Hunter's Private Press." *Journal of the History of Medicine and Allied Sciences* v. 25, no. 3 (July 1970): 262–269.

A. C. Piper. "Private Printing Presses in Sussex." *The Library* 3rd series, v. 5 (1914): 70–79.

Carroll D. Coleman. "The Parson-Printer of Lustleigh." *The Colophon* new series, v. 1 (1935): 221–226.

C. Davy. "A Memoir of the Life of the Rev. W. Davy." Prefixed to the latter's *Divinity, or Discourses on the Being of God. . . .* Exeter, 1827.

Ursula Radford. "William Davy, Priest and Printer." *Transactions of the Devonshire Association* v. 63 (1931): 325–339.

Roderick Cave. "The First Jamaican Private Press." *Private Library* 2nd series, v. 8, no. 3 (Autumn 1975): 115–119.

Sir Geoffrey Keynes. *William Blake: Poet, Printer, Prophet.* London, 1965.

Ruthven Todd. "The Techniques of William Blake's Illuminated Painting." *Print* v. 6 (1948): 53–65.

Robert Essick. *William Blake's Relief Inventions.* Los Angeles, 1978.

Roderick Cave. "Blake's Mantle: A Memoir of Ralph Chubb." *Book Design and Production* v. 3, no. 2 (1960): 24–28.

Anthony Reid. "Ralph Chubb, the Unknown." *Private Library* 2nd series, v. 3, no. 3 (Autumn 1970): 141–156; v. 3, no. 4 (Winter 1970): 193–213.

Roderick Cave. "GogMagog: The Private Press of Morris Cox." *The American Book Collector* v. 12, no. 9 (May 1962): 20–23.

David Chambers. "The Gogmagog Press." *Private Library* v. 5 (1964): 5–10.

CHAPTER 8: CLANDESTINE PRESSES I: MORAL

Thomas Edward Stonor. "The Private Printing Press at Stonor, 1581." *Bibliographical and Historical Miscellanies of the Philobiblon Society* v. 1 (1854).

———. "Description of a Copy of *Rationes Decem Campiani*." *Bibliographical and Historical Miscellanies of the Philobiblon Society* v. 9 (1865–1866).

Evelyn Waugh. *Edmund Campion*. London, 1935.

A. C. Southern. *Elizabethan Recusant Prose, 1559–1582*. London, 1950.

J. Dover Wilson. "The Marprelate Controversy." *The Cambridge History of English Literature* v. 3. Cambridge, 1909.

Piaras Béaslaí. *Michael Collins and the Making of a New Ireland*. Dublin, 1926.

James S. Dearden. "Printing at Brantwood." *Book Collector* v. 27, no. 4 (Winter 1978): 514–532; v. 28, no. 2 (Summer 1979): 236–251.

Jean Massart. *The Secret Press in Belgium*. Translated by Bernard Miall. London, 1918.

Douglas C. McMurtrie. "Joseph Skalda, Underground Printer." *New England Printer and Publisher* (January–February 1944).

Vercors. *Voices of Silence*. London, 1968.

Dirk de Jong. *Het Vrije Boek in Onvrije Tijd: Bibliografie van Illegale en Clandestiene Bellettrie, 1940–45*. Leiden, 1958.

J. Martinet. *Catalogue of the "Drucksel" Prints . . . by Hendrik Nicolaas Werkman*. Amsterdam, 1963.

L. G. A. Schlichting. "Dutch Underground Printing." *Print* v. 4, no. 3 (1946): 23–28.

Anna Simoni. "Dutch Clandestine Printing, 1940–1945." *The Library* 5th series v. 27, no. 1 (March 1972): 1–22.

CHAPTER 9: CLANDESTINE PRESSES II: IMMORAL

G. Legman. *The Horn Book*. New York, 1964.

Raymond Postgate. *That Devil Wilkes*. London, 1956.

Alec Craig. *The Banned Books of England*. 2nd ed. London, 1962.

Rigby Graham. "Potocki." *Private Library* v. 8 (1967): 8–26.

Geoffrey Potocki of Montalk. *Myself as Printer*. Wymondham, 1970.

CHAPTER 10: PRINTING FOR PLEASURE

James Mosley. "The Press in the Parlour: Some Notes on the Amateur Printer and His Equipment." *The Black Art* v. 2 (1963): 1–16. An outstandingly good survey, quoting extensively from the amateur printers' manuals of the nineteenth century. Some of these, such as Jabez Francis' *Printing at Home* (1870), or P. E. Raynor's *Printing for Amateurs* (1876), or the journal *Amateur Printing* (1895–1913) are also well worth consulting.

G. A. Snow. "Model T's of Printing." *Print* v. 5, no. 2 (1947): 7–14. Surveys the American production of presses designed for amateurs.

James Moran. *Printing Presses: History and Development from the Fifteenth Century to Modern Times*. London, 1973. Appendix I, "Miniature, 'Toy,' Amateur and Card Presses," on pp. 225–247, is particularly useful.

J. A. Fairley. "Peter Buchan, Printer and Ballad Collector." *Transactions of the Buchan Field Club* v. 7 (1902): 123–158.

A. C. Piper. "Private Printing Presses in Sussex." *The Library* 3rd. series, v. 5 (1914): 70–79.

Henry R. Plomer. "Some Private Presses of the Nineteenth Century." *The Library* 2nd series, v. 1 (1900): 407–428.

Charles Holtzapffel. *Printing Apparatus for the Use of Amateurs*. Reprinted from the third greatly enlarged edition of 1846 and edited by James Mosley and David Chambers. Pinner, 1971. Includes valuable notes on work undertaken on Parlour presses, as well as an immaculately edited text.

E. R. McClintock Dix. "The Private Press at Duncairn, Belfast." *The Irish Book Lover* v. 1 (1909–1910): 7–8, 25–26.

Truman J. Spencer. *History of Amateur Journalism*. Edited and revised by Edward A. Oldham. New York, 1947. Updating of his *Cyclopedia of the Literature of Amateur Journalism* (Hartford, Conn., 1891).

Carey S. Bliss. *The Willowdale Press, 1879: With Notes on the History of the Amateur Press in California*. Los Angeles, 1975.

The Daniel Press: Memorials of C. H. O. Daniel with a Bibliography of the Press, 1845–1919. Oxford, 1921.

Colin Franklin. "Garlands of Rachel." *Book Collector* v. 30, no. 4 (Winter 1981): 479–490.

Holbrook Jackson. *The Printing of Books*. London, 1938. Chapter VI, pp. 99–108, on Robert Bridges is suggestive for his influence on Daniel.

Bruce Dickins. "Samuel Page Widnall and His Press at Grantchester, 1871–1892." *Transactions of the Cambridge Bibliographical Society* v. 2, no. 5 (1958): 366–372. Addenda to this full account were published in *Transactions* v. 3, no. 1 (1959) and v. 3, no. 2 (1960): 176–178.

CHAPTER 11: PRINTING AS ONE OF THE FINE ARTS: WILLIAM MORRIS AND THE KELMSCOTT PRESS

The literature on the Kelmscott Press is of course very extensive. This list has deliberately been limited far more than for most other private presses.

H. Halliday Sparling. *The Kelmscott Press and William Morris, Master-craftsman.* London, 1924. Despite its age and over-adulatory approach, still a very useful book.

William Morris. *A Note on His Aims in Founding the Kelmscott Press: Together with a Short Description of the Press by S. C. Cockerell & an Annotated List of the Books Printed Thereat.* Hammersmith, 1898. The last of the Kelmscott books, reprinted in Sparling and in a photolithographic replica (1969).

William Morris Society. *The Typographical Adventure of William Morris.* London, 1957. An extremely good exhibition catalogue. The society's *Journal* also often contains material of interest.

Holbrook Jackson. *The Printing of Books.* London, 1938. "The Typography of William Morris," pp. 175–185, a paper originally read to the Double Crown Club's Morris Centenary Dinner and deliberately provocative, is a useful corrective to Sparling.

Duncan Robinson. *William Morris, Edward Burne-Jones and the Kelmscott Chaucer.* London, 1982.

Brown University. *William Morris and the Kelmscott Press: An Exhibition.* Providence, R.I., 1960.

Wilfred Blunt. *Cockerell.* London, 1964.

Pierpont Morgan Library. *William Morris and the Art of the Book: With Essays by Paul Needham, Joseph Dunlap and John Dreyfus.* New York, 1976. A superb, lavishly illustrated catalogue.

John Russell Taylor. *The Art Nouveau Book in Britain.* London, 1966.

CHAPTER 12: AFTER KELMSCOTT: THE FINE PRESS IN BRITAIN

Ruari Maclean. *Modern Book Design, from William Morris to the Present Day.* London, 1958.

Colin Franklin. *The Private Presses.* London, 1969.

A. J. A. Symons. "An Unacknowledged Movement in Fine Printing: The Typography of the Nineties." *The Fleuron* v. 7 (1930). Reprinted in *The Fleuron Anthology,* ed. by Francis Meynell and Herbert Simon, pp. 301–325. London, 1973.

Gillian Naylor. *The Arts and Crafts Movement.* London, 1971.

Holbrook Jackson. *The Printing of Books.* London, 1938. Chapter V, pp. 89–98, is on Whistler's influence on book design.

John Russell Taylor. *The Art Nouveau Book in Britain.* London, 1966.

Stephen Calloway. *Charles Ricketts, Subtle and Fantastic Decorator.* London, 1979.

Joseph Darracott. *The World of Charles Ricketts.* London, 1980. Pages 26–55 deal with the Vale Press.

Charles Ricketts. *A Defence of the Revival of Printing.* London, 1899.

———. *A Bibliography of the Books Issued by Hacon and Ricketts, 1896–1903.* London, 1904.

T. Sturge Moore. *A Brief Account of the Origin of the Eragny Press.* Hammersmith, 1903.

Lucien Pissarro. *Notes on the Eragny Press, and, A Letter to J. B. Manson.* Ed. with a supplement by Alan Fern. Cambridge, 1957.

W. S. Meadmore. *Lucien Pissarro.* London, 1962.

C. H. St. John Hornby and Arundel Esdaile. *A Descriptive Bibliography of the Books Printed at the Ashendene Press, MDCCCXCV–MCMXXXV.* London, 1935.

B. H. Newdigate. "Mr C. H. St. John Hornby's Ashendene Press." *The Fleuron* v. 2 (1924): 77–85.

Will Ransom, ed. *Kelmscott, Doves and Ashendene: The Private Press Credos.* New York, 1952.

Sir Sydney Cockerell. *Friends of a Lifetime.* Edited by Viola Meynell. London, 1940.

Priscilla Johnston. *Edward Johnston.* London, 1959.

T. J. Cobden-Sanderson. *Catalogue Raisonné of Books Printed at the Doves Press, 1900–1916.* Hammersmith, 1916. The last book from the press.

———. *Cosmic Vision.* London, 1922.

———. *Journals 1879–1922.* London, 1926.

John Henry Nash, ed. *Cobden-Sanderson and the Doves Press.* San Francisco, 1929.

C. Volmer Nordlunde. *Thomas James Cobden-Sanderson.* Copenhagen, 1957.

J. H. Mason. *A Selection from the Notebooks of a Scholar-Printer.* Leicester, 1961.

John R. Nash. "Mr Cobden-Sanderson's Two-handed Engine." *The Book Collector* v. 25, no. 4 (Winter 1976): 491–506.

C. R. Ashbee. *The Private Press, a Study in Idealism; To which Is Added a Bibliography of the Essex House Press.* Chipping Camden, 1909.

———. "The Essex House Press, and the Purpose or Meaning of a Private Press." *Book Collector's Quarterly* no. 11 (1933): 69–86.

CHAPTER 13: MORRIS IN AMERICA

Susan O. Thompson. *American Book Design and William Morris.* New York, 1977.

Robert Judson Clark, ed. *The Arts and Crafts Movement in America, 1876–1916.* Princeton, 1972.

Joseph Blumenthal. *The Printed Book in America.* Boston, 1977.

R. Malcolm Sills. "W. J. Linton at Yale—the Appledore Private Press." *Yale University Library Gazette* v. 12 (January 1938): 43–52.

Charles E. Hamilton. *As Bees in Honey Drown: Elbert Hubbard and the Roycrofters.* New York, 1973.

Philip John Schwarz. "Will Ransom: The Early Years." *Journal of Library History* v. 3 (1968): 138–55.

Vrest Orton. *Goudy: Master of Letters.* Chicago, 1939.

Peter Beilenson. *The Story of Frederic W. Goudy.* New York, 1939.

Bernard Lewis. *Behind the Types: The Life Story of Frederic W. Goudy.* Pittsburgh, 1941.

Melbert B. Cary. *Bibliography of the Village Press.* New York, 1938.

Rudolph Gjelsness. "Frank Holme: Newspaper Artist and Designer of Books." *The Colophon* new series, v. 1 (1935): 191–200.

Martin Gardner and Russell B. Nye. *The Wizard of Oz and Who He Was.* East Lansing, 1957.

Ralph Fletcher Seymour. *Some Went This Way.* Chicago, 1945.

George G. Booth. *The Cranbrook Press.* Detroit, 1902.

Paul McPharlin. "The Cranbrook Press." *The Dolphin* v. 4 (1941): 268–278.

Thomas A. Larremore and Amy Hopkins Larremore. *The Marion Press: A Survey and a Checklist.* Jamaica, N.Y., 1943.

CHAPTER 14: FINE PRINTING ON THE CONTINENT

A. M. Hammacher. *Die Welt Henry van der Velde.* Cologne, 1968.

Charles Van Halsbeke. *L'Art Typographique dans les Pays-Bas depuis 1892.* Brussels, 1929.

C. Reedijk. "The Renascence of Printing in the Netherlands." *Bibliotheekleven* v. 51 (1966): 437–457.

A. A. M. Stols. *Het Werk van S. H. de Roos.* Amsterdam, 1942.

A. M. Hammacher. *Jean François van Royen.* The Hague, 1947.

Museum Meermanno-Westreenianum. *Jean François van Royen, 1878–1942.* The Hague, 1964.

Julius Rodenberg. *Deutsche Pressen: Eine Bibliographie.* Zurich, 1925.

Willy Wiegand. "German Private Presses." *Imprimatur* v. 1 (1930): 101–107.

Fritz Kredel. "Rudolf Koch." In *Heritage of the Graphic Arts,* ed. by Chandler B. Grannis, pp. 91–102. New York, 1972.

Gordon Craig. "Edward Gordon Craig's *Hamlet.*" *Private Library* 2nd series, v. 10, no. 1 (Spring 1977): 35–48.

Hans Loubier. "Die Drucke der Ernst Ludwig Presse." *Archiv für Buchgewerbe und Graphik* v. 50 (1913): 3–23.

Albert Windisch. "Friedrich Wilhelm Kleukens, der Buch- und Schriftkünstler." *Gutenberg-Jahrbuch* (1950): 327–335.

Hans Schmoller. "Carl Ernst Poeschel." *Signature* new series, no. 11: 20–36.

Josef Lehnacker, ed. *Die Bremer Presse; Königin der deutschen Privatpressen.* Munich, 1964.

Bernhard Zeller and Werner Volke, eds. *Buchkunst und Dichtung: Zur Geschichte der Bremer Presse und der Corona.* Munich, 1966.

Friedrich Ewald. "The Officina Bodoni." *The Fleuron* no. 7 (1930): 121–131.

Hans Schmoller. "A Gentleman of Verona." *Penrose Annual* v. 52 (1958): 29–34.

John Dreyfus. *Giovanni Mardersteig: An Account of His Work.* Verona, 1966.

John Barr. *The Officina Bodoni.* London, 1978.

Giovanni Mardersteig. *Ein Leben den Büchern Gewidmet.* Mainz, 1968.

———. *The Officina Bodoni: An Account of the Work of a Hand Press, 1923–1977.* Introd. by Hans Schmoller. Verona, 1980. The definitive catalogue.

Franco Riva. *The Officina Bodoni.* Verona, 1968.

John Ryder. "The Officina Bodoni." *Private Library* 2nd series, v. 5, no. 4 (Winter 1972): 173–259.

CHAPTER 15: BETWEEN THE WARS IN BRITAIN I:
THE GREAT PRESSES

Malcolm Easton. *Claude Lovat Fraser (1890–1921): An Exhibition of the Printed Work.* Hull, 1968.

Oliver Simon. *Printer and Playground.* London, 1956.

The Nonesuch Century: An Appraisal by A. J. A. Symons, a Personal Note by Francis Meynell, and a Bibliography by Desmond Flower, of the First Hundred Books Issued by the Press, 1923–1934. London, 1936.

Ian Rogerson. *Sir Francis Meynell and the Nonesuch Press.* Manchester, 1979.

John Dreyfus. *The History of the Nonesuch Press.* London, 1981. A definitive history.

Chanticleer: A Bibliography of the Golden Cockerel Press, April 1921–August 1936. London, 1936.

Pertelote: Being a Bibliography of the Golden Cockerel Press, October 1936–April 1943. London, 1943.

Cockalorum: Being a Bibliography of the Golden Cockerel Press, June 1943–December 1948. London, 1949.

Cock-a-Hoop . . . Being a Bibliography of the Golden Cockerel Press, September 1949–December 1961, with a List of Prospectuses, 1920–1962. Pinner, 1978.

Loran Hurnscot. *A Prison, a Paradise.* London, 1958. A disguised account of the early days of Golden Cockerel by one of the original partners.

Roderick Cave. "The Lost Years of the Golden Cockerel Press." *Printing History* v. 4, no. 7/8 (1982): 3–15.

A. Mary Kirkus. *Robert Gibbings: A Bibliography.* London, 1962.

Thomas Jones. *The Gregynog Press.* Oxford, 1954.

Gwenllian Davies. "Memoirs of Gregynog." *Manchester Review* v. 8 (1959): 257–263.

Ewart Bowen. "Memoirs of Gregynog." *Manchester Review* v. 8 (1959): 264–268.

J. Michael Davies. *The Private Press at Gregynog.* Leicester, 1959.

Dorothy A. Harrop. *A History of the Gregynog Press.* Pinner, 1980. The definitive account of the press.

Loyd Haberly. *An American Bookbuilder in England and Wales: Reminiscences of the Seven Acres and Gregynog Press.* London, 1979.

CHAPTER 16: BETWEEN THE WARS IN BRITAIN II:
BACKWATERS AND TRIBUTARIES

Frank Sidgwick. *Frank Sidgwick's Diary: And Other Materials relating to A. H. Bullen and the Shakespeare Head Press.* Oxford, 1975.

Joseph Thorp. *B. H. Newdigate, Scholar-Printer, 1869–1944.* Oxford, 1950.

Paul Morgan. "A Pressman's Diary, 1927–1928, and the Shakespeare Head *Froissart*." *Matrix* no. 1 (1981): 12–16.

William Maxwell. *The Dun Emer Press and the Cuala Press.* London, 1932.

Liam Miller. *The Dun Emer Press, Later the Cuala Press.* Dublin, 1973.

Colin Smythe. "The Cuala Press, 1903–1973." *Private Library* 2nd series, v. 6, no. 3 (Autumn 1973): 107–113.

Leonard Woolf. *Beginning Again: An Autobiography of the Years, 1911–1918.* London, 1964.

————. *Downhill All the Way: An Autobiography of the Years, 1918–1939.* London, 1967.

————. *The Journey Not the Arrival Matters: An Autobiography of the Years, 1939–1969.* London, 1969.

Richard Kennedy. *A Boy at the Hogarth Press.* London, 1972.

John Lehmann. *Thrown to the Woolfs.* London, 1978. Lehmann's and Kennedy's memoirs give a rather different picture of the Hogarth Press from that to be gained from Leonard Woolf's spare account in the volumes of his autobiography.

Jean Peters, "Publisher's Imprints." In *Collectible Books: Some New Paths,* pp. 198–224. New York, 1979. Largely on the Hogarth Press.

Rigby Graham. "T. E. Lawrence and the Seizin Press." *Private Library* 2nd series, v. 6, no. 1 (Spring 1973): 16–21.

James Moran. "The Seizin Press of Laura Riding and Robert Graves." *The Black Art* v. 2 (1963): 34–39. Based largely on Graves's reminiscences, and differing in some details from Laura Riding's version.

Hugh Ford. "The Seizin Press." *Private Library* 2nd series, v. 5, no. 3 (Autumn 1972): 121–138. With a Postscript by Laura (Riding) Jackson on pp. 139–147; the other side of the story.

Martin Seymour-Smith. *Robert Graves: His Life and Work.* London, 1982.

H. C. D. Pepler. *The Hand Press.* Ditchling, 1934. A reprint was published by the Ditchling Press in 1952.

Brocard Sewell. *Three Private Presses: St. Dominic's Press, the Press of Edward Walters, St. Albert's Press.* Wellingborough, 1979.

Ann Barrett. "The Walpole Press of Old Costessey, Norwich." *Private Library* v. 8, no. 2 (1967): 38–43.

James A. Dearden. "The Raven Press." *Private Library* 2nd series, v. 6, no. 4 (Winter 1973): 158–191. Supplemented by his "Horace Walter Bray at the Raven Press" in v. 7, no. 3 (Autumn 1974): 122–123, and by Jeff Cooper's addendum in v. 7, no. 4 (Winter 1974): 170–171.

Cyril W. Beaumont. *The First Score: An Account of the Foundation and Development of the Beaumont Press.* London, 1927.

———. *Bookseller at the Ballet: Memoirs, 1891–1929.* London, 1975.

Nancy Cunard. *Those Were the Hours: Memories of My Hours Press Réanville and Paris, 1928–1931.* Carbondale, Ill., 1969.

———. "The Hours Press: Retrospect-Catalogue-Commentary." *The Book Collector* v. 13 (1964): 488–496.

Richard Lambert. "The Stanton Press: A Retrospect." *Private Library* 2nd series, v. 4, no. 2 (Summer 1971): 55–65.

Peter C. G. Isaac. "H. G. Dixey Press." *The Private Library* v. 6 (1962): 36–39.

CHAPTER 17: BETWEEN THE WARS IN THE U.S.A.

Joseph Blumenthal. *The Printed Book in America.* Boston, 1977. An excellent overview.

Chandler B. Grannis, ed. *Heritage of the Graphic Arts: A Selection of Lectures Delivered at Gallery 303.* New York, 1972. The lectures by Carolyn Reading Hammer on Victor Hammer (pp. 167–181) and by Roland Baughman on the Grabhorns (pp. 227–239) are particularly good.

Dard Hunter. *My Life with Paper.* New York, 1958.

Dard Hunter, II. *The Life Work of Dard Hunter: A Progressive Illustrated Assemblage of His Work as Artist, Craftsman, Author, Papermaker and Printer.* Chillicothe, 1981–   . For completion in a second volume 1983; a labor of devotion produced at Hunter's revived Mountain House Press.

Harry B. Weiss. "The Miniature Books of William Lewis Washburn." *The Book Collector's Packet* v. 3, no. 1 (1938): 20–22.

Gertrude H. Muir. "Edwin Bliss Hill, Pioneer Private Printer of the Southwest." *The American Book Collector* v. 18 (1967): 20–27. Includes an excellent checklist of the press's work, compiled by John M. Myers.

Herman Schauinger. *A Bibliography of Trovillion Private Press.* Herrin, Ill., 1943.

James Moran. "America's Oldest Private Press." *Book Design & Production* v. 1 (1958–1959): 17–19.

Marion C. Brown. *Joseph Ishill and the Oriole Press.* Berkeley Heights, N.J., 1960.

Mrs. Simon Mendelsohn. "A Complete Checklist of the Publications of Joseph Ishill and His Oriole Press." *American Book Collector* v. 25, no. 1 (September–October 1974): 14–25; v. 25, no. 2 (November–December 1974): 20–31; v. 25, no. 3 (January–February 1975): 16–23.

George Parker Winship. "Recollections of a Private Printer." *The Colophon* new series, v. 3, no. 2 (1938): 210–224.

Arthur W. Rushmore. "The Fun and Fury of a Private Press." In *Bookmaking and Kindred Amenities,* ed. by Earl S. Miers and Richard Ellis. Rutgers, 1942. (Reprinted with a postscript in *Books and Printing,* ed. by Paul A. Bennett. Cleveland, 1951.)

James Lamar Weygand. *Elmer F. Gleason and the Stratford Press.* Nappanee, Ind., 1965.

Sylvia Beach. *Shakespeare & Co.* London, 1960.

Hugh Ford. *Published in Paris: American and British Writers, Printers and Publishers in Paris, 1920–1939.* New York, 1975.

Robert D. Harlan. *John Henry Nash: The Biography of a Career.* Berkeley, 1970.

Elinor Raas Heller and David Magee. *Bibliography of the Grabhorn Press, 1915–1940.* San Francisco, 1940. Supplemented by Dorothy and David Magee's *Bibliography . . . 1940–1956* (San Francisco, 1957) and *Bibliography of the Grabhorn Press, 1957–1966, and Grabhorn-Hoyem, 1966–1973,* edited by Robert D. Harlan (San Francisco, 1977).

Ward Ritchie. *The Ward Ritchie Press, and Anderson, Ritchie & Simon.* Los Angeles, 1961.

Herbert Cahoon. *The Overbrook Press Bibliography, 1934–1959.* Stamford, Conn., 1964.

CHAPTER 18: WORLD WAR II AND THE AFTERMATH IN BRITAIN

B. E. Bellamy. *Private Presses & Publishing in England since 1945.* London, 1980.

B. Fairfax Hall. "The Stourton Press (from 1930–35)." *Private Library* 2nd series, v. 2 (1969): 54–67.

Lord Carlow. *A List of Books Printed at the Corvinus Press.* London(?), 1939(?).

Christopher Sandford. "Press Book Production, 1945–52." *Penrose Annual* v. 47 (1953): 31–34.

John Ryder. *Printing for Pleasure.* London, 1955.

Muriel Harris. "The Perpetua Press of Bland and Ridler." *Book Design & Production* v. 1 (1958): 15–17.

David Bland. "The Perpetua Press." *Private Library* 2nd series, v. 3, no. 2 (1970): 78–90.

Anthony Baker. "The Quest for Guido." *Private Library* 2nd series, v. 2, no. 4 (1969): 138–176. Supplemented by "The Latin Press: A Tentative Checklist," compiled by P. A. H. Brown and Anthony Baker, on pp. 180–187 of the same volume.

John Peters. "Notes on the Production of Vine Press Books." *Private Library* v. 7 (1966): 42–44.

The Times Bookshop. *Books from Stanbrook Abbey Press and the Vine Press.* With an introduction by John Dreyfus. London, 1965.

Stanbrook Abbey Press: Ninety-Two Years of Its History. Callow End, 1970.

Victoria & Albert Museum. *Stanbrook Abbey Press and Sir Sydney Cockerell: A Centenary Exhibition, 10 Nov. 1976–13 Feb. 1977.* London, 1976.

Alan Tarling. *Will Carter, Printer.* London, 1968.

Will Carter. *The Rampant Lions Press: A Printing Workshop through Five Decades.* Cambridge, 1983.

Roderick Cave. "Thomas Rae: A Modern Scottish Printer." *The American Book Collector* v. 12, no. 2 (1961): 18–21.

Thomas Rae. "The Signet Press." *The Black Art* v. 1 (1962): 86–90.

David Chambers. "The Cuckoo Hill Press." *Private Library* v. 4 (1963): 110–114.

CHAPTER 19: THE CONTEMPORARY SCENE IN BRITAIN

B. E. Bellamy. *Private Presses & Publishing in England since 1945.* London, 1980.

Juliet Standing. *The Private Press Today.* Wymondham, 1967.

Glasgow School of Art. *The Page Right Printed: An Exhibition of the Work of the Private Presses. . . .* Glasgow, 1973.

Victoria & Albert Museum. *The Open & Closed Book: Contemporary Book Arts—Catalogue of an Exhibition Held 12 September–18 November 1979.* London, 1979. A fascinating exhibition, including many fetish objects as well as real books.

Montague Shaw. "Private Presses." *Crafts* (May–June 1982): 28–33. A useful and shrewd, if sometimes wayward account; well illustrated.

Ann Morris. *The Private Press in Leicestershire.* Loughborough, 1976.

John Mason. "Adventurous Papermaking: The Founding of the Twelve by Eight Mill." *The Black Art* v. 2, no. 3 (Autumn 1963): 74–78.

———. *Twelve by Eight.* Leicester, 1958.

Rigby Graham. "The Pandora Press." *Private Library* v. 7 (1966): 5–10.

———. "The Orpheus Press." *The American Book Collector* v. 19, no. 5 (1969): 11–22.

Roderick Cave. "Printing at the Brewhouse." *The American Book Collector* v. 16, no. 9 (1966): 18–24.

Patricia Graham. *The Brewhouse Press at Wymondham.* Wymondham, 1974.

Geoffrey Wakeman. *The Plough Press, 1967–1981: Fifteen Years Printing in a Loughborough Garage.* Kidlington, Oxford, 1982.

David Butcher. *The Whittington Press: A Bibliography, 1971–1981.* Andoversford, 1982.

———. "The Whittington Press: The First Decade." *Private Library* 3rd series, v. 5, no. 3 (Autumn 1982): 136–160.

George Szirtes. "The Tern Press—Fine Books for Collectors." *Albion* v. 2, no. 3 (December 1978): 12–14.

B. S. Johnson. "The Gregynog Press and the Gregynog Fellowship." *Private Library* 2nd series, v. 6, no. 1 (Spring 1973): 4–15.

Michael Hutchins. "Gwasg Gregynog Lives." *Penrose Annual* v. 71 (1978–1979): 136–147.

Roger Burford Mason. "The Mandeville Press of Hitchin." *Private Library* 2nd series, v. 10, no. 1 (Spring 1977): 22–34.

John Cotton. "The Poet & Printer Press: Some Notes and a Checklist." *Private Library* 2nd series, v. 4, no. 3 (Autumn 1971): 128–139.

———. "The Fantasy Poets." *Private Library* 2nd series, v. 2, no. 1 (Spring 1969): 3–13.

Alan Tarling. "The Shoestring Press." *Small Printer* (January 1967): 5–8.

Richard Brown. "The Shoestring Press of Ben Sands." *Penrose Annual* v. 72 (1980): 163–172.

Rigby Graham. "Paul Peter Piech and the Taurus Press of Willow Dene." *The American Book Collector* v. 20, no. 6 (March-April 1970): 30–35.

Kenneth Hardacre. "The Private Press of Paul Piech." *Penrose Annual* v. 69 (1976): 98–112.

Ian Mortimer. *I M Imprimit: Catalogue of an Exhibition at Cheltenham Art Gallery, 1–29 October 1977.* Cheltenham, 1977.

Alan Anderson. *The Tragara Press, 1954–1979: A Bibliography.* Edinburgh, 1979.

R. T. Risk. "Alex Frizzell: Portrait of a Scottish Private Printer." *Private Library* 2nd series, v. 8, no. 2 (Summer 1975): 75–90.

———. "Stanislaw Gliwa: Private Printer." *Private Library* 3rd series, v. 2, no. 1 (Spring 1979): 2–26.

CHAPTER 20: THE UNITED STATES TODAY

Joseph Blumenthal. *The Printed Book in America.* Boston, 1977.

Frank J. Anderson. *Private Presswork: A Bibliographic Approach to Printing as an Avocation.* South Brunswick, N.J., 1977.

Leonard F. Bahr, ed. *Printing in Privacy: A Review of Recent Activity among American Private Presses.* Grosse Pointe Park, Mich., 1960.

Abe Lerner. "Assault on the Book: A Critique of Fine Printing at Private Presses in the U.S. Today." *Private Library* 3rd series, v. 1, no. 4 (Winter 1978): 148–170. This, together with Lerner's "Form and Content: The Books of the American Private Presses Today" [*Private Library* 3rd series, v. 2, no. 3 (Autumn 1979): 95–100], is a shrewd overview of the contemporary scene.

Michael Peich. "Small Press." In *Annual Report of the American Rare, Antiquarian and Out-of-Print Book Trade, 1978–79,* pp. 92–96. New York, 1979.

Printers' Choice: A Selection of American Press Books, 1968–1978—Catalogue of an Exhibition held at the Grolier Club . . . 1979. Compiled by Ruth E. Fine, William Matheson, and W. Thomas Taylor. Austin, 1983. Not yet available at press time, but on the basis of the exhibition itself, and advance information, a very important book.

Barbara Cash. *The Small Private Press, New England, 1979.* Mount Carmel, Conn., 1980.

Stephen Brook. *A Bibliography of the Gehenna Press, 1942–1975.* Northampton, Mass., 1976.

Dorothy King. "Notes on the Gehenna Press." *Printing & Graphic Arts* v. 7, no. 2 (1959): 33–48.

Joseph Low. "Notes on the Eden Hill Press." *Printing & Graphic Arts* v. 8, no. 2 (1960): 21–30.

Barbara Cash. "Warwick Press of Easthampton, Massachusetts." *American Book Collector* new series, v. 3, no. 4 (July-August 1982): 42–46.

James Fraser and Renée Weber. *John Anderson and the Pickering Press.* Madison, N.J., 1980.

Ruth Fine Lehrer. "The Janus Press." *Private Library* 2nd series, v. 7, no. 3 (Autumn 1974): 91–121.

Barbara Luck. "A Memoir of the Janus Press, Summer 1979." *Fine Print* v. 6, no. 4 (October 1980): 115–117.

Barbara Cash. "The Banyan Press of Pawlet, Vermont." *American Book Collector* new series, v. 3, no. 5 (September-October 1982): 26–31.

Kathryn Clark. "Twinrocker: Collaboration in Custom Papermaking." *Fine Print* v. 3, no. 4 (October 1977): 77–81.

Dennis C. Wendell. "The Private Press in Iowa." *Missouri Library Association Quarterly* v. 30 (1969): 4–9.

L. O. Cheever. "The Prairie Press: A Thirty Year Record." *Books at Iowa* no. 3 (1965): 15–33. Supplemented by "The Prairie Press: A Checklist, 1965–1975." *Books at Iowa* no. 23 (November 1975): 30–33.

[Carroll Coleman.] "Carroll Coleman on Printing: Excerpts from a 36-Year Correspondence with Emerson G. Wulling." *Books at Iowa* no. 23 (November 1975): 11–29.

Mary L. Richmond. "The Cummington Press." *Books at Iowa* no. 7 (1967): 9–31.

———. "Harry Duncan & the Cummington Press." *Fine Print* v. 4, no. 1 (January 1978): 1–4. Augmented by Kay Amert and Kim Merker, "Harry Duncan: Maker of Books," pp. 4–8, and "A Checklist of Books Printed by Harry Duncan," pp. 9–10, of the same issue.

Kay Amert et al. "Works printed by K. K. Merker: The Stone Wall Press, the Windhover Press, and Others." *Books at Iowa* no. 25 (November 1976): 21–33.

William Bright. "Juan Pascoe and His Taller Martín Pescador." *Fine Print* v. 7, no. 1 (January 1981): 12–13, 34.

Cynthia Bush. "The Perishable Press Limited." *Books at Iowa* no. 29 (November 1978): 36–52.

John Mason. "The Bird & Bull Press of Henry Morris." *The Black Art* v. 1 (1962): 114–118.

Henry Morris, ed. *Five on Paper.* North Hills, Pa., 1963.

W. Thomas Taylor and Henry Morris. *Twenty One Years of Bird & Bull: A Bibliography, 1958–1979.* North Hills, 1980.

Carolyn Reading Hammer, ed. *Victor Hammer: Artist and Printer.* Lexington, Ky., 1981.

Thomas A. Sutherland. "The Gravesend Press." *American Book Collector* v. 16, no. 8 (1966): 18–20.

Dwight Agner. *The Nightowl at Ten.* Baton Rouge, 1974.

Timothy Hawley. "Kay Michael Kramer and 'The Printery.'" *Private Library* (Autumn 1981): 92–115.

Bill Jackson. "Private Presses of Kansas." *Missouri Library Association Quarterly* v. 30 (1969): 10–15.

Gerald Lundeen. "Adagio: The Private Press of Leonard F. Bahr." *Private Library* (Summer 1973): 58–73.

Paul Hayden Duensing. *25: A Quarter Century of Triumphs and Disasters in the Microcosm of the Private Press and Type Foundry of. . . .* Vicksburg, Mich., 1976.

Book Club of California. *A Portfolio of Book Club Printers.* San Francisco, 1962.

Alastair Johnston. "Literary Small Presses since World War II in Europe and America." *American Book Collector* new series, v. 2, no. 3 (May-June 1981): 13–19.

Clif Rather and Lois Rather. *Ten Years of the Rather Press: A Bibliography, 1968–1978.* Oakland, 1978.

Lewis Allen. "The Evolution of an Edition de Luxe." *Quarterly News-Letter, Book Club of California* v. 27 (1962): 29–34.

The Allen Press Bibliography, MCMLXXXI: Produced by Hand with Art Work, Sample Pages from Previous Editions. Greenbrae, Calif., 1981.

Jane Wilson. "The Christmas Printer, or the Printing Career of James D. Hart." *Quarterly News-Letter, Book Club of California* v. 29, no. 1 (Winter 1963): 3–15.

Vicky Schreiber Dill. "The Books of William Everson." *Books at Iowa* no. 28 (April 1978): 9–24.

Linnea Gentry. "On William Everson as Printer." *Fine Print* v. 1, no. 3 (July 1975): 21–22.

William Everson. "The Poem as Icon—Reflections on Printing as a Fine Art." *Soundings* v. 8, no. 2 (December 1976): 7–21.

"American Bard: A Tale of Two Books." *Fine Print* v. 8, no. 2 (April 1982): 53, 68–69. A detailed account of the Lime Kiln edition, by Richard Bigus and Maureen Carey, and of the Viking Press edition, by Sandra Kirshenbaum.

Adrian Wilson. *The Work and Play of Adrian Wilson.* Austin, 1983. Not yet available at press time, but promises to be an important book on an outstanding typographer.

———. *Printing for Theater.* San Francisco, 1957.

Alastair Johnston. *A Bibliography of the Auerhahn Press & Its Successor Dave Haselwood Books.* Berkeley, 1977.

D. W. Davies. *Grant Dahlstrom and the First Fifty Years of the Castle Press.* Los Angeles, 1981.

Vance Gerry. *Some Fond Reminiscences of a Boy Printer at the Castle Press.* Pasadena, 1968.

Edwin H. Carpenter. *A Natural History of the Typestickers of Los Angeles: Compiled from the Letters of Wm. M. Cheney.* Los Angeles, 1960.

Mary Lutz Jones. *A Los Angeles Typesticker: William M. Cheney.* Los Angeles, 1981.

John Dreyfus. *Saul Marks and His Plantin Press.* Laguna Beach, Calif., 1975.

Lillian Marks. *Saul Marks and the Plantin Press.* Los Angeles, 1980.

J. Ben Lieberman. *The Whys and Therefores of a Chappel.* White Plains, N.Y., 1961.

Bernard Keelan. *A Bold Face on It: Or Three Quoins in the Fountain of Wisdom, Being an Account of Banter University Press.* London, 1964.

CHAPTER 21: CANADIAN PRIVATE PRESSES

Maureen Bradbury. "Fine Printing by Canadian Private Presses: A Descriptive Listing of the Holdings in Special Collections." *News from the Rare Book Room* (University of Alberta) no. 17 (June 1978); no. 18 (December 1980).

David B. Kotin and Marilyn Rueter. *Reader, Lover of Books, Lover of Heaven: A Catalogue Based on an Exhibition of the Book Arts in Ontario.* Willowdale, Ont., 1978.

Richard Pennington. *An Account of the Redpath Press.* Blanzac, 1977.

William Rueter. *Order Touched with Delight: Some Personal Observations on the Nature of the Private Press, with an Account of the Aliquando Press.* Toronto, 1976.

Marya Fiamengo. "Private Presses in Vancouver." *Canadian Literature* v. 22 (Autumn 1964): 24–28.

CHAPTER 22: FINE PRINTING DOWN UNDER

Philip Parr. *A History of Hobby Printing in Australasia.* Wellington, 1980. Also published in the *Bibliographical Society of Australia and New Zealand Bulletin* v. 4 (1980): 203–211.

Denis Glover. *Hot Water Sailor, 1912–1962, & Landlubber Ho! 1963–1980.* Auckland, 1981. An entertaining autobiography, with much on the Caxton Club and Caxton Press.

Ian Milner. "Denis Glover & The Caxton Club: A Memoir." *Islands* v. 3, no. 3 (Spring 1975): 265–270.

Dennis McEldowney. "The Typographical Obsession." *Islands* v. 8, no. 1 (March 1980): 59–70. A useful overview of good and fine printing in New Zealand.

Alan Loney. "Printing with the Handpress 'Pleases Eye and Mind and Hand.'" *Turnbull Library Record* v. 12, no. 2 (October 1979): 95–104.

George Mackaness. *Bibliomania: An Australian Book Collector's Essays.* Sydney, 1965. Chapter II, "Australian Private Presses," pp. 14–32.

Geoffrey Farmer. *Private Presses and Australia: With a Checklist.* Melbourne, 1972. A first supplement was issued in 1976.

———. "The Literature of Australian Private Presses and Fine Printing." *Bibliographical Society of Australia and New Zealand Bulletin* v. 5, no. 3 (1981): 93–108.

Harry F. Chaplin. *The Fanfrolico Press: A Survey.* Melbourne, 1976.

Jack Lindsay. *Fanfrolico and After.* London, 1962.

Richard Fotheringham. "Expatriate Publishing: Jack Lindsay and the Fanfrolico Press." *Meanjin Quarterly* v. 31, no. 1 (1972): 55–61.

———. "Expatriate Publishing: P. R. Stephensen and the Mandrake Press." *Meanjin Quarterly* v. 31, no. 2 (1972): 183–188.

Philip Lindsay. *I'd Live the Same Life Over.* London, 1941.

James Munro. "The Wattle Grove Press." *Private Library* v. 3, no. 7 (July 1961): 96–97.

Geoffrey Farmer. "Some Contemporary Australasian Presses." *Australian Library Journal* v. 28 (1979): 135–138.

Philip Roberts. "Ten Years on an Island." *Poetry Australia* no. 74–75 (July 1980): 101–108.

B. J. McMullin. "Bibliographical Presses in Australia and New Zealand." *Bibliographical Society of Australia and New Zealand Bulletin* v. 3 (1977): 55–64.

CHAPTER 23: SCHOOL AND TEACHING PRESSES

G. F. Barwick. "Books Printed at Sea." *The Library* 2nd series, v. 1 (1900): 163–166.

Octave Delepierre. "Essai Biographique sur l'Histoire Littéraire des Fous." *Miscellanies of the Philobiblon Society* v. 4 (1857–1858). 132 pp.

D. A. Doudney. *A Pictorial Outline of the Rise and Progress of the Bonmahon Schools.* Bunmahon, 1851.

E. R. McClintock Dix. "The Bonmahon Press." *The Irish Book Lover* v. 1 (1909–1910): 97–100.

L. C. Owens. *J. H. Mason, 1875–1951: Scholar-Printer.* London, 1976.

Edward Rainsberry. *Through the Lych Gate.* Kineton, 1969. Chapter 21, pp. 188–193, deals with the King's Stone Press.

L. J. Wallis. *Leonard Jay.* London, 1954.

David Chambers. "The Art Society Press." *Private Library* (Autumn 1969): 107–117.

Kenneth Day. "The Lion and Unicorn Press." *Book Design & Production* v. 3, no. 4 (1960): 16–24.

Lion & Unicorn Press: A Short History and List of Publications. London, 1978.

J. D. Van Trump. *Porter Garnett and the Laboratory Press: Catalogue of an Exhibition.* Pittsburgh, 1962.

Walter Leuba. "A Porter Garnett List." *The Black Art* v. 3 (1965–1964): 86–93.

Porter Garnett. *A Documentary Account of the Beginnings of the Laboratory Press.* Pittsburgh, 1927.

Russell T. Limbach. *Art Laboratory Impressions.* Middletown, Conn., 1960.

Philip Gaskell. "The First Two Years of the Water Lane Press." *Transactions of the Cambridge Bibliographical Society* v. 2 (1954–1958): 170–184.

———. "The Bibliographical Press Movement." *Journal of the Printing Historical Society* no. 1 (1965): 1–13.

PART TWO
PRIVATE PRESS TYPEFACES

CHAPTER 24: EARLY PRESSES AND THEIR TYPES

D. B. Updike. *Printing Types.* 2nd ed. Cambridge, Mass., 1937.

Talbot Baines Reed. *A History of the Old English Letter Foundries.* New ed., rev. and enlarged by A. F. Johnson. London, 1952.

M. Siddiq Khan. "William Carey and the Serampore Books, 1800–1834." *Libri* v. 11 (1961): 197–280.

J. S. L. Gilmour. "Julian Hibbert." Some Uncollected Authors xxvi. *The Book Collector* v. 9 (1960): 446–451.

Alexina Harrison. *A. M. Mackay: Pioneer Missionary of the Church Missionary Society to Uganda.* Photolitho ed. London, 1970.

James Evans Centennial Committee. *Birch Bark Talking: A Resumé of the Life and Work of the Rev. James Evans.* Toronto, 1940.

CHAPTER 25: MORRIS AND AFTER

Thomas Balston. *The Cambridge University Press Collection of Private Press Types.* Cambridge, 1951.

F. C. Avis. "Venetian Type Designs of the English Private Presses." *Gutenberg-Jahrbuch* (1965): 53–57.

Pierpont Morgan Library. *William Morris and the Art of the Book.* New York, 1976.

John Dreyfus. "New Light on the Design of Types for the Kelmscott Press and Doves Press." *The Library* 5th series, v. 29, no. 1 (March 1974): 36–41.

Colin Franklin. *Emery Walker: Some Light on His Theories of Printing and on His Relations with William Morris and Cobden-Sanderson.* Cambridge, 1973.

F. C. Avis. *Edward Philip Prince: Type Punchcutter.* London, 1968.

John Dreyfus. *Italic Quartet.* Cambridge, 1966.

Alan Fern. "The Count and the Calligrapher." *Apollo* v. 79 (1964): 214–220.

Joseph Blumenthal. *The Printed Book in America.* Boston, 1977.

Susan O. Thompson. *American Book Design and William Morris.* New York, 1977.

Frederic W. Goudy. *A Half-Century of Type Design and Typography.* New York, 1946.

Dard Hunter. *My Life with Paper.* New York, 1958.

Dard Hunter, II. *The Life Work of Dard Hunter.* Chillicothe, 1981–

CHAPTER 26: AFTER 1918

Robert Harling. "The Type Designs of Eric Gill." *Alphabet and Image* no. 6 (1948): 55–69.

James Mosley. "Eric Gill and the Golden Cockerel Type." *Matrix* no. 2 (1982): 17–22. Supplemented with a "Note on the Type" by Christopher Sandford, pp. 23–25.

Dorothy A. Harrop. *A History of the Gregynog Press.* Pinner, 1980.

Carolyn Reading Hammer. *Notes on the Two-Color Initials of Victor Hammer.* Lexington, Ky., 1966.

———. "Victor Hammer." In *Heritage of the Graphic Arts,* ed. by Chandler B. Grannis, pp. 167–181. New York, 1972.

———, ed. *Victor Hammer: Artist and Printer.* Lexington, Ky., 1981.

David Farrell. "Pursuit of the Ideal: The Uncial Letters of Victor Hammer." *Fine Print* v. 4, no. 4 (October 1978): 121–123.

Giovanni Mardersteig. *The Officina Bodoni: An Account of the Work of a Hand Press, 1923–1977.* Verona, 1980.

CHAPTER 27: THE CONTEMPORARY SCENE

Geoffrey Osborne. "An Unusual Type Specimen Book from India." *Matrix* no. 2 (1982): 100–102.

Roderick Cave. "Typefounding for Pleasure: A Note on the Grimalkin Press." *Book Design & Production* v. 4, no. 3 (1961): 184.

Eugene M. Ettenberg. "Paul Hayden Duensing's Private Type Foundry." *Inland Printer* (September 1967): 116–117.

The Private Press and Typefoundry of Paul Hayden Duensing. Kalamazoo, Mich., 1967.

25. A Quarter Century of Triumphs and Disasters in the Microcosm of the Private Press and Typefoundry of Paul Hayden Duensing. Vicksburg, Mich., 1976.

Paul Hayden Duensing. "Typefounding, Past and Future: The Oxford Conference." *Fine Print* v. 9, no. 1 (January 1983): 4–5.

Charles Bigelow. "On Type: Galliard." *Fine Print* v. 5, no. 3 (January 1979): 27–30.

Richard Brown. "Keeping the Presses in Condition." *Penrose Annual* v. 71 (1978–1979): 225–232.

Glenn Storhaug. "Three Proof Presses under an Oak Tree." *Matrix* no. 1 (1981): 28–34.

Tom Craig. "The Restoration of Iron Hand-Presses." *Matrix* no. 2 (1982): 63–68.

INDEX